Environmental Effects
On Cognitive Abilities

Environmental Effects On Cognitive Abilities

Edited by

ROBERT J. STERNBERG
Yale University

ELENA L. GRIGORENKO
Yale University and
Moscow State University

2001

LAWRENCE ERLBAUM ASSOCIATES, PUBLISHERS
Mahwah, New Jersey   London

Lawrence Erlbaum Associates, Inc., Publishers
10 Industrial Avenue
Mahwah, New Jersey 07430

Cover design by Kathryn Houghtaling Lacey

Library of Congress Cataloging-in-Publication Data

Environmental effects on cognitive abilities / edited by Robert J. Sternberg, Elena L. Grigorenko.
  p. cm.
  Includes bibliographical references and indexes.
  ISBN 0-8058-3183-5 (cloth : alk. Paper)
    1.   Intellect. 2. Nature and nurture. 3. Environmental psychology. I. Sternberg, Robert J.
  II. Grigorenko, Elena L.

  BF431 .E65 2001

                                                                00-051394

Books published by Lawrence Erlbaum Associates are printed on acid-free paper,
and their bindings are chosen for strength and durability.

Printed in the United States of America
10   9   8   7   6   5   4   3   2   1

Contents

Preface

It sometimes seems difficult to pick up a current newspaper or a magazine without reading about some behavioral characteristic for which it has been found that a gene is responsible. Even aspects of behavior that one would feel certain are environmentally controlled—such as divorce—are now being attributed in part to the effects of genes. But genes never act alone: Their effects are always filtered through the environment.

For example, it *is* ridiculous to view divorce as caused by a gene in itself. Indeed, some societies have no divorces whatsoever, for legal or other reasons, and no one would argue that their members lack some gene for divorce that is found in societies that do have divorce. Rather, what is most likely happening is that genetic predispositions, in interaction with the environment, can propel some people to be more likely to divorce than others, given that the environment (society) permits divorce. Thus, even in an age of interest in biology, the effects of the environment, however they may be partitioned, will always be with us.

The goal of this volume is to discuss how the environment influences the development and the maintenance of cognitive abilities. The volume is a successor, in many respects to the Sternberg–Grigorenko (1997) volume, *Intelligence, Heredity, and Environment.* The chapters in this volume supplement the chapters in that book with respect to the specific nature and range of environmental effects. This volume provides much greater detail. This book also serves as a companion volume to a book Grigorenko and Sternberg have edited, *Family Environment and Intellectual Functioning: A Life-Span Perspective,* on the effects of family environment, in particular, on cognitive abilities. Family effects are so broad-ranging and pervasive that they were believed to require a separate volume of their own. Taken together, the two-volume set comprises the most comprehensive existing work on the relation between the environment and cognitive abilities.

Why did we see a need for a book on environmental effects on cognitive abilities? There are several reasons.

1. *Genes always have their effect either in correlation with or in interaction with the environment.* As noted earlier, genes always filter their effects through the environment. So even those readers with a primarily biological orientation need to know how environment filters genetic effects.

2. *We can control environment, at least to some extent.* Whereas we can do relatively little about genes, we can do a great deal about the environment. Thus, to the extent that we wish to maximize the cognitive development both of children and adults, we need to understand environmental effects on cognitive abilities so as to have a basis for constructing optimal environments.

3. *Even if attributes are heritable, they can be modifiable.* Many people confuse heritability with modifiability. They believe that if something is heritable, it cannot be modifiable. This belief is false. Height is highly heritable, it has been highly modifiable. No matter what the heritability of a set of traits, these traits can develop very differently in different environments.

4. *Too much of what is written about the environment is vague.* Much of what people write about the environment is stated vaguely and without scientific support. "Environment" or "context" is said to matter, without further specification of just what the effects are or how they are manifested. This book concentrates on specifying these effects in detail, and on showing how they operate.

5. *The pendulum has swung too far in the direction of biology.* We believe that biological effects on cognitive development are important. But just as the 1970s placed too much emphasis on the environment, we believe that the 1990s placed too much emphasis on biology. Biological and environmental effects always work together. This book can help restore a more appropriate balance.

6. *The debate needs to go beyond specifying "environment" and "context" as important to specifying just what the environmental and contextual factors are.* The traditional debate is over what percentage of the variation in various cognitive abilities is inherited and what percentage of the variation is acquired through environment. The debate has begun to move beyond such relatively sterile characterizations to specification of what the genetic or environmental factors are that constitute each of these two large components. This book is the only one that systematically reviews such a broad range of environmental factors.

Why cover such a broad range of factors in one book? The reason is that, in the past, environmental approaches have been piecemeal, with articles and books tending to concentrate on one or two factors (e.g., parenting, birth order, schooling) without putting together all of the factors that contribute to environmental effects. A book is needed that serves as a handbook for those interested in the entire range of environmental effects. Thus, our goal is to integrate what formerly have been very diverse literatures that are seriously in need of integration and accessibility through a single volume.

No one author could possibly be an expert in all of the diverse environmental effects that contribute to individual differences in cognitive abilities. It is for this reason that an edited book is useful, with leading authorities commenting on effects in their own areas of expertise.

Chapter authors have been asked to make their chapters accessible to college-educated lay readers as well as professionals. As a result, this book has a wide-ranging potential audience:

1.   *Psychologists* in a variety of specializations, including (a) developmental, (b) cognitive, (c) differential, (d) health, (e) clinical, (f) counseling, (g) environmental, (h) behavior-genetic, (I) educational, and (j) school psychology are all likely to find this book of interest.

2.   *Educators* who teach, do research, or do administration will all be concerned with what they can do to establish the optimal possible environments for educating children.

3.   *Parents* will be interested in knowing what they can do to optimize children's environments.

4.   *Social workers* will also be interested in how environments can be arranged in order to facilitate the cognitive development of the people with whose best interests they are charged, for example, children placed in foster homes.

5.   *Employers* who want to create an environment at work that optimizes the cognitive work of their employees will find the book useful in suggesting what they can do to create an environment that stimulates high-level thinking.

ACKNOWLEDGMENTS

We are grateful to Judi Amsel for contracting the book, to Sai Durvasula for help with manuscript preparation, and to Grant R206R950001 from the U.S. Office of Education Research and Improvement, U.S. Department of Education, which has funded Sternberg's work on intelligence. The findings and opinions expressed in this book do not reflect the positions or policies of that agency.

Robert J. Sternberg
Elena L. Grigorenko

GENERAL ISSUES

1

Caste Status and Intellectual Development

John U. Ogbu
Pamela Stern
University of California, Berkeley

Social scientists have long observed that the racial stratification in the United States is organized along the principles of caste (Berreman, 1960, 1966; Davis, Gardner, & Gardner, 1965; Dollard, 1957; Lyman, 1973; Mack, 1968; Warner, 1965, 1970). In the 1970s, the first author of this chapter suggested that observed differences between Black and White Americans in cognitive development and IQ test scores could be explained by using the principle of caste organization (Ogbu, 1974, 1978). This was in response to the intensified nature–nurture debate that followed Jensen's (1969, 1971, 1972, 1973) statements regarding the profound influence of genetics in the determination of IQ. This debate continues to underlie much of the current research on intellectual development (cf. Benasich & Brooks-Gunn, 1996; Bouchard, 1997; Brody & Stoneman, 1992; Brooks-Gunn, Klebanov, & Duncan, 1996; Loehlin, Horn, & Willerman, 1997; Singh, 1996).

We remain dissatisfied with the conventional nature–nurture debate for three reasons. First, it is a debate with no possible resolution. Second, it is difficult, if not impossible, to separate White American beliefs about Black American intelligence from the "scientific theories" of differences in Black and White intelligence or IQ test scores. And finally, cross-cultural research increasingly casts doubt on both genetic and environmental explanations, but especially on the genetic explanation.

For these reasons, Ogbu offered the hypothesis that Black–White differences in IQ are due to different cognitive requirements of their respective positions or different ecocultural niches under an American caste system. The ascribed status of Black Americans (as a pariah caste), which until recently excluded most from participating fully in American technology, economy, and other institutions, also prevented Black Americans from developing to the same extent some of the cognitive or intellectual skills enhanced by the technological, economic, and other opportunities open to White Americans (Ogbu, 1974). Because IQ tests consist of the types of skills valued and promoted by middle-class, White culture, the scores of Blacks and other caste-like minorities tend to fall below the means of those in the majority. A cross-cultural study of caste-like minorities in six societies demonstrated that minority status rather than *race* was the critical factor in predicting IQ test scores. Across cultures, the caste-like minorities had lower IQ test scores than the dominant group both when the pariah caste and the dominant caste belong to the same race *and* when they belonged to different races (Ogbu, 1978).

Although some psychologists have taken note of our hypothesis (Herrnstein & Murray, 1994; Jensen, 1994; Neisser et al., 1996), no one has undertaken to test it. One difficulty we face in writing this chapter is the tendency of other researchers to confound caste with socioeconomic status. Consequently, one of our objectives is to clarify the difference between caste stratification and class stratification. Another objective is to discuss the social effects of caste positioning to the intellectual development of Black Americans.

The chapter is divided into six main sections: the relationship between intelligence and IQ; amplifiers of intelligence or origins of intellectual skills in a population; distinctions between caste, class, racial stratification, and minority statuses; Caste status, cognitive development, and IQ; the case of Black Americans; conclusions.

THE RELATIONSHIP BETWEEN INTELLIGENCE AND IQ

Conventional Definitions

A cursory examination of the psychological literature on the subject of intelligence and IQ might lead the naïve reader to conclude that there is little consensus among psychologists regarding what is meant by intelligence. This view, however, is somewhat erroneous. Although psychologists cannot agree as to what intelligence or IQ means, there is an overarching belief that the two are synonymous (Helms, 1992). Some, like Jensen (1969), consider IQ to be a technical term to label whatever intelligence tests test. To others, IQ reflects the "global ability to absorb complex information, or grasp and manipulate abstract concepts"(Travers, 1982, p. 235). Still other psychologists define intelligence as information processing (i.e., how people interpret or process the information they receive; Kyllonen, 1994). One thing that students of intelligence of virtually all persuasions agree on is that it can be measured. So, when they refer to intelligence they mean IQ, which is what they measure. As Jensen (1969) put it, "intelligence (i.e., IQ) is what intelligence tests test" (p. 5).

An Alternative "Intelligence"?

We propose an alternative definition of intelligence partly on the basis of suggestions from Baumrind (1972), Vernon (1969), and Greenfield (1998).[1] From a cross-cultural perspective, intelligence is a cultural system of thought, a cultural or group's repertoire of adaptive intellectual (or cognitive) skills. According to Vernon, there are three levels of intelligence: genotypic intelligence (Intelligence A), phenotypic intelligence (Intelligence B) and the intelligence measured by psychologists, IQ (Intelligence C). (See Fig. 1.1.)

Intelligence A, the genotype, is the innate capacity or potential (i.e., genetic endowment for intelligence) which individuals inherit from their parents. Intelligence A determines the level of intellectual abilities possible for individuals under given conditions. Similarly, the genetic potential of a population, Intelligence A, determines the extent of the intellectual skills of its members. *Intelligence A is a hypothetical construct that cannot be directly observed or measured by psychologists, behavioral geneticists, or anyone.* It only can be inferred or estimated from behavior, such as test scores (Jensen, 1994; Plomin, 1994; Vernon, 1969, p. 9; see also Ogbu, 1978, 1994a). What, we, following Vernon, also call Intelligence A is what Greenfield (1998, p. 81) chose to label *panhuman genotypic intelligence.* She defined it as the ability in all normal members of the human species to acquire competence in technology, linguistic communication, and social organization.

Intelligence B, the phenotype, is the observable behavioral manifestation of intelligence as defined in a culture. It refers to everyday observed behavior of an individual considered intelligent or not intelligent by members of his or her population. Intelligent behaviors reflect the adaptive repertoire of intellectual or cognitive skills in a population. Intelligence B is a product of both genetic potential (Intelligence A or nature) and environment. This is not the environment as defined in conventional environmental theory of IQ. Rather, environment consists of all social conditions and cultural activities in the ecocultural niche of a population that contribute to the intellectual skills of that population. Intelligence B is different for different populations partly because it is culturally defined and partly because it consists of intellectual skills adaptive to particular needs in each population's particular ecocultural niche. For example, the kinds of behaviors considered intelli-

---

[1]We should point out, however, that it is not necessary for these researchers to agree with our interpretation of their work or to continue to maintain the point of view we attribute to them. Rather, we find their ideas useful in the context of our own thinking on the matter.

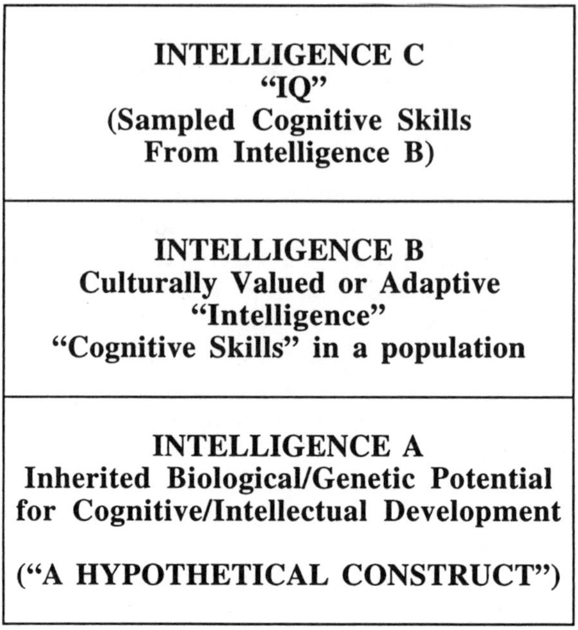

INTELLIGENCE C
"IQ"
(Sampled Cognitive Skills
From Intelligence B)

INTELLIGENCE B
Culturally Valued or Adaptive
"Intelligence"
"Cognitive Skills" in a population

INTELLIGENCE A
Inherited Biological/Genetic Potential
for Cognitive/Intellectual Development

("A HYPOTHETICAL CONSTRUCT")

FIG. 1.1.   Between phylogency and ontogeny: Genetic potential, cultural intelligence, and measured intelligence or IQ. Based on Vernon (1969) and Baumrind (1972).

gent, required, and valued in the ecocultural niche of White, middle-class Americans are somewhat different from behaviors required and valued as intelligent in the ecocultural niche of Igbo farmers of Nigeria or Inuit hunters in Canada. However, the extent and form of expression of Intelligence B in any population are determined by the same *biological potential* or *Intelligence A, the panhuman genotype.*

On the basis of the first author's experience, born to nonliterate parents in an Igbo village and now a professor at a major U.S. university, we accept Vernon's (1969) claim that *Intelligence B is not fixed.* It changes when the ecocultural niche of an individual or population changes. The first author's Intelligence B changed when he moved from his village and enrolled at a U.S. university. His experience is not unique. We are acquainted with many other individuals in similar and varying situations. Intelligence B of a population changes when its ecocultural niche changes. The introduction of formal, Western-style schooling is one type of this change. Employment by multinational manufacturing firms is another. What is important to bear in mind is that normal individuals and whole populations can and do acquire whatever intellectual skills are necessary because they possess the *panhuman genotype* (Greenfield, 1998).

Intelligence C, the IQ test scores or "Measured Intelligence," refers to a behavioral manifestation of intellectual skills selected from the adaptive intellectual skills of the White middle class. The selections are drawn from their specific Intelligence B. Intelligence C, IQ, is thus different from Intelligence B because it is only a part of the total intelligence of a population (White middle class, in this case). IQ also differs from intelligence because the intellectual skills included in IQ tests are selected for specific purposes, such as to predict academic achievement or job performance. The employment of IQ tests, in itself, is reflective of the social biases within a society, and IQ tests are often used to perpetuate social and economic inequalities (Fischer et al., 1996). In our view, IQ is NOT intelligence.

AMPLIFIERS OF INTELLIGENCE

Cultural Amplifiers

We designate as *cultural amplifiers* of intelligence activities or tasks in the *ecocultural niche*[2] of a population which require and enhance intellectual skills. Cultural activities are amplifiers when they require, stimulate, increase, or expand the quantity, quality, and cultural values of adaptive intellectual skills (see Fig. 1.2). Some obvious cultural amplifiers in Western middle-class ecocultural niche include handling technology, participation in a large-scale economy, negotiating bureaucracy, and urban life. These cultural activities require and enhance intellectual skills such as abstract thinking, conceptualization, grasping relations, and symbolic thinking that permeate other aspects of life (Vernon, 1969). Each ecocultural niche presents a wide array of cultural amplifiers of the intellectual skills that are required for success in that particular niche. Different ecocultural niches requires different repertoires of intellectual skills. Some skills enhanced by activities specific to one niche may also be of value in other ecocultural niches. Other examples of cultural amplifiers and the associated intellectual skills found in various ecocultural niches are pottery making–conservation (Price-Williams, 1961; Price-Williams, Gordon, & Ramirez, 1969), market trading–mathematics (Posner, 1982; Saxe & Posner, 1983), foraging–spatial perception (Dasen, 1974); video games–spatial perception (Greenfield, 1998); and verbal games–verbal abilities (Foster, 1974; Hannerz, 1969).

---

[2]Previously we used the term effective environment (Ogbu, 1981), macro-environment, and ecological niche (Ogbu, 1994a, 1994b) for the wider societal environment where activities or cultural tasks generated the cognitive problems for members of a population. In this chapter we are using the concept, ecocultural niche, borrowed from Greenfield (1998), as a better descriptive term.

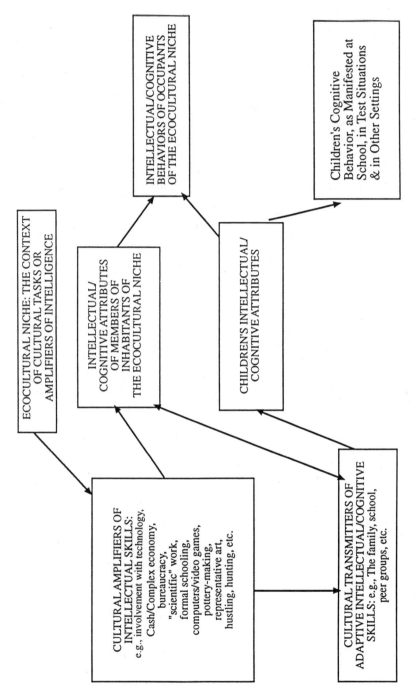

FIG. 12. Origins of intelligence-cognitive skills. Based on Ogbu (1978) and Whiting (1963).

The boxes contain the following text:

ECOCULTURAL NICHE: THE CONTEXT OF CULTURAL TASKS OR AMPLIFIERS OF INTELLIGENCE

INTELLECTUAL/COGNITIVE BEHAVIORS OF OCCUPANTS OF THE ECOCULTURAL NICHE

INTELLECTUAL/COGNITIVE ATTRIBUTES OF MEMBERS OF INHABITANTS OF THE ECOCULTURAL NICHE

Children's Cognitive Behavior, as Manifested at School, in Test Situations & in Other Settings

CHILDREN'S INTELLECTUAL/COGNITIVE ATTRIBUTES

CULTURAL AMPLIFIERS OF INTELLECTUAL SKILLS: e.g., involvement with technology, Cash/Complex economy, bureaucracy, "scientific" work, formal schooling, computers/video games, pottery-making, representative art, hustling, hunting, etc.

CULTURAL TRANSMITTERS OF ADAPTIVE INTELLECTUAL/COGNITIVE SKILLS: e.g., The family, school, peer groups, etc.

8

Cross-cultural studies of cultural amplifiers of intelligence suggest at least two conclusions. First, intellectual skills prevalent or considered important are not the same in all populations. They depend on the cultural amplifiers in the ecocultural niche. Second, normal members of all human populations can acquire new intellectual skills, including those included in IQ tests because all normal human beings possess the panhuman genotypic ability to do so. We observe this capability when individuals enter new ecocultural niches through migration, when formal Western schooling is introduced, and when social and economic circumstances change.

Commerce and Mathematical Skills. We might expect mathematical skills to be more prevalent and valued in a society whose economy is based on commerce than in a subsistence farming society. A comparative study of two West African communities found this to be the case (Posner, 1982; Saxe & Posner, 1983). The children of Dioula, a merchant population, had many opportunities through practice and observation to acquire mathematical skills whereas the children of the Baoule, an agricultural people, did not. Not surprisingly, when tested, Dioula children—even those who had not had Western-type schooling—performed better than Baoule children in tests of mathematical skills.

Video Games and Spatial Perception. Video games require and enhance the development of skills in visual–spatial representation and iconic imagery (Greenfield, 1998, p. 91), which are some of the skills tested by the nonverbal portions the Wechsler and Stanford-Binet intelligence scales. Presenting several examples from laboratory studies, Greenfield makes a convincing case that video games, films, and computers enhance perceptual–spatial skills in the contemporary United States.

Communicative Events (e.g., games, preaching, etc.) and Verbal Skills. Within the Black American speech community there are communicative events that serve as amplifier of verbal skills. These include games like playin' the dozen, toastin', as well as preaching, that require and enhance verbal skills. Thus, among Blacks, especially those in the inner city, verbal skills are among the most highly prized (Abraham, 1972; Foster, 1974; Kochman, 1972; Perkins, 1975; Ogbu, 1982, p. 119). The importance of verbal skills for ghetto residents is obvious in the following description of the role of verbal abilities in a Washington D.C. ghetto study by Hannerz (1969):

> The skill of talking well and easily is widely appreciated among ghetto men; although it is hardly itself a sign of masculinity, it can be very helpful in realizing one's wishes. "Rappin'," persuasive speech, can be used to manipulate others to give one's own advantage. (pp. 84–85)

This cultural amplifier of verbal skills may explain in part why Blacks do better on the verbal part of IQ tests than on the nonverbal tasks (Jensen 1994, p. 904).

Cultural Transmitters of Adaptive Intellectual Skills

The societal institutions responsible for transmitting to children the preexisting adaptive skills are distinct from the cultural amplifiers. We refer to these institutions as *cultural transmitters*. They include the family, school, peer groups, and other institutions. These institutions do not originate or invent the intellectual skills children acquire; *they are not the source of intelligence*. They merely transmit those in existence.

It is necessary to distinguish cultural transmitters, or where children acquire the adaptive intellectual skills of their population, *from* the ways the children acquire these skills. In other words, cultural institutions that transmit adaptive intellectual skills must be treated separately from the ways they perform their functions. For the latter, the process of transmission and acquisition, we turn to *formulae* that have evolved over time for this purpose. These formulae are not the same in all populations. In a comparative study one may discover that two populations use different formulae to transmit the same intellectual skills. For example, Australian Aborigines and White Australians may use different formulae to transmit perceptual–spatial skills. It is also quite likely that the Dioula and White middle-class Americans use different formulae to transmit mathematical knowledge and skills. The important thing to bear in mind is that the study of process of development is a study of *how* cultural transmitters transmit and *how* children acquire preexisting adaptive intellectual skills of their ecocultural niche.[3] There are usually many formulae in an ecocultural niche (see Ogbu, 1979, 1981, 1982). Some examples of formulae include childrearing practices, schooling, and theories of child development.

Family Childrearing Practices.   Family childrearing practices constitute one process or formula for transmitting adaptive intellectual skills to children. These are different among different populations. The difference in this formula can be seen in comparing the childrearing practices of White middle-class Americans with those of Chinese Confucian families in Hong Kong. Studies in the United States generally conclude that children whose parents emphasize *self-direction* (responsibility, consideration of others, curiosity) perform better on IQ tests than children whose parents emphasize *conformity* (obedience, neatness, good manners, and appropriate sex-role behaviors;

---

[3]Our concern here is not with "rate" or amount of development of particular skills by children. That is another matter.

Brody & Stoneman, 1992; Sameroff, Seifer, Baldwin, & Baldwin, 1993). In contrast, Ho (1994) found that Chinese parents in Hong Kong stress social control, are intolerant of deviancy, and *pressure their children to conform*. They also stress impulse control in early childhood and discourage the boisterous and highly verbal behaviors that are viewed as signs of superior intellect among middle-class American children. Yet, the Chinese children score as high as White American children on IQ tests and score higher than White American children in math tests.

Schooling. Another cultural formula used to transmit adaptive intellectual skills is formal schooling. The process of transmission and acquisition of intellectual skills through schooling can be best observed where formal schooling is newly introduced. An important feature of this formula is the prominent role given to spoken and written language. In populations without schooling, teaching and learning are primarily by demonstration and observation. The schooling formula uses explicit verbal formulation of what is to be learned and how it is to be learned. The linguistic formulations and other features of the formula have important cognitive consequences for enhanced language skills, decontexualized learning, information processing, and learning styles (Scribner & Cole, 1973).

Theories of Child Development. Cultural beliefs about child development lead parents to create environments in which children develop competence in certain intellectual skills (Harkness & Super, 1992; Sameroff et al., 1993). Sameroff et al. observed that parental beliefs accounted for group differences seen in the IQ scores of American children. The children whose parents believed that child development is the result of a single factor such as constitution or environment scored lower on IQ tests than the children whose parents held that child development resulted from the complex interplay of factors.

Ecocultural Context of IQ Tests

As we noted earlier, IQ tests measure a subset of the intellectual skills adaptive for and valued by White middle-class Americans. The psychologists and psychometricians who create IQ tests tend to come from the White middle-class ecocultural niche, and thus, view the skills required by the tests as natural and universal. Not only do the tests generally require specific knowledge from the White middle-class ecocultural niche, but more importantly they require problem-solving strategies specific to the White middle-class ecocultural niche such as speed and accuracy.

Greenfield (1998) illustrated the culture-specific nature of the knowledge for solving even nonverbal tasks in the IQ tests with an item from the Guilford–Zimmermann Aptitude Survey. This nonverbal task measures not only the spatial ability of the test taker but also his or her ability to shift visual perspective. "The test-taker is first asked to identify an upside-down alarm clock, rotate it mentally a quarter turn to the right, and then match the resulting visual perspective with one of 5 drawings." Greenfield concluded that this task is "extremely culture-specific." She continued:

> Note that it requires knowledge of what the back of an alarm clock looks like. It also requires knowledge of the arrow as a visual symbol as well as even more specific knowledge that the arrow as portrayed does not symbolize a horizontal direction on a flat plane but rather represents rotation in the third dimension. (pp. 110–111)

The ecocultural context of IQ tests is clearly observed in cross-cultural studies of classification abilities. Most Europeans and White Americans learn to classify or identify plants by their flowers. Western psychologists studying plant identification or classification among Africans assume that they also classify plants by flowers. On the contrary, most Africans identify plants by their leaves; and usually, Africans have difficulty distinguishing one flower from another (Bohannan & van der Elst, 1998, p. 18).

Some cross-cultural researchers have pointed out that it is erroneous to assume that IQ tests measure universal human abilities or that performance on the tests is determined by heredity or home environment. As with Intelligence B, all normal individuals in any human population can acquire the intellectual skills that are measured in IQ tests (Cole & Cole, 1993; Greenfield, 1998; Ogbu, 1978; Vernon, 1969). More importantly, as we discuss in the remainder of this chapter, the use of IQ tests is heavily burdened by the social and political context in which the tests are employed.

CASTE STRATIFICATION

Caste stratification is a system of *a hierarchy of endogamous groups whose membership is determined permanently at birth* (Berreman, 1966, p. 279, 1981). The groups in the hierarchy may be ranked on the basis of several criteria including ethnicity and traditional occupation, but, in general, the groups are associated with a level of ritual or social pollution–purity. Although no longer codified by statutes and although the traditional observance has been abolished by the state, caste structures continue to operate in India, Pakistan, among the Igbos of Nigeria, in Japan, in Rwanda and Burundi, and in the United States.

Berreman (1981) has described several distinguishing features of caste stratification. One is that membership in each group in a caste hierarchy is determined by birth; intermarriage and intercaste mating, when they occur, produce "mixed" offspring or "half-castes." Often, there is an explicit rule, by statute or custom, assigning mixed offspring to one caste. In the United States the rule, formerly by statute and now by custom, is that the offspring of Black–White mating, within or outside marriage, affiliate with Blacks. Another characteristic feature of the caste system is *high-status summation*. That is, group membership is a better predictor of the economic, political, and social positions of low-caste individuals than training (education), ability (IQ), or other qualification. Members of the lower caste are very often relegated to menial roles, regardless of individual ability and training. Still another feature of a caste system is that there is no vertical upward mobility between castes. There have been a small number of situations, however, where members of a higher caste were socially redefined as members of the lower caste because of intermarriage with the lower caste. This occurred in San Antonio, Texas, in the early part of the 20th century. Whites who married Mexicans were socially redefined as Mexicans and forced to associate only with Mexicans (Grebler, Moore, & Guzman, 1970, p. 323; see McBride, 1996, for another example). There are identity symbols that serve to mark group membership for both insiders and outsiders. These identity symbols include occupations, speech style, dress, social behaviors, religious or ritual activities, diet, lifestyle, residence, ancestry, and skin color.

Dominant and lower castes offer quite different explanations of their respective positions in society. The dominant castes tend to rationalize their subordination and exploitation of the lower castes through what DeVos (1984) called "caste thinking." This is the belief that caste positions are somehow natural because of unalterable biological, religious, social, or cultural differences that mark lower caste groups as inferior and set them apart from the rest of society. These beliefs have an intense emotional character and often possess religious rationales. The strong emotional beliefs that an indelible mark of inferiority characterizes members of the lower caste lead the dominant caste groups to take steps to protect themselves from contamination. These may include the prohibition of intermarriage, residential segregation, school segregation, and the like. A still commonly heard expression uttered by Whites in the American South regarding the unacceptability of Black–White intermarriage goes something like this: "If God had meant for people to mix, He wouldn't have made them different colors."[4]

---

[4]The second author heard this remark on several occasions in the 1990s while living in Arkansas (but never as a child growing up in Florida in the 1960s). On one occasion, while teaching undergraduates at the University of Arkansas, she asked the students if they, too, had heard the expression. Nearly all responded affirmatively.

Although lower caste members do not completely accept a dominant group's "caste thinking" as a rationalization for their subordination and exploitation, their own thinking and behaviors cannot help but be affected by it. Lower castes develop their own explanations for the caste system and especially their menial situation. These explanations or *institutionalized discrimination folk theories* tend to blame both dominant groups and "the system" for their menial condition (see Berreman, 1972; DeVos, 1984; Ogbu & Matute-Bianchi, 1986).

Social Class Stratification

Stratification by social class is different than caste stratification. To begin with, the primary basis of ranking groups as classes is economic, a criterion one may acquire *after* birth. An individual may qualify for class membership by birth or by his or her achievement (e.g., education, income, etc.; Berreman, 1981). Social mobility, both upward and downward across ranked groups is possible. The means for upward or downward mobility is also prescribed by culture and custom, and degree of social mobility in a class system depends on the degree of openness in that particular system. Where the class system is relatively open, status summation tends to be low for members of all groups. The identity symbols of people in different social classes are partly acquired (e.g., education, occupation, income) and partly bestowed or prescribed (e.g. behaviors and values attributed to members of different classes (Berreman, 1972, 1981; Ogbu, 1978).

Racial Stratification

Racial stratification in the United States, especially with regard to the position of Blacks, should be characterized as a form of caste stratification, not as class stratification. Categories or ranked groups are defined on the basis of ancestry, and membership is assigned on the basis of ancestry. There is currently no "intermediate" position for children of mixed parentage. Throughout history, American Blacks have been characterized by high-status summation. This partly accounts for the preoccupation of the civil rights movement with equal social, economic, and political opportunities. In more than 30 years of observation of American society, the first author has not witnessed a class-based civil rights struggle. White and Black Americans belong to *two different systems of class stratification.* The two class systems are not equal, and are qualitatively different due to unequal access to resources and differential opportunities for upward social mobility. Even when Blacks and Whites hold similar socioeconomic status Blacks rarely receive the same social recognition or subjective evaluation.

Involuntary Minority Status

In their countries of origins, lower castes are like involuntary minorities. Involuntary minorities are people who are part of a society, like the United States, against their will because they were conquered, colonized, or enslaved. They are considered inferior to the dominant group. They are mistreated and provided with inferior education, excluded from desirable jobs and social positions; their languages and ways of life are denigrated.

When caste minorities emigrate to other societies, they become immigrant or voluntary minorities. Immigrant minorities are people who have come to the United States by choice because they expected better opportunities (better jobs, more political freedom, and so) than they had in their homelands or places of origin. As immigrant minorities they are also mistreated by the dominant group of their new or host society: They may be provided with inferior education, excluded from desirable jobs and social positions, and their languages and ways of life despised. But their mistreatment as immigrant minorities has a different consequence for their performance on IQ tests than their mistreatment as caste or involuntary minorities.

CASTE STATUS, MINORITY STATUS, AND COGNITIVE DEVELOPMENT

The cognitive development of low-caste groups is affected by the social structure of the society, by individual and institutionalized discrimination, and by social and psychological responses to that discrimination. Institutionalized discrimination takes the form of both *expressive discrimination* and of *systematic exclusion* from cultural amplifiers.

By expressive discrimination we refer to beliefs by the dominant group that the subordinate caste is inferior. This generates the kind of "caste thinking" among the dominant caste described earlier. It is used by the higher caste to rationalize their superior position and exploitation of the lower caste. The belief reinforces the dominant group's claim to superior "culture," "blood," or "genes." In so doing social inequality is transformed into inequality of nature. This is true in India, in Rwanda, in Japan, and in the United States.

The beliefs that the subordinate castes are inferior are also used to rationalize their exclusion from education, jobs, and other positions in society that function as amplifiers of the intellectual skills. Before returning to a discussion of caste discrimination and intellectual development in the United States, it may be useful to survey the role of caste and performance on IQ tests in other societies.

Caste stratification as defined in this chapter exists in India, among the Igbos of Nigeria, in Japan, Nepal, Rwanda, South Africa, Sri Lanka, and in the

United States. However, in only a few of these societies have there been studies that can be used to understand the consequences of caste discrimination
on cognitive test performance. We focus here on data from India and Japan.

India.   Many IQ tests have been administered in India in order to assess
the relative performance of the various castes. Many methodological problems make it extremely difficult to interpret the results in terms of caste status and performance. For example, some researchers compare lower caste
subjects from rural background with upper caste children from the city
(Ghuman, 1978). In some cases, researchers confound caste status with
socioeconomic class or with various measures of deprivation (Das & Khurana, 1988). In their review of the relationship between IQ test scores and
caste membership, Das and Khurana (1988) found that results tend to vary
with the types of tests used. For example, there are no significant differences
between high castes (*Brahmin, Kshatriya, Vaishya*) and low castes (*Harijans*)
on Raven's Progressive Matrices or other nonverbal tests. Larger differences occur in tests requiring verbal skills. Socioeconomic status is the most
important sociological variable affecting IQ test performance of the caste
groups. That is, the caste group with the highest SES (but not the highest
caste group), namely, Vaishya, tends to have the highest IQ scores (see
Chopra, 1966, & Fig. 1.3).

Looking at the overall results of IQ testing in India we conclude that significant differences in cognitive test scores by caste status do not seem to exist.
One study that illustrates this was done by Rangari (1987), who found no sig-

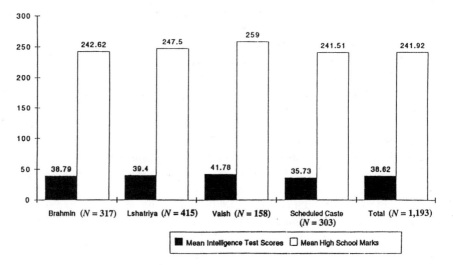

FIG. 1.3.   Mean intelligence test scores and mean high school marks for students from different castes. Based on Chopra (1966).

nificant differences in IQ test scores between the scheduled (low) castes and the unscheduled (high) castes. There are two possible reasons for this. One is that the tests do not measure the adaptive and valued intellectual skills of either the higher castes or the lower castes. Although the caste groups tend to be distinguished by their occupations, the latter are not necessarily differentiated by the types of intellectual skills measured in the tests. The other reason is that both the higher and lower castes are probably not familiar with the skills sought in the IQ tests and the questions or tasks used to elicit them. These skills do not come from ecocultural niches of any of the Indian castes but, rather, from Western White middle-class ecocultural niche.

Japan. The data from Japan are important in two ways. First, they show clearly that a large gap in IQ test scores exists between lower caste groups and the dominant group. Second, there are data with which we can compare the academic test scores of low-caste Japanese living in Japan with those living in the United States where they are not considered low caste. Although there are several caste minorities (e.g., Ainu, Burakumin, Hinin, Koreans, and so forth) in Japan, we discuss only two: the Burakumin and Koreans.

Burakumin are an outcaste or lower caste who belong to the same "race" as the dominant Ippan Japanese. They were declared untouchable in the 17th century and became a hereditary caste. Although they were "emancipated" and declared full citizens in 1871, Burakumin have remained largely segregated residentially in ghettos through informal and formal sanctions. They also remained confined to menial occupations and discriminated against in other ways (Ogbu, 1978). Since the early part of the 20th century the Buraku have been engaged in a civil rights struggle for equal educational and employment opportunities and for recognition and acceptance by the dominant group. Discrimination against the Burakumin persists, however (Kegard Prefecture, 1989; Fig. 1.4).

As a group, Burakumin score lower than the dominant Ippan on Tanaka–Binet IQ test (DeVos, 1973; DeVos & Wagatsuma, 1967; Fig. 1.5). *Time Magazine* had the following to say about the Buraku–Ippan gap in IQ test scores in 1973:

> The state proclaimed the outcaste system illegal in 1871, but prejudice did not yield to government fiat. On the average, Burakumin are less well educated than their countrymen, and their children test 16 IQ points lower than other Japanese. (Remarkably similar to the average 15-point difference between U. S. Blacks and Whites, which most experts attribute to environment influences). (*Time Magazine*, January 8, 1973, pp. 31–32)

The gap in IQ test scores persists even though the Japanese government has spent about $60 billion to improve the economic and social conditions, and

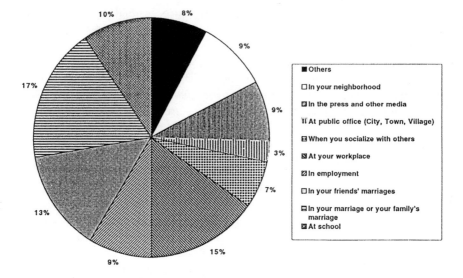

FIG. 1.4.   Discrimination in Kergard prefecture against Burakumin.

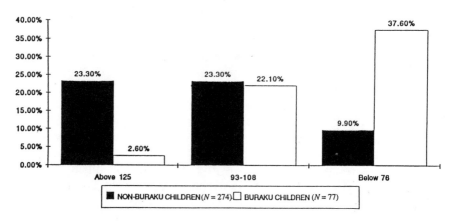

FIG. 1.5.   Burakumin IQ test scores. Based on data from DeVos (1973).

education of the Buraku since 1979 (Shimahara, 1991). By contrast, the Burakumin who emigrated to the United States perform just as well as or better in school as Ippan. We do not have comparative data on Burakumin and Ippan IQ test scores in the United States. However, the only study of Japanese immigrants to the United States that identified the Buraku shows that they do slightly better in school than the other Japanese immigrants (Ito, 1966).

Koreans in Japan arrived as forced labor under Japanese colonialism. Today, most of them are Japanese-born and speak no Korean, but continue to be treated as outcastes and foreigners. Japanese Koreans are required to be fingerprinted and to carry an identification card at all times. Job and school discrimination as well as other forms discrimination are common.

We do not have IQ test scores of Japanese Koreans, but results of other standardized tests show that they do not perform as well as the dominant Ippan Japanese or even as well as the Burakumin. For example, in 1976, 29.4% of the Ippan high school graduates and 18.7% of Burakumin but only 12.7% of Koreans in Hyogo Prefecture qualified to enter the University (Fig. 1.6; see Lee, 1991, p. 151). In contrast, Koreans in the United States perform as well as or better than White Americans on standardized tests (Lee, 1991, p. 152; see Fig. 1.7).

By comparing caste and IQ test scores in India, Japan, and the United States, we conclude that caste status per se does not explain the differences in IQ test scores between higher caste groups and lower caste groups in a society. IQ tests in India and the United States measure intellectual skills adaptive for and valued by Western White middle-class people. They do not necessarily measure the intellectual skills adaptive to any particular caste groups. Both high and low castes do poorly on the tests in India and differences between higher and lower castes are minor. In the United States and Japan differences between high castes and lower castes are quite large. But then, the lower castes in Japan do very well in the United States where they are members of a minority group rather than a low caste.

Based on these cross-cultural comparisons, we suggest that it is the manner in which caste and minority status combine rather than either minority position or low-caste status alone that lead to low cognitive or IQ test scores for low-status groups in complex, technological societies such as Japan and the United States. Often jobs and education require the adaptive intellectual skills of the dominant caste. In such societies, IQ tests discriminate against

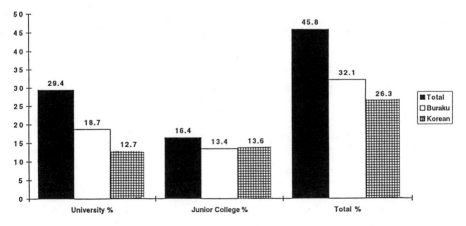

FIG. 1.6.   Korean school performance in Japan. Based on data from Lee (1991).

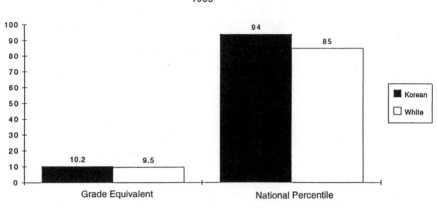

FIG. 1.7. Korean school performance in the United States. Based on data from Lee (1991).

all minorities, but how the minority groups perform on the tests depends on whether they became minorities by immigration or choice (voluntary minorities) or were forced by the dominant group into minorities status (involuntary minorities). The evidence indicates that immigrant minority status and nonimmigrant minority status have different implications for IQ test performance.

The distinction between voluntary and involuntary minorities is not by race or caste. Thus, in the United States, Afro-Caribbean, Asians, Jews, and Latinos from Central and South America are voluntary minorities; Black Americans, Native Americans and Native Hawaiians are involuntary minorities. Burakumin and Koreans are voluntary minorities in the United States, but are involuntary minorities in Japan. Voluntary or involuntary minority status, as we have noted, is largely a consequence of the way a group became a minority.

Voluntary or immigrant minorities in the United States, people who came to the United States by choice because they expected better opportunities, may differ from one another and from the majority White Americans by race or ethnicity, religion, or language. They include immigrants from Africa, the Caribbean, China, India, Japan, Korea, Mexico, the Philippines, and South America. *The important thing to bear in mind is that the people classified as voluntary minorities chose to move more or less permanently to and become minorities because they expected a better future for themselves or their children.* Although they may suffer discrimination, immigrants do not interpret their presence in the United States as forced on them by White Americans. In spite of the mistreatment, immigrant minorities, at least in the United States, generally do better than the nonimmigrants on IQ tests (Suzuki & Gutkin, 1994a; Vernon, 1982; Vraniak, 1994) for several reasons. These include a *preemigration experience* in which they participated in cultural amplifiers of the intellectual skills in the IQ; active *cognitive acculturation* during which they acquired the intellectual skills and know-how which enable them to participate in White middle-class cultural tasks, in school and the economy; and a *preemigration expectation and positive frame of comparison* such that immigrant minorities are strongly motivated to maximize their performance on IQ tests, other standardized tests, and in school, in general, immigrants see their chances of becoming successful through education (or test scores) as better in the United States than back home. They may also have a *folk theory of getting ahead in the United States* in which doing well in school (usually equated with high test scores) plays a central role (Ogbu, 1998). Finally, immigrant minorities employ a *pragmatic trust* in the helpful potential of authorities. Immigrant minorities do not necessarily think that the school personnel like them, but they view teachers and other school personnel as "useful experts" who can provide them with the skills and knowledge they need to succeed. They rarely question school authority, the curriculum, language, or IQ, and other standardized tests (Gibson, 1988).

Additionally, immigrants are *willing to accommodate* or adopt majority ways of behaving and talking. The immigrants are able to accommodate because the differences between their ways and the White ways are not oppositional— the differences predated emigration and did not emerge under oppression. And because they are not oppositional, the immigrants do not view accommodating to or adopting some White ways as threatening to their identities, cultures, and languages. Rather, they consider learning the White cultural skills, as acquiring new and necessary instrumental skills. They, therefore, take a pragmatic view in adopting majority ways and are willing to do whatever is necessary to succeed (Ogbu, 1991; Simons, Ogbu, & Bolton, n.d.).

Involuntary minorities in the United States, people who have been made a part of U.S. society against their will may be different from one another and from White Americans in terms of race, ethnicity, religion, or language. They include Native Alaskans, Native Americans, Native Hawaiians, Black Americans, early Mexicans in the American Southwest, and Puerto Ricans. *The important thing is that these minorities did not choose but were forced against their will to become a part of the U.S. society.* Unlike the immigrant minorities, involuntary minorities as a group do less well on IQ tests (Brand, 1996; Jensen, 1994; Suzuki & Gutkin, 1994b; Valencia & Aburto, 1991). The reasons include a longer history of mistreatment by White Americans, the absence of the incentive motivational factors that help the immigrants, and the psychological and social responses of involuntary minorities to their mistreatment. We turn now to a specific examination of Black Americans as involuntary minorities.

BLACK AMERICANS, INVOLUNTARY
MINORITY STATUS AND IQ

In 1972, Arthur Jensen reported to a U.S. Senate Committee that, unlike other ethnic groups, Black Americans had not achieved their expected representation in occupations requiring the intellectual skills of the White middle class. His explanation was that Blacks lack the adequate genetic endowment (i.e., the panhuman genotype) for such mental abilities. The occupations on Jensen's list included accounting, architecture, college professorship, engineering, law, natural sciences, proprietorship, and technical jobs (Jensen, 1972; see also Herrnstein & Murray, 1994). Jensen had also stated a few years earlier (1969, pp. 76–79) that Blacks failed to achieve their expected representation in these high-status occupations in spite of the elimination of employment barriers by the civil rights legislation of the 1960s.

The problem with Jensen's explanation is threefold. First, it erroneously assumes that the passage of the legislation to eliminate employment barriers immediately ended the barriers in practice (see Carnoy, 1994). Second, it fails to consider how the length of time it would take Blacks "to catch up" with Whites because of generations of exclusion *as a group* from White middle-class education and occupations. Third, it fails to consider the cognitive impacts of excluding generations of Black Americans from education and occupations that serve as amplifiers of middle-class intellectual skills.

We do not dispute the observation that American Blacks as a group achieve lower cognitive test scores than White Americans, but do dispute claims that either the genetic endowment of Blacks or that *mere cultural differences* between Blacks and Whites account for the observed differences. As we see it, three interrelated sets of factors account for the lower cognitive test scores attained by Black Americans. These are long-standing and ongoing social and economic discrimination by White Americans, the lack of historically induced incentive motivation, and Black cultural responses to involuntary minority status.

Discrimination falls into four categories: (a) exclusion from cultural amplifiers of White middle-class intellectual skills; (b) confinement to segregated and inferior education; (c) a job ceiling; and (d) expressive discrimination. The first three have been dealt with adequately elsewhere (Ogbu, 1978, 1981, 1986a, 1986b). We confine ourselves here to a discussion of role of expressive discrimination in the suppression of Black cognitive test scores.

Expressive discrimination includes both White people's beliefs that Black Americans are inferior to them in culture, language, and intelligence (Johnson, 1969/1939; Myrdal, 1944, p. 100) and White refusal to acknowledge and reward Black intellectual and other accomplishments (Myrdal, 1944, p. 100; *Newsweek*, February 26, 1979, p. 48; Ogbu, 1989). The publication of *The Bell Curve* in 1994 by Herrnstein and Murray is a reminder that the beliefs that

Blacks are inferior to Whites still exist even in White "scientific" mind. As described later in our discussion of Black responses, these views adversely affect Black performance on IQ tests in part because Blacks internalize the White beliefs.

Unlike voluntary minorities, the historical experiences of Black American does not suggest that assimilation is possible or that accommodation to White, middle-class practices would result in educational or economic success. Black Americans have *no prior expectation* that, for them, getting White education or high IQ test scores leads to "getting ahead." In general, Blacks have a *negative frame of comparison* and no "back home" situation to compare. Instead they compare their situation to that of White Americans and usually conclude that they are worse off than White people because of White discrimination. Unlike immigrants, if things do not work out in America, Blacks cannot return home. Blacks seem to have an *ambivalent belief* about the role of education (and test scores) in striving to get ahead in the United States. They wish they could get ahead through high test scores and good education, but, as we discuss next, many come to believe they cannot. Conscious and unconscious awareness of the dismal returns for their investment in education reduces the motivation to maximize their test scores.

Prior to changes in opportunity structure in the civil rights era of the 1960s, some Blacks were involved within their segregated ecological niche with amplifiers of intellectual skills similar to those of the White middle class. For example, some Blacks held professional jobs in segregated educational and health institutions. Others, such as preachers and hustlers also engaged in activities that required and enhanced "operational intelligence" or "smartness" similar to the intellectual skills of the White middle class. But it does not appear that their superior intellectual skills or smartness were reflected in cognitive test scores. Current studies suggest that, as a group, Blacks still score one standard deviation below White Americans on IQ tests. Furthermore, this gap between two racial groups remains even when those tested are from similar backgrounds. Thus, after an extensive review of the literature, Gordon and Bhattacharrya (1994) concluded that "When Blacks and White groups are matched for education, socioeconomic status, and residence, differences in intelligence test scores are only slightly reduced" (p. 896).

It appears that involvement in activities requiring and enhancing intellectual skills similar to those of White people or possessing such intellectual skills does not necessarily mean that Blacks will perform like Whites. Some psychologists have observed that the test scores Black children obtain in IQ tests like the WISC do not represent their true intellectual ability or the best they can do (Naiven, Hoffmann, & Bierbryer, 1969; cited in Dreger, 1973). Dreger (1973, p. 207) adds that this is in line with the experience of many psychologists who have dealt with young-sters, especially from deprived Black culture. In non-test situations (psychologists) observe the youngster communicating with his peers, solving problems, and utilizing conceptualizations that they are accustomed to associate with IQ of a Binet type ten to fifteen points higher than the youngster actually gets on a formal test.

Our own observations and our discussions with teachers, students, parents, and other adults in the Black community support this view, and lead us to conclude that the IQ test scores of Black Americans do not necessarily reflect "true ability" or "the best they can do."

In order to understand this phenomenon it is necessary to understand how individual and group experiences with IQ and other tests shape individuals' perceptions of the values and usefulness of tests. This is true for all groups—majority and minority, high status and low status. We focus on Blacks' perceptions of their *experiences with IQ test scores* rather than with education in general. By focusing on perceptions of the role of IQ test scores in their lives, we wish to emphasize the importance of the cultural meanings of IQ tests, not the meanings assigned to the tests by psychologists. How people behave in the tests is not determined by the beliefs of psychologists, but rather by the beliefs of the test takers.

Because cognitive and other tests were often used as instruments of racial discrimination, Blacks are unsure of the benefits of taking the tests or scoring well. They seem to perceive no connection between test scores and getting ahead. From an anthropological point of view, taking IQ and other "standard-ized" tests is a cultural and instrumental behavior which leads to predictable results that are either desirable or undesirable. People will continue or perse-vere in certain behaviors if the behaviors produce predictable and desirable results; they will discontinue the behaviors or reduce their efforts if the behav-iors produce predictable and undesirable results. The predictability is sup-ported by cultural beliefs that are acquired through socialization (Spindler, 1976). Such is the case with the cultural behavior of IQ test taking.

Black Americans did not become minorities in the United States with the expectation that in order to become successful in life they would have to get high IQ test scores. Furthermore, their individual and collective experiences have not enabled them to develop this belief. For many generations after slavery there was no connection between how well they did on IQ tests and their ability to get good jobs, earn decent wages, or achieve social recogni-tion and social positions, as individuals and as a group. This lack of connec-tion between performance on IQ tests and upward mobility continues today in some segments of the Black population.

Ethnographic research in Black communities suggests that the failure of individuals and the group to get ahead because of IQ test scores has, indeed, not generated a motivation to strive for the highest test scores. It has also not made "good performance" or scoring high on IQ tests a culturally valued behavior. In fact, it has sometimes resulted in the rejection of test scores as a criterion for employment or school admission. It is true that when questioned, Blacks say that they believe that good test scores are important for getting ahead, but many also believe that for them, *Black Americans,* good test scores are not enough. Some Blacks even interpret the test scores as a "White-made" rule unfair to Black people; and some suspect that IQ tests are designed to keep Black people from getting ahead. Partly for these reasons they sometimes attack test requirements for hiring and promotion and try to change them, rather than attempt to meet them.

The following cases from ethnographic research in Black communities in California suggest that Blacks perceive a dismal connection between their performance on IQ tests and their chances for economic advancement. The first incident is a dispute over the use of IQ test scores in hiring civil service employees in Stockton, California.

At several city council meetings in 1969, Blacks and Mexican Americans complained that they were systematically excluded from city jobs. Specifically, they complained that by requiring candidates for hiring or promotion to pass "biased" IQ tests the city effectively excluded them. They argued that because of the testing requirement only 30 out of 886 city employees in 1969 were Black. There were a similar number of Mexican American city workers.

Because of the repeated allegations the city council set up "a workshop in equality" to study the problem. Verbal and written presentations at the workshop indicated that the city charter written in 1935, stipulated tests for physical or mental abilities, but also required that tests should be job-related. Few Blacks "passed" the cognitive test required for employment and advanced to the interview stage of the hiring process. Of those Blacks who did pass, most were employed in manual labor jobs.

Whites and Blacks had very different opinions about the use of IQ test scores for hiring and promotions and very different explanations for the low test scores of minorities. City officials justified using the tests, claiming they provided an objective criterion to select people for city jobs, and that it placed civil service above politics and ensured high standard in city civil service. City officials explained that Black and Mexican Americans scored lower than Whites on the test because of their "disadvantaged" cultural and family backgrounds. The officials promised to establish remedial programs to prepare minorities to get higher scores on the tests.

Blacks and Mexican Americans insisted that the test was culturally biased, the designated minimum test score for eligibility for interviews excluded the average person from city jobs, and that so-called "unqualified" minorities obtained similar jobs in the private sector. Finally, they alleged that both city and county officials used prisoners (many of them minorities) who had not taken or passed the civil service tests to do some city jobs that minorities as ordinary citizens were denied because they failed the IQ tests.

There was a general feeling among Blacks that IQ tests for civil service jobs were used to exclude minorities. Furthermore, a high score on the tests did not translate into a job offer for Blacks. To obtain that they also had to pass an oral interview conducted by a White panel. Knowing that they would fail the oral interview even if they scored high on written IQ tests did not encourage them to try harder on the written tests. The informant below, a Black school counselor, described the outrage and distrust of many Blacks in Stockton about the civil service IQ examination process.

> The civil service test consists of a written IQ test, . . . a written examination area test, and it consists of an oral interview test. Now, unless they have changed it, the oral interview counts as much as the written. So, if three people would go down and take the test, see, you go take the IQ examination, the written examination, the oral examination. You pass 'em in that order. Now, we have eliminated and weeded out up to the oral examination; now 4 or 5 people go in for this oral examination. You're sitting down in front of 5 other, . . . White middle-class people for your oral examination. How would you feel? Would you feel that you would be on equal terms as the lily White boy that went up there and sit down in front of these five people for an oral examination? And that oral examination is counting as much as the written examination. You're gonna tell me that in the history of Stockton not one Black man has ever qualified and passed a fireman's examination. A Black man don't qualify on a fireman's test? Hell! I can't take a water hose and put out a fire. Not one has ever passed a fireman's test, oral examination!!"

Based on their own experiences some Stockton Blacks believed that taking or passing the IQ and other tests did not help Black people get ahead. Rather they believed that the tests intended to screen out Blacks.

> In my case they didn't allow me the opportunity. I went to the employment office (and) I passed this test. I made eighty,[5] the man (told me) when I came downstairs. He said, 'Oh, you didn't make it," he says, "you just made eighty." So, what is the passing mark? They didn't tell me. He told me, he said, "You made eighty, but you didn't pass it". Well, I went on and forgot it because, see, this White man had told me this. I then began to think about this. I said, "Eighty?" And the more I thought about (it). . . . Then one day I decided I would ask one of the men in the employment office. He said, "You passed that test." He told me I passed but I didn't get no job. Because at that time they only hired a White person, the Mexican and two or more Negroes to make it look good and that was all . . . This was only a gimmick to keep the Negro out of a job and

---

[5]70 points was the passing score.

he didn't really know what was really going on. That is one reason I didn't believe in this paper business when you go and look for a job.

Over the years we have interviewed many Blacks who described similar experiences of their own and of their friends and relatives. Some reported or believed that apprenticeship examinations in their communities were used to exclude Blacks; written IQ tests were used to screen out Blacks; and test score cutoffs were used to deny Blacks promotions on the job. Some informants gave examples of White people who were hired or promoted without taking IQ tests that were required of minorities. Children were often present during our interviews. Older children joined in discussing Black experiences with tests in school and for employment. They, too, reported on their own experiences with "unfair" tests and grading.

Employment and other opportunities for Blacks have improved since the civil rights legislation of the 1960s. However, these changes have not gone far enough or long enough and have not been experienced by a large enough number of Blacks to eliminate their doubts about the connection between getting high IQ test scores or doing well in school and getting ahead. Even as late as 1996 we continued to encounter and read about Black professionals—lawyers, doctors, and school administrators, who felt that they could not get jobs or were not paid appropriate wages in spite of their qualifications. They felt that despite accommodating to majority intellectual norms, they did not have the same opportunities as their White peers (see also Benjamin, 1991; Dill, 1982; Fashokun, 1996, personal communication; Matusow, 1989).

As a result of their experiences with IQ and other standardized tests it appears that many Blacks in Stockton and elsewhere do not see performance on IQ tests and, indeed, almost all other tests given by Whites as related to success. One also gains the impression from interviews and discussions with Black students, parents, and other members of the Black community that they have ambivalent beliefs about the instrumental value of the tests. In this situation it is difficult to imagine that parents encourage their children to maximize their IQ test scores. High test scores are not among the high cultural values. It is not surprising for some psychologists to observe Black youngsters behaving outside IQ test situation as if they had 10 points or more above their performance on the tests?

Another factor is the consequence of internalization of White Beliefs About Black Intellectual Ability. It is widely held in the Black community that White Americans believe that Blacks are intellectually inferior to them. The White beliefs have also become internalized in the thinking of many Blacks. Evidence of the internalization often shows up explicitly or implicitly during ethnographic interviews with Black school personnel, students, parents and others. One school counselor in Stockton, for example, said that White intellectual denigration of Blacks was prevalent in his school district just as it was in the college he attended in Arizona:

> If a kid is doing any work (in Stockton school district), he gets a C. If he does not do enough work he gets a C. And this isn't only found in elementary school. It's found in the junior and (senior) high schools. It's even found in our colleges. When I went to Arizona State, there were many teachers that said, "The most a Black person can get in my class is a C. I don't care what kind of work you do." . . . You know, the thing is, "Why it's just outright stereotypes of Black people. They feel there is no such a thing as an "A" Black person, a superior person. [What does the grade "A" mean? Superior?]. You can't give a Black person a superior grade when he's not a superior person. I've heard teachers say that. "I teach in North Stockton (mostly White area). (Therefore) I teach superior kids. I'm a superior teacher. You teach in South Stockton (mostly minority area). (Therefore) you teach below-normal kids and you're a below-normal teacher. "This is a status symbol that they attach to where they teach and where you work. In other words, White is good, Black is bad. Anyway it goes.

Our own study of the grading of one cohort of Black and Mexican American children in one elementary school in the same school district lent some support to the counselor's suggestion that teachers refused to reward minorities according to their intellectual accomplishments. We examined the grade records of 17 children over a 6-year period, from first to the sixth grade. Every year the children were given the same grade, C, regardless of their academic improvements or lack of it, all which were noted by teachers' in the children's files (Ogbu, 1977).

Black children become aware of the White beliefs quite early in life and begin to internalize them. In our study of more than 1,300 precollege Black students in Oakland, California, 82% reported that people in their families and community think that White Americans do not believe that Black Americans are as intelligent as White people (Ogbu, 1998). In contrast, only 14% of the immigrant Chinese and 50% of the semi-immigrant Mexican Americans in the same study reported similar family and community thinking (see Fig. 1.8). Further insight into Black students' sensitivity to the issue of intelligence can be seen in their response to other questions in the study. Black students "wished" they could prove to White Americans that they are wrong. Thus when asked why minorities went to school Blacks asserted nearly three times as often (18%) as Chinese (7%) and twice as often as Mexican Americans (9%) that they went to school *to show Whites that they are smart* (Simons, Ogbu, & Bolton, n.d.).

Many Black adults seem to live with the sense of intellectual inferiority because they were classified as "mentally retarded" in their schooldays. Take the case of one mother in the following interview excerpt:

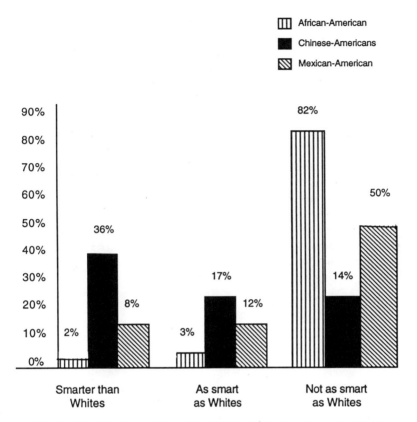

FIG. 1.8.   Minorities' perceptions of the beliefs of White Americans about their intellectual abilities vis-à-vis White intellectual abilities.

When I was a kid, it must have been in the 3rd or 4th grade, I was given a test. This White psychologist had come to the school to test the students . . . The test she gave me was like a little puzzle, another was a chart . . . I asked her, was I doing fine? She said I was doing fine . . . And so, then, a month later, my mother got the results and it said I was retarded . . . And it has affected me from my childhood, until adulthood, until now.

Another incident at a preschool–afterschool class during a Black history month program in February of 1996 suggests that children begin quite early to internalize the beliefs that Blacks are not as intelligent as White people. Three Black Americans from the San Francisco Health Department made a health presentation to 4 to 10 year olds, most of whom were Black. One of the three public health officials was a doctor who talked about what she and other doctors do. When asked what they wanted to be many children replied, "doctors, architects, dentists, and lawyers." Asked what they would do to achieve their goals they responded almost in unison, "Get good education." Finally, when questioned about what might make it difficult to attain their career goals a 7-year-old Black child said that Black people cannot be doctors because they are not good (i.e., not intelligent) enough. Several other Black children agreed. In a discussion later among the health officials and the staff of the day-care center, it was repeatedly noted by these adults that in their communities, Black children begin as early as 3 or 4 years of age to understand that White people discriminate against Black people and that White people do not believe that Blacks are as smart as they are. To further illustrate the serious-ness of the internalization problem, the doctor described a visit to her health center by a 3½ year old boy. The social worker who brought the boy had told him that it would be a good experience for him to see a Black doctor. The boy replied that there were no Black doctors. When the social worker introduced him to the narrator, the doctor, the boy repeatedly asked her if she was *a real doctor*. He said that "All doctors are supposed to be White."

One consequence of the internalization is self-doubt, coupled with resig-nation in intellectual performance. The phenomenon of self-doubt can be seen in this excerpt from our interview with a Black school administrator:

> The Black kids do not pay any attention to the test scores. They're resigned to the idea that (White) kids are smarter than they are. They've been told that they can't achieve and they accept it . . . The (Black) kids will say, talking about math and all, they'll say, "You know, we're not as smart as they (i.e., White stu-dents) are." When a girl made this statement, and we were talking about how smart they are in math, "You know, we aren't as smart as they are. They don't have any muscles, we have muscles (for sports and athletics)."

Self-doubt is also widespread among adults, including parents, as Luster (1992) discovered in her study in San Francisco. The women she studied, most of them parents of children in the public school, were attending a community school to prepare for the GED. Luster described her own effort and the effort of the school personnel to convince the women that they could pass their tests. A description of one incident illustrates the self-doubts of these parents (Luster, 1992, pp. 240–241).

> One day a woman who had been studying several months for the GED social studies test was in the lounge arguing with her instructor. The instructor was urging her to take the test, telling her she had studied enough, she had scored well on the pretests, she was ready and should go to the testing center and take the test. The woman kept insisting that she was not ready, that she did not know enough to take the test. This exchange turned into a shouting match—the teacher insisting, "You can!" the woman insisting, "I can't!" While the vehe-mence of the exchange may not have been typical, the essence was.

Because of their internalization of White belief that they are not as intelligent as White people and because of their intellectual treatment in school, some Blacks are highly suspicious of IQ tests; they also have self-doubts that they can do well on these tests. Many Black parents have difficulty effectively encouraging their children to perform well in IQ and other tests. Children themselves have difficulty striving to maximize their IQ test scores.

The need to maintain group identity also contributes to the low IQ test scores among some Blacks because it affects the ability and willingness of minority group members to accommodate to or adopt certain "White ways" (e.g., language) that are conducive to high test scores. As an involuntary minority group, the culture, dialect, and group identity of Black Americans have, to a large extent, been forged in opposition to those of White Americans. Partly for this reason some Blacks perceive accommodating to White ways as a subtractive process: they think that this requires them to give up their own ways of behaving and communicating and their collective identities. It is significant that some Black intellectuals consider it "assimilation" for Black children to learn the standard English (Steele, 1992). Ethnographic research in Black communities in California support this view. This interpretation results in opposition by peer groups to individuals who are accommodating to White ways; they are suspected of abandoning their Black identity and threatening racial solidarity in favor of Whites oppressors. Some Blacks avoid adopting White ways out of fear that they may, indeed, lose their Black identity and find themselves outside the Black community (see DeVos, 1984).

The target areas of opposition or avoidance include areas historically defined as White prerogatives, first by White people themselves and then conceded to by minorities. These are arenas in which White people long believed that only Whites could perform well, and where few Blacks were actually given the opportunity to perform or were adequately rewarded when they succeeded. These are also areas where the criteria for evaluation of performance and rewards are established and controlled by White Americans or their minority representatives. As Blacks see it, the criteria for evaluation of performance and rewards usually involve demonstration of the "right behavior," "proper speech," and the "right skills" which mean "White behaviors," "White speech," and "White skills." Performance on "intelligence" (IQ) tests and high-status jobs in the larger economy are examples of such arenas. For some, to do well in these arenas has acquired a secondary meaning; it has become a symbol of affiliating with White oppressors and a loss of Black collective identity. Those who think this way criticize their peers for accommodating to White ways and question their *bona fide identity*. The resistance to striving for high IQ test scores or good performance may be conscious or unconscious. In both Stockton (Ogbu, 1974) and in Oakland (Ogbu, 1998), many "smart" Black students did not show their smartness in class because they were afraid of being rejected by other Black students.

CONCLUSIONS

Neither heredity nor culture is adequate to explain the disparity in cognitive test scores of Black and White Americans. To understand the persistence of this disparity over time it is necessary to look at the full environment or ecocultural niche occupied by Whites and Blacks. It is not sufficient to define environment narrowly (as many have done) as the family, the neighborhood, or socioeconomic status. From that perspective, it is assumed that some people develop more or better intelligence because they come from a rich environment where they received better or more stimulation in early childhood. Rather, environment must be seen to also encompass the social conditions of the larger society. The social and economic position a group finds itself in affects not only access to the cultural amplifiers of cognitive skills, but the manner in which individuals approach the skills measured by cognitive tests, and their attitudes toward the tests themselves.

From this perspective, we have shown in this chapter that there is no "generic intelligence" that children develop through "generic socialization." Families stimulate or socialize their children to develop the adaptive intellectual skills in their ecocultural niche. And they do so according to formulae evolved in their culture. Family socialization itself is not the origin of intelligence.

Finally, findings from cross-cultural research support the view that cognitive development and intelligence is a life-long process. Changes in the ecocultural niche due to migration, economic change, the introduction of new technologies, or schooling often lead the development or enhancement of some cognitive skills. Even non-Western adults faced with new situations "develop" the Western middle-class intellectual skills associated with new activities (Cole, Gay, Glick, & Sharp, 1971; Cole & Scribner, 1974; Greenfield, 1966; Stevenson, 1982).

We are not saying that the family and early intellectual stimulation are not important for children's intellectual development. What we are saying is that the environment that influences the intellectual development of all children, including involuntary and caste-like minority children, include more than these. They include the amplifiers of intellectual skills available in the ecocultural niche of the children *and* the cultural meanings of IQ tests. To explain the differences between Blacks and Whites in cognitive development or IQ test performance, we must compare the two populations in terms of amplifiers of intelligence and cultural meanings of IQ tests.

ACKNOWLEDGMENT

Research for this chapter was supported by faculty research fund, University of California, Berkeley.

REFERENCES

Abraham, R. D. (1972). Joking: The training of the man of words in talking broad. In T. Kochman (Ed.), *Rappin' and stylin' out: Communication in urban Black America* (pp. 215–240). Urbana: University of Illinois Press.

Benasich, A. A., & Brooks-Gunn, J. (1996). Maternal attitudes and knowledge of child-rearing: Associations with family and child outcomes. *Child Development, 67*, 1186–1205.

Benjamin, L. (1991). *The Black elite: Facing the color line in the twilight of the twentieth century.* Chicago: Nelson-Hall.

Berreman, G. D. (1960). Caste in India and the United States. *American Journal of Sociology, LXI*, 120–127.

Berreman, G. D. (1966). Caste in cross-cultural perspective: Organizational components. In G. A. DeVos & H. Wagatsuma (Eds.), *Japan's invisible race: Caste in culture and personality* (pp. 275–307). Berkeley: University of California Press.

Berreman, G. D. (1972). Race, caste, and other invidious distinctions in social stratification. *Race, 13*, 385–414.

Berreman, G. D. (1981). Social inequality: A cross-cultural analysis. In G. D. Berreman (Ed.), *Social inequality: Comparative and developmental approaches* (pp. 3–40). New York: Academic Press.

Bohannan, P., & van der Elst (1998). *Asking and listening: Ethnography as personal adaptation.* Prospect Heights, IL: Waveland Press.

Bouchard, T. J., Jr. (1997). IQ similarity in twins raised apart: Findings and responses to critics. In R. J. Sternberg & E. L. Grigorenko (Eds.), *Intelligence, heredity, and environment* (pp. 126–160). Cambridge, England: Cambridge University Press.

Brand, C. (1996). 'g', Genes and pedagogy: A reply to seven (lamentable) chapters. In D. K. Detterman (Ed.), *Current topics in human intelligence: Vol. 5. The environment* (pp. 113–120). Norwood, NJ: Ablex.

Brody, G. H., & Stoneman, Z. (1992). Child competence and developmental goals among rural Black families: Investigating the links. In I. E. Sigel, A. V. McGillicuddy-Delisi, & J. J. Goodnow (Eds.), *Parental belief systems: The psychological consequences for children* (Vol. 2, pp. 415–431). Hillsdale, NJ: Lawrence Erlbaum Associates.

Brooks-Gunn, J., P. K. Klebanov, & G. J. Duncan (1996). Ethnic differences in children's intelligence test scores: Role of economic deprivation, home environment, and maternal characteristics. *Child Development, 67*, 396–408.

Carnoy, M. (1994). *Faded dreams: The politics and economics of race in America.* New York: Cambridge University Press.

Chopra, S. L. (1966). Relationship of caste system with measured intelligence and academic achievement of students in India. *Social Forces, 44*, 573–576.

Cole, M., & Cole, S. R. (1993). *The development of children.* New York: Scientific American Books.

Cole, M., Gay, J., Glick, J. A., & Sharp, D. W. (1971). *The cultural context of learning and thinking: An exploration in experimental anthropology.* New York: Basic Books.

Cole, M., & Scribner, S. (1974). *Culture and thought: A psychological introduction.* New York: Wiley.

Das, J. P., & Khurana, A. K. S. (1988). Caste and cognitive process. In S. H. Irvine & J. W. Berry (Eds.), *Human abilities in cultural context* (pp. 487–508). Cambridge, England: Cambridge University Press.

Dasen, P. (1974). The influence of ecology, culture and European contact on cognitive development in Australian Aborigines. In R. P. Dasen (Ed.), *Culture and cognition* (pp.). London: Methuen.

Davis, A., Gardner, B. B., & Gardner, M. R. (1965). *Deep south: Social anthropological study of caste and class* (Abridged ed.). Chicago: The University of Chicago Press.

DeVos, G. A. (1973). Japan's outcasts: The problem of the Burakumin. In B. Whitaker (Ed.), *The fourth world: Victims of group oppression.* New York: Schocken.

DeVos, G. A. (1984, April). *Ethnic persistence and role degradation: An illustration from Japan.* Paper presented at the American-Soviet Symposium on Contemporary Ethnic Processes in the USA and the USSR. New Orleans, LA.

DeVos, G. A., & Wagatsuma, H. (Eds.). (1967). *Japan's invisible race.* Berkeley: University of California Press.

Dill, K. (1992, December). *Getting good skills: Racism and the employment of African-American hospital workers.* Paper presented at the American Anthropological Association annual meeting, San Francisco, CA.

Dollard, J. (1957). *Caste and class in a southern town* (3rd ed.), Garden City, NY: Doubleday.

Dreger, R. M. (1973). Intellectual functioning. In K. S. Miller & R. M. Dreger (Ed.), *Comparative studies of Blacks and Whites in the United States* (pp. 185–229). New York: Seminar Press.

Fischer, C. S., Hout, M., Jankowski, M. S., Lucas, S. R., Swidler, A., & Voss, K. (1996). *Inequality by design: Cracking the bell curve myth.* Princeton, NJ: Princeton University Press.

Foster, H. L. (1974). *Ribbin', jivin' and playin' the dozens: The unrecognized dilemma of inner-city schools.* Cambridge, MA: Ballinger.

Ghuman, P. A. (1978). Nature of intellectual development of Punjabi children. *International Journal of Psychology, 13*(4), 282–294.

Gibson, M. A. (1988). *Accommodation without assimilation: Sikh immigrants in an American high school.* Ithaca, NY: Cornell University Press.

Gordon, E. W., & Bhattacharya, M. (1994). Race and intelligence. In R. J. Stenberg (Ed.), *Encyclopedia of intelligence, Vol. 2* (pp. 889–899). New York: Macmillan.

Grebler, L. Moore, J. W., & Guzman, R. (Eds.). (1970). *The Mexican-American people: The nation's second largest minority.* New York: Free Press.

Greenfield, P. M. (1966). On culture and conservation. In J. S. Bruner, R. R. Oliver, & P. M. Greenfield (Eds.), *Studies in cognitive growth.* New York: Wiley.

Greenfield, P. M. (1998). The cultural evolution of IQ. In U. Neisser (Ed.), *The rising curve: Long-term gains in IQ test scores and what they mean* (pp. 81–122). Washington, DC: American Psychological Association.

Harkness, S., & Super, C. M. (1992). Parental ethno-theories in action. In I. E. Sigel, A. V. McGillicuddy-Delisi, & J. J. Goodnow (Eds.), *Parental belief systems: The psychological consequences for children* (2nd ed., pp. 373–391). Hillsdale, NJ: Lawrence Erlbaum Associates.

Hannerz, U. (1969). *Soulside.* New York: Columbia University Press.

Helms, J. E. (1992). Why is there no study of cultural equivalence in standardized cognitive ability testing? *American Psychologist, 47,* 1083–1101.

Herrnstein, R. J., & Murray, C. (1994). *The bell curve: Intelligence and class structure in American life.* New York: Free Press.

Ho, D. Y. F. (1994). Cognitive socialization in Confucian heritage cultures. In P. A. Greenfield & R. R. Cocking (Eds.), *Cross-cultural roots of minority children* (pp. 285–313). Hillsdale, NJ: Lawrence Erlbaum Associates.

Ito, H. (1966). Japan's outcasts in the United States. In G. A. DeVos & H. Wagatsuma (Eds.), *Japan's invisible race.* Berkeley: University of California Press.

Jensen, A. R. (1969). How much can we boost IQ and scholastic achievement? *Harvard Educational Review, 39,* 1–123.

Jensen, A. R. (1971). The race x sex x ability interaction. In R. Cancro (Ed.), *Intelligence: Genetic and environmental influences* (pp. 107–161). New York: Grune and Stratton.

Jensen, A. R. (1972). *Statement of Dr. Arthur R. Jensen, Senate Select Committee on Education* (February 24, 1972). Unpublished manuscript.

Jensen, A. R. (1973). *Educability & group differences.* New York: Random House.

Jensen, A. R. (1994). Race and IQ scores. In R. J. Stenberg (Ed.), *Encyclopedia of intelligence* (pp. 899–907). New York: Macmillan.

Johnson, G. B. (1969/1939). The stereotype of the American Negro. In O. Klineberg (Ed.), *Characteristics of the American Negro* (pp. 1–22). New York: Harper.

Kegard Prefecture (1989). *The present situation of discrimination against Buraku. Research on the Conditions of Buraku.* Unpublished manuscript.

Kochman, T. (1972). *Rappin' and stylin out: Communication in urban Black America.* Urbana: University of Illinois Press.

Kyllonen, P. C. (1994). Information processing. In R. J. Stenberg (Ed.), *Encyclopedia of intelligence, Vol. 1* (pp. 580–588). New York: Macmillan.

Lee, Y. (1991). Koreans in Japan and the United States. In M. A. Gibson & J. U. Ogbu (Eds.), *Minority status and schooling: A comparative study of immigrant and involuntary minorities* (pp. 131–167). New York: Garland.

Loehlin, J. C., Horn, J. M., & Willerman, L. (1997). Heredity, environment, and IQ in the Texas adoption project. In R. J. Sternberg & E. L. Grigorenko (Eds.), *Intelligence, heredity, and environment* (pp. 105–125), Cambridge, England: Cambridge University Press.

Lyman, S. M. (1973). *The Black American in sociological thought: A failure of perspective.* New York: Capricorn Books.

Luster, L. (1992). *Schooling, survival, and struggle: Black women and the GED.* Unpublished doctoral dissertation, School of Eduction, Stanford University.

Mack, R. (1968). Functions of institutionalized discrimination. In R. Mack (Ed.), *Race, class and power* (pp. 341–344). New York: The American Book Company.

Matusow, B. (1989). Alone together: What do you do when the dream hasn't come true, when you're Black and middle-class and still shut out of White Washington, when it seems to quit trying? *The Washingtonian*, November, pp. 153–159, 282–290.

McBride, J. (1996). *The color of water: A Black man's tribute to his White mother.* New York: Riverhead Books.

Myrdal, G. (1944). *An American dilemma: The Negro problem and modern democracy* (Vol. 1). New York: Harper.

Naiven, B., Hoffmann, J., & Bierbryer (1969). The effects of subject's age, sex, race and socioeconomic status on psychologists' estimate of 'True IQ' from WISC scores. *Journal of Clinical Psychology, 25,* 271–274.

Neisser, U., Boodoo, G. Bouchard, T. J., Boykin, A. W. Brody, N., Ceci, S. J., Halpern, D. F., Loehlin, J. C., Perloff, R., Sternberg, R. J., & Urbina, S. (1996). Intelligence: Knowns and unknowns. *American Psychologist, 51,* 77–101.

Newsweek Magazine (1979). How Whites think about Blacks. February 26, p. 48.

Ogbu, J. U. (1974). *The next generation: An ethnography of education in an urban neighborhood.* New York: Academic Press.

Ogbu, J. U. (1977). Racial stratification and education: The case of Stockton, California. *ICRD Bulletin, 12*(3), 1–26.

Ogbu, J. U. (1978). *Minority education and caste: The American system in cross-cultural perspective.* New York: Academic Press.

Ogbu, J. U. (1979). Social stratification and socialization of competence. *Anthropology and Education Quarterly, 10*(1), 3–20.

Ogbu, J. U. (1981). Origins of human competence: A cultural-ecological perspective. *Child Development, 52,* 413–429.

Ogbu, J. U. (1982). Socialization: A cultural ecological perspective. In K. Borman (Ed.), *The socialization of children in a changing society* (pp. 251–265). Hillsdale, NJ: Lawrence Erlbaum Associates.

Ogbu, J. U. (1986a). Castelike stratification as a risk factor in intellectual development. In D. C. Farran & J. D. McKinney (Eds.), *The concept of risk in intellectual and psychological development* (pp. 83–119). New York: Academic Press.

Ogbu, J. U. (1986b). The consequences of the American caste system. In U. Neisser (Ed.), *The school achievement of minority children: New perspectives* (pp. 19–56). Hillsdale, NJ: Lawrence Erlbaum Associates.

Ogbu, J. U. (1989). Cultural boundaries and minority youth orientation toward work preparation. In D. Stern & D. Eichorn (Eds.), *Adolescence and work: Influences of social structure, labor markets, and culture* (pp. 101–140). Hillsdale, NJ: Lawrence Erlbaum Associates.

Ogbu, J. U. (1991). Low school performance as an adaptation: The case of Blacks in Stockton, CA. In M. A. Gibson & J. U. Ogbu (Eds.), *Minority status and schooling: A comparative study of immigrant and involuntary minorities* (pp. 249–286). New York: Garland Press.

Ogbu, J. U. (1994a). Culture and intelligence. In J. Sternberg (Ed.), *The encyclopedia of intelligence* (Vol. 1, pp. 228–238). New York: Macmillan.

Ogbu, J. U. (1994b). From cultural differences to differences in cultural frame of reference. In P. M. Greenfield & R. R. Cocking (Eds.), *Cross-cultural roots of minority child development* (pp. 365–391). Hillsdale, NJ: Lawrence Erlbaum Associates.

Ogbu, J. U. (1998). *Community forces and minority education strategies: The second part of the problem*. Unpublished manuscript, Department of Anthropology, University of California, Berkeley.

Ogbu, J. U., & Matute-Bianchi, M. E. (1986). Understanding sociocultural factors: Knowledge, identity, and school adjustment. *Beyond language: Social and cultural factors in schooling language minority students* (pp. 73–142), Bilingual Eduction Office, California State Department of Education. Evaluation, Dissemination & Assessment Center, California State University, LA.

Perkins, E. (1975). *Home is a dirty street*. Chicago, IL: Third World Press.

Plomin, R. (1994). Nature, nurture and development. In R. J. Sternberg (Ed.), *Encyclopedia of intelligence, Vol. 1* (pp. 754–764). New York: Macmillan.

Posner, J. K. (1982). The development of mathematical knowledge in two West African societies. *Child Development, 53*, 200–208.

Price-Williams, D. R. (1961). A study concerning concepts of conservation of quantities among primitive children. *Acta Psychological, 18*, 293–305.

Price-Williams, D. R., Gordon, W., & Ramirez, M. (1969). Skills and conservation: A study of pottery-making children. *Developmental Psychology, 1*, 769.

Rangari, A. (1987). Caste affiliation, sex, area of residence and socio-economic status as a source of variation in intelligence of students. *Indian Psychological Review, 32*(5–6), 43–49.

Sameroff, A. J., Seifer, Baldwin, & Baldwin (1993). Stability from pre-school to adolescence: The influence of social and family risk factors. *Child Development, 64*, 80–97.

Saxe, G. B., & Posner, J. (1983). The development of numerical cognition: Cross-cultural perspectives. In H. P. Ginsburg (Ed.), *The development of mathematical thinking* (pp. 291–317). New York: Academic Press.

Scribner, S., & Cole, M. (1973). Cognitive consequences of formal and informal education. *Science, 182*, 553–559.

Shimahara, K. N. (1991). Social mobility and education: Burakumin in Japan. In M. A. Gibson & J. U. Ogbu (Eds.), *Minority status and schooling: A comparative study of immigrant and involuntary minorities* (pp. 342–353). New York: Garland Press.

Simons, H. D., Ogbu, J. U., & Bolton, K. (n.d.). *Ogbu theory for teachers*. Unpublished manuscript, Department of Anthropology, School of Education, University of California, Berkeley.

Singh, B. R. (1996). The genetic-environmental influences on individual cognitive functioning or IQ. *Educational Studies, 22*, 41–56.

Spindler, G. D. (1976). From omnibus to linkages: Cultural transmission models. In J. I. Roberts & S. K. Akinsanya (Eds.), *Educational patterns and cultural configurations: The anthropology of education* (pp. 177–102). New York: David McKay.

Steele, C. (1992). Race and the schooling of Black Americans. *The Atlantic Monthly*, April, pp. 68–75.
Stevenson, H. W. (1982). Influences of schooling on cognitive development. In D. A. Wagner & H. W. Stevenson (Eds.), *Cultural perspectives on child development* (pp. 208–224). San Francisco: W. H. Freeman.
Suzuki, L. A., & Gutkin, T. B. (1994a). Asian Americans. In R. J. Sternberg (Ed.), *Encyclopedia of intelligence, Vol. 1* (pp. 140–144). New York: Macmillan.
Suzuki, L. A., & Gutkin, T. B. (1994b). Hispanic. In R. J. Sternberg (Ed.), *Encyclopedia of intelligence, Vol. 1* (pp. 539–545). New York: Macmillan.
Time Magazine (1973). Japan: The invisible race. pp. 311–32, January 8.
Travers, J. R. (1982). Testing in educational placement: Issues and evidence. In K. Heller, W. H. Holtzman, & S. Messick (Eds.), *Placing children in special education: A strategy for equity* (pp. 230–261). Washington, DC: National Academy Press.
Valencia, R. R., & Aburto, S. (1991). The uses and abuses of educational testing: Chicanos as a case in point. In R. R. Valencia (Ed.), *Chicano school failure and success* (pp. 203–251). New York: The Falmer Press.
Vernon, P. E. (1969). *Intelligence and cultural environment.* London: Methuen.
Vernon, P. E. (1982). *The abilities and achievements of Orientals in North America.* New York: Academic Press.
Vraniak, D. A. (1994). Native Americans. In R. J. Sternberg (Ed.), *Encyclopedia of intelligence, Vol. 2* (pp. 747–754). New York: Macmillan.
Warner, W. L. (1965). Introduction. In A. Davis, B. B. Gardner, & M. R. Gardner, *Deep south: A social anthropological study of caste and class* (pp. 3–14). Chicago: University of Chicago Press.
Warner, W. L. (1970). A methodological note. In St. Clair Drake & H. R. Cayton (Eds.), *Black metropolis: A study of Negro life in a northern city, Vol. 2* (pp. 769–782). New York: Harcourt, Brace & World.

Family Matters: A Systems View of Family Effects on Children's Cognitive Health

Barbara H. Fiese
Syracuse University

Recently, the American family has come under attack by researchers and the popular press alike. On the one hand, the decline of the family as an institution has been blamed for the increase in troubled youth (e.g., Popenoe, 1993). On the other hand, outside of their genetic contribution and choice of neighborhood, parents have been cast out as major contributors to their children's social and cognitive development (e.g., Harris, 1995). Despite these claims, many parents believe that they do indeed have a positive effect on their children's lives (Miller, 1988). Parents invest their time and money into raising children, in part, because they feel that they make a difference. Why, then, is it difficult to accept the family as a distinct socializing agent? This question becomes particularly poignant when considering children's cognitive development and their future as intelligent shapers of society. Considerable attention has been paid to family factors that increase the child's risk for poor outcomes such as conduct disorder, mental health problems, and delinquency (e.g., Fiese, Wilder, & Bickham, 2000; Patterson, DeBaryshe, & Ramsey, 1989; Wagner & Reiss, 1995). However, less attention has been paid to how the family context may serve as a positive resource in fostering children's cognitive development and performance in academic settings.

In order to accurately portray the family in relation to child development it is necessary to clearly describe what constitutes family effects. Families are complex and highly organized groups that attempt to find meaning in their collective lives. Families come in different sizes, have different heritages, and endorse different values. In this chapter, a model of family process is proposed that takes into account the complexity of family effects in developmental context. It is argued that families are composed of different relationships that operate as subsystems of an organized group (e.g., marital, parent–child, sibling relationships). Furthermore, family relationships are created and maintained through observable interactions and detectable beliefs that directly and indirectly influence child development.

This necessarily brief overview focuses on child cognitive health as an outcome of family process. Cognitive development is considered from the perspective that intelligence stems from the ability to adapt to or modify the environment (Sternberg, 1997). Beyond infancy, children's cognitive competence is typically measured through academic achievement and on occasion through IQ scores. This chapter considers how the family context affects the child's preparedness to learn as well as more standard assessments of school performance.

FAMILIES ARE ORGANIZED SYSTEMS

Organized systems share three characteristics: wholeness, boundaries, and hierarchical structure. Wholeness is summarized by the axiom; the whole is greater than the sum of its parts, which takes on additional meaning when relationships between parts are added (Sameroff, 1995). This principle suggests that the functioning of a child at any point in time can not be adequately explained by characteristics of the child or parents alone, but the transactional processes that arise when parents and children assemble as a family. Wholeness may be accessed through such concepts as family cohesion, flexibility, dominance, and control (Markman & Notarius, 1987).

The second aspect of family organization is the concept of boundaries. In families, marital, parental, and sibling relationships constitute subsystems that are distinct from but also influence each other. Families can be described in terms of the degree of permeability evident in their subsystem boundaries. Healthy families are characterized by semipermeable boundaries. Information exchange is neither so rigid as to prevent dialogue among the subsystems, nor so fluid as to lose definitional boundaries. When boundaries become either too rigid or too permeable, the wholeness of the system is threatened and there may be a cost to individual functioning. For example, effective problem solving has been identified as a central feature of intellectual development (Sternberg, 1997). Families that have clear boundaries between the parent and child subsystem are able to directly communicate with each other such that successful problem solving is fostered. When boundaries are blurred it is more difficult to communicate and thus poor models of problem solving are a part of the family context (Vuchinich, Vuchinich, & Wood, 1993).

Boundaries are also created between the family and larger systems. The degree to which families are open to the outside social world and engage in neighborhood, school, and community activities, also reflect the relative permeability of family boundaries. This feature will be particularly important in considering how families interact with schools that may foster the child's cognitive development. Families that have rigid boundaries between themselves and the outside world are less likely to seek information about other social institutions, relying more on idiosyncratic beliefs (Reiss, 1981). Ultimately, these rigid boundaries may prevent important information (such as expectations for children's performance) from being incorporated into the family's world. This filtering of information may then place the child at a disadvantage when asked to compete with children whose families are more open to and seek information.

The third aspect of organization is hierarchical structure. Families are composed of subsystems that are organized in a hierarchical fashion and influence each other. Hierarchies are characterized by a distribution of power such that healthy family systems include a strong parental subsystem that influences the child and sibling subsystems. The relative health of each subsystem may influence subsystems lower in the hierarchy. For example, high levels of hostility in the marital relationship may be related to harsh discipline in the parent–child relationship, suggesting a system that is organized around the regulation of negative affect.

Family Balance

If there is one thing that can be said with certainty it is that families change. However, families also attempt to keep things "running smoothly" by balancing the different demands of each part of the system. One of the ways in which families maintain wholeness is through homeostatic regulation. Families typically have a "set point" of comfort; when an internal or external stressor threatens balance within the family, family members are mobilized to act in such a way that the system's balance is restored.

Although families are regulated to maintain balance, they are also developmental systems that undergo change. On a daily, or even moment to moment basis, families make minor adjustments in their response to change using preexisting patterns of behavior (Watzlawick, Weakland, & Fisch, 1974) but must also redefine roles throughout the family life cycle (McGoldrick, Heiman, & Carter, 1993). The developmentalist will recognize that these types of change are similar to Piaget's notions of assimilation and accommodation (Lyddon, 1990). Just as the child's development may be characterized by the interplay between assimilation and accommodation, families maintain patterns of organization until faced with a challenge that calls for reorganization.

Early adolescence has been identified as a transition period for children as well as the family as a whole (Grotevant, 1983). This important developmental period coincides for most youth with the transition to middle school. The new school environment is marked by an increase in academic rigor and expectations for independent learning (Eccles & Midgley, 1989). The family must alter its *set point* of comfort in regard to the adolescent's striving for autonomy. Families that are able to attune to their adolescent's need for independence have children who make a smoother transition to middle school than adolescents from less democratic families (Lord, Eccles, & McCarthy, 1994).

Family Subsystems

Families are organized through their practices and representations to maintain balance and to face change. The enactment of these alterations comes about through the interplay of different subsystems within the family that influence each other. These subsystems include marital, parent–child, sibling, and the family as a whole group. In regard to children's cognitive development, the parent–child subsystem has received the greatest attention. Selected portions of this research are highlighted. However, family effects extend beyond how mothers (the most widely studied parent) interact with their children. The direct and indirect influences of marital, sibling, and whole family relationships are also reviewed. This nonexhaustive review focuses on how the practices and representations of family subsystems add to the puzzle of family effects on child cognitive development and academic performance.

FAMILY PRACTICES AND REPRESENTATIONS

A common thread running throughout many family theories is that behavior and beliefs are two equally important domains in understanding family effects on child adaptation. Whether referred to as family style and world view (Minuchin, 1988), parenting practices and style (Darling & Steinberg, 1993), or the representing and practicing family (Reiss, 1989), these descriptions share the perspective that family life is organized around interactions and beliefs that extend across generations and are altered with time. Reiss' (1989) distinction between the practicing and representing family is especially pertinent to understanding family effects on children. Family practices stabilize and regulate family members through directly observed interaction patterns. The interaction patterns are repetitive and serve to provide a sense of family coherence and identity. Family interaction patterns may remain relatively stable until there is a perturbation such as an adolescent's striving for autonomy or a change in family composition such as death or divorce. Adolescents, for example, are undergoing rapid physical and cognitive changes that may alter their position in the family. As adolescents mature, family adaptation requires that interaction patterns that once revolved around close monitoring of children's behavior to be altered to include adolescents as more independent members of the family (Grotevant & Cooper, 1985). Should the previous family patterns persist, adolescents may not develop the autonomy necessary to successfully transition into young adulthood (Allen & Hauser, 1996; Barber, 1996). Families reorganize their interaction patterns until stability is once again reached, thus reflecting the joint roles of change and stability in the family system.

Family beliefs are representations that guide behavior as well as are created by family practices. Representations are relatively stable but may be altered through developmental changes in the family and through individual changes experienced in reconstructing past experiences. The surge in programs and apparatus for infant stimulation may be motivated, in part, by parents' beliefs that early stimulation may lead to a more cognitively competent child. As is demonstrated, families hold beliefs about children's abilities to learn which in turn may affect children's performance.

In the following sections, the contribution of family practices and representations to children's cognitive development and academic performance are reviewed. The marital, parent–child, sibling, and whole family subsystems are examined for the direct and indirect influence on children's development.

Family Practices

Marital Interaction and Child Cognitive Performance. Resolving conflict is part of family life. Husbands and wives disagree with each other, parents and children don't always see eye to eye, and sibling relationships frequently involve rivalry. The characteristic ways in which families resolve conflict are an important part of the practicing family and influence child development (Downey & Coyne, 1990). Children are sensitive to marital conflict even during infancy (Easterbrooks, Cummings, & Emde, 1994). Children visually track the back-and-forth exchanges between parents when they are engaged in a disagreement and may respond differentially to maritally satisfied versus dissatisfied fathers (Dickstein & Parke, 1988). The degree to which couples are satisfied with their marriages indirectly affects the child through alterations in parent–child interaction patterns. For example, fathers who report being satisfied in their marriages are more responsive and affectionate with their infants than maritally dissatisfied fathers (Belksy & Volling, 1986).

Persistent marital conflict may affect the child's ability to perform in school settings. Cowan and colleagues (Cowan, Cowan, Schulz, & Heming, 1994) reported on a longitudinal study of family factors associated with child outcome in the preschool and early school years. When couples describe their marriage as unsatisfactory over a period of several years and are openly critical of one another, their children have lower academic achievement scores in kindergarten than children whose parents are relatively satisfied with their marital relationship and resolve conflict in a constructive manner. The effects of marital conflict on academic achievement in the early school years may be mediated, in part, by ineffective parenting style. Parents who are experiencing distress in their marriage may be ill-equipped to be sensitive to their child's needs and engage in more controlling and harsh parenting styles.

The marital relationship can affect child academic performance throughout the early school years and into adolescence. Children in their early teen years who come from families where there is a high degree of marital conflict were rated lower by their teachers on cognitive competence and had lower G.P.A.'s than low conflict comparison children (Long, Forehand, Fauber, & Brody, 1987). These effects extend to families who have undergone a divorce and conflict between exspouses remains high (Long, Slater, Forehand, & Fauber, 1988).

It is unclear whether the pathways between marital interaction and child cognitive performance are direct or indirect. Several models have been proposed linking marital distress to children's behavior problems: spill-over effects of marital conflict have been proposed to compromise parenting (Easterbrooks & Emde, 1988); the tendency to focus singular negative attention on an individual child results in "scapegoating" and "detours" the family's attention away from marital conflict (Minuchin, Rosman, & Baker, 1978); and an affectively charged family environment has been found to impair the child's coping strategies (Grych & Fincham, 1990). It is likely that all of these features play a role in the child's cognitive development. Children exposed to heightened levels of marital distress may also experience inconsistent parenting that would otherwise foster cognitive growth and development. In order to maintain balance in the family and distract parents from fighting, children may turn their attention away from school activities and focus on saving their parent's marriage (Katz & Gottman, 1995). Children who are raised in households marked by marital conflict may be exposed to heightened levels of negative affect that creates negative perceptions of self (Cummings, 1987). Taken together, the marital subsystem is one part of the family context that affects child competence. Family environments that are distinguished by satisfied marriages and the ability to resolve conflict in a constructive manner support children's cognitive development through accessible and consistent parenting and an atmosphere that values personal relationships. Family environments that are characterized by high levels of marital conflict provide poor models for effective problem solving, compromise effective parenting, and create an atmosphere of personal disappointment.

Parent–Child Practices. Considerable attention has been directed toward the characteristic ways that parents interact with their children and child outcome. Parents who are responsive to their infants, provide emotional support, supply their children with varied stimulating toys and objects, and a variety of out of home experiences have children who have strong academic and intellectual performance in first grade (Bradley & Caldwell, 1984). Once children are in elementary school, warmth, involvement, and calm discussion aids academic performance (Petit, Bates, & Dodge, 1997). During the high-school years, hostile exchanges between parents and adolescents are related to poorer academic performance (Melby & Conger, 1996).

The area that has received the most attention in regard to children's academic performance is that of parenting style. Warmth and control have been identified as two qualities of parent–child interaction that affect child outcome (Maccoby & Martin, 1983). Baumrind (1978) proposed that the interplay of these two dimensions results in different parenting styles. Parents who are warm but also exert reasonable control are referred to as authoritative. Parents who exert firm control but are relatively cold in their interactions are referred to as authoritarian. Parents who are warm but do not exert control over their children are classified as permissive. These parenting styles have been found to be related to children's academic performance, particularly during adolescence with children of authoritative parents performing at higher academic levels than children of authoritarian or permissive parents (e.g., Baumrind, 1978; Dornbush, Ritter, Leiderman, Roberts, & Farleigh, 1987; Steinberg, Elmen, & Mounts, 1989). There are several caveats to this relation, however. Factors such as ethnicity, socioeconomic background, and community context have been found to effect the relation between parenting style and academic achievement (e.g., Baldwin, Baldwin, & Cole, 1990; Lamborn, Dornbush, & Steinberg, 1996). These differential findings highlight the importance of studying the family in cultural context when considering effects on child cognitive development. Conclusions drawn from the studies on parenting style are also limited by the methodology used to ascertain the different classifications. Generally, adolescents report on parenting behaviors. Although it has been argued that adolescent perception of parenting is an important contributor to academic performance (Steinberg, Mounts, Lamborn, & Dornbusch, 1991), it may be more reasonably identified as child beliefs about parenting practices rather than an observable form of parent–child interaction.

Direct observation of parent–child interaction and its effect on academic achievement has been conducted by Patterson and colleagues. In longitudinal studies of parent discipline and child antisocial behavior, it has been demonstrated that ineffective discipline when children were in Grade 6 directly affected the child's engagement in academic activities which in turn was related to academic achievement in Grade 7 (DeBaryshe, Patterson, &

Capaldi, 1993). The authors conclude that parents who use effective discipline strategies provide effective adult models that emphasize the connection between behaviors and outcomes, a characteristic necessary for on-task behavior in school settings.

With rare exception (e.g., Melby & Conger, 1996) the majority of parent–child interaction studies have been restricted in focusing on the mother–child dyad and child cognitive outcomes. Although the call to include fathers as part of the parent subsystem has been heeded in studies of children's social development (e.g., Parke & Tinsley, 1987) this is still a serious limitation when considering cognitive growth. There is some evidence that mothers and fathers may make distinct contributions to children's cognitive performance. Grolnick and Slowiaczek (1994) reported that children who have involved mothers also tend to have involved fathers. Whereas the mother's involvement directly predicted school success, father's involvement indirectly influenced child school success by increasing the child's perceived self-competence. The authors conclude that mothers' and fathers' involvement may motivate children to succeed in school, but through different pathways.

Although the effects of mother–child interaction on child cognitive competence has been extensively studied, there have been several limitations to this approach including viewing the family outside of its cultural context, reliance on child report, and exclusion of fathers. With an expanded scope of the family context, parent–child interaction may be seen as one part of the practicing family that influences child development. Parents who engage in consistent and warm interactions with their children while setting developmentally appropriate limits have children who are prepared to learn. As the effects of the marital interaction on child competence could be considered direct as well as indirect, the same pattern holds for parent–child interaction. Children may directly model interactions they experience with their parents that are associated with success in school such as connecting outcomes to behavior (DeBaryshe et al., 1993). Distinct parent–child interaction patterns may indirectly affect performance by fostering self-confidence and motivation to perform (Grolnick & Slowiaczek, 1994). Finally, a good fit between child needs for autonomy and parental fostering of independence may place the child on a positive developmental trajectory (Eccles & Midgley, 1989).

Sibling Interaction. Siblings can be a valuable resource and have been found to have important influences on child development (for a review see Brody, 1998). Siblings may have the strongest influence on children's cognitive development through practicing roles of teacher and learner. Older siblings have been found to act as teachers while placing their younger siblings in the role of learner (Brody, Stoneman, & MacKinnon, 1985). In structured teaching situations it has been found that siblings give more detailed explanations than peers and that learners are more active when interacting with their sibling than with a peer (Azmitia & Hesser, 1993). Relatively little attention has been paid to direct effects of sibling interaction on children's school performance. Preliminary accounts suggest that siblings that engage in teaching roles have younger siblings who perform better on reading and language achievement tests (Smith, 1993). Until more extensive research is conducted linking sibling interaction and school performance, it can be said that practices between siblings may affect children's academic achievement indirectly by reinforcing the role of teacher and learner.

Whole Family Interaction. Whereas the examination of the marital, parent–child, and sibling relationships relies on dyadic exchanges, it is also important to consider the family as a group. One way to access whole family organization is through the study of family rituals. Family rituals range from highly stylized religious observances, such as first communion, to less articulated daily interaction patterns such as dinnertime. Two dimensions have been identified as important in understanding family rituals; the degree to which roles and routines are an integral part of the ritual and the degree to which the rituals include symbolic meaning and are an important part of family life (Fiese, 1995; Fiese & Kline, 1993). During the childrearing years, creating and maintaining family rituals on a daily basis can be a central part of family life (Bennett, Wolin, & McAvity, 1988) and change over time (Fiese, Hooker, Kotary, & Schwagler, 1993). For example, families with preschool age children established more dinnertime, weekend, and annual celebration rituals than families whose oldest child was an infant. Furthermore, families of preschool age children reported more meaning associated with their rituals including greater occurrence, a stronger attachment of affect and symbolic significance to family rituals, more deliberate planning around ritual events, and a stated commitment to continue the family rituals into the future than families of infants.

Family rituals may be one way that families organize their busy lives that can foster academic achievement and cognitive growth. As part of a longitudinal study of family practices and beliefs in relation to child competence, fifty-four parents completed the Family Ritual Questionnaire (FRQ; Fiese & Kline, 1993) when their child was 4 years old and again when the child was 8 years old. The FRQ is a 56-item forced choice questionnaire that assesses family routines across seven different settings (dinnertime, weekends, annual celebrations, vacations, special celebrations, religious celebrations, and cultural traditions) and eight dimensions (occurrence, roles, routines, attendance, affect, symbolic significance, continuation, and deliberateness). Summary scores may be calculated for a routine dimension reflecting the degree to which family rituals are practiced in a regular and predictable manner and a second dimension referred to as the meaning dimension reflecting the degree to which family rituals are a significant and meaningful component of family life. For the purposes of this chapter, the relation between family rituals practiced at ages 4 and 8 years in predicting child academic competence (as measured by the Kaufmann Test of Educational Achievement) is presented. As can be seen in Table 2.1, the child's math, spelling, and total achievement scores at age 8 were significantly related to mothers' and fathers' report of the degree to which the family engaged in routine and predictable rituals when the child was 4 years old. Spelling and total achievement scores at age 8 were related to the degree to which family rituals were seen as an important and meaningful aspect of family life for mothers and fathers when their child was 4 years old. A similar pattern held when considering the contemporaneous report of family rituals when the child was 8 except that mother's report of the routine aspect was no longer significantly related to the child's total academic achievement scores.

There was considerable stability of family ritual scores across the two periods although the stability was stronger for fathers (meaning $r = .73$, rou-

TABLE 2.1
Relation Between Family Rituals and Child Academic Achievement at Eight Years

	Academic Achievement Score			
	Math	*Reading*	*Spelling*	*Total Achievement*
Parent Ritual Report				
Time 1 (4 years)				
Mother				
Routine	.35**	.21	.31*	.37**
Meaning	.20	.13	.33**	.31*
Father				
Routine	.32*	.22	.42**	.45***
Meaning	.23	.12	.35**	.30*
Time 2 (8 years)				
Mother				
Routine	.20	.06	.28	.25
Meaning	.33*	.12	.31*	.35**
Father				
Routine	.30*	.26	.36**	.41**
Meaning	.30*	.22	.40**	.39**

Note. *$p < .05$; **$p < .01$; ***$p < .001$

tine $r = .62$) than for mothers (meaning $r = .36$, routine $r = .50$). When the effects of Time 2 scores were partialled out, father's routine score at 4 years of age remained a predictor of child academic achievement at age 8 ($r = .28$, $p < .06$). These preliminary results suggest that the degree to which the family practices predictable routines when the child is 4 and continues to consider family gatherings as a source of meaningful interactions when the child is school age, have children who score higher on academic achievement tests than families who have less predictability and meaning associated with their family routines.

Family rituals may have direct and indirect effects on child cognitive competence. A ritualized family environment that includes predictability of routines and deliberate planning of events also supports activities that are important for school success such as regular attendance, incorporating homework into a daily routine, and planning for the future. The meaning ascribed to family gatherings may also foster a sense of belonging to a group and feelings of personal self-worth (Fiese, 1995). This positive family environment may then foster self-confidence associated with success in the school environment.

Family Representations

Family representations include working memories of relationships and family experiences that serve to regulate behavior. Just as the domain of family practices may be examined according to the relative influence of different subsystems, it is possible to consider the domain of family representations across different relationships and their relation to child cognitive competence. Children's representations of the marital relationship, parenting beliefs, perceptions of sibling relationships, and representational processes evident in the whole family will serve as examples of the represented family.

Children's Perceptions of Marital Conflict. Children who create images of warm and responsive caregiving tend to consider themselves as worthy of love and affection and develop a sense of confidence in relating to others. When children are exposed to marital conflict, feelings of anger, shame, and fear often evolve. Children may then create images of themselves as either potential mediators or provocateurs of the marital conflict. In this regard, the child places blame on themselves which may then be integrated into a view of the self as unworthy of rewarding relationships and feelings of shame and guilt predominate self-perceptions (Grych & Fincham, 1990). Wierson, Forehand, and McCombs (1988) reported that children's perceptions of marital conflict was related to teacher-rated cognitive competence and G.P.A.

Grych and Fincham (1990) proposed that marital conflict affects the child's cognitive coping strategies. Children who are able to reduce emotional upset through effective coping styles will be less affected by marital distress and better equipped to focus on school-related activities. Children who employ coping strategies that focus on interrupting marital conflict may eventually be drawn further into the conflict and have fewer emotional resources available for coping outside of the family context. In this regard, representations of the marital relationship as conflictual may have an indirect effect on the child's cognitive competence by deploying ineffective coping strategies.

Parenting Beliefs and Child Cognitive Competence. Considerable attention has been directed toward how the beliefs that parents hold about childrearing may influence child development. In general, parents hold interactionist views of the effects of heredity and environment on child development. However, these views are modified by age of child (Miller, 1988), culture (Palacios, Gonzalez, & Moreno, 1992), and socioeconomic status (Sameroff & Feil, 1985). It is likely that many of these beliefs are rooted in the parents' own upbringing (Cowan et al., 1994) as well as the explicit values endorsed by the dominant culture (Harkness, Super, & Keefer, 1992).

The link between parenting beliefs and children's cognitive performance is a relatively weak one. Maternal beliefs have been found to make a significant contribution to IQ (Sameroff, Seifer, Barocas, Zax, & Greenspan, 1987) and to cognitive performance (Sigel, 1992). However, these relations are modified by the domain in which parent beliefs are assessed (Sigel, 1992) and personal characteristics of the parent. For example, McGillicuddy-Delisi (1992) reported that mothers who believe that the course of development is different for boys and girls had children who performed more poorly on academic achievement tests. Whether these beliefs are enacted in differential treatment of boys and girls has yet to be determined. Sigel (1992) concluded that parent beliefs are multidetermined phenomena that must take into account culture, socioeconomic status, and parent personality characteristics before a link to child performance can be drawn.

Perceptions of Siblings Relationships. Siblings do not always see eye to eye on family life. Indeed, siblings often report that they are treated differently by their parents (e.g., Daniels & Plomin, 1985). It appears, however, that the perception of differential treatment may extend beyond differences in personality characteristics. The interplay between the marital and sibling subsystem influences how siblings perceive their relationships and the likelihood that conflict with develop. In families where there is heightened marital conflict and hostile interchanges, there is a greater likelihood for siblings to engage in conflict with each other and to view the other as an irritant (e.g., Brody, Stoneman, & MacKinnon, 1986; Dunn & Kendrick, 1982). In this regard, interactional aspects of the marital system may affect representational aspects of the sibling subsystem. As studies have not been conducted linking sibling representation of relationships and cognitive performance, any discussion would be speculative at best. It is likely that, as in the case of marital conflict, a child who is distracted by angry exchanges will not be developing prosocial behaviors often associated with being a good student and active learner.

Family Stories.   One way to access whole family representational process-es is through the study of family stories. Family stories deal with how the family makes sense of its world, express rules of interaction, and create beliefs about relationships that have implications for child development (Fiese, Sameroff, Grotevant, Wamboldt, Dickstein, & Fravel, 2000). When family members are called upon to recount an experience they set an interpretive frame reflecting how individuals grapple with understanding events, how the family works together, and how the ascription of meaning is linked to beliefs about relationships in the family and social world. It is possible to consider family stories from a variety of perspectives including their thematic content, the coherence of the narrative, and the ways in which relationships are depicted to reflect expectations in social settings. It is the thematic content that may be most pertinent in considering effects on child competence.

The formation of close personal relationships and striving for success are two central themes in adult and child development (Erikson, 1963; Gilligan, 1982; McAdams & de St. Aubin, 1992). How the family goes about imparting val-ues of relationships and achievement is tempered by the developmental stage of the family and the personal values held by the family. Mothers and fathers tell stories with different themes to children at different developmental levels (Fiese, Hooker, Jenkins, Schwagler, & Rimmer, 1995). Fathers tend to talk about their childhood experiences with an emphasis on achievement themes and mothers tend to talk about childhood experiences with an emphasis on affili-ation themes. Furthermore, parents of infants have been found to tell family stories with strong affiliation themes and parents of preschool age children to tell family stories with achievement themes. Representations of family events may alter with the developmental demands of the family. Families with infants, focused on intense caregiving and nurturing demands, may impart images that revolve around close relationships with others. Families with preschool age children, on the other hand, may be preparing their children for the role of achiever and student and relay messages that emphasize the importance of success of persistence in the face of obstacles.

There is also some evidence that boys and girls are told different types of stories based on the gender-type of their parents (Fiese & Skillman, 1997). Parents who are traditionally gender typed (either masculine or feminine) tend to tell family stories that emphasize achievement to their sons and affil-iation to their daughters. Parents who endorse more androgynous gender roles were just as likely to share stories of personal achievement with their daughters as with their sons.

Family stories are one way that values are imparted to children. However, the act of telling family stories also involves the child. Themes are altered according to age and gender of child. It is likely that personal characteristics of the child may also call forth different types of family stories. A child who is struggling with school may elicit stories of success from their parents as a way to encourage the child to persevere. It is unlikely that family stories have a direct effect on children's cognitive competence except perhaps through an enriched language environment. However they may serve as representations of success (or failure) that become integrated into the child's personal schemas for success (or failure).

INTEGRATING FAMILY PRACTICES AND REPRESENTATIONS

The family is a complex system that includes characteristic ways of interacting with its members and representations that may guide behavior. Families are part of ongoing developmental processes that reflect the changing nature of individuals as well as the changing nature of family relationships. It is possible to consider how family practices and representations transact with one another to create a context that supports cognitive competence. Figure 2.1 depicts a series of transactions between the representational and practicing components of the family system. It is assumed that each aspect is comprised of different family relationships including marital, parent–child, sibling, and whole family. The starting point of this transactional journey is an arbitrary one. Indeed, family representations and practices may be affected by generational as well as current context. Across time, the child is involved in family practices and creates representations that can foster cognitive health. Directly, practices may provide models that link outcomes with behavior, promote effective problem solving, and create predictable routines. Indirectly, practices may affect the child's ability to engage in schoolwork and create representations of a self that is confident to perform in challenging situations. It appears that family practices affect cognitive health through *preparing* the child to adapt to environments that foster intellectual growth. Families that interact with each other in warm and responsive ways, engage in effective problem solving, and adjust to meet the developmental needs of individual members prepare their children to be attentive, actively engage in seeking solutions to problems, and adapt to new challenges. Family representations affect cognitive health through *reinforcing* values that are consistent with the child as a competent learner. Families that create environments where relationships are viewed as rewarding and the group is considered a resource reinforce to their children their ability to learn and foster self-confidence.

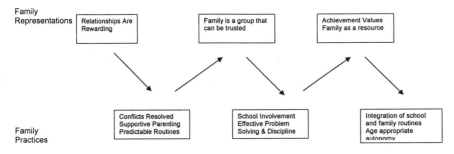

FIG. 2.1. Transactions between the represented and practicing family.

To consider children's cognitive health without attending to the family context is to minimize the very environment in which they are raised. The family context is not a simple one and demands a multidimensional approach in understanding family effects on child development. These effects can not be summarized into a singular correlation or comparison of effect sizes across studies (Cowan, 1997). Given that families are systems that undergo change, attempt to maintain stability, are composed of different relationships, and exert influence through observable practices as well as detectable representations is it any wonder that a singular approach to explaining family effects would fail? It is not families that have failed to contribute to children's development it is the reliance on simplistic notions of family life that obscures the fact that families do make a difference. A careful examination of family effects can paint an optimistic picture when considering children's cognitive health. There are multiple pathways through multiple relationships that can be accessed to support children's intellectual growth. These identifiable pathways can serve as models for early intervention aimed at fostering success and academic achievement. Future efforts are warranted to aid families in their efforts to raise healthy children because families do matter.

ACKNOWLEDGMENT

Preparation of this manuscript was supported, in part, by a grant from the National Institute of Mental Health.

REFERENCES

Allen, J. P., & Hauser, S. T. (1996). Autonomy and relatedness in adolescent-family interactions as predictors of young adults' states of mind regarding attachment. *Development and Psychopathology, 8,* 793–809.

Azmitia, M., & Hesser, J. (1993). Why siblings are important agents of cognitive development: A comparison of siblings and peers. *Child Development, 64,* 430–444.

Baldwin, C., Baldwin, A., & Cole, R. (1990). Stress-resistant families and stress-resistant children. In J. Rolf, A. Masten, D. Cicchetti, K. Neuchtherlin, & S. Weintraub (Eds.), *Risk and protective factors in the development of psychopathology* (pp. 257–280). New York: Cambridge University Press.

Barber, B. K. (1996). Parental psychological control: Revisting a neglected construct. *Child Development, 67,* 3296–3319.

Baumrind, D. (1978). Parental disciplinary patterns and social competence in children. *Youth and Society, 9,* 239–276.

Belsky, J., & Volling, B. L. (1986). Mothering, fathering, and marital interaction in the family triad: Exlporing family systems processes. In P. Berman & F. Pederson (Eds.), *Men's transition to parenthood: Longitudinal studies of early family experience.* Hillsdale, NJ: Lawrence Erlbaum Associates.

Bennett, L. A., Wolin, S. J., & McAvity, K. J. (1988). Family identity, ritual and myth: A cultural perspective on lifecycle transitions. In C. J. Falicov (Ed.), *Family transitions* (pp. 211–234). New York: Guilford Press.

Bradley, R. H., & Caldwell, B. M. (1984). The relation of infants' home environments to achievement test performance in first grade: A follow-up study. *Child Development, 55,* 803–809.

Brody, G. H. (1998). Sibling relationship quality: Its causes and consequences. *Annual Review of Psychology, 49,* 1–24.

Brody, G. H., Stoneman, Z., & MacKinnon, C. E. (1985). Role relationships and behavior among preschool-aged and school-aged sibling pairs. *Developmental Psychology, 21,* 124–129.

Brody, G., Stoneman, Z., & MacKinnon, C. (1986). Contributions of maternal child rearing practices and play contexts to sibling interactions. *Journal of Applied Developmental Psychology, 7,* 225–236.

Cowan, P. A. (1997). Beyond meta-analysis: A plea for a family systems view of attachment. *Child Development, 68,* 601–604.

Cowan, P. A., Cowan, C. P., Schulz, M. S., & Heming, G. (1994). Prebirth to preschool family factors in children's adaptation to kindergarten. In R. D. Parke & S. G. Kellam (Eds.), *Exploring family relationships with other social contexts* (pp. 75–114). Hillsdale, NJ: Lawrence Erlbaum Associates.

Cummings, E. M. (1987). Coping with background anger in early childhood. *Child Development, 58,* 976–984.

Daniels, D., & Plomin, R. (1985). Differential experience of siblings in the same family. *Developmental Psychology, 21,* 747–760.

Darling, N., & Steinberg, L. (1993). Parenting style as context: An integrative model. *Psychological Bulletin, 113,* 487–496.

DeBaryshe, B. D., Patterson, G. R., & Capaldi, D. M. (1993). A performance model for academic achievement in early adolescent boys. *Developmental Psychology, 29,* 795–804.

Dickstein, S., & Parke, R. (1988). Social referencing: A glance at fathers and marriage. *Child Development, 59,* 506–511.

Dornbusch, S., Ritter, P., Leiderman, P., Roberts, D., & Farleigh, M. (1987). The relation of parenting style to adolescent school performance. *Child Development, 58,* 1244–1257.

Downey, G., & Coyne, J. C. (1990). Children of depressed parents: An integrative review. *Psychological Bulletin, 108,* 50–76.

Dunn, J., & Kendrick, C. (1982). *Siblings: Love, envy, and understanding.* London: Grant McIntyre.

Easterbrooks, M. A., Cummings, E. M., & Emde, R. N. (1994). Young children's responses to constructive marital disputes. *Journal of Family Psychology, 8,* 160–169.

Easterbrooks, M. A., & Emde, R. N. (1988). Marital and parent-child relatioships: The role of affect in the family system. In R. A. Hinde & J. S. Hinde (Eds.), *Relationships within families: Mutual influences* (pp. 83–103). New York: Oxford University Press.

Eccles, J. S., & Midgley, C. (1989). Stage/environment fit: Developmentally appropriate classrooms for early adolescence. In R. E. Ames & C. Ames (Eds.), *Advances in motivation and achievement Vol. 3* (pp. 139–186). New York: Academic Press.

Erikson, E. H. (1963). *Childhood and society*. New York: Norton.

Fiese, B. H. (1995). Family rituals. In D. Levinson (Ed.), *Encyclopedia of marriage and the family* (pp. 275–278). New York: Macmillan.

Fiese, B. H., Hooker, K. A., Jenkins, L., Schwagler, J., & Rimmer, M. (1995). Family stories in the early stages of parenthood. *Journal of Marriage and the Family, 57*, 763–770.

Fiese, B. H., Hooker, K. A., Kotary, L., Schwagler, J. (1993). Family rituals in the early stages of parenthood. *Journal of Marriage and the Family, 55*, 633–642.

Fiese, B. H., & Kline, C. A. (1993). Development of the Family Ritual Questionnaire: Initial reliability and validity studies. *Journal of Family Psychology, 6*, 290–299.

Fiese, B. H., Sameroff, A. J., Grotevant, H. D., Wamboldt, F., Dickstein, S., & Fravel, S. (2000). The stories that families tell: Narrative coherence, narrative interaction and relationship beliefs. *Monographs of the Society for Research in Child Development, 64*(2).

Fiese, B. H., & Skillman, G. (1997, April). *Getting the story straight: Congruence between parent story theme and gender role in relation to child behavior*. Presented in B. H. Fiese (Chair) Defining family heritage through rituals and stories, Society for Research in Child Development, Washington DC.

Fiese, B. H., Wilder, J., & Bickham, N. (2000). Family context in developmental psychopathology. In M. Lewis & A.J. Sameroff (Eds.). *Handbook of developmental psychopathology* (2nd ed., pp. 115–134). New York: Plenum.

Gilligan, C. (1982). *In a different voice: Psychological theory and women's development*. Cambridge, MA: Harvard University Press.

Grolnick, W. S., & Slowiaczek, M. L. (1994). Parents' involvement in children's schooling: A multidimensional conceptualization and motivational model. *Child Development, 65*, 237–252.

Grotevant, H. D. (1983). The contribution of the family to the facilitation of identity formation in early adolescence. *Journal of Early Adolescence, 3*, 225–237.

Grotevant, H. D., & Cooper, C. R. (1985). Patterns of interaction in family relationships and the development of identity exploration in adolescence. *Child Development, 56*, 415–428.

Grych, J. H., & Fincham, F. D. (1990). Marital conflict and children's adjustment: A cognitive-contextual framework. *Psychological Bulletin, 108*, 267–290.

Harkness, S., Super, C. M., & Keefer, C. H. (1992). Learning to be an American parent: How cultural models gain directive force. In R. G. D'Andrade (Ed.), *Human motives and cultural models* (pp. 163–178). Cambridge, England: Cambridge University Press.

Harris, J. R. (1995). Where is the child's environment? A group socialization theory of development. *Psychological Review, 102*, 458–489.

Katz, L. F., & Gottman, J. M. (1995). Marital interaction and child outcomes: A longitudinal study of mediating and moderating processes. In D. Cicchetti & S. L. Toth (Eds.), *Emotion, cognition, and representation. Rochester Symposium on Developmental Psychopathology* (pp. 301–342). New York: University of Rochester Press.

Lamborn, S. D., Dornbusch, S. M., & Steinberg, L. (1996). Ethnicity and community context as moderators of the relations between family decision making and adolescent adjustment. *Child Development, 67*, 283–301.

Long, N., Forehand, R., Fauber, R., & Brody, G. (1987). Self-perceived and independently observed competence of young adolescents as a function of parental marital conflict and recent divorce. *Journal of Abnormal Child Psychology, 15*, 15–27.

Long, N., Slater, E., Forehand, R., & Fauber, R. (1988). Continued high or reduced interparental conflict following divorce: Relation to young adolescent adjustment. *Journal of Consulting and Clinical Psychology, 56*, 467–469.

Lord, S. E., Eccles, J. S., & McCarthy, K. A. (1994). Surviving the junior high school transition: Family processes and self perceptions as risk and protective factors. *Journal of Early Adolescence, 14*, 162–199.

Lyddon, W. J. (1990). First- and second-order change: Implications for rationalist and constructivist cognitive therapies. *Journal of Counseling and Development, 69*, 122–127.

Maccoby, E., & Martin, J. (1983). Socialization in the context of the family: Parent-child interaction. In E. M. Hetherington (Ed.), P. H. Mussen (Series Ed.), *Handbook of child psychology: Vol 4. Socialization, personality, and social development* (pp. 1–101). New York: Wiley.

Markman, H. J., & Notarious, C. I. (1987). Coding marital and family interaction: Current status. In T. Jacob (Ed.), *Family interaction and psychopathology* (pp. 329–390). New York: Plenum.

McAdams, D. P., & de St. Aubin, E. (1992). A theory of generativity and tis assessment through self report, behavioral acts, and narrative themes in autiobiography. *Journal of Personality and Social Psychology, 62,* 1003–1015.

McGillicuddy-Delisi, A. V. (1992). Parents' beliefs and children's personal-social development. In I. E. Sigel, A. V. McGillicuddy, & J. J. Goodnow (Eds.), *Parental belief systems: The psychological consequences for children* (2nd ed., pp. 115–142). Hillsdale, NJ: Lawrence Erlbaum Associates.

McGoldrick, M., Heiman, M., & Carter, B. (1993). The changing family life cycle: A perspective on normalcy. In F. Walsh (Ed.), *Normal family processes* (2nd ed., pp. 405–443). New York: Guilford.

Melby, J. N., & Conger, R. D. (1996). Parental behaviors and adolescent academic performance: A longitudinal analysis. *Journal of Research on Adolescence, 6,* 113–137.

Miller, S. A. (1988). Parents' beliefs about children's cognitive development. *Child Development, 59,* 259–285.

Minuchin, P. (1988). Relationships within the family: A systems perspective on development. In R. A. Hinde & J. Stevenson-Hinde (Eds.), *Relationships within families* (pp. 7–26). Oxford: Clarendon Press.

Minuchin, S., Rosman, B., & Baker, L. (1978). *Psychosomatic families.* Cambridge, MA: Harvard University Press.

Palacios, J., Gonzalez, M., & Moreno, M. (1992). Stimulating the child in the zone of proximal development: The role of parents' ideas. In I. E. Sigel, A. V. McGillicuddy-Delisi, & J. J. Goodnow (Eds.), *Parental belief systems: The psychological consequences for children* (2nd ed., pp. 71–94). Hillsdale, NJ: Lawrence Erlbaum Associates.

Parke, R., & Tinsely, B. (1987). Family interaction in infancy. In J. Osofsky (Ed.), *Handbook of infant development* (2nd ed., pp. 579–641). New York: Wiley.

Patterson, G. R., DeBaryshe, B. D., & Ramsey, E. (1989). A developmental perspective on anti-social behavior. *American Psychologist, 44,* 329–335.

Petit, G. S., Bates, J. E., & Dodge, K. A. (1997). Supportive parenting, ecological context, and children's adjustment: A seven-year longitudinal study. *Child Development, 68,* 908–923.

Popenoe, D. (1993). American family decline, 1960–1990: A review and appraisal. *Journal of Marriage and the Family, 55,* 527–542.

Reiss, D. (1981). *The family's construction of reality.* Cambridge, MA: Harvard University Press.

Reiss, D. (1989). The practicing and representing family. In A. J. Sameroff & R. Emde (Eds.), *Relationship disturbances in early childhood* (pp. 191–220). New York: Basic Books.

Sameroff, A. J. (1995). General systems theories and developmental psychopathology. In D. Cicchetti & D. Cohen (Eds.), *Developmental Psychopathology, Vol 1* (pp. 659–695). New York: Wiley.

Sameroff, A. J., & Feil, L. (1985). Parental concepts of development. In I. Sigel (Ed.), *Parental belief systems: The psychological consequences for children* (pp. 83–104). Hillsdale, NJ: Lawrence Erlbaum Associates.

Sameroff, A. J., Seifer, R., Barocas, B., Zax, M., & Greenspan, S., (1987). I.Q. scores of 4-year-old children: Social-environmental risk factors. *Pediatrics, 79,* 343–350.

Sigel, I. (1992). The belief-behavior connection: A resolvable dilemma? In I. E. Sigel, A. V. McGillicuddy-DeLisi, & J. J. Goodnow (Eds.), *Parental belief systems: The psychological consequences for children* (2nd ed., pp. 433–456). Hillsdale, NJ: Lawrence Erlbaum Associates.

Smith, T. E. (1993). Growth in academic achievement and teaching yournger siblings. *Social Psychology Quarterly, 56,* 77–85.

Steinberg, L., Elmen, J. D., & Mounts, N. S. (1989). Authoritative parenting, psychosocial maturity, and academic success among adolescents. *Child Development, 60*, 1424–1436.

Steinberg, L., Mounts, N. S., Lamborn, S. D., & Dornbusch, S. M. (1991). Authoritative parenting and adolescent adjustment across varied ecological niches. *Journal of Research on Adolescence, 1*, 19–36.

Sternberg, R. J. (1997). The concept of intelligence and its role in lifelong learning and success. *American Psychologist, 52*, 1030–1037.

Vuchinich, S., Vuchinich, R. A., & Wood, B. (1993). The interparental relationship and family problem solving with preadolescent males. *Child Development, 64*, 1389–1400.

Wagner, B. M., & Reiss, D. (1995). Family systems and developmental psychopathology: Courtship, marriage or divorce? In D. Cicchetti & D. J. Cohen (Eds.), *Developmental psychopathology Vol 1: Theory and methods* (pp. 696–730). New York: Wiley.

Watzlawick, P., Weakland, J., & Fisch, R. (1974). *Change: Principles of problem formation and problem resolution.* New York: Norton.

Wierson, M., Forehand, R., & McCombs, A. (1988). The relationship of early adolescent functioning to parent-reported and adolescent-perceived interparental conflict. *Journal of Abnormal Child Psychology, 16*, 707–718.

3

Socioeconomic Status, Multiple Risks, and Development of Intelligence

Ronald Seifer

Brown University School of Medicine

The association of socioeconomic status (SES) and intelligence is among the strongest and longstanding effects studied in the behavioral sciences. In fact, although this association remains a topic of discussion (Neisser et al., 1996; Williams & Ceci, 1997), it is rarely examined empirically in recent studies because the effect is so expectable (instead, appropriate measures are applied in research designs so that bias attributable to SES is minimized). Still, many questions remain about the association of SES and intelligence that have import for behavioral scientists as well as for larger questions of social and public policy. In this chapter, I review some basic facts about the SES–intelligence association, focusing primarily on North American work. A discussion of some definitional issues that pertain to this association follows. Next is review of speculation, along with empirical support where available, about why this association exists. Following this, I describe related approaches to examining the role of social position in intellectual performance that attempt to integrate several different characteristics of social context. Finally, I provide summary statements and brief commentary.

SOCIOECONOMIC STATUS AND INTELLIGENCE: BASIC FACTS

Starting about 1910, when the first wide-scale use of intelligence testing was instituted in the U.S. military, a strong and consistent association between SES and intelligence has been observed. Typically, if one compares upper social strata (professionals and managers) with lower social strata (skilled and unskilled workers, individuals on public assistance), differences of about 1 standard deviation (*SD*) or 15 IQ points are found; in designs using continuous measures of both SES and intelligence, correlations of about .40 are usually found (Neisser et al., 1996; White, 1982). These effects are large in the context of behavioral science research (Cohen, 1988).

There is little evidence that the specific test examined, or that different classes of tests (e.g., verbal vs. nonverbal) substantially affect this result. There do appear to be larger effect sizes for IQ tests when compared with their close cousin, achievement tests, where typical correlations are more in the .25–.30 range. Of further interest is that correlations of core SES measures (education, occupation, income, and combinations) lag behind those of less traditional measures such as household atmosphere (White, 1982).

This difference in intelligence test scores appears early in life, but not immediately during infancy (Golden & Birns, 1976). During the first year of life, there is no reliable difference between SES groups on test performance (see subsequent section on developmental issues in the definition of intelligence). In fact, there is some evidence that African American children, who on average are of lower SES in the United States, may have some advantage on the early measures of intelligence (Sameroff, Seifer, & Zax, 1982). It is only between 18 and 24 months that the large association of SES and intelligence is found in repeated studies. Of particular note is that this is the period when language emerges developmentally, and the time when intelligence tests begin to use language skills as an integral part of the assessment.

Furthermore, it is around the end of the second year of life when stability of intelligence test performance emerges in a major way. By age 2, stability coefficients of at least .40–.50 are typical, and rise swiftly across the rest of the preschool period until stability approximates that of older children and adults by about 5 years of age; coefficients approach .90 for short intervals and are only slightly lower for longer intervals (Jensen, 1980).

Implications of SES–Intelligence Association

Why should we care about this difference in intellectual performance across SES groups? Is it anything more than some groups having bragging rights over other groups? First, it is important to remember that the two strongest validation criteria of intelligence tests are educational and occupational attainment. Across many studies, the typical correlation of intelligence with these validation criteria is about .50. This includes school performance, level of education attained, type of occupation, and success in job performance (Gottfredson, 1997; Neisser et al. 1996).

Differences of 1 *SD* may be crucial in accessing postsecondary education, or at least the type of postsecondary education, as some form of college education is becoming the norm in the United States. For example, 1 *SD* differentiates the mean of college graduates from those with a 50–50 chance of passing an academic high-school curriculum (Jensen, 1980). Furthermore, the 1 SD differences are mimicked in 100-point differences in the closely related Scholastic Assessment Test (SAT), which can determine whether or not students are admitted to the more prestigious public and private universities. All of these factors taken together are reflected in differences in the number of years of schooling attained, the type of schooling (including both form and status of postsecondary education), and the performance of students in these various settings.

Schooling is, of course, related to occupational success, particularly in terms of initial entry into the workforce. Access to the more prestigious and economically rewarding occupations is often dictated by formal educational training. Even within the same occupation or job category, competition for the better paying jobs with better employers is often determined by the type of school attended and performance in that education setting.

Although the prior discussion is necessarily limited to averages and group effects, the individuals in these groups will certainly have higher or lower probability of attaining a wide variety of life goals based on their measured intelligence. Still, it must be kept in mind that when examining the association of SES and intelligence along with the consequences in everyday life circumstances, it is not possible to attribute all differences in educational and occupational attainment to the differences in SES. It may well be that other factors confounded with, or independent of, SES may affect performance in school, number of years of schooling, choice of postsecondary schooling, and ultimate occupational success.

DEFINITIONAL ISSUES REGARDING SES AND INTELLIGENCE

To this point, I have proceeded without defining the basic terms fundamental to the discussion. In part, this is possible because both constructs (SES and intelligence) are well established in both the scientific and popular cultures, with much shared meaning across individuals. Still, there remain important issues surrounding how each construct is defined, but perhaps more important, how far the connotational structure of each construct is taken. It is beyond the scope of this chapter to address all definitional issues; instead I will highlight those that affect our understanding of the association of SES and intelligence (a thorough treatment of these issues may be found in Sternberg, 1990).

Defining Intelligence

Perhaps as much as any issue in behavioral science, the meaning of intelligence has sparked enormous controversy both in terms of what behaviors should be considered within the realm of intelligence and how those chosen behaviors should be understood (Herrnstein & Murray, 1994; Sternberg, 1990). Two roots leading to controversy are the complexity of human behavior (with the attendant problems of combining diverse functions in a single construct) and the important social implications of intelligence. With respect to the SES–intelligence association, several issues warrant special attention.

Operational Versus Conceptual Definition of Intelligence

One of the most quoted statements about intelligence is Boring's (1923) "intelligence is what the tests test." The author himself did not fully endorse this notion and virtually all scholars reject this pure operational definition to some extent. Still, the main body of evidence regarding SES and intelligence is derived from psychometric testing. This testing tradition has relied on the historical construction of tests, in that new forms of intelligence tests are required to correlate highly with old forms of the tests. Thus, it has been difficult to incorporate the large body of cogent theorizing about intelligence (beyond the operational definition) into the databases used to evaluate the types of questions addressed here. One is then left with the task of describing what the existing tests contain as the definition of intelligence at the conceptual level. For example, processing speed has been identified as a major substrate of IQ test performance (Neisser et al., 1996); Jensen (1980) elaborates the themes of mental manipulation, choice, decision, invention, memory, and distinguishing relevant information.

In a more pragmatic sense, the operational definition of intelligence could have been created (had historical events unfolded differently) so as to make this chapter nonsensical. Current intelligence tests are normed in such a way that they have similar properties for males and females and for individuals of all ages. That is, test developers decided that any final tests (and often any items) that discriminated males from females should be removed from the pool used to construct the test (Matarazzo, 1972). In a similar manner, standardized test scores are constructed and tabled for different age groups so that any individual taking the test will fall into the same distribution (M of 100, SD of 15). It is just as conceivable that in the beginning of this century test developers could have had a special sensitivity for the demographic factors of social position or racial group membership and created the same criteria for those variables (i.e., items that discriminated would not be allowed in the test). Had this been the case (and if it proved feasible) the discussions surrounding intelligence testing would have a very different flavor.

Unitary Intelligence Versus Multiple Intelligences

An offshoot of the predominantly operational definition of intelligence manifest in current standardized tests is the emphasis on a unitary construct of intelligence. Beginning with Spearman's (1904) analysis of ability tests and continuing through the factor analysis traditions and current conceptual analyses of intelligence, there has been strong emphasis on a single factor (sometimes called *g*) to explain intellectual performance (Herrnstein & Murray, 1994; Jensen, 1980; Spearman, 1904; Thurstone & Thurstone, 1941). This is in contrast to models that posit multiple intelligences, which may have widely varied characteristics (Gardner, 1983; Guilford, 1956; Sternberg, 1990).

Intelligence tests, and particularly those used in the literature assessing the SES–intelligence association, have relied on the unitary construct of intelligence. One the one hand, this has allowed for efficiency in the design and interpretation of research. On the other hand, many would argue this methodology has limited our understanding of the phenomenon of intelligence in general, and the understanding of how SES plays a role in particular (Fischer et al., 1996; Gardner, 1983). If indeed a multiple-intelligences perspective is pursued, then the basic facts regarding the association of SES and intelligence would be far more obscure at the present time, as examination by SES has not been a major focus of the work.

Heritability and Malleability of Intelligence

The most contentious issue in the popular debate regarding intelligence has been the issue of heritability (the proportion of variance in a measured trait attributable to genes). This was at the center of controversy around the publications that have spurred most public debate (Herrnstein & Murray, 1994; Jensen, 1969). Many studies have been conducted using family and adoption designs to address the issue of heritability in intelligence and estimates have ranged from .40 to .80 using standard behavior genetics methods.

The methods of behavior genetics typically examine directly the genetic influences, such as degree of family relationships (i.e., the amount of average shared genetic material). In large part, the methods *infer* sources of variance attributable to nongenetic influences, and typically assign the amount of environmental influence using indirect methods (such as subtracting genetic variance and gene by environment interactions from total variance). This begs the question of how the estimates of genetic influence would fare using an analogous approach where genetic influences were estimated by similarly indirect methods without directly examining their characteristics.

All of this is important as one attempts to understand the meaning of SES–intelligence associations for larger questions of social policy. Herrnstein's (1971) essay asserting that social position was largely attributable to the merits of performance based on IQ highlighted the issue of direction of effect in understanding SES–intelligence associations. Explicit in most arguments positing a direction of IQ causing social position is that intelligence is largely inherited, with little opportunity for environmental modification (this issue is explored in more detail shortly).

The flip side of the heritability issue is the degree to which intelligence is malleable across the life span. It is logically possible that intelligence could be 100% environmentally determined, yet still be highly resistant to change after certain periods in development. In fact, most evidence suggests there is little movement in individual test scores, particularly when viewed from the perspective of the ordering of individual differences. As already noted, stability coefficients generally exceed .80 after 5 years of age. Still, in the fewer studies that have reported patterns of individual performance over time, there are meaningful numbers of individuals who do show substantial changes (on the order of 1 *SD*) over periods of time (Neisser et al., 1996). Of most interest with regard to malleability is whether specific interventions might serve to systematically change the intellectual performance of individuals. Evidence that this is possible comes from several sources, including interventions with impoverished children demonstrating substantial IQ gains (Ramey et al., 1993), cross-racial adoption studies where average IQ's of blacks were one standard deviation above expected population norms (Werner et al., 1981), and secular trends indicating changes of several IQ points every decade across a wide range of countries and cultures (Flynn, 1987; Neisser, 1998). On the negative side, several environmental conditions are believed to result in lower IQ scores, such as lead exposure, nutrition, perinatal insult, and prenatal substance exposure (Lester, Lagasse, & Seifer, 1998; Neisser et al., 1996).

Developmentally Changing Functions in the Assessment of Intelligence

Intelligence is not a static phenomenon. The methods used to assess intelligence, and more important the mental processes and behaviors indicative of intelligence, vary widely across childhood. From a purely testing perspective, the types of tasks used to assess intelligence change dramatically over the first years of life and less quickly across middle childhood and adolescence (Bayley, 1993; Wechsler, 1991). From a more theoretical perspective, the fundamental nature of how children perceive and think about the physical and social world changes in systematic (and nonsystematic) ways across development (Beilin, 1992; Flavell, 1963; Piaget, 1972). When viewed in the context of unitary models of intelligence, the ever-changing fabric of abilities across childhood should be taken into account. In fact, one might conclude it is remarkable that such a high degree of stability in intelligence exists when many of the fundamental properties of the measurement strategy are changing across the period when stability is being assessed.

Definition of SES

Shifting focus to definitional issues regarding SES, there is some level of disagreement of how best to measure this construct, although this issue has captured neither the public nor professional attention focused on IQ. One approach to SES is to identify who associates with whom (Hollingshead & Redlich, 1958). Other approaches focus more directly on economic and education variables (Entwistle & Astone, 1994). Regardless of how SES is conceptualized, there is a common set of indicators used to arrive at a final determination of an individuals' social position. These include highest educational attainment, type of occupation, household income, or neighborhood of residence (usually in terms of census information). Also, some closely derived indicators from the previous list are used when they are more easily available, such as receiving public assistance, medicaid eligibility, or income below the poverty level.

There is no full consensus regarding the best measurement of SES (Entwistle & Astone, 1994; Hauser, 1994). In the psychology literature, the Hollingshead (1957, 1975) index of social position is by far the most widely used measure. This approach considers the education and occupation of the head of household (and in the more recent version, the other adult partner in the household), and combines these factors in a single weighted index, yielding five social status groups. Another widely used measure has been the Duncan index, which focuses solely on occupational status (Duncan, Featherman & Duncan, 1972); more recently, the U.S. Census groupings of occupation have been employed. In most circumstances, these different indicators of SES are highly correlated and provide similar information about this demographic characteristic of individuals and families, although there is some evidence that examining neighborhood adds additional information to the education–occupation based indicators of SES (Brooks-Gunn, Duncan, Klebanov, & Sealand, 1993; Greenberg et al., 1999). There is also theoretical (if not empirical) movement toward simultaneously examining multiple indicators of social position, including financial capital (income), human capital (education), social capital (household structure), poverty status, and occupation (Entwistle & Astone, 1994).

The major point to keep in mind when considering SES is that, as operationalized, it is a very indirect measure of any individual's real standing in the social order. No direct assessment is made of how an individual interacts with or is perceived by neighbors, coworkers, or other community members. Rather, these measures rely on historical trends on how American culture has segmented itself across economic boundaries. Thus, as typically used, they fail to consider such factors as lower SES families living in better or worse neighborhoods and the implications that might have.

HOW SHOULD WE UNDERSTAND THE ASSOCIATION OF INTELLIGENCE AND SES

Thus far, I have concentrated on some basic facts about the SES–intelligence association and some background issues affecting any interpretation. In this section, I note some of the interpretations that have been offered (which inevitably have counterinterpretations) and provide an overall assessment of how certain we can be about the utility of any of these explanations.

Intelligence Has Driven a Merit-Based Sorting Into Social Classes

One of the reasons for the continuing interest in SES and intelligence, despite the fact that little new empirical data is available, is the debate over direction of effect in explaining the association of these two variables. As noted earlier, Herrnstein (1971) reinvigorated the debate with his contention that our current class structure has derived from the sorting of individuals based on their abilities and talents (often termed *meritocracy*). The argument offered (fully described in Herrnstein & Murray, 1994) is relatively straightforward. First, the basic assumptions are that intelligence is unitary and well measured by standard indexes of IQ or *g*, and that heritability of IQ is high. Second, population data are examined to identify where IQ predicts various aspects of social position. Third, similar population data are examined to identify where IQ better predicts outcomes than a wide variety of *single* indicators such as children born out of wedlock, children experiencing parental divorce, parental SES, or quality of home environment (I return to this issue of single indicators in a subsequent section). From this series of analyses, the conclusion is drawn that IQ is the major determining factor on the eventual social position of individuals—if the analyses are taken at face value, such conclusions are quite reasonable.

From this basic conclusion, Herrnstein and Murray (1994) then draw a wide range of inferences. These are useful to consider as they encompass the controversial issues that frequently arise when the implications of SES–intelligence associations are addressed. Among the inferences are:

1. We should embrace the idea that IQ may (partially) emanate from genetic differences among individuals and races (but that this should not affect how the races deal with one another).

2. There exist dysgenic trends in American IQ resulting from differential birth rates among high and low IQ mothers (see also Lynn, 1998a, 1998b).

3. Solutions to crime and other problems need to be targeted at low-IQ individuals, as this is where most of these problems are apparent.

4. Intervention attempts to raise cognitive ability are misguided.

5. Emphasis in education should be shifted from attempts to serve below-average students to identifying the gifted and embracing the "ideal of the educated man."

6. Affirmative action programs should be drastically scaled back and applied only when "equal ability" is established.

7. Immigration of people with below-average IQ is placing strain on America's cognitive structure.

8. Government rules should be simplified (i.e., there should be less government regulation) to make the system equally accessible to low-IQ individuals.

9. Marriage should return as the legal and ethical centerpiece of American values and culture.

10. Individual initiative should be identified and rewarded in all areas of social and economic life.

Responses to Meritocracy Explanations. When considering this well-integrated description of conservative politics in 1990s America, the first question raised is whether the more evidence-based conclusion (of IQ leading to sorting on social position) necessarily leads to one set of political beliefs. For example, if one starts from the premise that the basic unit of analysis for making policy decisions should be the culture and not the individual, then many different inferences might flow from the basic scientific conclusion. Rather than setting individuals of different abilities free to find their own place in a highly competitive social–economic environment, policy might be directed at optimizing the chances of low-IQ individuals receiving the education and training necessary to be competent in occupations requiring technical or managerial skills—so that the society as a whole might benefit from the largest number of people performing the highest level of occupation. Similarly, attempting to reduce economic inequality through a more complex set of tax structures, economic incentives, affirmative action policies, or government-sponsored programs would serve the function of increasing inclusion of low-IQ individuals in a more integrated cultural system. Thus, it is important to differentiate the scientific argument (i.e., whether the direction of effect in the SES–intelligence association is that IQ drives social position) from the inferred policy implications.

The other important question to consider is whether the basic scientific conclusion (that IQ causes social position) is in fact correct. One comprehensive treatment of these issues may be found in Fischer et al. (1996), where the authors contested the meritocracy argument on two basic grounds—that some of the analyses are flawed (which when corrected tell a different picture), and that the basic assumptions about intelligence, social position, and the role of public policy are incorrect. In addressing the first issue (specifics of analyses) Fischer et al. demonstrated that when slightly more sophisticated indexes of social context are employed, the relative importance of social context and IQ in predicting poverty are about equivalent. [Note that much of the meritocracy argument rests upon the notion that if something is the single best predictor (to the exclusion of other candidate predictors) than it is the causal predecessor—a logic that is easily challenged.] The simple changes made by Fischer et al. were to aggregate a few basic social context variables, a theme I elaborate later in the chapter. Thus, a central aspect of the Fischer et al. (1996) argument (when the basic assumptions of Herrnstein & Murray are accepted) is that that the association of IQ and ultimate outcome looks very much like the same outcomes plotted against neighborhood, school, and home characteristics (p. 85). Furthermore, IQ accounts for only a small portion of the variance of ultimate social position (about 10%), begging the question of what other factors are operative.

On the interpretation side, Fischer et al. presented evidence in opposition to the assumption that IQ is relatively resistant to modification by identifying the importance of schooling and other "enrichment" programs on cognitive performance. This evidence draws on the work of Bryk and Raudenbush (1988) in examining individual learning trajectories using hierarchical linear modeling (Bryk & Raudenbush, 1992), and Entwistle and Alexander's (1992, 1994) studies of test performance in school year versus summer vacation periods. With these different premises and conclusions, Fischer et al. inferred a very different set of policy implications than was derived from the meritocracy. It is worth noting again that the scientific assumptions and conclusions advanced by Fischer et al. could be interpreted to support those policies advanced by Herrnstein and Murray (1994), emphasizing the importance of separating the science from the political conclusions.

Contextual Factors Covarying With Social Class Influence Intelligence

In discussing the meritocracy interpretation of the SES–intelligence association, we have touched upon features of the next explanation examined—that factors associated with social position affect the test performance of individuals. In this realm, there is far less reliance on the large-scale survey studies that form the basis of arguments for (and against) meritocracy, and much more reliance on smaller scale studies of behavioral development.

Parenting. Parenting practices vary by social class and they are also related to children's IQ. Several decades of research have documented that self-reported styles of parenting are typical of middle- versus lower-class parents. The major dimension examined has been the authoritarian style, with lower SES families more frequently endorsing practices that emphasize control, position within the family, and restrictiveness (Baumrind, 1971). These findings parallel those with respect to parenting values, where child conformity (obedience, good manners, sex-role conformity, neatness) is most highly valued in low-SES families, wheras independence (curiosity, responsibility) is more highly valued in higher SES families (Kohn, 1977).

These self-reported parenting practices and values are reflected in directly observed parenting behavior (although three is often low correlation between the two, especially if SES is covaried from analyses). Lower SES parents are more controlling, restrictive, punitive, and negative in their parenting styles (Bee, Van Egeren, Streissguth, Nyman & Leckie, 1969; Hoff-Ginsberg, 1991; Seifer, Sameroff, Anganostopolou, & Elias, 1992). Furthermore, when teaching practices are examined, these same characteristics are found in addition to less emphasis on providing a "big-picture" cognitive context for their children—they use fewer orienting statements, fewer attempts to engage children in the problem-solving process, and more directive statements (Barocas et al., 1991; Hess & Shipman, 1965).

These parenting practices, in turn, have some effect on child cognitive outcomes. In fact, the original studies of parenting were motivated by attempt to discern those qualities of parenting that were related to better intellectual performance (Hess & Shipman, 1965). These studies were ultimately confronted with the problem of SES confounds, which in turn led to numerous investigations of SES-related characteristics of parenting. More recently, studies appropriately accounting for SES in their research designs have demonstrated that more child centered, or scaffolding (Wood, Bruner, & Ross, 1976) parenting styles are associated with higher cognitive performance. Work in our own lab identified such parenting behavior (in a teaching task) that mediated the SES–IQ association when child attention was examined in the model (Barocas et al., 1991).

Schooling. Another domain where social context affects intelligence is schooling. It is well-established that in the United States there are many ways that schools reflect the SES of their students. Per-pupil spending, class size, quality of physical plants, quality and experience of teachers, and proportions attending private versus public schools are among the factors that reflect SES backgrounds of students. Although studies are inherently difficult to perform because of the segmentation of students in our schools by SES, some complex analyses have shed light on the issue. Jencks et al.'s (1972) classic analyses of survey data came to the conclusion that differences among schools made little difference in the cognitive ability of students, but that amount of education attained did have some effect. When effects of interventions were examined, a somewhat different picture emerged.

For example, Head Start and other preschool programs for children in poverty have resulted in demonstrable gains in children's IQ (Lazar, Darlington, Murray, Royce, & Snipper, 1982; Ramey et al., 1993), with the main issue being whether these gains can be maintained when the enriched educational environment is discontinued.

In a related domain, among those who hold the view of multiple intelligences, the construct of emotional intelligence has become a major source of investigation (Goleman, 1995; Weissberg & Greenberg, 1998). Many different intervention programs have produced gains in observed behaviors and teacher reports of social–cognitive abilities, conduct problems, social planning, impulsivity, and general adaptation to school social environments. These aspects of intelligence (if one accepts the premise they are indeed part of intelligence) may prove to be an important adjunct to traditional cognitive skills in predicting school success (Elias et al., 1997; Kushe & Greenberg, 1995).

Nutrition. Basic nutrition is essential for physical and behavioral development, and in the current context has attracted attention regarding whether it is associated with intellectual performance. Again, in the United States, poor nutrition is largely reflective of poverty; on a global basis the quality of nutrition reflects the overall economic status of nations. Although intuitively appealing, the empirical evidence about the role of nutrition in intelligence is more equivocal. Improvement in nutrition among children in developing countries results in sporadic gains in mental tests, which appear more consistent when motor development is the focus (Martorell, 1998; Sigman & Whaley, 1998). Still, these findings have led Lynn (1998a, 1998b) to conclude that the well-described secular increases in intelligence test scores (Flynn, 1987) are due entirely to rises in world-wide nutrition levels. In a related vein, intestinal parasites (which interfere with absorption of nutrients) also affect intelligence, but again the effects were present only when infection was very severe and improvements were not consistent when infection was treated (Watkins & Pollitt, 1997).

Neighborhoods. There is increasing attention to the role of neighborhoods in influencing various indicators of competence in developing children. In the United States, one major characteristic that distinguishes neighborhoods is the average social and economic position of the residents, with associated differences in resources such as housing, density, crime, or schools. Of interest when focusing on neighborhood is there does *not* exist a perfect match between individual socioeconomic factors and the aggregate levels in neighborhoods, thus allowing some ability to examine unique sources of variance at the individual and neighborhood levels. In the realm of intelligence, there is good evidence that neighborhoods indeed make a difference, at times above and beyond the influence of other social–demographic factors or individuals (Brooks-Gunn et al., 1993; Greenberg et al., 1999). This body of research is still relatively new, and analysis of neighborhood is relatively gross (e.g., areas defined by the U.S. Census). As more research becomes available, the specific characteristics of neighborhoods that affect individual functioning will likely become more evident.

Responses to Context Driven Explanations. Despite the fact that many aspects of social and physical contexts characteristic of different SES strata are related to intelligence, proponents of the intelligence-causes-SES argument contend that these associations are artifacts of the true underlying relations—that the associations we see in context factors related to intelligence are artifacts of the fact that intrinsic intelligence has in fact driven the social position of the individuals studied. Again, depending on whose analyses one regards as the final word, the ultimate decision regarding correct model will be vastly different (Fischer et al., 1996; Herrnstein & Murray, 1994; Neisser et al., 1996).

Intelligence Derives From A Dynamic Interplay of Individual and Contextual Factors

A very different perspective of the explanations for the SES–intelligence association is apparent when the construct of intelligence is broadened beyond the unitary view. Sternberg (1990) proposed looking at intelligence from a dynamic systems view, looking at the interplay of child-centered internal analytic characteristics, external synthetic experiential factors, and the developmental–contextual relation of practical application of individual and experiential components. In this approach (in addition to studying internal mental processes), emphasis is placed on understanding how experience is internalized, how individuals adapt to environments, and how individuals select environments.

Thus, instead of viewing intelligence as a characteristic firmly rooted in the individual where the question of group differences requires simple comparisons among individuals, it is viewed in a way that intrinsically unifies individual and context. In this more systems oriented view, the standard nature–nurture dichotomy becomes less relevant. Instead, questions are more of the form "How has the individual's cultural milieu become incorporated in adaptive intelligent behavior" rather than "How do groups of individuals differ in their intellectual performance?" This more relativist view requires greater complexity in how questions about social position and intelligence are framed.

As such theoretical formulations are relatively new, the research base for identifying how they ultimately differ with respect to SES differences is generally not in place. As noted earlier, when considering one aspect of an expanded view of intelligence, emotional competence, there are evidently specific mechanisms by which environmental context may play a role in its development (Weissberg & Greenberg, 1998). Within the more systemically oriented theory, the behaviors and operations targeted by emotional competence interventions would fall under Gardner's (1983) rubrics of *interpersonal* and *intrapersonal* intelligence.

Response to Systems Explanations. The distinctions between those who support a single-factor of intelligence as a fundamental property of individuals and those who support more systemically integrated multifaceted views of intelligence probably are reflective of fundamental paradigm differences than of arguments about the basic empirical data. Attempts to reconcile theories that grapple with phenomena at different levels of systemic organization (in this case *individual* versus the *integration of individual and social context*) are always fraught with difficulty. Until we have operational models of human behavior and development that truly incorporate multiple levels of systemic organization, we are likely to remain in a position where such fundamentally different types of arguments provide parallel explanations of phenomena such as intelligent human behavior (Sameroff, 1983).

Historical Factors in the Measurement of Intelligence

Taking one more step away from the individual person as the focus of analysis for understanding intelligence, another alternative to understanding the SES–intelligence association is that it results from a set of historical events, often colored by the social–political zeitgeist during the period when the use of intelligence testing was experiencing its greatest expansion. Two major social processes in the United States were dominant during the early part of the 20th century (when intelligence testing was first becoming a significant part of the culture): World War I and the large-scale population movements from Europe to the United States. Some analysts (e.g., Kamin, 1974) have argued that in both cases the intelligence test movement was strongly influenced by some of the more restrictive needs of the dominant culture to maintain its control over resources. In the case of testing in the military, the early tests used were excellent discriminators of upper and lower class recruits, and simultaneously clearly differentiated officers from enlisted personnel. In the realm of immigration, the tests likewise discriminated Northern Europeans from Southern Europeans, which in turn was consistent with legislatively imposed quotas of the time favoring Northern over southern Europeans.

In the military, intelligence testing became a major tool in selection for officer training and other specialized duties, whereas it did *not* become an integral part of the selection process for immigrants. Still, the legacy of the tests themselves may remain in that their utility in these tasks (a form of construct and instrument validation) may have skewed the development of a technology so interwoven with the differentiation of social classes and ethnic–racial groups that it is inevitable that any descendants of the early tests would continue to make these same distinctions (Kamin, 1974). This line of reasoning typically concludes with a call for elimination of broad-based use of the tests in education or occupation selection, as they simply serve to perpetuate a non-merit-based class structure. In some respects, this type of analysis frames meritocracy arguments in a new light. Rather than simply analyzing information from tools developed in a dispassionate context, the contention is that the tools themselves are so riddled with the expected answer that there are no opportunities for objective science.

Responses to Essential Bias Explanations. Of course, such social–political arguments have been as vehemently countered as they have been supported. Herrnstein's (1971) essay articulating the meritocracy position revitalized the opposing view in modern discourse, and his view was fully articulated (and connected to a large body of empirical evidence) in the Herrnstein and Murray (1994) volume—a book that went on to became a public sensation. When approaching this issue from the perspective of inherent bias in intelligence tests, Jensen (1980) concluded that bias does indeed exist when the definition is limited to a consistent finding that different groups perform at different levels. Jensen argued that this is not a flaw in the tests, but reflective of real, and likely genetic, differences in the populations considered.

In some respects, evaluation of the essential bias argument and its counterpoint rests on which assumptions are accepted at the outset. Under the assumption of multiple intelligences (where single indicators of g are viewed a flawed) and the belief that decisions to limit equality in standardization of tests to age and sex were too narrow, the case for merit-based differences in social position driven by intelligence has many conceptual flaws that render most current evidence irrelevant. Conversely, under the assumptions of intelligence being well measured by g and the soundness of behavior genetic approaches, then there is a case to be made for the intelligence-driven ordering of social position. Still, even given the assumptions as articulated by Jensen (1980) and Herrnstein and Murray (1994), there may sill be empirical flaws in the meritocracy arguments, with a comprehensive treatment of such an argument found in Fischer et al. (1996).

SOCIOECONOMIC STATUS AS A MARKER: GENERALIZATION TO MULTIPLE RISKS

At this point, I shift gears and discuss an approach somewhat different from SES in organizing the social context and position of individuals. Socioeconomic status is an indicator measure in social science research. That is, knowledge about SES provides little information about any psychological or social process that might be affecting thoughts or behaviors. Instead, what SES tells us is something very broad about a large aggregate of individuals. Because SES has been such a good predictor in behavioral research (although some might call it a nuisance) there has often been little interest among psychologists in pursuing the issues further as they are not in the basic realm of behavioral processes.

For those of us interested in how SES differences and poverty affect the development of children, the agenda of more fully understanding the processes by which SES might operate has become compelling. In particular, when considering the association of SES and intelligence, the public policy debate that has flared across many decades requires better understanding of the phenomena if we are to move beyond rhetoric and into the realm of scientifically driven appreciation of the phenomena in question.

One approach we have taken in our laboratory (along with many others in the field) is to examine simultaneously the many factors at different levels of social organization that are intrinsic to social position in U.S. culture. In addition to the status measures of education and occupation, there are numerous other characteristics that are known to be more or less prevalent in different social classes but are more proximally related to individual and social behavior. These include (but are not limited to) number of people in households, life events experienced by individuals, parenting practices, symptoms of psychopathology, parenting values, quality of home environment, marital conflict, family functioning, parental substance use, parental criminal behavior, and perceived neighborhood quality.

We were motivated by early findings from Rutter (1979) and Parmelee (Parmelee & Haber, 1973) that demonstrated the statistical power of aggregating multiple indicators of risk in the prediction of child outcomes. These studies were of very different domains, focusing on delinquency and psychopathology (Rutter, 1979) and on early developmental status in preterm infants (Parmelee & Haber, 1973). Common to both was vastly increased predictive power when multiple indicators were brought together in a single index compared to any of the individual predictors alone.

From a content perspective, Rutter's (1979) work was closer to our own in attempting to examine multiple social–contextual risks (as opposed to perinatal pregnancy, labor, and delivery risks). Rutter examined six risk factors— marital distress, low SES, large family size, paternal criminal behavior, maternal psychopathology, and care by local authorities. When used in prediction, there was a tenfold increase in detection (from 2% in families with zero or one risk to 20% in families with four or more risks) of psychiatric problems among 10-year-olds.

As our interest was in examining SES differences, we began with the premise that poverty co-occurs with many other risks (as already enumerated). We considered 10 risk factors: household occupation, maternal education, maternal psychopathology, maternal anxiety, family size, minority status, family composition, life events, parenting values, and quality of observed parenting behavior. To reduce data to a manageable form, each risk factor was dichotomized to yield a higher risk and a lower risk group. The final aggregate was the number of assignments to a higher risk group (Samerof, Seifer, Baldwin, & Baldwin, 1993). Two qualities of this index are noteworthy. First, it is psychometrically unsophisticated; second, it uses only measures of context—there are no direct indicators of child behavior.

This risk index was used to address three basic questions. What was the degree of association with IQ? What was the stability of this index? Did the multiple risk index add to our prediction of IQ beyond SES and race? The risk index was correlated with IQ around .60 at ages 4 and 13. This is in line with the effect size described in White's (1982) meta-analysis for the home atmosphere measures. Children in families with no risk factors compared with those in families with seven or more risks differed by about 30 IQ points at both 4 and 13 years of age. Stability of the risk index was .77 across the 9-year period, compared with a stability of child IQ of .72—there is an equivalent level of stability for the individual factor of IQ as for the contextual factor of multiple risks. Finally, when the context-IQ association was examined with SES and minority status covaried, the differences remained significant with the extreme risk groups differing by about 15 points at each age. Note that these types of effects are not unique to our own research program (e.g. Shaw et al., 1996; Greenberg et al., 1999).

These findings are important for several reasons. First, they tell us the traditional SES indicators may not be the best summary descriptors of the social and economic context in which children's intellectual skills develop. Second, there are many features of the social context that have substantial explanatory power beyond that explained by SES alone (in fact, the leftover portions still reveal 1 *SD* differences between the extreme multiple risk groups). Third, the power of aggregation is emphasized. Although IQ when used in practice is a single variable, it is actually an aggregation of many measured abilities. Thus, in analyses comparing predictive power (especially when policy conclusions are drawn) it is important to use the same power of aggregation in the social context as is used in the description of individual abilities. Such comparative predictive power (as in the types of analyses offered by Herrnstein and Murray [1994] and in the behavior genetics literature) might yield very different conclusions when more powerful social–contextual variables are used (cf. Fischer et al, 1996).

CONCLUSION AND COMMENTARY

Almost since the inception of intelligence testing, large and reliable effects of SES on intelligence have been detected. The only restriction on this statement would be that it applies to the psychometric view positing a unitary factor describing ability level in individuals. Other areas of cognitive research have been remarkably inattentive to the issue of SES in their research (a simple review of recent studies on cognition outside the realm of intelligence often reveal a failure to describe the SES of participants, let alone design of studies to evaluate its effects).

As described throughout, the explanation for the SES–intelligence association has generated longstanding controversies, most of which are not yet definitively resolved. Despite many available datasets and many analyses and re-analyses, fundamental questions about direction of effect remain unanswered. Of special note here is that little evidence is derived from experiments, as most of the desired experiments would be unethical. Instead, most information is from the few natural experiments that occur (such as adoption studies) as well as large survey datasets. The main exceptions to this rule are those studies where the question is asked, "Can environmental interventions change the intellectual performance of individuals?"

Some Noticeable Trends

There are several trends in the literature on SES and intelligence worth emphasizing. First, there is very little new empirical evidence being collected to directly address this issue. Given the degree to which group differences in IQ is perhaps the most widespread publicly debated question regarding the science of psychology, the lack of new research is surprising. Our science has progressed over the years and new approaches might yield better answers to the challenging questions before us.

In the realm of test construction, most effort is being directed to providing new updates to old standards such as the Wechsler series, the Stanford–Binet, and the many widely used achievement tests. As with most other aspects of American life, this part of our technology seems primarily driven by commercial interests, with little attention to what the next generation of tests (will there be a next generation?) might look like. Instead, the disciplines devoted to understanding cognitive, perceptual, and emotional processes are diverging more and more from the technology of psychometric test development for detection of individual differences. The strongest efforts in applying cognitive science findings to applied detection of individual differences may be in the domain of neuropsychology, which typically addresses issues of pathology and lags behind the most current knowledge in the field.

There appears to be renewed attention to dysgenic arguments regarding intelligence. These likely add little to scientific or popular debate, particularly when applied to immigration. The question of population trends in an inherited characteristic as a function of differential birth rates certainly has some academic interest. When the factor of immigration is included, however, little of interest to behavioral science can be learned. The peculiar issues about who chooses to live in which country tells us nothing about processes by which intelligence is transmitted across generations. Such arguments only serve to amplify tensions associated with national boundaries, which seem to have no positive scientific value nor utility in improving the social fabric in an increasingly shrinking world.

Finally, there appears to be declining interest in broadening views of intelligence (either in the realm of testing practices or general theory), perhaps indicating a discipline that has grown weary of addressing some important basic theoretical issues. During my graduate training in the mid-1970s, the debate following Jensen's (1969) critique of early compensatory education programs was at its height, which substantially informed my work at that time—intelligence testing and popular conceptualization of the construct. It is striking in that in this new century the same arguments are being debated with few theoretical or scientific additions, except perhaps some added perspective on how we should conduct the argument. Obviously, there remains a group of researchers and theoreticians working diligently on these problems (e.g., Detterman, 1998; Sternberg, 1988), but this has become a highly specialized area of behavioral science. In particular, there is little interest in the field of basic human development research to identify processes conceived within the framework of intelligence. One notable exception is the applied study emotional intelligence conducted primarily within an intervention framework (Elias et al., 1997).

A Look to the Future

Where does the field move from here? How should the more casual observer of SES and intelligence (behavioral scientist or not) make sense of things? The issue of SES and intelligence, particularly direction of effect, continues to be of interest and will not disappear. What will be most interesting in future years is research designed to explicitly explore the question. Secondary analyses of existing datasets have likely exhausted their utility, and new datasets brought into the secondary analysis enterprise will likely fail to include the necessary design and control features to advance the science beyond its present state.

Those studies where behavioral scientists critically examine the utility of their intelligence measures will likely be of special interest. When we use a standardized intelligence test, why are we using it? How does it relate to our research hypotheses? How might we be misinterpreting our results because we are attending only to the names of our instruments and not to their valid measurement characteristics? It is all too easy to pull a standardized instrument off the shelf, when more thought and care might produce a better study. Related to this is critical examination of the validation criteria for intelligence tests. Are educational and occupational attainment the only important products of cognitive activity? What other factors in the adaptive realm might be incorporated in intelligence constructs when attempting to predict these and other criteria?

Moving to applications of the science, we should be wary of inferences about policy labeled as scientific conclusions. Instead, healthy debate would be better served by clear labeling of these policy pronouncements as speculation and statements of personal values. On all sides of the debates around intelligence (whether they be about SES, race, use in school placement, evaluation of teacher performance, and so on) the science lags far behind that necessary to be useful in forming public policy (Gottfredson, 1997). What currently happens is that individual commentators cite selected findings or analyses to support their positions, rather than invoking a broad scientific consensus, which ultimately supports a distrust of science among the general public and a tuning out of the important policies being debated. As citizens, we should embrace the policy debate and take an active role in supporting our personal values and desires. As behavioral scientists, we should minimize the use of our work beyond the point where it has reached substantive conclusions.

As much of the policy debate has rested on arguments about inheritance of intelligence, I would suggest further that debates about nature and nurture are in large part an entertaining distraction. Although the quantitative estimate of genetic or environmental influences on specific behaviors is a legitimate scientific enterprise, such research should not be a bottom line in behavioral science, but should perhaps set the stage for where to look first when asking more process oriented questions about the development of behavioral systems of individuals in context. It is a fundamental characteristic of human behavior that it has a biological substrate and that it develops in context. More systemic conceptualization of intelligence as multiple abilities developed in context should lead us to ask better questions about processes underlying the development of the skills necessary to lead successful lives.

ACKNOWLEDGMENT

This author was supported by grants from the National Institute of Mental Health.

REFERENCES

Barocas, R., Seifer, R., Sameroff, A. J., Andrews, T. A., Croft, R. T., & Ostrow, E. (1991). Social and interpersonal determinants of developmental risk. *Developmental Psychology, 27,* 479–488. Reprinted in Annual progress in *Child Psychiatry and Child Development* (25th Edition).

Baumrind, D. (1971). Current patterns of paternal authority. *Developmental Psychology Monographs, 4*(1, 2).

Bayley, N. (1993). *The Bayley scales of infant development (Version II).* San Antonio, TX: Psychological Corporation.

Bee, H. L., Van Egeren, L. F., Streissguth, A. P., Nyman, B. A., & Leckie, M. S. (1969). Social class differences in maternal teaching strategies and speech patterns. *Developmental Psychology, 1,* 726–734.

Beilin, H. (1992). Piaget's enduring contribution to developmental psychology. *Developmental Psychology, 28*(2), 191–204.

Boring, E. G. (1923). Intelligence as the tests test it. *New Republic, 35,* 35–37.

Brooks-Gunn, J., Duncan, G. J., Klebanov, P. K., & Sealand, N. (1993). Do neighborhoods influence child and adolescent development? *American Journal of Sociology, 99*(2), 353–395.

Bryk, A. S., & Raudenbush, S. R. (1988). Toward a more appropriate conceptualization of research on school effects: A three-level hierarchical linear model. *American Journal of Education, 97,* 65–108.

Bryk, A. S., & Raudenbush, S. W. (1992). *Hierarchical linear models: Applications and data analysis methods.* Newbury Park, CA: Sage.

Cohen, J. (1988). *Statistical power analysis for the social sciences* (2nd ed.). Hillsdale, NJ: Lawrence Erlbaum Associates.

Detterman, D. (1998). Kings of men: Introduction to a special issue. *Intelligence, 26,* 175–180.

Duncan, O. D., Featherman, D. L., & Duncan, B. (1972). *Socioeconomic background and achievement.* New York: Seminar Press.

Elias, M. J., Zins, J. E., Weissberg, R. P., Frey, K. S., Greenberg, M. T., Haynes, N. M., Kessler, R., Schwab-Stone, M. E., & Shriver, T. P. (1997). *Promoting social and emotional competence.* Alexandria, VA: Association for Supervision and Curriculum Development.

Entwistle, D. R., & Alexander, K. L. (1992). Summer setback: Race, poverty, school composition, and mathematics achievement in the first two years of school. *American Sociological Review, 57,* 72–84.

Entwistle, D. R., & Alexander, K. L. (1994). Winter setback: The racial composition of schools and learning to read. *American Sociological Review, 59,* 446–460.

Entwistle, D. R., & Astone, N. M. (1994). Some practical guidelines for measuring youth's race/ethnicity and socioeconomic status. *Child Development, 65,* 1521–1540.

Fischer, C. S., Hout, M., Jankowski, M. S., Lucas, S. R., Swidler, A., & Voss, K. (1996). *Inequality by design: Cracking the bell curve myth.* New Jersey: Princeton University press.

Flavell, J. H. (1963). *The developmental psychology of Jean Piaget.* New York: D. Van Nostrand Company.

Flynn, J. R. (1987). Massive IQ gains in 14 nations: What IQ tests really measure. *Psychological Bulletin, 101,* 171–191.

Gardner, H. (1983). *Frames of mind: The theory of multiple intelligences.* New York: Basic Books.

Golden, M., & Birns, B. (1976). Social class and infant intelligence. In M. Lewis (Ed.), *Origins of intelligence: Infancy and early childhood* (pp. 299–351). New York: Plenum.

Goleman, D. (1995). *Emotional intelligence.* New York: Bantam.

Gottfredson, L. S. (1997). Mainstream science on intelligence: An editorial with 52 signatories, history, and bibliography. *Intelligence, 24,* 13–23.

Greenberg, M. T., Lengua, L. J., Coie, J. D., Pinderhughes, E. E., & The Conduct Disorders Prevention Research Group. (1999). Predicting developmental outcomes at school entry using a multiple-risk model: Four American communities. *Developmental Psychology, 35,* 403–417.

Guilford, J. P. (1956). The structure of intellect. *Psychological Bulletin, 53,* 267–293.

Hauser, R. M. (1994). Measuring socioeconomic status in studies of child development. *Child Development, 65,* 1541–1545.

Herrnstein, R. J. (1971). IQ. *Atlantic Monthly,* September, 43–64.

Herrnstein, R. J., & Murray, C. (1994). *The bell curve: Intelligence and class structure in American life.* New York: The Free Press.

Hess, R. D., & Shipman, V. C. (1965). Early experience and the socialization of cognitive modes in children. *Child Development, 36,* 869–886.

Hoff-Ginsberg, E. (1991). Mother-child conversation in different social classes and communicative settings. *Child Development, 62,* 782–796.

Hollingshead, A. B. (1957). *Two factor index of social position.* Unpublished manuscript. Available from the author (Yale University, New Haven, CT).

Hollingshead, A. B. (1975). *Four factor index of social status.* Unpublished manuscript. Available from the author (Yale University, New Haven, CT).

Hollingshead, A. B., & Redlich, F. C. (1958). *Social class and mental illness: A community study.* New York: Wiley.

Jencks, C., Smith, M., Acland, H., Mane, M. J., Cohen, D., Gintis, H., Heyns, B., & Michelson, S. (1972). *Inequality: A reassessment of the effect of family and schooling in America.* New York: Basic Books.

Jensen, A. R. (1969). How much can we boost IQ and scholastic achievement? *Harvard Educational Review, 39,* 1–123.

Jensen, A. R. (1980). *Bias in mental testing.* New York: The Free Press.

Kamin, L. J. (1974). *The science and politics of IQ.* Hillsdale, NJ: Lawrence Erlbaum Associates.

Kohn, M. L. (1977). *Class and conformity: A study in values* (2nd ed.). Chicago: University of Chicago Press.

Kushe, C. A., & Greenberg, M. T. (1995). *The PATHS curriculum.* Seattle: Developmental Research and Programs.

Lazar, I., Darlington, R., Murray, H., Royce, J., & Snipper, A. (1982). Lasting effects of early education: A report from the Consortium of Longitudinal Studies. *Monographs of the Society for Research in Child Development, 47*(Serial No. 195).

Lester, B. M., Lagasse, L., & Seifer, R. (1998). Prenatal cocaine exposure: The meaning of subtle effects. *Science, 282,* 633–634.

Lynn, R. (1998a). The decline of genotypic intelligence. In U. Neisser (Ed.), *The rising curve: Long-term gains in IQ and related measures* (pp. 335–364). Washington, DC: American Psychological Association.

Lynn, R. (1998b). In support of the nutrition theory. In U. Neisser (Ed.), *The rising curve: Long term gains in IQ and related measures* (pp. 207–215). Washington, DC: American Psychological Association.

Martorell, R. (1998). Nutrition in the worldwide rise in IQ scores. In U. Neisser (Ed.), *The rising curve: Long term gains in IQ and related measures* (pp. 183–206). Washington, DC: American Psychological Association.

Matarazzo, J. D. (1972). *Wechsler's measurement and appraisal of intelligence.* New York: Oxford University Press.

Neisser, U. (Ed.). (1998). *The rising curve: Long term gains in IQ and related measures.* Washington, DC: American Psychological Association.

Neisser, U., Boodo, G., Bouchard, T. J., Boykin, A. W., Brody, N., Ceci, S. J., Halpern, D. F., Loehlin, J. C., Perloff, R., Sternberg, R. J., & Urbina, S. (1996). Intelligence: Knowns and unknowns. *American Psychologist, 51,* 77–101.

Piaget, J. (1972). *The psychology of intelligence.* Totowa, NJ: Littlefield Adams.

Ramey, C. T., Bryant, D. M., Wasik, B. H., Sparling, J. J., Fendt, K. H., & LaVange, L. M. (1993). Infant Health and Development Program for low birth weight, premature infants: Program elements, family participation, and child intelligence. *Pediatrics, 89*, 454–465.

Rutter, M. (1979). Protective factors in children's response to stress and disadvantage. In M. W. Kent, & J. E. Rolf (Eds.), *Primary prevention of psychopathology (Vol. 3): Social competence in children* (pp. 49–74). Hanover, NH: University Press of New England.

Sameroff, A. J. (1983). Developmental systems: contexts and evolution. In W. Kessen (Ed.), *Handbook of child psychology (4th Ed.): History, theories and methods* (pp. 237–294). New York: Wiley.

Sameroff, A. J., Seifer, R., Baldwin, A., & Baldwin, C. P. (1993). Stability of intelligence from preschool to adolescence: The influence of social and family risk factors. *Child Development, 64*, 80–97.

Sameroff, A. J., Seifer, R., & Zax, M. (1982). Early development of children at risk for emotional disorder. *Monographs of the Society for Research in Child Development, 47*(serial no. 199).

Seifer, R., Sameroff, A. J., Anganostopolou, R., & Elias, P. K. (1992). Mother-infant interaction during the first year: Effects of situation, maternal mental illness and demographic factors. *Infant Behavior and Development, 15*, 405–426.

Shaw, D. S., Owens, E. B., Vondra, J. I., Keenan, K., & Winslow, E. B. (1996). Early risk factors and pathways in the development of early disruptive behavior problems. *Development and Psychopathology, 8*, 679–699.

Sigman, M., & Whaley, S. E. (1998). The role of nutrition in the development of intelligence. In U. Neisser (Ed.), *The rising curve: Long term gains in IQ and related measures* (pp. 155–183). Washington, DC: American Psychological Association.

Spearman, C. (1904). General intelligence, objectively determined and measured. *American Journal of Psychology, 15*, 201–293.

Sternberg, R. J. (1988). *The triarchic mind: A new theory of human intelligence*. New York: Viking Press.

Sternberg, R. J. (1990). *Metaphors of mind: Conceptions of the nature of intelligence*. New York: Cambridge University Press.

Thurstone, L. L., & Thurstone, T. G. (1941). *Factorial studies of intelligence*. Chicago: University of Chicago Press.

Watkins, W. E., & Pollitt, E. (1997). "Stupidity or worms": Do intenstinal worms impair mental performance? *Psychological Bulletin, 121*, 171–191.

Wechsler, D. (1991). *Wechsler Intelligence Scale for Children* (3rd ed.). New York: Psychological Corporation.

Weissberg, R. P., & Greenberg, M. T. (1998). School and community competence-enhancement programs. In I. E. Sigel, & K. A. Renninger (Eds.), *Handbook of child psychology (5th Ed.). Vol 4: Child Psychology in Practice* (pp. 877–954). New York: Wiley.

Werner, J., Lane, D., Mohanty, A., Nichols, R. C., McNemar, Q., Scarr, S., Weinberg, R. A., Oden, C. W., & MacDonald, W. S. (1981). IQ test performance of black children adopted by white families. In S. Scarr (Ed.), *Race, social class, and individual differences in IQ* (pp. 109–135). Hillsdale, NJ: Lawrence Erlbaum Associates.

White, K. R. (1982). The relation between socioeconomic status and academic achievement. *Psychological Bulletin, 91*, 461–481.

Williams, W. M., & Ceci, S. J. (1997). Are Americans becoming more or less alike? Trends in race, class, and ability differences in intelligence. *American Psychologist, 52*, 1226–1235.

Wood, D., Bruner, J., & Ross, G. (1976). The role of tutoring in problem solving. *Journal of Child Psychology and Psychiatry, 17*, 89–100.

4

Intelligence and Experience

Craig T. Ramey
Sharon Landesman Ramey
Robin Gaines Lanzi
University of Alabama at Birmingham

EARLY EXPERIENCE PARADIGM

The idea that an individual's early experiences are of particular consequence for later development is an old one, dating to biblical writings. Yet the significance of early experience has been advanced only intermittently in the history of Western thought. Other concepts have more frequently provided the dominant models of human development. In the 19th century, predeterminism was advanced by Galton, and other proponents of the primacy of heredity in development.

Predeterminism, unlike the earlier notion of preformationism, acknowledged maturational changes in form as well as size, but held that these changes were relatively encapsulated and consequently relatively unaffected by early experiences (Gottlieb, 1971). In the first half of the 20th century, the predeterministic view induced two empirical traditions that denied the contribution of early experience to later development: the study of instincts as unlearned patterns of behavior, and the investigation of behavioral development as controlled by the child's rate of biological maturation (Hunt, 1979).

The early experience paradigm replaced the concept of predeterminism in development with that of *probabilistic epigenesis*. Whereas predeterminism assumed that the maturational process is relatively unaffected by experience, probabilistic epigenesis emphasized the importance of sensory stimulation and voluntary movement for subsequent development (Gottlieb, 1971). The early experience paradigm further held that the presence or absence of stimulation at *critical periods* in development could permanently alter the individual's pattern of developmental or what today we refer to as developmental trajectories.

Hebb (1949) provided a neuropsychological theory for the existence of critical periods in intellectual *and* social development. Investigations with animals revealed that variations in early experiences affected both the organization and the biological bases of subsequent behavior (e.g., Kretch, Rosenweig, & Bennett, 1960; Thompson & Heron, 1954).

The educational implications of this empirical background were assimilated in the works of J. McVicker Hunt and Benjamin Bloom. Hunt's (1961) *concept of the match* put forth in *Intelligence and Experience* was an application of Piaget's dialectical model of development and assigned a greater role in intellectual development to the characteristics of the environment than to the hereditary make-up of the individual. Developmental outcomes were seen as the cumulative result of the child's successive interactions with increasingly complex stimuli (i.e., experience). Hence, adequate intellectual development depended upon the child's receiving *appropriate stimulation at the appropriate point in development*. Although Hunt's general thesis did not postulate critical periods in development, it implied that early experiences were particularly important.

In *Stability and Change in Human Characteristics*, Bloom (1964) made two major points that provided a major impetus for preschool interventions designed to affect intellectual development. First, he posited that intellectual growth occurred most rapidly in the first 4 or 5 years of life, and began tapering off by the time the child entered grade school. Second, Bloom argued that the first 5 years of life were a critical period for intellectual development from an educational perspective. Intellectual development was, in his opinion, characterized by plasticity only during the early years of life. Consequently, the first few years provided the only opportunity for facilitating intellectual development by enriching the child's environment. Bloom's ideas figured prominently in the creation of Head Start—the U.S. early intervention policy remedy to increase school readiness for children from low-income families.

EARLY INTERVENTION RESEARCH AS A CRUCIAL TEST OF THE EARLY EXPERIENCE PARADIGM

Race, Education, and Intelligence

Early intervention to improve intellectual development, as a concept, was born in the shadow of *Brown vs. the Board of Education*. In that 1954 Supreme Court desegregation case, the right to a decent education in the United States was affirmed. Not only were separate and unequal education systems disavowed, but separate educational systems for African Americans were judged to be inherently unequal because of the negative effects on child development due to social stigma and its associated negative psychological consequences. Racial integration within school systems was chosen as the instrument to promote educational equity.

For generations the institution of slavery systematically denied access to schooling and literacy. *De facto* segregation, after slavery was abolished, reinforced this outcome through neglect and underfunding of Black schools. Not surprisingly, in the wake of *Brown vs. Board of Education*, psychologists and educators discovered that African American children were entering integrated public schools at an intellectual and educational disadvantage relative to their White classmates. The pernicious race card was immediately played and some social scientists used psychology's bad penny—the nature *versus* nurture, either–or concept of development as an explanatory construct for these educational and cognitive inequalities. African Americans were judged as intellectually inferior to Whites due to genetic limitations (see Jensen, 1969). That this crude explanation is alive and socially influential can be seen in the popularity and reactions to Herrnstein and Murray's (1994) recent and fundamentally flawed book, *The Bell Curve*.

Another stream of evidence flowed into this general argument about intellectual potential in such a way as to apparently soften the perniciousness of the race card. Namely, the induction proceedings for World Wars I and II, that included the use of intelligence assessments for conscription and assignments. These assessments detected systematic inequalities among Whites. Whites from poorer, less educated sections of the country performed less well on standardized measures of intelligence than did Whites from more affluent and better educated sections of the country (Ginzberg, 1965). In 1959, during the presidential campaign, the then highly popular *Life Magazine* ran a haunting portrait of life in the Appalachian mountains depicting the terrible cognitive and social life-situations of poor White families in West Virginia and other states in the Appalachian chain. This time, instead of the race card being played, it was the social class card that was played. Many of the early settlers in the Appalachian chain—which until relatively recently was quite remote and inaccessible—were descendants of impoverished and lower class English, Scottish, Irish, and Welsh immigrants. The lower class children from the hardscrabble farms and hollows were often undernourished, undereducated, and cognitively delayed. Again, a convenient hereditary explanation was combined with social Darwinism to provide a psychological explanation for this state of affairs. This explanation fit well with the then dominant conception of heredity associated with the psychometric conception of intelligence.

Against this hereditary and maturationally dominated view of development, a small group of experimentally and clinically trained psychologists, who frequently had been grounded in learning theory, began to explore the role and consequences of early experience in rats, lower primates, and later, humans. Prominent theorists in early experience included: Hebb (1949), Hunt (1961), and Harlow (1958), all of whom emphasized the importance of early experience for brain and behavioral development. Although recognizing the importance of genetics in development, each of these theorists worked on explicating the roles that early experiences play in cognitive, social, and emotional development.

Another group of investigators conceptualized and conducted systematic studies involving young children and their families. Many of these investigators were influenced by the work at Iowa of Skeels and Dye (1939) who, in a methodologically controversial but seminal study, argued for the power of early experience to alter the development of intelligence and the life-course in institutionalized retarded children. The findings by Skeels—especially when contrasted with the dominant view of intelligence as determined primarily by hereditary forces—set the stage for larger scale systematic early intervention studies with conventionally accepted research designs including random assignment to treatment and control groups. Prominent among this group of researchers was Gray and Klaus (e.g., 1970), Weikart (e.g., Schweinhart & Weikart, 1993) and Caldwell (e.g., 1973). This work, collectively, and especially Gray's work with 3 and 4 year olds in Tennessee, laid the cornerstones for Project Head Start, which began in 1964 (see Zigler & Valentine, 1979).

Social Class as a Risk Factor for Intellectual Development

One of the most consistent findings by psychologists has been the predictable relationship between socioeconomic status (SES) and performance on cognitive and linguistic tasks. Lower class children, as a group, almost invariably demonstrate slower and lower intellectual trajectories than those of the general population. The classic works by Galton (1869) and Burt, Jones, Miller, and Moodie (1934) attributed these differences in intellectual performance to hereditary factors. Beginning with Hunt's (1961) influential book, *Intelligence and Experience*, however, it became academically respectable to consider that these social class differences might have a strong experiential component. During the 1970s and 1980s there was considerable research concerning environmental influences on intelligence, in general, and more recently on language development, in particular. Two major questions have guided research on environmental influences concerning performance by the different social classes. First, investigators have attempted to specify the earliest ages at which social class differences in cognitive and linguistic performance become significant. Second, researchers have tried to identify the psychological mechanisms related to different developmental trajectories (cf. Burchinal, Campbell, Bryant, Wasik, & Ramey, 1997). A brief synopsis of the empirical literatures for each of these research areas is presented next.

Intellectual Development
and Social Risk Mechanisms

If the various social classes begin life with similar physical and mental potential, the age at which they begin to diverge will provide some clues for possible causal mechanisms underlying that divergence. In general, researchers have consistently failed to show social class differences in intelligence during the first 6 months of life using standardized tests of infant development (Bayley, 1965; Golden & Birns, 1968; Hindley, 1960; Knoblock & Pasamanick, 1953; Lewis & Wilson, 1972; Ramey, Farran, & Campbell, 1979). Significant differences in intellectual performance (with lower SES children scoring lower) have consistently been reported during the second year of life (Golden & Birns, 1968, 1971; Knoblock & Pasamanick, 1953; Ramey et al., 1979). A vast literature concerning the school years consistently indicates major social class differences in intelligence (Ceci, 1991; Hess, 1970).

Item analyses of performance on intelligence tests have been used to identify the particular components of intelligence most strongly associated with social class. From an item analysis of intelligence test results for school-age children reported by Eells, Davis, Havighurst, Herrick, and Lyler (1951), it was concluded that "mean SES differences were largest for verbal items and smallest for picture, geometric-design, and stylized-drawing items" (Hess, 1970, p. 507). A more recent item analysis of the performance of lower class children at 18 months using the Bayley Mental Development Index and at 24 and 36 months using the Stanford–Binet has been reported by Ramey and Campbell (1977). In comparing an educationally treated preschool group of low-SES children with a control group not receiving systematic preschool education, they found that the control group's lower scores were due to their higher rate of failure on language items. This finding was also supported by the control group's relative inferiority (and below average performance) at 30 months of age on the Verbal Scale of the McCarthy Scales of Children's Abilities. The implication of language as a major component in the relatively lower intellectual performance of very young lower class children is consistent with previously reported deficits in the verbal abilities of older children from lower class families (Deutsch, 1967). If language is, as it seems to be, a major factor, to what do we attribute the linguistic differences and how early do the differences begin?

Language and Intellectual Development

Language is a social medium and is acquired, at least initially, in social situations. Therefore, the social situations of children must be examined to understand the learning of specific languages features. Throughout the world virtually all biologically healthy children develop a language system.

In this country, however, there are substantial differences in the specific elements of the language learned by lower class children. Furthermore, these differences exist before the children enter public school. Given that preschool-age children typically spend more time with their parents than others, and more typically with mothers than fathers (Rebelsky & Hanks, 1971), the mother–child behavioral interactional system becomes a likely candidate for close scrutiny concerning the development of language.

The current research on social class differences in mother–child interactions during the preschool years flows from classic studies by Hess and Shipman (1965) and by Bernstein (1961). Hess and Shipman (1965) demonstrated that middle-class mothers used more effective teaching strategies than lower class mothers and that the quality of the mother's teaching strategy was related to the child's level of cognitive functioning. Bernstein (1961) demonstrated that the speech of lower and middle-class parents differed with lower class mothers using a more "restricted code" in communicating; whereas, middle-class mothers used a more "elaborated code" characterized by greater flexibility.

Bee, VanEgeren, Streissguth, Nyman, and Leckie (1969) extended these findings with 4- and 5-year-olds and reported that middle-class mothers used longer and more complex sentences, more adjectives, and fewer personal referents than lower class mothers. With the realization that substantial linguistic differences in interactional styles existed by the end of the preschool years, investigators began to identify the earliest ages of those differences. Thus, Lewis and Wilson (1972) studied 12-week-old infants who represented five socioeconomic levels. They reported that although lower and middle-class mothers vocalized in equal amounts to their infants, the middle-class mothers were more likely to respond to their infant's vocalizations with a vocalization of their own; whereas, lower class mothers were more likely to touch their infants in response to infant vocalizations. Tulkin and Kagan (1972), working with 10-month-old first-born girls, found that middle-class mothers exceeded working-class mothers on every verbal measure they used, including total amount of vocalization and reciprocal vocalizing. Cohen and Beckwith (1975) reported that better educated mothers vocalized more to their infants at 1, 3, and 8 months and that they were more likely than undereducated mothers to address positive comments to their infants.

Observations of 6-month-old infants and their mothers by Ramey and Mills (1977) showed that lower SES mothers talked less to their infants and that their infants vocalized less than their middle-class comparison sample. These results supported an earlier report by Ramey, Mills, Campbell, and O'Brien (1975), which showed that lower SES mothers were observed to be less warm and verbally responsive, more punitive, and less involved with their 6-month-old infants than were middle-class mothers.

That verbal responsivity and involvement by mothers with their infants is important to the child's subsequent intellectual status is supported by results from longitudinal studies. Clarke-Stewart (1973) investigated the mothering styles of 36 lower SES mothers and their first-born children between 9 and 18 months. She found that "the amount of verbal stimulation directed toward the child significantly related to the child's intellectual development, particularly the ability to comprehend and express language" (p. 92). Clarke-Stewart also stated that, "it was strongly suggested that maternal responsiveness to the child's social signals was enhancing the child's later intellectual and social performance." More recently, longitudinal finding by Hart and Risley (1998) and Huttenlocher et al. (1991) have extended these findings on the importance of maternal responsiveness to young children's language development. Figure 4.1 from Huttenlocher's research illustrates the development of the relationship during the second year of life. The eightfold difference in children's vocabularies by age 2 years bears a striking relationship to the language input to the children from their mothers. Given these striking individual differences, the question naturally arises: Can they be modified by systematic interventions?

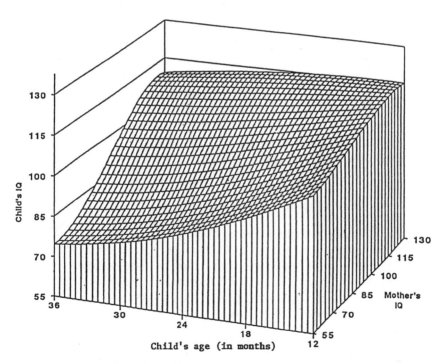

FIG. 4.1.   Effects of mothers' speech on infant vocabulary.

A THEORY OF EARLY INTERVENTION

Can *Intellectual* Development be Enhanced?

The test of intellectual malleability has come to be called *early intervention*. Early intervention, in aggregate, represents a broad array of programs, treatments, and strategies designed to enhance the development of children. Early intervention refers to a systematic process that begins with developmental concerns for high-risk children and extends through the delivery of supports, services, and therapies to eligible children and their families.

In early intervention, "early" typically refers to the first 5 years of life—the postnatal period when brain growth and development is most rapid and when young children acquire language, a sense of self, and the social skills essential for their everyday lives and, especially, their social interactions with adults and peers. Currently most federal funds for early intervention come through the Department of Education or though the Head Start program under the Department of Health and Human Services.

Advocates for early intervention generally agree that the earlier intervention begins, the more likely it is to produce desired results for children and their families. Currently there is much concern among developmental neurobiologists who study brain growth that if certain kinds of early stimulation are not experienced, the brain may later be unable to compensate for the earlier loss of critical experience (see Carnegie Task Force Report, 1994, 1996; Shore, 1997; Ramey & Ramey, 1998, 1999).

The term *early intervention* refers to both the process of planning and the actual delivery of services that are designed to meet each child's intellectual developmental needs. A central component of many early intervention programs is a child development center and/or a structured home visiting program designed to facilitate the child's intellectual, communicative, and social development.

The Logic of Early Intervention

Each year 10% to 20% of children enter kindergarten unprepared to meet the typical intellectual demands of school (Alexander & Entwistle, 1988). Lack of cognitive readiness bodes ill for their future school performance. Poor school readiness predicts increased likelihood of low levels of academic achievement and high levels of retention in grade, special education placement, and school dropout (Ramey et al., 2000). In turn, school dropouts are at much elevated risk for unemployment, teen pregnancy, juvenile delinquency, social dependency, and poor parenting practices. Their children all too frequently repeat this pattern (cf. Carnegie Report, 1996).

Poor school performance is foreshadowed by subaverage performance on cognitive and social functioning during the years prior to kindergarten. Epidemiological catchment-area surveys reveal that risk for both mental retardation and poor school readiness is highest among children from the lowest SES families and particularly those with low maternal education (e.g., Boyle, Decoufle, & Yeargen-Allsopp, 1994; Ramey, Stedman, Borders-Patterson, & Mengel, 1978).

Remedial special education to improve cognitive development and academic achievement that is begun in the elementary school years faces an enormous challenge. In essence, the rate of development must be altered if the progressive gap between normal and subaverage cognitive development is to be arrested and intellectual development is to be returned to normative trajectories. If genuine *catch-up* is to occur, then for a given period of intervention, the rate must actually exceed the normative rate. This point is illustrated in Fig. 4.2.

Little is currently known about how to actually accelerate general cognitive development beyond normative or typical rates. Clearly this realization adds further support for the rationale of beginning systematic intervention

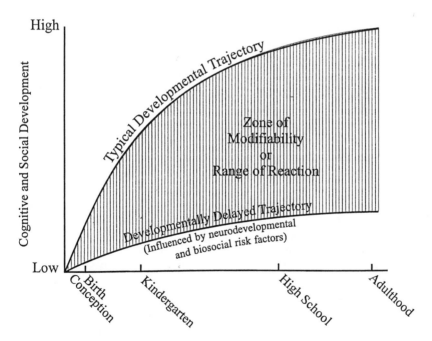

FIG. 4.2. Hypothetical range of reaction for experience-driven cognitive neurodevelopment.

early in a child's life, but how should we judge the success of early intervention programs?

Criteria for the Success of Early Intervention Programs

The criteria for the success of early intervention must be understood within several important contexts. *First*, the criteria are a function of the developmental period or epoch within which the intervention occurred *and* when outcomes are being judged. Thus, an intervention, that began at age 3 with children who were already developmentally delayed would have different expected outcomes 1 year later than an intervention that began at birth for high-risk infants who were being assessed at age 1 year. Similarly, if the intervention has ceased and follow-up is being conducted, then it is important to note the content and duration of the intervention as well as the developmental time that has elapsed since the intervention was terminated and what experiences the participants have had in the meantime. For example, what quality schools have the children been attending, what quality of home life have the children experienced, and who are the children's peers and what level of influence have they exerted. All of these factors are amenable to empirical documentation.

Second, the context of what epidemiologists, call *host factors* is important. That is, why were the children considered as eligible for early intervention? For example, current eligibility for early intervention from birth to age 3 under PL 99-457 emphasizes enrolling children with established disabilities such as Pervasive Developmental Delay or syndromes frequently associated with poor developmental progress such as autism or Down syndrome. There is a strong press for children with severe biological disorders to be enrolled early as opposed to children with social risk factors. Head Start is primarily for children from poverty level families and it typically begins at age 4, although an Early Head Start program for children under age 3 is now being tried on an experimental basis. Clearly, programs that begin later in the preschool years emphasize prevention of *secondary conditions or remediation* rather than *prevention* of delays and deficits that have their roots in poverty, family insufficiency, or family dysfunction.

Third, success for children typically revolves around *assessments of cognitive, linguistic, social, and emotional functioning* as well as later school performance, peer relations, and constructive social contribution. Complementing this child focus many early intervention programs emphasize appropriate parent involvement, family functioning, and integration into the community. Historically, however, the only consistently available information across experimentally adequate early intervention programs has been IQ scores, and they are the focus of this chapter. But first, we feel the need to pull the various threads discussed so far into a practically useful conceptual framework concerning early intervention, which we do in the next section.

Biosocial Developmental Contextualism as a Guiding New Conceptual Framework

Conceptualizing and implementing early intervention programs is a challenging task laden with logistical, conceptual, ethical, and legal problems. Because the task is complex we have found the following general conceptual framework to be useful. This framework has been presented in greater detail by Ramey, Ramey, Gaines, and Blair (1995) and Ramey and Ramey (1998) and is presented only briefly here. Figure 4.3 depicts the key sources of influence on the cognitive, linguistic, social, and emotional development of parents and children and specifies broad categories of early intervention services that have been included in previously reported early intervention programs. Within this framework the *current* biological and behavioral status of children and adults reflects the cumulative effects of their personal experiences. Influences on these experiences include developmental genetics, quality of the prenatal environment, variation in the pervasive sociocultural norms and practices, and special characteristics and circumstances of local communities. In addition, each family has particular supports and stressors that affect individual members and these effects may be conditional by the age sophistication, cognitive acumen, and other factors for family members that, nominally, inhabit the same environment. The source of supports and stressors may exist both within and outside the family such as divorce (within), or as job loss due to the local economy (outside).

At the start of an early intervention program, information is usually collected to contextualize the family within the larger social ecology. For example, are parents longtime members of the community, or not? What characteristics (e.g., beliefs, resources) do they feel they share with their neighbors or that set them apart? How do they regard local institutions such as schools (i.e., as potential sources of stress or support)? Furthermore, when conducting an initial needs assessment, a balanced view of the family that recognizes the presence of both supports (or strengths) and stressors (or problem areas) is frequently used to avoid inaccurate stereotypic attributions. Such in-depth knowledge allows early intervention program personnel to build on the family's natural support systems, and to allocate limited program resources in an efficient and, we hope, effective manner. In philosophy, most early intervention programs are highly contextualized and, therefore, individualized.

Next, this framework illustrates how resources and activities may be used to produce changes in adults, children, and the family's general environment. These changes may include those targeted primarily to: (a) the family as a unit,

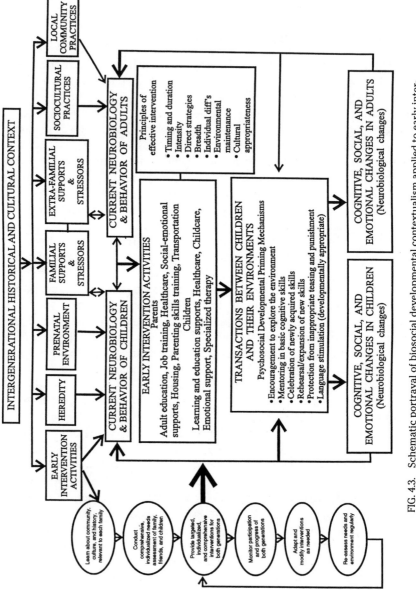

FIG. 4.3. Schematic portrayal of biosocial developmental contextualism applied to early intervention.

such as those related to adequacy of income, housing, utilities, food, clothing, safety, health care, transportation, cultural and recreational activities, and healthy lifestyles; (b) the adults, including adult education, job training, employment, social and emotional supports, parenting and family management skills; and (c) the children, such as early childhood educational supports, high-quality child care, effective social and emotional supports, and needed neurodevelopmental therapies. These resources and supports may be provided via many routes, including direct provision by the early intervention program, the program's referral of families to existing services and agencies (case management), and other means (such as by empowering friends and natural helpers, enabling pre-existing supports like churches and schools, or increasing family-initiated activities or self-referrals, or by effective use of the media).

For an individual family, the decisions about allocating programmatic resources and activities in an early intervention program frequently are made after a needs assessment or intake process. Almost all early intervention programs have developed some form of "case management" system—that is, a way to establish a trusting and continuous relationship between program staff and the family, so that as additional information is gathered about the family's life circumstances and progress, appropriate changes in the family's service plan can be made.

In this conceptual framework, changes in a child's intellectual status are mediated by specific *psychosocial developmental priming mechanisms* (described shortly). That is, the supports and services have their effect on individual children by potentially producing changes in their experiences. Social transactions within and outside the family and their cognitive mediation by the child is construed as the primary mechanism of developmental change for the individual child.

The cognitive, linguistic, social, and emotional developmental changes are, or course, interrelated and neurobiologically mediated. In short, these changes are registered in brain tissue and affect neuroanatomy, neurophysiology, and neurocircuitry. Important developmental neurobiological mediators implicated in early experience and early intervention include, neurotransmitter changes (such as in the serotonin, dopamine, and the endorphin systems), synaptic pruning as a function of experience (particularly response-contingent neural network development), and gene activation associated with experience. It is very interesting to note that approximately 60% of currently known genes are related to brain development and functioning and that in many, and perhaps the majority of cases, their expression is dependent on specific environmental inputs and experiences. This exquisite developmental cascade, although only partially understood, has led developmental neuroscientists and early experience researchers as well as early intervention practioners to reframe the overly simplistic nature versus nurture debate. According to a recent consensus report integrating the latest developmental neuroscience and early intervention thinking entitled *Rethinking the Brain* (Families and Work Institute, 1996):

> All of this evidence—and a great deal more that is beyond the scope of this report—leads to a single conclusion: how humans develop and learn depends critically and continually on both nature (an individual's genetic endowment) and nurture (the surroundings, care, stimulation, and teaching that are provided or withheld). The roles of nature and nurture in determining intelligence cannot be weighted quantitatively; genetic and environmental factors have a more dynamic, qualitative interplay that cannot be reduced to a simple equation. And both are crucial. New knowledge about brain function has ended the "nature *or* nurture" debate once and for all.

In Fig. 4.3, the provision of early intervention activities includes monitoring the participation and progress of both children and parents and adapting and modifying interventions as needed. These programmatic activities serve to increase positive outcomes by ensuring that those supports that are valued and used will be continued, those that are not will be discontinued or modified, and new supports in response to developmental changes in the child or family members will be obtained in a timely manner. Given the philosophical breadth of most early intervention programs and the individual differences in families when they are enrolled, few (if any) of a program's activities can be completely prespecified (such as when a mother will complete her education or job training and be ready for competitive employment; when health care that is not routine will be needed; or when a child is ready for more advanced books and learning activities). By reassessing needs regularly, with active involvement of program participants in this reassessment, and then adapting and modifying supports, early intervention programs become engaged in an iterative developmental process. To the degree that early intervention programs systematically document this process, and the associated neurodevelopmental and behavioral changes in children and adults, then a cumulative knowledge base about a program's operation and impact on families can be developed. This knowledge can help guide the program's future activities and resource allocation process, as well as to inform other programs and professionals working with similar types of families in comparable community and cultural contexts.

Psychosocial Developmental Priming Mechanisms. We recently summarized from the empirical literature six psychosocial mechanisms associated with neurodevelopmental changes in the status of children and adults pertinent to cognitive, linguistic, social, and emotional outcomes (Ramey & Ramey, 1998). We have labeled these *developmental priming mechanisms* to emphasize both their role in altering the course of human development and the fact that they help individuals be primed or "to get ready" for subsequent developmental opportunities. Admittedly, maturational and neurodevelopmental processes are complex and far from adequately understood. What is well established, however, is that what an individual does (behavioral activities) influences the development of the central nervous system (in turn, setting the stage for future learning and social functioning), just as neurobiological development itself influences the likelihood of particular behaviors in particular situations.

The six developmental priming mechanisms, identified in Fig. 4.3 are:

- exploring and gathering information,
- being mentored in new skills,
- having developmental advancements celebrated,
- reviewing and rehearsing new skills and knowledge,
- avoiding inappropriate punishment and ridicule for developmental advances, and
- being supported for language development and symbolic functioning.

We identified these developmental priming mechanisms based on our own empirical work and a review of the child development literature (Ramey & Ramey, 1992). Further, we hypothesize a positive relationship between the summed frequencies of occurrence of these developmental priming mechanisms and individual differences in intellectual status as measured by standardized IQ tests. We hypothesize that all of these priming mechanisms must be present in children's everyday lives, on a frequent and predictable basis, to promote normal, healthy development.

Early intervention, as a systematic social policy, is one mechanism to provide supplementary developmental priming mechanisms to facilitate more adequate development for high-risk children. In the next section we briefly review results of intellectual assessments of children that have been conducted to evaluate various early intervention programs that were designed to enhance intellectual development in high-risk lower SES children. All of these programs appear to have focused on some or all of these priming mechanisms as part of their early childhood education programs although the labeling of concepts from study to study is not consistent.

EMPIRICAL EVIDENCE I: SHORT-TERM RESULTS FROM RANDOMIZED TRIALS OF EARLY INTERVENTION

This review is limited to early intervention programs that used random assignment of participants to early intervention or control groups because that is the only scientifically defensible way to create initial equivalence of groups that will then be treated differently to ascertain if a given treatment regimen produces an hypothesized effect. If there has been an unbiased initial equivalence of groups; and, if the treatments are substantially and credibly different; and, if sample attrition over time is low and unbiased among groups; then, under the logic of sampling theory and experimental design, differences between treated and control participants are plausibly attributable to some or all of the treatment components. Thus, by restricting this review to studies with minimally adequate research designs, we are deliberately injecting a conservative criterion about the magnitude of effects of early intervention on intellectual development. As such we can be reasonably sure that the effects of early intervention are not artifacts of flawed or biased research designs. Because of the straightforward extrapolation of research to public policy in this field of inquiry (e.g., Head Start) we believe that this conservative approach is prudent.

Early Intervention Programs

Two reviews of the early intervention literature for high-risk, low-SES children have recently been written and we refer people to them for a more comprehensive and detailed treatment of particular programs (Bryant & Maxwell, 1997; Ramey & Ramey, 1998). In this section we present a brief summary of 11 early intervention projects that began intervention in the first year of life and three early childhood education programs that began intervention during the preschool years (3–5 years). All programs involved random assignment to intervention groups and were intensive, multi-pronged programs. The focus of the projects that begun in the first year of life was on the prevention of intellectual disabilities as assessed by IQ tests.

The eleven early intervention projects generally used one of three early intervention strategies: (1) a home-visiting program that was parent focused, (2) a center-based early childhood education program that was focused on parenting skills, or (3) a combination of a center-based early childhood education program and a home visiting program that is parent focused. A brief description of the characteristics of the subjects, research design, and intervention strategy is provided below in two sections: the first section addresses the programs that began intervention during *infancy* and the second section addresses the programs that began intervention during the *preschool years* (Note: the reader is referred to Ramey, Bryant, and Suarez (1985) for a fuller description of these projects). Following these sections, IQ results are presented.

Infancy

Home Visiting Programs. Four projects comprise the home visiting programs: Mobile Unit for Child Health, Family Oriented Home Visiting, Florida Parent Education Project, and the Ypsilanti–Carnegie Infant Education Project.

The *Mobile Unit for Child Health Project* focused on teenage, unmarried African American mothers in an urban setting (Washington, DC). The mothers' scores were greater than 20 on the Peabody. The grandmother was the head of the household in the majority of the families. The 3-year program began when the mother was 7 months pregnant. The experimental group received at least 20 medical services and 24 infant stimulation services at home for 1 hour and participants in the control group were referred to other available health services. At the end of the project, there were 44 participants in the experimental condition and 45 in the control condition. The *Family-Oriented Home Visiting Project* was conducted in an urban setting (Nashville, Tennessee) and focused on mothers who met the following criteria: less than 10 years of education, average income less than $4,137, and nonworking or working at night to ensure home visits could be made. Approximately half of the mothers were White and half were African American, with 72% of them having a spouse. The program was initiated with families in which the mother had a 17 to 24 month old and another child between 2 and 5 years. The experimental group received 30 weekly (60–90 min) home visits for 9 months and the control group received four social visits, photographs of children, and noneducational presents. There were 20 children in the experimental group and 17 children in the control group at the end of the project. The *Florida Parent Education Project* concentrated on families below the poverty level as defined by the hospital criteria. It was conducted in urban, small town, and rural communities (Gainesville, Florida and surrounding 12 counties). Approximately 80% of the mothers were African American and 20% were White. The program was initiated when the child was 3 months old. The experimental group received 1 of 6 home visit and/or playgroup combinations of 1 , 2, or 3 years duration and the control group received testing only. Children in the experimental condition received weekly 1-hour home visits for 3 years and participated in a playgroup for 2 hours twice a week in the third year. At the end of the study, there were a total of 192 children in the study, with 50 in the control condition and 142 in the experimental condition (83 for 1 year, 35 for 2 years, and 24 for 3 years). The *Ypsilanti–Carnegie Infant Education Project* primarily worked with families who were unemployed, parental education was less than 10 years, and approximately six people in the home. The program was conducted with both White and African American families in an urban setting (Ypsilanti, Michigan). The children were 3, 7, or 11 months old when they entered the program. The program lasted 16 months, with the experimental group ($n = 22$ at the end of the study) receiving weekly 60–90 minute home visits and the control group being tested only ($n = 22$ at the end of the study).

Center-Based Early Childhood Education Programs. Five programs comprise the center-based early childhood education programs: Abecedarian, Project CARE, Birmingham–Parent Child Development Center, New Orleans–

Parent Child Development Center, and Houston–Parent Child Development Center. The *Abecedarian Project* was conducted in a small town community (Chapel Hill, North Carolina) with African American families. The participants' average income was $1,455, with mother's education 10 years or less and their average IQ was 85. One out of four of the mothers was single. The program was initiated with families when the child was 3 months old and lasted a minimum of 5 years. The control group received free nutritional supplements for the infants along with social services and free or low-cost pediatric follow-up services and the experimental group received these same nutrition, social, and pediatric services *plus* participation in a full-day, year-round high-quality preschool program from the ages of 6 weeks to 5 years old. Half of the group also received additional support for 3 years after they entered public school. There were 49 children in the experimental group and 47 children in the control group at the end of the study. Participants in *Project CARE* had the following characteristics: $6,500 average family income; 11 years of education for both mothers and fathers; average maternal IQ of 87. About a quarter of the families were two-parent families. The program was conducted largely with African American families (95% African American, 5% White) in a small town community (Chapel Hill, North Carolina) and was initiated when the child was 3 months old and were followed longitudinally, as in the Abecedarian Project. Project CARE systematically compared two forms of intervention, a home-based program of weekly home visits for the first 3 years of life, followed by biweekly visits for the next 2 years and a center-based program identical to the Abecedarian Project. Children were randomly assigned to one of three conditions: child care plus home visits, home visits only, or control. All Project CARE children assigned to either the child care plus home visit or home visit only groups also received the home–school resource teacher treatment during the first 3 years of elementary school. There were 14 children in the first experimental condition, 25 in the second experimental condition, and 22 in the control condition at the end of the study. The *Birmingham–Parent Child Development Center* program participants had the following characteristics: $4,000 annual income, mean maternal education level of approximately 11 years; approximately 5 people in the home, with 50% of them having the father as head of the household. The majority of the families lived in public housing, with less than 50% receiving welfare. The program was conducted in an urban setting (Birmingham, Alabama) with African American families. The program was initiated when the child was between 3 and 5 months old and lasted for 31 to 33 months. The experimental group received daycare, parent training and work experience in day-care settings ($n = 71$ at the end of the study) and the control group received a small stipend for testing ($n = 65$ at the end of the study). The intensity of services varied from 12 hours a week when the children were between 3 and 11 months of age to 20 hours a week when the children were between

12 and 17 months of age to 40 hours a week when the children were between 18 and 36 months of age. The *New Orleans–Parent Child Development Center* program participants had the following characteristics: $4,000 average income; approximate maternal education of 10 to 11 years; approximately 5 person in the home, with 50% having the father as the head of the household. The program was conducted in an urban setting (New Orleans, Louisiana) with African American families. The program was initiated when the child was 2 months old and lasted 34 months. The experimental group received day care, parent training, and family services twice a week for 3 hours and the control group were offered health services and a stipend for testing. There were 67 children in the experimental group and 59 children in the control group at the beginning of the study. The *Houston–Parent Child Development Center* family characteristics were as follows: $6,000 average annual income; mean maternal education of 7.5 years, with one third of the mothers speaking solely Spanish; approximately six people in the home, with 90% of the families having the father present. The majority of the families lived in a house. The program operated in an urban setting (Houston, Texas) with Mexican American families. The program began with families when their child was 1 year old and lasted 24 months. The first year, the program was conducted in the family's home; the second year the program was conducted at the center. The experimental group received home visits, day care, and family services ($n = 44$ at end of study) and the control group received testing only ($n = 58$ at the end of the study). For the experimental group, families received 90-minute home visits for 30 weeks and four family workshops in the first year and 2- to 3-hour sessions 4 days a week for 8 months and nightly meetings in the second year.

Home-Visiting and Center-Based Programs. Two programs offered both home visiting and center-based programs: the Milwaukee Project and the Infant Health and Development Program. The *Milwaukee Project* targeted African American mothers from an economically depressed urban community (Milwaukee, Wisconsin) as defined by the census tract, with mothers who have an IQ of less than 75. The program began when the child was between 3 and 6 months of age. Many hours of home visits were conducted in the first 4 months of the program and then full-day, year-round day care was offered to the child for 6 years at the center and the mother received 2 years of vocational and social education. The control group received testing only. There were 17 participants in the experimental group and 18 in the control group at the end of the project. The *Infant Health and Development Program* targeted population was low birth weight (2,500 g), premature (< 37 weeks) infants born in Level III hospitals, with no major congenital anomalies. The program was conducted in eight sites across the country with great demographic diversity. There was great ethnic diversity in the infants as well: 53% were African American, 10% White–non-Hispanic, and 37% were White, Asian, or other. Families in the experimental condition received home visits beginning at hospital discharge weekly for the first year, biweekly visits until 36 months corrected age; children attended a full-day, 5-day-per-week child development center beginning at 12 months corrected age; parent group meetings occurred bimonthly, beginning at 12 months. All children, both control and experimental, received pediatric follow-up. At the beginning of the study, there were 377 children assigned to the experimental group and 608 assigned to the control group.

Early Intervention Programs: Preschool Years.   Three early childhood education programs began their programs during the preschool years: Perry Preschool Project, Early Training Project, and the Academic Preschool Project. The *Perry Preschool Project* program participants had the following characteristics: 53% of the families were two-parent families, approximately seven people were in the home, 70% of the families had at least one parent employed, the mean maternal education was 9.7 years, and the mean paternal education was 8.8 years. The program was conducted with African American families in an urban setting (Ypsilanti, Michigan) and was initiated when the child was 4 years old for the first cohort and when the child was 3 years old for the remaining cohorts (total of five cohorts). The program lasted 30 weeks for the first cohort and 60 weeks for cohorts 2 through 5. The experimental group received 2 years of preschool (12½ hours per week) and weekly 90-minute home visits. The control group received testing only. There were 58 children in the experimental condition and 65 children in the control condition at the end of the study. The *Early Training Project* was conducted with families who were: in unskilled or semiskilled occupations, average income less $3,000, and mother's education less than 8 years. Approximately six or seven people were in the homes, with 67% of the families being two-parent families. The program was conducted in small town communities (Tennessee) with African American families. The program was initiated when the child was between 3 and 4 years of age. There were two experimental conditions: Group one received 3 years of summer school and home visits and Group two received 2 years of summer school and home visits. The summer program was offered 4 hours daily for 10 weeks and the winter program consisted of weekly 1-hour home visits for 9 months. The control group participants were given gifts, picnics, and twice weekly play periods in the last summer. At the end of the study, 19 children were in experimental condition one, 19 children in experimental condition two, and 18 children in the control group. The *Academic Preschool* project was conducted in an urban setting (Champaign, Illinois) with mostly African American families when the child was 4 years of age. Thirty-forty percent of the families were receiving welfare and were usually in unskilled or semiskilled occupations. The experimental group received 2 years of Academic Preschool 2 hours a day and the control group received 1 year of traditional preschool and 1 year of public school kindergarten. At the beginning of the study, there were 15 children in the experimental condition and 28 children in the control condition.

Birth to Age 3 Results

Table 4.1 presents age 3-year IQ findings. (Note: Table 4.1 is an updated version of an analysis originally reported by Ramey, Bryant, and Suarez [1985]). Tests of IQ are highly relevant to these projects because general intelligence is what they sought to influence and IQ tests are the best measure of general intelligence that have been developed for young children.

When the 11 relevant studies are arrayed based on the magnitude of treatment effects, they seem to cluster into four groups: 32 IQ point difference (Group one); 12 to 17 IQ point difference (Group two); 6 to 8 IQ point difference (Group three); and 3 to 4 IQ point difference (Group four). *Group One:* The Milwaukee Project, with the most intensive treatment, showed the largest treatment–control group difference at age 3 (32 points) and forms a

TABLE 4.1
Stanford–Binet Scores at Three Years of Age From Early Intervention (EI) Programs for High-Risk Children That Used Randomized Designs

	Intervention – Control IQ Difference	Treatment Mean	Control Mean	Type of Program*
Milwaukee Project[1]	32	126	94	Both
Abecedarian Project[2]	17	101	84	Center –Parent
Infant Health and Development Project[3] 2000 –2500 gram birthweight	13	98	85	Both
Project CARE[4]	12	105	93	Center –Parent
Mobile Unit[5]	8	99	91	Home Visit
Family-Oriented Home Visiting[6]	8	93	85	Home Visit
Birmingham Parent –Child Development Center[7]	7	98	91	Center –Parent
PCDC –New Orleans[8]	6	105	99	Center –Parent
PCDC –Houston[9]	4	108	104	Center –Parent
Florida Parent Education[10]	4	95	91	Home Visit
Ypsilanti –Carnegie Infant Project[11]	3	104	101	Home Visit
Average IQ effect of IQ	10.4	103.5	93.1	

Note. [1]Garber (1988). [2]Ramey et al. (1999). [3]Ramey et al. (1992). [4]Wasik, Ramey, Bryant, & Spalling (1990). [5]Gutelius et al. (1997). [6]Gray & Ruttle (1980). [7-9]Andrews et al. (1982). [10]Gordon & Guinagh (1978). [11]Epstein & Weikart (1979)

*Center-Parent = a center-based early childhood education program that was focused on parenting skills; Home Visit = home visiting program; Both = a combination of a center-based early childhood education program and a home visiting program.

category of its own. *Group Two:* For the other three, full-day, early childhood projects (Abecedarian, Infant Health and Development, and Project CARE), treatment–control differences of about three fourths to one standard deviation (17, 13, 12 respectively) were observed. These three projects form a second cluster in terms of magnitude of effect. *Group Three:* The third group of studies includes four programs that had practically important group differences, but differences of somewhat more modest magnitude 6 to 8 IQ points. Two of these were Parent Child Development Centers (PCDCs in Birmingham and New Orleans) that were center-based, parent-focused interventions. The other two (Mobile Unit and Family-Oriented Home Visiting) were home-visit, parent-focused projects. *Group Four:* The fourth group of projects all have mean differences in the predicted direction but of quite modest magnitude (3 or 4 points). They also tended to be the least intensive programs.

Among the studies, general support is provided for an *intensity of treatment hypothesis.* That is, more intensive treatments produced larger intellectual benefits for high-risk children? Further, it appears that a variety of modes of operation can successfully alter the course of intellectual development during the first 3 years of life for high-risk children. Taken collectively, these 11 projects average approximately 10 IQ point boast as a function of early intervention, but range from 3 to 32 IQ points. Further, the function of the interventions was to maintain the treated groups at or above national average.

Ages 3 to 5 Years Results

The database for discussion of IQ changes in the so-called preschool years (ages 3–5) is composed of fewer studies than were available for the period through age 3. In part, this reflects the historical awareness that early intervention needed to begin *earlier* if it is to be preventive rather than remedial. Interventions that began at age 3 or later typically occurred in the 1950s and 1960s. The more recent studies tend to begin at younger ages.

As previously discussed, three studies used random assignment to treatment or control groups and intervened for 1 to 3 years beginning at age 3 or 4: Perry Preschool, Early Training Project, and Academic Preschool and three other studies began intervention in infancy and continued treatment through the preschool years (Milwaukee Project, Abecedarian Project, and Project CARE). Results from these studies are presented in Table 4.2. In some studies, IQ tests were given before and after the preschool intervention rather than on the child's birthday, so the ages are approximately 3 and 5 years.

Two studies showed a remarkable improvement in IQ scores of the treated group after intervention. Treated children in the Academic Preschool improved 17 points, and treated children in the Perry Preschool improved 16 points. Perry Preschool children were initially selected based on IQ scores of less than 85, whereas Academic Preschool children were selected from a

TABLE 4.2
Change in Children's IQ Scores From Ages Three to Five Years for Intervention That Began in Infancy and Preschool

	Early Intervention			Control		
	3 Years	5 Years	Change	3 Years	5 Years	Change
Interventions That Began in Infancy						
Milwaukee Project	126	118	-8	94	93	-1
Abecedarian Project	101	101	0	84	94	+10
Project CARE	105	103	-2	93	95	+2
Interventions That Began in Preschool						
Perry Preschool	79	95	+16	78	84	+6
Early Training Project	90	97	+7	95	88	-7
Academic Preschool	95	112	+17	95	102	+7

disadvantaged population but with an average IQ of 95 upon entry. Scores of the control-group children in both of these studies also improved about 6 or 7 points. Both of these studies involved at least one full school term of intervention and succeeded in producing significant treatment–control groups differences.

The Early Training Project intervened most intensely during 10-week, summer sessions with home visits occurring during the year. This study also produced significant treatment–control group differences at 5 years, and differences of about the same magnitude as the Perry Preschool Program. In absolute gains, the treatment group children in the Early Training Project gained 7 IQ points over 2 years of intervention, but, because the control group children decreased 7 points over the same time period, the outcome at age 5 looked very similar to the Perry Preschool results.

Results from the three studies that continued preventive intervention up to school entry, the Milwaukee Project, the Abecedarian Project, and Project CARE, showed significant treatment-comparison differences at age 5. The Milwaukee early intervention children still average far above the mean (Stanford–Binet IQ = 118) whereas the Abecedarian treated children scored right at the national mean (WPPSI IQ = 101). The intensity differences between these treated studies have been discussed in detail in a previous publication (Campbell & Ramey, 1995) and may be the reason for the difference in the absolute treatment group mean scores.

Overall, the preschool results seem to show that continuous interventions continued to have positive effects on intelligence, and that programs that began at age 3 or 4 were also able to raise IQ levels. No studies experimentally addressed the issue of timing of the intervention, but the Perry Preschool and the Early Training Project, which began at age 3, and the Academic Preschool, which began at age 4, were all able to produce significant IQ gains by age 5 in the children who received the educational treatment. Thus, it is clear from multiple high-quality early education experiments that school readiness as assessed by standardized measurements of intellectual performance, can be improved to a practically important degree.

EMPIRICAL EVIDENCE II: LONG-TERM RESULTS

IQ Results

Because all the projects we have mentioned can be construed as school readiness projects, it is naturally of interest to learn how treated and control group children have fared later in school. Long-term follow-up has been widely regarded as a major part of the test of the early experience paradigm. Although we harbor reservations about the theoretical soundness of this expectation (which we elaborate in a later section) it is apparently commonsensical to hope that an investment in early education (all other things being equal) will result in later school benefits for children from high-risk families. The later the measurement occasions, the more stringent tends to be.

The latest occasion on which directly comparable data exist is age 15— and at that assessment occasion these are now three relevant projects that have had random assignment to treatment and control conditions: the Abecedarian Project; the Milwaukee Project, and the Perry Preschool Project. All three treated children from economically disadvantaged families, primarily African American, but their selection criteria varied somewhat. The Milwaukee study sample was limited to children born to very low IQ mothers (IQ < 75); the Perry Preschool Project enrolled children aged 3 years or 4, with 3-year IQs between 70 and 85; the Abecedarian study used a weighted combination of 13 risk—social risk factors reflecting family sociodemographic circumstances. Also, the programs in which children were enrolled varied. The Perry Preschool provided a half-day center-based educational program for children aged 3 to 5, with family visits in the afternoons. The Milwaukee and Abecedarian programs provided child and parent focused, full-day educational intervention within a preschool setting, from infancy through age 5. The Milwaukee project continued its educational program through the children's kindergarten year. Midadolescent intellectual and academic outcomes are available for all three programs, although the academic data from the Milwaukee Project have not been published yet.

Table 4.3 contains means for midadolescent IQ scores reported by all three intervention studies. The Abecedarian and Milwaukee programs appear to have had a more enduring impact on the IQ performance of treated individuals than did the Perry Preschool Project. Subjects treated in the Perry Preschool no longer showed a significant IQ advantage over controls by age 15. The groups differ by less than one IQ point at age (81.0 vs. 80.7) and are significantly below the national average. In contrast, the children treated in the Milwaukee study consistently outscored controls through age 15. At that time, the last occasion for which scores are available, they maintained a 10-point IQ advantage over the Milwaukee controls (101.1 vs. 91.1). Abecedarian children treated in preschool also outscored controls through age 15, but not as dramatically. To provide a more comparable contrast between the Milwaukee and Abecedarian studies, the treatment–control difference in IQ for Abecedarian treatment and control participants born to with IQ < 70 mothers was calculated. Thirteen of the Abecedarian mothers had IQ scores of 70 or below. It is interesting to note that, when mean IQ scores are compared for the 12 of these Abecedarian subjects (6 in the preschool treatment group, 6 in the preschool control group) for whom age-15 child IQ data are available, the preschool treatment–control difference is 11.7 IQ points, very comparable to the age 15 Milwaukee treatment–control IQ difference.

TABLE 4.3

Adolescent Mean Intellectual Test Scores for the Abecedarian, Milwaukee, and Perry Preschool Early Educational Programs and Academic Test Scores for the Abecedarian and Perry Preschool

Programs	Early Intervention Group	Control Group
Mean IQ score		
Abecedarian[a]	95.00	90.3
Perry Preschool[b]	81.00	80.7
Milwaukee[b]	101.1	91.1
California Achievement Test (range of percentile scores)		
Abecedarian	40	28
Perry Preschool	16	<10

Note. aBased on the Wechsler Intelligence Scale for Children–Revised (WISC–R)

Academic Achievement Results

Both the Abecedarian study and the Perry Preschool Project obtained California Achievement Test (CAT) percentile scores for academic achievement in Reading, Mathematics, and Language at eighth grade. Abecedarian children earned higher average scores than did the Perry Preschool Project subjects: CAT percentile scores averaged 40th percentile for Abecedarian preschool Experimental subjects, those of the preschool controls were at the 28th percentile. In contrast, subjects treated in the Perry Preschool Project earned academic achievement scores between the 15th and 17th percentiles and their controls earned scores below the 10th percentile (L. J. Schweinhart, personal communication, May, 1993). Thus, for the Abecedarian and Perry Preschool studies, statistically significant academic benefits related to preschool programs were maintained into adolescence, long after treatment had ended. The absolute levels of performance between the Abecedarian and Perry Preschool participants at eighth grade was probably influenced by the quality of schools that they attended, although this cannot be established definitively. The Perry children attended inner-city schools, whereas, the Abecedarian children attended top ranking schools in North Carolina, schools that had, on average, relatively few at-risk children and very substantial resources for them. The Milwaukee study reportedly found no treatment–control differences in academic performance by 7 years in school (H. Garber, personal communication, June, 1992). Even if one concedes that intervention in early childhood had a more powerful effect, it is still necessary to explain the fact that midadolescent academic test scores and indices of progress through school (or of failing to made satisfactory progress) still showed positive effects from an intervention that happened so many years earlier. The most parsimonious explanation appears to be that the early cognitive gains reflected in higher preschool IQ scores were associated with greater mastery of academics from the start, which led, in turn, to better performance thereafter. At least, through age 15, early mastery has continued to be associated with higher scores on tests of reading and mathematics. There does appear to be support for the suggestion by Zigler, Abelson, Trickett, and Seitz (1982) that early academic success is associated with continued success. It does not appear to be entirely dependent upon continued enhancement of IQ. In the Abecedarian study, IQ differences were less pronounced at age 15 than were academic benefits, and the Perry Preschool study found midadolescent academic benefits in the absence of any demonstration of lasting IQ benefits.

Woodhead (1988) speculated that, even in the absence of enduring IQ or achievement test differences, early intervention may change the psychosocial functioning of treated children, leading teachers to perceive them in more positive ways, and influencing the teacher's decisions about nominating the child for grade retention or assignment to special classes. In the Abecedarian study, there were both academic test score benefits and indices of enhanced school progress. These were fewer instances of retention in grade and Special Education placement for students treated in preschool as indicated in Fig. 4.4. The latter Abecedarian finding is consistent with the report by the Consortium for Longitudinal Studies of better school progress for students with preschool treatment (Lazar, Darlington, Murray, Royce, & Snipper, 1982).

EMPIRICALLY ESTABLISHED GENERAL PRINCIPLES OF EARLY INTERVENTION

Clearly, variation exists in the degree and extensiveness of the effects of early intervention as well as the likely duration of benefits. Following are seven principles derived from the literature by Ramey and Ramey (1998), that represent a short-hand summary of the early intervention literature.

1. *Principle of developmental timing.*   Generally, interventions that begin earlier in development and continue longer afford greater benefits to the participants than do those that begin later and do not last as long.

2. *Principle of program intensity.*   Programs that are more intensive, as indexed by the number of hours per day, days per week, and weeks per year of contact with children and their families, produce larger positive effects

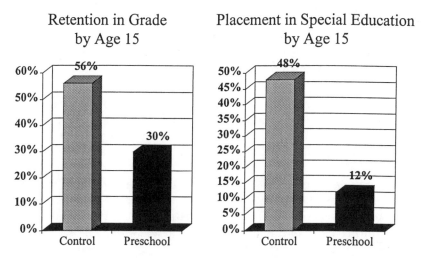

FIG. 4.4. Retention in grade and special education placements in the Abecedarian project.

than do interventions that are less intensive. Further, children and parents who participate the most actively and regularly are the ones who show the greatest overall progress.

3. *Principle of direct provision of learning experiences.* Children receiving interventions that directly alter their daily learning experiences have larger and longer lasting results than do those that rely primarily on indirect routes to change children's competencies (e.g., parent training only).

4. *Principle of program breadth and flexibility.* Interventions that provide more comprehensive services and use multiple routes to enhance children's development generally have stronger effects, compared to interventions that are narrower in their focus.

5. *Principle of individual differences in risk and response.* Some children show greater benefits from participation in educational interventions than do other children. Thus far, these individual differences appear to relate to aspects of the children's initial risk condition.

6. *Principle of ecological dominion and environmental maintenance of development.* Over time, the initial positive effects of early interventions will diminish to the extent that there are not adequate environmental supports to maintain children's positive attitudes and behavior and to encourage continued learning relevant to the children's lives.

7. *Principle of Cultural Congruence.* To achieve desired outcomes, interventions provided for children and families must recognize and build upon cultural beliefs, traditions, and practices. To the extent that interventions are perceived as culturally relevant and welcomed, they are more likely to be valued, used, and incorporated into participants' everyday lives.

CONTEMPORARY RESEARCH NEEDS AND POLICY ISSUES

There are many program development, scientific, and public policy issues of contemporary importance concerning early experience and early intervention. We will comment briefly on four issues that we judge to be crucial to continued progress in the field.

1. Timing and content variations in early intervention programs. The question of the efficacy of early intervention has now been answered in the affirmative. Yes, early intervention *can* improve the course of early human development during its application and is associated with long-term positive outcomes. This answer begs for systematic, theoretically explicit comparisons of various intervention approaches. Of particular practical and theoretical importance are variations in intervention content and intensity during the first 3 years. It is during the first 3 years that intervention efforts generally must change from a preventive to a remedial focus. We must better understand why and the relative effectiveness of different and differently timed approaches. Answers to these issues have obvious implications for the cost effectiveness of early intervention.

2. *Differential risk and differential response to early interventions.* The selection criteria for early intervention participants are currently relatively crude. In Head Start, for example, the only eligibility criterion is income below the federal poverty line when the child is age appropriate. We have argued elsewhere (Landesman & Ramey, 1989) that such procedures are likely to lead to over-identification of children for early intervention services thus driving up public costs by providing unnecessary services to some children and families. We now know that there are wide variations in developmental risks and outcomes tied to different types of families who are below the poverty line (Ramey, Ramey, & Gaines-Lanzi, 1998). Therefore, better targeting of early intervention services deserves closer scrutiny. Similarly, some children and families respond better to particular early interventions than do others. Some apparently do not benefit in measurable ways. This knowledge needs to be incorporated, into policy decisions about programs.

3. *Lasting effects (or not) and mediating mechanisms.* First, contrary to opinion as expressed recently in *The Bell Curve* (Herrnstein & Murray, 1994) relatively few early intervention programs have received long-term follow-up. Thus, the knowledge base of long term effects needs to be expanded via high-quality follow-up of effective, experimentally adequate studies.

Second, the issue of "lasting effects" in the context of early intervention must be understood as maintenance of a *rate of acquisition* in intellectual development after intervention has ceased, as opposed to simple retention of previously learned material. For example, preschool programs may provide experiences relevant to basic quantitative concepts such as size or number but these must be understood as prerequisites to the formal operations required for addition or multiplication and these, in turn, as prerequisites for mastery of algebra. Without postulation of specific mediating or carrier mechanisms it is unwarranted to expect even an excellent preschool program which had an emphasis on mathematical fundamentals to result in relative superiority, in a normative sense, in facility with algebra at, say, ninth grade. That is not to say that such continuities are impossible but simply that there must be some bridging or mediating mechanism to provide the scaffolding for such a relationship. What are plausible mediating mechanisms for long-term positive effects such as higher cognitive performance, school achievement, and reduced grade retention and special education placement?

We discern four major types of likely long-term mediating mechanisms: (a) An increase in a child's *intellectual skills* that allows the child to control exposure of him or herself to new development-enhancing experiences, for example, through increased reading facility and accompanying access to developmentally appropriate books. (b) A *motivational* change in the child such that the child seeks out or creates advantageous learning experiences, for example, by successful competition for scholarships or their equivalent. (c) An enhanced knowledge base that results in the child being selected for enhanced *educational tracking* (into broader or higher planes of experience) or *avoidance of circumstances that punish developmental advances* (e.g., peer groups that devalue success in school) and (d) The child has access to more accomplished *mentors* than otherwise would have occurred (e.g., improved parenting, better teachers, more accomplished peers) who possess and use skills that provide a more optimal match between the child's developmental level and the experiences that will enhance the child's acquisition of additional intellectual breadth and development. These mediating mechanisms and their neurobiological substrates warrant systematic inquiry as a high research priority.

4. The relation of developmental science and public policy formulation. Biosocial Developmental Contextualism as a conceptual framework is as germane to the analysis of public policy as to the development of individual children and their families. The demands of scientific rigor must be combined with the ever-changing and multiple constituencies that drive public policy debate and development. Historically, developmental scientists and children's advocates have been uneasy companions concerning the development of a usable knowledge base for early intervention. Nevertheless, a usable knowledge-base currently exists and the way to expand it is clear. The primary issues for early intervention now is one of political will to aid intellectually vulnerable children and to compare the developmental impact of alternative intervention methods. Through such research and development society will likely achieve a great return in its investment and we, as scientists, will, in turn, learn more about the factors that regulate the development of intelligence—a much needed commodity in an increasingly complex world.

REFERENCES

Alexander, K., & Entwistle, D. (1988). *Achievement in the first 2 years of school: Patterns and processes.* Monograph of the Society for Research in Child Development, *53*, Chicago.

Andrews, S. R., Blumenthal, J. B., Johnson, D. L., Kahn, A. J., Ferguson, C. J., Lasater, T. M., Malone, P. F., & Wallace, D. B. (1982). The skills of mothering: A study of parent–child development centers. *Monographs of the Society for Research in Child Development, 47*(6, Serial No. 198).

Bayley, N. (1965). Comparisons of mental and motor test scores for ages 10–15 months by sex, birth order, race, geographical location and education of parents. *Child Development, 36*, 379–441.

Bee, H. L., VanEgeren, L. F., Streissguth, A. P., Nyman, B. A., & Leckie, M. S. (1969). Social class differences in maternal teaching strategies and speech patterns. *Developmental Psychology, 1*, 726–734.

Bernstein, B. (1961). Social class and linguistic development: A theory of social learning. In A. H. Halsey, J. Floud, & C. A. Anderson (Eds.), *Economy, education and society* (pp. 228–314). New York: Free Press.

Bloom, B. (1964). *Stability and change in human characteristics.* New York: Wiley.

Burchinal, M. R., Campbell, F. A., Bryant, D. M., Wasik, B. H., & Ramey, C. T. (1997). Early intervention and mediating processes in cognitive performance of children of low-income African American families. *Child Development, 68*, 935–954.

Boyle, C. A., Decoufle, P., & Yeargen-Allsopp, M. (1994). Prevalence and health impact of developmental disabilities in US children. *Pediatrics, 93*, 399–403.

Burt, C., Jones, E., Miller, E., & Moodie, W. (1934). How the mind works. New York: Appleton-Century-Crofts.

Caldwell, B. M. (1973). Infant day care—The outcast gains respectability. In P. Robey (Ed.), *Child care—Who cares? Foreign and domestic infant and early child development policies.* New York: Basic Books.

Campbell, F. A., & Ramey, C. T. (1995). Cognitive and school outcomes for high risk students at middle adolescence: Positive effects of early intervention. *American Educational Research Journal, 32*, 743–772.

Carnegie Task Force on Meeting the Needs of Young children (1994). *Starting points: Meeting the needs of our youngest children.* New York: Carnegie Corporation of New York.

Carnegie Task Force on Learning in the Primary Grades (1996). *Years of promise: A comprehensive learning strategy for America's children.* New York: Carnegie Corporation of New York.

Ceci, S. J. (1991). How much does schooling influence general intelligence and its cognitive components? A reassessment of the evidence. *Developmental Psychology, 27*, 703–720.

Clarke-Stewart, K. A. (1973). Interactions between mothers and their young children: Characteristics and consequences. *Monographs of the Society for Research in Child Development, 38*, 6–7.

Cohen, S. E., & Beckwith, L. (1975, August). *Maternal language input in infancy.* Paper presented at the annual meeting of the American Psychological Association, Chicago.

Deutsch, M. (1967). *The disadvantaged child.* New York: Basic Books.

Eells, N. W., Davis, A., Havighurst, R., Herrick, V., & Lyler, R. (1951). *Intelligence and cultural differences.* Chicago: University of Chicago Press.

Epstein, A. S., & Weikart, D. B. (1979). *The Ypsilanti-Carnegie Infant Education Project: Longitudinal follow-up.* Ypsilanti, MI: High/Scope Educational Research Foundation.

Families and Work Institute (1996, June). *Rethinking the brain: New insights into early development.* Conference report, Brain development in young children: New frontiers for research, policy and practice. New York.

Galton, F. (1869). *Hereditary genius: An inquiry into its laws and consequences.* London: MacMillan.

Ginzberg, E. (1965). The mentally handicapped in a technological society. In S. F. Osler & R. E. Cooke (Eds.), *The biosocial basis of mental retardation* (pp. 1–15). Baltimore, MD: Johns Hopkins University Press.

Golden, M., & Birns, B. (1968). Social class and cognitive development in infancy. *Merrill-Palmer Quarterly, 14*, 139–149.

Gordon, I. J., & Guinagh, B. J. (1978). A home learning center approach to early stimulation. *JSAS Catalogue of Selected Documents in Psychology, 8*(6), No. 1634.

Gottlieb, G. (1971). *Development of species identification in birds.* Chicago: University of Chicago Press.

Gray, S., & Klaus, R. A. (1970). The early training project: A seventh year report. *Child Development, 41*, 909–924.

Gray, S., & Ruttle, K. (1980). The family-oriented home visiting program: A longitudinal study. *Genetic Psychology Monographs, 102*, 299–316.

Gutelius, M. F., Kirsch, A. D., MacDonald, S., Brooks, M. R., & McErlean, T. (1977). Controlled study of child health supervision: Behavioral results. *Pediatrics, 60,* 294–304.

Harlow, H. F. (1958). The nature of love. *American Psychologist, 13,* 673–685.

Hebb, D. O. (1949). *The organization of behavior.* New York: Wiley.

Herrnstein, R. J., & Murray, C. (1994). *The bell curve. Intelligence and class structure in American life.* New York: The Free Press.

Hess, E. H. (1970). Ethology and development psychology. In P. H. Mussen (Ed.), *Carmichael's manual of child psychology, Vol. 1.* New York: Wiley.

Hess, R. D., & Shipman, V. C. (1965). Early experience and the socialization of cognitive modes in children. *Child Development, 34,* 869–886.

Hindley, C. B. (1960). The Griffiths scale of infant development: Scores and predictions from 3 to 18 months. *Child Psychology and Psychiatry, 1,* 99–112.

Hunt, J. McV. (1961). Intelligence and experience. New York: Ronald Press.

Hunt, J. McV. (1979). Psychological development: Early experience. *Annual Review of Psychology, 30,* 103–143.

Jensen, A. R. (1969). How much can we boost IQ and scholastic achievement? *Harvard Educational Review, 39,* 1–123.

Knoblock, H., & Pasamanick, B. (1953). Further observation on the behavioral development of Negro children. In J. Genet (Ed.), *Psychology, 83,* 137–157.

Kretch, D., Rosenwig, M. R., & Bennett, E. L. (1960). Effects of early environmental complexity and training on brain chemistry. *Journal of Comparative and Physiological Psychology, 53,* 509–519.

Landesman, S., & Ramey, C. T. (1989). Developmental psychology and mental retardation: Integrating scientific principles with treatment practices. *American Psychologist, 44,* 409–415.

Lazar, I., & Darlington, R., Murray, H., Royce, J., & Snipper, A. (1982). Lasting effects of early education: A report from the consortium of longitudinal studies. *Monographs of the Society for Research in Child Development, 47*(2–3, Serial No. 195).

Lewis, M., & Wilson, C. D. (1972). Infant development in lower-class American families. *Human Development, 15,* 112–127.

Ramey, C. T., Bryant, D. M., & Suarez, T. M. (1985). Preschool compensatory education and the modifiability of intelligence: A critical review. In D. Detterman (Ed.), *Current topics in intelligence* (pp. 247–296). Norwood, NJ: Ablex.

Ramey, C. T., Bryant, D. M., Wasik, B. H., Sparling, J. J., Fendt, K. H., & LaVange, L. M. (1992). Infant Health and Development Program for low birth weight, premature infants: Program elements, family participation, and child intelligence. *Pediatrics, 89,* 454–465.

Ramey, C. T., & Campbell, F. A. (1977). The prevention of developmental retardation in high-risk children. In P. Mittler (Ed.), *Research to practice in mental retardation: Vol. 1. Care and intervention* (pp. 157–164). Baltimore: University Park Press.

Ramey, C. T., Campbell, F. A., Burchinal, M., Skinner, M. L., Gardner, D. M., & Ramey, S. L. (2000). Persistent effects of early intervention on high-risk children and their mothers. *Applied and Developmental Science, 4,* 2–14.

Ramey, C. T., Farran, D., & Campbell, F. A. (1979). Predicting IQ from mother-infant interactions. *Child Development, 50,* 804–814.

Ramey, C. T., & Mills, P. J. (1977). Social and intellectual consequences of day care for high-risk infants. In R. Webb (Ed.), *Social development in childhood: Day care programs and research.* Baltimore, MD: John Hopkins University Press.

Ramey, C. T., Mills, P. J., Campbell, F., & O'Brien, C. (1975). Infants' home environments: A comparison of high-risk families and families from the general population. *American Journal of Mental Deficiency, 80,* 40–42.

Ramey, S. L., & Ramey, C. T. (1992). Early educational intervention with disadvantaged children—To what effect? *Applied and Preventive Psychology, 1,* 131–140.

Ramey, C. T., & Ramey, S. L. (1998). Early intervention and early experience. *American Psychologist, 53*, 109–120.

Ramey, C. T., & Ramey, S. L. (1999). *Right from birth: Building your child's foundation for life.* New York: Goddard Press.

Ramey, C. T., Ramey, S. L., Gaines, R., & Blair, C. B. (1995). Two-generation early intervention programs: A child development perspective. In S. Smith (Ed.), *Two-generation programs for families in poverty: A new intervention strategy. Vol. 9: Advances in applied developmental psychology* (pp. 199–228). Norwood, NJ: Ablex.

Ramey, C. T., Ramey, S. L., & Gaines-Lanzi, R. G. (1998). Differentiating developmental risk levels for families in poverty: Creating a family typology. In M. Lewis & C. Feiring (Eds.), *Families, risk, and competence* (pp. 187–205). Mahwah, NJ: Lawrence Erlbaum Associates.

Ramey, C. T., Stedman, D. S., Borders-Patterson, A., & Mengel, W. (1978). Predicting school failure from information available at birth. *American Journal of Mental Deficiency, 82*, 525–534.

Rebelsky, F., & Hanks, C. (1971). Father's verbal interaction with infants in the first three months of life. *Child Development, 42*, 63–68.

Schweinhart, L. J., & Weikart, D. P. (1993). Success by empowerment: The High/Scope Perry Preschool Study though age 27. *Young Children, 49*, 54–58.

Shore, R. (1997). *Rethinking the brain: New insights into early development.* New York: Families and Work Institute.

Skeels, H. M., & Dye, H. A. (1939). A study of the effects of differential stimulation in mentally retarded children. *Proceedings of the American Association of Mental Deficiency, 44*, 114–136.

Thompson, W. R., & Herron, W. (1954). The effects of early restriction on activity in dogs. *Journal of Comparative and Physiological Psychology, 47*, 77–82.

Tulkin, S., & Kagan, J. (1972). Mother-child interaction in the first year of life. *Child Development, 43*, 31.

Woodhead, M. (1988). When psychology informs public policy: The case of early childhood intervention. *American Psychologist, 43*, 443–454.

Zigler, E., Abelson, W. D., Trickett, P. K., & Seitz, V. (1982). Is an intervention program necessary in order to improve economically disadvantaged children's IQ scores? *Child Development, 53*, 340–348.

Zigler, E., & Valentine, J. (1979). *Project Head Start: A legacy of the war on poverty.* New York: Free Press.

PUBLIC AND PERSONAL
HEALTH ISSUES

5

The Role of Nutrition in Intellectual Development

Sally Grantham-McGregor
Cornelius Ani
Lia Fernald
Institute of Child Health
University College London

Child development is affected by many environmental factors both psychosocial and biological. The biological factors include poor health and nutrition which frequently occur together—the one predisposing to the other. Poor nutrition can affect human development from early in pregnancy throughout childhood and probably throughout adulthood. The effects depend on which nutrient or nutrients are deficient, the severity and duration of the deficiency, and the stage of development of children.

Poor health and nutrition usually occur in conditions of poverty, particularly in developing countries. These conditions themselves affect children's development and may exacerbate the effects of undernutrition. When considering the effects of poor nutrition it is important to consider the context in which it occurs.

In this chapter we selectively review the evidence on nutritional deficiencies affecting children's development. We discuss conditions that affect large numbers of people and are thus of public health importance. We review the following topics: protein–energy–malnutrition, breastfeeding, iron, iodine, and zinc deficiencies, and short-term hunger. Undernutrition and infection in pregnancy are common and result in children who are low birth weight and small for their gestational age. The effects of being small for gestational age on children's development have been comprehensively reviewed at a recent workshop and therefore are not reviewed here (Goldenberg, Hoffman, & Cliver, 1998; Grantham-McGregor, 1998; Hack, 1998). The main findings were that these children tend to have poorer developmental levels at least through to adolescence and an increased incidence of minor neurological deficits and behavioral problems. The size of the deficit is usually small and varies by quality of environment, however, there is extremely little data from developing countries.

PROTEIN-ENERGY-MALNUTRITION

Protein–energy–malnutrition (PEM) is not a specific disease but rather a collection of clinical signs. Furthermore, protein and energy are not the only deficiencies that are present and many micronutrient deficiencies often occur at the same time. PEM is usually caused by diets inadequate in quantity or quality, or both. Infections, especially those that cause diarrhea, also contribute to its etiology. PEM is most likely to occur in the first 2 to 3 years of life when the child is growing rapidly and demands for nutrients and energy are high. The timing of an episode of malnutrition may be critical in determining its effect on children's development.

The diagnosis of PEM depends on having weights, heights, or weights-for-height below a certain cut-off level when compared with internationally accepted references (Hamill, Drizd, Johnson, Reed, & Roche, 1977) . There are several different ways of classifying PEM. The Wellcome classification (Lancet, 1970) classifies severe malnutrition into kwashiorkor, marasmus, or marasmic kwashiorkor. Marasmus comprises having weight below 60% of the expected value for age, and kwashiorkor indicates the presence of edema (excess of watery fluid in intercellular spaces and body cavities) with weight below 80% of expected value. Children with marasmic kwashiorkor have weight below 60% of expected value in addition to edema.

A more recent classification defines malnourished children by low height-for-age (stunting) and low weight-for-height (wasting) (Waterlow & Rutishauser, 1972). Stunting reflects poor nutrition over a reasonably long period whereas wasting reflects current or recent undernutrition. It is likely that duration and severity affect child development differently. Weight-for-age represents a combination of stunting and wasting. The use of standard scores (Z scores) of the reference value rather than percentage of the reference values is now recommended because these scores have the same meaning across different nutritional indices and over the age range.

Prevalence

Protein energy malnutrition remains a major public health problem. The World Health Organization (WHO, 1997) estimates that 31% of children under 5 years old in developing countries are underweight (i.e., weight for age < −2SD of the reference). The prevalence of wasting in developing countries is estimated to be 9%, and to be as high as 15.2% in parts of Asia. Stunting is more common than wasting (Keller, 1988) and WHO estimates that 38.1% of children under 5 years in developing countries, and up to 49.6% of children in south-central Asia are moderately stunted (height-for-age < −2SD). Considering the enormous numbers of children affected by malnutrition, if it affects children's development, the implications both for the individual and national development are extremely serious.

In the following section we first discuss the studies of severely malnourished children who were hospitalized with marasmus, kwashiorkor, or marasmic kwashiorkor followed by studies of mild to moderate malnutrition.

Effects of Acute Episode of Severe Malnutrition

An in-depth review of the effects of severe malnutrition on children's development has recently been published (Grantham-McGregor, 1995), so only a brief description is given here.

Short-Term Effects. Children's developmental level in the acute stage of malnutrition is extremely poor compared with children in hospital with other illnesses (Cravioto & Robles, 1965; Grantham-McGregor, Schofield, & Desai, 1978; Yatkin & McLaren, 1970). Although they improve with refeeding this improvement is no more than that found in sick adequately nourished children who are also in hospital. The malnourished children thus fail to reduce their deficits (Brockman & Ricciuti, 1971; Grantham-McGregor et al., 1978; Pollitt & Granoff, 1967; McLaren, Yatkin, Kanawati, Sabbagh, & Kadi, 1973).

Malnourished children's behavior is also abnormal in the acute stage and they are more apathetic, less active, and less exploring than other hospitalized children. On refeeding these behaviors return to normal except for the quality of exploration, which probably reflects their lower developmental levels (Grantham-McGregor, Powell, Walker, & Himes, 1991). Their return to normal behavior contrasts with their failure to catch up in developmental levels.

Long-Term Effects of Acute Malnutrition on Intellectual Development. Studies of the long-term effects of severe childhood malnutrition have usually had case control designs comparing the formerly malnourished children with their own siblings or matched controls. The major limitation of matched nonsibling comparisons is the difficulty of finding exact matches for all social and environmental confounders that occur with malnutrition and may independently affect children's development (Richardson, 1974). Sibling comparisons are also imperfect as the siblings themselves are likely to have suffered from undernutrition in early childhood, although lacking an acute episode.

With these limitations in mind, most studies using matched controls (Champakam, Srikantia, & Gopalan, 1968; Galler, Ramsey, Solimano, Lowell,

& Mason, 1983; Hertzig, Birch, Richardson, & Tizard, 1972; Hoorweg & Stanfield, 1976; Nwuga, 1977; Richardson, Birch, & Hertzig, 1973) and some using sibling (Birch, Pineiro, Alcalde, Toca, & Cravioto, 1971; Carmona da Mota, Antonio, Leitao, & Porto, 1990; Hertzig et al., 1972; Nwuga, 1977; Pereira, Sundararaj, & Begum, 1979) comparisons have found poorer intellectual development and or school achievement in children who suffered from an acute episode of severe malnutrition in childhood. The findings are less consistent in sibling comparison studies with some studies (Bartel, Griesel, Burnett, Freiman, Rosen, & Geefhuysen, 1978; Evans, Moodie, & Hansen, 1971; Graham & Adrianzen, 1979; Moodie, Bowie, Mann, & Hansen, 1980) showing no or only small differences. Differences were more likely to be found in tests of cognitive function than of school achievement (Richardson et al., 1973). The latter is closely associated with family characteristics, which may explain the lack of differences with sibling comparisons.

There is insufficient data to identify specific cognitive deficits although they may exist. However, motor function has frequently been found to be poor (Galler, Ramsey, Solimano, Kucharski, & Harrison, 1984; Hoorweg & Stanfield, 1976). Formerly severely malnourished children have usually been found to have behavior differences (Hoorweg, 1976). They have poor attention, and make poorer relationships with peers and teachers than their classmates. They have also been found to have less emotional control (e.g., more emotional outbursts, crying in the class, attacking other children; Galler, Ramsey, Solimano, & Lowell, 1983; Richardson, Birch, & Ragbeer, 1975; Richardson, Birch, Grabie, & Yoder, 1972).

The Role of Environment

In the foregoing studies most of the children continued to live in generally poor homes and most likely continued to have poor diets. Under these circumstances, the children were unable to improve in cognitive and behavioral development. However, when children were moved to enriched environments through adoption vast improvements have occurred (Winick, Mayer, & Harris, 1975). In a study in Chile (Colombo, de la Parra, & Lopez, 1992) children who were adopted had normal IQs at follow-up. In contrast, children who returned to poor homes or remained in a residential institution continued to have extremely low IQs (Fig. 5.1). One study showed that an intervention with psychosocial stimulation in the children's own homes produced modest but sustained improvements (Grantham-McGregor, Powell, Walker, Chang, & Fletcher, 1994).

It appears that the quality of the environment largely determines the long-term outcome of severe malnutrition. Unfortunately, most severely malnourished children in developing countries continue to live in extremely poor circumstances.

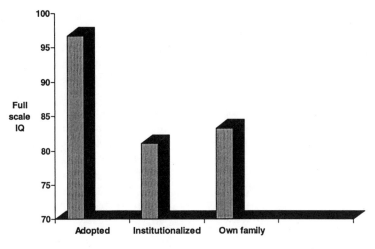

FIG. 5.1. Comparison of WISC scores at school age of severely malnourished children who were adopted, institutionalized, or remained with their family. From "Intellectual and Physical Outcome of Children Undernourished in Early Life is Influenced by Later Environmental Conditions" by M. Colombo, A. de la Parra, and I. Lopez, 1992, *Developmental Medicine and Child Neurology, 34*, p. 617. Copyright 1992 by Mac Keith Press. Adapted with permission.

In conclusion, there is reasonably consistent evidence that children who were severely malnourished in early childhood continue to have poor cognitive and motor function and behavior problems if they return to poor environments. Marked improvements can occur with enriched environments.

The Effects of Stunting and Wasting on Intellectual Development

Although the etiology of linear growth retardation is multifactorial (Neumann & Harrison, 1994; Waterlow, 1994), poor nutrition appears to play a major role in children in developing countries. The data implicating deficiencies of zinc (Prentice & Bates, 1994) and protein (Golden, 1988) are strongest although energy and iron deficiencies (Allen, 1994) are thought to contribute. Repeated or chronic infection especially diarrhea also contributes. Stunting usually occurs in the first 3 years of life and catch-up growth can occur in good conditions. However, in many developing countries the children remain short throughout childhood (Martorell, Kahn, & Schroeder, 1994).

Studies of the effect of stunting on intellectual development have used cross-sectional, longitudinal, and interventional designs.

Observational Studies. Most cross-sectional observation studies have found significant associations between height-for-age and IQ, cognitive function, and school achievement in school-aged children even after controlling for socioeconomic conditions (Agarwal, Upadhyay, Tripathi, & Agarwal, 1987; Clarke, Grantham-McGregor, & Powell, 1991; Florencio, 1988; Huda, Grantham-McGregor, Rahman, & Tompkins, 1999; Johnston, Low, de Baessa, & MacVean, 1987; Moock & Leslie, 1986; Sigman, Neumann, Jansen, & Bwibo, 1989), although not in all cases (Bogin & MacVean, 1983; Colombo, de Andraca, & Lopez, 1988; Wachs et al., 1992). Similarly, height-for-age was related to psychomotor development in studies of younger children (Lasky, Klein, Yarbrough, Engle, Lechtig, & Martorell, 1981; Powell & Grantham-McGregor, 1985; Sigman, Neumann, Baksh, Bwibo, & McDonald, 1989). Wasting has less often been found to be associated with mental development (Lasky et al., 1981; Popkin & Lim-Ybanez, 1982; Sigman, Neumann, Baksh, Bwibo, & McDonald, 1989). Growth in the first 2 to 3 years has been shown to be related to change in developmental levels in Guatemala (Lasky et al., 1981) and Jamaica (Powell, Walker, Himes, Fletcher, & Grantham-McGregor, 1995).

Intervention Studies

Intervention Studies Beginning in Pregnancy.   Intervention studies provide the strongest evidence of a causal relationship between nutrition and development. Several studies have been conducted in areas where undernutrition is endemic. In one study in Taiwan (Joos, Pollitt, Mueller, & Albright, 1983) women were given nutritional supplements during pregnancy and lactation but their offspring were not supplemented. Benefits were found to the children's motor but not mental development at 8 months of age. In three studies, pregnant women and their offspring were given nutritional supplements and in all of them the children showed concurrent benefits to growth, cognitive, and motor development: Bogota, Colombia (Waber et al., 1981); Guatemala (Freeman, Klein, Townsend, & Lechtig, 1980); Mexico (Chavez & Martinez, 1982). Subsequent follow-up studies of the children were carried out. No benefit was found in the Taiwan study to the children's IQ at 5 years of age but only the mothers had been supplemented. Benefit was shown in all studies in which children were also supplemented. In Bogota (Super, 1991), at 7 years of age the supplemented children showed benefits on reading readiness, however, the details have not been reported and there was a large loss of subjects at follow-up. In the Mexican study, the boys but not girls showed benefits on the Ravens Progressive Matrices at 18 years of age (Chavez, Martinez, Soberanes, Dominguez, & Avila, 1994). The Guatemalan study had the most comprehensive follow-up and the children between 11 and 24 years of age showed benefits in a range of achievement and cognitive tests (Pollitt, Gorman, Engle, Martorelle, & Rivera, 1993). The children from the poorest homes showed the most benefits.

Interventions With Undernourished Children

Several supplementation studies have been conducted with undernourished children. In Indonesia, underweight children who were supplemented for 3 months showed benefits to their motor but not mental development (Pollitt, Watkins, & Husaini, 1997). At follow-up 8 years later the children were given a battery of cognitive tests and those who had been supplemented before 18 months of age showed benefits in one test of working memory.

In Cali, Columbia (McKay, Sinisterra, McKay, Gomez, & Lloreda, 1978) nutritional supplementation alone of undernourished children produced no benefit, but supplementation combined with stimulation produced comprehensive benefits that were proportional to the duration of the intervention. After intervention ceased the children had higher IQs at 8 years of age and showed benefits in school performance measures up to age 10 (McKay & McKay, 1983). There was no group that received stimulation alone so it is not possible to separate the effects of stimulation from supplementation.

In a Jamaican study (Grantham-McGregor et al., 1991) stunted children were randomly assigned to four groups: stimulation, supplementation, both interventions, or no treatment. Stimulation and supplementation had independent benefits on the children's development and the effects were additive. Only the group receiving both treatments caught up to a group of nonstunted children who were also studied (Fig. 5.2). Four years after intervention there was no longer an additive effect but all intervened groups showed a very small benefit on a wide range of cognitive tests (Grantham-McGregor, Walker, Chang, & Powell, 1997).

Conclusions From Intervention Studies

There are many problems in interpreting supplementation studies. Perhaps the most important problems are that in the early studies treatment was not always assigned by randomization, placebos were often not given, and the actual increase in dietary intake was often small. In spite of these problems, concurrent benefits were consistently found in the supplemented groups. It appears that the best results come from interventions that include stimulation and supplementation.

Where the mothers in pregnancy and their offspring were supplemented for about 3 years, small long-term benefits were also found. But only one of these studies had comprehensive data up to adolescence from a reasonably large sample (Pollitt et al., 1993). The evidence of long-term benefits to development from supplementation given to undernourished children is weaker. Two studies of follow-up to primary school age have shown very small benefits (Grantham-McGregor et al., 1997; Pollitt et al., 1997). There are no reports from older children.

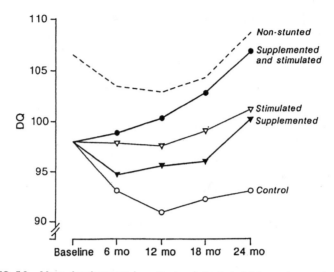

FIG. 5.2. Mean developmental quotients of stunted children who received stimulation, supplementation, both, or none (controls), adjusted for initial age and score compared with those on non stunted group adjusted for age only. From "Nutritional Supplementation, psychosocial stimulation, and mental development of stunted children: The Jamaican Study" by S. M. Grantham-McGregor, C. A. Powell, S. P. Walker, and J. H. Himes, 1991, *Lancet, 338*, p. 3. Copyright 1991 by Elsevier Science Ltd. Reprinted with permission.

Malnourished Children's Increased Vulnerability

The cognitive functions of malnourished children appear to remain more vulnerable to further nutritional stress or infection. For example, short-term food deprivation was shown to affect malnourished children's cognitive abilities whereas adequately nourished children were not affected (Chandler, Walker, Connolly, & Grantham-McGregor, 1995; Simeon & Grantham-McGregor, 1989). Similarly, parasitic infection is more likely to affect undernourished children than adequately nourished children (Simeon, Grantham-McGregor, & Wong, 1995). It is likely they are also more affected by poor psychosocial environments.

Critical Period

There is limited evidence that mental development is most vulnerable to poor nutrition in the first 2 to 3 years of life. Several investigators have shown that height at 3 years (Martorell, Rivera, Kaplowitz, & Pollitt, 1992), 18 to 30 months (Sigman, McDonald, Neumann, & Bwibo, 1991), 1 year (Richardson, 1979), and 9 to 24 months (Grantham-McGregor et al., 1997) all predicted later intellectual development at school age sometimes better than concurrent height (Grantham-McGregor et al., 1997). Pollitt and colleagues found that children supplemented before 24 months did better than those supplemented after 24 months (Pollitt et al., 1997). However, there were fewer children in the latter group. McKay et al. (1978) showed that among children receiving combined supplementation and stimulation, the youngest starters (at 42 months) showed the most benefits. However, the finding was confounded by intervention duration. Lucas, Morley, and Cole (1998) showed that suboptimal early nutrition in preterm babies affects later cognitive development. However, the implication of this finding for the long-term mental development of children undernourished in early childhood is not clear.

Mechanism

The precise mechanism by which malnutrition compromises intellectual development is not fully understood, although there are several plausible hypotheses. One possibility is the "functional isolation" hypothesis (Levitsky, 1979), which suggests that undernutrition delays children's motor development and reduces available energy which impairs their ability to explore the environment and acquire skills. Meeks-Gardner, Grantham-McGregor, Himes, and Chang (1999) showed that stunted children were more apathetic and explored their environment with less enthusiasm. This behavior in turn may reduce the stimulation provided by the caretaker.

Another possibility is that malnutrition may cause permanent changes to the maturing brain of a young child. There is evidence from animal studies that malnutrition induces small structural and neurochemical changes in the brain which are sustained after refeeding (Levitsky & Strupp, 1995; Smart, 1998). Electroencephalographic abnormalities such as high evoked potential indices, and changes to latency and amplitude of certain wave complexes have also been demonstrated in malnourished children compared with normal controls (Barnet et al., 1978).

Implications

The evidence confirms that children who suffer from severe or moderate malnutrition in the first 3 years of life are at high risk of poor cognitive development, particularly if living in a poor environment. This has serious implications for the development of countries where malnutrition is highly prevalent. It appears that interventions involving food supplementation integrated with child care and stimulation will produce the greatest current benefits.

BREASTFEEDING

There are many research supported claims that breastfeeding benefits children's development (e.g., Lanting, Filder, Huisman, Touwen, & Boersma, 1994; Lucas, Morley, Cole, & Gore, 1994; Lucas, Morley, Cole, Lister, & Leeson Payne,

1992). There are several possible mechanisms whereby breastfeeding may affect development. First, the nutrient content of breast milk is thought to be optimal. For example, breast milk contains more and a wider range of essential fatty acids (Crawford, 1993) than formula milk, and these fatty acids are necessary for brain development (Innis, 1993). In addition, poor populations often cannot afford to buy sufficient formula milk so that the children are given diluted formula which leads to malnutrition and detrimentally affects development.

Another possible mechanism is that breastfeeding is associated with a reduced number of infections (Howie, Forsyth, Ogston, Clark, & Florey, 1990). This reduction is due to breast milk having a direct effect on infant's immune response (Pabst, Spady, Pilarski, Carson, Beeler, & Krezolek, 1997) as well as a lower risk of infection being introduced with contaminated bottle feeds. In addition, breastfeeding promotes maternal–child responsivity (Morrow Tlucak, Haude, & Ernhart, 1988), which benefits the children's development.

Problems With Studies on Breastfeeding

There are many problems with interpreting studies on breastfeeding and child development. More educated mothers are likely to breastfeed than less educated ones. Maternal education is associated with many environmental factors that directly affect children's development and it is difficult to control for all these variables. It is usually not possible to do a randomized treatment trial.

Different investigators have used different definitions for breastfeeding. The duration of breastfeeding and whether other foods are given are often not recorded. The nutrient content of milk formula given to the control groups may be critical but this is rarely recorded. Another problem is that children at high risk of poor development, such as premature infants, are less likely to breast feed, but this has not always been taken into account.

Studies of Development

Studies comparing breast fed with bottle fed babies were recently reviewed in detail (Grantham-McGregor, Fernald, & Sethuraman, 1999) and only a brief summary is given here.

Most studies of children's development during the time of breastfeeding have shown a small but consistent benefit in breast fed compared with bottle fed babies. Eight studies of children 24 months and under and 14 studies of subjects 3 to 50 years of age were located. Practically all of these studies found small benefits to the cognitive function of the breast fed group. The benefits remained significant after controlling for some socioeconomic factors in most studies (e.g., Fergusson, Beautrais, & Silva, 1982; Horwood & Fergusson, 1998; Lucas et al., 1992; Niemela & Jarvenpaa, 1996; Ounsted, Moar, Cockburn, & Redman, 1984; Rodgers, 1978; Rogan & Gladen, 1993; Taylor & Wadsworth, 1984). However, the benefit lost significance following controlling for confounding factors in other studies (e.g., Gale & Martyn, 1996; Jacobson & Jacobson, 1992; Malloy & Berendes, 1998). A few studies did not control for any background factors (e.g., Broad, 1979; Hoefer & Hardy, 1929; Pollock, 1994).

Conclusion

Although most of these studies used correlational analysis, the consistency of the findings suggest that breastfeeding provides a small benefit. Extremely few studies have come from developing countries where benefits are likely to be greater.

IRON DEFICIENCY

Anemia affects 20%–25% of young children globally, with a prevalence of 46%–51% in developing countries and 7%–12% in developed countries (DeMaeyer & Adiels-Tegman, 1985). It is most common in children between 6 and 24 months. The major cause of anemia is iron deficiency resulting from inadequate dietary intakes of bioavailable iron (e.g., meat products such as liver and beef), or high intakes of substances that inhibit absorption (e.g., phytates in wheat bran and maize, and polyphenols in tea; British Nutrition Foundation, 1995). In older children parasitic infections that cause blood loss such as hookworm also contribute to anemia.

Iron deficiency affects work productivity in adults (Scrimshaw, 1984) and children (Bhatia & Seshadri, 1987). There is growing concern that iron deficiency also affects children's cognitive, motor, and behavioral development. In the following section we review the literature on the relationship between iron and behavior in children. We first discuss possible mechanisms linking iron deficiency to poor development, followed by observational studies and then treatment trials.

Mechanisms

Possible mechanisms whereby iron deficiency affects development were reviewed recently by Lozoff (1998). Animal studies have shown that iron deficiency in early development causes irreversible changes to the central nervous system (CNS). These changes include alterations to neurotransmitters, especially the dopaminergic system, which are thought to contribute to changes in learning and arousal. In addition, hypomyelination and reduced brain iron occur. If iron deficiency occurs in early development the changes to the brain persist despite treatment (Ben Shachar, Ashkenazi, & Youdim,

1986; Dallman & Spirito, 1977; Youdim, 1990). Behavioral changes also occur in young animals and persist after treatment.

Research in iron deficient infants has shown that they have prolonged latency in auditory brain stem responses and prolonged central conduction time which could be due to hypomyelination (Roncagliolo, Garrido, Walter, Peirano, & Lozoff, 1998). The altered responses persist after treatment and provide the first evidence of a direct link between changes in the CNS and behavior in iron deficient infants (Roncagliolo et al., 1998).

It is also possible that iron deficiency affects development through changes to children's behavior. Iron deficient children have been observed to be wary, hesitant, easily tired, to stay closer to their mothers, and be less happy and playful (Lozoff, Klein, Nelson, McClish, Manuel, & Chacon, 1998). In turn, adults also differ in their behavior when interacting with iron deficient children. There is an interesting analogy with children with PEM who show similar behavioral changes (Meeks-Gardner et al., 1999). It has been hypothesized that these behaviors "functionally isolate" children from their environment and contribute to their poor development (Levitsky, 1979).

To summarize, iron deficiency could affect children's development through several different mechanisms including changes to the CNS, and behavior. In addition, iron deficient children generally come from poor environments, which probably contribute to their poor development, and may exacerbate the effect of iron deficiency.

Observational Studies

Cross-Sectional Studies. Many correlational studies have shown that children who are iron deficient have poorer developmental levels or school achievement than children who are iron sufficient (e.g., Clarke et al., 1991; Ivanovic, Vasquez, Marambio, Ballester, Zacarias, & Aguayu, 1991; Popkin & Lim-Ybanez, 1982; Walker, Grantham-McGregor, Himes, Williams, & Duff, 1998; Webb & Oski, 1973). In addition pretreatment measures from treatment trials have also shown associations between iron deficiency anemia and poor mental and motor development (e.g., Lozoff, Brittenham, & Wolf, 1987; Soemantri, Pollitt, & Kim, 1985). The severity of anemia affects the association with development. Lozoff et al. (1987) showed in children from Costa Rica that deficits on the Bayley scales became apparent in infants with hemoglobin levels below 10 to 10.5g/dl. Also deficits in developmental levels are greater in children who had been anemic longest (Walter, de Andraca, Chadud, & Perales, 1989).

Longitudinal Studies. We located four studies in which babies who were anemic in the first 2 years of life and successfully treated were re-examined several years later. In three studies children who were previously anemic had poorer scores in different cognitive tests (de Andraca, Walter, Castillo,

Pino, Rivera, & Cobo, 1990; Lozoff, Jimenez, & Wolf, 1991; Palti, Pevsner, & Adler, 1983) or school achievement (Palti, Meijer, & Adler, 1985). In the fourth study (Cantwell, 1974) the previously anemic children had more signs of neurological delay than nonanemic children. In an epidemiological study, Hurtado, Claussen, and Scott (1999) examined records of the WIC program (a national program of nutritional supplementation for high-risk children and mothers) in Dade County, Florida. They found that children who were anemic on enrollment to the program in the first four years of life were more likely to be receiving special education at age 10.

Conclusions From Observational Studies. It is clear that iron deficiency anemia in early childhood identifies children at risk of poor development, not only concurrently but also in the longer term. However, it is well recognized that iron deficiency tends to occur in poor environments, which themselves could be responsible for the children's poor development. The response to treatment either prophylactically or therapeutically should give an indication as to what extent iron deficiency alone is implicated.

Treatment Trials With School-Aged Children

Trials with school-aged children have generally shown consistent benefits. Watkins and Pollitt (1998) have reviewed these studies. In randomized controlled trials in Egypt (Pollitt, Soemantri, Yunis, & Scrimshaw, 1985) and Indonesia (Soemantri, Pollitt, & Kim, 1985), anemic school-aged children who were treated improved more than nontreated anemic children in scores on tests of cognition and achievement. In four trials of iron treatment in India, the treated anemic groups all showed improvements in tests of cognition or IQ compared with the nontreated groups (Seshadri & Gopaldes, 1989). However, in the first two studies, as well as iron treatment, folic acid was given, which may have played a role.

Shrestha (1994) found that anemic children in Malawi who had been treated had higher scores in cognitive tests than nontreated children. However, scores were not reported for the test conducted before treatment so the results are difficult to interpret.

The only study we located of school-aged children that showed no improvement from treatment was one from Thailand, where treated children showed no benefit to school achievement levels (Pollitt, Hathirat, Kotchabhakdi, Missell, & Valyasevi, 1989). It may be that school achievement is less sensitive to small changes in the child's biological state because so many other family and school factors affect it.

Conclusion From Treatment Trials in School-Aged Children. These studies in school-aged children indicate that iron treatment usually benefits anemic children's cognitive function.

Treatment Trials in Children Under Two Years

The results of treatment trials in infants and toddlers have been somewhat different from those in school-aged children, and have had inconsistent results. The first treatment trials lasted less than 2 months and no significant benefits were found in trials which had both iron and placebo treated anemic groups (Lozoff et al., 1987; Lozoff, Brittenham, Viteri, Wolf, & Urrutia, 1982; Oski & Honig, 1978; Walter et al., 1989). Most of the longer lasting trials with young children failed to have an anemic placebo group. The iron treated anemic group was therefore compared with nonanemic children. In three such treatment trials (Lozoff, de Andraca, Walter, & Pino, 1996; Lozoff et al., 1987; Walter et al., 1989) the anemic children initially had lower development scores but did not improve more than the nonanemic children after 2 to 6 months of treatment. In one study, children showing complete hematological correction showed the most improvements (Lozoff et al., 1987) but not in another study (Walter et al., 1989).

We could find only two randomized treatment trials lasting more than 2 months in this age group. Treated anemic children in England (Aukett, Parks, Scott, & Wharton, 1986) failed to show greater improvements than a placebo treated group on the Denver Test. However this test was developed to screen for developmental abnormalities and is unlikely to be sensitive to small changes. The proportion of iron treated children attaining normal rates of development was greater than in the placebo treated group. A randomized treatment trial in Indonesia was the only study to show an unequivocal improvement with iron treatment (Idjradinata & Pollitt, 1993). A group of anemic children was randomly assigned to iron or placebo treatment. After 4 months the iron treated group showed dramatic improvements on both the Bayley motor and mental scale compared with the placebo treated group.

Conclusions From Treatment Trials of Anemic Children

The three trials that showed no benefit suggest that either the deficit shown by anemic children is irreversible at least in the short term or that the deficit is not attributable to iron but to other environmental factors. However, the interpretation has to be cautious because the studies were not randomized controlled trials and therefore inadequate to infer causal relationships. In contrast, the study with the most rigorous design showed clear benefits. However, one study with 51 anemic children (26 treated, 25 placebo) is insufficient to extrapolate globally and more randomized trials are needed to determine whether iron treatment reverses the poor development of anemic children.

Preventive Trials

Several trials have been conducted in which iron was given to very young children before anemia occurred in order to prevent it, and a placebo was given to a control group.

Two of the trials are difficult to interpret. In one study in Papua, New Guinea (Heywood, Oppenheimer, Heywood, & Jolley, 1989) many of the children had malaria at the posttreatment assessment and this altered their performance. There was no significant treatment effect. The other study was in Chile (Walter et al., 1989) and the results were not reported by treatment group. Instead all groups were combined and the anemic children were found to have poorer developmental levels than the nonanemic ones.

Two large preventive studies have recently been carried out in England (Morley, 1998) and in Chile (de Andraca, Castillo, & Walter, 1997). In Chile, children who were not anemic at 6 months of age were assigned to receive iron supplements or noniron supplements and at 12 months no benefit was found to their developmental levels. In England, children were enrolled at 9 months and supplemented until age 18 months when no benefits were found. It is impossible to evaluate these studies until full details are reported. However, it is likely that the placebo children in these countries were only mildly anemic, if at all.

Two studies show clear benefits, although they were only transient in one of them. In Canada (Moffatt, Longstaffe, Besant, & Dureski, 1994), babies who were bottle fed from poor Amerindian families were given iron fortified or nonfortified formula from 2 months of age. The children's performance on the Bayley motor scale improved with fortification at 9 and 12 months compared with nonfortified children, but the benefit was no longer apparent at 15 months. The differences between the fortified and nonfortified groups in prevalence of anemia was maximum at 6 months (19%). The difference in prevalence of anemia fell by 15 months to 7.8%. Unfortunately, there was also a large loss of subjects by 15 months of age.

In a recent English study (Williams et al., 1999), poor children, some of whom were already anemic were assigned to iron-fortified formula or unfortified cows' milk from 7 to 18 months of age. The fortified and unfortified groups had similar levels of development up to 18 months of age when the treatments stopped. However, at 24 months the fortified group had significantly higher scores on all subscales of the Griffith's test except the locomotor one. The difference was mainly due to a decline in scores in the untreated group (Fig. 5.3). The prevalence of anemia in the placebo group reached a peak of 33% at 18 months compared with 2% in the treated group. There would have been other differences in nutrients between the fortified formula and cows' milk and these may have contributed to the results.

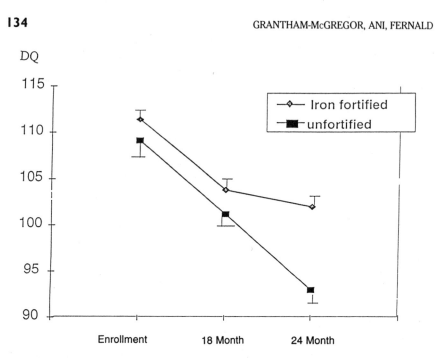

FIG. 5.3.   Developmental quotients of children who received iron fortified formula milk compared with those who received cows milk. From "Iron Supplemented Formula Milk Related to Reduction in Psychomotor decline in Infants From Inner City Areas: Randomized Study" by J. Williams, A. Wolff, A. Daly, A. MacDonald, A. Aukett, and I. W. Booth, 1999, *British Medical Journal, 318*, p. 695. Copyright 1999 by British Medical Journal, Adapted with permission.

In conclusion, findings from the preventive trials suggest that where anemia is highly prevalent in the placebo group, iron supplementation may be beneficial to children's development. However, the evidence is not robust. When full details of the studies are published, it will be easier to identify factors that modify the results. The duration and severity of iron deficiency and the age of the children may all be critical.

Conclusions From Studies on Iron Deficiency

In younger children there is only limited evidence that iron deficiency causes developmental lags from two preventive trials and one treatment trial; however, there are many trials showing no benefits. It is probable that iron deficiency detrimentally affects young children's development but it is unclear why some children benefit from treatment and others do not. It may be that the context in which iron deficiency occurs plays a role as well as the severity and duration of anemia.

There is reasonably good evidence that iron treatment benefits cognition in anemic school-aged children. The situation in younger children is unclear and more data are needed before firm conclusions can be made.

IODINE DEFICIENCY

Introduction, Prevalence and Epidemiology

Iodine is required for the synthesis of thyroxin, a hormone involved in key metabolic reactions in humans (Hetzel, Potter, & Dulberg, 1990). Approximately 90% of the world's population live in countries with significant iodine deficiency (Dunn, 1996). Although commoner in developing countries, the list includes developed countries like Germany, France, and Italy (Dunn, 1996). Worldwide, it is estimated that iodine deficiency is responsible for 5.7 million cases of cretinism and another 43 million cases of lesser degrees of intellectual impairment (Nelson, 1996). In addition to intellectual compromise, the health and social consequences of iodine deficiency have enormous economic implications (Gutekunst, 1993).

Iodine deficiency occurs mostly in regions where leaching by rain, flooding, and glaciation reduces the iodine content of soil. Thus, man's dietary sources in the food chain, which includes plants and herbivorous animals, become iodine deficient. There is a high prevalence of iodine deficiency in countries around the Himalayas (e.g., China, India, Nepal), and the Andes (e.g., Ecuador).

Manifestations of Iodine Deficiency

Goiter is the most obvious sign of iodine deficiency although its effects on brain development are more far reaching (Dunn, 1996). The term *Iodine Deficiency Disorders* (IDD) describes the spectrum of effects of iodine deficiency and includes goiter, endemic cretinism, neuromotor delays, and increased pre and postnatal mortality (Hetzel, 1983).

Endemic cretinism is the most serious form of IDD and results from severe iodine deficiency during brain development (Ebrahim, 1995). The two major types of this disorder are neurological and myxoedematous cretinism (Delange, 1994). Neurological cretinism is characterized by intellectual retardation, impaired hearing and speech, and movement disorders (Delong, Stanbury, & Fierro-Benitez, 1985). Myxoedematous cretins are retarded both intellectually and in growth and may manifest other signs of hypothyroidism like coarse dry skin (Hetzel, 1989). However, both types of cretins may show similar neurological deficits (Halpern, 1994).

Observational Studies

Investigators of the effect of iodine on intellectual development have conducted both observational studies and treatment trials. The observational studies usually involved comparing inhabitants of iodine deficient areas with those in iodine sufficient ones. Although most comparisons found that children had better intellectual development in iodine sufficient areas (Azizi et al., 1993; Bleichrodt, Garcia, Rubio, Morreale de Escobar, & Ecobar de Rey, 1987; Boyages, Collins, Maberly, Jupp, Morris, & Eastman, 1989; Fenzi et al., 1990; Mehta, Pandav, & Kochupillai, 1987; Querido, Bleichrodt, & Djokomoeljanto, 1978; Tiwari, Godbole, Chattopadhyay, Mandel, & Mithal, 1996; Vermiglio et al., 1990), their interpretation is limited by the possibility that other factors unrelated to iodine may be wholly or partly responsible for these differences. Iodine deficient areas are usually more remote and have fewer facilities than iodine sufficient areas. In view of such potential confounders, the subsequent discussions are based only on treatment trials because they provide stronger evidence for causal associations. The treatment trials in which iodine was given to women before or during pregnancy are discussed separately from those in which children were supplemented.

Iodine Supplementation in Pregnancy

Perhaps the most scientifically rigorous study was a randomized double blind controlled treatment trial in Papua, New Guinea begun in 1966 (Connolly & Pharaoh, 1989; Connolly, Pharaoh, & Hetzel, 1979; Pharoah & Connolly, 1987, 1989, 1991, 1994; Pharoah, Buttfield, & Hetzel, 1971; Pharoah, Connolly, Hetzel, & Ekins, 1981; Pharoah, Connolly, Ekins, & Harding, 1984). The investigators clearly demonstrated that intramuscular iodized oil given to mothers before conception was effective in preventing endemic cretinism (Fig. 5.4). In addition, when the remaining children were 10 years old, those whose mothers received the iodized oil were found to have better cognitive and motor function compared with control children. They also showed significant positive correlations between the intellectual abilities of the children and their maternal thyroxin levels.

In an early study in Ecuador (Ramirez, Fierro-Benitez, Estrella, Jaramillo, Diaz, & Urresta, 1969), pregnant women in one village were supplemented with iodine and those in a matched control village were not. Subsequently, children born to mothers supplemented prior to conception had better developmental levels than children in the control village. However, the lack of random assignment of treatment and other differences between the villages make interpretation of this study difficult.

In another study in Peru (Pretell, Torres, Zenteno, & Cornejo, 1972), investigators compared children in three iodine deficient villages whose mothers

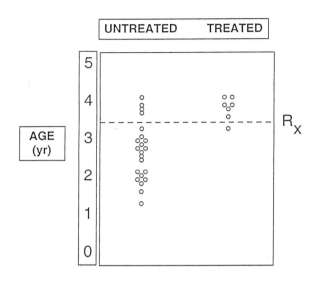

FIG. 5.4. Number of cretins born to women who received an injection of iodized oil compared with those who received placebo in Papua New Guinea. From "Neurological damage to the Fetus Resulting From Severe Iodine Deficiency During Pregnancy" by P. O. D. Pharoah, I. H. Buttfield, and B. S. Hetzel, 1971, *Lancet, 1*, p. 309. Copyright 1971 by Elsevier Science Ltd. Reprinted with permission.

received iodine prior to pregnancy with children born by unsupplemented mothers in the same villages. The developmental quotient of children of supplemented mothers was higher at all ages although the differences were not statistically significant. This lack of statistical significance may be due to the relatively small size of the study sample.

In 1980, Thilly and colleagues treated 115 pregnant women in a severely iodine deficient area of Zaire with iodized oil, and another 104 pregnant women with vitamins in a double blind randomized trial (Thilly, Lagasse, Roger, Bourdoux, & Ermans, 1980). When assessed at 4 to 25 months of age, babies born to the iodine group had significantly higher developmental quotients than the noniodine group.

Following the robust findings of the these studies, it was no longer ethical to do further randomized trials of iodine in pregnant women. So in 1994, Cao et al. administered iodine to 295 pregnant women in an iodine deficient area of China. They found that babies whose mothers were supplemented up to the end of the second trimester had significantly fewer neurological abnormalities than those whose mothers were supplemented from the third trimester and those supplemented after birth. These findings not only supported the previous studies in confirming the role of iodine in the development of fetal brains, but it also suggests a critical time scale when the damage occurs.

In summary, it is clear that iodine deficiency in pregnancy causes cretinism, and cognitive and motor deficits in children.

Iodine Supplementation in Childhood

Fewer supplementation studies have been conducted with iodine deficient children and most have failed to have a randomized design. The earliest iodine trial in children was by Dodge and colleagues (Dodge, Palkes, Fierro-Benitez, & Ramirez, 1969). They injected 51 children (aged 6–10 years) from an iodine deficient village in Ecuador with iodized oil and compared them 2 years later with children from a control village. They found a higher average intelligence in the treated group, but this was only statistically significant in girls. Bleichrodt, Escobar del Rey, Morreale de Escobar, Garcia, and Rubio (1989) compared 103 Spanish children from iodine deficient areas who were treated with oral iodized oil 32 months before with 102 nontreated children from iodine deficient areas and 82 children from iodine sufficient areas. They found no significant differences in tests of manual dexterity and reaction speed among the three groups. However, the prolonged interval between the treatment and test administration may have attenuated the effect of iodine.

A randomized controlled trial with Bolivian children using iodized oil found no treatment effect on their intellectual function (Bautista, Barker, Dunn, Sanchez, & Kaiser, 1982). However, the iodine status of the nontreated group also improved during the trial, which would have reduced the possibility of finding a treatment benefit. In another randomized trial involving children in an iodine deficient area of Malawi, Shrestha and colleagues found better fluid and crystallized intelligence and better perceptual skills in the treated group (Shrestha, 1994). The findings are again inconclusive because there were no valid pretreatment measures on the children.

In a study in China (Yan-You & Shu-Hua, 1985), investigators treated 115 children aged 7 to 11 years from severe iodine deficient areas with iodine for 3 years and compared their mean hearing at different frequencies with 30 control children from matched but nonendemic areas. They found that children from the deficient areas had significantly lower mean hearing threshold which improved following treatment. However, the control village was slightly more prosperous and the controls were only given one test. The improvements in the treated group could therefore have been a practice effect.

We are unaware of studies of iodine supplementation and cognition of adults. In summary, there is no consistent clear evidence that iodine supplementation in school-aged children benefits their cognition.

Mechanisms

Animal experiments have shown that iodine deficiency in utero causes reduced brain weight, delayed maturation of the cerebellum, and reduced dendritic interconnections in the cerebrum (Hetzel & Mano, 1989). The brain areas mostly affected are the neocortex, the cochlea, and basal ganglia, which are known to grow fast during the second trimester and to be vulnerable to iodine deficiency (Delong, 1989). Thus the mental retardation, deaf-mutism, and spasticity seen in cretinism may be explained by the respective involvement of these regions of the brain.

The exact timing of developmental injury from iodine deficiency has not been clearly identified (Cao et al., 1994). However, findings that the cut-off point for the efficacy of iodine supplementation is the end of the first (Pharoah, Buttfield, & Hetzel, 1972) or second (Cao et al., 1994) trimesters of pregnancy suggest that these are the critical periods. The exact pathogenesis of brain damage in iodine deficiency is still unclear (Dumont, Corvilain, & Contempre, 1994; Cao et al., 1994). Connolly and Pharoah (1989) found significant correlations between maternal thyroxin levels in pregnancy and their children's cognitive and motor function at 14 to 16 years. This is one of the few studies linking maternal biochemical parameters with long-term child developmental outcome.

In children and adults concurrent hypothyroidism may cause cognitive and behavior changes. In a recent study in Bangladesh, children's cognitive function was significantly associated with thyroxin levels after controlling for a comprehensive range of psychosocial, economic, and biological variables (Huda, Grantham-McGregor, Rahman, & Tompkins, 1999).

In adults, hypothyroidism from other causes can produce cognitive deficits which improve with thyroxin treatment (Osterweil et al., 1992). It is likely that hypothyroidism secondary to iodine deficiency would also affect cognition.

Conclusions

Evidence from treatment trials of iodine in pregnant women is strong enough to establish that iodine deficiency during intrauterine life (especially first and second trimesters) causes cretinism and impairs cognitive and motor development.

Evidence from iodine supplementation of children in iodine deficient areas is less consistent concerning the role of iodine in the intellectual development of older children. However, supplementing children prevents goiter and ensures that adolescent girls become iodine sufficient before they commence child bearing, thereby reducing the likelihood of fetal neurological damage.

Policy Implications

The usual preventive strategy is iodination of cooking salt, however, alternatives include using iodized water or taking iodized oil capsules by mouth. The enormous public health significance of iodine deficiency has recently been re-echoed by the 49th World Health Assembly which passed a resolution in 1996 urging countries to increase their efforts toward eliminating iodine deficiency disorders. It is clear that concerted and sustained efforts by individual countries and international agencies can eliminate iodine deficiency.

ZINC DEFICIENCY

Zinc deficiency has been described in many countries (Sandstead, 1995). However, it is difficult to identify this deficiency and no statistics are available on its prevalence. Zinc deficiency occurs when diets are poor in flesh foods but high in substances such as phytates and fiber which inhibit absorption. This type of diet is widespread in many developing countries and zinc deficiency is now thought to be a public health problem (Sandstead, 1995). Zinc deficiency is associated with growth retardation, impaired immune function, and an increased incidence and duration of diarrhea. There is also concern that it affects children's cognitive and behavioral development.

Several studies in primates have shown that zinc deficiency reduces activity level and impairs attention (Golub, Takeuchi, Keen, Hendrickx, & Gershwin, 1996). Only few studies have been conducted in children. In Canada (Friel et al., 1993), very low birth weight children who were given zinc and copper had better motor scores on the Bayley test at 6 months of age than unsupplemented children. In another treatment trial in Brazil, low birth weight term babies were given zinc for the first 2 months of life. They showed no benefit in Bayley scores at 6 and 12 months compared with a non-supplemented matched group born a year earlier. However, the supplemented group was rated as being more responsive to the examiner and showing more activity and vocalization, and more happiness and cooperation with the tester (Ashworth, Morris, Lira, & Grantham-McGregor, 1998).

In two randomized controlled trials of zinc, supplemented toddlers were found to be more active (Golub, Keen, Gershwin, & Hendrickx, 1995), and to lie down less often (Bentley et al., 1997) than unsupplemented ones.

Three randomized controlled trials were conducted in school-aged children. In two (Cavan, Gibson, Graziosa, Isalgue, Ruz, & Solomons, 1993; Gibson, Smit Vanderkooy, MacDonald, Goldman, Ryan, & Berry, 1989) no differences were found on a limited number of cognitive tests. In a third study in China, supplemented children showed benefits on a wide range of cognitive tests (Penland et al., 1997). However, the analysis was problematical.

In conclusion, there is limited and inconsistent evidence that zinc deficiency affects behavior, motor, and cognitive function. The data is insufficient to draw conclusions.

SHORT-TERM HUNGER

Introduction

Hunger is difficult to define. The term can be used to describe a recurring condition lasting for months or years; or an occasional transient condition.

A recent review (Grantham-McGregor & Walker, 1998) identified six studies in developing countries reporting associations between poor school achievement or cognitive function in children and reduced dietary intakes, skipping breakfast, or feelings of hunger (Clarke, 1989; Florencio, 1988; Popkin & Lim-Ybanez, 1982; Sigman, Neumann, Jansen, & Bwibo, 1989; Wilson, 1970). In one study, a rating of the number of days with insufficient food in the home was associated with school achievement levels. We are aware of only one study that looked at the effect of famine on children's behavior (McDonald, Sigman, Espinosa, & Neumann, 1994). During a famine in Kenya, a study was in progress and children were found to spend more time "off task" in the classroom than either before or after the famine. However, it is possible that other stressors played a role.

Most research on the effects of hunger and cognition has focused on the effects of missing or giving breakfast to school-aged children. We focus here on the more rigorous of these studies.

Prevalence of Short-Term Food Deprivation

Short-term food deprivation affects children in developed and developing countries. However, data from developing countries are scanty. A South African study showed that almost one fourth of children did not routinely have breakfast, and about the same number reported being hungry when they came to school (Jooste, Wolmarans, & Oelofse, 1993). A survey of 12 schools in a London borough in the late 1970s showed that 4% of children in infant schools, 9% in junior schools, 13% in middle schools, and 21% in senior schools did not eat breakfast (Bender, Harris, & Getreuer, 1977). Another study of inner-city London schools found that one third of the children missed breakfast (Doyle, Jenkins, Crawford, & Puvandendran, 1994). A U.S. study of midwestern inner-city school children showed that 6.6% were hungry and 32.7% were at risk for hunger (Cutts, Pheley, & Geppert, 1998). The Community Childhood Hunger Identification Project has identified 8% of all children in the United States under 12 to be hungry and an additional 21% to be at risk for hunger (Kleinman et al., 1998).

Organized food distribution in schools dates back to the late 18th century in Europe, and to the 1890s in the United States. Many developing countries also have initiated school feeding programs (Levinger, 1986). Initially, the evaluations of school breakfast programs rested mainly on nutritional benefits resulting from supplementation. However, inspired by the anecdotal testimony of parents and teachers, researchers in the past few decades have been evaluating the effects of school feeding programs on cognition, school achievement, and behavior. Studies evaluating the effects of missing or giving breakfast, have been conducted under laboratory conditions and in schools.

Mechanisms

Our hypotheses of how breakfast may benefit school achievement is illustrated in Fig. 5.5. In poor populations providing free meals may improve attendance and enrollment. It may also improve children's attitude toward school. Consistent and regular attendance ensures the sequence of instruction is maintained and should facilitate learning. Breakfast may also improve the time children spend on task, concentrating on their work, as well as their cognitive ability, especially memory. It is also possible that school meals can improve the children's nutritional status and subsequently improve their cognitive ability.

Laboratory Studies

The best studies of the effects of breakfast on cognitive function have used a rigorous cross-over design in which a child's performance after receiving breakfast was compared with her or his performance after receiving a placebo (e.g., a cup of tea sweetened with aspartame). Most of these studies have shown that missing breakfast can have a direct, negative impact on performance. In two U.S. studies, children who received breakfast had improvements in performance on a test of visual perception and problem solving (Pollitt, Leibel, & Greenfield, 1981; Pollitt, Lewis, Garcia, & Shulman, 1983). In a Jamaican study, children were given a battery of seven cognitive tests in the morning following a breakfast or placebo (Simeon & Grantham-McGregor, 1989). When not receiving breakfast, children who were stunted (low height for their age) deteriorated in two tests. Children who were wasted (low weight for height) deteriorated in another two tests. In contrast, adequately nourished children were not detrimentally affected by missing breakfast in any test. The fourth study, conducted in Peru, also showed that memory in undernourished children was detrimentally affected by missing breakfast, but was not affected in adequately nourished children. Two studies failed to show the effects of missing breakfast on a child's cognitive per-

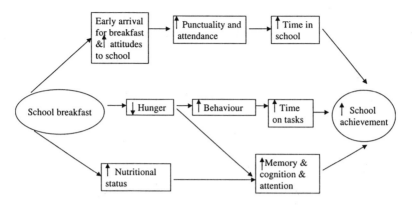

FIG. 5.5. Possible mechanisms of the effect of school breakfast on school achievement.

formance (Lopez, de Andraca, Perales, Heresi, Castillo, & Colombo, 1993; Upadhyay, Agarwal, Agarwal, Srivasta, & Adhikari, 1988). However, these studies were not so rigorously controlled as the others.

Several studies have examined the effects of glucose drinks. Benton and Parker (1998) in a study of university students found that missing breakfast adversely affected memory and this was corrected by glucose drinks. In another study, glucose drinks were found to reduce frustration and to increase attention when children were asked to do a difficult task (Benton, Brett, & Brain, 1987).

Experimental Studies of Providing Breakfast in Schools

Investigators have studied the effects of providing breakfast in school usually for short periods using experimental designs. School achievement and attendance, cognition, and classroom behavior have all been examined.

Behavior.   In South Africa, children who were given a school breakfast for 6 weeks showed reduced "off task" and "out of seat" behavior compared with preintervention measures (Richter, Rose, & Griesel, 1997). However, changes might occur over time regardless of breakfast and the control group was not well matched.

In a Jamaican study, the quality of the classroom organization appeared to modify how the children responded to receiving breakfast (Chang, Walker, Himes, & Grantham-McGregor, 1996). When the classrooms were well organized, spacious, and well equipped, the children were more on task and moved around less when they received breakfast. In contrast, in disorganized overcrowded classrooms children's behavior actually deteriorated when they had breakfast and they were less on task and talked more to their peers. In a U.S. study, there was some suggestion that the type of task may also modify children's behavioral response to breakfast (Bro, Shank, McLaughlin, & Williams, 1996).

Cognition. Two cross-over studies looked at the effect on cognitive function. One was in Jamaica (Chandler et al., 1995) where undernourished children were found to have higher scores in tests of verbal fluency when they received breakfast than when they did not receive breakfast. In contrast, adequately nourished children were not affected by breakfast. The other study was in Sweden (Wyon, Abrahamsson, Jartelius, & Fletcher, 1997), and children who were given adequate breakfasts improved in tests of arithmetic, creativity, and physical perseverance compared with when they received inadequate breakfasts.

Other investigators have looked at school achievement and attendance.

School Achievement and Attendance. In an early Jamaican study (Powell, Grantham-McGregor, & Elston, 1983), the progress of a class of children over one semester when they received breakfast was compared with two other classes in the same school and grade level who did not receive breakfast. The breakfast class improved in attendance and arithmetic compared with the other two classes. The findings remained when the rate of progress in the previous semester was controlled. Because the children did not improve in nutritional status over the same period, the investigators hypothesized that the improvements were attributed directly to the relief of short-term hunger.

A Peruvian study of 10 schools randomly assigned either to receive breakfast for 6 weeks or to receive no breakfast, found that children who were heavier for their height improved in vocabulary if they had received breakfast. Also the children who received breakfast improved in attendance. It is not clear why children with high weights for height were more affected.

In a U.S. study comparing children who participated in a school breakfast program for 3 months with those who did not participate, improvements were evident in a school achievement test consisting of language, mathematics, and reading (Myers, Sampson, Weitzman, Rogers, & Kayne, 1989). Absenteeism and tardiness were also reduced in the participants. It is possible that the choice to eat breakfast identified special children.

We could find only one study that lasted more than 3 months. This was a randomized controlled trial in Jamaica which ran for one school year. The children receiving breakfast improved in attendance and nutritional status and the younger children improved in arithmetic (Powell, Walker, Chang, & Grantham-McGregor, 1998).

In conclusion, it appears that most studies have shown improvements in school attendance and cognition. There is limited evidence of improvements to school achievement. Only one study lasted more than 3 months and more long-term evaluations are needed. Improvements in behavior may depend on the classroom environment. In children who are frequently hungry, the effect on their ability to learn in school is potentially serious. However, if marked improvements to school achievement are required it will be necessary to have integrated interventions including educational as well as nutritional components.

CONCLUSIONS FROM REVIEW

In conclusion, there is substantial evidence that nutrition affects children's development. The effects vary from *devastating and permanent* as in iodine deficiency in utero to *mild and transient* as in short-term food deprivation at school age. All stages of development from conception to puberty appear vulnerable to nutritional deficits, although there is some suggestion that the first 3 years are the most vulnerable.

Many different nutritional deficiencies (e.g., protein–energy–malnutrition, low birth weight, iron and zinc deficiency) appear to have similar effects on children's behavior causing reduced activity and exploration, less happiness, and more fussing. A wide range of cognitive and motor functions appear to be affected. Some long-term outcomes appear to be modified by the environment.

REFERENCES

Agarwal, D. K., Upadhyay, S. K., Tripathi, A. M., & Agarwal, K. N. (1987). *Nutritional status, physical work capacity and mental function in school children*, No. 6. New Delhi: Nutrition Foundation of India.

Allen, L. H. (1994). Nutritional influences on linear growth: a general review. *European Journal of Clinical Nutrition, 48*(Suppl. 1), S75–S89.

Ashworth, A., Morris, S. S., Lira, P. I., & Grantham-McGregor, S. M. (1998). Zinc supplementation, mental development and behavior in low birth weight term infants in northeast Brazil. *European Journal of Clinical Nutrition, 52*, 223–227.

Aukett, M., Parks, Y., Scott, P., & Wharton, B. (1986). Treatment with iron increases weight gain and psychomotor development. *Archives of Disease in Childhood, 61*, 849–857.

Azizi, F., Nafarabadi, M., Ghazi, A., Kimiagar, M., Noohi, S., Rahbar, N., Bahrami, A., & Kalantari, S. (1993). Impairment of neuromotor and cognitive development in iodine-deficient school-children with normal physical growth. *Acta Endocrinlogica, 129*, 501–504.

Barnet, A. B., Weiss, I. P., Sotillo, M. V., Ohlrich, E. S., Shkurovich, M., & Cravioto, J. (1978). Abnormal auditory evoked potentials in early infancy malnutrition. *Science, 201*, 450–452.

Bartel, P., Griesel, R., Burnett, L., Freiman, I., Rosen, E., & Geefhuysen, J. (1978). Long-term effects of kwashiorkor on psychomotor development. *South African Medical Journal, 53*, 360–362.

Bautista, A., Barker, P. A., Dunn, J. T., Sanchez, M., & Kaiser, D. L. (1982). The effects of oral iodized oil on intelligence, thyroid status, and somatic growth in school-age children from an area of endemic goiter. *American Journal of Clinical Nutrition, 35,* 127–134.

Ben Shachar, D., Ashkenazi, R., & Youdim, M. B. (1986). Long-term consequence of early iron-deficiency on dopaminergic neurotransmission in rats. *International Journal of Developmental Neuroscience, 4,* 81–88.

Bender, A. E., Harris, M. C., & Getreuer, A. (1977). Feeding of school children in a London borough. *British Medical Journal, 1,* 757–759.

Bentley, M. E., Caulfield, L. E., Ram, M., Santizo, M. C., Hurtado, E., Rivera, J. A., Ruel, M. T., & Brown, K. H. (1997). Zinc supplementation affects the activity patterns of rural Guatemalan infants. *Journal of Nutrition, 127,* 1333–1338.

Benton, D., Brett, V., & Brain, P. (1987). Glucose improves attention and reaction to frustration in children. *Biological Psychology, 24,* 95–100.

Benton, D., & Parker, P. Y. (1998). Breakfast, blood glucose, and cognition. *American Journal of Clinical Nutrition, 67,* 772S–778S.

Bhatia, D., & Seshadri, S. (1987). Anemia, undernutrition and physical work capacity of young boys. *Indian Pediatrics, 24,* 133–139.

Birch, H. G., Pineiro, C., Alcalde, E., Toca, T., & Cravioto, J. (1971). Relation of kwashiorkor in early childhood and intelligence at school age. *Pediatric Research, 5,* 579–585.

Bleichrodt, N., Escobar del Ray, F., Morreale de Escobar, G., Garcia, I., & Rubio, C. (1989). Iodine deficiency, implications for mental and psychomotor development in children. In G. R. Delong, J. Robbins, & P. G., Condliffe (Eds.), *Iodine and the brain.* New York: Plenum.

Bleichrodt, N., Garcia, I., Rubio, C., Morreale de Escobar, G., & Ecobar del Rey, F. (1987). Developmental disorders associated with severe iodine deficiency. In B. Hetzel, J. Dunn, & J. Stanbury (Eds.), *The prevention and control of iodine deficiency disorders* (pp. 65–84). Amsterdam: Elsevier.

Bogin, B., & MacVean, R. B. (1983). The relationship of socioeconomic status and sex to body size, skeletal maturation, and cognitive status of Guatemala City schoolchildren. *Child Development, 51,* 115–128.

Boyages, S. C., Collins, J. K., Maberly, G. F., Jupp, J. J., Morris, J., & Eastman, C. J. (1989). Iodine deficiency impairs intellectual and neuromotor development in apparently-normal persons. *Medical Journal of Australia, 150,* 676–682.

British Nutrition Foundation (1995). *Iron: Nutritional and physiological significance.* The report of the British Nutrition Foundation's Task Force. London: Chapman & Hall.

Bro, R. T., Shank, L. L., McLaughlin, T. F., & Williams, R. L. (1996). Effects of a breakfast program on on-task behaviors of vocational high school students. *Journal of Educational Research, 90,* 111–115.

Broad, F. E. (1979). Early feeding history of children with learning disorders [letter]. *Developmental Medicine and Child Neurology, 21,* 822.

Brockman, L. M., & Ricciuti, H. N. (1971). Severe protein calorie malnutrition and cognitive development in infancy and early childhood. *Developmental Psychology, 54,* 312–319.

Cantwell, R. J. (1974). The long term neurological sequelae of anemia in infancy. *Pediatric Research, 342,* 68.

Cao, X. -Y., Jiang, X. -M., Dou, Z. -H., Murdon, A. R., Zhang, M. -L., O'Donnell, K., Tai, M., Amette, K., DeLong, N., & Delong, G. R. (1994). Timing of vulnerability of the brain to iodine deficiency in endemic cretinism. *New England Journal of Medicine, 331*(26), 1739–1744.

Carmona da Mota, H., Antonio, A. M., Leitao, G., & Porto, M. (1990). Late effects of early malnutrition [letter]. *Lancet, 335,* 1158.

Cavan, K. R., Gibson, R. S., Graziosa, C. F., Isalgue, A. M., Ruz, M., & Solomons, N. W. (1993). Growth and body composition of peri-urban Guatemalan children in relation to zinc status: a longitudinal zinc intervention trial. *American Journal of Clinical Nutrition, 57,* 344–352.

Champakam, S., Srikantia, S. G., & Gopalan, C. (1968). Kwashiorkor and mental development. *American Journal of Clinical Nutrition, 21,* 844–852.

Chandler, A. K., Walker, S. P., Connolly, K., & Grantham-McGregor, S. M. (1995). School breakfast improves verbal fluency in undernourished Jamaican children. *Journal of Nutrition, 125,* 894–900.

Chang, S. M., Walker, S. P., Himes, J., & Grantham-McGregor, S. M. (1996). Effects of breakfast on classroom behavior in rural Jamaican school children. *Food Nutrition Bulletin, 17,* 248–257.

Chavez, A., & Martinez, C. (1982). *Growing up in a developing community.* Guatemala City: Institute of Nutrition in Central America and Panama.

Chavez, A., Martinez, C., Soberanes, B., Dominguez, L., & Avila, A. (1994). *Early nutrition and physical and mental development in Mexican rural adolescent families.* Washington, DC: International Center for Research on Women.

Clarke, N. (1989). *The health and nutritional determinants of academic achievement in Jamaican primary school children.* Unpublished doctoral dissertation, University of the West Indies.

Clarke, N., Grantham-McGregor, S. M., & Powell, C. (1991). Nutrition and health predictors of school failure in Jamaican children. *Ecology of Food and Nutrition, 26,* 1–11.

Colombo, M., de Andraca, I., & Lopez, I. (1988). Mental development and stunting. In J. Waterlow (Ed.), *Linear growth retardation in less developed countries* (pp. 201–214). New York: Raven Press.

Colombo, M., de la Parra, A., & Lopez, I. (1992). Intellectual and physical outcome of children undernourished in early life is influenced by later environmental conditions. *Developmental Medicine and Child Neurology, 34,* 611–622.

Connolly, K. J., & Pharoah, P. O. D. (1989). Iodine deficiency, maternal thyroxin levels in pregnancy and developmental disorders in the children. In G. R. Delong, J. Robbins, & P. G. Condliffe (Eds.), *Iodine and the brain* (pp. 317–331). New York: Plenum Press.

Connolly, K. J., Pharoah, P. O. D., & Hetzel, B. S. (1979). Fetal iodine deficiency and motor performance during childhood. *Lancet, II,* 1149–1151.

Cravioto, J., & Robles, B. (1965). Evolution of adaptive and motor behavior during rehabilitation from kwashiorkor. *American Journal of Ortho-Psychiatry, 35,* 449–464.

Crawford, M. A. (1993). The role of essential fatty acids in neural development: implications for perinatal nutrition. *American Journal of Clinical Nutrition, 57,* 703S–709S.

Cutts, D. B., Pheley, A. M., & Geppert, J. S. (1998). Hunger in midwestern inner-city young children. *Archives of Pediatrics and Adolescent Medicine, 152,* 489–493.

Dallman, P. R., & Spirito, R. A. (1977). Brain iron in the rat: Extremely slow turnover in normal rats may explain long-lasting effects of early iron deficiency. *Journal of Nutrition, 107,* 1075–1081.

de Andraca, I., Castillo, M., & Walter, T. (1997). Psychomotor development and behavior in iron-deficient anemic infants. *Nutrition Reviews, 55,* 125–132.

de Andraca, I., Walter, T., Castillo, M., Pino, P., Rivera, P., & Cobo, C. (1990). Iron deficiency anemia and its effects upon psychological development at preschool age: A longitudinal study. *Nestle Foundation Annual Report,* 53–62.

Delange, F. (1994). The disorders induced by iodine deficiency. *Thyroid, 4,* 107–128.

Delong, R. (1989). Observations of the neurology of endemic cretinism. In G. R. Delong, J. Robbins, & P. G. Condliffe (Eds.), *Iodine and the brain* (pp. 231–238). New York: Plenum.

Delong, G. R., Stanbury, J. B., & Fierro-Benitez, R. (1985). Neurological signs in congenital iodine-deficiency disorder (endemic cretinism). *Developmental Medicine & Child Neurology, 27,* 317–324.

DeMaeyer, E., & Adiels-Tegman, M. (1985). The prevalence of anemia in the world. *World Health Statistics Quarterly, 38,* 302–316.

Dodge, P. R., Palkes, H., Fierro-Benitez, R., & Ramirez, I. (1969). Effect on intelligence of iodine in oil administered to young Andean children—A preliminary report. In J. B. Stanbury (Ed.), *Endemic goiter* (pp. 378–380). Washington, DC: Pan American Health Organization.

Doyle, W., Jenkins, S., Crawford, M. A., & Puvandendran, K. (1994). Nutritional status of school children in an inner city area. *Archives of Diseases of Childhood, 70,* 376–381.

Dumont, J. E., Corvilain, B., & Contempre, B. (1994). Endemic cretinism: The myxedematous and neurological forms of a disease caused by severe iodine deficiency. In J. B. Stanbury (Ed.), *The damaged brain of iodine deficiency: Cognitive, behavioral, neuromotor, education aspects* (pp. 259–263). New York: Cognizant Corporation.

Dunn, J. T. (1996). Extensive personal experience: Seven deadly sins in confronting endemic iodine deficiency, and how to avoid them. *Journal of Clinical Endocrinology and Metabolism, 81*(4), 1332–1335.

Ebrahim, G. J. (1995). Hypothyroidism in the newborn. *Journal of Tropical Pediatrics, 41*, 256–257.

Evans, D., Moodie, A., & Hansen, J. (1971). Kwashiorkor and intellectual development. *South African Medical Journal, 45*, 1413–1426.

Fenzi, G. F., Giusti, L. F., Aghini-Lombardi, F., Marcocci, C., Santini, F., Bargagna, S., Brizzolara, D., Ferretti, G., Falciglia, G., Monteleone, M., Marcheschi, M., & Pinchera, A. (1990). Neuropsychological assessment in school children from an area of moderate iodine deficiency. *Journal of Endocrinological Investigation, 13*, 427–431.

Fergusson, D. M., Beautrais, A. L., & Silva, P. A. (1982). Breast-feeding and cognitive development in the first seven years of life. *Social Science and Medicine, 16*, 1705–1708.

Florencio, C. (1988). *Nutrition, health and other determinants of academic achievement and school-related behavior of grades one to six pupils.* Quezan City, Phillipines: University of the Phillipines.

Freeman, H. E., Klein, R. E., Townsend, J. W., & Lechtig, A. (1980). Nutrition and cognitive development among rural Guatemalan children. *American Journal of Public Health, 70*, 1277–1285.

Friel, J. K., Andrews, W. L., Matthew, J. D., Long, D. R., Cornel, A. M., Cox, M., McKim, E., & Zerbe, G. O. (1993). Zinc supplementation in very-low-birth-weight infants. *Journal of Pediatric Gastroenterology and Nutrition, 17*, 97–104.

Gale, C. R., & Martyn, C. N. (1996). Breastfeeding, dummy use, and adult intelligence. *Lancet, 347*, 1072–1075.

Galler, J. R., Ramsey, F., Solimano, G., Kucharski, L. T., & Harrison, R. (1984). The influence of early malnutrition on subsequent behavioral development. IV. Soft neurologic signs. *Pediatric Research, 18*, 826–832.

Galler, J. R., Ramsay, F., Solimano, G., & Lowell, W. E. (1983). The influence of early malnutrition on subsequent behavioral development II. Classroom behavior. *Journal of the American Academy of Child Psychiatry, 22*, 16–22.

Galler, J. R., Ramsey, F., Solimano, G., Lowell, W., & Mason, E. (1983). The influence of early malnutrition on subsequent behavioral development. I. Degree of impairment of intellectual performance. *Journal of the American Academy of Child Psychiatry, 22*, 8–15.

Gibson, R. S., Smit Vanderkooy, P. D., MacDonald, A. C., Goldman, A., Ryan, B. A., & Berry, M. (1989). A growth-limiting, mild zinc deficiency syndrome in some Southern Ontario boys with low height percentiles. *American Journal of Clinical Nutrition, 49*, 1266–1273.

Golden, M. H. N. (1988). The role of individual nutrient deficiencies in growth retardation of children as exemplified by zinc and protein. In J. C. Waterlow (Ed.), *Linear growth retardation in less developed countries* (pp. 143–164). New York: Raven Press.

Goldenberg, R. L., Hoffman, H. J., & Cliver, S. P. (1998). Neurodevelopmental outcome of small-for gestational-age infants. *European Journal of Clinical Nutrition, 52*, S54–S58.

Golub, M. S., Keen, C. L., Gershwin, M. E., & Hendrickx, A. G. (1995). Developmental zinc deficiency and behavior. *Journal of Nutrition, 125*, 2263S–2271S.

Golub, M. S., Takeuchi, P. T., Keen, C. L., Hendrickx, A. G., & Gershwin, M. E. (1996). Activity and attention in zinc-deprived adolescent monkeys. *American Journal of Clinical Nutrition, 64*, 908–915.

Graham, G., & Adrianzen, B. (1979). Status at school of Peruvian children severely malnourished in infancy. In J. Brozek (Ed.), *Behavioral effects of energy and protein deficits* (pp. 185–194). Washington, DC: US Department of Health, Education and Welfare.

Grantham-McGregor, S. M. (1995). A review of studies of the effect of severe malnutrition on mental development. *Journal of Nutrition, 125*, 2233S–2238S.

Grantham-McGregor, S. M. (1998). Small for gestational age, term babies, in the first six years of life. *European Journal of Clinical Nutrition, 52*(S1), S59–S64.

Grantham-McGregor, S. M., Fernald, L. C., & Sethuraman, K. (1999). The effects of health and nutrition on cognitive and behavioral development in children in the first three years of life. Part 1: Low birth weight, breast feeding and protein-energy-malnutrition. *Food Nutrition Bulletin, 20*, 53–75.

Grantham-McGregor, S. M., Powell, C., Walker, S., Chang, S., & Fletcher, P. (1994). The long-term follow-up of severely malnourished children who participated in an intervention program. *Child Development, 65*, 428–439.

Grantham-McGregor, S. M., Powell, C. A., Walker, S. P., & Himes, J. H. (1991). Nutritional supplementation, psychosocial stimulation, and mental development of stunted children: The Jamaican Study. *Lancet, 338*, 1–5.

Grantham-McGregor, S. M., Schofield, W., & Desai, P. (1978). A new look at the assessment of mental development in young children recovering from severe malnutrition. *Developmental Medicine and Child Neurology, 20*, 773–778.

Grantham-McGregor, S. M., Stewart, M., & Powell, C. (1991). Behavior of severely malnourished children in a Jamaican hospital. *Developmental Medicine and Child Neurology, 33*, 706–714.

Grantham-McGregor, S. M., & Walker, S. (1998). Health and nutritional determinants of school failure. In S. M. Grantham-McGregor (Ed.), *Nutrition, health, and child development. Research advances and policy recommendations* (pp. 82–90). Washington, DC/Kingston, Jamaica: Pan American Health Organization, The World Bank, and Tropical Metabolism Research Unit of University of the West Indies.

Grantham-McGregor, S. M., Walker, S. P., Chang, S. M., & Powell, C. A. (1997). Effects of early childhood supplementation with and without stimulation on later development in stunted Jamaican children. *American Journal of Clinical Nutrition, 66*, 247–253.

Gutekunst, R. (1993). Iodine deficiency costs Germany over one billion dollars per year. *IDD Newsletter, 9*(3), 29–31.

Hack, M. (1998). Effects of intrauterine growth retardation on mental performance and behavior: outcomes during adolescence and adulthood. *European Journal of Clinical Nutrition, 52*, S65–S71.

Halpern, J. -P. (1994). The neuromotor deficit in endemic cretinism and its implications for the pathogenisis of the disorder. In J. B. Stanbury (Ed.), *The damaged brain of iodine deficiency* (pp. 15–24). New York: Cognizant Communication.

Hamill, P. V., Drizd, T. A., Johnson, C. L., Reed, R. B., & Roche, A. F. (1977). NCHS growth curves for children birth-18 years. *United States Vital. Health Stat., 11*, i–iv, 1–74.

Hertzig, M., Birch, H., Richardson, S., & Tizard, J. (1972). Intellectual levels of school children severely malnourished during the first two years of life. *Pediatrics, 49*, 814–824.

Hetzel, B. S. (1983). Iodine deficiency disorders (IDD) and their eradication. *Lancet, 12*, 1126–1129.

Hetzel, B. S. (1989). *The story of iodine deficiency: An international challenge in nutrition.* New York: Oxford University Press.

Hetzel, B. S., & Mano, A. T. (1989). A review of experimental studies of iodine deficiency during fetal development. *Journal of Nutrition, 119*, 145–151.

Hetzel, B. S., Potter, B. J., & Dulberg, E. M. (1990). The iodine deficiency disorders: Nature, pathogenesis and epidemiology. In G. H. Bourne (Ed.), *Aspects of some vitamins, minerals and enzymes in health and disease* (pp. 59–119). Basel: S. Karger.

Heywood, A., Oppenheimer, S., Heywood, P., & Jolley, D. (1989). Behavioral effects of iron supplementation in infants in Madang, Papua New Guinea. *American Journal of Clinical Nutrition, 50*, 630–637.

Hoefer, C., & Hardy, M. C. (1929). Later development of breast fed and artificially fed infants: Comparison of physical and mental growth. *Journal of the American Medical Association, 92*(8), 615–619.

Hoorweg, J. (1976). *Protein-energy malnutrition and intellectual abilities: A study of teen-age Ugandan children.* The Hague, Netherlands: Mouton.

Hoorweg, J., & Stanfield, J. (1976). The effects of protein-energy malnutrition in early childhood on intellectual and motor abilities in later childhood and adolescence. *Developmental Medicine and Child Neurology, 18,* 330–350.

Horwood, L. J., & Fergusson, D. M. (1998). Breastfeeding and later cognitive and academic outcomes. *Pediatrics, 101,* e9.

Howie, P. W., Forsyth, J. S., Ogston, S. A., Clark, A., & Florey, C. D. (1990). Protective effect of breast feeding against infection. *British Medical Journal, 300,* 11–16.

Huda, S. N., Grantham-McGregor, S. M., Rahman, K. M., & Tomkins, A. (1999). Biochemical hypothyroidism secondary to iodine deficiency is associated with poor school achievement and cognition in Bangladeshi children. *Journal of Nutrition, 129,* 980–987.

Hurtado, E. K., Claussen, A. H., & Scott, K. G. (1999). Early childhood anemia and mild or moderate mental retardation. *American Journal of Clinical Nutrition, 69,* 115–119.

Idjradinata, P., & Pollitt, E. (1993). Reversal of developmental delays in iron-deficient anemic infants treated with iron. *Lancet, 341,* 1–4.

Innis, S. M. (1993). Essential fatty acid requirements in human nutrition. *Canadian Journal of Physiology and Pharmacology, 71,* 699–706.

Ivanovic, D., Vasquez, M., Marambio, M., Ballester, D., Zacarias, I., & Aguayo, M. (1991). Nutrition and education. II. Educational achievement and nutrient intake of Chilean elementary and high school graduates. *Archivos Latinoamericanos de Nutricion, 41,* 499–515.

Jacobson, S. W., & Jacobson, J. L. (1992). Breastfeeding and intelligence [letter; comment]. *Lancet, 339,* 926.

Johnston, F. E., Low, S. M., de Baessa, Y., & MacVean, R. B. (1987). Interaction of nutritional and socioeconomic status as determinants of cognitive development in disadvantaged urban Guatemalan children. *American Journal of Physical Anthropology, 73,* 501–506.

Joos, S. K., Pollitt, E., Mueller, W. H., & Albright, D. L. (1983). The bacon chow study: Maternal nutritional supplementation and infant behavioral development. *Child Development, 54,* 669–676.

Jooste, P. L., Wolmarans, P., & Oelofse, A. (1993). *Needs assessment for school feeding programs in low socio-economic areas.* Cape Town: Medical Research Council.

Keller, W. (1988). The epidemiology of stunting. In J. C. Waterlow (Ed.), *Linear growth retardation in less developed countries* (pp. 17–40). New York: Raven.

Kleinman, R. E., Murphy, J. M., Little, M., Pagano, M., Wehler, C. A., Regal, K., & Jellinek, M. S. (1998). Hunger in children in the United States: Potential behavioral and emotional correlates. *Pediatrics, 101,* e3.

Lancet (1970). Editorial. "Classification of infantile malnutrition." *Lancet, 2,* 303.

Lasky, R. E., Klein, R. E., Yarbrough, C., Engle, P. L., Lechtig, A., & Martorell, R. (1981). The relationship between physical growth and infant behavioral development in rural Guatemala. *Child Development, 52,* 219–226.

Levinger, B. (1986). *Schoolfeeding programs in developing countries: An analysis of actual and potential impact. USAID, Washington,* 30th ed. AID Evaluation Special Study: USAID, Washington DC.

Levitsky, D. A. (1979). Malnutrition and hunger to learn. In D. A. Levitsky (Ed.), *Malnutrition, environment and behavior* (pp. 161–179). Ithaca, NY: Cornell University Press.

Levitsky, D. A., & Strupp, B. J. (1995). Malnutrition and the brain: Changing concepts, changing concerns. *Journal of Nutrition, 125,* 2245S–2254S.

Lopez, I., de Andraca, I., Perales, C. G., Heresi, E., Castillo, M., & Colombo, M. (1993). Breakfast omission and cognitive performance of normal, wasted and stunted school children. *European Journal of Clinical Nutrition, 47,* 533–542.

Lozoff, B. (1998). Explanatory mechanisms for poorer development in iron-deficient anemic infants. In S. M. Grantham-McGregor (Ed.), *Recent advances in research on the effects of health and nutrition on children's development and school achievement in the Third World: Policy implications* (pp. 162–178). Washington, DC: Pan American Health Organization.

Lozoff, B., Brittenham, G. M., Viteri, F. E., Wolf, A. W., & Urrutia, J. J. (1982). The effects of short-term oral iron therapy on developmental deficits in iron deficient anemic infants. *Journal of Pediatrics, 100,* 351–357.

Lozoff, B., Brittenham, G. M., & Wolf, A. W. (1987). Iron deficiency anemia and iron therapy: Effects on infant developmental test performance. *Pediatrics, 79,* 981–995.

Lozoff, B., de Andraca, I., Walter, T., & Pino, P. (1996). Does preventing iron-deficiency anemia (IDA) improve developmental test scores? *Pediatric Research, 39,* 136(A).

Lozoff, B., Jimenez, E., & Wolf, A. W. (1991). Long-term developmental outcome of infants with iron deficiency. *New England Journal of Medicine, 325,* 687–694.

Lozoff, B., Klein, N. K., Nelson, E. C., McClish, D. K., Manuel, M., & Chacon, M. E. (1998). Behavior of infants with iron-deficiency anemia. *Child Development, 69,* 24–36.

Lucas, A., Morley, R., & Cole, T. J. (1998). Randomized trial of early diet in preterm babies and later intelligence quotient. *British Medical Journal, 317,* 1481–1487.

Lucas, A., Morley, R., Cole, T. J., Lister, G., & Leeson Payne, C. (1992). Breast milk and subsequent intelligence quotient in children born preterm. *Lancet, 339,* 261–264.

Malloy, M. H., & Berendes, H. (1998). Does breast-feeding influence intelligence quotients at 9 and 10 years of age? *Early Human Development, 50,* 209–217.

Martorell, R., Khan, L. K., & Schroeder, D. G. (1994). Reversibility of stunting: Epidemiological findings in children from developing countries. *European Journal of Clinical Nutrition, 48*(Suppl 1), S45–S57.

Martorell, R., Rivera, J., Kaplowitz, J., & Pollitt, E. (1992). Long term consequences of growth retardation during early childhood. In M. Hernandez & J. Argenta (Eds.), *Human growth: Basic and clinical aspects* (pp. 143–149). Amsterdam: Elsevier.

McDonald, M. A., Sigman, M., Espinosa, M. P., & Neumann, C. G. (1994). Impact of a temporary food shortage on children and their mothers. *Child Development, 65,* 404–415.

McKay, A., & McKay, H. (1983). Primary school progress after preschool experience: Troublesome issues in the conduct of follow-up research and findings from Cali, Colombia Study. In K. King & R. Meyers (Eds.), *Preventing school failure: The relationship between preschool and primary education* (pp. 32–42). Ottawa: International Development Research Center.

McKay, H., Sinisterra, L., McKay, A., Gomez, H., & Lloreda, P. (1978). Improving cognitive ability in chronically deprived children. *Science, 200,* 270–278.

McLaren, D., Yatkin, U., Kanawati, A., Sabbagh, S., & Kadi, Z. (1973). The subsequent mental and physical development of rehabilitated marasmic infants. *Journal of Mental Deficiency Research, 17,* 273–281.

Gardner, J. M., Grantham-McGregor, S. M., Himes, J. H., & Chang, S. M. (1999). Behavior and development of stunted and non-stunted Jamaican children. *Journal of Child Psychology and Psychiatry, 40,* 819–827.

Mehta, M., Pandav, C. S., & Kochupillai, N. (1987). Intellectual assessment of school children from severely iodine deficient villages. *Indian Pediatrics, 24,* 467–473.

Moffatt, M. E. K., Longstaffe, S., Besant, J., & Dureski, C. (1994). Prevention of iron deficiency and psychomotor decline in high-risk infants through use of iron-fortified infant formula: A randomized clinical trial. *Journal of Pediatrics, 125,* 527–523.

Moock, P. R., & Leslie, J. (1986). Childhood malnutrition and schooling in the Teri region of Nepal. *Journal of Development Economics, 20,* 33–52.

Moodie, A., Bowie, M., Mann, M., & Hansen, J. (1980). A prospective 15-year follow-up study of kwashiorkor patients. Part II. Social circumstances, educational attainment and social adjustment. *South African Medical Journal, 58,* 677–681.

Morley, R. (1998). Food for the infant's brain. *British Nutrition Foundation Bulletin, 23,* 65–76.

Morrow Tlucak, M., Haude, R. H., & Ernhart, C. B. (1988). Breastfeeding and cognitive development in the first 2 years of life. *Social Science and Medicine, 26*, 635–639.⁻

Myers, A., Sampson, A., Weitzman, M., Rogers, B., & Kayne, H. (1989). School breakfast program and school performance. *American Journal of Diseases of Childhood, 143*, 1234–1239.

Nelson, K. G. (1996). Salt solution for Ghana's plague of goitres. *Lancet, 348*, 883.

Neumann, C. G., & Harrison, G. G. (1994). Onset and evolution of stunting in infants and children. Examples from the Human Nutrition Collaborative Research Support Program. Kenya and Egypt studies. *European Journal of Clinical Nutrition, 48*(Suppl 1), S90–S102.

Niemela, A., & Jarvenpaa, A. L. (1996). Is breastfeeding beneficial and maternal smoking harmful to the cognitive development of children? *Acta Paediatrica, 85*, 1202–1206.

Nwuga, V. C. B. (1977). Effect of severe kwashiorkor on intellectual development among Nigerian children. *American Journal of Clinical Nutrition, 30*, 1423–1430.

Oski, F. A., & Honig, A. S. (1978). The effects of therapy on the developmental scores of iron-deficient infants. *Journal of Pediatrics, 92*, 21–25.

Osterweil, D., Syndulko, K., Cohen, S. N., Pettler-Jennings, P. D., Hershman, J. M., Cummings, J. L., Tourtellotte, W. W., & Solomon, D. H. (1992). Cognitive function in non-demented older adults with hypothyroidism. *Journal of American Geriatric Society, 40*(4), 325–335.

Ounsted, M., Moar, V. A., Cockburn, J., & Redman, C. W. (1984). Factors associated with the intellectual ability of children born to women with high risk pregnancies. *British Medical Journal Clinical Research Edition, 288*, 1038–1041.

Pabst, H. F., Spady, D. W., Pilarski, L. M., Carson, M. M., Beeler, J. A., & Krezolek, M. P. (1997). Differential modulation of immune response by breast- or formula-feeding of infants. *Acta Paediatrica, 86*, 1291–1297.

Palti, H., Meijer, A., & Adler, B. (1985). Learning achievement and behavior at school of anemic and non-anemic infants. *Early Human Development, 10*, 217–223.

Palti, H., Pevsner, B., & Adler, B. (1983). Does anemia in infancy affect achievement on developmental and intelligence tests? *Human Biology, 55*, 183–194.

Penland, J. G., Sandstead, H. H., Alcock, N. W., Dayal, H. H., Chen, X. C., Li, J. S., Zhao, F., & Yang, J. J. (1997). A preliminary report: Effects of zinc and micronutrient repletion on growth and neuropsychological function of urban Chinese children. *Journal of American College of Nutrition, 16*, 268–272.

Pereira, S. M., Sundararaj, R., & Begum, A. (1979). Physical growth and neuro-integrative performance of survivors of protein-energy malnutrition. *British Journal of Nutrition, 42*, 165–171.

Pharoah, P. O. D., Buttfield, I. H., & Hetzel, B. S. (1971). Neurological damage to the fetus resulting from severe iodine deficiency during pregnancy. *Lancet, 1*, 308–310.

Pharoah, P. O., Buttfield, I. H., & Hetzel, B. S. (1972). The effect of iodine prophylaxis on the incidence of endemic cretinism. *Advances in Experimental Medicine and Biology, 30*, 201–221.

Pharoah, P. O. D., & Connolly, K. J. (1987). A controlled trial of iodinated oil for the prevention of endemic cretinism: a long term follow-up. *International Journal of Epidemiology, 16*(1), 68–73.

Pharoah, P. O. D., & Connolly, K. J. (1989). Maternal thyroid hormones and fetal brain development. In G. R. Delong, J. Robbins, & P. G. Condliffe (Eds.), *Iodine and the brain* (pp. 333–354). New York: Plenum Press.

Pharoah, P. O. D., & Connolly, K. J. (1991). Effects of maternal iodine supplementation during pregnancy. *Archives of Disease in Childhood, 66*, 145–147.

Pharoah, P. O. D., & Connolly, K. J. (1994). Iodine deficiency in Papua New Guinea. In J. B. Stanbury (Ed.), *The damaged brain of iodine deficiency* (pp. 299–308). New York: Cognizant Communication.

Pharoah, P. O. D., Connolly, K. J., Ekins, R. P., & Harding, A. G. (1984). Maternal thyroid hormone levels in pregnancy and the subsequent cognitive and motor performance of the children. *Clinical Endocrinology, 21*, 265–270.

Pharoah, P. O. D., Connolly, K. J., Hetzel, B. S., & Ekins, R. P. (1981). Maternal thyroid function and motor competence in the child. *Developmental Medicine and Child Neurology, 23*, 76–82.

Pollitt, E., Gorman, K. S., Engle, P. L., Martorell, R., & Rivera, J. (1993). Early supplementary feeding and cognition. *Mon Soc Child Dev, 58*, 1–99.

Pollitt, E., & Granoff, D. (1967). Mental and motor development of Peruvian children treated for severe malnutrition. *Revista Interamericana de Psicologia, 1*(2), 93–102.

Pollitt, E., Hathirat, P., Kotchabhakdi, N. J., Missell, L., & Valyasevi, A. (1989). Iron deficiency and educational achievement in Thailand. *American Journal of Clinical Nutrition, 50*, 687–697.

Pollitt, E., Leibel, R. L., & Greenfield, D. (1981). Brief fasting, stress and cognition in children. *American Journal of Clinical Nutrition, 34*, 1526–1533.

Pollitt, E., Lewis, N., Garcia, C., & Shulman, R. (1983). Fasting and cognitive funciton. *Journal of Psychological Research, 17*, 169–174.

Pollitt, E., Soemantri, A. G., Yunis, F., & Scrimshaw, N. S. (1985). Cognitive effects of iron-deficiency anemia. *Lancet, 19*, 158.

Pollitt, E., Watkins, W. E., & Husaini, M. A. (1997). Three-month nutritional supplementation in Indonesian infants and toddlers benefits memory function 8 y later. *American Journal of Clinical Nutrition, 66*, 1357–1363.

Pollock, J. I. (1994). Long-term associations with infant feeding in a clinically advantaged population of babies. *Developmental Medicine and Child Neurology, 36*, 429–440.

Popkin, B., & Lim-Ybanez, M. (1982). Nutrition and school achievement. *Social Science and Medicine, 16*, 53–61.

Powell, C. A., & Grantham-McGregor, S. (1985). The ecology of nutritional status and development in young children in Kingston, Jamaica. *American Journal of Clinical Nutrition, 41*, 1322–1331.

Powell, C. A., Grantham-McGregor, S., & Elston, M. (1983). An evaluation of giving the Jamaican government school meal to a class of children. *Human Nutrition: Clinical Nutrition, 37*, 381–388.

Powell, C. A., Walker, S. P., Chang, S. M., & Grantham-McGregor, S. M. (1998). Nutrition and education: a randomized trial of the effects of breakfast in rural primary school children. *American Journal of Clinical Nutrition, 68*, 873–879.

Powell, C. A., Walker, S. P., Himes, J. H., Fletcher, P. D., & Grantham-McGregor, S. M. (1995). Relationships between physical growth, mental development and nutritional supplementation in stunted children: the Jamaican study. *Acta Paediatrica, 84*, 22–29.

Prentice, A., & Bates, C. J. (1994). Adequacy of dietary mineral supply for human bone growth and mineralisation. *European Journal of Clinical Nutrition, 48*, S161–S177.

Pretell, E. A., Torres, T., Zenteno, V., & Cornejo, M. (1972). Prophylaxis of endemic goiter with iodized oil in rural Peru. *Advances in Experimental Medicine and Biology, 30*, 249–265.

Querido, A., Bleichrodt, N., & Djokomoeljanto, R. (1978). Thyroid hormones and human mental development. *Progress in Brain Research, 48*, 337–344.

Ramirez, I., Fierro-Benitez, R., Estrella, E., Jaramillo, C., Diaz, C., & Urresta, J. (1969). Iodized oil in the prevention of endemic goiter and associated defects in the Andean region of Ecuador. II. Effects on neuromotor development and somatic growth before two years. In J. B. Stanbury (Ed.), *Endemic goiter* (pp. 341–359). Washington, DC: Pan American Health Organization.

Richardson, S. A. (1974). The background histories of schoolchildren severely malnourished in infancy. *Advances in Pediatrics, 21*, 167–195.

Richardson, S. A. (1979). Severity of malnutrition in infancy and its relation to later intelligence. In J. Brozek (Ed.), *Behavioral effects of energy and protein deficits* (pp. 172–184). Washington, DC: National Institute of Arthritis, Metabolism, and Digestive Diseases. U.S. Department of Health, Education, and Welfare.

Richardson, S. A., Birch, H. G., & Hertzig, M. (1973). School performance of children who were severely malnourished in infancy. *American Journal of Mental Deficiency, 77*, 623–632.

Richardson, S. A., Birch, H. G., Grabie, E., & Yoder, K. (1972). The behavior of children in school who were severely malnourished in the first two years of life. *Journal of Health and Social Behavior, 13*, 276–284.

Richardson, S. A., Birch, H., & Ragbeer, C. (1975). The behavior of children at home who were severely malnourished in the first two years of life. *Journal of Biosocial Science, 7*, 255–256.

Richter, L. M., Rose, C., & Griesel, R. D. (1997). Cognitive and behavioral effects of a school breakfast. *South African Medical Journal, 87*, 93–100.

Rodgers, B. (1978). Feeding in infancy and later ability and attainment: a longitudinal study. *Developmental Medicine and Child Neurology, 20*, 421–426.

Rogan, W. J., & Gladen, B. C. (1993). Breast-feeding and cognitive development. *Early Human Development, 31*, 181–193.

Roncagliolo, M., Garrido, M., Walter, T., Peirano, P., & Lozoff, B. (1998). Evidence of altered central nervous system development in infants with iron deficiency anemia at 6 mo: Delayed maturation of auditory brainstem responses. *American Journal of Clinical Nutrition, 68*, 683–690.

Sandstead, H. H. (1995). Is zinc deficiency a public health problem? *Nutrition, 11*, 87–92.

Scrimshaw, N. S. (1984). Functional consequences of iron deficiency in human populations. *Journal of Nutritional Science and Vitaminology, 30*, 47–63.

Seshadri, S., & Gopaldes, T. (1989). Impact of iron supplementation on cognitive functions in preschool and school-aged children: the Indian experience. *American Journal of Clinical Nutrition, 50*, 675–686.

Shrestha, R. M. (1994). *Effect of iodine and iron supplementation on physical, psychomotor and mental development in primary school children in Malawi.* Wageningen: Grafisch Service Centrum.

Sigman, M., Neumann, C., Baksh, M., Bwibo, N., & McDonald, M. A. (1989). Relationship between nutrition and development in Kenyan toddlers. *Journal of Pediatrics, 115*, 357–364.

Sigman, M., Neumann, C., Jansen, A. A., & Bwibo, N. (1989). Cognitive abilities of Kenyan children in relation to nutrition, family characteristics, and education. *Child Development, 60*, 1463–1474.

Sigman, M., McDonald, M. A., Neumann, C., & Bwibo, N. (1991). Prediction of cognitive competence in Kenyan children from toddler nutrition, family characteristics and abilities. *Journal of Child Psychology and Psychiatry, 32*, 307–320.

Simeon, D. T., & Grantham-McGregor, S. (1989). Effects of missing breakfast on the cognitive functions of school children of different nutritional status. *American Journal of Clinical Nutrition, 49*, 646–653.

Simeon, D. T., Grantham-McGregor, S. M., & Wong, M. S. (1995). *Trichuris trichiura* infection and cognition in children: results of a randomized clinical trial. *Parasitology, 110*, 457–464.

Smart, J. L. (1998). Malnutrition, Learning, and Behavior: Recent Advances in Laboratory Animal Research. In S. M. Grantham-McGregor (Ed.), *Nutrition, health, and child development. Research advances and policy recommendations* (pp. 1–13). Washington, DC: Pan American Health Organization, Tropical Metabolism Research Unit University of the West Indies, and The World Bank Scientific Publication No. 566.

Soemantri, A. G., Pollitt, E., & Kim, I. (1985). Iron deficiency anemia and educational achievement. *American Journal of Clinical Nutrition, 42*, 1221–1228.

Super, C. M. (1991). *Cognitive outcomes of early nutritional intervention in the Bogata study.* Paper presented at the meeting of the Society for Research in Child Development, Seattle.

Taylor, B., & Wadsworth, J. (1984). Breast feeding and child development at five years. *Developmental Medicine and Child Neurology, 26*, 73–80.

Thilly, C. H., Lagasse, R., Roger, P., Bourdoux, P., & Ermans, A. M. (1980). Impaired fetal and postnatal development and high perinatal death-rate in a severe iodine deficient area. In J. R. Stockigt & S. Nagataki (Eds.), *Thyroid research VIII* (pp. 20–23). Oxford: Pergamon Press.

Tiwari, B. D., Godbole, M. M., Chattopadhyay, N., Mandal, A., & Mithal, A. (1996). Learning disabilities and poor motivation to achieve due to prolonged iodine deficiency. *American Journal of Clinical Nutrition, 63*, 782–786.

Upadhyay, S. K., Agarwal, D. K., Agarwal, K. N., Srivastava, K. B., & Adhikari, G. S. (1988). Brief fasting and cognitive functions in rural school children. *Indian Paediatrics, 25*, 288–289.

Vermiglio, F., Sidoti, M., Finocchario, M. D., Battiato, S., Lo Presti, V. P., Benvenga, S., & Trimarchi, F. (1990). Defective neuromotor and cognitive ability in iodine-deficient schoolchildren of an endemic goiter region in Sicily. *Journal of Clinical Endocrinology and Metabolism, 70*(2), 379–384.

Waber, D. P., Vuori-Christiansen, L., Ortiz, N., Clement, J. R., Christiansen, N. E., Mora, J. O., Reed, R. B., & Herrera, M. G. (1981). Nutritional supplementation, maternal education, and cognitive development of infants at risk of malnutrition. *American Journal of Clinical Nutrition, 34*, 807–813.

Wachs, T. D., Sigman, M., Bishry, Z., Moussa, W., Jerome, N., Neumann, C., Bwibo, N., & McDonald, M. (1992). Caregiver child interaction patterns in two cultures in relation to nutritional intake. *International Journal of Behavioral Development, 15*, 1–18.

Walker, S. P., Grantham-McGregor, S. M., Himes, J. H., Williams, S., & Duff, E. M. (1998). School performance in adolescent Jamaican girls: Associations with health, social and behavioral characteristics, and risk factors for dropout. *Journal of Adolescence, 21*, 109–122.

Walter, T., de Andraca, I., Chadud, P., & Perales, C. G. (1989). Iron deficiency anemia: adverse effects on infant psychomotor development. *Pediatrics, 84*, 7–17.

Waterlow, J. C. (1994). Introduction. Causes and mechanisms of linear growth retardation (stunting). *European Journal of Clinical Nutrition, 48*(Suppl 1), S1–S4.

Waterlow, J. C., & Rutishauser, I. (1972). Malnutrition in man. In J. Cravioto, L. Hambraeus, & B. Vahlquist (Eds.), *Early malnutrition and mental development* (pp. 13–26). Stockholm: Almqvist and Wiksell.

Watkins, W. E., & Pollitt, E. (1998). Iron deficiency and cognition among school-age children. In S. M. Grantham-McGregor (Ed.), *Nutrition, health, and child development. Research advances and policy recommendations* (pp. 179–197). Wahington, DC: Pan American Health Organization, Tropical Metabolism Research Unit of the University of the West Indies, and The World Bank.

Webb, T. E., & Oski, F. A. (1973). Iron deficiency anemia and scholastic achievement in young adolescents. *Journal of Pediatrics, 82*, 827–830.

WHO (1997). *WHO Global Database on Child Growth and Malnutrition.* Geneva: World Health Organization—Program of Nutrition.

Williams, J., Wolff, A., Daly, A., MacDonald, A., Aukett, A., & Booth, I. W. (1999). Iron supplemented formula milk related to reduction in psychomotor decline in infants from inner city areas: Randomized study. *British Medical Journal, 318*, 693–698.

Wilson, A. (1970). Longitudinal analysis of diet, physical growth, verbal development, and school performance. In J. Balderston, A. Wilson, M. Freire, & M. Simonen (Eds.), *Malnourished children of the rural poor* (pp. 39–81). Boston, MA: Auburn House.

Winick, M., Meyer, K. K., & Harris, R. C. (1975). Malnutrition and environmental enrichment by early adoption. *Science, 190*, 1173–1175.

Wyon, D. P., Abrahamsson, L., Jartelius, M., & Fletcher, R. J. (1997). An experimental study of the effects of energy intake at breakfast on the test performance of 10-year-old children in school. *International Journal of Food Sciences and Nutrition, 48*, 5–12.

Yan-You, W., & Shu-Hua, Y. (1985). Improvement in hearing among otherwise normal schoolchildren in iodine-deficient areas of Guizhou, China, following use of iodized salt. *Lancet, 7*, 518–520.

Yatkin, V. S., & McLaren, D. S. (1970). The behavioral development of infants recovering from severe malnutrition. *Journal of Mental Deficiency Research, 14*, 25–32.

Youdim, M. B. (1990). Neuropharmacological and neurobiochemical aspects of iron deficiency. In J. Dobbing (Ed.), *Brain, behavior, and iron in the infant diet* (pp. 83–106). London: Springer-Verlag.

6

Environmental Pollutant Exposures and Children's Cognitive Abilities

David C. Bellinger
Harvard Medical School

Heather Foley Adams
Brigham Young University

Since the Industrial Revolution, our society's accelerating dependence on technology has resulted in the employment of large numbers of synthetic and natural chemicals in myriad contexts. Some of the chemicals purposely dispersed into the environment in large quantities, such as organophosphate pesticides, were specifically designed to be nervous system poisons. Unfortunately for us, to these chemicals, a human nervous system is indistinguishable from an insect nervous system. As a result of production processes, improper use (in some cases, proper use), and careless disposal, the potential for human exposures to industrial chemicals has increased dramatically in recent decades. In 1996, the U.S. Environmental Protection Agency listed approximately 15,000 uncontrolled hazardous waste sites in the United States. Approximately 11 million people, of whom nearly one third are children, live within 1 mile of one of the 1,371 sites on the National Priorities List, which consists of those sites considered to pose the greatest public health threat (ATSDR, 1997).

Only in the last three decades has the wisdom of our complacence about environmental chemicals and their potential effects on human health been seriously challenged. This effort has been slowed, however, by the dearth of empirical evidence available. Although an estimated 70,000 chemicals are presently in use (National Research Council, 1992), data on the human health effects of long-term exposure are available for a remarkably small number. The Integrated Risk Information System (IRIS) of the U.S. Environmental Protection Agency, the repository of that agency's consensus scientific opinions on pollutant health effects, contains information on a mere 500 chemicals. In view of the fact that the nervous system is one of the primary organ systems in which the toxicity of many chemicals is expressed, it is a matter of considerable societal importance to characterize the dose–response relationships for these chemicals, and in particular the threshold dose. After all, as Paracelsus observed nearly 500 years ago, even therapeutic chemicals are toxic if given in sufficient doses (Casarett & Bruce, 1980).

In this chapter, we summarize the evidence regarding the impact of selected sources of chemical intoxication on children's cognitive abilities. Table 6.1 summarizes our assessment of current knowledge, jointly classifying chemicals (or classes of chemicals) according to the amount of information available, first, on the extent to which exposures occur to the general population of children and, second, on neurodevelopmental effects. For only a single chemical, inorganic lead, are estimates available of population exposures based on a nationally representative sample of children (the National Health and Nutrition Examination Survey-III or NHANESIII; Brody et al., 1994). For all other chemicals, exposure estimates are based solely on targeted surveys, often carried out on groups considered to be at high risk. Similarly, only for inorganic lead can the database available for deriving estimates of developmental effects be characterized as "considerable" for both high dose and low dose (or "subclinical") exposures. For other major neurotoxicants, such as methyl mercury and polychlorinated biphenyls (PCB's), considerable data are available on the effects of acute high-dose poisoning, but knowledge of low-dose exposures is limited to at best a handful of epidemiological studies. For other compounds, such as pesticides, some information is available on exposures, but little on developmental effects. Finally, for other types of exposures, including some that command considerable public attention, such as municipal incinerators and hazardous waste sites, virtually no information is available either on the extent of exposure or developmental effects. In accord with the available data, this chapter focuses primarily on the impact of high-dose and, wherever information is available, on low-dose exposures to lead, methyl mercury, and PCB's.

The biological bases for concern about the impact of exposure to environmental chemicals on cognitive development are well established. This is generally attributed to the extensive central nervous system development that extends into the postnatal period, involving precisely timed sequences of cell proliferation, migration, and differentiation. Disruption of these processes or their coordination prior to completion can result in irreparable damage. Different toxicants tend to affect different aspects of these processes (although, of course, the impact of a given toxicant may differ depending on the developmental stage of the organism at the time of exposure). For example, X-irradiation impairs call proliferation, methyl mercury impairs cell migration, and chemicals such as PCB's and dioxins which suppress the

TABLE 6.1
Classification of Environmental Chemicals According to Availability of Data Regarding Childhood Exposure and Developmental Effects

Amount of Information on Childhood Exposures	Amount of Information on Developmental Effects		
	Little or None	Some	Considerable
Little or none	hazardous waste sites municipal incinerators arsenic solvents manganese		
Some	pesticides cadmium inorganic mercury fluoride	PCB's (low dose)1 methyl mercury (low dose)2	PCB's (high dose) methyl mercury (high dose)
Considerable			inorganic lead (high/low dose)3

1. *PCB's (polychlorinated biphenyls):* PCB's are a diverse class of polycyclic hydrocarbon chemicals, now banned in the United States, but once use in a wide variety of industrial processes and products, including dielectric fluids in capacitors and transformers, hydraulic fluids, plasticizers, and adhesives. Current exposures are due primarily to residual contamination of soils and water. The consumption of sport fish taken from contaminated water bodies is a major pathway of exposure.

2. *Methyl Mercury:* Mercury is a heavy metal that occurs naturally in the earth's crust and is released into the atmosphere by geologic processes such as volcanoes. The primary human activities that result in dispersal of mercury into the environment are emissions from power plants and waste incinerators, smelting processes, and industries such as paper mills and cement production. Dental amalgam, the material traditionally used to restore caries, contains 50% elemental mercury and may produce chronic low-dose exposure. Inorganic mercury can be biotransformed to the organic form, methyl mercury, by bacteria in water body sediments. Methyl mercury undergoes "biomagnification," with tissue concentrations highest among organisms near the top of the food chain. Thus, fish consumption is the primary pathway of human exposure to methyl mercury.

3. *Lead:* Lead is a heavy metal that has been mined and smelted for thousands of years. For decades, lead was added to residential paint to increase its durability and to gasoline to boost octane rating. The current primary sources and pathways include leaded paint still in place within homes, soil, and dust contamination resulting from these past uses, drinking water (primarily plumbing fixtures), industrial point sources such as smelters, and food processing procedures.

action of thyroid hormones impair cell differentiation (Rodier, 1994). Some chemicals affect synaptogenesis and thus the cytoarchitecture of the developing brain. Lead, for example, disrupts both the stimulated and unstimulated release of neurotransmitters, affecting the processes by which neuronal circuitry is established as well as the processes that regulate receptor numbers. It is also important to note, however, children may be less vulnerable than adults to some neurotoxicant exposures, as when immaturity of key metabolic pathways results in reduced absorption and thus increased excretion of a chemical.

Identifying and characterizing the effects of high-dose exposures that produce clinical signs and symptoms is usually relatively straightforward insofar as they are outside of the bounds of "normal limits" of function and tend to be clearly linked in time and space to a known exposure. Identifying and characterizing any effects of low-dose exposures to environmental chemicals poses more formidable challenges, being complicated by several factors. First, implicit in the concept of "subclinical" effects is the recognition that they will be subtle in magnitude and within the range of normal variation. Whereas single case studies of poisoned children can aid in the characterization of high-dose effects, large population studies are required to identify low-dose effects. Second, except for the rare clinical trial of a pharmacologic treatment, nearly all studies of low-dose exposures are non-experimental (observational) in design. As the chapters in this volume demonstrate, cognition is multidetermined, representing the final common pathway for the expression of many biological, psychological, and sociological influences. Exposure to a neurotoxicant may be confounded by exposure to other risk factors for poor neurodevelopmental outcome, such as poor nutrition, a less stimulating home environment, and poor schools, seriously complicating the task of drawing causal inferences about the contribution of the target exposure to poor outcome. Third, although most studies focus on a single toxicant exposure, an individual is generally exposed to complex mixtures of chemicals (Lewis, Worobey, Ramsey, & McCormack, 1992). Some chemical combinations appear to work synergistically (Cassee, Groten, von Bladeren, & Feron, 1998), such that their joint impact is more than additive. Other combinations may be antagonistic, with individuals exposed to both chemicals paradoxically appearing to suffer fewer adverse effects than those exposed only to one of the chemicals (e.g., lead and cadmium—Nation, Grover, Bratton, & Salinas, 1990; lead and cocaine—Burkey, Nation, Grover, & Bratton, 1997). In some cases, an effect may be erroneously attributed to a particular chemical when it actually reflects the influence of a correlated exposure. For example, children exposed to higher levels of pollutants such as methyl mercury and PCBs by virtue of their consumption of breast milk have, in some studies, been found to achieve developmental milestones more rapidly than children who, ingesting only cow's milk, had lower exposures to these chemicals (Grandjean, Weihe, & White, 1995). It is likely that other constituents of breast milk, possibly n-3 long-chain fatty acids or selenium, are responsible for the enhanced development of the breast-fed children. Fourth, the impact of a toxicant exposure on cognition may be indirect rather than direct. For example, exposure to the estrogenic organochlorine pesticide DDT appears to reduce the length of time that a woman is able to nurse her infant (Gladen & Rogan, 1995). Thus, slower development of the children of more highly exposed women may not reflect so much a toxic effect of this chemical on brain development as much as the fact that these infants are less able to reap the cognitive benefits of prolonged breastfeeding. Fifth, in all human studies, exposure assessments rest on a chain of toxicokinetic assumptions linking measurement of surrogate biomarkers, such as blood lead or hair methyl mercury, to estimates of toxicant concentration at the brain, the critical target organ for neurodevelopmental effects. At present, noninvasive measurement of toxicant dose in the brain is not possible, creating fertile conditions for exposure misclassification and thus imprecision in estimating dose-effect relationships and associated features such as the threshold dose at which adverse effects can be detected. The strategy for estimating internal exposure must take into account the specific biokinetic characteristics of a chemical. For chemicals such as lead that accumulate in mineralized tissues, the concentrations in bone or shed deciduous teeth are useful biomarkers of total body burden (Hu, Rabinowitz, & Smith, 1998). For lipophilic (i.e., fat-soluble) chemicals such as PCBs, the concentrations in blood serum, adipose tissue aspirates or breast milk may be useful biomarkers of exposure (Sim & McNeil, 1992). Some compounds, such as organophosphate pesticides and organic solvents, have very short biological residence times providing few options for direct assessment of body burden after exposure ends. Past exposure must, instead, be estimated by indirect measures such as duration of residence in a contaminated area, distance of residence from a point source of contamination, airborne levels of contaminants, or amount of contaminated food or water consumed.

INORGANIC LEAD

Lead is the most thoroughly studied environmental pollutant in terms of its impact on children's health in general and cognitive development in particular. It is unique among environmental pollutants in the breadth and depth of the human database available, which obviates the need to estimate the public health impact by extrapolating from studies of health effects in animal models. Moreover, whereas exposure to many toxicants is limited to specific population subgroups with relatively unusual occupations or habits, all members of the general population have been exposed to the lead due to its many applications. For more than a century, until the 1970s, lead was added to the paint used in most homes. For six decades beginning in the 1920s, grams of lead were added to each gallon of gasoline to boost octane rating, with the result that enormous quantities of this heavy metal were emitted from the tailpipes of automobiles, essentially making automobiles a ubiquitous mobile source of exposure. Lead-based paint continues to be the primary source of exposure for children who develop clinical lead poisoning (Schwartz & Levin, 1991), especially among children who practice pica, the pathological form of hand-to-mouth activity. Among children who are not clinically poisoned, however, lead-contaminated housedust is consistently demonstrated to be the strongest predictor of blood lead level (Lanphear, Burgoon, Rust, Eberly, & Galke, 1998). This is because the lead loading or concentration in a sample of housedust represents the integration of lead from several other sources or pathways, such as deteriorated paint, soil lead carried into the house, and airborne deposition of atmospheric lead. In a contaminated environment, a young child's normal exploration by means of hand-to-mouth and object mouthing can produce excess lead exposure (Lanphear & Roghmann, 1997). Among many other common sources of exposure are lead carried home on the shoes or clothing by a parent who is occupationally exposed, lead in water due to lead-soldered pipes or lead connectors, consumption of imported foods or foods prepared or served in improperly fired lead-glazed pottery, and folk medicines and practices (U.S. CDC, 1991). The disturbance of leaded surfaces in the course of home renovation and remodeling can represent a serious hazard to children, as well as other family members (U.S.CDC, 1997a). Despite the success of recent legislative measures to reduce population exposures to lead from paint, gasoline, and other sources with highly centralized distribution systems, lead continues to occupy the first rank on the priority list of 275 hazardous substances compiled annually by the Agency for Toxic Substances and Disease Registry and the Environmental Protection Agency.

The biologic plausibility of the hypothesis that lead adversely affects the central nervous system (CNS) rests on an enormous basic science literature that spans histopathologic, physiologic, cellular, subcellular, and molecular levels of analysis (Finkelstein, Markowitz & Rosen, 1998). Although no unifying theory of the mechanism(s) of lead neurotoxicity has yet been developed, this is not due to a lack of candidates. Dose-dependent effects have been identified on cell adhesion processes that regulate neuronal fiber outgrowth and synapse formation, on glial differentiation and the trophic and pathway supports provided by these cells, on mitochondrial function (specifically on oxidative metabolism) and thus on energy-dependent transport mechanisms within and between cells, and on many neurotransmitter systems and processes critical to the morphological organization of the brain. At a molecular level, these likely reflect lead's impact on gene expression, signal transduction, and the calcium messenger systems. Lead also interferes in several ways with the glutamate–dopamine mesocorticolimbic system, including the NMDA receptor complex, providing a possible mechanism for its impact on long-term potentiation and other forms of synaptic plasticity that underlie learning and memory (Cory-Slechta, 1997). This may help to account for the finding of Trope, Lopez-

Villegas, and Lenkinski (1998), using magnetic resonance spectroscopy to assess in vivo brain metabolism in a 10-year-old lead-poisoned child, that the ratios of N-acetylaspartate to creatine were reduced in both frontal gray and white matter. Two aspects of lead toxicokinetics contribute to its impact on cognitive development, namely the ease with which it crosses both the placenta and the immature blood–brain barrier. These processes thus allow exposure of the fetal central nervous system to this heavy metal during sensitive periods. The fetal brain is less able than the mature brain to form the lead-protein complexes in astrocytes that appear to sequester lead and restrict its access to mitochondria (Tiffany-Castiglioni, Sierra, Wu, & Rowles, 1989).

High Dose Exposure

Childhood lead poisoning was first described in the 1890s in Australia, although it was not until the 1920s that it received much attention in the United States. For several decades, the admission of a child presenting with signs of lead encephalopathy was a frequent occurrence in the emergency rooms of urban hospitals. These signs, which include hyperirritability, ataxia, confusion, stupor, and coma, usually become evident only when blood lead levels exceed 80 to 100 micrograms per 100 milliliters of whole blood (referred to as ug/dL), although individual variability in susceptibility is substantial. Prior to the development of chelation therapy, the use of pharmacologic agents to promote the excretion of lead from the body, approximately 65% of children presenting with a lead encephalopathy died. Neuropathological findings often included interstitial cerebral edema, hypertrophy and hyperplasia of the endothelial cells in capillaries, focal neuronal necrosis, and perivascular glial proliferation (U.S. EPA, 1986). Damage to the blood–brain barrier and increased permeability of brain capillaries are viewed as likely mechanisms of at least some of these effects (Goldstein, 1992). It is fortunate that cases of symptomatic lead poisoning are now rare, because the neurologic prognosis for survivors of lead encephalopathy is poor. In one case series, 54 of 59 children (82%) who presented with an encephalopathy had persistent sequelae, evident as long as 10 years later, including recurrent seizures, mental retardation, cerebral palsy (usually spastic hemiplegia), and optic atrophy (blindness; Perlstein & Attala, 1966). Among the children in this case series who did not present with encephalopathy, but instead with seizures (nonfebrile or febrile), ataxia, gastrointestinal complaints, or, indeed, no clinical signs, 67% were reported to have recovered "completely" from lead intoxication, although the results of formal assessments were not reported. The more acute the onset of lead poisoning and the younger the child was at the time, the greater was the mortality and the more severe the neurologic sequelae among survivors. The prognosis was especially dire for children who had survived one episode of lead poisoning only to suffer another.

Until the 1940s, clinicians generally believed that children who recovered from lead encephalopathy suffered no residual neurologic sequelae. This assumption was challenged by a landmark study of a clinical case series of 20 children, none of whom had signs and symptoms of encephalopathy upon initial presentation (Byers & Lord, 1943). Nevertheless, all but one child suffered persistent, posttreatment cognitive difficulties that seriously interfered with their success in school. Among the behavioral problems noted in these children were impulsivity, aggression, and short attention span. These findings were confirmed by numerous later studies. Mellins and Jenkins (1955) followed up 15 survivors of lead poisoning, reporting that 14 of them were "markedly retarded in some way," with linguistic abilities and fine motor coordination being the most common domains of weakness. Nearly all had behavior problems that compromised their sibling and peer relationships, and they were described as distractible and emotionally unstable. In a 50-year follow-up study, White, Diamond, Proctor, Morey, and Hu (1993) reported that individuals who were lead poisoned prior to age 4 years performed worse than controls matched on age, gender, race, and neighborhood on tests of IQ, attention, executive function, visuomotor tracking, motor speed, reasoning, and short-term memory. Their occupational achievements were also significantly more modest.

In an effort to discern whether age at lead poisoning is related to the profile of neuropsychological sequelae, Shaheen (1984) compared 18 lead poisoned children, identified at 14 to 42 months of age and tested at 4 to 6 years of age, to control children matched for sex, age, socioeconomic status, and residential community. Poisoning that occurred prior to 24 months of age was associated with primarily linguistic deficits, whereas later poisoning that occurred between 24 and 36 months of age was associated with primarily visuospatial deficits. Children who were poisoned after 36 months of age presented a mixed neuropsychological picture. In accounting for this pattern of findings, Shaheen referred to differences in the timing of myelination of the cortical areas that subserve linguistic and visual–spatial skills.

Low Dose Exposure

The report of Byers and Lord marked the beginning of a tradition of epidemiological studies seeking to determine how much lead children can tolerate before adverse central nervous system effects can be detected. In the United States, this research has helped to motivate a series of gradual but, viewed in aggregate from an historical perspective, dramatic downward revisions in the level at which intervention is recommended. Pediatric textbooks from the 1960s identified a blood lead level of 60 ug/dL as the upper limit of normal and thus, implicitly, as the threshold for neurotoxicity. In contrast, by the early 1990s a blood lead level of 10 ug/dL or higher was established as the definition of lead poisoning (U.S. CDC, 1991). What is most striking about the recent shift in perspective about low-level lead toxicity is that until quite recently most U.S. children had a blood lead level that exceeded this value. For instance, in Second National Health and Nutrition Examination Survey (NHANES II), conducted from 1976 to 1980, the median blood lead level among preschool children was 15 ug/dL, and 88% had a level greater than 10 (Mahaffey, Annest, Roberts, & Murphy, 1982). Fortunately, recent regulatory initiatives promulgated to reduce population exposures have been spectacularly successful, so that the mean blood lead level of preschool children is now 2.7 ug/dL, with only 4.4% having levels exceeding 10 ug/dL (U.S. CDC, 1997b). Although this absolute decline in prevalence is remarkable, it is also remarkable that more than 1 in 25 preschool children still meet the definition of lead poisoning. Figure 6.1 summarizes what are currently considered to be the "lowest observed effect levels" for a variety of health endpoints that are sensitive to lead.

The process by which this consensus was eventually reached was attended by considerable controversy due to the substantial economic stakes involved in regulatory control over lead sources and exposure pathways (Bellinger & Matthews, 1998). This was due in large part to the difficulties, mentioned earlier, that attend the attempt to draw inferences about causality from nonexperimental, epidemiological studies. Several recent efforts to apply meta-analytic techniques to this literature have concluded that an increase of 10 ug/dL in blood lead level is associated with a decline of 1 to 3 points in full-scale IQ (WHO, 1995). No threshold for the inverse association has been identified, which is perhaps not surprising given that even the very low body lead burdens of today are at least two orders of magnitude greater than natural or "background" body lead burdens (Owen & Flegal, 1998). Ages 1 to 3 years appear to be a period of particular vulnerability to lead exposure. Although the question of whether lead-induced cognitive changes are reversible once exposure ceases is extremely difficult to answer, in several studies modest elevations of exposure in the early postnatal period were inversely associated with IQ measured as late as 10 to 13 years of age (Bellinger, Stiles & Needleman, 1992; Tong, Baghurst, McMichael, Sawyer, & Mudge, 1996; Wasserman et al., 1997), and late neuropsychological and academic difficulties have been identified in adolescence and early adulthood (Fergusson, Horwood, & Lynskey, 1997; Needleman, Schell, Bellinger, Leviton, & Allred, 1990). Studies using experimental animal models, in which more precise control of potential confounding factors is possible, provide strongly concordant evidence for the long-term persistence and probable irreversibility of exposure effects (Rice, 1993). Although pharmacologic agents, called chelating agents, have been used for half a century to facilitate

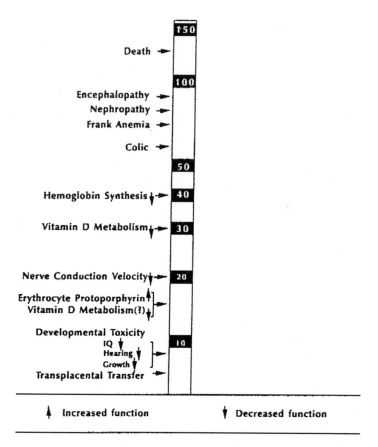

FIG. 6.1. Lowest observed effect levels of inorganic lead in children. The levels in this diagram do not necessarily indicate the lowest levels at which lead exerts an effect. These are the levels at which studies have adequately demonstrated an effect. From Agency for Toxic Substances and Disease Registry. *Case Studies in Environmental Medicine: Lead Toxicity.* Atlanta: GA: ATSDR, 1990.

the excretion of lead from a child's body (at least at blood lead levels exceeding 40 ug/dL), only nonexperimental evidence can be marshaled to support the hypothesis that such treatments either reverse lead's effects on the central nervous system or at least prevent additional damage (Ruff, Bijur, Markowitz, Ma, & Rosen, 1993). Despite impressive interstudy consistency in the magnitude of the lead-associated reduction in IQ scores, no "neuropsychological signature injury" has consistently been identified (Bellinger, 1995). As the small study conducted by Shaheen (1984) suggested, the specific sequelae of childhood lead poisoning may depend on factors such as the age at poisoning, as well as on factors such as the chronicity of exposure and the dose incurred.

METHYL MERCURY

Mercury, which occurs naturally in the earth's crust, is used in a wide variety of products, including light bulbs, batteries, thermometers, paints, and pesticides. Other so-called "anthropogenic" (man-made) sources include emissions from powerplants, waste incinerators, electrical and paper industries, and smelting operations. When mercury is released into the environment it accumulates in bodies of water where microorganisms transform it into methyl mercury (Bakir et al., 1973; Clarkson, 1997). It ascends the aquatic food chain, concentrating in predatory fish such as shark, swordfish, tuna, bass, and pike. The bioaccumulation factor may exceed 10 million (Clarkson, 1992). Fish consumption is thus the primary method of human exposure to this chemical (Wheeler, 1996). Methyl mercury and inorganic mercury are both well absorbed by the human body and cross the placental and blood–brain barriers (Cernichiari et al., 1995). Although chelating agents can be administered once exposure has occurred, as with lead, the effectiveness of these treatments in reversing central nervous system damage is likely to be modest (Bakir et al., 1973).

The precise mechanism of methyl mercury neurotoxicity is unknown and, in all likelihood, involves multiple and overlapping pathways. Many of the best candidates involve aspects of the interactions between neurons and astrocytes, a type of glial cell. Among the observed effects are inhibition of protein synthesis and mitochondrial respiration, disturbance of intracellular calcium homeostasis and neurotransmitter release and uptake, oxidative stress injury (free-radical injury and membrane lipoperoxidation), and microtubule disorganization (Verity, 1997). The impairments in neuroblast genesis, growth, differentiation, migration, and organization caused by in utero exposure to methyl mercury provide the basis for the conclusion that the developing nervous system is especially vulnerable to this toxicant. Depending on the gestational age at exposure, dose, and chronicity of exposure, the neuropathological findings in cases of in utero methyl mercury poisoning include reduction in brain weight, abnormal gyri, heterotopias and heterotaxias, hypoplasia of the corpus callosum, disorganized cortical laminae, neuronal death, glial proliferation (astrocytosis), and abnormal myelination (Choi, 1989).

High-Dose Exposure

Two relatively well-documented epidemics of high-dose methyl mercury exposure in humans have been described. The first episode occurred in Minamata, Japan in the 1950's when the inhabitants of surrounding areas ingested fish and shell fish contaminated with methyl mercury that was attributable to waste from an acetaldehyde plant in which inorganic mercury salts were used as a catalyst. The high-dose exposures were probably chronic, extending over a period of 7 or 8 years. In May 1956, Minamata Disease was recognized as a disease of adults characterized by sensory disturbances (glove and sock), ataxia, dysarthria, constricted visual fields, auditory disturbance, and tremor. More than 2,000 people were diagnosed with this disease, but the true prevalence was probably at least six times higher. A striking increase in reproductive morbidity was also noted. In 1963, 42.9% of pregnancies resulted in miscarriages or stillbirths (Fujino et al., 1985, cited in Harada, 1995). Among live borns, the incidence rates of several adverse outcomes were reported to be elevated, including cerebral palsy, mental retardation, cerebellar ataxia, pyramidal dysfunctions, seizures, dysarthria, sensory disturbances (especially vision), primitive reflexes, limb deformity, and other disturbances of physical development (Watanabe & Satoh, 1996). By 1974, 40 cases of Fetal Minamata Disease had been identified. The risk appeared to be related to the concentration of mercury in umbilical cord blood (Harada, 1995). One survey reported that 29% of children born between 1955 and 1958 in heavily contaminated areas were mentally retarded and 7% had signs consistent with cerebral palsy (Harada, 1995; Watanabe & Satoh, 1996). For many children manifesting clinical impairments, only transient paresthesias were observed in their mothers, demonstrating the heightened sensitivity of the fetus to methyl mercury. Many developmental milestones were late in exposed children including head control, rolling over, crawling, sitting, standing, walking, speaking, and other adaptive and social movements. By the age of 3, none could understand a word and many could not yet recognize their mothers. When followed up as adolescents, half were considered to be incapable of learning. Only among children who were more mildly affected did cognitive ability seem to improve with time (Tsubaki & Irukayama, 1977).

The second well-documented mass exposure to methyl mercury occurred in Iraq in the winter of 1971–1972. In this episode, exposure resulted from the ingestion of seed grain that had been treated with a fungicide that contained methyl mercury and a small amount of inorganic mercury (Bakir et al., 1973). Within 4 months, 6530 cases of mercury poisoning were reported, including males and females of all ages. Although 459 mercury-related deaths were reported to health authorities, it is almost certainly the case that many more went unreported. Among adults, symptoms commonly included loss of sensation in extremities and mouth, loss in coordination, slurred speech, and loss of hearing and vision (Bakir et al., 1973).

Amin-Zaki et al. (1974) investigated the effects of prenatal exposure by examining 15 infants who had been exposed to mercury as fetuses. Five of the fifteen had severe clinical symptoms, including blindness, hearing impairment, increased or decreased muscle tone, general paralysis, hyperactive reflexes, and/or evidence of impaired mental development. Cerebral palsy in infancy was reported to be associated with third trimester exposure and related to higher maternal hair concentration of mercury during pregnancy (Amin-Zaki et al., 1979).

Several follow-up studies of children exposed *in utero* have been reported (Amin-Zaki et al., 1979; Marsh et al., 1980; Marsh et al., 1987). In both studies, the level of prenatal exposure was estimated from maternal hair using x-ray fluorescence spectrometry. This is a good exposure biomarker for methyl mercury because the concentration in hair is highly correlated with the concentration in blood at the time of hair formation. In addition, using autopsy material, Cernichiari et al. (1995) found a high correlation between maternal hair mercury level and infant brain mercury level. In the cohort studied by Marsh et al., higher maternal hair mercury levels were associated with increased rates of delayed achievement of developmental milestones, psychomotor delay, mental retardation, and seizures. Delays in motor and speech development were defined as a child being unable to walk or talk by 18 and 24 months, respectively. These effects appeared to be dose-related and more prominent in boys than in girls. Amin-Zaki and colleagues followed 32 children from infancy to age 5. The children were divided into two groups based on the presence or absence of signs and symptoms in infancy. Because an IQ test standardized for use with nomadic Iraqi children was not available, estimates of the children's mental abilities were based on maternal and physician reports. All of the children who were symptomatic in infancy subsequently exhibited neurological signs and substantial delays in speech, cognitive, and motor skills. Among the children who did not have symptoms as infants, more than half were judged to be developmentally delayed at age 5, a rate that was significantly higher than what would be expected among nonexposed children in the general Iraqi population.

The nervous system impact of early postnatal exposure to methyl mercury is probably less severe than the impact of prenatal exposure. Iraqi infants who were exposed to methyl mercury only via the consumption of contaminated breast milk appeared to be unaffected (Bakir et al., 1973). Some children who had eaten contaminated bread developed symptoms such as ataxia, weakness, and visual and sensory changes (Amin-Zaki, Majeed, Clarkson, & Greenwood, 1978). After 2 years, all the children with mild to moderate poisoning had improved, with most considered to be "normal." However, 7 of the 18 children with severe poisoning remained mentally and physically handicapped at the time of the 2-year follow-up evaluation.

Because of the significant economic and social consequences of methyl mercury toxicity associated with the consumption of contaminated seafood, efforts have been made to establish specific dose-response curves for the adverse effects of prenatal exposure to methyl mercury so that permissible daily intakes can be estimated. Based on the mercury concentrations in archived umbilical cord tissue samples for patients diagnosed with Minamata Disease, Akagi, Grandjean, Takizawa, and Weihe (1998) estimated that the hair concentrations of the mothers of these children during pregnancy was approximately 41 parts per million (ppm) (25th–75th percentile: 20–59). (Analyses of neonatal autopsy material suggest that maternal hair mercury concentration is a reasonably good surrogate index of the exposure of the fetal brain to methyl mercury; Cernichiari et al., 1995.) Using data from several different study cohorts, the minimum methyl mercury levels in maternal hair at which adverse effects are seen in offspring appear to lie in the range of 10 to 20 ppm (Harada, 1997). For a variety of reasons, this figure must be viewed as tentative, however. Recent re-analyses of the Iraqi data, for instance, have revealed the presence of a small number of influential data points with disproportionate influence on the estimate of population threshold (Cox, Marsh, Myers, & Clarkson, 1995; Crump et al., 1995). The current World Health Organization guideline identifies 5 ppm as the upper tolerable level of mercury in hair. This was derived by applying a safety factor of 10 to the hair level considered to be the lowest level at which fetal toxicity is observed (50 ppm) (WHO, 1990).

Low-Dose Exposure

Several studies on low dose mercury exposure have been conducted in an effort to determine a threshold or "safe" level of methyl mercury exposure. For instance, although assessments of the Iraqi exposure suggested the threshold may be around 10 ppm, the estimates of exposure timing, intensity, and duration were subject to large error. Furthermore, it is likely that the acute, high-dose exposures experienced by the Iraqi population are not representative of the chronic, low-level methyl mercury exposures that are more typical of the general fish-eating population (Egeland & Middaugh, 1997; Myers et al., 1997).

In order to investigate whether lower level but chronic exposures are associated with adverse outcomes in children, several cohorts of children have been assembled in which fish consumption, the major source of methyl mercury exposure in humans, is relatively high (Clarkson, 1997). A study conducted in Peru (Marsh, Turner, Smith, Allen, & Richdale, 1995) included 131 mother–infant pairs in whom the peak maternal hair level during pregnancy was between 1 and 30 ppm, with an average of about 8 ppm. Higher maternal hair levels were not associated with an increased prevalence of abnormalities in the children on neurological examination in the children or with delays in sitting, standing, walking, or talking. A study of 234 12- to 30-month-old Cree Indian children in Quebec, in whom the mean maternal methyl mercury concentration in hair was 6 ppm, found an association between methyl mercury exposure and tendon reflex abnormalities in boys but not in girls (McKeown-Eyssen, Ruedy, & Neims, 1983). The risk was not dose-related, however. No associations were found between prenatal methyl mercury and other parts of the neurologic examination or the Denver Developmental Screening Test (which included assessments of motor, language, and personal/social skills development). In a fish-eating population in New Zealand, children whose maternal methyl mercury hair levels were above 10 ppm achieved lower scores than children with lower exposures on a variety of tests at age 6, including the WISC–R, the McCarthy Scales of Children's Abilities, and the Test of Language development (Kjellstrom, 1989). It appeared that even the performance of children whose maternal hair levels were as low as 6 to 10 ppm during pregnancy may have been reduced relative to the controls.

Two large studies of fetal methyl mercury exposure attributable to maternal consumption of seafood are currently being conducted in the Faroe Islands (North Atlantic) and the Seychelles Islands (Indian Ocean) (Grandjean et al., 1997; Myers et al., 1995). Both studies have many methodological advantages over previous research, including a longitudinal design, large sample sizes, rigorous and comprehensive exposure estimates, and comprehensive batteries for assessing neurological and neuropsychological functioning.

In a pilot study of more than 789 1 to 25 month old Seychellois children in whom the median maternal hair methyl mercury level was 6.6 ppm (0.6 to 36), an inverse association was found between children's scores on the Denver Developmental Screening Test–Revised, but only if a nonstandard method of scoring this test was employed (combining children who failed the test with children whose performance was considered "questionable") (Myers et al., 1995). The main Seychelles study cohort consists of 779 women in whom the median methyl mercury hair level during pregnancy was 5.9 ppm (range 0.5 to 26.7) (Myers et al., 1995). A thorough general medical exam and neurological examination as well as the Fagan Test of Infant Intelligence and the Revised Denver Developmental Screening Test (DDST–R) were administered when the infants were 6.5 months old. Level of prenatal methyl mercury exposure was not significantly associated with any of the outcome measures. The findings of the Iraqi studies, linking level of prenatal methyl mercury exposure and the ages at which children achieved important developmental milestones, were not replicated in the Seychelles cohort (Myers et al., 1997).

More than 700 infants from the same group were followed up at 19 and 29 months of age (Davidson et al., 1995) using the Bayley Scales of Infant Development, including the Bayley Infant Behavior Record. At neither age were children's Bayley Scales scores associated with their levels of prenatal methyl mercury exposure. At 29 months of age, more highly exposed boys, but not girls, were rated as being less active by the Bayley Scales examiners. Most recently, similar results have been reported for assessments conducted at 66 months (Davidson et al., 1998). No significant associations with methyl mercury were found for outcomes that included the McCarthy Scales of Children's Abilities, the Preschool Language Scale, the Bender–Gestalt Test, and selected subtests of the Woodcock–Johnson Psycho-Educational Battery.

In the Faroe Islands, a cohort of more than 1,000 mother–infant pairs were sampled from a population exposed to methyl mercury primarily from the consumption of pilot whale meat (Grandjean et al., 1997). Methyl mercury levels were measured in the cord blood (geometric mean 23 ug/L, interquartile range 13 to 41), maternal hair at delivery (geometric mean 4 ppm, interquartile range 3 to 8), and child hair at 12 months (geometric mean 1, interquartile range 1 to 2) and 7 years (geometric mean 3, interquartile range 2 to 6). In a cohort of 583 infants, those with high concentrations of methyl mercury in their hair at 12 months of age were not slower to attain developmental milestones such as sitting, creeping, and standing (Grandjean, Weihe, & White, 1995). In fact, higher levels were associated with earlier milestone development. Because both factors were associated with duration of breastfeeding, the investigators concluded that any negative effects of mercury exposure that occur as a result of breastfeeding are outweighed by the benefits of breastfeeding on infant development.

At age 7, 917 children from the original cohort were assessed by means of a functional neurological exam, neurophysiological tests, and neuropsychological tests (Grandjean et al., 1997). The neuropsychological battery included: finger tapping, hand–eye coordination, reaction time on a continuous performance test, Tactual Performance Test, WISC–R subtests (digit span, similarities, block design), Bender Gestalt Test, Boston Naming Test, and the California Verbal Learning Test (Children). No neurological or neurophysiological abnormalities were found. Higher cord methyl mercury levels were associated with subtle deficits in language, attention, and memory and to a lesser extent in visuospatial and motor abilities. The inverse associations were apparent even when children whose mothers had hair methyl mercury concentrations greater than 10 ppm were excluded. Children's hair methyl mercury concentrations at 12 months and 7 years of age were generally not associated with their scores on the cognitive tests, supporting the hypothesis that central nervous system vulnerability to this metal is greater in the prenatal than the postnatal period.

Important differences between the Faroes Islands and Seychelles Islands cohorts may be responsible for the apparent lack of concordance in the findings of the two studies. First, methyl mercury exposure in the Seychelles tends to result from consumption of ocean fish in which the methyl mercury levels is one tenth the levels in the pilot whale meat consumed by the population of the Faroes. In addition, whereas exposure in the Seychelles appears to be relatively constant over time, exposure in the Faroes may be more episodic, coinciding with the periodic harvesting and consuming of pilot whales. Second, the two study populations differ in many respects, including cultural and genetic characteristics that may be relevant to methyl mercury metabolism. For instance, dietary differences, such as selenium intake, or certain genetic polymorphisms relevant to methyl mercury pharmacokinetics (perhaps involving glutathione) may affect the neurotoxicity of methyl mercury at low dose. Third, pilot whale meat, especially blubber, tends to harbor higher concentrations of other contaminants, especially organochlorine compounds such as PCB's, dibenzofurans, dioxins, and pesticides. It may be exposure to these chemicals and not methyl mercury that is responsible for the associations reported by Grandjean et al. (1997). Fourth, the Seychelles study used only maternal hair to measure exposure while the Faroe Islands study found stronger associations with cord blood than maternal hair levels (Davidson et al., 1998; Grandjean & Weihe, 1993). Cord blood concentration may be a better measure of the methyl mercury that crosses the placenta and reaches the fetal brain.

POLYCHLORINATED BIPHENYLS

Polychlorinated biphenyls (PCBs) are a group of polycyclic synthetic hydrocarbons that were used for decades in many industrial processes, and products, including hydralic fluids, plasticizers, adhesives, and perhaps most importantly, dielectric fluids in capacitors and transformers. PCBs degrade extremely slowly. Being lipophilic (fat soluble) and hydrophobic, they tend to bioconcentrate, with body burdens tending to increase as one ascends the food chain. No treatment is available for PCB poisoning. Recognition of PCB toxicities led to restrictions on their use in the United States during the 1970s, but this merely reduced new inputs of PCBs into the environment. Residual contamination dating from past uses remains largely unaddressed.

PCBs are actually a class of chemicals, which consists of 209 different congeners differing in degree of chlorination. This results in differences in the rate at which they are degraded in the environment and metabolized in the body. They are readily transferred to the fetus via the placenta, although because of the high rate of lipid mobilization during lactation, most of the PCBs transferred from a woman to her offspring occurs postnatally during breastfeeding. The mechanism of PCB neurotoxicity is not well understood. It is hypothesized that disruption of endocrine functions may be involved, as the class of dioxin-like (co-planar) congeners appear to have antiestrogenic properties. Another possibility is disruption of binding sites associated with tyrosine hydroxylase activity and, hence, dopamine synthesis (McKinney, 1993).

High-Dose Exposure

Data on high-dose PCB exposure derive largely from studies of two populations that experienced mass poisonings as a result of exposure to rice oil contaminated with PCBs used as heat exchangers during production. In 1968, 1,788 people living in Western Japan and, in 1979, 2,060 people in Taiwan were exposed in this manner. In both incidents, other heat-degraded by-products also contaminated the rice oil, specifically polychlorinated dibenzofurans (PCDFs) and polychlorinated quarterphenyls (PCQs) (Masuda, 1985).

Studies of the health effects in adults from the two sites yielded similar findings. The initial effects consisted mostly of dermal and mucosal signs, such as skin pigmentation changes, eye discharge, and severe acne. Longer lasting effects included cough, fatigue, and neurological symptoms such as limb numbness and headache (Masuda, 1985). The severity of physical symptoms appeared to be dose-related. The clinical disease came to be known by the words for cooking oil in each language (Yusho in Japanese, Yucheng in Taiwanese). The concentrations of PCBs in the oils differed at the two sites but total PCB intakes were thought to be comparable (Masuda, 1985).

In Taiwan, rates of miscarriage, stillbirth, and infant mortality were significantly higher among women exposed to PCBs than in the general population (Yen, Lan, Ko, & Chen, 1989). In addition, birth weight was significantly lower in the exposed group, although the children's somatic growth appeared to catch up in early childhood (Yen et al., 1989). In both countries, a distinctive set of physical findings characterized infants with in utero PCB exposure: dark brown pigmentation of skin and nails (leading them to be called "cola babies"), early eruption of teeth, gingival hyperplasia, abnormal calcification of the skull, increased rate of bronchitis, and swollen eyelids (Rogan et al., 1988; Yamashita & Hayashi, 1985).

Follow-up evaluations of the children exposed *in utero* revealed high rates of cognitive morbidities. In Japan, they were described as dull and apathetic, with IQ's in the 70's. The study on which this conclusion was based had several weaknesses, however, including the absence of controls and the possibility that the exposed children who were followed up were not representative of the entire group of exposed children, resulting in overrepresentation of children with the most severe handicaps (Harada, 1976). In addition, the absence of solid measurements of dose for children in the Japanese cohort precluded the determination of the dose–response relationships for different health endpoints.

The follow-up studies of the Taiwanese children exposed *in utero* are much stronger methodologically than the studies of the Japanese children. A cohort of 118 children were followed for 6 years (Chen, Guo, Hsu, & Rogan, 1992; Chen, Yu, Rogan, Gladen, & Hsu, 1994; Guo, Lai, Chen, & Hsu, 1995; Yu, Hsu, Gladen, & Rogan, 1991). All children were born after their mothers' ingestion of PCB-contaminated oil and between the years of 1978 and 1985. Serum PCB levels of exposed women ranged from 2 to 456 ppm (median of 26 ppm). Each exposed child was matched to a control child in terms of age, sex, neighborhood, maternal age, parental education, and occupational class. Exposed children lagged behind their controls on 32 of 33 developmental milestones, as assessed by parental reports and neurologic examination (Rogan et al., 1988; Yu et al., 1991). Severity of delay did not appear to be related to level of maternal exposure, although the estimates of dose were not considered to be highly reliable. Not all children had detectable levels of PCBs in their blood, although those who did tended to have lower developmental scores. It appeared that prenatal exposure had the greatest impact on development insofar as the developmental scores of children exposed to PCBs via breast milk did not differ from the scores of children who were bottle fed (Rogan et al., 1988; Yu et al., 1991).

Developmental delays were still apparent in children born 7 to 12 years after maternal PCB exposure, presumably because of the long half-life of PCBs in their mothers' bodies (Guo, Chen, Yu, & Hsu, 1994). Exposed children scored on average 5 points lower than controls on the Stanford–Binet at ages 4 and 5 and 5 points lower on the Wechsler Intelligence Scale for Children at ages 6 and 7 (Chen et al., 1992). This deficit was still apparent when the children were 11 years old (Lai, Guo, Yu, Ko, Hsu, 1994). A mother's PCB level was not related to her child's cognitive outcome. The performance of the older siblings of the children exposed *in utero*, who themselves were exposed to PCBs only postnatally, was similar to the performance of the control group, again suggesting that the cognitive effects of prenatal exposure to PCBs are greater than the effects of postnatal exposure to PCBs (Chen et al., 1992).

Raven's Colored Progressive Matrices (CPM) were given to 118 of the children in this cohort at ages 6, 7, and 8, and Raven's Standardized Progressive Matrices (SPM) at 9 years (Guo et al., 1995). Exposed children scored lower than matched controls at all ages, although the group difference on the SPM was not significant. In addition, scores were not correlated to serum PCB levels, although these levels were not available for all children. The difference between the scores of the exposed and unexposed children was attributable largely to exposure-related differences in the scores of boys. As was the case with other endpoints, the magnitude of the deficit did not decrease with age, nor was it related to the interval between a woman's exposure and her child's birth. The investigators speculated that gender differences in effect may be the result of a PCB-related antiandrogenic effect involving perturbation of the levels of sex hormones during prenatal development.

Two parent-completed questionnaires, the Rutter's Child Behavior Scale A and a modified Werry–Weiss–Peters Activity Scale, were used to collect information about the behavior of exposed children and their controls between the ages of 3 and 12. Yucheng children born up to 6 years after maternal intoxication had significantly higher activity levels and "mildly disordered behavior" (Chen et al., 1994). However, children born 7 to 12 years after maternal exposure did not have more behavior problems than unexposed controls (Guo et al., 1994).

It is not clear whether the behavioral and cognitive deficits among the exposed children were attributable to permanent changes induced in the central nervous system during fetal development or to continued internal exposure to PCB mobilized from long-term fat stores (Chen et al., 1994). Neither is it clear whether the toxicities expressed were attributable to specific PCB congeners or, indeed, whether they were due to PCBs at all or to other contaminants in the oils, including PCQs and PCDFs. PCDFs are thought to be much more toxic than PCBs, and thus may have been responsible for the adverse outcomes of the children (Yu et al., 1991; Guo, Yu, & Ryan, 1996).

Low-Dose Exposure

Knowledge of the neurobehavioral effects of low-dose prenatal exposure to PCBs comes largely from two large population-based longitudinal studies conducted in Michigan and North Carolina. In both cohorts, exposures were near background levels for the U.S. population, so the results may be broadly generalizable. In addition, measurements of PCB dose are more accurate and comprehensive in these studies than in the studies of the Yusho and Yucheng cohorts.

The Michigan study recruited 242 infants at birth whose mothers had been exposed to PCB-contaminated lake fish and 71 control subjects whose mothers had not been exposed. A woman's PCB exposure was estimated from her reported fish consumption before and during pregnancy. PCB concentration in cord serum provided another index of fetal exposure. Using fish consumption and cord serum level as indices of exposure, higher PCB levels were associated with lower birth weight, smaller head size, and shorter gestational period (Fein, Jacobson, Jacobson, Schwartz, & Dowler, 1984). Subtle neonatal behavioral deficits, assessed using Brazelton's Neonatal Behavior Assessment Scale (NBAS), were related to the consumption of contaminated fish including increased startle, depressed responsiveness, and poor motor, reflex, and neuromuscular function (Jacobson, Jacobson, Fein, Schwartz, & Dowler, 1984).

At the age of 7 months, the Fagan Test of Infant Intelligence, which employs a visual recognition memory paradigm, was administered to 123 children from the original cohort. Increased cord serum PCB levels (highest quartile: 3.6 to 7.9 ng/mL) and consumption of contaminated fish were associated with poorer visual recognition memory (Jacobson, Fein, Jacobson, Schwartz, & Dowler, 1985).

At 4 years of age, children in the cohort were administered a battery of tests that included the McCarthy Scales of Children's Abilities, the Beery

Test of Visual-Motor Integration, PPVT–R (Jacobson, Jacobson, & Humphrey, 1990). Modest dose-dependent deficits on the McCarthy Verbal and Memory scales, specifically the short-term verbal and numerical memory, were seen over the range of 0 to 12.3 ng/mL of PCBs in cord serum. No exposure-related effects were seen on the other McCarthy scales, the VMI, or the PPVT–R. Tests of cognitive processing efficiency and sustained attention were also administered. Higher levels of umbilical cord PCB were related to an increase in short-term memory errors and less efficient visual discrimination processing. Sustained attention was not associated with prenatal PCB exposure (Jacobson, Jacobson, Padgett, Brumitt, & Billings, 1992).

At age 11, children were administered the WISC–R and achievement tests (WRAT–R and subtests of the Woodcock Reading Mastery test). Children with the highest prenatal exposures (i.e., > 4.7 ng/mL in cord serum, > 9.7 ng/mL in maternal serum, > 1.25 ug/g of breast milk fat) had slightly lower Full Scale and Verbal IQ scores, with lower performance on the subtests that measure memory and attention contributing most to these overall differences (Jacobson, & Jacobson, 1996). The more highly exposed children also had somewhat decreased word and reading comprehension. It is noteworthy that in none of these studies were cognitive or behavioral outcomes found to be associated with exposure to PCBs after birth through breast milk, even the amount of PCB's transferred to a child via lactation is most likely substantially greater than the amount transferred to the fetus via the placenta. This strongly suggests that the sensitivity of the nervous system to PCB toxicity is greater prenatally than postnatally.

The second study designed to study low-dose PCB effects recruited 912 infants from the general population in North Carolina. PCB concentrations were determined in maternal serum, cord blood, placenta, and breast milk. No relationships were found between PCB concentrations and either birth weight or head circumference (Rogan et al., 1986). More highly exposed infants were, however, found to display hypotonicity and hyporeflexia on the Brazelton NBAS. More than 800 of the children were administered the Bayley Scales of Infant Development at 6, 12, 18, and 24 months of age (Gladen et al., 1988; Rogan & Gladen, 1991). Psychomotor Development Index (PDI) scores at 6, 12, and 24 months were inversely related to prenatal PCB exposure, although Mental development Index (MDI) scores were not. For most endpoints, the effect sizes were modest, corresponding to approximately half of a standard deviation, and the association was largely limited to children with transplacental PCB exposures greater than the 95th percentile in this population (> 3.5 ug/g in breast milk fat). The McCarthy Scales of Children's Abilities were administered to 712 children in this cohort at 3, 4, and 5 years of age (Gladen & Rogan, 1991). Neither prenatal PCB exposure nor breast milk exposure was significantly associated with scores on the McCarthy Scales or with school grades.

An additional study of low-dose prenatal PCB exposure was conducted in the Netherlands (Koopman-Esseboom et al., 1996). Neonatal neurological optimality scores were inversely related to levels of PCBs in breast milk, but not to levels in maternal or cord blood. The Bayley Scales were administered to the children at 3, 7, and 18 months of age. As in the North Carolina cohort, higher PCB levels in maternal serum were associated with lower PDI (but not MDI) scores at 3 months of age, although by 18 months of age, neither MDI nor PDI scores were associated with level of PCB exposure.

In summary, the effect size relating low-level PCB exposures to children's cognitive functioning ranges from *none* to *moderate*, depending on the study. Difficulties in estimating exposure as well as the use of different analytical methods for measuring PCB levels may contribute to the inconsistency of the results. Other potential reasons for discrepant results across studies include differences in exposure profiles (e.g., rate, timing, chronicity) and in the specific mix of PCB congeners to which cohorts were exposed (Jacobson, & Jacobson, 1997; Rogan et al., 1986).

PESTICIDES

A substantial literature documents the adverse effects of high-dose pesticide exposures on the neurobehavioral function of adults (e.g., Stephens, Spurgeon, & Berry, 1996). Given the mechanism of actions of most pesticides, the number and volume of pesticides used worldwide, and the chronic exposures incurred by the general population as a result of normal patterns of consumption, it is surprising that very few data are available on the long-term health impacts of pesticides on children (NRC, 1993). Children are considered to be a subgroup at high risk because the greater representation of fruit and vegetable products in their diets compared to adults results in greater relative exposures to pesticide residues (Bellinger, 1998). Although long-term prospective studies of children's pesticide exposures are being planned as part of the Border XXI Program, a United States–Mexico project focusing on environmental quality issues, the literature is presently limited largely to case reports characterized by small sample sizes and potential bias in patient ascertainment (Weiss, 1997). Undue exposure to pesticides is not uncommon, however. In 1995, more than 77,000 cases of pesticide exposure among children less than 19 years of age were reported to U.S Poison Control Centers, with 85% of cases occurring in children less than 6 years of age (Blondell, 1997). Exposure to the two major cholinesterase-inhibiting classes of insecticides, organophosphates and carbamates, were the most frequent, followed by exposure to rodenticides and disinfectants. Because of the nonspecificity of the presenting signs and symptoms, it is likely that pesticide poisoning is underdiagnosed (Weiss, 1997). Although children of agricultural workers involved in pesticide application are at greatest risk of exposure to these chemicals, either directly or as the result of "take home" exposures, most cases of childhood poisoning are the result of exposure to pesticides used in the home (Blondell, 1997).

Case reports provide compelling evidence that pesticide exposures that are sufficient to induce clinical signs of central nervous system toxicity are associated with serious neurologic sequelae, especially when exposure occurs during the prenatal period. A fetus exposed to the organophosphate oxydemeton-methyl in the fifth week of gestation was born with cerebral and cerebellar atrophy, in addition to a variety of major cardiac and ocular malformations and several minor anomalies (Romero, Barnett, & Midtling, 1989). Four fetuses exposed to chlorpyrifos (an organophosphate) presented with CNS malformations that included corpus callosum defects, enlarged choroid plexus, and absence of the septum pellucidum (Sherman, 1996). All four were growth retarded, while three were microcephalic and mentally retarded. Angle, McIntire, and Meile (1968) conducted follow-up evaluations of children reported to the Nebraska Master Poison Control Center as having been exposed to chlorinated hydrocarbon or organophosphate insecticides. The subgroup that presented with an acute intoxication characterized by seizures and signs such as ataxia, incoherence, loss of consciousness, lethargy, pupillary changes, and abnormal reflexes had significantly lower IQ scores and greater deficits in visual–motor integration than a control group of children who presented without CNS signs.

In one small ecologic study that did not include measurement of any exposure biomarkers, children living in a rural area in which a variety of pesticides are routinely applied were similar to children from a control area in terms of physical growth but scored significantly worse on tests of balance, eye-hand coordination, short-term memory, and draw-a-person (Guillette, Meza, Aquilar, Soto, & Garcia, 1998).

OTHER ENVIRONMENTAL EXPOSURES

Plausible arguments can be marshaled in support of the hypothesis that population exposures to heavy metals other than lead and mercury also adversely affect children's cognition and behavior. Comprehensive and rigorous evaluations of these possibilities have not, in most instances, been conducted, however.

Although the primary targets of cadmium are thought to be the renal and hepatic systems, inverse associations have been reported between hair cadmium levels and aspects of children's cognitive function (Bonithon-Kopp, Huel, Moreau, & Wendling, 1986; Thatcher, Lester, McAlaster, & Horst, 1982). In addition, in case-control studies, higher hair cadmium levels have been associated with the occurrence of mentally retardation (Jiang, Han, & He, 1990; Marlowe, Errera & Jacobs, 1983) and learning disabilities (Capel, Pinnock, Dorrell, Williams, & Grant, 1981; Pihl & Parkes, 1977).

Manganese neurotoxicity is well-recognized based on studies of adult occupational exposure, producing a Parkinson's-like syndrome of abnormalities in the motor system as well as various cognitive and behavioral dysfunctions (Mergler & Baldwin, 1997). After the practice of adding tetraethyl lead to boost gasoline octane was phased out in the United States in the 1980s, the Ethyl Corporation began to use methylcyclopentadienyl manganese tricarbonyl in its place. It would be a public health tragedy, indeed, and one that is entirely foreseeable, if widespread contamination of the environment by manganese were permitted, a perverse repetition of the ecological disaster created by a similar use of lead earlier in the last century. Serious manganese neurotoxicity has been reported in children whose exposure occurs as the result of undergoing parenteral nutrition (Fell et al., 1996), and two studies conducted in China suggest that elevated levels of manganese in drinking water are associated with poorer school function (He et al., cited by Mergler & Baldwin, 1997; Zhang, Liu, & He, 1995).

Elemental mercury is another heavy metal known to be neurotoxic at high doses. Yeates and Mortensen (1994) described two acutely poisoned adolescent siblings who manifested long-term deficits in visuoperceptual and constructional skills, nonverbal memory, and conceptual abstraction. Similarly, Diamond, White, Gerr, and Feldman (1995) reported the case of a 19 year old, chronically exposed to elevated mercury between the ages of 4 and 9 years, who still experienced difficulties in the domains of executive function, visuospatial orientation, fine motor control, verbal fluency, and word retrieval. In the general population, the major source of exposure to elemental mercury is silver amalgam, the standard-of-care material for restoring dental caries, which contains 50% mercury (Lorschedier, Vimy, & Summers, 1995). This concern issues from the fact that small amounts of mercury vapor are released by the mechanical stresses placed on restorations by everyday activities such as chewing and brushing. Behavioral studies of dentists and dental hygienists chronically exposed through work activities to low doses of silver amalgam provide some justification for concern over the use of this material. Subtle signs of CNS toxicity have been observed at urinary mercury levels of 4 ug/L and below, levels that are not uncommon among the general population (Echeverria et al., 1998). The National Institute of Dental Research is currently funding two large randomized clinical trials to evaluate whether the use of mercury-containing amalgam causes neurobehavioral dysfunctions in children.

Recent animal studies suggest that a fluoride body burden that does not greatly exceed that accumulated by means of normal dietary and hygiene practices may be neurotoxic (Mullenix, Denbesten, Schunior, & Kernan, 1995). Although rigorous studies have not been conducted in human populations to test this hypothesis, studies of populations in China exposed to high levels of fluoride in drinking water suggest that children's IQ scores may be adversely affected (Li, Zhi, & Gao, 1995).

Because endogenous hormones play many critical roles during development, including brain differentiation and ultimately the expression of sexually dimorphic behaviors and characteristics (Whitten & Naftolin, 1994), it has been hypothesized that exogenous chemicals that mimic or block hormones, especially estrogen but thyroid hormone, androgens, and glucocorticoids as well, can have long-lasting effects on reproduction, growth, behavior, and immunologic function (Kavlock et al., 1996). The class of potential "endocrine disrupters" is large, with chlorinated hydrocarbon compounds (e.g., PCB, DDT, DDE) being the most important. The hypothesis that, at environmental levels of exposure, endocrine disrupting chemicals affect children's cognition, although plausible, is largely speculative at this point.

CONCLUSION

Many human organ systems have a tremendous capacity to repair or compensate for damage, or at least have sufficient reserve capacities to tolerate a partial loss of function. Elaborate hepatic detoxification systems have evolved to protect other organ systems from exogenous biological and chemical insults. CNS plasticity, especially in the developing organism, also provides some measure of protection from the effects of such insults. Nevertheless, these systems have limits. An important aspect of our current exposures to environmental neurotoxicants is that many of the chemicals are synthetic, manufactured only in the past few decades to meet specific technological needs. Thus, we are expecting biological defense and repair mechanisms that evolved in response to certain types of threats to protect us, as well, from entirely new classes of threats that they had never "seen" until very recently and were not designed to address. It may be wishful thinking to assume that these mechanisms will be equally effective in meeting these novel challenges.

Historically the endpoints used to identify chemical toxicities have been rather crude, including the LD50 (the dose required to kill 50% of experimental animals), recognizable birth defects, and tumors. The CNS is increasingly recognized as one of the organs most sensitive to environmental chemicals (Kilburn, 1989). It was not until 1995, however, that the U.S. Environmental Protection Agency developed Proposed Guidelines for Neurotoxicity Risk Assessment (U.S. EPA, 1995). These establish common procedures for deciding, for regulatory purposes, whether or not a chemical should be considered neurotoxic. At present the infrastructure for monitoring for environmentally induced disease in the United States is inadequate. One of the objectives of the

Healthy People 2000 initiative of the U.S. Public Health Service is to monitor several nonoccupational "sentinel" environmental diseases, including asthma, heatstroke, hypothermia, heavy metal poisoning, pesticide poisoning, acute chemical poisoning, and methemoglobinemia. According to a recent survey of the 52 state or district epidemiologists by the U.S. Centers for Disease Control (U.S. CDC, 1998), only 174 environmental public health surveillance systems are currently in place. The number of systems monitoring each of the chemical diseases is as follows: Childhood lead poisoning–51; pesticide poisoning–20; mercury poisoning–15; arsenic poisoning–11; cadmium poisoning–11, acute chemical poisoning–8. Only about two thirds of the systems include case investigation, with the others limited only to data collection and review.

Work clearly needs to be done to insure the protection of citizens, particularly children, from chemical exposures that are sufficient in magnitude to adversely affect CNS development and function. High-dose exposures warrant the greatest concern but recent studies of low-dose exposures indicate that it would be prudent for us to be concerned, as well, about potential adverse effects of low-dose chronic exposures to environmental chemicals. The lead story is particularly instructive in this regard. In the late 1970s, when 88% of U.S. preschoolers had blood lead levels greater than 10 ug/dL, and a substantial percentage had levels two or three times this level, few entertained the hypothesis that a level around 10 is associated with deleterious effects. Indeed, how would an investigator interested in testing this hypothesis have been able to identify a suitable control group? As we now know, the high prevalence of blood lead levels of 10 and greater in that era notwithstanding, a blood lead level of 10 is not "physiologically normal." Because low-dose effects are necessarily subtler than those that result from clinical intoxication, they will not be identified unless studies are conducted for the express purpose of identifying them. For most chemicals, we have little idea what the "no observed adverse effect level" is. Weiss (1983) speculated that thalidomide might still be used to reduce the nausea of early pregnancy if, instead of causing phocomelia (limb reduction), it caused a 5-point drop in offspring IQ. Although 5 IQ points is modest when viewed as the impact on an individual, Weiss demonstrated that, on a population basis, such a shift in mean IQ has enormous implications, approximately doubling the number of individuals with IQ scores below 70, and halving the number with IQ scores above 130 (Weiss, 1997). It is at our own peril that we fail to take seriously the possibility that the cognitive health of our population can be adversely affected by environmental chemical exposures.

REFERENCES

Agency for Toxic Substances and Disease Registry. (1997). *Healthy children-toxic environments. Acting on the unique vulnerability of children who dwell near hazardous waste sites. Report of the child health workgroup.* Atlanta, GA: U.S. Department of Health and Human Services.

Akagi, H., Grandjean, P., Takizawa, Y., & Weihe, P. (1998). Methylmercury dose estimation from umbilical cord concentrations in patients with Minamata Disease. *Environmental Research, 77*, 98–103.

Amin-Zaki, L., Elhassani, S., Majeed, M. A., Clarkson, T. W., Doherty, R. A., & Greenwood, M. (1974). Intra-uterine methylmercury poisoning in Iraq. *Pediatrics, 54*, 587–595.

Amin-Zaki, L., Majeed, M. A., Clarkson, T. W., & Greenwood, M. R. (1978). Methylmercury poisoning in Iraqi children: clinical observations over two years. *British Medical Journal, 1*, 613–616.

Amin-Zaki, L., Majeed, M. A., Elhassani, S. B., Clarkson, T. W., Greenwood, M. R., & Doherty, R. A. (1979). Prenatal methylmercury poisoning. *American Journal of Diseases of Children, 133*, 172–177.

Angle, C., McIntire, M., & Meile, R. (1968). Neurologic sequelae of poisoning in children. *Journal of Pediatrics, 73*, 531–539.

Bakir, F., Damluji, S. F., Amin-Zaki, L., Murtadha, M., Khalidi, A., Al-Rawi, N. Y., Tikriti, S., Dhahir, H. I., Clarkson, T. W., Smith, J. C., & Doherty, R. A. (1973). Methylmercury poisoning in Iraq. *Science, 181*, 230–241.

Bellinger, D. (1995). Interpreting the literature on lead and child development: The neglected role of the "experimental system". *Neurotoxicology and Teratology, 17*, 201–212.

Bellinger, D. (1998). What are the unique susceptibilities of children to environmental pollutants? *Health and Environment Digest, 12*, 9–11.

Bellinger, D., & Matthews, J. (1998). Social and economic dimensions of environmental policy: Childhood lead poisoning as a case study. *Perspectives in Biology and Medicine, 41*, 307–326.

Bellinger, D., Stiles, K., & Needleman, H. (1992). Low-level lead exposure, intelligence, and academic achievement: A long-term follow-up study. *Pediatrics, 90*, 855–861.

Blondell. J. (1997). Epidemiology of pesticide poisonings in the United States, with special reference to occupational cases. *Occupational Medicine Reviews, 12*, 209–220.

Bonithon-Kopp, C., Huel, G., Moreau, T., & Wendling, R. (1986). Prenatal exposure to lead and cadmium and psychomotor development of the child at 6 years. *Neurobehavioral Toxicology and Teratology, 8*, 307–310.

Brody, D., Pirkle, J., Kramer, R., Flegal, K., Matte, T., Gunter, E., & Paschal, D. (1994). Blood lead levels in the US population. Phase 1 of the Third National Health and Nutrition Examination Survey (NHANES III, 1988 to 1991). *Journal of the American Medical Association, 272*, 277–283.

Burkey, R. T., Nation, J. R., Grover, C. A., & Bratton, G. R. (1997). Effects of chronic lead exposure on cocaine-induced disturbance of fixed-interval behavior. *Pharmacology, Biochemistry and Behavior, 56*(1), 117–121.

Byers, R., & Lord, E. (1943). Late effects of lead poisoning on mental development. *American Journal of Diseases of Children, 66*, 471–494.

Capel, I. D., Pinnock, M. H., Dorrell, H. M., Williams, D. C., & Grant, E. C. (1981). Comparison of concentrations of some trace, bulk, and toxic metals in the hair of normal and dyslexic children. *Clinical Chemistry, 27*, 879–881.

Casarett, L. J., & Bruce, M. C. (1980). Origin and scope of toxicology. In J. Doull, C. D. Klassen, & M. D. Amdur (Eds.), *Casarett and Doull's toxicology: The basic science of poisons* (pp. 3–10). New York: Macmillan.

Cassee, F. R., Groten, J. P., van Bladeren, P. J., & Feron, V. J. (1998). Toxicological evaluation and risk assessment of chemical mixtures. *Critical reviews in Toxicology, 28*, 73–101.

Cernichiari, E., Brewer, R., Myers, G. J., Marsh, D. O., Lapham, L. L., Cox, C., Shamlaye, C. F., Berlin, M., Davidson, P. W., & Clarkson, T. W. (1995). Monitoring methylmercury during pregnancy: Maternal hair predicts fetal brain exposure. *Neurotoxicology, 16*, 705–710.

Chen, Y. J., Guo, Y., Hsu, C., & Rogan, W. J. (1992). Cognitive development of yu-cheng ('oil disease') children prenatally exposed to heat-degraded PCBs. *Journal of the American Medical Association, 268*, 3213–3218.

Chen, Y. J., Yu, M. M., Rogan, W. J., Gladen, B. C., & Hsu, C. (1994). A 6-year follow-up of behavior and activity disorders in the Taiwan yu-cheng children. *American Journal of Public Health, 84*, 415–421.

Choi, B. (1989). The effects of methylmercury on the developing brain. *Progress in Neurobiology*, *32*, 447–470.

Clarkson, T. W. (1992). Mercury: Major issues in environmental health. *Environmental Health Perspectives, 100*, 31–38.

Clarkson, T. W. (1997). The toxicology of mercury. *Critical Reviews in Clinical Laboratory Sciences, 34*, 369–403.

Cory-Slechta, D. (1997). Relationships between Pb-induced changes in neurotransmitter system function and behavioral toxicity. *Neurotoxicology, 18*, 673–688.

Cox, C., Marsh, D., Myers, G., & Clarkson, T. (1995). Analysis of data on delayed development from the 1971-72 outbreak of methylmercury poisoning in Iraq: assessment of influential points. *Neurotoxicology, 16*, 727–730.

Crump, K., Viren, J., Silvers, A., Clewell, H., Gearhart, & Shipp, A. (1995). Reanalysis of dose-response data from the Iraqi methylmercury poisoning episode. *Risk Analysis, 15*, 523–531.

Davidson, P. W., Myers, G. J., Cox, C., Shamlaye, C. F., Marsh, D. O., Tanner, M. A., Berlin, M., Sloane-Reeves, J., Cernichiari, E., Choisy, O., Choi, A., & Clarkson, T. W. (1995). Longitudinal neurodevelopmental study of Seychellois children following in utero exposure to methylmercury from maternal fish ingestion: outcomes at 19 and 29 months. *Neurotoxicology, 16*, 677–688.

Davidson, P., Myers, G., Cox, C., Axtell, C., Shamlaye, C., Sloane-Reeves, J., Cernichiari, E., Needham, L., Choi, A., Wang, Y., Berlin, M., & Clarkson, T. (1998). Effects of prenatal and postnatal methylmercury exposure from fish consumption on neurodevelopment: Outcomes at 66 months of age in the Seychelles Child Development Study. *Journal of the American Medical Association, 280*, 701–707.

Diamond, R., White, R., Gerr, F., & Feldman, R. (1995). A case of developmental exposure to inorganic mercury. *Child Neuropsychology, 1*, 140–149.

Echeverria, D., Aposhian, H., Woods, J., Heyer, N., Aposhian, M., Bittner, A., Mahurin, R., & Cianciola, M. (1998). Neurobehavioral effects from exposure to dental amalgam Hg°: New distinctions between recent exposure and Hg body burden. *FASEB Journal, 12*, 971–980.

Egeland, G. M., & Middaugh, J. P. (1997). Balancing fish consumption benefits with mercury exposure. *Science, 278*, 1904–1905.

Fein, G. G., Jacobson, J. L., Jacobson, S. W., Schwartz, P. M., & Dowler, J. K. (1984). Prenatal exposure to polychlorinated biphenyls: Effects on birth size and gestational age. *Journal of Pediatrics, 105*, 315–320.

Fell, J., Reynolds, A., Meadows, N., Khan, K., Long, S., Quaghebeur, G., Taylor, W., & Milla, P. (1996). Manganese toxicity in children receiving long-term parenteral nutrition. *Lancet, 347*, 1218–1221.

Fergusson, D., Horwood, L., & Lynskey, M. (1997). Early dentine lead levels and educational outcomes at 18 years. *Journal of Child Psychology and Child Psychiatry, 38*, 471–478.

Finkelstein, Y., Markowitz, M., & Rosen, J. (1998). Low-level lead-induced neurotoxicity in children: An update on central nervous system effects. *Brain Research Reviews, 27*, 168–176.

Gladen, B. C., & Rogan, W. J. (1991). Effects of perinatal polychlorinated biphenyls and dichlorodiphenyl dichloroethene on later development. *Journal of Pediatrics, 119*, 58–63.

Gladen, B., & Rogan, W. (1995). DDE and shortened duration of lactation in a northern Mexican town. *American Journal of Public Health, 85*, 504–508.

Gladen, B. C., Rogan, W. J., Hardy, P., Thullen, J., Tingelstad, J., & Tully, M. (1988). Development after exposure to polychlorinated biphenyls and dichlorodiphenyl dichloroethene transplacentally and through human milk. *Journal of Pediatrics, 113*, 991–995.

Goldstein, G. (1992). Developmental neurobiology of lead toxicity. In H. L. Needleman (Ed.), *Human lead exposure* (pp. 125–135). Boca Raton, FL: CRC Press.

Grandjean, P., & Weihe, P. (1993). Neurobehavioral effects of intrauterine mercury exposure: potential sources of bias. *Environmental Research, 61*, 176–183.

Grandjean, P., Weihe, P., & White, R. F. (1995). Milestone development in infants exposed to methylmercury from human milk. *Neurotoxicology, 16*, 27–34.

Grandjean, P., Weihe, P., White, R. F., Debes, F., Araki, S., Yokoyama, K., Murata, K., Sorensen, N., Dahl, R., & Jorgensen, P. J. (1997). Cognitive deficit in 7-year-old children with prenatal exposure to methylmercury. *Neurotoxicology and Teratology, 19*, 417–428.

Guillette, E., Meza, M., Aquilar, M., Soto, A., & Garcia, I. (1998). An anthropological approach to the evaluation of preschool children exposed to pesticides in Mexico. *Environmental Health Perspectives, 106*, 347–353.

Guo, Y. L., Yu, M. L., & Ryan, J. J. (1996). Different congeners of PCBs/PCDFs may have contributed to different health outcomes in the Yucheng cohort. *Neurotoxicology and Teratology, 18*, 255–256.

Guo, Y. L., Chen, Y., Yu, M., & Hsu, C. (1994). Early development of Yu-cheng children born seven to twelve years after the Taiwan PCB outbreak. *Chemosphere, 29*(9–11), 2395–2404.

Guo, Y. L., Lai, T. J., Chen, S. J., & Hsu, C. C. (1995). Gender-related decrease in Raven's Progressive Matrices scores in children prenatally exposed to polychlorinated biphenyls and related contaminants. *Bulletin of Environmental Contamination and Toxicology, 55*, 8–13.

Harada, M. (1976). Intrauterine poisoning: Clinical and epidemiological studies and significance of the problem. *Bulletin of the Institute of Constitutional Medicine, 25* (Suppl).

Harada, M. (1995). Minamata disease: methylmercury poisoning in Japan caused by environmental pollution. *Critical Reviews in Toxicology, 25*, 1–24.

Harada, M. (1997). Neurotoxicity of methyl-mercury: Minamata and the Amazon. In M. Yasui, M. J. Strong, K., Ota, & M. A. Verity (Eds.), *Mineral and metal neurotoxicology* (pp. 177–188). Boca Raton, FL: CRC Press.

Hu, H., Rabinowitz, M., & Smith, D. (1998). Bone lead as a biological marker in epidemiologic studies of chronic toxicity: Conceptual paradigms. *Environmental Health Perspectives, 106*, 1–8.

Jacobson, S. W., Fein, G. G., Jacobson, J. L., Schwartz, P. M., & Dowler, J. K. (1985). The effect of intrauterine PCB exposure on visual recognition memory. *Child Development, 56*, 853–860.

Jacobson, J. L., & Jacobson, S. W. (1996). Intellectual impairment in children exposed to polychlorinated biphenyls in utero. *New England Journal of Medicine, 335*, 783–789.

Jacobson, J. L., & Jacobson, S. W. (1997). Evidence for PCBs as neurodevelopmental toxicants in humans. *Neurotoxicology, 18*(2), 415–424.

Jacobson, J. L., Jacobson, S. W., Fein, G. G., Schwartz, P. M., & Dowler, J. K. (1984). Prenatal exposure to an environmental toxin: A test of the multiple effects model. *Developmental Psychology, 20*, 523–532.

Jacobson, J. L., Jacobson, S. W., & Humphrey, H. E. B. (1990). Effects of in utero exposure to polychlorinated biphenyls and related contaminants on cognitive functioning in young children. *Journal of Pediatrics, 116*, 38–45.

Jacobson, J. L., Jacobson, S. W., Padgett, R. J., Brumitt, G. A., & Billings, R. L. (1992). Effects of prenatal PCB exposure on cognitive processing efficiency and sustained attention. *Developmental Psychology, 28*, 297–306.

Jiang, H. M., Han, G. A., & He, Z. L. (1990). Clinical significance of hair cadmium content in the diagnosis of mental retardation of children. *Chinese Medical Journal, 103*, 331–334.

Kavlock, R., Daston, G., DeRosa, C., Fenner-Crisp, P., Gray, E., Kattari, S., Lucier, G., Luster, M., Mac, M., Maczka, C., Miller, R., Moore, J., Rolland, R., Scott, G., Sheehan, D., Sinks, T., & Tilson, H. (1996). Research needs for the risk assessment of health and environmental effects of endocrine disruptors: A report of the U.S. EPA-sponsored workshop. *Environmental Health Perspectives, 104 (Suppl. 4)*, 715–740.

Kilburn, K. (1989). Is the human nervous system most sensitive to environmental toxins? *Archives of Environmental Health, 44*, 343–344.

Kjellstrom, T., Kennedy, P., Wallis, S., Stewart, A., Friberg, L., Lind, B., Wutherspoon, T., & Mantell, C. (1989). *Physical and mental development of children with prenatal exposure to mercury from fish.* National Swedish Environmental Protection Board. Report 3642.

Koopman-Esseboom, C., Weisglas-Kuperus, N., de Riddert, M. A. J., Van der Paauws, C. G., Tuinstra, L. G. M. Th., & Sauer, P. J. J. (1996). Effects of polychlorinated biphenyl/dioxin exposure and feeding type on infants' mental and psychomotor development. *Pediatrics, 97*, 700–706.

Lai, T., Guo, Y., Yu, M., Ko, H., & Hsu, C. (1994). Cognitive development in Yucheng children. *Chemosphere, 29*(9–11), 2405–2411.

Lanphear, B., Burgoon, D., Rust, S., Eberly, S., & Galke, W. (1998). Environmental exposures to lead and urban children's blood lead levels. *Environmental Research, 76*, 120–130.

Lanphear, B., & Roghmann, K. (1997). Pathways of lead exposure in urban children. *Environmental Research, 74*, 67–73.

Lewis, M., Worobey, J., Ramsay, D. R., & McCormack, M. K. (1992). Prenatal exposure to heavy metals: Effects on childhood cognitive skills and health status. *Pediatrics, 89*, 1010–1015.

Li, X. S., Zhi, J. L., & Gao, R. O. (1995). Effect of fluoride exposure on intelligence in children. *Fluoride, 28*, 189–192.

Lorscheider, F., Vimy, M., & Summers, A. (1995). Mercury exposure from "silver" tooth fillings: Emerging evidence questions a traditional dental paradigm. *FASEB Journal, 9*, 504–508.

Mahaffey, K., Annest, J., Roberts, J., & Murphy, R. (1982). National estimates of blood lead levels: United States 1976-1980. *New England Journal of Medicine, 307*, 573–579.

Marlowe, M., Errera, J., & Jacobs, J. (1983). Increased lead and cadmium burdens among mentally retarded children and children with borderline intelligence. *American Journal of Mental Deficiency, 87*, 477–483.

Marsh, D. O., Clarkson, T. W., Cox, C., Myers, G. J., Amin-Zaki, L., & Al-Tikriti, S. (1987). Fetal methylmercury poisoning: Relationship between concentration in single strands of maternal hair and child effects. *Archives of Neurology, 44*, 1017–1022.

Marsh, D. O., Myers, G. J., Clarkson, T. W., Amin-Zaki, L., Tikriti, S., & Majeed, M. A. (1980). Fetal methylmercury poisoning: clinical and toxicological data on 29 cases. *Annals of Neurology, 7*, 348–353.

Marsh, D. O., Turner, M. D., Smith, J. C., Allen, P., & Richdale, N. (1995). Fetal methylmercury study in a Peruvian fish-eating population. *Neurotoxicology, 16*, 717–726.

Masuda, Y. (1985). Health status of Japanese and Taiwanese after exposure to contaminated rice oil. *Environmental Health Perspectives, 60*, 321–325.

McKeown-Eyssen, G., Ruedy, J., & Neims, A. (1983). Methylmercury exposure in northern Quebec: Neurologic findings in children. *American Journal of Epidemiology, 118*, 470–479.

McKinney, J. (1993). PCB-structure-activity relationships and developmental toxicity. *Workshop Report on Developmental Neurotoxic Effects Associated with Exposure to PCBs*. U.S. Environmental Protection Agency, EPA/630/R-92/004, ch. 2, pp. 2–13.

Mellins, R., & Jenkins, D. (1955). Epidemiological and psychological study of lead poisoning in children. *Journal of the American Medical Association, 158*, 15–20.

Mergler, D., & Baldwin, M. (1997). Early manifestations of manganese neurotoxicity in humans: An update. *Environmental Research, 73*, 92–100.

Mullenix, P., Denbesten, P., Schunior, A., & Kernan, W. (1995). Neurotoxicity of sodium fluoride in rats. *Neurotoxicology and Teratology, 17*, 685–688.

Myers, G. J., Davidson, P. W., Shamlaye, C. F., Axtell, C. D., Cernichiari, E., Choisy, O., Choi, A., Cox, C., & Clarkson, T. W. (1997). Effects of prenatal methylmercury exposure from a high fish diet on developmental milestones in the Seychelles child development study. *Neurotoxicology, 18*, 819–830.

Myers, G. J., Marsh, D. O., Davidson, P. W., Cox, C., Shamlaye, C. F., Tanner, M., Choi, A., Cernichiari, E., Choisy, O., & Clarkson, T. W. (1995). Main neurodevelopmental study of Seychellois children following in utero exposure to methylmercury from a maternal fish diet: outcome at six months. *Neurotoxicology, 16*, 653–664.

Nation, J., Grover, C., Bratton, G., & Salinas, J. (1990). Behavioral antagonism between lead and cadmium. *Neurotoxicology and Teratology, 12*, 99–104.

National Research Council. (1992). *Environmental neurotoxicology.* Washington, DC: National Academy Press.

National Research Council. (1993). *Pesticides in the diets of infants and children.* Washington, DC: National Academy Press.

Needleman, H., Schell, A., Bellinger, D., Leviton, A., & Allred, E. (1990). Long term effects of childhood exposure to lead at low dose: An eleven-year follow-up report. *New England Journal of Medicine, 322,* 83–88.

Owen, B., & Flegal, A. (1998). Blood lead concentrations in marine mammals validate estimates of 100 to 1000-fold increases in human blood lead concentrations. *Environmental Research, 78,* 134–139.

Perlstein, M., & Attala, R. (1966). Neurologic sequelae of plumbism in children. *Clinical Pediatrics, 5,* 292–298.

Pihl, R. O., & Parkes, M. (1977). Hair element content in learning disabled children. *Science, 198,* 204–206.

Rice, D. (1993). Lead-induced changes in learning: Evidence for behavioral mechanisms from experimental animal studies. *Neurotoxicology, 14,* 167–178.

Rodier, P. (1994). Vulnerable periods and processes during central nervous system development. *Environmental Health Perspectives, 102* (Suppl. 2), 121–124.

Rogan, W. J., & Gladen, B. C. (1991). PCBs, DDE, and child development at 18 and 24 months. *Annals of Epidemiology, 1,* 407–413.

Rogan, W. J., Gladen, B. C., McKinney, J. D., Carreras, N., Hardy, P., Thullen, J., Tinglestad, J., & Tully, M. (1986). Neonatal effects of transplacental exposure to PCBs and DDE. *Journal of Pediatrics, 109,* 335–341.

Rogan, W. J., Gladen, B. C., Hung, K., Koong, S., Shih, L., Taylor, J. S., Wu, Y., Yang, D., Ragan, B., & Hsu, C. (1988). Congenital poisoning by polychlorinated biphenyls and their contaminants in Taiwan. *Science, 241,* 334–336.

Romero, P., Barnett, P., & Midtling, J. (1989). Congenital anomalies associated with maternal exposure to oxydemeton-methyl. *Environmental Research, 50,* 256–261.

Ruff, H., Bijur, P., Markowitz, M., Ma, Y. -C., Rosen, J. (1993). Declining blood lead levels and cognitive change in moderately lead-poisoned children. *Journal of the American Medical Association, 269,* 1641–1646.

Shaheen, S. (1984). Neuromaturation and behavior development: the case of childhood lead poisoning. *Developmental Psychology, 20,* 542–550.

Sherman, J. (1996). Chlorpyrifos (Dursban)-associated birth defects: Report of four cases. *Archives of Environmental Health, 51,* 5–8.

Sim, M., & McNeil, J. (1992). Monitoring chemical exposure using breast milk: A methodological review. *American Journal of Epidemiology, 136,* 1–11.

Stephens, R., Spurgeon, A., & Berry, H. (1996). Organophosphates: The relationship between chronic and acute exposure effects. *Neurotoxicology and Teratology, 18,* 449–453.

Thatcher, R. W., Lester, M. L., McAlaster, B., & Horst, R. (1982). Effects of low-levels of cadmium and lead on cognitive functioning in children. *Archives of Environmental Health, 37,* 159–166.

Tiffany-Castiglioni, E., Sierra, E. M., Wu, J. N., & Rowles, T. K. (1989). Lead toxicity in neuroglia. *Neurotoxicology, 10*(3), 417–443.

Tong, S., Baghurst, P., McMichael, A., Sawyer, M., & Mudge, J. (1996). Lifetime exposure to environmental lead and children's intelligence at 11-13 years: The Port Pirie cohort study. *British Medical Journal, 312,* 1569–1575.

Trope, I., Lopez-Villegas, D., & Lenkinski, R. (1998). Magnetic resonance imaging and spectroscopy of regional brain structure in a 10-year-old boy with elevated blood lead levels. *Pediatrics, 101,* E7.

Tsubaki, R., & Irukayama, K. (Eds.). (1977). *Minamata Disease.* New York: Elsevier.

U.S. Centers for Disease Control. (1991). *Preventing lead poisoning in young children: A statement by the Centers for Disease Control.* Atlanta, GA: U.S. Department of Health and Human Services.

U.S. Centers for Disease Control. (1997a). Children with elevated blood lead levels attributed to home renovation and remodeling activities—New York, 1993–1994. *Morbidity and Mortality Weekly Report, 45,* 1120–1123.

U.S. Centers for Disease Control. (1997b). Update: Blood lead levels—United States, 1991–1994. *Morbidity and Mortality Weekly report, 46,* 141–146.

U.S. Centers for Disease Control. (1998). Monitoring environmental disease—United States, 1997. *Morbidity and Mortality Weekly Report, 47,* 522–525.

U.S. Environmental Protection Agency. (1986). *Air quality criteria for lead, Vol. IV.* Research Triangle Park, NC: Environmental Criteria and Assessment Office, EPA-600/8-83/028dF.

U.S. Environmental Protection Agency. (1995). Proposed guidelines for neurotoxicity risk assessment. *Federal Register, 60,* 52032–52056.

Verity, A. (1997). Pathogenesis of methyl mercury neurotoxicity. In M. Yasui, M. Strong, K. Ota, & A. Verity (Eds.), *Mineral and metal neurotoxicology* (pp. 159–167). Boca Raton, FL: CRC Press.

Wasserman, G., Liu, X., Lolacono, N., Factor-Litvak, P., Kline, J., Popovac, D., Morina, N., Musabegovic, A., Vrenezi, N., Capuni-Paracka, S., Lekic, V., Preteni-Redjepi, E., Hadzialjevic, S., Slavkovich, V., & Graziano, J. (1997). Lead exposure and intelligence in 7-year-old children: The Yugoslavia Prospective Study. *Environmental Health Perspectives, 105,* 956–962.

Watanabe, C., & Satoh, H. (1996). Evolution of our understanding of methylmercury as a health threat. *Environmental Health Perspectives, 104,* 367–379.

Weiss, B. (1983). Behavioral toxicology and environmental health science: Opportunity and challenge for psychology. *American Psychologist, 91,* 1174–1186.

Weiss, B. (1997). Pesticides as a source of developmental disabilities. *MRDD Research Reviews, 3,* 246–256.

Wheeler, M. (1996). Measuring mercury. *Environmental Health Perspectives, 104,* 826–831.

White, R., Diamond, R., Proctor, S., Morey, C., & Hu, H. (1993). Residual cognitive deficits 50 years after lead poisoning during childhood. *British Journal of Industrial Medicine, 50,* 613–622.

Whitten, P., & Naftolin, F. (1994). Xenoestrogens and neuroendocrine development. In H. Needleman & D. Bellinger (Eds.), *Prenatal exposure to toxicants: Developmental consequences* (pp. 268–293). Baltimore: The Johns Hopkins University Press.

World Health Organization. (1990). *Environmental health criteria 101: Methylmercury.* Geneva, Switzerland: WHO.

World Health Organization. (1995). *Environmental health criteria 165: Inorganic lead.* Geneva, Switzerland: World Health Organization.

Yamashita, F., & Hayashi, M. (1985). Fetal PCB syndrome: clinical features, intrauterine growth retardation and possible alteration in calcium metabolism. *Environmental Health Perspectives, 59,* 41–45.

Yeates, K., & Mortensen, M. (1994). Acute and chronic neuropsychological consequences of mercury vapor poisoning in two early adolescents. *Journal of Clinical and Experimental Neuropsychology, 16,* 209–222.

Yen, Y. Y., Lan, S. J., Ko, Y. C., & Chen, C. J. (1989). Follow-up study of reproductive hazards of multiparous women consuming PCBs- contaminated rice oil in Taiwan. *Bulletin of Environmental Contamination and Toxicology, 43,* 647–655.

Yu, M., Hsu, C., Gladen, B. C., & Rogan, W. J. (1991). In utero PCB/PCDF exposure: relation of developmental delay to dysmorphology and dose. *Neurotoxicology and Teratology, 13,* 195–202.

Zhang, G., Liu, D., & He, P. (1995). Effects of manganese on learning abilities in school children. *Chinese Journal of Preventive Medicine, 29:* 156–158.

7

Prenatal Drug Exposure and Cognitive Development

Linda C. Mayes
Thomas Fahy
Yale Child Study Center

Concerns about the long-term effects of prenatal exposure to drugs and other environmental toxins stem from ancient traditions regarding the vulnerability of the fetus and the inherent value in protecting a mother's pregnancy. Today's scientific interest in neurobehavioral teratology was preceded by centuries of warnings about the enduring effects of presumed harmful toxins ingested during a pregnancy. As early as Hippocrates, there are documented warnings about "uterine Suffocation" with maternal opiate use and cautions in the Old Testament to (Hans, 1992; Zagon & McLaughlin, 1984) "drink not wine nor any strong drink" during pregnancy (Judg. 13:7, cited in Heath, 1991). Scientific studies have taken their tone, if not their cue, in part from longstanding cultural fears regarding the believed harmful and insidious effects of drugs such as alcohol or opium and deep seated biases that fetuses would pay the price of their mothers' ill ways and misfortunes. Indeed, in many instances, hypotheses take shape first in the emotional climate of public fear and conviction about how a given drug affects the adult addict and thus, how it must by downward extension affect the fetus, infant, and young child. Out-of-control, dangerous addicts must have children with the same constitutional predisposition, marked for life as it were by the shadow of their parents' wrongdoing.

Because of the effects of public opinion and social standards on the shape and emphasis of scientific studies, the first reports about the consequences of prenatal exposure to a given drug or related environmental toxin often describe far more deleterious and severe outcomes than are true once larger and more heterogeneous samples are examined. Later hypotheses are also usually revised based on neurobiologic models for the mechanism of action of the drug or toxin and the pendulum often swings toward more cautious appraisals of the effects, if any, of a particular prenatal exposure. Thus, the first probands of any epidemic or new illness are often the most severe, most obvious, and least representative of the natural history of a condition. This observation is not limited to behavioral teratology, but nonetheless is particularly relevant to considerations of the effects of drugs such as alcohol, opiates, or cocaine. Studies of the teratologic effects of nearly every drug of abuse have shown this swing in emphasis with the most recent, and perhaps most dramatic example being cocaine (Day & Richardson, 1993; Hutchings, 1993; Mayes, Granger, Bornstein, & Zuckerman, 1992).

To date, more than 20 drugs have clearly demonstrated teratogenic and postnatal toxic effects (Levy & Koren, 1992); for many others, concern persists but data are inconclusive. The thalidomide tragedy notwithstanding, in most instances, demonstrated links in humans between prenatal drug exposure and immediate physical., neurological., or later developmental and psychological outcomes are fraught with significant methodologic problems. These include determining frequency, dose, and duration of exposure, associated conditions (e.g., poor nutrition, polydrug use, parental stress, and psychiatric illness) that also impact on development, and the developmentally toxic effects of a postnatal substance-abusing environment. Animal models provide some basis for comparison (e.g., Kosofsky & Wilkins, 1998; Morris, Binienda, Gillam, et al., 1996; Spear, 1993, 1995; Stanton & Spear, 1990), particularly about neurobiological and physical effects and do provide directional hypotheses for effects on aspects of learning, attention, and information processing. The drugs for which there is an increasing literature about both physical and behavioral teratologic effects include alcohol, heroin, marijuana, and cocaine (for reviews, see Day, 1992; Hans, 1992; Mayes, 1992; Mayes & Granger, 1995; Streissguth, 1992; Zuckerman & Frank, 1992). We focus our review on these four drugs in human infants and young children with particular attention to relationships between prenatal exposure and effects on cognition and related processes. Any discussion of the effects of any one in utero drug exposure should also be contextualized by the effects of growing up in a substance using home, that is, by the effects of the postnatal substance-using environment. We discuss the effects of the postnatal substance-using environment for these four drugs as a group. First, we turn to a general methodologic review of critical design issues regarding studies of prenatal drug exposure in human models.

METHODOLOGIC ISSUES IN STUDIES
OF PRENATAL DRUG EXPOSURE

Several crucial methodologic issues cut across all studies of prenatal drug exposure regardless of the specific drug being studied. Some of these issues are inherent to a longitudinal study design that examines the relationship between later and early events. All are particularly crucial and problematic in studies of prenatal exposure to drugs (for more detailed methodologic reviews, see Brooks-Gunn, McCarton, & Hawley, 1994; Carroll, 1995; Griffith & Freier, 1992; Lester, Freier, & LaGasse, 1995; Neuspiel, 1995). These methodologic issues fall into the following broad areas: (a) Definition and ascertainment of the independent exposure variable; (b) Sampling strategies and potential recruitment biases that may affect the generalizability of study findings; (c) Identification of crucial covariates often associated with substance abuse and exploring interactive as well as main effects models; (d) Definition of hypothesis driven outcome variables; (e) Distinguishing between short and long-term effects, later effects not apparent early on, and transient effects that nonetheless may influence other developmental functions downstream.

Defining the Exposure Variable. Human models of prenatal drug exposure usually present complicated dilemmas regarding definitions of the exposure variable. This issue alone may be the single most problematic one in neurobehavioral teratologic studies. Substance abusers typically do not report consistently or reliably the frequency or amount of their drug use (Babor, Brown, & DelBoca, 1990; Chasnoff, Landress, & Barrett, 1990; Grissom, 1997; Weiss et al., 1998). Various strategies have been devised to improve the reliability of self-reports of substance use including use of timelines, careful training of interviewers, and narrow windows for retrospective recall (Callahan et al., 1992; Carey, 1997; Richardson & Day, 1994; Rogers & Kelly, 1997). Even with these more sophisticated interviewing strategies, self-report of single or polydrug use typically although not uniformly (e.g., Richardson, Day, & McGauhey, 1993) underestimates the amount of exposure particularly of illicit drugs.

Frequency of exposure obtained through self-report histories is usually expressed as a number of days per unit time (e.g., per month, use in last 30 days, use per week). Self-reports are typically although not universally augmented with toxicologic sampling of urine for drugs such as cocaine, marijuana, or opiates. Repeated toxicology screening through a pregnancy may provide some confirmation or identification of users and not uncommonly toxicologic screens are obtained from both infant and mother at the time of delivery. Urine toxicology provides a relatively narrow window on use. For example, for cocaine users, a urine toxicology is typically positive no longer than 36 hours after use and that window varies for other drugs. For cocaine, infants' meconium and hair (infant's or mother's) have gained some support as particularly good samples to ascertain or confirm infant exposure because they provide a longer window for ascertaining exposure. Some data suggest that meconium or hair from the newborn may be a reliable measure of exposure as far back as mid-first trimester (Callahan et al., 1992; Graham et al., 1989; Kline, Ng, Schittini, Levin, & Susser, 1997; Ostrea, 1995). However, despite early enthusiasm for these kinds of longer window measures and despite their obvious utility, they do not provide a reliable quantitative estimate of exposure.

Indeed, quantity or amount of exposure is particularly difficult to estimate reliably. Estimates of amount of drug per time of use are as problematic as frequency of use when obtained by self-report. Toxicologic assays typically do not provide sufficiently accurate quantitative assays to permit the definition of a more quantitative exposure variable. But it is an important variable because between individuals and for any one person, "dose" or amount per use varies enormously. There are obviously no standards for how illicit drugs are sold—how pure or how diluted with other ingredients that may be active or inert. Thus, even if an addict presents a more or less accurate account of frequency and amount of use, there are few to no reliable indices of how concentrated or not the drug was and what the carrier or substance for cutting the pure drug might have been.

With these various problems in obtaining accurate estimates of frequency and amount of exposure, the majority of studies of prenatal exposure to date have defined the independent exposure variable as a dichotomous one—exposed or not exposed. Potential dose-related effects are obscured by grouping all exposed infants and children together, and the likelihood of detecting exposure effects may be reduced by including those only minimally exposed in the exposed group. Thus, a growing number of studies are attempting to create some metric of heavy, moderate, and light use to examine dose related effects that follow either linear or nonlinear models (e.g., Frank, Augustyn, & Zuckerman, 1998; King et al., 1995; Tronick, Frank, Cabral, Mirochnick, & Zuckerman, 1996).

Route of use presents a third problem in defining the severity or amount of exposure. Although total amount is always an important metric in defining severity of exposure, amount of time above a certain peak blood level may also be important in some models of teratogenicity. Stated another way, the teratogenic effect is carried not by total amount of exposure time but only by those times when the level of exposure is above a certain threshold. Certain aspects of fetal alcohol effects may follow this threshold rather than a linear dose-related model. Blood levels peak at different levels following use depending on the preferred route of use. Intravenous use as with heroin or smoking crack with rapid absorption through the pulmonary vascular bed provide rapid and large peak blood levels to both mother and fetus. Few to no studies, particularly of cocaine where the routes of use may be quite varied, have examined differences in outcome depending on preferred method of use.

A fourth problem in the definition of exposure variables is polydrug use. Rarely do addicts use one drug only. Although they may consider one drug of abuse their primary drug, polydrug use and exposure is the rule rather than the exception. For example, for cocaine users, a very typical combination is alcohol and tobacco in combination with cocaine. The same issues of defining frequency and amount of use for each drug pertain but also there are questions of interactive effects among drugs such as alcohol with cocaine and the resulting metabolite cocethylene. And a fifth problem specific to studies of prenatal exposure is obtaining reliable estimates of frequency and amount of exposure by trimester. Different drugs have different effects during the three trimesters of pregnancy. For example, in the first trimester, prenatal cocaine exposure may have a direct effect on neuronal migration and brain structure formation whereas in the third trimester the central nervous system (CNS) effect may be on synaptogenesis in specific brain regions (Dow-Edwards, Freed, & Milhorat, 1988; Frank, Augustyn, & Zuckerman, 1998; Mayes & Bornstein, 1995). Related to breaking down exposure by trimester is continued exposure postnatally. Particularly among agents that may be inhaled passively (e.g., crack, tobacco, marijuana), postnatal exposure is relatively common (e.g., Bender et al., 1995; Kjarasch, Glotzer, Vinci, Weitzman, & Sargent, 1991; Lustbader, Mayes, McGee, Jatlow, & Roberts, 1998).

Sampling Strategies.   How samples are identified, recruited, and maintained are crucial questions for any longitudinal study but with a special valence in studies of substance abuse and prenatal exposure. The valence relates to severity of exposure and compliance with the study. Samples recruited from substance abuse clinics while practical and convenient present several potential detection biases. For one, patients attending substance abuse clinics or seeking help for their addiction may represent a group of more motivated or more distressed addicts. There is no readily available way to compare those recruited to substance users from the same population not recruited. More general screening strategies such as through a prenatal care or pediatric clinic afford a broader based sampling approach that may include mild to moderate as well as heavy users.

Identification of Covariates and Development of Interactive Models.   Substance abuse of one or multiple drugs rarely occurs isolated from other developmentally salient variables. Parental health during pregnancy is usually compromised and more often than not, substance using mothers receive little to no prenatal care. Nearly all drugs of abuse during pregnancy may at the very least influence fetal growth and contribute to intrauterine growth retardation and perhaps prematurity (see the following for detailed discussions under individual drugs). Postnatally, important covariates include those broadly describing parental–caregiving function. Indeed, variables such as ongoing parental substance use, neglect and abuse, parental depression, exposure to violence as witness or victim, homelessness, parental separation, and loss are common events for children growing up in substance using homes (see also next section). It is naïve conceptually and statistically to discuss all of these events simply as covariates of prenatal substance exposure. Although they usually co-occur with substance use, they may or may not be related to the outcome of interest. On the other hand, many of these variables probably serve as either mediators or moderators of the relation between prenatal exposure and later neurocognitive outcome (Baron & Kenny, 1986; Frank, Bresnahan, & Zuckerman, 1993). For example, infants exposed prenatally to cocaine (see next section) appear more likely to have disorders of arousal or emotional regulation (e.g., Mayes, Grillon, Granger, & Schottenfeld, 1998). The strength of the relationship between prenatal cocaine exposure and the expression of this particular vulnerability may be mediated by the quality of postnatal care the infant and young child receives.

Considering mediating and moderating variables also brings up the issue of interactive as well as main effect models. Traditionally, behavioral teratology studies have relied on main effect conceptualizations: How much of the variance of a given neurodevelopmental outcome is explained by the prenatal exposure status? Although important and a first step, most developmental questions relating to prenatal exposure are probably better addressed as interactions. For example, as already cited, interactions between caregiving and prenatal exposure may more explain more of the variance in neurodevelopmental outcome than main effects alone. Interactions among a given genetic predisposition (e.g., for attentional disorders), exposure to drugs in utero, and postnatal neglect define another cluster of effects that are both more generalizable than single effect, exposure models, and more biologically plausible.

Definition of Outcome and Windows of Effect.   Outcome variables and timing of outcome measurement have varied widely in traditional behavioral teratology studies. Traditional models of teratology address both categories of outcome and window of effect (e.g., Abel, 1989; Vorhees, 1989). Typically, teratologic outcomes are expressed as CNS effects (including neurochemical, neuroanatomical, cognitive, behavioral, social–emotional), physical growth deficits (including brain growth), and malformations, and these outcomes are typically more manifest as the dose of exposure increases. At lower doses, CNS effects may still be apparent even in the absence of morphologic changes. Some effects on the CNS may only be manifest at later stages of development. These are often referred to as latent or "sleeper" effects and examples of these are found both in studies of prenatal alcohol and marijuana exposure (e.g., Day et al., 1994). Certain developmental periods mark periods of neurological reorganization (e.g., puberty, early school age, second half of the first year) and often prove to be important times to look for either latent or exacerbated effects of prenatal exposure. Within latent effects are those functional impairments that are apparent only under stressful, challenging, or novel conditions. In the work on cocaine in animal models, a considerable body of evidence has accumulated that this pattern may be particularly relevant to the neurotoxicity of cocaine (Spear, 1998).

Just as profiles of first cohorts may present a picture of more severe impairment, so are the initial outcome variables of study often more globally defined and less linked to hypotheses about pharmacologic action of the drug. Besides physical or morphologic impairment, neurobehavioral studies of prenatal drug exposure have most often focused on global measures of intelligence and general developmental functions such as memory, school performance, and incidence of maladaptive behavior. More recently, studies of in utero drug exposure have begun to utilize more functional measures such as reaction time and to focus on individual components of more general functions (e.g., visual vs. auditory attention). Outcome measures such as these may be more reflective of hypotheses that are directly linked to understanding the site of action of the drug in the CNS.

Finally, it is important to make explicit that potential teratogens may exert their effects through different mechanisms. Most often assumed is a direct effects model in which the teratogen directly impairs a specific area of function in the CNS or otherwise. (And parenthetically, even stating a "direct" effect on CNS is far too global a statement that does not allow for the remarkable complexity of any effect on developing neural tissue. The levels of effect in the CNS span direct toxicity to developing cells, impaired synapse or connectivity, to facilitated or impaired induction of genes that in turn regulate neural development.)

A second, less often explicitly discussed model is one in which the potential teratogen contributes to a domain of vulnerability that is expressed or not depending on environmental conditions. A third model particularly relevant to conditions in which the potential teratogen is also a drug of abuse is that the drug itself may not be teratogenic for the developing child. Rather in this third model, it may be that the context of drug abuse so alters the child's caregiving environment that any presumed teratogenicity is actually expressed through the effects of environmental chaos and deprivation.

PRENATAL ALCOHOL EXPOSURE

Studies of the teratologic effects of prenatal alcohol exposure have been ongoing for many years since the initial reports of fetal alcohol syndrome (FAS; Jones & Smith, 1973, Jones, Smith, Ulleland, & Streissguth, 1973). Alcohol acts as a direct neuroteratogen, affecting not only fetal facial morphology and overall physical growth but also more specifically brain growth, structure, and function through mechanisms not yet clearly elucidated (Goodlett & West, 1992; Schenker et al., 1990). In infancy, FAS is characterized by (a) intrauterine growth retardation with persistent postnatal poor growth in weight or height; (b) a pattern of specific minor physical anomalies that include a characteristic facial appearance; and (c) CNS deficits including microcephaly, delayed development, hyperactivity, attention deficits, intellectual delays, learning disabilities, and in some cases, seizures (Claren & Smith, 1978; Smith, 1982). The characteristic facial features include microphthalmia, short palpebral fissures, a thin upper lip, midface hypoplasia, and a smooth and long philtrum. Children with a history of in utero alcohol exposure who have either the characteristic physical appearance or CNS dysfunction are given the diagnostic label of having fetal alcohol effects (Claren & Smith, 1978). Even in the absence of FAS, infants born to alcoholic mothers show an increased incidence of intellectual impairments congenital anomalies, and decreased birth weight (Aronson, Kyllerman, Sabel, Sandin, & Olegård, 1985; Day, 1992; Sokol, Miller, & Reed, 1980). Partial expression of FAS and the issue of fetal alcohol effects have led to a number of studies relating amount of exposure to the presence or absence of diagnostic criteria and to the severity of CNS manifestations.

In the general population, the syndrome occurs in approximately one or two live births per 1,000, and the incidence of FAS among alcoholic women is between 2.5 and 10% (Sokol et al., 1980). Although in general the more severe effects on physical growth are associated with more severe intellectual impairments (Streissguth, 1992) and heavier alcohol use is associated with more severe physical effects, the relationships are not entirely consistent, and dose-response and duration of exposure questions remain significant unresolved issues in the study of prenatal alcohol exposure (Day, 1992; Streissguth, Barr, Sampson, & Darby, 1990). For example, in one study of newborn behavior (Smith, Coles, & Lancaster, 1986), differences in orientation responses on the Brazelton Neonatal Behavioral Assessment Scale (NBAS) were related to differences in the duration of prenatal alcohol exposure, whereas differences in autonomic regulation were related to both duration and amount of exposure. Others however have failed to find similar relations between prenatal alcohol exposure and NBAS performance (e.g., Ernhart et al., 1985).

Hundreds of reports of children with FAS are now available documenting the delayed development in the first 2 to 3 years of life for children exposed to alcohol prenatally (e.g., Coles, Smith, Lancaster, & Falek, 1987; Gusella & Fried, 1984; O'Connor, Brill, & Sigman, 1986). However, significantly fewer studies describe follow-up findings through school age and adolescence (Streissguth, 1992). Coles et al. (1991), studying children at age 70 months who were exposed to alcohol throughout gestation, reported deficits in sequential processing and on some measures of academic skills including reading and mathematics. Streissguth (1976) reported on a 7-year follow-up of 23 children of alcoholic mothers compared with 46 children of nonalcoholic mothers matched for socioeconomic status, age, education, race parity, and marital status. At 7 years, children of the alcoholic mothers had significantly lower IQ scores and poorer performance on tests of reading, spelling, and arithmetic, and 44% of the children of alcoholic mothers compared with 9% in the control group had IQ scores in the borderline to retarded range. Significant differences in height, weight, and head circumference were also apparent. In a study of 21 children of alcoholic mothers again compared with a matched control sample, Aronson et al. (1985) described significantly greater problems with distractibility, hyperactivity, and short attention spans in the alcohol-exposed group. Similar behavior problems have been described for other cohorts (e.g., Steinhausen, Nestler, & Spohr, 1982), and impairments in concentration and attention, social withdrawal., and conduct problems continue to be described for adolescents and young adults (Streissguth et al., 1991).

PRENATAL OPIATE EXPOSURE

In contrast to those exposed to alcohol, infants exposed prenatally to opiates (heroin or methadone) are born passively addicted to the drug and exhibit withdrawal symptoms in the first days to weeks after delivery (Desmond & Wilson, 1975). Numerous studies have now replicated the finding that prenatal opioid exposure reduces birth weight and head circumference (Finnegen, 1976; Hans, 1992; Jeremy & Hans, 1985, Kaltenbach & Finnegen, 1987; Wilson, Desmond, & Wait, 1981). Similar findings in animal models that control for exposure to other drugs such as alcohol or tobacco and for poor maternal health support the finding of an opiate effect on fetal growth (Zagon & McLaughlin, 1984). Prenatal exposure to opiates also contributes significantly to an increased incidence of sudden infant death syndrome (SIDS). In some studies, the incidence of SIDS is eight times that reported for non-opiate-exposed infants (Finnegan, 1979; Hans, 1992; Rosen & Johnson, 1988; Wilson et al., 1981).

On neurobehavioral assessments in the newborn period, opiate-exposed infants are more easily aroused and irritable (Hans, 1985; Marcus & Hans, 1982; Strauss, Starr, Ostrea, Chavez, & Stryker, 1976). They exhibit proportionately less quiet compared with active sleep and show increased muscle tone and poor motor control (e.g., tremulousness and jerky movements). Opiate-exposed infants are less often in alert states and are more difficult to bring to an alert state. The dramatic neurobehavioral abnormalities seen in the newborn period generally diminish over the first month of life (Jeremy &

Hans, 1985) for the majority of infants and are thus assumed to reflect the transitory symptoms of narcotic withdrawal rather than evidence of permanent neurological dysfunction (Hans, 1992).

Past the neonatal period, a number of studies have documented small, and not usually statistically significant, delays in the acquisition of developmental skills as measured by the Bayley Scales of Infant Development (1969, 1993; Hans, 1989; Hans & Jeremy, 1984; Rosen & Johnson, 1982; Wilson et al., 1981). However, much more consistent and significant across studies have been the findings of persistent problems in poor motor coordination, high activity level, and poor attentional regulation among opiate exposed infants in the first year of life (Hans & Marcus, 1983; Hans et al., 1984). These state and motor regulatory difficulties make it hard for even a well-functioning adult in a relatively nonstressed environment to care for the infant, and present significant problems for an opiate addicted adult experiencing his or her own state and attentional problems (Hans, 1992).

Follow-up studies through early childhood of opiate-exposed compared with non-opiate-exposed children have continued to report few to no differences in cognitive performance (Kaltenbach & Finnegan, 1987, Strauss et al., 1976; Wilson, McCreary, Kean, & Baxter, 1979). However, opiate-exposed school-age children show higher activity levels, are often impulsive with poor self-control, show poor motor coordination, and have more difficulty with tasks requiring focused attention (Oloffson, Buckley, & Andersen, 1983). There is also an increased incidence of attention deficit disorder (ADD) among opiate-exposed school-age children (Hans, 1992). Most recently, two studies have described altered sexually dimorphic behavior in opiate-exposed males (Sandberg, Meyer-Bahlburg, Rosen, & Johnson, 1990; Ward, Kopertowski, Finnegin, & Sandberg, 1989). Opiate-exposed boys showed more stereotypically feminine behavior than nonexposed boys, but there were no differences between exposed and nonexposed girls. These findings are consistent with similar observations of male rats exposed to opioid drugs in utero (Ward, Orth, & Weisz, 1983).

Past the years of early childhood, there are few studies of the long-term effects of prenatal opiate exposure, and those available usually lack a nonexposed control group or are not based on a longitudinal design (Hans, 1992). The data from these studies suggest that, by adolescence, opiate-exposed children exhibit an increased incidence of behavior and conduct problems including impulsivity, involvement in criminal activities or in early substance abuse, more antisocial behavior, and increased school dropout (Bauman & Levine, 1986; Sowder & Burt, 1980; Wilson, 1989). It is not altogether clear how much these problems in conduct and impulse regulation are attributable to persistent effects of prenatal opiate exposure and how much they are the consequence of cumulative exposure to the discord and dysfunction often characterizing substance-abusing households.

PRENATAL MARIJUANA EXPOSURE

After alcohol, marijuana is the most commonly abused drug in the United States, and like alcohol, marijuana abuse cuts across different socioeconomic groups and strata. Marijuana, also known as cannabis, is obtained from the flower tops of the hemp plant from which more than 300 natural compounds including at least 61 different cannabinoids are extracted. Of these, tetrahydrocannabinol (THC), or marijuana, is the most potently psychoactive (Levy & Koren, 1992). THC readily crosses the placenta, and among heavy users, is also concentrated in breast milk (Blackard & Tennes, 1984; Perez-Reyes & Wall, 1982). THC has a strong affinity for lipids and is stored in fatty tissue through out the body (Kruez & Axelrod, 1973). Thus, a single dose of THC in humans has a half-life of 7 days but may take up to 30 days to be excreted completely and accumulates throughout the body with chronic use (Nahas, 1976).

The rate of women reporting marijuana use during pregnancy varies from 5% to 34% (Zuckerman, 1988). During pregnancy, THC has documented effects in animals and humans on pituitary ovarian function, prolactin secretion, and uterine contractility (Harclerode, 1980). However, no relation has been documented between marijuana use and length of gestation or birth weight (Fried, Buckingham, & Von Kulmitz, 1983). It should be noted that birth weight reductions associated with marijuana use have been described by others studying higher risk, lower income families (Hingson et al., 1989) and the results are conflicting (Zuckerman et al., 1989). Marijuana has an indirect effect on fetal oxygenation through the high levels of carbon monoxide found in marijuana smoke (higher than that of cigarette smoke [Wu, Tashkin, Djahed, & Rose, 1988]), which in turn results in fetal hypoxia. This type of effect may influence fetal growth, particularly in instances of heavy use (Zuckerman & Frank, 1992).

Few physical anomalies have been reported with marijuana exposure (O'Conel & Fried, 1984), although several studies have suggested a link between prenatal marijuana exposure and features similar to those of FAS (Hingson et al., 1989; Qazi, Mariano, Beller, Millman, & Crombleholme, 1982). In one study, the incidence of fetal alcohol-like features was estimated to be five times higher in users of THC. It is quite likely, however, that heavy marijuana users are also abusing alcohol, and thus, the similarity to fetal alcohol effects is more likely to reflect the accompanying alcohol use (Fried, Innis, & Barnes, 1984). Several neurobehavioral findings in the newborn period point to decreased responsiveness on the Brazelton NBAS, particularly in visual., but not auditory, responsiveness to both animate and inanimate stimulation (Fried, 1980, 1982) and a higher pitched cry (Fried & Makin, 1987). Another characteristic of newborns exposed to heavy maternal THC use are tremors and increased startle in the first 7 to 14 days of life (Levy &

Koren, 1992). Changes in sleep patterns have also been reported including a decrease in the amount of trace alternans quiet sleep (Scher, Richardson, Coble, Day, & Stoffer, 1988) and lower sleep efficiency and maintenance as measured by sleep EEG by as late as 3 years of age (Day & Richardson, 1991).

Postnatally, marijuana has been identified in the urine of breast-fed infants whose mothers continue to use after delivery (Perez-Reyes & Walls, 1982). However, no acute toxic effects have been identified with this level of passive exposure although a few studies suggest possible developmental effects related to heavy postpartum exposure via breast milk (Zuckerman & Frank, 1992). In one study, marijuana exposure via breast milk in the 1st postpartum month was related to decreased motor development at 1 year, and there appeared to be a dose-related pattern to the level of association between exposure and motor delay (Astley & Little, 1990). Longer term studies of the outcome of prenatal marijuana exposure are few in number. In one study, no association was found between prenatal marijuana use and developmental scores at 12 and 24 months (Fried & Watkinson, 1988). When these children were 4 years old, heavy prenatal use (more than six joints per week) was associated with lower scores on memory and verbal subscales of standard preschool intelligence tests. These findings pertained in comparison with the scores of children whose mothers had not used marijuana and after controlling for factors such as the home environment (Fried & Watkinson, 1990). A second study (Streissguth, Bookstein, Sampson, & Barr, 1989) found no correlation with IQ scores at age 4. The paucity of long-term follow-up studies and the few findings make it difficult to conclude whether or not prenatal marijuana exposure has a direct effect on later developmental functions such as memory.

PRENATAL COCAINE EXPOSURE

In many inner-city populations, nearly 50% of women giving birth report or test positive for cocaine use at the time of delivery (Amaro, Fried, Cabral, & Zuckerman, 1990; Osterloh & Lee, 1989). A recent study of consecutively recruited women in routine prenatal care reported that 17% used cocaine during pregnancy (Frank et al., 1988), and national estimates across all socioeconomic groups suggest that 10% to 20% of all infants are exposed to cocaine prenatally (Chasnoff et al., 1990). Most often, infants exposed prenatally to cocaine are also exposed to a number of other risk factors that may also contribute to impaired development (Mayes, 1992). These include exposure to other substances of abuse including alcohol and tobacco as well as opiates, marijuana, and amphetamines. Mothers who abuse cocaine often have associated health problems including a higher incidence of HIV-positive titers with or without AIDS-related illnesses, and they have pregnancies more often complicated by preterm delivery and intrauterine growth retardation. Postnatally, infants exposed to cocaine continue to be exposed to ongoing parental substance abuse, they are more often neglected and abused, and they have parents with more frequent depression and higher overall stress and anxiety (Mayes, 1995). Any one of these factors may influence the development of early attentional and arousal regulatory functions, later language, and potentially overall developmental competency.

Although the reports to date have been essentially inconclusive as to the presence of one or more cocaine-specific effects or to critical issues such as the timing or dose of exposure, there is accumulating evidence that cocaine may have an effect on attention and arousal regulation. Cocaine and crack are CNS stimulants that act through the monoaminergic neurotransmitter systems including dopamine, norepinephrine, and serotonin (5-HT; Gawin & Ellinwood, 1988; Wise, 1984). The primary CNS action of cocaine occurs at the level of neurotransmitter release, reuptake, and recognition at the synaptic junction. Cocaine blocks the reuptake of dopamine, norepinephrine, and 5-HT by the presynaptic junction (Swann, 1990), a process that is primarily responsible for the inactivation of neurotransmitters. Blocking reuptake leaves more dopamine, norepinephrine, and 5-HT available within the presynaptic space (and thus, in the peripheral blood as well) and results in enhanced activity of these agents in the CNS (Goeders & Smith, 1983) with associated physiologic reactions (e.g., tachycardia and vasoconstriction with hypertension) and behavioral response (e.g., euphoria and increased motor activity). Within the various dopamine-rich areas of the brain, certain areas of the prefrontal cortex are somewhat insensitive to the effects of cocaine on dopamine reuptake whereas parts of the limbic system and basal ganglia (regions that regulate emotion and locomotion) are 100% sensitive to the effect (Hadfield & Nugent, 1983). The dopamine-rich nigrostriatal system projects from cell bodies in the brain stem (e.g., substantia nigra) to the subcortex region called the corpus striatum and innervates the prefrontal cortex and regions of the limbic system (Goeders & Smith, 1983; Shepherd, 1988). Each of these areas is involved in a number of basic neuropsychological functions including arousal and attentional modulation, the regulation of anxiety and other emotional states, and in the reinforcing properties basic to stimulant addiction in adults.

In fetal brain development, dopamine, serotonin, and norepinephrine play critical roles in defining brain structure and neuronal formation by influencing cell proliferation, neural outgrowth, and synaptogenesis or connections between neurons (Lauder, 1988; Mattson, 1988). Cocaine readily crosses the placenta as well as the blood–brain barrier, and brain concentrations of cocaine have been reported as high as four times that of peak plasma levels (Farrar & Kearns, 1989). Thus, cocaine may affect the formation and remodeling of brain structures through this effect on the release and metabolism of monoamines. Additionally, cocaine may influence the actual ontogeny of the neurotransmitter systems and thus again modify a number of critical processes in brain development. In prenatally cocaine-exposed animal models, several structures associated with dopamine activity, including those regions cited earlier, show significant changes in dopaminergic activity compared with that of controls (Dow-Edwards, 1989; Dow-Edwards et al., 1988). Effects on developing monoaminergic neurotransmitter systems have wide-reaching implications, for they may lead to mistimed neurogenesis between the affected and unaffected areas of the brain with resultant changes in synpatic connections (Lauder, 1991). By altering monoaminergic neurotransmitter control of morphogenesis, chronic exposure to cocaine in utero may adversely affect autonomic function, state regulation, and regulation of attention in the developing nervous system. (For a detailed review of the effects of cocaine on neural ontogeny, see Mayes, 1999.)

The effect of cocaine on fetal development may also be expressed through the norepinephrine-related effects of cocaine on vascular tone. These consist of decreased uteroplacental flow with resulting acute and chronic impairment in placental function and a relative state of fetal hypoxia (Moore et al., 1986; Woods, Plessinger, & Clark, 1987). Moreover, in humans, cocaine use has been associated with spontaneous abortions, premature labor, and abruptions (Bingol et al., 1987; Cherukuri et al., 1988; Lindenberg et al., 1991). The effect of cocaine use on placental blood flow probably contributes to the reported relation between cocaine and fetal growth (low birth weight and microcephaly; Fulroth, Phillips, & Durand, 1989; Hadeed & Siegel, 1989; Hurt et al., 1995; MacGregor et al., 1987; Oro & Dixon, 1987; Ryan, Ehrlich, & Finnegan, 1987). Additionally, because of the effect of cocaine on overall adult nutrition, compliance with prenatal care and the usual association between cocaine use and the use of other drugs such as alcohol, tobacco, and opiates (Amaro, Zuckerman, & Cabral, 1989; Frank et al., 1988), women using cocaine while pregnant are in an overall poorer state of health, which in turn increases the risk of impaired fetal outcome and fetal growth retardation. Intrauterine growth-retarded, small-for-gestational age infants show persistent problems with irritability and distractibility well into the first year of life (Watt, 1990; Watt & Strongman, 1985).

Studies of relation between prenatal cocaine exposure and indices of developmental competency and cognition in infants and preschool-aged children have reported mixed findings; and in contrast to studies of alcohol, opiates, or marijuana, there are very few data for in utero cocaine exposure for children older than 7 years. Mayes, Bornstein, Chawarska, and Granger (1995) reporting on 3-month-olds, Jacobson et al. (1996) studying 13-month-olds, Graham et al. (1992) studying 20-month-olds and Hurt et al. (1995)

reporting on 6, 12, 18, 24, and 30-months-olds all found no effects of prenatal cocaine exposure on standard developmental metrics (e.g., the Bayley Scales of Infant Development) or on language development at 30 months (Hurt et al., 1997). On the other hand, Alessandri, Bendersky, and Lewis (1998) reported that prenatal cocaine exposure was related to lower scores on the Bayley index at 18 months. Similarly, Richardson, Day, and Gold-schmidt (1995) found second trimester exposure related to lower motor scores at 12 months, and Singer et al. (1997) reported both lower mental and motor scores at varying times between 6 and 24 months. Other findings from the first 2 years of life have included increased irritabilty and questions of impaired arousal regulation at 3 months (Alessandri et al., 1993; Mayes et al., 1995; Mayes et al., 1996) and poorer performance on tests of visual recognition memory and processing speed at 13 months (Jacobson et al., 1996).

For children 3 years and older, findings remain mixed, although more consistently reporting some relationship to in utero cocaine exposure. Hurt et al. (1997) reported no differences between cocaine-exposed and nonexposed 4-year-old children on the Weschler Preschool and Primary Scales of Intelligence (WPPSI–R) scales after controlling for other drug use and prenatal care. Another group reported that children 3 years of age exposed prenatally to cocaine had significantly lower verbal reasoning scores on the Stanford–Binet (Azuma & Chasnoff, 1993; Griffith, Azuma, & Chasnoff, 1994). Importantly, the difference in scores was between cocaine-exposed and no-drug-exposed but not when cocaine-exposed children were compared to those exposed to alcohol or marijuana but not cocaine. Both drug-exposed groups has significantly lower scores on the abstract–visual reasoning score compared with the nonuser group but did not differ from one another and there were no differences on overall composite cognitive performance scores. Others have reported significant cocaine-related differences on the Stanford–Binet composite and short-term memory scores (Richardson, 1998). At ages 4 and 6, Bender et al. (1995) examined children exposed to crack/cocaine both pre- and postnatally, only prenatally, and a nonexposed group. Children who were exposed both pre- and postnatally did more poorly on tests of receptive language ability and visual motor integration than the other two groups when other potentially confounding variables were controlled.

However, in contrast to the relatively inconclusive or at the least tentative findings regarding cognitive performance and in utero cocaine exposure, several lines of work point more consistently to a relation between prenatal cocaine-exposure and disruption in arousal and attention regulation (Jacobson et al., 1996; Karmel & Gardner, 1996; Mayes et al., 1996). Few studies to date have examined these functions in children past the preschool-age period. For example, at 6 years, Richardson, Conroy, and Day (1996) reported first trimester cocaine exposure associated with more errors of omission on standard computerized attention tasks. Similarly, Mayes et al. (1998) reported decreased reaction time and increased impulsive responding among 5-year-old prenatally cocaine exposed children.

As a caveat, it is important to note that establishing cause–effect relations between prenatal cocaine exposure and attentional deficits is problematic given the number of additional variables that might affect vulnerability for such neurodevelopmental outcomes. In addition to a direct effect on developing monoaminergic neurotransmitter systems in fetal brain, prenatal cocaine exposure may potentially affect attentional and arousal regulation indirectly because of effects on fetal growth. Exposure to alcohol, tobacco, and marijuana in addition to cocaine is a common profile as well. Also, continued maternal postnatal use of cocaine affects the child's caregiving environment at minimally two levels, which may contribute to attention regulation. Adults who are under the influence of cocaine are less able to respond adequately to their children at any given time (Bauman & Dougherty, 1983; Mayes, 1995). The effect of cocaine on memory and attention impair the adult's ability to care for a child. More generally, because of the lifestyle adjustments necessary with cocaine use—including for example, prostitution, crime, exposure to violence, and the overwhelming power of the addiction, the overall environment for these children is often chaotic, violent, and neglectful (Black & Mayer, 1980; Regan, Leifer, & Finnegan, 1984). Specific outcomes in children such as attentional regulation are also influenced by maternal interactive style (Bornstein, 1985; Bornstein & Tamis-LeMonda, 1990; Tamis-LeMonda & Bornstein, 1989). Similarly, the psychological–personality factors that lead an adult to substance abuse may have genetic as well as experiential implications for the fetus. For example, attention deficits or chronic affective disorders in the adult, both of which may be partially alleviated by cocaine (Khantzian, 1983; Khantzian & Khantzian, 1984; Rounsaville, Weissman, Wilber, & Kleber, 1982) are associated with genetic risks for similar disorders in the child, and these disorders, particularly depression, also impinge on the adult's capacity to care adequately for the child (Fendrick, Warner, & Weisman, 1990; Field, 1995).

Thus, prenatal exposure to alcohol, heroin, marijuana, or cocaine may contribute to specific short- and long-term impairments or vulnerabilities in arousal modulation, activity level, or attention regulation, which may make it more difficult for an adult to parent the child. Moreover, when that adult is involved in substance abuse, his or her addiction and the associated environmental., psychiatric, and neuropsychological effects may further impair the interactions between the child and parent assessed through both indirect measures of the incidence of abuse and neglect and direct observational measures of parenting attitudes and behaviors.

POSTNATAL SUBSTANCE-ABUSING ENVIRONMENT

Each of these presumed effects relating prenatal drug exposure to neurobehavioral and developmental dysfunctions must be viewed in the context of the postnatal substance-abusing environment in which many prenatally drug-exposed children remain (Mayes & Granger, 1995). As already alluded to, the postnatal drug-using world carries a number of risks to children's development. These include exposure to extreme, often chronic violence, virtual homelessness, poverty, parental neglect and abuse, and parental depression and associated psychopathology. Each of these factors, in turn, influences the parenting behaviors of adults who are also substance abusers.

Addiction to any substance (or condition) points to personality characteristics, disabilities, or impairments, each of which may have significant implication for an adult's ability to parent a child. Moreover, all substances of abuse alter in varying degree an individual's state of consciousness, memory, affect regulation, and impulse control and may become so addictive that the adult's primary goal is to be able to supply his or her addiction to the exclusion of all else and all others in his or her life. These alterations may influence at any given moment the adult's capacity to sustain contingent, responsive interactions with an infant and young child. For example, neuropsychological impairments in concentration and memory associated with chronic cocaine abuse (O'Malley, Adamse, Heaton, & Gawin, 1992) might be expected to influence certain parenting behaviors such as the capacity to sustain an interaction.

There are differences in the behavioral and personality characteristics of substance-abusing adults according to tile specific substance of abuse. Systematic studies of psychopathology among substance abusers find, for example, that abuse of cocaine versus opiates is associated with a different spectrum of psychological disorders (Khantzian, 1985). Heroin addicts are generally considered a more psychiatrically deviant group than cocaine abusers (Rounsaville et al., 1991), but there are higher incidences of drug abuse and alcoholism among the relatives of cocaine abusers than among the relatives of heroin addicts (Rounsaville & Luthar, 1992). These factors influence treatment issues according to the specified drug of abuse and probably also affect the adult's parenting capacities. Moreover, abused drugs differ markedly in their psychological and physiological effects on the user, and these effects, in turn, differentially influence the adult's capacity to respond to a child. Agents such as alcohol, marijuana, heroin, or antianxiety drugs such as Valium tend to depress mood, whereas stimulants such as cocaine or amphetamines increase activity and contribute to a sense of euphoria and elation. In either case, the adult's moment-to-moment responsiveness to children's needs is impaired, but in one case the impairment is toward depression and withdrawal and in the other toward unpredictable activity and impulsivity. Although the distinctions are not absolute, because, for example, chronic cocaine abusers often experience depression and alcoholics may be quite agitated, the child's experience will differ depending on whether or not the parent is predominantly withdrawn or unpredictably agitated. Moreover, as cited earlier, for a proportion of substance-abusing adults, the individual's drug of choice may also in part indirectly reflect different preexisting conditions that the drug use may be intended to self-medicate (Khantzian, 1985; Khantzian & Khantzian, 1984). These conditions such as depressive or anxiety disorders not only carry potential genetic risks for the child but will also surely influence parenting in the domains of affective availability, capacity to foster the child's independence, and the parent's tolerance for the child's aggression.

The social context of the particular abused substance varies markedly, and these factors also indirectly influence parenting. Alcohol, when abused, poses major health and psychological problems, but it is legally available, and its use is more socially acceptable for women and men than cocaine, heroin, or even marijuana abuse, all of which are illegal. Abuse of cocaine far more often involves the user directly or indirectly in criminal activities such as prostitution, theft, or drug dealing (Boyd & Mieczkowski, 1990) and exposes the user, as well as his or her children, to personal and property violence. Because of these activities, cocaine-abusing adults are more likely to be arrested and incarcerated repeatedly, exposing their children to multiple episodes of parental separation and placements usually with different foster families or with other (often substance-abusing) neighbors or relatives (Lawson & Wilson, 1980). Additionally, substance-abusing parents often report feeling more isolated and lonely with few friends or relatives in their neighborhoods or immediate communities whom they identify as supportive and helpful (Tucker, 1979). Feelings of isolation and self-denigration may reflect both premorbid and postmorbid states related to the adult's substance abuse, but, in any case, parents who experience isolation and separateness when their isolation is compounded by the psychological effects of their addiction.

Multiple studies from substance abuse treatment programs also document the high incidence of unemployment and less than a high school education among participating substance-abusing women (Hawley & Disney, 1992). Among this population, the rate of unemployment has been shown as high as 96% (Suffet & Brotman, 1976). The level of violence in substance-abusing families, particularly between women and their spouses or male friends, is markedly high and exposes children to a considerable amount of witnessed violence (Regan et al., 1982). Studies have repeatedly documented the markedly increased occurrence of severe, often multigenerational., impairments in parenting physical and sexual abuse, neglect, abandonment, and foster placement (Black & Mayer, 1980; Lawson & Wilson, 1980; Wasserman & Leventhal, 1993). Neglect and out-of-home placement are extremely common among the children of opiate-using adults. In a sample of heroin-exposed children followed through school age (Wilson, 1989), only family or friends, and 25% have been adopted. By their first birthday, nearly half (48%) of these children as infants were living away from their biological mothers.

There are suprisingly few direct observational studies of parent–child interactions among substance-abusing mothers and their children and most of these have involved adults addicted to alcohol or opiates (Mayes, 1995). In 1985, Lief presented a series of clinical descriptions of interactions between mothers in treatment and their infants and toddlers. Described as points for intervention were the impoverished use of language between substance-abusing mothers and their infants, restriction of exploration that was seen as the infant's "getting into things" (Lief, 1985, p. 76), and a diminished responsiveness to the infant's bids for social interaction. Few studies have systematically investigated the interactive behaviors between substance-abusing mothers and their infants. The measures employed have been quite variable both in the amount of interactive detail studied and in the aspects of interaction considered potentially impaired by substance abuse.

Most studies have reported impairments in a number of interactive domains, although these differences have not always been attributed to substance abuse only. Householder (1980, cited in Hans, 1992), reported on the interactions between opioid-using mothers and their 3-month-old infants, described more physical activity, less emotional involvement with the infant, and less direct gaze toward the infant than non-opioid-using mothers. Opiate-addicted mothers tended either to withdraw completely from the interaction or to be persistently physically intrusive. In a study of 15 mothers in a methadone maintenance clinic compared to 15 non-opiate-addicted women interacting with 2- to 6-year-old children (Bauman & Dougherty, 1983), addicted women were more likely to use a threatening, commanding, or provoking approach to discipline and "to reinforce a disruptive method of attention seeking" (Bauman & Dougherty, 1983, p. 301) in comparison with nonaddicted mothers who relied more on positive reinforcement. The 2- to 6-year-old children of the substance-abusing mothers in that study also were significantly more provocative and complaining with their mothers.

Studies of attachment profiles among prenatally and postnatally substance-exposed children are, to date, few. Goodman (1990, cited in Hans, 1992) studied attachment patterns in 35 methadone-exposed and 46 nonexposed 1-year-old infants. Methadone-exposed infants more often showed disorganized (Group D; Main & Solomon, 1986) or mixed insecure attachment patterns. Similarly, Rodning and colleagues (Rodning, Beckwith, & Howard, 1989, 1991), studying 13-month-old children prenatally exposed to cocaine, phencyclidine (PCP), heroin, or methadone compared with socioeconomic status (SES)-matched preterm children, showed that drug-exposed toddlers were more likely to be insecurely attached to their mothers, whereas most of the non-drug-exposed premature infants were securely attached. In addition, the drug-exposed children showed higher rates of disorganized attachment behaviors. In a similar study of maternal alcohol use (O'Connor et al., 1990, reported in Griffith & Freir, 1992), maternal interactions and maternal prenatal alcohol use significantly predicted infant attachment behaviors at 1 year of age.

Importantly, several studies have emphasized that, although the substance-abusing mothers had apparently more impaired interactions than comparison groups, a number of associated (e.g., comorbid) factors in addition to, or instead of, their substance use seemed to predict poor parenting. Jeremy and Bernstein (1984), reporting on the dyadic interactions of a cohort of 17 methadone-maintained women and their 4-month-old infants compared to 23 non-opiate-using mothers (Bernstein, Jeremy, Hans, & Marcus, 1984; Bernstein, Jeremy, & Marcus, 1986), found that drug use status alone did not significantly predict maternal interactive behavior. Instead, maternal psychological and psychosocial resources, as measured by assessments of maternal IQ and semistructured, diagnostic psychiatric interviews, were more predictive of the quality of the maternal–infant interaction than was drug-use status. Indeed, maternal drug use when analyzed together with other maternal variables was not a significant predictor of mothers' interactive performance. However, coexisting maternal psychopathology contributes to greater impairments in parenting interactions among substance-abusing adults compared with non-substance abusers and with those substance abusers with no coexisting psychiatric disturbance. Hans and colleagues (Hans et al., 1990 reported in Griffith & Freier, 1992) reported that mothers using methadone who were also diagnosed as having antisocial personality disorders were significantly more dysfunctional in their interactions with their 24-month-olds than were methadone-maintained mothers either having no significant psychopathology or affective disorders alone. Moreover, the latter group did not differ in their interactions from drug-free mothers. Findings such as these, albeit from small cohorts, point to the importance of not considering drug use alone as the single determining variable for observed differences in maternal interactive behaviors, but rather as a marker for several predictor variables that are more often associated with substance abuse (Mayes, 1995).

CONCLUSIONS

The field of behavioral and developmental teratology focuses on identifiable effects of prenatal exposure to substances such as alcohol, heroin, marijuana, and cocaine. Children developing amid the violence, substance abuse, poverty, and discord increasingly common in inner-city neighborhoods are at risk for dysfunctional development on a number of accounts. Although specific syndromes such as that associated with maternal alcoholism during pregnancy have been clearly identified, controversy, and conflicting findings still pertain regarding long-term effects of any one of these agents on cognitive and intellectual development. Suggestive findings, particularly with prenatal cocaine exposure, point to impairments in more basic neurodevelopmental domains of attention and arousal regulation, functions that underlie learning and information processing. However, the postnatal substance-abusing environment, both in its more general factors of poverty, homelessness, and violence and in the specific dysfunctions of parenting that accompany substance abuse, almost certainly exacerbate the effects of prenatal substance exposure.

Remediation for the attention and learning impairments described in this review is not specific to the particular prenatal exposure but rather to the profile of developmental delay or impairment. Indeed, there has been considerable discussion and debate about whether or not, for example, cocaine-exposed children need special educational programs tailored specifically to their needs or can already existing special education curricula and teaching approaches be appropriately tailored and revised (e.g., Lesar, 1992; Sinclair, 1998; Smith, 1993). Issues of labeling haunt the first approach and issues of inadequate educational fit are problems for the second. There has been no empirical work regarding different educational approaches for drug-exposed children with special needs though descriptions of model programs are available (e.g., Tanner-Halverson, 1997; Crites, Fischer, McNeish-Stengel, & Clare, 1992). These programs also include early childhood intervention approaches often working with parents and children together (e.g., Kaplan-Sanoff & Leib, 1995; Chapman, Mayfield, Cook, & Chissom, 1995) Similarly, there have been no carefully conducted psychopharmacologic studies of the use of stimulants or other psychoactive drugs for the behavioral and psychiatric–psychological difficulties that are more common among children from substance using homes and with prenatal exposure. Each of these areas is of considerable importance for future work with these populations.

REFERENCES

Abel, E. (1989). *Behavioral teratogenesis and behavioral mutagenesis.* New York: Plenum Press.
Alessandri, S. M., Bendersky, M., & Lewis, M. (1998). Cognitive functioning in 8- to 18-month-old drug-exposed infants. *Developmental Psychology, 34,* 565–573.
Alessandri, S. M., Sullivan, M. W., Imaizumi S., & Lewis, M. (1993). Learning and emotional responsivity in cocaine-exposed infants. *Developmental Psychology, 29,* 989–997.
Amaro, H., Fried, L. E., Cabral, H., & Zuckerman, B. (1990). Violence during pregnancy and substance use. *American Journal of Public Health, 80,* 575–579.
Amaro, H., Zuckerman, B., & Cabral, H. (1989). Drug use among adolescent mothers: Profile of risk. *Pediatrics, 84,* 144–151.

Aronson, M., Kyllerman, M., Sabel, K. G., Sandin, B., & Olegård, R. (1985). Children of alcoholic mothers: Developmental, perceptual, and behavioral characteristics as compared to matched controls. *Acta Paediatrica Scandinavica, 74*, 27–35.

Astley, S. J., & Little, R. E. (1990). Maternal marijuana use during lactation and infant development at one year. *Neurotoxicology Teratology, 12*, 161–168.

Azuma, S., & Chasnoff, I. (1993). Outcome of children prenatally exposed to cocaine and other drugs. A path analysis of three-year data. *Pediatrics, 92*, 396–402.

Babor, T. F., Brown, J., & delBoca, F. K. (1990). Validity of self-reports in applied research on addictive behaviors: Fact or fiction? *Behavioral Assessment, 12*, 5–31.

Baron, R., & Kenny, D. (1986). The moderator-mediator variable distinction in social psychological research: Conceptual, strategic, and statistical considerations. *Journal of Personality and Social Psychology, 51*, 1173–1182.

Bauman, P. S., & Dougherty, F. E. (1983). Drug-addicted mothers' parenting and their children's development. *International Journal of Addiction, 18*, 291–302.

Bauman, P., & Levine, S. A. (1986). The development of children of drug addicts. *International Journal of Addiction, 21*, 849–863.

Bayley, N. (1969). *Manual for the Bayley scales of infant development.* New York: Psychological Corporation.

Bayley, N. (1993). *Manual for the Bayley Scales of Infant Development* (2nd ed.). New York: Psychological Corporation.

Bender, S. L., Word, C. O., DiClemente, R. J., Crittenden, M. R., Persaud, N. A., & Ponton, L. E. (1995). The developmental implications of prenatal and/or postnatal crack cocaine exposure in preschool children: A preliminary report. *Journal of Developmental and Behavioral Pediatrics, 16*, 418–424.

Bernstein, V., Jeremy, R. J., Hans, S. L., & Marcus, J. (1984). A longitudinal study of offspring born to methadone-maintained women. II: Dyadic interaction and infant behavior at four months. *American Journal of Drug and Alcohol Abuse, 10*, 161–193.

Bernstein, V., Jeremy, R. J., & Marcus, J. (1986). Mother-infant interaction in multiproblem families: Finding those at risk. *Journal of the American Academy of Child and Adolescent Psychiatry, 25*, 631–640.

Bingol, N., Fuchs, M., Diaz, V., Stone, R. K., & Gromisch, D. S. (1987). Teratogenicity of cocaine in humans. *Journal of Pediatrics, 110*, 93–96.

Black, R., & Mayer, J. (1980). Parents with special problems: Alcoholism and opiate addiction. *Child Abuse and Neglect, 4*, 45–54.

Blackard, C., & Tennes, K. (1984). Human placental transfer of cannabinoids. *New England Journal of Medicine, 311*, 797.

Bornstein, M. H. (1985). How infant and mother jointly contribute to developing cognitive competence in the child. *Proceedings of the National Academy of Sciences of the United States of America, 85*, 7470–7473.

Bornstein, M. H., & Tamis-LeMonda, C. S. (1990). Activities and interactions of mothers and their firstborn infants in the first six months of life: Covariation, stability, continuity, correspondence, and prediction. *Child Development, 61*, 1206–1217.

Boyd, C. J., & Miecskowski, T. (1990). Drug use, health, family, and social supports in "crack" cocaine users. *Addictive Behaviors, 15*, 481–485.

Brooks-Gunn, J., McCarton, C., & Hawley, T. (1994). Effects of in utero drug exposure on children's development. Review and recommendations. *Archives of Pediatrics and Adolescent Medicine, 148*(1), 33–39.

Callahan, C. M., Grant, T. M., Phipps, P., Clark, G., Novack, A. H., Streissguth, A. P., & Raisys, V. A. (1992). Measurement of gestational cocaine exposure: Sensitivity of infants' hair, meconium, and urine. *Journal of Pediatrics, 120*, 763–768.

Carey, K. (1997). Clinical rating scales for substance abuse. *Psychiatric Services, 48*, 106–107.

Carmichael Olson, H., Grant, T., Martin, J. C., & Streissguth, A. P. (1995). A cohort study of prenatal cocaine exposure: Addressing methodological concerns. In M. Lewis & M. Bendersky (Eds.), *Mothers, babies and cocaine: The role of toxins in development* (pp. 129–162). Hillsdale, NJ: Lawrence Erlbaum Associates.

Carroll, K. M. (1995). Methodological issues and problems in the assessment of substance use. *Psychological Assessment, 7*, 349–358.

Chapman, J. K., Mayfield, P. K., Cook, M. J., & Chissom, B. S. (1995). Service patterns and educational experiences between two groups who work with young children prenatally exposed to cocaine: A study across four states. *Infant-Toddler Intervention, 5*, 31–49.

Chasnoff, I. J., Landress, H. J., & Barrett, M. E. (1990). Prevalence of illicit drugs or alcohol abuse during pregnancy and discrepancies in mandatory reporting in Pinellas County, Florida. *New England Journal of Medicine, 322*, 1202–1206.

Cherukuri, R., Minkoff, H., Feldman, J., Parekh, A., & Glass, L. (1988). A cohort study of alkaloidal cocaine ("crack") in pregnancy. *Obstetrics and Gynecology, 72*, 147–151.

Claren, S. K., & Smith, D. W. (1978). The fetal alcohol syndrome. *New England Journal of Medicine, 298*, 1063–1067.

Coles, C. D., Brown, R. T., Smith, I. E., Platzman, K. A., Erickson, S., & Falek, A. (1991). Effects of prenatal alcohol exposure at school age. I: Physical and cognitive development. *Neurotoxicology and Teratology, 13*, 357–367.

Coles, C. D., Smith, I. E., Lancaster, J. S., & Falek, A. (1987). Persistence over the first months of neurobehavioral differences in infants exposed to alcohol prenatally. *Infant Behavior and Development, 10*, 23–37.

Crites, L. S., Fischer, K. L, McNeish-Stengel, M. S., & Clare, J. (1992). Working with families of drug-exposed children: Three model programs. In L. M. Rossetti (Ed.), *Developmental problems of drug-exposed infants* (pp. 13–23). San Diego, CA: Singular Publishing Group.

Day, N. L. (1992). Effects of prenatal alcohol exposure. In I. S. Zagon & T. A. Slotkin (Eds.), *Maternal substance abuse and the developing nervous system*. San Diego, CA: Academic Press.

Day, N. L., & Richardson, G. A. (1991). Prenatal marijuana use: Epidemiology, methodologic issues, and infant outcome. *Clinics in Perinatology, 18*, 77.

Day, N. L., & Richardson, G. A. (1993). Cocaine use and crack babies: Science, the media, and miscommunication. *Neurotoxicology and Teratology*, 293–294.

Day, N. L., Richardson, G., Goldschmidt, L., Robles, N., Taylor, P., Stoffer, D., Cornelius, M., & Geva, D. (1994). The effect of prenatal marijuana exposure on the cognitive development of offspring at age three. *Neurotoxicology and Teratology, 16*, 169–175.

Desmond, M. M., & Wilson, G. S. (1975). Neonatl abstinence syndrome: Recognition and diagnosis. *Addictive Diseases, 2*, 113–121.

Dow-Edwards, D. (1989). Long-term neurochemical and neurobehavioral consequences of cocaine use during pregnancy. *Annals of the New York Academy of Sciences, 562*, 280–289.

Dow-Edwards, D. (1991). Cocaine effects on fetal development: A comparison of clinical and animal research findings. *Neurotoxicology and Teratology, 13*, 347–352.

Dow-Edwards, D., Freed, L. A., & Milhorat, T. H. (1988). Stimulation of brain metabolism by perinatal cocaine exposure. *Developmental Brain Research, 42*, 137–141.

Ernhart, C. B., Wolf, A. W., Linn, P. L., Sokol, R. J., Kennard, M. J., & Filipovich, H. F. (1985). Alcohol-related birth defects: syndromal anomalies, intrauterine growth retardation, and neonatal behavioral assessment. *Alcoholism: Clinical & Experimental Research, 9*, 447–453.

Farrar, H. C., & Kearns, G. L. (1989). Cocaine: Clinical pharmacology and toxicology. *Journal of Pediatrics, 115*, 665–675.

Fendrick, M., Warner, V., & Weisman, M. (1990). Family risk factors, parental depression, and psychopathology in offspring. *Developmental Psychology, 26*, 40–50.

Field, T. M. (1995). Psychologically depressed parents. In M. H. Bornstein (Ed.), *Handbook of parenting. Vol III: Status and social conditions of parenting*. Hillsdale, NJ: Lawrence Erlbaum Associates.

Finnegan, L. P. (1976). Clinical effects of pharmacologic agents on pregnancy, the fetus, and the neonate. *Annals of the New York Academy of Sciences, 281*, 74–89.

Finnegan, L. P. (1979). In utero opiate dependence and sudden infant death syndrome. *Clinics in Perinatology, 6*, 163–180.

Frank, D. A., Augustyn, M., & Zuckerman, B. (1998). Neonatal neurobehavioral and neuroanatomic correlates of prenatal cocaine exposure. Problems of dose and confounding. *Annals of the New York Academy of Science, 846*, 40–50.

Frank, D. A., Bresnahan, K., & Zuckerman, B. S. (1993). Maternal cocaine use: Impact on child health and development. *Advanced Pediatrics, 40*, 65–99.

Frank, D. A., Zuckerman, B. S., Amaro, H., Aboagye, K., Bauchner, H., Cabral, H., Fried, L., Hingson, R., Kayne, H., Levenson, S. M., Parker, S., Reece, H., & Vinci, K. (1988). Cocaine use during pregnancy: Prevalence and correlates. *Pediatrics, 82*, 888–895.

Fried, P. A. (1980). Marijuana use by pregnant women: Neurobehavioral effects in neonates. *Drug and Alcohol Dependence, 6*, 415–424.

Fried, P. A. (1982). Marijuana use by pregnant women and effects on offspring: An update. *Neurobehavioral Toxicology & Teratology, 4*, 451–454.

Fried, P. A., Buckingham, M., & Von Kulmitz, P. (1983). Marijuana use during pregnancy and perinatal risk factor. *American Journal of Obstetrics and Gynecology, 144*, 922–924.

Fried, P. A., Innes, K. S., & Barnes, M. V. (1984). Soft use prior to and during preganancy: A comparison of samples over a four year period. *Drug and Alcohol Dependence, 13*, 161–176.

Fried, P. A., & Makin, J. E. (1987). Neonatal behavioral correlates of prenatal exposure to marijuana, cigarettes, and alcohol in a low-risk population. *Neurotoxicology and Teratology, 9*, 1–7.

Fried, P. A., & Watkinson, B. (1988). 12- and 24-month nerobehavioral follow-up of children prenatally exposed to marijuana, cigarettes, and alcohol. *Neurotoxicology and Teratology, 10*, 305–313.

Fried, P. A., & Watkinson, B. (1990). 36-and 48-month neurobehavioral follow-up of children prenatally exposed to marijuana, cigarettes, and alcohol. *Journal of Developmental and Behavioral Pediatrics, 11*, 49–58.

Fulroth, R., Phillips, B., & Durand, D. J. (1989). Perinatal outcome of infants exposed to cocaine and/or heroin in utero. *American Journal of Diseases of Children, 143*, 905–910.

Gawin, F. H., & Ellinwood, F. H. (1988). Cocaine and other stimulants. *New England Journal of Medicine, 318*, 1173–1182.

Goeders, N. E., & Smith, J. E. (1983). Cortial dopaminergic involvement in cocaine reinforcement. *Science, 221*, 773–775.

Goodlet, C. R., & West, J. R. (1992). Alcohol exposure during brain growth spurt. In I. S. Zagon & T. A. Slotkin (Eds.), *Maternal substance abuse and the developing nervous system* (pp. 45–75). San Diego, CA: Academic Press.

Goodman, G. (1990). *Identifying attachment patterns and their antecedents among opioid-exposed 12-month-old infants.* Unpublished doctoral dissertation, Northwestern University Medical School, Chicago, IL.

Graham, K., Feigenbaum, A., Pastuszak, A., Nulman, I., Weksberg, R., Einarson, T., Goldberg, S., Ashby, S., & Koren, G. (1992). Pregnancy outcome and infant development following gestational cocaine use by social cocaine users in Toronto, Canada. *Clinical and Investigative Medicine, 15*, 384–394.

Graham, K., Koren, G., Klein, J., Schneiderman, J., & Greenwald, M. (1989). Determination of gestational cocaine exposure by hair analysis. *Journal of the American Medical Association, 262*, 3328–3330.

Griffith, D. R., Azuma, S., & Chasnoff, I. (1994). Three-year outcome of children exposed prenatally to drugs. *Journal of the American Academy of Child and Adolescent Psychiatry, 33*, 20–27.

Griffith, D. R., & Freier, C. (1992). Methodological issues in the assessment of the mother-child interactions of substance-abusing women and their children. In M. M. Kilbey & K. Asghar (Eds.), *Methodological issues in epidemiological, prevention, and treatment research on drug-*

exposed women and their children. Rockville, MD, National Institute on Drug Abuse, Research Monograph, *117*, 228–247.

Grissom, G. (1997). Treatment outcomes in inpatient and substance abuse programs. *Psychiatric Annals, 27*, 113–118.

Gusella, J., & Fried, P. (1984). Effects of maternal social drinking and smoking on offspring at 13 months. *Neurobehavioral Toxicology & Teratology, 6*, 13–17.

Hadeed, A. J., & Siegel, S. R. (1989). Maternal cocaine use during pregnancy: Effect on the newborn infant. *Pediatrics, 84*, 205–210.

Hadfield, M. G., & Nugent, E. A. (1983). Cocaine: Comparative effect on dopamine uptake in extrapyramidal and limbic systems. *Biochemical Pharmacology, 32*, 744–746.

Hans, S. L. (1989). Developmental consequences of prenatal exposure to methadone. *Annals of the New York Academcy of Science, 562*, 195–207.

Hans, S. L. (1992). Maternal opioid use and child development. In I. S. Zagon & T. A. Slotkin (Eds.), *Maternal substance abuse and the developing nervous system* (pp. 177–214). San Diego, CA: Academic Press.

Hans, S. L., & Jeremy, R. J. (1984). Post-neonatal motoric signs in infants exposed in utero to methadone. *Infant Behavior and Development, 7*, 158.

Hans, S. L., & Marcus, J. (1983). Motor and attentional behavior in infants of methadone maintained women. *National Institute on Drug Abuse Research Monogram, 43*, 287–293.

Hans, S. L., Marcus, J., Jeremy, R. J., et al. (1984). Neurobehavioral development of children exposed in utero to opioid drugs. In J. Yanai (Ed.), *Neurobehavioral teratology* (pp. 249–273). New York: Elsevier.

Harclerode, J. (1980). The effect of marijuana on reproduction and development. *National Institute on Drug Abuse Research Monograph, 31*, .

Hawley, T. L., & Disney, E. R. (1992). Crack's children: The consequences of maternal cocaine abuse. *Social Policy Report of the Society for Research in Child Development, 6*(4), 1–22.

Heath, D. B. (1991). Women and alcohol: Cross-cultural perspectives. *Journal of Substance Abuse, 3*, 175–185.

Hingson, R., Alpert, J. J., Day, N., Dooling, E., Kayne, H., Morelock, S., Oppenheimer, E., & Zuckerman, B. (1989). Effects of maternal drinking and marijuana use on fetal growth and development. *Pediatrics, 70*, 539–542.

Hurt, H., Brodsky, N., Betancourt, L., Braitman, L., Malmud, E., & Giannetta, J. (1995). Cocaine-exposed children: Follow-up through 30 months. *Journal of Developmental and Behavioral Pediatrics, 16*, 29–35.

Hurt, H., Malmud, E., Betancourt, L., Braitman, L., Brodsky, N., & Giannetta, J. (1997). Children with in utero cocaine exposure do not differ from control subjects on intelligence testing. *Archives of Pediatric and Adolescent Medicine, 151*, 1237–1241.

Hurt, H., Malmud, E., Betancourt, L., Brodsky, N., & Giannetta, J. (1997). A prospective evaluation of early language development in children with in utero cocaine exposure and in control subjects. *Journal of Pediatrics, 130*, 310–312.

Hutchings, D. E. (1993). The puzzle of cocaine's effects following maternal use during pregnancy: Are there reconcilable differences? *Neurotoxicology and Teratology, 15*, 281–286.

Isenberg, S. J., Spierer, A., & Inkelis, S. H. (1987). Ocular signs of cocaine intoxication in neonates. *American Journal of Ophthalmology, 103*, 211–214.

Jacobson, J., Jacobson, S., Sokol, R., Nartier, S., & Chiado, L. (1996). New evidence for neurobehavioral effects of in utero cocaine exposure. *Journal of Pediatrics, 129*, 581–590.

Jeremy, R. J., & Bernstein, V. (1984). Dyads at risk: Methadone-maintained women and their four-month-old infants. *Child Development, 5*, 1141–1154.

Jeremy, R. J., & Hans, S. L. (1985). Behavior of neonates exposed in utero to methadone as assessed on the Brazelton scale. *Infant Behavior and Development, 8*, 323–336.

Jones, K. L., & Smith, D. W. (1973). Recognition of the fetal alcohol syndrome in early infancy. *Lancet, 2*, 999–1001.

Jones, K. L., Smith, D. W., Ulleland, C. N., & Streissguth, A. P. (1973). Pattern of malformation in the offspring of chronic alcoholic mothers. *Lancet, 1*, 1267–1271.

Kaltenbach, K., & Finnegan, L. P. (1987). Perinatal and developmental outcome of infants exposed to methadone in-utero. *Neurotoxicology & Teratology, 9*, 311–3.

Kaplan-Sanoff, M., & Leib, S. A. (1995). Model intervention programs for mothers and children impacted by substance abuse. *School Psychology Review, 24*, 186–199.

Karmel, B. Z., & Gardner, J. M. (1996). Prenatal cocaine exposure effects on arousal-modulated attention during the neonatal period. *Developmental Psychobiology, 29*, 463–480.

Khantzian, E. J. (1983). An extreme case of cocaine dependence and marked improvement with methylphenidate treatment. *American Journal of Psychiatry, 140*, 784–785.

Khantzian, E. J. (1985). The self-medication hypothesis of addictive disorders: Focus on heroin and cocaine dependence. *American Journal of Psychiatry, 142*, 1259–1264.

Khantzian, E. J., & Khantzian, N. J. (1984). Cocaine addiction: Is there a psychological predisposition. *Psychiatric Annals, 14*, 753–759.

King, T. A., Perlman, J. R., Laptook, A. R., Rollins, N., Jackson, G., & Little, B. (1995). Neurologic manifestations of in utero cocaine exposure in near-term and term infants. *Pediatrics, 96*, 259–264.

Kjarasch, S. J., Glotzer, D., Vinci, R., Wietzman, M., & Sargent, T. (1991). Unsuspected cocaine exposure in children. *American Journal of Diseases of Children, 145*, 204–206.

Kline, J., Ng, S., Schittini, M., Levin, B., & Susser, M. (1997). Cocaine use during pregnancy: Sensitive detection by hair assay. *American Journal of Public Health, 87*, 352–358.

Kosofsky, B. E., & Wilkins, A. S. (1998). A mouse model of transplacental cocaine exposure. Clinical implications for exposed infants and children. In J. Harvey & B. E. Kosofsky (Eds.), *Cocaine: Effects on the developing brain* (pp. 248–261). New York: New York Academy of Sciences.

Kruez, D., & Axelrod, J. (1973). Delta-9-tetrahydrocannabinol: Localization in body fat. *Science, 179*, 391–393.

Lauder, J. M. (1988). Neurotransmitters as morphogens. *Progress in Brain Research, 73*, 365–387.

Lauder, J. M. (1991). Neuroteratology of cocaine: Relationship to developing monamine systems, *National Institute on Drug Abuse Research Monograph, 114*, 233–247.

Lawson, M., & Wilson, G. (1980). Parenting among women addicted to narcotics. *Child Welfare, 59*, 67–79.

Lesar, S. (1992). Prenatal cocaine exposure: The challenge to education. In L. M. Rossetti (Ed.), *Developmental problems of drug-exposed infants* (pp. 37–52). San Diego, CA: Singular Publishing Group.

Lester, B. M., Freier, K., & LaGasse, L. (1995). Prenatal cocaine exposure and child outcome: What do we really know? In M. Lewis & M. Bendersky (Eds.), *Mothers, babies, and cocaine: The role of toxins in development* (pp. 19–40). Hillsdale, NJ: Lawrence Erlbaum Associates.

Levy, M., & Koren, G. (1992). Clinical toxicology of the neonate. *Seminars in Perinatology, 16*, 63–75.

Lief, N. R. (1985). The drug user as parent. *International Journal of the Addictions, 20*, 63–97.

Lindenberg, C. S., Alexander, E. M., Gendrop, S. C., Nencioli, M., & Williams, D. G. (1991). A review of the literature on cocaine abuse in pregnancy. *Nursing Research, 40*, 69–75.

Lustbader, A. S., Mayes, L. C., McGee, B. A., Jatlow, P., & Roberts, W. L. B. (1998). Incidence of passive exposure to crack/cocaine and clinical findings in infants seen in an outpatient service. *Pediatrics, 102*(1), e5.

MacGregor, S. N., Keith, L. G., Chasnoff, I. J., Rosner, M. A., Chisum, G. M., Shaw, F., & Minogue, J. P. (1987). Cocaine use during pregnancy: Adverse perinatal outcome. *American Journal of Obstetrics and Gynecology, 157*, 686–690.

Main, M., & Solomon, J. (1986). Discovery of an insecure-disorganized/disoriented attachment pattern. In T. B. Brazelton & M. Yogman (Eds.), *Affective development in infancy* (pp. 95–124). Norwood, NJ: Ablex.

Marcus, J., & Hans, S. L. (1982). Electromyographic assessment of neonatal muscle tone. *Psychiatric Research, 6*, 31–40.

Mattson, M. P. (1988). Neurotransmitters in the regulation of neuronal cytoarchitecture. *Brain Research Review, 13*, 179–212.

Mayes, L. C. (1992). Prenatal cocaine exposure and young children's development. *Annals of the American Academy of Politics & Social Science Journal, 521*, 11–27.

Mayes, L. C. (1995). Substance abuse and parenting. In M. Bornstein (Ed.), *The handbook of parenting* (pp. 101–125). Hillsdale, NJ: Lawrence Erlbaum Associates.

Mayes, L. C. (1999). Developing brain and in-utero cocaine exposure: Effects on neural ontogeny. *Development and Psychopathology, 11*, 685–714.

Mayes, L. C., & Bornstein, M. H. (1995). Developmental dilemmas for cocaine-abusing parents and their children. In M. Lewis & M. Bendersky (Eds.), *Mothers, babies and cocaine: The role of toxins in development* (pp. 251–272). Hillsdale, NJ: Erlbaum Associates.

Mayes, L. C., & Bornstein, M. H. (1996). The context of development for young children from cocaine-abusing families. In P. Kato & T. Mann (Eds.), *Handbook of diversity issues in health psychology* (pp. 69–95). New York: Plenum.

Mayes, L. C., Bornstein, M. H., Chawarska, K., & Granger, R. H. (1996). Regulation of arousal in infants exposed prenatally to cocaine. *Development and Psychopathology, 8*, 29–42.

Mayes, L. C., Bornstein, M., Chawarska, K., & Granger, R. H. (1995). Information processing and developmental assessments in three-month-old infants exposed prenatally to cocaine. *Pediatrics, 95*, 539–545.

Mayes, L. C., & Granger, R. H. (1995). Teratologic and developmental effects of prenatal drug exposure: Alcohol, heroin, marijuana, and cocaine. In M. Lewis (Ed.), *A comprehensive textbook of child and adolescent psychiatry* (pp. 374–382). Philadelphia, PA: Williams and Wilkins.

Mayes, L. C., Granger, R. H., Bornstein, M. H., & Zuckerman, B. (1992). The problem of prenatal cocaine exposure: A rush to judgment. *Journal of the American Medical Association, 267*, 406–408.

Mayes, L. C., Grillon, C., Granger, R., & Schottenfeld, R. (1998). Regulation of arousal and attention in preschool children exposed to cocaine. In J. A. Harvey & B. E. Kosofsky (Eds.), *Cocaine: Effects on the developing brain* (pp. 126–143). New York: New York Academy of Sciences.

Moore, T. R., Sorg, J., Miller, L., et al. (1986). Hemodynamic effects of intravenous cocaine on the pregnant ewe and fetus. *American Journal of Obstetrics and Gynecology, 155*, 883–888.

Morris, P., Binienda, Z., Gillam, M. P., Harkey, M. R., et al. (1996). The effect of chronic cocaine exposure during pregnancy on maternal and infant outcomes in the rhesus monkey *Neurotoxicology and Teratology, 18*, 147–154.

Nahas, G. (1976). *Marijuana: Chemistry, biochemistry, and cellular effects.* New York: Springer-Verlag.

Neuspiel, D. R. (1995). The problem of confounding in research on prenatal cocaine effects on behavior and development. In M. Lewis & M. Bendersky (Eds.), *Mothers, babies, and cocaine: The role of toxins in development* (pp. 95–110). Hillsdale, NJ: Lawrence Erlbaum Associates.

O'Connell, C. M., & Fried, P. A. (1984). An investigation of prenatal cannabis exposure and minor physical anomalies in a low risk population. *Neurobehavioral Toxicology and Teratology, 6*, 345–350.

O'Connor, M. J., Brill, N., & Sigman, M. (1986). Alcohol use in elderly primips: Relation to infant development. *Pediatrics, 78*, 444–450.

O'Connor, M. J., Kasari, C., & Sigman, M. (1992). *The influence of mother-infant interaction on attachment behavior of infants exposed to alcohol prenatally.* Paper presented at the Seventh International Conference on Infant Studies, Montreal.

O'Malley, S., Adamse, M., Heaton, R. K., & Gawin, F. H. (1992). Neuropsychological impairment in chronic cocaine abuse. *American Journal of Drug and Alcohol Abuse, 18*, 131–144.

Oloffson, M., Buckley, W., & Andersen, G. E. (1983). Investigation of 89 children born by drug-dependent mothers: Follow-up 1–19 years after birth. *Acta Paediatrica Scandinavica, 72*, 407–410.

Oro, A. S., & Dixon, S. D. (1987). Perinatal cocaine and methamphetamine exposure: Maternal and neonatal correlates. *Journal of Pediatrics, 111*, 571–578.

Osterloh, J. D., & Lee, B. L. (1989). Urine drug screening in mothers and newborns. *American Journal of Diseases of Children, 143*, 791–793.

Ostrea, E. M. (1995). Meconium drug analysis. In M. Lewis & M. Bendersky (Eds.), *Mothers, babies and cocaine: The role of toxins in development* (pp. 179–202). Hillsdale, NJ: Lawrence Erlbaum Associates.

Perez-Reyes, M., & Wall, M. E. (1982). Presence of 8^9-tetrahdrocannabinol in human milk. *New England Journal of Medicine, 307*, 819–820.

Qazi, Q. H., Mariano, E., Beller, E., Millman, D., & Crombleholme, W. (1982). Is marijuana smoking terotoxic? *Pediatric Research, 16* (272A).

Regan, D. O., Leifer, B., & Finnegan, L. P. (1984). Depression, self-concept, and violent experience in drug abusing women and their influence upon parenting effectiveness. *NIDA Research Monograph, 49*, 332.

Richardson, G. (1998). Prenatal cocaine exposure: A longitudinal study of development. In J. Harvey & B. Kosofsky (Eds.), *Cocaine: Effects on the developing brain.* New York: Annals of the New York Academy of Sciences.

Richardson, G., Conroy, M., & Day, N. (1996). Prenatal cocaine exposure: Effects on the development of school-age children. *Neurotoxicology & Teratology, 18*, 627–634.

Richardson, G., & Day, N. (1994). Detrimental effects of prenatal cocaine exposure: Illusion or reality? *Journal of the American Academy of Child and Adolescent Psychiatry, 33*, 28–34.

Richardson, G., Day, N., & Goldschmidt, L. A. (1995). *Longitudinal study of prenatal cocaine exposure: Infant development at 12 months.* Paper presented at SRCD Annual Meeting, Indianapolis, Indiana.

Richardson, G., Day, M., & McGauhey, P. (1993). The impact of prenatal marijuana and cocaine use on the infant and child. *Clinical Obstetrics and Gynecology, 36*, 302–318.

Richie, J. M., & Greene, N. M. (1985). Local anesthetics. In A. G. Gilman, L. S. Goodman, T. N. Rall, & F. Murad (Eds.), *The pharmacologic basis of therapeutics* (7th ed., pp. 309–310). New York: Macmillan.

Rodning, C., Beckwith, L., & Howard, J. (1989). Characteristics of attachment organization and play organization in prenatally drug-exposed toddlers. *Development and Psychopathology, 1*, 277–289.

Rodning, C., Beckwith, L., & Howard, J. (1991). Quality of attachment and home environments in children prenatally exposed to PCP and cocaine. *Development and Psychopathology, 3*, 351–366.

Rogers, R., & Kelly, K. S. (1997). Denial and misreporting of substance abuse. In R. Rogers (Ed.), *Clinical assessment of malingering and deception* (pp. 108–129). New York: Guilford Press.

Rosen, T. S., & Johnson, H. L. (1982). Children of methadone-maintained mothers: Follow-up to 18 months of age. *Journal of Pediatrics, 101*, 192–196.

Rosen, T. S., & Johnson, H. L. (1988). Drug-addicted mothers, their infants, and SIDS. *Annals of the New York Academy of Sciences, 533*, 89–95.

Rosett, H. L., Weiner, L., & Lee, A., Zuckerman, B., Dooling, E., & Oppenheimer, D. (1983). Patterns of alcohol consumption and fetal development. *Obstetrics and Gynecology, 61*, 539–546.

Rounsaville, B. J., Anton, S. F., Carroll, K., Budde, D., Prusoff, B. A., & Gawin, F. (1991). Psychiatric disorders of treatment-seeking cocaine abusers. *Archives of General Psychiatry, 48*, 43–51.

Rounsaville, B. J., & Luthar, S. S. (1992). Family/genetic studies of cocaine abusers and opioid addicts. In T. R. Kosten & H. D. Kleber (Eds.), *Clinician's guide to cocaine addiction* (pp. 206–221). New York: Guilford Press.

Rounsaville, B. J., Weissman, M. M., Wilber, C. H., & Kleber, H. D. (1982). Pathways of opiate addiction: An evaluation of differing antecedents. *British Journal of Psychiatry, 141*, 437–466.

Ryan, L., Ehrlich, S., & Finnegan, L. (1987). Cocaine abuse in pregnancy: Effects on the fetus and newborn. *Neurotoxicology and Teratology, 9*, 295–299.

Sandberg, D. E., Meyer-Bahlburg, H. F. L., Rosen, T. S., & Johnson, H. L. (1990). Effects of prenatal methadone exposure on sex-dimorphic behavior in early school-age children. *Psychoneuroendocrinology, 15*, 77–82.

Schenker, S., Becker, H. C., Randall, C. L., Phillips, D. K., Baskin, G. S., & Henderson, G. I. (1990). Fetal alcohol syndrome: Current status of pathogensis. *Alcoholism: Clinical and Experimental Research, 14*, 635–647.

Scher, M. S., Richardson, G. A., Coble, P. A., Day, N. L., & Stoffer, D. S. (1988). The effects of prenatal alcohol and marijuana exposure: Disturbances in neonatal sleep cycling and arousal. *Pediatric Research, 24*, 101–105.

Shepherd, G. M. (1988). *Neurobiology* (2nd ed.). New York: Oxford University Press.

Sinclair, E. (1998). Head Start children at risk: Relationship of prenatal drug use exposure to identification of special needs and subsequent special education kindergarten placement. *Behavioral Disorders, 23*, 125–133.

Singer, L., Arendt, R., Farkas, K., Minnes, S., Huang, J., & Yamashita, T. (1997). Relationship of prenatal cocaine exposure and maternal postpartum psychological distress to child developmental outcome. *Development and Psychopathology, 9*, 473–489.

Smith, D. W. (1982). *Recognizable patterns of human malformation: Genetic, embryologic, and clinical aspects* (3rd ed.). Philadelphia: Saunders.

Smith, G. H. (1993). Intervention strategies for children vulnerable for school failure due to exposure to drugs and alcohol. *International Journal of the Addictions, 28*, 1435–1470.

Smith, I. E., Coles, C. D., Lancaster, J. (1986). The effect of volume and duration of prenatal ethanol exposure on neonatal physical and behavioral development. *Neurobehavioral Toxicology & Teratology, 8*, 375–381.

Sokol, R. J., Miller, S., & Reed, G. (1980). Alcohol abuse during pregnancy: An epidemiological study. *Alcoholism: Clinical and Experimental Research, 4*, 135–145.

Sowder, B. J., & Burt, M. R. (1980). *Children of heroin adddicts: An assessment of health, learning, behavioral, and adjustment problems.* New York: Praeger.

Spear, L. (1993). Missing pieces of the puzzle complicate conclusions about cocaine's neurobehavioral toxicity in clinical populations: Importance of animal models. *Neurotoxicology and Teratology, 15*, 307–309.

Spear, L. (1995). Neurobehavioral consequences of gestational cocaine exposure: A comparative analysis. In C. Rovee-Collier & L. Lipsitt (Eds.), *Advances in infancy research* (pp. 56–102). Norwood, NJ: Ablex.

Spear, L. P., Campbell, J., Snyder, K., Silveri, M., & Katovic, N. (1998). Animal behavioral models. Increased sensitivity to stressors and other environmental experiences after prenatal cocaine exposure. *Annals of the New York Academy of Science, 846*, 76–88.

Stanton, M., & Spear, L. (1990). Workshop on the qualitative and quantitative comparability of human and animal developmental neurotoxicity, Work Group I report: Comparability of measures of developmental neurotoxicity in humans and laboratory animals. *Neurotoxicology and Teratology, 12*, 261–267.

Steinhausen, H. C., Nestler, V., & Spohr, H. L. (1982). Development and psychopathology of children with the fetal alcohol syndrome. *Developmental and Behavioral Pediatrics, 3*, 49–54.

Strauss, M. E., Starr, R. H., Ostrea, E. M., Jr., Chavez, C. J., & Stryker, J. C. (1976). Behavioral concomitants of prenatal addiction to narcotics. *Journal of Pediatrics, 89*, 842–846.

Streissguth, A. P. (1976). Psychologic handicaps in children with fetal alcohol syndrome. *Annals of the New York Academy of Science, 273*, 140–145.

Streissguth, A. P. (1992). Fetal alcohol syndrome and fetal alcohol effects: A clinical perspective on later developmental consequences. In I. S. Zagon & T. A. Slotkin (Eds.), *Maternal substance abuse and the developing nervous system* (pp. 5–26). Boston: Academic Press.

Streissguth, A. P., Aase, J. M., Clarren, S. K., Randels, S. P., LaDue, R. A., & Smith, D. F. (1991). Fetal alcohol syndrome in adolescents and adults. *Journal of the American Medical Association, 265*, 1961–1967.

Streissguth, A. P., Barr, H. M., Sampson, P. D., & Darby, B. L. (1990). IQ at age 4 in relation to maternal alcohol use and smoking during pregnancy. *Developmental Psychology, 25*, 3–11.

Streissguth, A. P., Bookstein, F. L., Sampson, P. D., & Barr, H. M. (1989). Neurobehavioral effects of prenatal alcohol: Part III. PLS analyses of neuropsychologic tests. *Neurotoxicology & Teratology, 11*(5), 493–507.

Suffet, F., & Brotman, R. (1976). Employment and social disability among opiate addicts. *American Journal of Drug and Alcohol Abuse, 3*, 387–395.

Swann, A. C. (1990). Cocaine: Synaptic effects and adaptations. In N. D. Volkow & A. C. Swann (Eds.), *Cocaine in the brain* (pp. 58–94). New Brunswick, NJ: Rutgers University Press.

Tamis-LeMonda, C. S., & Bornstein, M. H. (1989). Habitation and maternal encouragement of attention in infancy as predictors of toddler language, play, and representation competence. *Child Development, 60*, 738–751.

Tanner-Halverson, P. (1997). A demonstration classroom for young children with FAS. In A. Streissguth & K. Jonathan (Eds.), *The challenge of fetal alcohol syndrome: Overcoming secondary disabilities* (pp. 78–88). Seattle: University of Washington Press.

Teske, M. P., & Trese, M. T. (1987). Retinopathy of prematurity-like fundus and persistent hyperplastic primary vitreous associated with maternal cocaine use. *American Journal of Ophthalmology, 103*, 719–720.

Tronick, E. Z., Frank, D. A., Cabral, H., Mirochnick, M., & Zuckerman, B. (1996). Late dose-response effects of prenatal cocaine exposure on newborn neurobehavioral performance. *Pediatrics, 98*(1), 76–83.

Tucker, M. B. (1979). A descriptive and comparative analysis of the social support structure of heroin addicted women. *Addicted women: Family dynamics, self-perceptions, and support systems* (pp. 37–76). Washington, DC: National Institute of Drug Abuse, Superintendent of Documents, U.S. Government Printing Office.

Vorhees, C. (1989). Concepts in teratology and developmental toxicology derived from animal research. In D. Hutchings (Ed.), *Prenatal abuse of licit and illicit drugs: Annals of the New York Academy of Sciences, 562*, 31–41.

Ward, O. B., Kopertowski, D. M., Finnegan, L. P., & Sandberg, D. E. (1989). Gender-identity variations in boys prenatally exposed to opiates. *Annals of the New York Academy of Sciences, 562*, 365–366.

Ward, O. B., Orth, T. M., & Weisz, J. (1983). A possible role of opiates in modifying sexual differentiation. *Monographs in Neural Sciences, 9*, 194–200.

Wasserman, D. R., & Leventhal, J. M. (1993). Maltreatment of children born to cocaine-dependent mothers. *American Journal of Diseases of Children, 147*, 1324–1328.

Watt, J. (1990). Interaction, intervention, and development in small for gestational age infants. *Infant Behavior and Development, 13*, 273–286.

Watt, J. E., & Strongman, K. T. (1985). The organization and stability of sleep stages in fullterm, preterm, and small-for-gestational age infants: A comparative study. *Developmental Psychobiology, 18*, 151–162.

Weiss, R. D., Najavits, L. M., Greenfield, S. F., Soto, J. A., Shaw, S. R., & Wyner, D. (1998). Validity of substance use self-reports in dually diagnosed outpatients. *American Journal of Psychiatry, 155*, 127–128.

Wilson, G. S. (1989). Clinical studies of infants and children exposed prenatally to heroin. *Annals of the New York Academy of Sciences, 562*, 183–194.

Wilson, G. S., Desmond, M. M., & Wait, R. B. (1981). Follow-up of methadone-treated and untreated narcotic-dependent women and their infants: Health, development, and social implications. *Journal of Pediatrics, 98*, 716–722.

Wilson, G. S., McCreary, R., Kean, J., & Baxter, J. (1979). The development of preschool children of heroin-addicted mothers: A controlled study. *Pediatrics, 63*, 135–141.

Wise, R. A. (1984). Neural mechanisms of the reinforcing action of cocaine. *National Institute of Drug Abuse Research Monogram, 50*, 15–33.

Woods, J. R., Plessinger, M. A., & Clark, K. E. (1987). Effect of cocaine on uterine blood flow and fetal oxygenation. *Journal of the American Medical Association, 257*, 957–961.

Wu, T., Tashkin, D., Djahed, B., & Rose, J. E. (1988). Pulmonary hazards of smoking marijuana as compared to tobacco. *New England Journal of Medicine, 318*, 347–351.

Zagon, I. S., & McLaughlin, P. (1984). An overview of the neurobehavioral sequelae of perinatal opioid exposure. In J. Yanai (Ed.), *Neurobehavioral teratology* (pp. 197–233). Amsterdam, Elsevier.

Zuckerman, B. (1988). Marijuana and cigarette smoking during pregnancy: Neonatal effects. In I. Chasnoff (Ed.), *Drugs, alcohol, pregnancy and parenting* (pp. 73–89). London: Kluwer.

Zuckerman, B., & Frank, D. A. (1992). Prenatal cocaine and marijuana exposure: Research and clinical implications. In I. S. Zagon & T. A. Slotkin (Eds.), *Maternal substance abuse and the developing nervous system* (pp. 125–154). Boston, MA: Academic Press.

Zuckerman, B., Frank, D. A., Hingson, R., Amaro, H., Levenson, S., Kayne, H., Parker, S., Vinci, R., Aboagye, K., Fried, L. E., Cabral, H., Timperi, R., & Bauchner, H. (1989). Effects of maternal marijuana and cocaine use on fetal growth. *New England Journal of Medicine, 320*, 762–768.

8

The Impact of Infectious Disease on Cognitive Development

Katherine J. Alcock
Donald A. P. Bundy
University of Oxford, England

Infectious diseases are among the commonest of biological insults or disease states, particularly in children. All of us are continuously exposed to infectious diseases, and are at risk of infection. This is true both In the poorest communities of low income countries, where malaria and parasitic infections are endemic, and in the richest countries where we continue to experience pandemics of colds and influenza, epidemics of meningitis and our preschool children experience chronic and repeated middle ear infections.

Children can be even more vulnerable to infection because of transmission from mother to infant at the time of birth, or by breastfeeding, and they may be more vulnerable to factors affecting neurocognitive functioning because of the differing vulnerability of an infant or young child's nervous system. Research into the effects of brain injury appears to show that a younger child can withstand an injury or impact to the central nervous system (CNS) better than an older child or an adult (Kolb & Wishaw, 1990); however other studies suggest that some effects are more pronounced in infants and young children, due either to increased vulnerability of the nervous system during development, or to disruption of cognitive development during a "critical period" (a period during which a particular ability must develop, or it will never do so; see Spreen, Risser, & Edgell, 1995).

Maternal infection is an important field of study in its own right. Several diseases have been shown to cause severe mental retardation when the mother is infected while pregnant, including rubella, syphilis, and cytomegalovirus (Gentile, Boll, Stagno, & Pass, 1989). These diseases are not considered in this review, which instead focuses on infection in the infant and childhood diseases that may cause deficits in cognitive development.

In many studies of cognitive and neural development, some aspects of development that may be considered part of neurological function (e.g., the development of motor skills) are included under the umbrella of "cognitive development." Although strictly these should be excluded from a review concentrating on purely cognitive abilities, where neurological or neuromotor aspects of development are relevant to the topic at hand, or help to elucidate the types of functions that may be affected by a particular disease, they are considered.

The importance of infectious disease for physical development is widely recognized and there have been several efforts to quantify the health burden that these diseases present (e.g., World Bank, 1993). But the impact on cognitive development of the world's children has yet to be effectively quantified. This impact arises in part through constraints on early child development; infection in preschool children and infants can constrain developmental milestones and inhibit readiness to learn (Young, 1997). Infection at school age can prevent children from attending school or can constrain their ability to learn while in school (Bundy, 1996; Partnership for Child Development, 1997; Pollitt, 1990). Such effects are important in any society, but for the child in the poorest society, infection at school age may prevent the child from taking advantage of what may be the only opportunity to receive formal education in his or her lifetime. If infectious disease is important for cognition and learning, then it would be difficult to overstate the importance for human development both at the individual level and in terms of the development of society.

Prior Research on Effects on Cognitive Functioning

The effects of infectious diseases on cognitive functioning and development have, however, received proportionally little research interest. There may be several reasons for this. Smith, Tyrrell, Coyle, and William (1987) suggested that one commonly held view is that there is little point in investigating the effect of infectious disease on cognitive functioning because, by definition, if you are ill you cannot be functioning properly. In addition, it is often assumed that all illnesses will make the patient perform equally badly on all aspects of cognitive functioning. This assumption implies that illnesses do not differ and, hence, if it has been shown that one illness can cause a problem with cognitive development, there is little point in investigating any other diseases. This assumption holds true particularly for diseases directly affecting the brain and meninges, such as encephalitis, meningitis, and cerebral malaria.

Conversely, because so many infectious diseases are either common or "minor," or both, it is assumed that they cannot have an effect on cognitive functioning or development (Smith et al., 1987). This assumption of little or no effect is often held for diseases that are widespread and not life threatening, such as respiratory tract infections, intestinal parasites, but sometimes is also held with respect to malaria, as this too is common in some populations.

However both these standpoints ignore well-established research showing that infectious diseases do affect cognitive functioning and development, and differ in their effects on cognitive functioning and development. In addition, those diseases that are more prevalent or have higher intensity in children have extra relevance for inquiry, especially those that have even greater effects on children than on adults. It is during the early years of development and the years of formal schooling that children have the greatest cognitive demands placed on them, and hence their cognitive functioning is of greatest importance. There is also evidence that cognitive development is fastest during infancy and early childhood, so any disruption during this period could lead to cognitive delay. School children too are at particular risk from infectious diseases, because during the years of formal schooling cognitive demands are high.

In measuring the effect of infectious diseases on cognition and development it is important to consider not only the type of infection and its severity but several other factors too. First, it is important to distinguish between effects at the individual and at the population level. For example, a relatively rare infection such as a viral encephalitis may have a very significant and severe impact on cognitive functioning within the individual, whereas the common cold or influenza, although having relatively minor effects on cognition in the individual may have a significant impact at the population level in terms of reduced ability to learn at school, or reduced productivity. Hence the incidence of a disease is important as well as the severity of any effect.

Environment plays a large part too, with both sociocognitive environment (loosely, socioeconomic status, stimulation from and interaction with the environment) and the general health of the child being important mediators of the impact of a disease. Additionally, different diseases may share similar symptoms; or the same or similar etiological agents may cause different symptoms, depending on a number of factors including route of infection (e.g., HIV). For example, many of the acute infectious diseases, such as encephalitis, meningitis, and cerebral malaria, can cause fever, convulsions and loss of consciousness. Meningitis can have exactly the same symptoms but with different microbiological causes. Conversely, meningitis can present with or without neurological complications. Well-designed studies can disentangle the effect of different aetiological agents and the effect of the symptoms themselves (Grimwood et al., 1996; Rorabaugh et al., 1993).

Experimental Design

Before progressing, it is worth mentioning something about this issue as it is crucial in the interpretation of study data and may be the underlying reason for the ambiguity of results in some cases. Although a correlational or cross-sectional design, where the cognitive functioning of an infected group of children is compared with an uninfected group can be appealing, such a design does not permit the causal nature of the relationship to be determined because the two groups may differ in several respects other than infection status. Studies that use retrospective accounts of infections are subject to extra bias through their reliance on people's memory or on medical records, which are not as accurate as systematic diagnosis.

For diseases that may be treated, the most appropriate study design is a double blind, randomized, placebo controlled, treatment trial. The basic procedure is for a group of infected children to be tested for cognitive functioning at baseline and then randomized to receive either treatment or placebo. Neither the tester nor child knows which preparation was given, hence double blind. The two treated groups are then retested and the cognitive functioning compared again. Because randomization should have equally distributed any confounding factors between the two groups, any improvement in the treatment group over the placebo group (after controlling for baseline scores) may be because the treated group is no longer infected. An uninfected group can also be included to examine baseline differences between infected and uninfected, and determine how close to the performance of uninfected children is that of treated, formerly infected children.

For some diseases and in some situations a placebo controlled study design is not appropriate. This might be because postponement of treatment during the period of the study may be considered unethical, or because the prescribed treatment is not very effective, or perhaps the effects on cognitive development are not thought to be reversible following treatment. In such instances, a prospective study design may be more appropriate. Here a cohort of children at risk of infection is followed, in some cases from birth. Those who go on to develop the disease are compared on measures of cognitive functioning with those who do not develop the disease. Other measures such as general nutrition and home environment are also measured in order that they can be controlled for statistically at the end.

This review does not seek to be exhaustive, but instead focuses on certain infectious diseases for which there are useful data concerning impact on cognition. We consider first those diseases that affect neurocognitive functioning directly, either by infecting the central nervous system (CNS) itself or by causing pathological changes. For example, encephalitis is a disease that directly infects the CNS and hence can cause neurological damage. Even among those diseases rigorous experimental design and technique is necessary to disentangle environmental and general health effects from direct effect of an infection. Next, we examine those infections that affect functioning through some as yet unrecognized mechanism, possibly via the general health and well-being of the child, or the child's interactions with the environment. In this group we find diseases such as parasitic helminth infections, which cause anemia and malnutrition, which are known to affect cognitive development; and otitis media, which may have an effect on cognitive and linguistic development due to its effect on hearing.

DISEASES THAT DIRECTLY AFFECT THE CENTRAL NERVOUS SYSTEM (CNS)

Encephalitis, Including Herpes Simplex Encephalitis

Encephalitis is an infection that leads to an inflammation of the brain, and, as such, is the most obvious example of an infection directly affecting the CNS. The symptoms of encephalitis include fever, headache, stiff neck, vomiting and, in severe cases, coma. The most common infectious agent is generally accepted to be the herpes simplex virus (HSV). However, a cohort study by Rantala, Uhari, Uhari, Saukkonen, and Sorri (1991) found that in the population of a Finnish town the virus varicella (chicken pox) was the most common cause, followed by the mumps virus (both common childhood illnesses which rarely lead to encephalitis) and HSV.

HSV encephalitis can cause a variety of severe neurological and cognitive impairments in children but memory, motor, and expressive difficulties predominate. Deficits found include autistic symptoms (Ghaziuddin, Tsai, Eilers, & Ghaziuddin, 1992), dense amnesia (Wood, Brown, & Felton, 1989), and language deficits very closely resembling adult fluent aphasia (Greer, Lyons-Crews, Mauldin, & Brown, 1989; Van Hout & Lyon, 1986). HSV has a high mortality rate and even in surviving patients it tends to cause either temporal lobe or frontal lobe damage, which can be visible on computerized tomography (CT) scan (Greer et al., 1989); this is in line with the findings that memory, motor, and expressive difficulties predominate.

It has greatly been assumed that if encephalitis did not cause frank neurological deficits then children who had been infected would follow a normal developmental pattern. The study of Rantala et al. (1991) confirmed this by reporting generally good long-term outcomes for infected children. However they found that the children with a history of encephalitis had a lower mean IQ when compared to controls for the general population, although the IQ scores for both groups (infected and control) were in the normal range. This implies that any study without controls would have failed to find any effect due to disease. Performance IQ was particularly affected in this group of infected children; school achievement was also worse and more abnormal EEGs were found in the infected group. These results suggest that even where a frank neuropsychological syndrome is not found, encephalitis has a detrimental effect on general cognitive development. In general, it appears that those cognitive functions affected again fall on the motor and performance side, with some effect on memory; the study design including uninfected controls has brought these effects to light.

Meningitis

Meningitis, an infection of the meninges of the brain and spinal cord, can be caused by a number of different bacteria or by a virus. Symptoms of both bacterial and viral meningitis are similar, and similar to those of encephalitis, including fever, headache, vomiting, stiff neck, and convulsions in severe cases, with some other neurological symptoms including vision disturbances and muscle weakness in some cases.

Annually in the United States there are an estimated 4.6 to 10 cases of bacterial meningitis per 100,000 population; and more than 2,000 deaths are attributable to meningitis each year. Seventy percent of cases occur in children under 5 years (Wilson & Harrison, 1991). The most common infectious agent is bacterial, *Haemophilus influenzae*, especially in children aged 2 months to 3 years of age. Aseptic or viral meningitis, in contrast, accounts for many fewer cases. There are a variety of infectious agents including CMV, HSV, HIV, and the Epstein–Barr virus. Ninety percent of cases of aseptic meningitis are found in those under 30 and so both types of meningitis, if they have potential consequences for cognitive functioning, are relevant to children and adolescents. To date, most studies of the cognitive consequences of meningitis have looked at bacterial meningitis in younger children, and have found some effects on generalised cognitive development (Taylor, Barry, & Schatschneider, 1993; Taylor & Schatschneider, 1992; Taylor, Schatschneider, Petrill, Barry, & Owens, 1996). These studies, however, found differences between children who had experienced complications (loss of consciousness, seizures, and other neurological symptoms) with meningitis, and those with uncomplicated meningitis. The group with complications were found to score worse on IQ measures, particularly performance scale items, as well as some differences on school achievement tests (spelling, arithmetic, reading for comprehension, and oral reading). Teacher and parent-rated behavior showed no differences, and there were no differences between noncomplicated cases and siblings. Behavior problems are not frequently associated with this disease, unlike other causes of early brain injury, such as trauma.

Studies of aseptic (viral) meningitis have not tended to find any such group differences. Rorabaugh et al. (1992, 1993) compared infants under 2 years with and without complications on developmental scales (the Bayley at a younger age and the Kaufmann at a second time point). There were some differences at the first time point but these had disappeared by 18 months of age.

Hence one disease can have differing effects on cognitive development depending both on the symptoms present—neurological complications or absence of such complications—and the aetiological agent—bacterial or viral—responsible for the disease. As described later in studies of other diseases, where younger, mainly preschool, children are assessed, it is difficult to differentiate specific cognitive effects; rather, a generalized lowering of cognitive developmental scores tends to be found.

Cerebral Malaria

Malaria is a major public health problem, infecting around 200 million people each year and causing an estimated 1 million deaths per year (Wools, 1997). Symptoms of cerebral malaria include but are not limited to fever, convulsions, and unconsciousness; again it resembles the other fevers affecting the CNS such as encephalitis or meningitis. The vast majority of these cases are found in tropical, low-lying areas of poorer countries. In areas where malaria is holoendemic, most members of the population have malaria parasites in their blood much of the time. *Plasmodium falciparum*, one of four malaria parasites, is the only one that can cause cerebral malaria, and it is this type of malaria that is most likely to have consequences for cognitive functioning, with neurological complications including coma and seizure representing risk factors.

Most cases of cerebral malaria are in young children. In developing countries it is responsible for approximately one fourth of all deaths of children aged 1 to 4 years and half of hospital admissions in this group (Brewster, Kwiatkowski, & White, 1990). Neurological sequelae occur in about 10% of children with the disease. Damage to the nervous system is caused by hemorrhage around the cerebral capillaries, and erythrocytes packing into the capillaries; many of these erythrocytes contain parasites, and it is thought that the parasites adhere to the lining of the capillaries (Wools, 1997).

Neurocognitive consequences of cerebral malaria can vary in severity although in general they do seem to be restricted to motor and executive functioning. Brewster et al. (1990) found that 11% of children who survived cerebral malaria had some neurological sequelae, with a transient hemiparesis being the most common. Of those with such consequences, 26% or 6 cases were left with major handicaps after 6 months. Two of these were suffering from aphasia and two from cortical blindness.

Subtler impairments are also found in groups of children who have suffered from cerebral malaria with some neurological complications such as loss of consciousness. These are generally found to be in motor and executive functions (Dugbartey & Spellacy, 1997; Holding, Peshu, Stevenson, & Marsh, submitted; Muntendam, Jaffar, Bleichrodt, & Van, 1996). They can include differences in reaction time, executive tasks such as the Trails task (Dugbartey & Spellacy, 1997), attention and planning skills, expressive language and behavioural measures, but no differences are commonly found in information-processing tasks more similar to those found on general intelligence scales (Holding et al., submitted). Muntendam et al. (1996) also found differences between children who had had cerebral malaria and their controls on two sensorimotor tasks, out of a large battery of neuropsychological tests. The frequency of significant lasting neurocognitive deficits (10%) found in this group was higher than that found in the group of children studied by Brewster, Kwiatkowski, and White (1990).

It is unknown, however, what the consequences of cerebral malaria might be for children who do not have such severe neurological complications; as with meningitis, it might be possible that there is no effect on cognitive functioning unless there are neurological complications. Moreover, it is also possible that clinical falciparum malaria, without obvious cerebral symptoms, may affect cognitive development, particularly if there are repeated episodes. In holoendemic areas, many children and adults have high levels of parasitaemia that appear to be asymptomatic; again it is not known if this may affect cognitive functioning. Further research is needed in these areas. Again, it is possible that the same etiological agent giving rise to differing patterns of symptoms may have differing effects on cognitive functioning.

The Human Immunodeficiency Virus and the Acquired Immune Deficiency Syndrome (HIV and AIDS)

It is currently estimated there are 15,000 to 20,000 cases of pediatric HIV infection in the United States. This is only a very small proportion of those to be found worldwide, and it is estimated that by the year 2000 ten million children will have been born infected (Belman, 1997). Most children who are currently HIV positive were infected in utero or perinatally, from an HIV positive mother, and virtually all new cases are infected by this route. Some older cases were infected from unscreened blood transfusions, or clotting factors in the case of children with hemophilia. The latter two causes are decreasing in incidence as blood and blood products are regularly screened, although some studies on these groups have proved useful in disentangling the various causes for HIV- and AIDS-related cognitive difficulties. In the early stages HIV is asymptomatic, and children and infants are only found to be carrying the virus following testing. Infants of infected mothers can be found to be carrying antibodies to the virus without actually being infected, but can revert from being seropositive to seronegative by around the age of 10 months.

After summarizing what is known about the neurocognitive effects of the HIV virus in adults, we discuss studies on younger children and infants, which are the majority of those available, highlighting the importance of good study design that minimizes confounding variables. We follow this review with a discussion of the available data on older children and on the effect of treatment.

The Picture in Adults

In adults, AIDS dementia is common and is sometimes due to opportunistic infections of the CNS. Poor cognitive functioning can be found in addition in HIV-positive adults who are not suffering from severe dementia, although on the whole this is limited to patients with symptoms of AIDS, and not to asymptomatic HIV-seropositive individuals (Egan, Crawford, Brettle, & Goodwin, 1990; Selnes et al., 1990); any cognitive impairments in the latter tend to be due to other factors such as drug use (Egan et al., 1990). Antiretroviral drugs seem to be effective to some extent against the cognitive effects of HIV (Schmitt et al., 1988) although this has not been found to be the case in all studies (Heseltine et al., 1998).

Opportunistic infections of CNS are rare in infants and young children (Armstrong, Seidel, & Swales, 1993; Mintz, 1992). This may be due to the short time between infection and illness and death, or examination, so that there is not sufficient time for such infections to be acquired after birth. Opportunistic infections are thought in many cases to be recurrences of those that were acquired before the HIV infection was acquired; obviously it is not so likely that a child who is infected *in utero* or perinatally will have acquired other infections before the HIV infection. Rather, any effects on neurocognitive functioning in children are thought to be due to a direct infection of the CNS with the virus.

The effects of HIV infection on cognition are complex as there may be both direct cerebral effects as well as indirect effects resulting from the wide range of sequelae from infection and socioeconomic conditions.

Studies of Infants and Young Children Infected by Vertical Transmission

Early studies of children with AIDS or AIDS related complex (ARC, which is less severe) have tended to find a high rate of neurological abnormalities and developmental delay, with estimates as high as 60% to 90%. However as mentioned earlier, there may be multiple causes contributing to the cognitive–developmental effects observed. Commonly, brain abnormalities and signs of neurological impairment were found in most children and no developmental milestones were attained in any child once AIDS was diagnosed (Iannetti, Falconieri, & Imperato, 1989; Ultmann et al., 1985). Children with ARC tended to fare better than those with AIDS (Ultmann et al., 1985). However low birthweight, prematurity, and prenatal exposure to drugs are additional factors that may induce such developmental delays (Armstrong et al., 1993), as well as nutritional and metabolic deficits and hypoxia due to lung disease, all of which are known to cause developmental delay in some circumstances (Grantham-McGregor, Powell, Walker, & Himes, 1991; Newburger, Silbert, Buckley, & Fyler, 1984).

Further research has confirmed that environmental factors such as prenatal drug exposure, general health status, and sociocognitive environment need to be taken into consideration in determining whether a HIV infection has an impact on cognitive development. In addition, the stage of the disease—in other words, the presence or absence of symptoms and the viral load—and the age at which the infection was acquired seem to be important.

Turning first to the degree of symptoms present, generally studies of children with asymptomatic HIV infection do not find any major developmental delay. In some children with AIDS or ARC there are signs of encephalopathy, and generally difficulties are found in the area of motor and expressive skills rather than perceptual or comprehension abilities (Epstein et al., 1986; Ultmann et al., 1985). Early opportunistic infections and encephalopathy (degree of impairment of cognitive development and gross motor function) both seem to predict well the course of the disease (Blanche et al., 1990).

However some of this research is flawed owing to poor study design, in particular an absence of appropriate controls. When a group of seronegative children of infected mothers is included in such studies the importance of controlling for environmental factors, in order to isolate the unique effects of HIV infection, is made very clear.

Neurological soft signs and generalized cognitive delay can be found in both infected and seronegative groups of children, although these signs are more common in the infected group (Diamond et al., 1990). This is not very surprising given that cerebral palsy is common in children born to mothers who abuse drugs, the main source of maternal infection in most studies.

In infants, the main finding tends to be generalized developmental delay (Aylward, Butz, Hutton, Joyner, & Vogelhut, 1992), such that infected children perform worse than uninfected children whether the uninfected children were born to HIV positive or negative mothers, and both levels of the virus that are present and physical growth can predict motor or cognitive functioning. However, uninfected children from the same high-risk groups also tend to be developmentally delayed although not to the same extent (Pollack et al., 1996).

Studies on Infants and Young Children With Mothers Infected Solely Through Heterosexual Transmission

The presence of a developmental delay in uninfected infants and children has led researchers to look at children whose mothers became infected, or were at risk of infection, through high rates of heterosexual transmission in a particular population. In such studies the effects of drug abuse are eliminated and it is generally found that there is a lower rate of neurological and cognitive deficits (Gay et al., 1995; Msellati et al., 1993). This is another example of how careful study design can distinguish artefacts from genuine effects.

Both infected and uninfected children of infected Haitian mothers in the United States, who had no prenatal drug exposure, were found to deteriorate on the mental subscale of the Bayley scales after the ages of 9 to 12 months; this is probably because more language-based items are included at this stage and the primary language in the home was not English. Neither group was found to deteriorate to the same extent on the performance scale. The seropositive group was however found to perform worse than the seroreverters, and these differences increased with age (Gay et al., 1995).

Similarly, in Kigali, Rwanda, seronegative children born to seropositive mothers performed no worse than children born to uninfected mothers. This may mean that seronegative children of infected mothers lead a more "normal" life, perhaps because children born to mothers who then become ill can be cared for by members of the extended family. This study also found a much lower rate of neurological abnormalities than reported in many previous studies—at 12 months 31% of infants and at 18 months 40% of infants were considered delayed but few children with asymptomatic HIV had any delay. In contrast, among the children with frank AIDS the proportions were 87% and 70%. Again, this is thought to be due to these children having fewer negative environmental influences than many children in other studies (Msellati et al., 1993).

Studies on Older, Vertically Infected Children

Studies on children of school age tend to have similar findings. Again, children born to mothers who have a history of intravenous drug abuse tend to have worse outcomes than those whose mothers have no such history (Brouwers et al., 1995a; Brouwers et al., 1995b). However, the incidence of neurological abnormalities and cognitive deficits seems to be lower in this age group, compared to younger age groups (Levenson, Mellins, Zawadzki, Kairam, & Stein, 1992; Mayes et al., 1996; Whitt et al., 1993). This could be due to the fact that more severely affected children tend to die at a younger age than those with less severe symptoms, or to some special factors associated with the age at infection.

Studies that only include vertically infected children are rare in this age group, because the primary means of infection among older children has in the past been transfusion. If the route of infection, or associated environmental factors, is indeed important, this could make a difference to the results of studies with this age group. As vertically infected children grow older and survive longer, and with the advent of universal blood screening, this ratio can be expected to change.

In contrast to the generalized developmental delays and motor difficulties found in infants, studies of older, vertically infected children tend to show more specific problems, including visuospatial and neurological abnormalities and school achievement problems (Tardieu et al., 1995) and differences on measures of short-term memory and number reasoning (Havens, Whitaker, Feldman, Alvarado, & Ernhardt, 1993). This may result from an artificial bias in analysis of results—subtests of IQ tests carried out on older children tend to be analysed separately, but not those used with younger children.

Studies Comparing Older Children Infected by Differing Routes

Comparing older vertically infected children with those infected via transfusion, among all infected children, 81% were found to have some brain abnormalities on CT, which mainly consisted of atrophy. Some calcifications were also found but these were only present in vertically infected children. There was a correlation between IQ and the CT rating which was again stronger for the vertically infected children but present in the children infected via transfusion as well. The stage of the disease and the presence of brain abnormalities were correlated, while no abnormalities were found in the milder stages. Abnormalities tended to be generalized with no bias to frontal or dorsal, or laterality effects. Counterintuitively, brain abnormalities were negatively correlated with hyperactivity; the authors suggest that the more impaired patients have severe motor problems that preclude any behavioral problems (Brouwers et al., 1995a; Brouwers et al., 1995b). In other studies basal ganglia calcifications have been found to be particularly common, and these could account for motor impairments commonly found in these children (Armstrong et al., 1993).

Among children who had blood transfusions at birth, differences were found between infected and uninfected on motor tasks and educational achievement (Cohen et al., 1991). In contrast, two studies of children with hemophilia infected later in life found no differences between HIV infected and uninfected (Mayes et al., 1996; Whitt et al., 1993). It seems possible that children who are infected early in life, whether or not they have other risk factors such as maternal drug use or nutritional deficits, are at a disadvantage when compared to children who are infected at an older age. Among both perinatally and *in utero* infected children, even where there is not maternal drug use, poorer performance on cognitive testing has been found (Cohen et al., 1991; Gay et al., 1995; Msellati et al., 1993). There is also some suggestion that intrauterine infection has a poorer prognosis than perinatal infection. These differences in outcome based on the timing of infection may reflect the greater vulnerability of the very young nervous system, or may simply be due to the time course of the disease having longer to progress in children infected early.

Effects of Drug Treatments for HIV

This type of study has been more common with HIV than with many other diseases, partly because of the recent introduction of such drugs and the fact that their efficacy in general, as well as their impact on cognitive deficits, is still under investigation. As with some other infectious diseases, it is possible to assess whether cognitive impairment is genuinely due to a disease if they are reversible following treatment for the disease; however, caution must be exercised if there is no treatment effect, as this may not mean that cognitive deficits are unrelated to the disease, but that they are irreversible or unaffected by treatment.

From the evidence to date, it seems that some effects on cognitive development of HIV and AIDS can be improved by some drug regimes, but not in all circumstances. Three to six months of treatment with the antiretroviral agent Zidovudine (AZT) may be able to improve the lowered IQ found in children with symptomatic AIDS, with the most dramatic improvements being in those with signs of encephalopathy (Pizzo et al., 1988). AZT may, however, have some side effects and drug resistance is also found, so that different drug regimes involving a combination of drugs are commonly used. A combination of dideoxycytidine (ddC) and AZT is used in some cases; with this mixture neuropsychological test scores may become stable, which can be considered a positive outcome given the normal tendency of these scores to fall in children with AIDS (Nozyce et al., 1994; Wolters, Brouwers, Civitello, & Moss, 1997); however, on ddC alone test scores tended to fall (Pizzo et al., 1990). It seems that AZT is more effective than ddC either alone or in drug combinations in improving scores on cognitive measures.

The mechanism of action of the drug could be via general improvements in health and nutrition, or a specific antiviral action within the brain. The latter seems to be more likely, as nutritional gains are not always associated with cognitive gains (Brouwers et al., 1996), and where there is individual variation in response to the drug these variable outcomes were associated with penetration of the drug into the CNS. Improvement in immunological status, in contrast, does not depend on penetration into CNS (Brouwers et al., 1994).

In summary, it seems that as in adults, infants and children suffering from AIDS, but not those with asymptomatic HIV infection, can have a global intellectual deficit accompanied by cerebral atrophy, focal cerebral lesions, and other neurological abnormalities. Generally, motor and expressive skills seem to be more affected than perceptual or sensory abilities, especially in older children; some of the deficits seem to improve following antiretroviral treatment. However, there is great individual variability in the effects seen, and this can be due to environmental factors such as the home environment and prenatal exposure to drugs; the stage of the disease and the amount of virus to be found; and the age at infection and route of infection. Of course all these factors are interdependent and it is not possible to isolate, for example, specific effects of environment and of route of infection. It is more likely that cognitive outcome varies with route of infection due to other effects of environmental differences, than that the route of infection directly affects outcome.

It also seems that in children in roughly similar circumstances, general health and nutritional status is not as important as the above environmental factors, neither are improvements in health and nutrition following treatment always directly associated with improvements in cognitive functioning.

Lyme Disease

Lyme borreliosis is a tick-borne spirochetal disease which predominantly affects the population of the eastern United States, and the Rocky Mountain states (Coyle, 1997). Around 1,000 people acquire the disease each summer. A proportion of those complain of neurological and cognitive symptoms several weeks or months after the onset of disease. These are usually those patients who present themselves, or are selected, for inclusion in studies of these effects. The disease affects both children and adults but the majority of research has been carried out in adult patients; this research is only briefly summarized here.

In studies carried out with children, some definite effects of infection on neurological status and cognitive functioning do seem to be found. These include white matter abnormalities seen on magnetic resonance imaging (MRI) scan (Belman, Coyle, Roque, & Cantos, 1992; Belman, Iyer, Coyle, & Dattwyler, 1993); and clinical deficits in "auditory and visual processing" including digit span, following sequential commands, and rhythm discrimination, as well as the Trail Making task (with alternate letters and numbers; Bloom, Wyckoff, Meissner, & Steere, 1998); these tasks seem to be related to working memory and executive function. However, these studies were carried out in patients who had been preselected as presenting with difficulties in cognitive or neurological functioning. When an unselected group of patients who had already been treated with antibiotics was compared to healthy controls and children with arthritis, no differences were found on any cognitive tests used (Adams, Rose, Eppes, & Klein, 1994).

In some studies on adults white matter abnormalities and their associated cognitive problems seem to be reversible following antibiotic treatment, as shown by Halperin (1989; Halperin, Pass, Anand, Luft, & Volkman, 1988) in adults. It therefore seems possible that cognitive deficits do exist in a subset of Lyme disease patients. Biased selection of patients makes the task of determining what these deficits might be more difficult, as studies where only those patients who complain of neurocognitive problems are included are evidently flawed. Similar intervention studies have yet to be undertaken in children.

DISEASES THAT DO NOT DIRECTLY INFECT THE CNS

Parasitic Helminth Infections

Infections with helminths, including worms that are found in the intestines and schistosomes, which infect the blood vessels around the bladder and intestines, are among the most common infections in the world, especially in developing countries, and are estimated to affect one fourth of the world's population (WHO, 1987).

The prevalence of infection with helminths begins to rise rapidly as soon as children begin to explore their environment, and in highly endemic areas remains high throughout adulthood. An important feature of these parasitic infections is that the intensity of infection (i.e., the worm burden or number of worms in the host) is what largely determines the degree of morbidity. The intensity of infection shows a different pattern to that of prevalence because it peaks in children aged 10 to 15 years, depending on the species. This has important implications because children of school age are not only more likely to be infected, they are also more likely to be heavily infected and experiencing most illness during their years at school (Cooper & Bundy, 1988).

Parasitic infections are readily treated with drugs that have no serious side effects, and the high prevalence of these infections can be attributed to poor environmental conditions and low levels of health care provision in endemic areas, leading to high rates of infection and low rates of treatment. In the studies quoted here, some studies have examined treatment effects and where these confirm findings from correlational or cross-sectional studies this can indicate the effect is relatively robust. Because many studies include both comparison of infected and uninfected children and comparison of treated and untreated infected children, these two study types have been examined together in this section. We discuss first the domains of cognitive functioning that parasitic infection might have an impact on, followed by a discussion of the mediating effects that may alter such an impact.

Effects on Cognitive Functioning

The specific cognitive domains that are associated with parasitic infection have not been clearly defined but could be important for understanding the implications of the effects on children's educational achievement and development. It has been suggested by some authors that it may be more profitable to examine lower level skills such as memory and attention, rather than high level, conceptual skills (Watkins & Pollitt, 1997); others suggest that examining specific cognitive abilities will be more profitable than examining general intellectual ability (Connolly & Kvalsvig, 1993).

These suggestions have been borne out by the data. The main effects observed have been on working memory and executive functions (e.g. Boivin et al., 1993; Nokes et al., 1992; Simeon, Grantham-McGregor, & Wong, 1995). Other studies have observed effects on sustained attention, search tasks, and reaction time (Kimura et al., 1992; Kvalsvig, Cooppan, & Connolly, 1991; Simeon, Grantham-McGregor, & Wong, 1995). However, some effects have also been observed on long-term memory (Simeon, Grantham-McGregor, & Wong, 1995), and analogical reasoning (Sternberg, Powell, McGrane, & Grantham-McGregor, 1997).

The lack of consistency in the domains of cognitive functioning affected is possibly due to differing effects of different parasitic species. For example, iron deficiency anemia has a particularly strong link with impaired cognitive functioning in primary school children (Grantham-McGregor, 1990) and is a common component of the clinical picture of hookworm disease, schistosomiasis, and intense *T. trichiura*. Low height-for-age (stunting) has been associated with poorer performance in tests of cognitive function, mental development, behavior, and educational achievement (Simeon & Grantham-McGregor, 1989) and is also a feature of intense trichuriasis, ascariasis, and *S. japonicum* infection. Low weight-for-age (wasting) and low weight-for-height, two common consequences of *A. lumbricoides* and schistosome infection, have also, though more rarely, been associated with poorer performance on tests of cognitive function and school achievement (Simeon & Grantham-McGregor, 1989). This evidence suggests that different helminth infections could have a detrimental and differential effect on children's performance on tests of cognitive function.

If it is true that working memory and executive function are particularly affected by helminth infections, then it may be possible to look at the mechanism that might be causing this. Some areas of the cerebral hemispheres have been shown to develop postnatally, and the prefrontal cortex may continue to develop into adolescence and even early adult life (Goldman-Rakic,

1984). Stunting of growth due to helminth infection could then lead to differential effects on these areas, which are thought to play a large part in working memory and executive functions (Passingham, 1993).

Effects on School Performance

Studies looking at academic achievement and attendance have tended to be somewhat contradictory. There is some evidence for poorer school performance by children who have a parasitic infection (Nokes & Bundy, 1993) and some additional evidence for improvement of this following treatment (Jordan & Randall, 1962; Simeon et al., 1995a), suggesting the effect is robust and reversible. However, the evidence is mixed, with some studies finding that infected children do not perform any more poorly (Ekanem et al., 1994; Watkins, Cruz, & Pollitt, 1996).

Interactions With Other Factors

There is also strong evidence that not all children infected with helminths are likely to score lower on tests of cognitive function and educational achievement (Simeon et al., 1995a; Simeon, Grantham-McGregor, & Wong, 1995; Watkins, Cruz, & Pollitt, in preparation). Only those with the most intense infections (highest worm burdens) are probably affected to a sufficient degree for their performance to be affected (Kimura et al., 1992; Kvalsvig et al., 1991; Watkins et al., in preparation). Also, it is likely that the duration of infection is important for this will also be associated with the degree of iron deficiency anaemia and undernutrition.

Similarly, evidence is growing that it is probably the more vulnerable children who are likely to be most affected and thus likely to benefit most from treatment. Younger children have been seen to be more affected amongst those children with a combination of intense *S. japonicum* infection and low haemoglobin levels or high *S. japonicum* infection and low height-for-age (long-term undernutrition; Nokes et al., 1999). Simeon and coworkers (1995a) also found that the children who benefited most from treatment of *T. trichiura* in terms of improved scores on tests of spelling and fluency, were those who were not only the most heavily infected but were also the most undernourished.

In many cases children can be shown to improve in tests of cognitive functioning following anthelminthic treatment (Boivin & Giordani, 1993; Boivin et al., 1993; Callender et al., 1992; Nokes et al., 1992), but although anthelminthic treatment is cheap, easily administered to children, safe and effective, it is probably not enough to give this alone with the expectation of improving children's cognition and ultimately their school performance (Bundy & de Silva, 1998). Ironically, children who already have an advantage socioeconomically or cognitively may benefit more from treatment. Boivin et al. (1993) found greater improvement in test scores following treatment in children who came from higher SES homes. If little is being taught in the schools, or if there is little stimulation at home, the full benefit of treatment may not be realized.

Hence, it appears that having a parasitic infection has some effects on cognitive functioning in school age children, and having additional nutritional deficits may exacerbate these. Poorer performance seems to be found primarily in the areas of working memory and of scanning of long-term memory, as well as of speed of information processing (Watkins & Pollitt, 1997). Possible mechanisms that have been suggested by various researchers include lassitude (Kvalsvig et al., 1991), discomfort (Watkins & Pollitt, 1997), anemia (Nokes et al., 1992) and undernutrition (Simeon, Grantham-McGregor, & Wong, 1995). It seems certain that a wide variety of factors modify this effect, including severity and type of infection, health status, and sociocognitive environment.

Chronic Fatigue and Postinfectious Fatigue Syndrome

With fatigue, muscle weakness, headaches, and complaints of cognitive and neurological problems, the pattern of symptoms of chronic fatigue syndrome and the related syndrome, postinfectious fatigue syndrome, resembles closely the cluster of symptoms found in Lyme disease. Postinfectious fatigue syndrome, found in a subset of patients suffering from chronic fatigue syndrome, is thought to be caused by the Epstein–Barr virus (Krupp, 1997). There have been, however, some doubts about the infectious etiology of the syndromes in children and adolescents (Smith et al., 1991), and some researchers have suggested one of a number of other viruses as potential etiological agents (Smith, 1990a). An estimated 50% of children have been infected with the Epstein–Barr virus by adolescence in industrialised countries, with the rate being higher in developing countries (Wilson et al., 1991). Early infection seems to have milder consequences than infection later in life, but there are still a number of children who appear to have an infection that is serious enough to cause chronic fatigue syndrome. As the division between chronic fatigue and postinfectious fatigue syndromes is not clear, studies of either or both are reported here. The clinical definition of chronic fatigue in adults includes a duration of at least 6 months; it should be noted that in many studies on children, this time period is not strictly adhered to in diagnosis (Carter et al., 1995).

Patients with chronic fatigue (CF) complain of cognitive difficulties including memory loss. Studies in adults have shown in some cases that these can be subjective, with CF patients rating their performance as worse than other groups and worse than objective measures suggest (Cope, Pernet, Kendall,

& David, 1995). Other studies, however, seem to provide convincing evidence for the reality of these problems (Smith, A., 1990a).

In children there seems to be little evidence that CF affects cognitive functioning. Carter et al. (1995) matched healthy children, CF patients, and depressed children and found no differences between the healthy and CF children on a general intelligence test. The depressed controls, in fact, performed worse than the CF patients.

In fact, there is some evidence that children with CF misperceive their own activity and abilities, similarly to adults. Fry and Martin (1996) looked at actual and perceived activity in children with chronic fatigue, using an activity monitor and questionnaires. Surprisingly they found that children with CF actually had the same activity level as the normal controls, but in line with the results of Cope et al. (1995) judged their own activity level to be lower than it actually was. In addition they tended to desire a higher level of activity in the future than control children.

In summary, it seems that there is little evidence that CF syndrome has an overall effect on cognitive functioning in children, whereas the evidence for such effects in adults is somewhat more conclusive; in children it seems possible that the syndrome may lead to misperceptions of self-performance. It is of interest that the two diseases, Lyme disease and CF syndrome, have similar symptoms, and may appear to present in the same manner, but with different aetiological agents, very different patterns of neurocognitive outcome can be found.

Colds and Flu

Taken together these are probably the most common of all infectious diseases, with each person catching an estimated 1 to 3 colds every year (Smith et al., 1987); the impact on attendance at and ability to benefit from school is therefore potentially huge. The number of viruses that cause colds and flu is also large, possibly as many as 200 are in existence, and hence any differential effects found may be due to this variability (Smith, 1990b).

One prospective study in children showed that visual perception and verbal working memory (repeating nonsense words) were found to be significantly poorer in children who were tested both before and during a cold, and compared to controls from the same grade. Reading comprehension was also affected, although not as much (Heazlett & Whaley, 1976).

In adults, experimentally induced colds, naturally occurring colds, and flu have all been studied. Experimentally induced infection with flu impaired visual search, whereas a cold primarily impaired motor tasks. The impairments were several orders of magnitude greater than those found when moderate doses of alcohol are given to healthy subjects, or when the performance at night time of healthy subjects is compared to their own daytime performance (Smith et al., 1987; Smith et al., 1988). Performance on memory tasks has also been shown to be impaired, but primarily due to lack of attention to relevant aspects of the material to be remembered (Smith, 1990b). When naturally occurring colds were examined (Hall & Smith, 1996) tracking and reaction time were found to be impaired, but there were no differences found on motor tasks. Naturally occurring colds result from many differing viruses, and the virus used in the experimental studies reported earlier is not common in adults; again this may be an instance where study design could affect results. The researchers suggest that this may be one reason why no differences in motor function were found in this study.

It is possible that many of the effects of colds and flu are due to the effect on the immune system of a interferon. When this is administered directly similar psychomotor deficits are observed (Smith, 1990b). However, it remains true that many different viruses which all cause immune reactions do seem to cause impairments in different cognitive abilities, despite very similar symptoms.

Febrile Convulsions

High fever is common in childhood infection and this can be accompanied by febrile convulsions; with any neurological complication there is always a question of whether this could have consequences for cognitive development. Febrile convulsions are defined as convulsions associated with fever but not associated with any infection that directly affects the CNS, such as meningitis, encephalitis, or cerebral malaria. Hence, this syndrome is essentially the same as these diseases symptomatically, but has a different etiological agent.

Convulsions do not seem to affect long-term cognitive outcomes adversely (Knudsen, 1996). Farwell et al. (1990) found that rather, children who were given phenobarbital—a common antiseizure medication—had depressed IQ, as measured with the Stanford–Binet scale, following 2 years of prophylactic administration of the drug, compared to untreated children with a similar history of seizures. Their IQ remained depressed even after treatment was discontinued, while the recurrence of seizure did not differ significantly between the treated and placebo groups. Using a different drug, benzodiazepine, which is administered only on signs of fever or seizure, Knudsen et al. (1996) found that not only were there no differences in cognitive performance between the treatment groups (administration at fever or administration at seizure) but that even children with potentially serious complex seizures (longer lasting and possibly with neurological complications) showed no adverse cognitive or educational outcomes, compared to the children with simple seizures.

Here again, it seems that even where symptoms are similar, different etiological agents lead to very different cognitive outcomes.

Otitis Media

Otitis media (infection of the middle ear) has affected two thirds of all children before their third birthday, with boys more often affected than girls (Black & Sonnenschein, 1993). Of children who are treated, 70% still have fluid (effusion) in their ears after 2 weeks of treatment. This fluid can lead to hearing loss. Of children that have one such episode, 15% still have a hearing loss after 6 months (Kirkwood & Kirkwood, 1983). Otitis media with effusion (OME) is hence a potentially huge problem, partly due to the numbers of children affected and partly due to the timing of such hearing loss, at the age when language development is peaking. It is also unusual among infectious diseases in that any potential effect it may have on cognitive development is potentially via a sensory mechanism, rather than through a direct infection of the CNS or an effect on general health. Although some treatments are possible for OME, these tend to be preventative rather than curative, including long-term courses of antibiotics and drains in the ear canal; there have not been any studies distinguishing the impact on children who have naturally different levels of infection from those who have been given prophylaxis.

Differing studies on the effects on cognitive and behavioral development of children with OME have tended to have conflicting results. For example, significant relationships with intelligence or cognitive outcomes are more often seen where parental report or medical records were used to assess whether children had suffered from OME, compared to studies that used an otological examination. Studies finding such a significant relationship have also tended to be those that have relied on retrospective assessment of children's infection status, rather than studying a group of children prospectively (Roberts & Schuele, 1990). It is important to bear these differences in study design in mind when interpreting results. As in the section on HIV, this section deals first with studies on younger children, as well as possible interactions with developmental delay, and then moves on to studies of older children and those that have followed groups of children through their childhood.

Studies of Infants and Younger Children

In early life, some effects of OME on language and cognitive development can be seen. Looking at children aged 1 to 3 years, the incidence of developmental delay can be seen to be relatively high in infants with OME; however it is possible that this is due to two distinctive groups of children with OME occurring in different proportions to the normal population—the group of children with severe developmental delay being larger proportionally in the group with OME than in the uninfected group, with the other children with a history of OME having broadly normal development (Black & Sonnenschein, 1993). Receptive language (comprehension of spoken language) can be particularly vulnerable to OME and subsequent hearing loss (Roberts et al., 1995b); however some research finds a general effect on language development as a whole (Teele et al., 1984). This may depend on the age at which assessment is carried out.

In these studies on infants, some researchers found that home environment and mother–child interactions can be just as important, if not more important, than presence or absence of infection in predicting cognitive and linguistic outcomes (Black & Sonnenschein, 1993; Roberts et al., 1995b). Similarly, Owen et al. (1996), looking at hearing abilities, found that children with poor home environments and longer duration of OME were those with the poorest auditory discrimination scores. A possible explanation for these findings is that parents caring for children in a poor home environment frequently miss signs of OME, or that the environment itself is associated with increased incidence or severity of infection. In contrast, Teele et al. (1984) found that children from high SES families with frequent OME performed worse on all language subtasks compared to those with very infrequent OME from a similar home background, but no differences were found for those from low SES families. It is possible that parents from high SES homes may bring their children to the clinic more frequently or more immediately than parents from low SES homes, and hence infection is diagnosed more often for their children, and this likelihood of clinic attendance may increase further if the parents also perceive a language or hearing problem that is in fact unrelated to OME.

Interactions With Developmental Delay

OME infection also appears to interact with some types of developmental delay. The majority of such studies are correlational, retrospective studies so it is difficult to determine the direction of causality. For example, among children who had already been labeled as having learning difficulties, those with a diagnosis of hyperactivity were more likely to have a history of OME (Hagerman & Falkenstein, 1987) than those with another type of learning disability; and differences have also been found between a group of developmentally delayed children with a history of OME, and a group of children with similar developmental delay but without such a history, on measures of "sequential processing" (digit span, symbol, and arithmetic subtests of the WISC; Secord, Erickson, & Bush, 1988). The children in this study, however, had a mean full-scale IQ of 102, which is not in the learning disabled range.

Studies of Older Children

Differences found at older ages tend to be much smaller and less clear cut. Some differences on behavioral measures have been found at in some ages of children in school, especially if these measures were rated by the children's teacher (Roberts, Burchinal, & Campbell, 1994; Roberts et al., 1989). Recurrent bouts of OME were found to have a greater effect than a continuous infection on behavior at age 9, but differences vanished by the time a later follow-up was carried out at age 12 (Roberts, Burchinal, & Clarke-Klein, 1995). Similarly, although differences in language, behavior, and general cognitive development were found at 5 years of age, the only differences seen were in verbal expression at age 7 and there were no group differences by age 9 (Chalmers et al., 1989). It seems that early OME is the important factor; the duration of OME in the first year of life has been found to correlate significantly with scores on the WISC-R at age 7, as well as school achievement, and speech and language abilities, whereas OME at a later age did not contribute at all to performance (Klein et al., 1988; Teele et al., 1990). Children with more episodes of OME however tended to be overrepresented in later follow-ups in these studies, meaning that the study group was somewhat biased in composition.

From these studies, it seems that OME in early life, particularly if it is frequent, can have some effect on cognitive and behavioral development. However, the general assumption that OME will frequently lead to major learning disabilities may be overstated. Some confounding of results can also be attributed to a variety of factors related to study design; correlational studies in particular cannot really be relied on for many reasons. For example, studies where communicative or cognitive delay is found to be associated with OME cannot necessarily be taken to prove that OME causes these delays; instead children with these delays may have OME for longer or more frequently because they communicate their state of health less well to caretakers. Children with poor home environments may be more at risk for OME, or more likely to suffer from associated cognitive delays. In many studies to date, the direction of causality remains to be established.

GENERAL SUMMARY

Overall, this review of studies examining the effect of infectious diseases on cognitive development upholds the view that such diseases can have a significant effect, and that effects differ depending on which disease is studied.

Some diseases have a direct effect on the CNS and others have some different, less well understood, mechanism of action. In the former case, a direct effect can take the form of either an infection of the CNS or inflammation or other CNS damage. In the latter case, the mechanisms are more varied. They can be through immunological effects, such as for the common cold; through probable effects on nutritional status, such as with parasitic infections; or through effects on sensory perception, such as in the case of otitis media with effusion.

One disease can also affect cognitive functioning through more than one mechanism; for example, parasitic infections probably have an impact on both general nutritional status and iron status, both of which can be shown to have an effect on cognitive functioning (Boivin & Giordani, 1993; Simeon, Grantham-McGregor, & Wong, 1995).

Mediating Factors in the Impact of a Disease on Cognitive Development

Even once a mechanism is known by which a disease might have an impact on cognitive development, it is still necessary to examine all the other influences that might alter this impact. Many of these influences are interactive, that is to say that not only can the outside influences and the disease both affect cognitive development independently, but the influences can be affected by the disease, and vice versa.

Both general health and the sociocognitive environment have been shown to be important mediating factors in the effects of disease on cognitive functioning. However, the child's general health, in the form of nutritional status, iron status, and general feeling of well-being, is obviously closely linked to their infection status. In some cases, poor general health can lead to an increased probability of becoming infected. This can be true of, for example, colds and flu. In other cases having an infection commonly leads to poorer general health. This is especially true of chronic conditions such as HIV or parasitic infections, but can also be true of acute infections such as malaria.

The Relationship Between Etiology and Symptoms

The relationship between infection and cognitive effect is hence variable and not well understood. Different diseases can present with very similar symptoms, and the same disease can have varying symptoms or aetiological agents. All these variables can be seen to be important in predicting the effect a disease will have on cognitive functioning. For example, as discussed earlier, Lyme disease and chronic fatigue have very similar symptoms but different underlying causes, and seem to have very different effects on cognitive functioning. Similarly, high fevers causing neurological side effects seem to have long-term implications for cognitive functioning in cases of encephalitis and cerebral malaria, and some cases of meningitis. Febrile convulsions without direct infection of the CNS do not seem to have any long-term impact. Meningitis provides an example of how even within one disease, both symptoms and aetiology can be important. Viral meningitis, whether or not it presents with complications, seems to have no long-term effects on cognitive functioning. Bacterial meningitis with complications can have a long-term impact on cognitive functioning, although the same disease with no complications does not have such an impact.

The Impact of the Environment

Social factors are an important determinant of both risk of infection and cognitive development. Children who have poorer sociocognitive environments may in some cases be more likely to become infected, or to stay infected. For example, in developing countries, children who have no latrines in their homes are more likely to acquire an intestinal helminth infection, and to become reinfected (Bundy, 1988). In the West, children who become infected with HIV are more likely to come from homes with a drug-using parent, and are very likely to have had some prenatal exposure to drugs. Hence any effects of the infection on cognitive development must be disentangled from environmental effects. In East Africa, where most HIV transmission is unrelated to drug abuse, it has been shown that the incidence of developmental delay in uninfected children of infected mothers is no greater than that in children of uninfected mothers, where all other environmental factors can be held constant. Hence it is possible to disentangle the effect of the environment from that of the disease.

Not only can an adverse environment lead to higher probability of becoming infected, but also an infection can feed back into reduced social and cognitive interactions and hence make a child's environment less supportive of normal cognitive development. As discussed earlier, children with otitis media with effusion are often found to interact less with their caregivers. It is difficult to say whether this is a result of the disease, an incidental finding due to the different home environments of children more and less at risk of infection, or even a possible cause of prolongation of the disease, if children do not complain about their illness.

The Aspects of Cognitive Functioning That Are Affected

Different diseases have an impact on different aspects of cognitive development. Some limited generalization is however possible. When a comparison is made between effects on perceptual and sensory skills, effects on motor and performance measures (including simple measures of memory), and effects on conceptual, higher order skills (including measures of reasoning), overall more diseases seem to affect basic performance and motor skills than other areas of cognitive development. For example, most effects of parasitic infection are found in working memory and speed of processing, whereas effects of HIV and AIDS tend to be on motor and expressive language development. Similarly, encephalitis tends to affect memory as well as motor and expressive language skills.

An exception to this generalization seems to be otitis media with effusion, in which effects seem to be smaller than originally thought, but are probably on language—including receptive language—and attentional–behavioral functioning. This apparently anomalous finding may reflect the mechanism by which OME is thought to affect behavioural and cognitive development, via an effect on auditory input and processing, whereas, in most infectious diseases, there is either a general systemic effect or a direct neural effect.

Summary and Future Directions

In the case of many of the diseases reviewed here, different studies have presented widely varying findings, so that it is sometimes difficult to arrive at a consensus of opinion. In particular, it is difficult to compare studies that do not find any effects on cognitive functioning with those finding differences between groups based on infection status. Here again, an examination of study design and group size is important. Good studies tend to be those with relatively large numbers, a relatively severe infection, and a clean design (e.g., using prospective rather than retrospective reporting of infection status, and assessing treatment effects where relevant). If this type of study is examined, then for some diseases the effect that was thought to exist can be seen to be an artefact. Looking at studies with differing study design, we can see that the effect of OME may be less than was once thought, and the fact that asymptomatic HIV does not seem to affect cognitive development can be disentangled from the potentially severe effects of AIDS.

In the case of other diseases, when study design is clearer effects can be revealed that previously may not have been apparent or may have been in question. Larger studies of the effect of parasitic infections, again in children with more severe infections, tend to show that these children are at risk for some cognitive deficits; and in particular, the effect of meningitis with neurological complications, and the effect of an encephalitis infection which does not lead to a frank neuropsychological deficit, may not have been noticed but for this type of study.

It is possible that further such studies on other infectious diseases, such as cerebral malaria, will bring to light similar effects that have not been noticed in smaller studies. Therefore, it seems that further research in this area is warranted, in particular to determine if those diseases that have been little researched may have some unnoticed effect on cognitive development; and in addition for the possible impact on public health and medical treatment strategies to be assessed. If children with a specific disease suffer not only from poor physical health but also cognitive delay, then any treatment measures may need to take this into account and include some provision for stimulation or rehabilitation to overcome this delay.

The overall conclusion of this review must be that the effects of infectious disease on cognitive development are potentially very great, but little studied and little understood. Given the developmental importance of these effects there is a clear need for more focused investigation.

REFERENCES

Adams, W. V., Rose, C. D., Eppes, S. C., & Klein, J. D. (1994). Cognitive effects of Lyme disease in children. *Pediatrics, 94*(1), 185–189.

Armstrong, F. D., Seidel, J. F., & Swales, T. P. (1993). Pediatric HIV infection: a neuropsychological and educational challenge. *Journal of Learning Disabilities, 26*, 92–103.

Aylward, E. H., Butz, A. M., Hutton, N., Joyner, M. L., & Vogelhut, J. W. (1992). Cognitive and motor development in infants at risk for human immunodeficiency virus. *American Journal of Disease in Childhood, 146*, 218–222.

Belman, A. L. (1997). Neurological disorders associated with HIV infections in children. In K. L. Roos (Ed.), *Central nervous system infectious diseases and therapy* (pp. 45–78). New York: Dekker.

Belman, A. L., Coyle, P. K., Roque, C., & Cantos, E. (1992). MRI findings in children infected by *B burgdorferi. Pediatric Neurology, 18*, 428–431.

Belman, A. L., Iyer, M., Coyle, P. K., & Dattwyler, R. (1993). Neurologic manifestations in children with North American Lyme disease. *Neurology, 43*, 2609–2614.

Black, M. M., & Sonnenschein, S. (1993). Early exposure to otitis media: a preliminary investigation of behavioral outcome. *Journal of Developmental and Behavioural Pediatrics, 14*, 150–155.

Blanche, S., Tardieu, M., Duliege, A., Rouzioux, C., Le, D. F., Fukunaga, K., Caniglia, M., Jacomet, C., Messiah, A., & Griscelli, C. (1990). Longitudinal study of 94 symptomatic infants with perinatally acquired human immunodeficiency virus infection. Evidence for a bimodal expression of clinical and biological symptoms [see comments]. *American Journal of Disease in Childhood, 144*, 1210–1215.

Bloom, B. J., Wyckoff, P. M., Meissner, H. C., & Steere, A. C. (1998). Neurocognitive abnormalities in children after classic manifestations of Lyme disease. *Pediatric Infectious Disease Journal, 17*, 189–196.

Boivin, M. J., & Giordani, B. (1993). Improvements in cognitive performance for schoolchildren in Zaire, Africa, following an iron supplement and treatment for intestinal parasites. *Journal of Pediatric Psychology, 18*, 249–264.

Boivin, M. J., Giordani, B., Ndanga, K., Maky, M. M., Manzeki, K. M., Ngunu, N., & Muamba, K. (1993). Effects of treatment for intestinal parasites and malaria on the cognitive abilities of school children in Zaire, Africa. *Health Psychology, 12*, 220–226.

Brewster, D. R., Kwiatkowski, D., & White, N. J. (1990). Neurological sequelae of cerebral malaria in children. *The Lancet, 336*, 1039–1043.

Brouwers, P., DeCarli, C., Civitello, L., Moss, H., Wolters, P., & Pizzo, P. (1995a). Correlation between computed tomographic brain scan abnormalities and neuropsychological function in children with symptomatic human immunodeficiency virus disease. *Archives of Neurology, 52*, 39–44.

Brouwers, P., DeCarli, C., Heyes, M. P., Moss, H. A., Wolters, P. L., Tudor-Williams, G., Civitello, L. A., & Pizzo, P. A. (1996). Neurobehavioral manifestations of symptomatic HIV-1 disease in children: can nutritional factors play a role? *Journal of Nutrition, 126*(Suppl.), 2651S–2662S.

Brouwers, P., DeCarli, C., Tudor-Williams, G., Civitello, L., Moss, H., & Pizzo, P. (1994). Interrelations among patterns of change in neurocognitive, CT brain imaging, and CD4 measures associated with antiretroviral therapy in children with symptomatic HIV infection. *Advances in Neuroimmunology, 4*, 223–231.

Brouwers, P., Tudor-Williams, G., DeCarli, C., Moss, H. A., Wolters, P. L., Civitello, L. A., & Pizzo, P. A. (1995b). Relation between stage of disease and neurobehavioral measures in children with symptomatic HIV disease. *AIDS, 9*, 713–720.

Bundy, D. A. P. (1988). Population ecology of intestinal helminth infections in human communities. *Philosophical Transactions of the Royal Society of London B, 321*, 405–420.

Bundy, D. A. P. (1994). The global burden of disease due to intestinal nematode infection. *Transactions of the Royal Society of Tropical Medicine and Hygiene, 88*, 259–261.

Bundy, D. A. P., & de Silva, N. R. (1998). Can we deworm this wormy world? *British Medical Bulletin, 54*(2), 421–432.

Callender, J. E. M., Grantham-McGregor, S., Walker, S., & Cooper, E. S. (1992). Trichuris infection and mental development in children. *The Lancet, 339*, 181.

Carter, B. D., Edwards, J. F., Kronenberger, W. G., Michalczyk, L., & Marshall, G. S. (1995). Case control study of chronic fatigue in pediatric patients. *Pediatrics, 95*, 179–186.

Chalmers, D., Stewart, I., Silva, P., & Mulvena, A. (1989). *Otitis media with effusion—the Dunedin study*. London: MacKeith Press.

Cohen, S. E., Mundy, T., Karassik, B., Lieb, L., Ludwig, D. D., & Ward, J. (1991). Neuropsychological functioning in human immunodeficiency virus type 1 seropositive children infected through neonatal blood transfusion. *Pediatrics, 88*, 58–68.

Connolly, K. J., & Kvalsvig, J. D. (1993). Infection, nutrition and cognitive performance in children. *Parasitology, 107*, S187–S200.

Cooper, E. S., & Bundy, D. A. P. (1988). Trichuris is not trivial. *Parasitology Today, 4*, 301–306.

Cope, H., Pernet, A., Kendall, B., & David, A. (1995). Cognitive functioning and magnetic resonance imaging in chronic fatigue. *British Journal of Psychiatry, 167*, 86–94.

Coyle, P. K. (1997). Lyme disease. In K. L. Roos (Ed.), *Central nervous system infectious diseases and therapy* (pp. 213–236). New York: Dekker.

Diamond, G. W., Gurdin, P., Wiznia, A. A., Belman, A. L., Rubinstein, A., & Cohen, H. J. (1990). Effects of congenital HIV infection on neurodevelopmental status of babies in foster care. *Developmental Medicine and Child Neurology, 32*, 999–1004.

Dugbartey, A. T., & Spellacy, F. J. (1997). Simple reaction time and cognitive processing ability after cerebral malaria in Ghanaian children. *Neurological Infections and Epidemiology, 2*, 141–144.

Egan, V., Crawford, J. R., Brettle, R., & Goodwin, G. (1990). The Edinburgh Cohort of HIV-positive drug users: Current intellectual function is impaired, but not due to early AIDS dementia complex. *AIDS, 4*, 651–656.

Ekanem, E. E., Asindi, A. A., Ejezie, G. C., & Antia-Obong, O. E. (1994). Effect of *Schistosoma haematobium* infection on the physical growth and school performance of Nigerian children. *Central African Journal of Medicine, 40*, 38–44.

Epstein, L. G., Sharer, L. R., Oleske, J. M., Connor, E. M., Goudsmith, J., Bagdon, L., Guroff, M. R., & Koenigsberger, M. R. (1986). Neurological manifestations of HIV infection in children. *Pediatrics, 78*, 678–687.

Farwell, J. R., Lee, Y. J., Hirtz, D. G., Sulzbacher, S. I., Ellenberg, J. H., & Nelson, K. B. (1990). Phenobarbital for febrile seizures—effects on intelligence and on seizure recurrence. *The New England Journal of Medicine, 322*, 364–369.

Fry, A. M., & Martin, M. (1996). Cognitive idiosyncrasies among children with the chronic fatigue syndrome: anomalies in self-reported activity levels. *Journal of Psychosomatic Research, 41*, 213–223.

Gay, C. L., Armstrong, F. D., Cohen, D., Lai, S., Hardy, M. D., Swales, T. P., Morrow, C. J., & Scott, G. B. (1995). The effects of HIV on cognitive and motor development in children born to HIV-seropositive women with no reported drug use: birth to 24 months. *Pediatrics, 96*, 1078–1082.

Gentile, M. A., Boll, T. J., Stagno, S., & Pass, R. F. (1989). Intellectual ability of children after perinatal cytomegalovirus infection. *Developmental Medicine and Child Neurology, 31*, 782–786.

Ghaziuddin, M., Tsai, L. Y., Eilers, L., & Ghaziuddin, N. (1992). Brief report: autism and herpes simplex encephalitis. *Journal of Autism and Developmental Disorders, 22*, 107–113.

Goldman-Rakic, P. S. (1984). Modular organization of prefrontal cortex. *Trends in Neurosciences, 7*, 419–429.

Grantham-McGregor, S. M. (1990). Malnutrition, Mental Function and Development. In R. M. Suskind (Ed.), *Workshop Series, Vol. 19* (pp. 197–212). New York: Raven Press.

Grantham-McGregor, S., Powell, C., Walker, S., Chang, S., & Fletcher, P. (1994). The long-term follow-up of severely malnourished children who participated in an intervention program. *Child Development, 65*, 428–439.

Grantham-McGregor, S. M., Powell, C. A., Walker, S. P., & Himes, J. H. (1991). Nutritional supplementation, psychosocial stimulation, and mental development of stunted children: The Jamaican study. *The Lancet, 338.*

Greer, M. K., Lyons-Crews, M., Mauldin, L. B., & Brown, F. R., III. (1989). A case study of the cognitive and behavioral deficits of temporal lobe damage in herpes simplex encephalitis. *Journal of Autism and Developmental Disorders, 19*, 317–326.

Grimwood, K., Nolan, T. M., Bond, L., Anderson, V. A., Catroppa, C., & Keir, E. H. (1996). Risk factors for adverse outcomes of bacterial meningitis. *Journal of Pediatrics and Child Health, 32*, 457–462.

Hagerman, R. J., & Falkenstein, A. R. (1987). An association between recurrent otitis media in infancy and later hyperactivity. *Clinical Pediatrics, 26*, 253–257.

Hall, S., & Smith, A. (1996). Investigation of the effects and aftereffects of naturally occurring upper respiratory tract illnesses on mood and performance. *Physiology of Behaviour, 59*, 569–577.

Halperin, J. J. (1989). Abnormalities of the nervous system in Lyme disease: response to antimicrobial therapy. *Review of Infectious Diseases, 11*(Suppl. 6), S1499–S1504.

Halperin, J. J., Pass, H. L., Anand, A. K., Luft, B. J., & Volkman, D. J. (1988). Nervous system abnormalities in Lyme disease. *Annals of the New York Academy of Sciences, 539*, 24–34.

Havens, J., Whitaker, A., Feldman, J., Alvarado, L., & Ehrhardt, A. (1993). A controlled study of cognitive and language function in school-aged HIV-infected children. *Annals of the New York Academy of Sciences, 693*, 249–251.

Heazlett, M., & Whaley, R. F. (1976). The common cold: Its effect on perceptual ability and reading comprehension among pupils of a seventh grade class. *Journal of School Health, 46*, 145–147.

Heseltine, P. N., Goodkin, K., Atkinson, J. H., Vitiello, B., Rochon, J., Heaton, R. K., Eaton, E. M., Wilkie, F. L., Sobel, E., Brown, S. J., Feaster, D., Schneider, L., Goldschmidts, W. L., & Stover, E. S. (1998). Randomized double-blind placebo-controlled trial of peptide T for HIV-associated cognitive impairment. *Archives of Neurology, 55*, 41–51.

Holding, P. A., Stevenson, J., Peshu, N., & Marsh, K. (1999). Cognitive sequelae of severe malaria with impaired consciousness. *Transactions of the Royal Society of Tropical Medicine and Hygiene, 93*(5), 529–534.

Iannetti, P., Falconieri, P., & Imperato, C. (1989). Acquired immune deficiency syndrome in childhood. Neurological aspects. *The Child's Nervous System, 5*, 281–287.

Jordan, P., & Randall, K. (1962). Bilharziasis in Tanganyika: Observations on its Effects and the Effects of Treatment in Schoolchildren. *Journal of Tropical Medicine and Hygiene, 65*, 1–7.

Kimura, E., Moji, K., Uga, S., Kiliku, F. M., Migwi, D. K., Mutua, W. R., Muhoho, N. D., & Aoki, Y. (1992). Effects of Schistosoma Haematobium Infection on Mental Test Scores of Kenyan School Children. *Annals of Tropical Medicine and Parasitology, 43*, 155–158.

Kirkwood, C. R., & Kirkwood, M. E. (1983). Otitis media and learning disabilities: The case for a causal relationship. *Journal of Family Practise, 17*, 219–227.

Klein, J., Chase, C., Teele, D., Menyuk, P., & Rosner, B. (1988). Otitis media and the development of speech, language and cognitive abilities at seven years of age. In D. Lim, C. Bluestone, J. Klein, & J. Nelson (Eds.), *Recent advances in otitis media*. Philadelphia: Decker.

Knudsen, F. U. (1996). Febrile seizures—treatment and outcome. *Brain Development, 18*, 438–449.

Knudsen, F. U., Paerregaard, A., Andersen, R., & Andresen, J. (1996). Long term outcome of prophylaxis for febrile convulsions. *Archives of Disease in Childhood, 74*, 13–18.

Kolb, B., & Wishaw, I. Q. (1990). *Fundamentals of Human Neuropsychology* (3rd ed.). New York: Freeman.

Krupp, L. B. (1997). Postinfectious neurological syndromes. In K. L. Roos (Ed.), *Central nervous system infectious diseases and therapy* (pp. 455–480). New York: Dekker.

Kvalsvig, J. D., Cooppan, R. M., & Connolly, K. J. (1991). The effects of parasite infections on cognitive processes in children. *Annals of Tropical Medicine and Parasitology, 85*, 551–568.

Levenson, R. L., Jr., Mellins, C. A., Zawadzki, R., Kairam, R., & Stein, Z. (1992). Cognitive assessment of human immunodeficiency virus-exposed children. *American Journal of Disease in Childhood, 146*, 1479–1483.

Mayes, S. D., Handford, H. A., Schaefer, J. H., Scogno, C. A., Neagley, S. R., Michael-Good, L., & Pelco, L. E. (1996). The relationship of HIV status, type of coagulation disorder, and school absenteeism to cognition, educational performance, mood, and behavior of boys with hemophilia. *Journal of Genetic Psychology, 157*, 137–151.

Mintz, M. (1992). Neurologic abnormalities. In R. Yogev & E. Connor (Eds.), *Management of HIV infection in infants and children*. St Louis, MO: Mosby-Year Book Inc.

Msellati, P., Lepage, P., Hitimana, D., Van Goethem, C., Van de Perre, P., & Dabis, F. (1993). Neurodevelopmental testing of children born to HIV type 1 seropositive and seronegative mothers: a prospective cohort study in Kigali, Rwanda. *Pediatrics, 92*, 843–848.

Muntendam, A. H., Jaffar, S., Bleichrodt, N., & van Hensbroek, M. B. (1996). Absence of neuropsychological sequelae following cerebral malaria in Gambian children. *Transactions of the Royal Society of Tropical Medicine and Hygiene, 90*, 391–394.

Newburger, J. W., Silbert, A. R., Buckley, L. P., & Fyler, D. C. (1984). Cognitive function and age at repair of transposition of the great arteries in children. *The New England Journal of Medicine, 310*, 1495–1499.

Nokes, C., & Bundy, D. A. P. (1993). Compliance and absenteeism in school children: implications for helminth control. *Transactions of the Royal Society of Tropical Medicine and Hygiene, 87*, 148–152.

Nokes, C., Grantham-McGregor, S. M., Sawyer, A. W., Cooper, E. S., Robinson, B. A., & Bundy, D. A. P. (1992). Moderate to heavy infections of Trichuris trichiura affect cognitive function in Jamaican school children. *Parasitology, 104*, 539–547.

Nokes, C., McGarvey, S. T., Shiue, L., Wu, G., Liu, C., Wu, H., Bundy, D. A. P., & Olds, G. R. (1999). Evidence for an improvement in cognitive function following treatment of Schistosoma japonicum infection in Chinese primary school children. *American Journal of Tropical Medicine and Hygiene, 60*(4), 556–565.

Nozyce, M., Hoberman, M., Arpadi, S., Wiznia, A., Lambert, G., Dobroszycki, J., Chang, C. J., & St, L. Y. (1994). A 12-month study of the effects of oral zidovudine on neurodevelopmental functioning in a cohort of vertically HIV-infected inner-city children. *AIDS, 8*, 635–639.

Owen, M. J., Johnson, D. L., Swank, P. R., Baldwin, C. D., Aker, J., & Howie, V. M. (1996). Duration of otitis media with effusion from birth to 3 years of age related to language and cognitive scores at 5 years. In D. J. Lim (Ed.), *Recent advances in otitis media* (pp. 329–331). Oxford: Blackwell Science.

Partnership for Child Development (1997). Better health, nutrition and education for the school aged child. *Transactions of the Royal Society of Tropical Medicine and Hygiene, 91*, 1–2.

Passingham, R. (1993). *The frontal lobes and voluntary action*. Oxford, England: Oxford University Press.

Pizzo, P. A., Butler, K., Balis, F., Brouwers, E., Hawkins, M., Eddy, J., Einloth, M., Falloon, J., Husson, R., Jarosinski, P., Meer, J., Moss, H., Poplack, D. G., Santacroce, S., Weiner, L., & Wolters, P. (1990). Dideoxycytidine alone and in an alternating schedule with zidovudine in children with symptomatic HIV infection. *Journal of Pediatrics, 117*, 799–808.

Pizzo, P. A., Eddy, J., Falloon, J., Balis, F. M., Murphy, R. F., Moss, H., Wolters, P., Brouwers, P., Jarosinski, P., Rubin, M., Broder, S., Yarchoan, R., Brunetti, A., Maha, M., Nusinoff-Lehrman,

S., & Poplack, D. G. (1988). Effect of continuous intravenous infusion of zidovudine (AZT) in children with symptomatic HIV infection. *New England Journal of Medicine, 319*, 889–896.

Pollack, H., Kuchuk, A., Cowan, L., Hacimamutoglu, S., Glasberg, H., David, R., Krasinski, K., Borkowsky, W., & Oberfield, S. (1996). Neurodevelopment, growth, and viral load in HIV-infected infants. *Brain Behaviour and Immunology, 10*, 298–312.

Pollitt, J. (1988). Clinical-pharmacology in psychiatry—selectivity in psychotropic-drug action—promises or problem. Dahl, S. G., Gram, L. F., Paul, S. M., Potter, W. Z. *British Journal of Psychiatry, 152*, 444–445.

Pollitt, E. (1990). *Malnutrition and infection in the classroom.* UNESCO, Paris.

Rantala, H., Uhari, M., Uhari, M., Saukkonen, A., & Sorri, M. (1991). Outcome after childhood encephalitis. *Developmental Medicine and Child Neurology, 33*, 858–867.

Roberts, J. E., Burchinal, M. R., & Campbell, F. (1994). Otitis media in early childhood and patterns of intellectual development and later academic performance. *Journal of Pediatric Psychology, 19*, 347–367.

Roberts, J. E., Burchinal, M. R., & Clarke-Klein, S. M. (1995). Otitis media in early childhood and cognitive, academic, and behavior outcomes at 12 years of age. *Journal of Pediatric Psychology, 20*, 645–660.

Roberts, J. E., Burchinal, M. R., Collier, A. M., Ramey, C. D., Koch, M. A., & Henderson, F. W. (1989). Otitis media in early childhood and cognitive, academic and classroom performance of the school-aged child. *Pediatrics, 83*, 477–485.

Roberts, J. E., Burchinal, M. R., Medley, L. P., Zeisel, S. A., Mundy, M., Roush, J., Hooper, S., Bryant, D., & Henderson, F. W. (1995). Otitis media, hearing sensitivity, and maternal responsiveness in relation to language during infancy. *Journal of Pediatrics, 126*, 481–489.

Roberts, J. E., & Schuele, C. M. (1990). Otitis media and later academic performance: The linkage and implications for intervention. *Topics in Language Disorders, 11*, 43–62.

Rorabaugh, M. L., Berlin, L. E., Heldrich, F., Roberts, K., Rosenberg, L. A., Doran, T., & Modlin, J. F. (1993). Aseptic meningitis in infants younger than 2 years of age: acute illness and neurologic complications. *Pediatrics, 92*, 206–211.

Rorabaugh, M. L., Berlin, L. E., Rosenberg, L., Rossman, M., Allen, M., & Modlin, J. F. (1992). Absence of neurodevelopmental sequelae from aseptic meningitis. *Pediatric Research, 31*, 177A.

Schmitt, F. A., Bigley, J. W., McKinnis, R., Logue, P. E., Evans, R. W., & Drucker, J. L. (1988). Neuropsychological outcome of zidovudine (AZT) treatment of patients with AIDS and AIDS-related complex. *The New England Journal of Medicine, 319*, 1573–1578.

Secord, G. J., Erickson, M. T., & Bush, J. P. (1988). Neuropsychological sequelae of otitis media in children and adolescents with learning disabilities. *Journal of Pediatric Psychology, 13*, 531–542.

Selnes, O. A., Miller, E., McArthur, J. C., Gordon, B., Munoz, A., Sheridan, K., Fox, R., Saah, A. J., & Multicenter AIDS Cohort Study. (1990). HIV-1 infections—no evidence of cognitive decline during the asymptomatic period. *Neurology, 40*, 204–208.

Simeon, D. T., & Grantham-McGregor, S. (1989). Effects of missing breakfast on the cognitive functions of school children of differing nutritional status. *The American Journal of Clinical Nutrition, 49*, 646–653.

Simeon, D. T., Grantham-McGregor, S. M., Callender, J. E., & Wong, M. S. (1995). Treatment of Trichuris trichiura infections improves growth, spelling scores and school attendance in some children. *Journal of Nutrition, 125*, 1875–1883.

Simeon, D. T., Grantham-McGregor, S., & Wong, M. S. (1995). *Trichuris trichiura* infection and cognition in children: Results of a randomised clinical trial. *Parasitology, 110*, 457–464.

Smith, A. (1990a). Chronic Fatigue Syndrome and performance. In A. P. Smith & D. M. Jones (Eds.), *Handbook of Human Performance* (pp. 261–268). New York: Harcourt Brace Jovanovich.

Smith, A. P. (1990b). Colds, influenza and performance. In A. P. Smith & D. M. Jones (Eds.), *Handbook of Human Performance* (p. 1117). New York: Harcourt Brace Jovanovich.

Smith, A. P., Tyrrell, D. A. J., Al-Nakib, W., Coyle, K. B., Dovovan, C. B., Hoggins, P. G., & William, J. S. (1988). The effect of experimentally induced respiratory virus infections on performance. *Psychological Medicine, 18*, 65–71.

Smith, A. P., Tyrrell, D. A. J., Coyle, K. B., & William, J. S. (1987). Selective effects of minor illnesses on performance. *British Journal of Psychology, 78*, 183–188.

Smith, M. S., Mitchell, J., Corey, L., Gold, D., McCauley, E., Glover, D., & Tenover, F. C. (1991). Chronic fatigue in adolescents. *Pediatrics, 88*, 195–202.

Spreen, O., Risser, A. H., & Edgell, D. (1995). *Developmental neuropsychology.* Oxford, England: Oxford University Press.

Sternberg, R., Powell, C., McGrane, P., & Grantham-McGregor, S. (1997). The effect of parasitic infection on cognitive development. *Journal of Experimental Psychology–Applied, 3*, 67–76.

Tardieu, M., Mayaux, M. J., Seibel, N., Funck-Brentano, I., Straub, E., Teglas, J. P., & Blanche, S. (1995). Cognitive assessment of school-age children infected with maternally transmitted human immunodeficiency virus type 1. *Journal of Pediatrics, 126*, 375–379.

Taylor, H. G., & Schatschneider, C. (1992). Academic achievement following childhood brain disease: Implications for the concept of learning disabilities. *Journal of Learning Disabilities, 25*, 630–638.

Taylor, H. G., Barry, C. T., & Schatschneider, C. W. (1993). School-age consequences on Haemophilus influenzae Type b meningitis. *Journal of Clinical Child Psychology, 22*, 196–206.

Taylor, H. G., Schatschneider, C., Petrill, S., Barry, C. T., & Owens, C. (1996). Executive dysfunction in children with early brain disease: outcomes post *haemophilus influenzae* meningitis. *Developmental Neuropsychology, 12*, 35–51.

Teele, D. W., Klein, J. O., Chase, C., Menyuk, P., & Rosner, B. A. (1990). Otitis media in infancy and intellectual ability, school achievement, speech, and language at age 7 years. Greater Boston Otitis Media Study Group. *Journal of Infectious Disease, 162*, 685–694.

Teele, D., Klein, J., Rosner, B., & Greater Boston Otitis Media Study Group. (1984). Otitis media with effusion during the first three years of life and development of speech and language. *Pediatrics, 74*, 282–287.

Ultmann, M. H., Belman, A. L., Ruff, H. A., Novick, B. E., Cone-Wesson, B., Cohen, H. J., & Rubinstein, A. (1985). Developmental abnormalities in infants and children with acquired immune deficiency syndrome (AIDS) and AIDS-related complex. *Developmental Medicine and Child Neurology, 27*, 563–571.

Van Hout, A., & Lyon, G. (1986). Wernicke's aphasia in a 10-year-old boy. *Brain and Language, 29*, 268–285.

Watkins, W. E., Cruz, J. R., & Pollit, E. (1996). The effects of deworming on indicators of school performance in Guatemala. *Transactions of the Royal Society of Tropical Medicine and Hygiene, 90*, 156–161.

Watkins, W. E., Cruz, J. R., & Pollitt, E. (in preparation). *Whether deworming improves or impairs memory and reaction time depends on intensity of ascaris infection.*

Watkins, W. E., & Pollitt, E. (1997). "Stupidity or worms": do intestinal worms impair mental performance? *Psychological Bulletin, 121*, 171–191.

Whitt, J. K., Hooper, S. R., Tennison, M. B., Robertson, W. T., Gold, S. H., Burchinal, M., Wells, R., McMillan, C., Whaley, R. A., Combest, J., & Hall, C. D. (1993). Neuropsychologic functioning of human immunodeficiency virus-infected children with hemophilia. *Journal of Pediatrics, 122*, 52–59.

WHO. (1987). Technical Report Series: 749. *Prevention and control of intestinal parasitic infections.* Geneva: World Health Organization.

Wilson, J. D., & Harrison, B. T. R. (Eds.). (1991). *Harrison's Principles of Internal Medicine.* New York: McGraw Hill.

Wolters, P. L., Brouwers, P., Civitello, L., & Moss, H. A. (1997). Receptive and expressive language function of children with symptomatic HIV infection and relationship with disease parameters: a longitudinal 24-month follow-up study. *AIDS, 11*, 1135–1144.

Wood, F. B., Brown, I. S., & Felton, R. H. (1989). Long-term follow-up of a childhood amnesic syndrome [see comments]. *Brain and Cognition, 10,* 76–86.

Wools, K. K. (1997). Cerebral malaria. In K. L. Roos (Ed.), *Central nervous system infectious diseases and therapy* (pp. 601–618). New York: Dekker.

World Bank (1993). *World Development Report: Investing in Health.* Oxford, England: Oxford University Press.

Young (1997, April). Early Child Development: Investing in our Children's Future. *Proceedings of a World Bank Conference on Early Child Development: Investing in the Future,* Atlanta, Georgia, New York: Elsevier Science.

9

The Invisible Danger: The Impact of Ionizing Radiation on Cognitive Development and Functioning

Elena L. Grigorenko
Yale University and Moscow State University

It happened again. On September 30, 1999, a worker of the Tokaimura nuclear plant near Tokyo, Japan, mixed too much uranium with nitric acid in a storage tank (16 kilograms [35 pounds], instead of 2.4 kilograms [5 pounds], were used), and started a fission reaction. Nuclear fission, the principle behind the atomic bomb, happens when neutrons hit uranium, causing atoms to split and releasing huge amounts of energy. The accident involving fission was due totally to human error.

Rescue teams said at least 55 people were suffering from radiation exposure in Tokaimura, including two workers who were in critical condition (state of shock with fever and diarrhea), and later died. Three paramedics who treated the workers also were found to be contaminated and were hospitalized. The workers at the plant reported seeing a blue light and then becoming ill. They were taken to a local hospital, then flown to a hospital that specializes in radiation sickness. The accident spewed a gas containing α, β, and γ radiation into the atmosphere. Radiation levels soared as high as 10,000 times above normal shortly after the accident. The village of Tokaimura has a population of around 34,000. In the immediate aftermath of the accident, officials reacted slowly and made many poor decisions exposing many people to needless risk. Schools and transportation services in the region ultimately were shut down for days. More than 300,000 people were affected by the order to restrict their activities and to stay in their homes with windows and vents closed for 4 days. About 150 people were evacuated from the immediate vicinity of the plant, one of 15 nuclear-related plants in Tokaimura.

By now, the list of major nuclear accidents is not, by any means, short. The first major nuclear accident took place near Toronto (Chalk River), Canada, on December 12, 1952. The reactor core was nearly demolished when a technician opened valves, melting some uranium fuel and boiling coolant. In November, 1955, an experimental reactor near Idaho Falls, Idaho, partially melted down during a test. In October, 1957, a fire caused by a plutonium production reactor in the northwest of England (Windscale/Sellafield) burned 11 tons of uranium and killed 32 people. The March 1958 explosion at a nuclear plant in Fyshtym, the former Soviet Union, devastated the region for hundreds of square miles. January 1961 brought another tragedy to Idaho Falls: A reactor exploded, emitting extremely high levels of radiation. October 5, 1966, another nuclear accident in the United States: An experimental reactor near Detroit partially melted down. The December 1975 fire at the Lubmin nuclear power complex near Greifswald on the Baltic coast in former East Germany caused near meltdown. The Three Mile Island (Middletown, PA) tragedy of March, 1979, led to partial meltdown of the nuclear plant. The plant had opened just six months earlier. In April, 1986, explosion and fire at the Chernobyl nuclear reactor near Kiev, Ukraine, spewed radiation over much of Europe. This tragedy was followed by another Russian accident: In 1992, loss of pressure in the reactor channel released radioactive iodine and inert gases into the atmosphere near St. Petersburg. A November, 1995, reactor accident in Japan leaked two to three tons of sodium from the cooling system. This accident was followed by fire and explosion at a power reactor and nuclear fuel plant in Tokaimura (Japan).

How many more additions to this list can be expected? The answer is: We do not know, but most likely it will happen again. Modern society is dependent on nuclear energy and probably this dependency will increase. Our life contains a large variety of both benefits and potential risks due to technological development. Energy produced in nuclear power plants is but one example. Technologically based benefits are easy to welcome and adapt to, whereas related risks are hard to understand, consider, and digest. Ionizing radiation is one of the potentially hazardous agents of technological progress, a central nervous system (CNS) teratogen, whose impact on human cognitive development and functioning deserves as much attention as researchers can give it.

Modern knowledge of the impact of ionizing radiation on cognitive functioning is derived from three major sources: animal irradiation studies, clinical studies of patients treated with radiation, and disaster studies. Thus, this chapter reviews the data on links between irradiation and cognitive functioning, considering evidence from animal studies, clinical studies, and disaster research.

EVIDENCE FROM ANIMAL STUDIES

Animal models have been used productively to investigate the mechanisms of irradiation-induced brain damage since the beginning of this century. Most of these studies have focused on histopathological rather than behavioral changes. Yet, there is a considerable number of studies addressing behavioral changes caused by irradiation. The following brief review of these studies is structured by the time of irradiation, that is, whether it was carried out prenatally or postnatally.

Fetal Irradiation

Animal experiments have shown that fetal exposure to radiation can result in functional abnormalities of the central nervous system. Specifically, the sequelae are expressed in the form of motor functional disorders, electroencephalogram (EEG) aberrations, and learning and behavioral defects (UNSCEAR, 1993). There is a distinct link between the degree of impairment, the dose of exposure, and the time of exposure.

Exposure to 1 Gray[1] (Gy) or above of X- or γ-radiation[2] during the fetal gestational days has been reported to produce behavioral changes in adult rats (Jensch, Eisenman, & Brent, 1995; Kimler & Norton, 1988; Norton & Kimler,

---

[1]The annual dose limit range for occupational exposure recommended by the International Commission on Radiation Protection is 0.5 Gy.

[2]Radiation is energy in the form of electromagnetic waves or particles with kinetic energy. Radiation is emitted from radioactive (unstable) atoms, generated during the interaction of radiation with matter or from a radiation producing machine (such as an X-ray machine). Radiation sometimes has enough energy to separate electrons from their atoms when the energy is absorbed in matter. The positively charged atom is called an ion and the process is ionization. Ionizing radiation includes α, β particles, γ (and x) rays, and neutrons. α-particles are charged particles containing two protons and two neutrons that are emitted from the nucleus of certain heavy atoms, such as uranium, when they decay. An α-particle can be stopped or shielded by a sheet of paper, but can be very damaging when inside the body. β-particles are electrons emitted with high energy from many different radioactive atoms. β(s) with a positive charge are called positrons. β-particles are likely to interact and deposit their energy as they pass through surrounding matter. Those emitted from the decay of a radioactive atom can easily be shielded by using thin metals or plastic. β-particles are usually stopped by the skin, but they can cause serious injury to the skin and eyes. γ (and x) rays are electromagnetic radiation with no mass or charge. γ-rays are generally emitted from the nucleus of an atom during radioactive decay, and x rays are emitted from the electron shells. Electromagnetic radiation may also be emitted by a charged particle accelerating or decelerating in an electric field. Electromagnetic waves are very penetrating forms of radiation, and dense materials such as lead or depleted uranium are used for shielding. Neutrons are particles that are emitted from the nucleus during fission, emitted as part of radioactive decay, and are emitted as secondary radiation from the interaction of other high energy particles with matter. Neutrons are a very penetrating form of radiation. Shielding that is most effective for neutrons includes water, paraffin, boron, and concrete.

1987; Schull, Norton, & Jensh, 1990; Tamaki, Hoshino, & Kameyama, 1989) and mice (Sienkeiwicz, Haylock, & Sounders, 1994; Sienkeiwicz, Saunders, & Butland, 1992).

For example, Norton, Kimler, and Mullenix (1991) conducted a gait analysis and photographic analysis of sequences of behavioral acts at 1 and 3 months postnatally on rats exposed to ionizing radiation *in utero* and no-treatment controls. Experimental fetuses were exposed to 0.75 Gy of ionizing radiation on gestational day 15 through the whole-body exposure of pregnant rats. Body weight and thickness of the cerebral cortex of the exposed rats were 10%–25% below those of the controls. Behavior in all tests was more affected at 3 months than at 1 month of age. Gait widened less in the irradiated rats than in the control rats from 1 to 3 months. In photographic analysis of behavior, controls increased their time spent standing significantly more than did irradiated rats. Some behavioral alterations from perinatal exposure to radiation become more marked with maturation, suggesting that deleterious effects of ionizing radiation on the developing brain may be not only prolonged but also progressive.

Gigi, Mintz, Ben-Elyahu, and Myslobodsky (1997) reported the findings on tail asymmetry in neonate rats exposed to radiation (1.5 Gy) on Days 15, 17, and 19 of prenatal development. This study was based on 601 pups—368 exposed and 233 sham-irradiated controls (i.e., they were administered "placebo" radiation). On Day 2, pups were weighed and subjected to axial symmetry testing. The data showed that exposed and sham pups had about identical incidences of postural asymmetry: 70% of exposed pups and 66% of sham-irradiated controls showed tail asymmetry. No side bias was found to be statistically significant in either of the exposed or sham-irradiated groups, males or females; however, when all asymmetry data were pooled, a slight (58%) but significant left-side preference emerged. Exposed pups showed a small but statistically significant weight reduction, and pups exposed on Days 15 and 17 were significantly more affected. These findings are consistent with the view that weight is an important variable in revealing the effects of prenatal radiation.

Mintz, Yovel, Gigi, and Myslobodsky (1998) explored the role of prenatal radiation-related trauma in disordered gating. Pregnant rats were exposed

---

Radiation exposure is a quantity, originally developed to determine the output of medical x-ray machines, and the unit of measure is the Roentgen (R). The Roentgen is defined by the amount of electrical charge produced when x-ray or γ radiation "exposes" a specific volume of air. When ionizing radiation passes through matter, some or all of its energy is imparted to the matter. The amount of energy absorbed per unit mass is called the absorbed dose. The absorbed dose is measured using the unit rad, which is equal to 100 ergs/gram deposited by an ionizing radiation in any type of material. The standard unit for the absorbed dose is the gray (Gy), where 1 Gy = 100 rad.

to 1.5 Gy (0.15 Gy/min) of whole-body γ-radiation on Days 15, 17, or 19 of gestation. Controls were sham-exposed during 10 minutes in the same conditions. Exposed and control offspring were evaluated for the auditory startle response and its gating. The tests were conducted when the animals reached 27 and 57 days of age. A noticeable hyperresponding and delayed habituation of startle were found in rats exposed on Day 15, with meager effects in rats exposed on Days 17 and 19. Maximal deficit was obtained on tests conducted on the 57th day of life but not on the 27th day of life. However, in rats pretreated with amphetamine, dysfunctional startle was shown already on the Day 27 test. These findings correspond to findings from earlier studies, where progeny of rats irradiated on Days 14–16 have been shown to demonstrate hyperresponding and hyperactivity (Furchgott, Tacker, & Draper, 1968).

In line with the previously described results, researchers (Devi, Hossain, & Bisht, 1999) registered significant dose-dependent decreases in locomotor and exploratory activities in progeny of mice irradiated on Day 17 of gestation. These researchers exposed pregnant mice to 0.3–1.5 Gy of γ radiation. When offspring were 6 months old, they were subjected to tests of locomotor and exploratory activities, learning, and memory. After all tests, 10 males and 10 females from each group were sacrificed, and their brain weights were measured. Learning and memory functions showed a significant impairment, even at 0.3 Gy, with dose-dependent decrements in behavioral tests, conditioned avoidance response, and maze-learning efficiency. Brain weight showed a linear dose-dependent decrease, but brain:body weight ratio was not significantly different.

Thus, studies consistently show a linear dose-dependent increase in the radiation-induced changes in animal locomotor and exploratory activities, with the threshold at about 0.2–0.3 Gy at late fetal age in rats and mice (Devi et al., 1999; Minamisawa & Hirokaga, 1996). The time-based difference in the impact of irradiation at late fetal age is remarkable—the behavioral manifestations vary from excessive to suppressed emotionality and from hyper- to hypoactivity. The earlier period of fetal mammalian development is considered to be comparatively resistant to the teratogenic effect of radiation (Devi et al., 1999). Schull et al. (1990) discussed ionizing radiation as a CNS teratogen and reviewed animal studies of the effects of radiation exposure. Sensitivity to radiation (dose-response) is similar among all mammalian species when developmental periods are compared. At exposure levels of 1.0 Gy and above, serious consequences (e.g., mental retardation) occur with high probability when fetuses are exposed during the period of neuronal migration to the cortical plate of the developing telencephalon. At the same exposure levels, many behavioral tests in animals show significant alterations when fetuses are exposed during cortical plate formation.

Postnatal Irradiation

Research on behavioral deficits following X-irradition in animals has revealed some inconsistencies, both for irradiation for a strong single dose and for fractionated doses of radiation.

For example, one study has showed that, in the rat brain, a single dose of about 20 Gy of x-rays induced predominantly vascular lesions, which appeared after a latent period of approximately 12 months (Calvo, Hopewell, Reinhold, & Yeung, 1988). The researchers stressed that higher single doses resulted in more pronounced damage in white-matter areas and that the latency for the development of such lesions was significantly shorter. In contrast, Walters et al. (1995) examined the possible bioeffects of an acute exposure to high peak power ultra-wide-band electromagnetic radiation using male rats and found no significant differences between irradiated and non-irradiated animals on any of the measured behavioral and cognitive parameters.

Chen, Lamproglou, Poisson, Le Ponchin, and Delattre (1992) applied fractionated doses of radiation (30 Gy/10 fractions/12 days) in young rats and found no learning deficits. Explaining their results, Chen et al. suggested that the lack of effect on cognition of their fractionated dose of radiation may have occurred because young animals were more resistant to the effects of irradiation than were older animals. Lamproglou et al. (1995) followed up on this hypothesis and demonstrated a progressive deterioration of memory function over a 7-month period after a course of whole-brain irradiation (30 Gy/10 fractions/12 days) in elderly rats based on performance on avoidance and water maze tasks.

Hodges et al. (1998) assessed the delayed consequences of radiation damage on learning and memory in rats over a period of 44 weeks (starting 26 weeks after local irradiation of the whole brain with single doses of x-rays). Doses were set at levels known to produce vascular changes alone (20 Gy) or vascular changes followed by necrosis (25 Gy). Experimental tests included assessments of working memory and spatial learning in various maze tasks. Findings demonstrated that local cranial irradiation with these doses produced delayed impairment (at least 26 weeks after irradiation) of spatial learning and working memory. The extent of these deficits appears to be task- and dose-related, because rats treated with 25 Gy showed marked impairments in all measures, whereas rats treated with the lower dose showed less impairment in water-maze learning and no deficits in water-maze working memory, despite significant disruption of working memory in the T-maze.

Maier and Landauer (1990) assessed the effects of acute (10 Gy) radiation exposure on aggressive behavior, locomotor activity, and body weight in two experiments with individually housed male mice. Irradiated and sham-irradiated resident animals did not differ significantly in the amount or type of offensive aggressive behavior that they displayed until 7 days postirradiation, when a decrease was observed in irradiated mice. Ambulation and activities in an open field were suppressed, beginning on the day of irradiation. Body weight significantly decreased by 4 days postirradiation, showing either that food consumption had dropped because of radiation-induced anorexia or that animals were no longer physiologically capable of deriving the full nutritional value of their food due to erosion of gastrointestinal cells. These results have been supported in subsequent research. Miyachi and Yamada (1996) examined the effects of low-dose x-ray irradiation (x-irradiation) on aggressive behavior, using a resident-intruder paradigm. Male inbred mice became gradually calm and showed remarkably quiet behavior 7–10 days after whole-head .05- or .15-Gy X-irradiation. Targeted exposure of the anterior part of the head (olfactory system including orbits) also induced a remarkable suppression of aggressive behavior. The olfactory system has direct access to the limbic system, a central part of the brain concerned with emotion; it is plausible that low-dose x-irradiation of the olfactory system results in some changes in the limbic system which, in turn, lead to suppression of aggressive behavior. The researchers also presented data on brain biochemistry that further support the observed low-dose effects on mouse behavior: The carnosine content (the brain-produced chemical determining the function and sensitivity of the olfactory system) and its production in the olfactory bulbs decreased significantly after targeted exposure of the anterior part of the head. Higher doses (.25–.35 Gy), however, did not induce such effects. Results suggest that the depression of aggressive behavior is limited to animals irradiated with smaller doses. Sudakov et al. (1995) studied the effects of chronic γ-irradiation on rats' reactions to conflict situations producing emotional stress. The results of Sudakov were similar to those of Miyachi and Yamada: Low-to-medium dosage of radiation suppressed open-field behaviors and calmed the animals.

To summarize, radiation damage appears to be restricted to the white matter and is characterized by a number of histopathological changes (e.g., vascular lesions, edema, necrosis, and demyelination). The radiation dose and time appear to be crucial in determining extent, location, type of damage, and latent period between exposure and appearance of lesions (Calvo, Hopewell, Reinhold, Van Den Berg, & Yeung, 1987; Calvo et al., 1988; Diaz-Granados, Greene, & Amsel, 1994; Shtemberg, 1999). There is also some evidence that although high-dose irradiation-induced white matter necrosis is associated with substantial impairment, cognitive deficits not associated with the development of necrosis may be detected after a lower dose (Hodges et al., 1998). Joseph (1992), for example, in his research with rats, supported the concept that low-dose radiation exposure can induce "accelerated aging" (e.g., Ainsworth et al., 1976; Upton, 1959), as observed in memory and motor performance.

Taken together, the pre- and postnatal irradiation studies indicate the impairing impact of radiation, but suggest that the dose and duration of radiation, the age of the animal, and the type of task all interact in determining the degree of cognitive impairment induced by irradiation.

EVIDENCE FROM MEDICAL STUDIES INVOLVING RADIATION

Radiation therapy is widely used in the treatment of brain tumors and acute lymphoblastic leukemia. The curative effectiveness of therapeutic radiation is well established. Specifically, the use of ionizing radiation therapy in the medical treatment of children with acute lymphoblastic leukemia has resulted in dramatically higher recent survival rates than even a dozen years ago (Margolin & Poplack, 1997).

Oncology treatment usually involves some combination of chemotherapy and radiation therapy. Patients with leukemia conventionally receive low-dose whole-brain irradiation; patients with tumors are usually treated with local irradiation at a higher dose. Since the first years of radiation therapy, there has been an issue of a trade-off between the helpful and the harmful impacts of radiation therapy on patients suffering from various cancers. With improved patient survival, attention has focused on delayed adverse side effects (e.g., Iaconetta et al., 1994). The question, specifically, is the neuropsychological cost of this radiation therapy. To address this question, researchers have utilized a number of research designs.

First, they compared irradiated and nonirradiated survivors of leukemia. The results revealed no significant intellectual differences between irradiated and nonirradiated groups of children who were 6.5 years or older at diagnosis (Stehbens et al., 1994). However, mild isolated deficits have been found in patients who were between ages of 3 and 6.5 at diagnosis (MacLean et al., 1995). It is important to know whether irradiated or nonirradiated survivors of leukemia show significant declines on measures of verbal IQ and arithmetic achievement over a period of approximately 5 years following treatment (Ochs et al., 1991). In a prospective study designed to investigate late neurocognitive functioning in leukemia patients who received treatment with chemotherapy but without radiotherapy, researchers (Copeland, Moore, Francis, Jaffe, & Gulbert, 1996) documented a lack of significant deleterious effects of chemotherapy on neuropsychological status. Yet mild academic declines were noted for this nonirradiated sample. Lockwood, Bell, and Colegrove (1999) retrospectively examined the long-term effects of cranial radiation therapy (CRT) on attention functioning. Survivors of childhood leukemia who had been randomly assigned to a treatment regimen of chemotherapy with or without 1,800 cGy CRT were administered a neuropsychological test battery, including the Wechsler Intelligence Scale for Children–Third Edition, the California Verbal Learning Test, and the Controlled Oral Word Association Test, among other tests. Significant differences were found between the irradiated and nonirradiated groups on three of four attentional components. An interaction between treatment type and age at diagnosis was significant on one attentional component. Further, the mean scores of participants irradiated in early childhood (prior to the age of 54 months) were significantly lower relative to published norms for age-standard scores on the majority of task variables, while the other groups showed rare deviations from average scores. Thus, these findings indicate that early irradiation was associated with significant impairment in attentional filtering, focusing, and automatic shifting. Computerized tomography studies and postmortem studies have demonstrated white matter necrosis and alterations in arterial function following cranial irradiation (Fletcher & Copeland, 1988; Maurer et al., 1988). Irradiated leukemia survivors have been observed to demonstrate symptoms resembling those of attention deficit or hyperactivity disorder (Brouwers & Poplack, 1990).

Second, researchers evaluated and described behavioral and cognitive characteristics of leukemia survivors as a group. It has been shown that long-term leukemia survivors often show learning disabilities (Fogarty et al., 1988). Ciesielski et al. (1994) investigated whether there are consistent morphologic changes in the cerebellums of young children treated with radiation and chemotherapy for acute lymphoblastic leukemia and whether these changes are related to any consistent pattern of cognitive deficits. Participants were asked to perform a battery of 9 neuropsychological tests and underwent magnetic resonance imaging (MRI). Results found consistent and variable structural changes in the brains of survivors of leukemia. It was also suggested that the neurodevelopmental mechanism of cerebellar abnormality may be multifactorial, and that the complex relationship between structure, processes, and behavior has a reciprocal character. Computer tomography scans have linked cranial radiotherapy to demyelination of subcortical regions and subsequent ventricular enlargement (Feltcher & Copeland, 1988). To determine the pathways between treatment intensity (high-dose cranial radiation and chemotherapy) and various psychosocial outcomes, researchers (Chen et al., 1998) reviewed medical records and carried out structured interviews with young adult survivors of childhood leukemia (aged 18–33 years). Survivors' moods, health-compromising behaviors, perceived limitations, educational achievements, and medical variables were assessed. Structural equation modeling showed that higher treatment intensity during childhood predicted more health-compromising behaviors as adults through lower educational achievement. Additionally, higher childhood treatment intensity predicted current negative mood, both directly and via changes in perceived limitations.

Third, researchers compared cognitive performance of irradiated leukemia survivors to that of their relatives. For example, Haupt et al. (1994) demonstrated a significantly high rate of placement in special education and learning disabled programs for irradiated survivors relative to their siblings. Moreover, the risk for special placement was mediated by age at diagnosis and dose received during therapy.

Fourth, they compared performance of irradiated children to that of the general population. Specifically, patients irradiated in early childhood were found to demonstrate lower academic performance than was shown by the general population (Goff, Anderson, & Cooper, 1980).

Fifth, intellectual functioning in children with leukemia was compared at pre- and posttreatment stages. Specifically, there is some evidence of a significant decline in IQ functioning as measured after radiational treatment (Stehbens & Kisker, 1984). Little is known about cognitive outcomes in irradiated adults, although studies provide some evidence of intellectual decline occurring after cranial irradiation (Imperato, Paleologos, & Vicky, 1990; Roman & Sperduto, 1995).

Comparable data have been collected in studies of brain tumor patients. For example, researchers followed for 3 to 4 years a group of children with noncortical brain tumors, primarily medulloblastoma (Radcliffe et al., 1994). All participants of this study received craniospinal irradiation, and 79% received chemotherapy as well. For the group as a whole, Full Scale IQ fell from 104 at baseline to 91 at final follow-up. Children younger than 7 years at diagnosis showed a significant decrease in IQ as early as Year 1, and all changes from baseline to Years 3 and 4 were significant. In contrast, children older than 7 years at diagnosis did not show a significant IQ change from baseline to Year 3 or 4. In another study, a group of children and adolescents with tumors in various brain sites completed the Wechsler Intelligence Scale for Children (WISC) and memory tests (recognition, content, and sequence memory) (Dennis et al., 1992). Fifty percent of these children had received radiation therapy and 7% had received chemotherapy and radiation therapy. Verbal intelligence varied positively with age at radiation treatment. Memory for word meanings appeared to be unrelated to radiation history or to hormone status. Severe deficits in working memory were associated with a history of radiation and a principal tumor site that involved thalamic–epithalamic brain regions. The researchers concluded that radiation treatment affected later cognitive functioning in recipients of the treatment. Christianson, Neppe, and Hoffman (1994) presented the case of a 43-year-old man with a brain tumor who developed a syndrome of amnestic disorder (frequent forgetting and difficulties remembering) and vegetative (somatic) abnormalities after undergoing brain surgery and tumor irradiation. The man showed extremely poor long-term memory of both visually and verbally presented material and of autobiographical events that occurred after the onset of the illness. However, the patient showed preserved memory functions on short-term memory tasks, semantic-memory tasks, and implicit-memory tasks. Fossen (1995) reviewed the long-term neuropsychological aftereffects of the treatment of brain tumors in children. According to Fossen's interpretation of the literature, most negative consequences of brain-tumor treatment are linked to radiation treatment. The resulting impairments include those of intellectual functions, speech, attention, concentration, and memory. Psychophysiological sequelae are hypoactivity, visuomotor disorders, and physical-development disorders. Similarly, Iaconetta et al. (1994) reviewed the literature related to the development of long-term side effects (such as the syndrome of dysfunction in neurobehavioral abilities, induction of new tumors, visual disturbances, and brain necrosis) in adult patients who had been treated with radiation therapy for brain tumors. The researchers arrived at the conclusion that, although the risk–benefit ratio is considered acceptable in the treatment of malignant tumors, there is uncertainty as to whether it is acceptable in the management of benign tumors.

Hypothesizing on the nature of neuropsychological impairments caused by radiation, researchers have pointed to hippocampal damage following radiation-induced vasculopathy (a vascular disorder) and hypoxia (a deficiency of oxygen reaching the tissues of the body; Abayomi, Chun, & Kelly, 1990), generalized CNS atrophy (Ladavas, Missiroli, Rosito, Serra, & Vecchi, 1983), and hemispheric disconnection via damage to the corpus callosum and anterior commisure (Jenkins, 1991). Autopsy studies linked a slow onset of dementia, speech, and movement disturbance following CNS radiation and chemotherapy in children to degeneration of cerebral white matter and, in some cases, of grey matter around the basal ganglia (Fletcher & Copeland, 1988).

Thus, it appears that radiation-therapy-induced somatic improvements have been associated with long-term neuropsychological consequences (Brouwers, 1987; Moss, Nannis, & Poplack, 1981; Rowland et al., 1984). These conclusions, however, are not certain: Repeated cranial irradiation to children does not necessarily lead to impaired cognitive function (Davidson, Childs, Hopewell, & Tait, 1994). Moreover, it is interesting to note that there is some evidence suggesting that behavioral and social adjustment of children treated with radiation appears to be similar to population norms and shows no "dose response" related to radiation intensity (Noll et al., 1997).

Whole-brain irradiation (typically used in treatment of leukemia) carries a greater risk for neuropsychological impairment than does local-brain irradiation (typically used in tumor treatment) (Mumby & Pinel, 1994). Reflecting on the incidence of learning disabilities in children treated with irradiation, researchers suggest that the most pronounced side effect of irradiation is impaired attention and memory rather than low intellectual level (Abayomi et al., 1990; Dennis et al., 1992; Roman & Sperduto, 1995). In general, the findings suggest that higher radiation treatment intensity during childhood may serve as a risk factor for adult survivors' neuropsychological functioning.

EVIDENCE FROM DISASTER STUDIES

Nuclear disasters of this century have meant many things for many people. For those who happened to be in the immediate proximity to these tragedies, they meant loss of life, destroyed communities, chronic health illnesses, sterility, miscarriages, an increase in congenital malformations, spontaneous abortions, fetal resorptions, low birth weight, increase in childhood cancers, developmental, neurobehavioral, neuroendocrine, and neurochemical abnormalities, and forever changed life pathways. For those concerned with issues of the effects of technological disasters on public attitudes and behaviors, communicating risks, and managing massive health hazards, these events provided opportunities to verify and modify their theories and practices. For those responsible for health care of the irradiated, these tragedies provided opportunities to learn, even though the cost of these lessons was very high.

Nuclear health is largely uncharted territory, because we have little direct experience with the epidemiological links between people and radiation. Paradoxically, monitoring the human health consequences of nuclear disasters leaves us wiser and better informed. In its short history, the field of nuclear health has accumulated enough data to classify the data into two categories, addressing the direct and the indirect impacts of irradiation.

Direct Impacts of Irradiation

According to the Law of Bergonie and Tribondeau, cells are radiosensitive if they have a high mitotic rate; they undergo many cell divisions; and they are of a primitive type (Casarett, 1968). The CNS in adult humans consists of fully differentiated cells that are incapable of dividing. So the CNS is one of the most radioresistant organs. Small-to-moderate radiation exposure is rarely reported to produce any detectable morphological changes in nervous tissue. Very high doses of several ten Gy result in a "delayed radionecrosis" of the CNS, which occurs after a latent period of months or years (Casarett, 1968). Similarly, electrophysiological studies have also suggested that ionizing radiation can induce changes in the bioelectric properties of nerve cells only at superlethal doses (as cited in Miyachi & Yamada, 1996). Some researchers have demonstrated an enhancement of neuroexcitability at x-ray dose of more than 100 Gy (Gunther & Hug, 1974). Other researchers have shown that radiation doses below 100 Gy have no effect on action potentials, conduction velocity, or membrane resistance (Gaffey, 1971a, 1971b). It is well documented that an acute high dose of ionizing radiation produces a decrement in behavioral and cognitive performance. There is now also some evidence suggesting a detrimental impact of low-dose extended irradiation.

High-Dose Acute Irradiation. Irrefutable evidence of the potentially devastating effects of *in utero* ionizing radiation exposure on neurological development has been accumulated since early history of radiology. As far back as in the early 1930s, researchers (Goldstein & Murphy, 1929) noticed higher rates of mental retardation in children exposed to radiation *in utero*. Dekeban (1968) reported data collected in a group of 26 infants who had been exposed to therapeutic radiation. Eighty-five percent of these children, irradiated between 3 and 20 weeks of gestation, were microcephalic, mentally retarded, or both.

There is also abundant evidence suggesting that parental exposure to radiation results in elevated incidence of Down's syndrome (e.g. , Strigine, Sansone, Carobbi, & Pierluigh, 1990). Bound, Francis, & Harvey (1995) have analyzed a prevalence of Down's syndrome in Lancashire, England, with particular reference to low-dose ionizing radiation. The researchers registered a significant increase in the prevalence of Down's syndrome in all cases conceived in 1963 and 1964, and a lesser peak in 1958 that did not quite reach significance. The 1963–1964 peak coincided with the maximum estimated radiation dose; the 1958 peak coincided with increased exposure to radiation from fallout, possibly enhanced by ground deposits after a fire at the Windscale reactor in October 1957.

Much of our current knowledge of the effects of prenatal ionizing radiation exposure on neuropsychological development and functioning has been gained through research with survivors of *in utero* radiation exposure at Hiroshima and Nagasaki[3] and various nuclear accidents (e.g., the Chernobyl tragedy[4]). Given that all of these tragedies happened to their victims unexpectedly, there are no accurate data on either the true numbers of *in utero* exposures or survivors of *in utero* exposures from the nuclear bomb-

---

[3]In August 1945, two atomic bombs were dropped on the cities of Hiroshima and Nagasaki, Japan. In all, more than 200,000 peopled died from the blast and the radiation released by the bombs. Those who lived through the atomic bombs are referred to as Hibakusha. Their offspring are referred to as second-generation Hibakusha (or Hibakusha Nisei).

[4]In April 1986, the Chernobyl Nuclear Power Reactor Number Four exploded, the core began to melt, and a conflagration ignited that spread a cloud of radioactivity over large parts of Russia and neighboring countries. The conditions that led to the explosion began on April 25 and the explosion occurred on April 26, 1986. The explosion and fire blew the top off the reactor, caused a tremendous release of radioactive substances into the atmosphere, and sent a radioactive plume across the former Soviet Union and some parts of Europe. This release of radiation into the environment posed a serious risk to human health. The fallout from the Chernobyl accident was unevenly distributed, unlike the fallout from nuclear bomb testing in the

ings/accidents. The samples are usually based on national census data whose accuracy varies from country to country. The bulk of the data comes from Japan, where the magnitude of the tragedy and the intensity of radiation exposure resulted in the largest sample of survivors of *in utero* exposures (2,310 in Hiroshima and 1,562 in Nagasaki).

The early studies (e.g., Plummer, 1952; Yamazaki, Wright, & Wright, 1954) were based on opportunistic samples. These studies showed higher rates of both microcephalia and mental retardation in children exposed to radiation *in utero*. The later studies have been much more systematic in (a) ascertaining the exposed sample, (b) matching its members with controls, (c) carefully recording the gestational age at exposure, and (d) including dosimetric data (e.g., Dunn, Yoshimaru, Otake, Annegers, & Schull, 1990; Otake & Schull, 1984). These newer studies have revealed the differential impact of radiation on cognitive functioning outcome depending on both dose and gestational age at the exposure.

Specifically, prior to the pioneer study by Otake and Schull (1984), researchers believed that ionizing radiation kills cells in the brain, resulting in small head size, and, when severe enough, mental retardation. Otake and Schull demonstrated the differential impact of radiation based on dose and time of exposure. Specifically, Otake, Schull, and Yoshimaru (1991) showed that children exposed to atom bomb radiation in the range of 0.12–0.23 Gy during the most sensitive stage of 8 to 15 weeks of gestation developed mental retardation. Otake and Schull (1984) suggested that exposure to ionizing radiation during weeks 8 to 15 impairs the process of cortical neurons proliferating or migrating to the cortex from areas near the ventricles. The first period of the brain development (0–8 weeks) is marked by the emergence of the two principal types of cells from which the nervous system develops— neurons and neuroglia. Cells killed before the 8th week of gestational age can result in small head size without mental retardation, because the neurons that will form the cerebrum are at a stage that is not susceptible to impairment by radiation. What is susceptible to reduction at this very early stage of brain development is the glial cells, which provide structural support for the brain (Miller, 1990). The patterns of outcomes of the newer studies suggests that either one or both processes of proliferation and migration can be adversely affected by radiation. This does not appear to be the cir-

---

1960s. An invisible cloud of radiation floated freely overhead, moving to wherever the winds carried it (Bailey, 1989). After the decay of short-lived radionuclides, ^{137}Cs and [134]Cs are the most significant nuclides. One particular concern is Cesium-137, a radioactive particle that can accumulate in body tissues. It was present in the Chernobyl cloud; its half-life is 30 years, and as a result of atmospheric movements, it poisoned large areas of Russia. Overall, Russian territories were affected by the catastrophe in such a way that the density of poisoning higher than 1 Ci over a squared Km is about 55.1 Km^2. These areas are inhabited by approximately 1,209,929 people, who now live in an environment of low-dose irradiation.

cumstance when the radiation occurred during 0 to 8 weeks. Thus, the effects of radiation on cell migration during Weeks 8 to 15 may be the crucial histopathologic insult (Sever, 1993). It is apparent that small head size is related to reduction in cell number. However, the nature of the reduction is not clear—it can originate from impairment of neuronal proliferation, massive cell death, or a combination of these two processes. Mental retardation has been found in children with normal head size; thus, it might result from a proliferation of glial cells in the brain after radiation exposure. Animal research has demonstrated (D'Amato & Hicks, 1965) the ability of glial cells to regenerate after radiation exposure.

As for the dosage of the exposure, there is an increasing frequency of neuropsychological endpoints (i.e., microcephaly, mental retardation, and seizure disorders) at 0.50 Gy. The findings for exposures below this dosage are more ambiguous, although some studies show an effect at 0.10–0.19 Gy (Sever, 1993).

Similarly to results of Japanese epidemiological studies of children exposed to radiation *in utero*, studies in Belorussia, the Ukraine, and Russia revealed higher rates of mild mental retardation in children irradiated prenatally than in children from control samples (WHO, 1996). Researchers (Kolominsky, Igumnov, & Drozdovitch, 1999) examined psychological development in children at the ages of 6 to 7 and 10 to 11 years who had suffered prenatal radiation exposure at the time of the Chernobyl accident in 1986. These children were compared to an age-matched control group of children from noncontaminated areas of Belarus. Included were neurological and psychiatric examinations, intellectual assessment, and clinical psychological investigation of parents, as well as the estimation of thyroid exposure *in utero*. The exposed group manifested a relative increase in psychological impairment compared with the control group, with increased prevalence in cases of specific developmental speech-language disorders (18.1% vs. 8.2 % at 6–7 years; 10.1% vs. 3.3% at 10–11 years) and emotional disorders (20.3% vs. 7.4% at 6–7 years; 18.1 vs. 7.4% at 10–11 years). The mean IQ of the exposed group was lower than that of the control group, and there were more cases of borderline IQ. No correlation was found between individual thyroid doses and IQ at age 6 to 7 years or 10 to 11 years. There was a moderate correlation between high personal anxiety in parents and emotional disorders in children.

It is rather striking that there are virtually no psychological studies of the survivors of the Hiroshima–Nagasaki tragedy and their offspring; most research is on the biological consequences of the atomic bombing (e.g., Plummer, 1995; Neal et al., 1953; Russell et al., 1973; Wakabayashi, 1995). In one of the rare studies on the neuropsychological impact of the atomic bombing, Yamada et al. (1999) examined the prevalence rate of dementia and its subtypes and investigated the relationship of risk factors (age, gender, attained education, history of head trauma, and history of cancer) to the prevalence of Alzheimer's disease (AD) or vascular dementia in the Adult Health Study (AHS) cohort consisting of atomic-bomb survivors and their controls, selected from residents in Hiroshima and Nagasaki. Since 1958, AHS members have been followed through biennial medical examinations. In addition to the biennial medical exams, a screening test for cognitive impairment was conducted between 1992 and 1996. Results show that the prevalence of dementia was 7.2% and did not differ from that in the control sample. The prevalence of AD was 2.0% in men and 3.8% in women, and the prevalence of vascular dementia was 2.0% in men and 1.8% in women (these rates also did not differ from those in the control sample). Odds ratios of AD for age (in 10-year increments), attained education (in 3-year increments), history of head trauma, and history of cancer were 6.3, 0.6, 7.4, and 0.3, respectively. Odds ratios of vascular dementia for age, history of stroke, and history of hypertension were 2.0, 35.7, and 4.0, respectively. Neither type of dementia showed any significant effect of radiation exposure.

A number of studies address the issue of the psychological status of those who participated in the containment of the Chernobyl accident. These people (called Liquidators in Russia) got highest dosages of radiation. Specifically, Chikina and Torubarov (1991) conducted a clinical psychological study of a group of men who developed acute radiation sickness of various degrees of severity following the disaster at the Chernobyl Atomic Power Station. The men were observed at different times (right after the irradiation and at multiple time points during the recovery period). These men's performance was compared to that of aged-matched controls. The multiple exposures to stress and acute radiation sickness led to severe anxiety, depression, modifications of the structure of self-awareness, reduction of mental working capacity, and specific changes in the structure of the personality. Tarabrina, Lazebnaya, and Zelenova (1994) studied the incidence of posttraumatic stress disorder in workers who were involved for 1 to 2 months in the clean-up following the Chernobyl nuclear disaster. The incidence of the posttraumatic stress disorder in this sample was elevated as compared to the general population. Similarly, Zhavoronkova et al. (1995) examined the psychoneurological status of a group of Liquidators, comparing them to a group of healthy controls. The data revealed higher incidence of headaches, rapid onset of fatigue, sleep disturbances, bone pain, emotional instability, intolerance to solar radiation, and disturbed EEG patterns in the group of Liquidators. In a different study, indices of sensorimotor reactivity, functional lability of the nervous processes, capacity for mental work, and short-term visual memory were determined among the Chernobyl clean-up crew members 6 years after the accident (Makarenko, Voronovskaya, & Sprin', 1996). The psychophysiological indices under study were below the population standards and deteriorated with age. It is important to know that, as a group, the Liquidators performed worse at the 6-year follow-up than at the baseline assessment during or immediately after the clean-up operation. Moreover, at the 6-year follow-up, there were no differences in performance of those Liquidators who were diagnosed with acute radiation sickness afterward and those without radiation sickness who had, however, been exposed to radiation, even though there was a significant difference at the baseline. This finding suggests the possibility of progressive neuropsychological deterioration caused by irradiation. Similarly, progressive neuropsychological deficits were registered in a 4-year longitudinal study of Liquidators of various ages (Novikov, Tsygan, Borisova, & Rybina, 1997).

A number of researchers (Bazylevich, Aseyev, Bodunov, & Guseva, 1993; Terestchenko, Lyaginskaya, & Burtzeva, 1991; Tkachenko & Vlasov, 1995) have attempted to study individuals and families affected by the Chernobyl fallout. The general conclusion of this research is that, as a group, these individuals differ from the general population on a number of mental-health variables—primarily, demonstrating elevated anxiety and depression and some psychomotor dysfunctioning. These data, however, do not permit the formulation of any causal conclusions—immediate victims of the tragedy, on top of receiving a dose, have experienced a number of adverse life events due to evacuation, relocation, lose of a sense of belonging, and so on.

Continuous Low-Dose Irradiation. The symptoms of radiation trauma, described as the result of long-term poisoning with low doses of ionized radiation, appeared in the Chernobyl-related literature in the early 1990s. Specialists pointed to three major types of symptoms of radiation trauma— disturbances in the blood circulatory system, disturbances in the digestive system, and psychological and psychiatric reactions. The presence of a psychological component of radiation trauma was initially noted by psychiatrists who worked with people affected by the Chernobyl catastrophe. This component was described in clinical reports as an elevation of depression and anxiety in the population living under conditions of higher level of radiation. These reports were scattered throughout related literature and there were no relevant broad-scale epidemiological studies. Obviously, the etiology of this phenomenon is unclear, and stress-related and pure radiation-related (if any) causes of this phenomenon are confounded.

Unfortunately, very little behavioral data have been collected in contaminated regions. As for adults, Lakosina and colleagues (1992) studied clinical features of mental disorders among employees of a large industrial enterprise and of some institutional collectives in a radiation-polluted area (Novozybkov, Russia). As compared to the general population, this sample demonstrated higher incidence of neuroses, asthenoneurotic states of complex etiology, organic disorders of the CNS, somatogenic disorders, endogenous disorders, alcoholism, and psychopathic disorders.

In a study of the impact of the Chernobyl catastrophe on the mental health of children living in the poisoned territories of Russia, Grigorenko and Kuznetsova (1999) collected maternal reports on behaviors of 6 to 8 and 9 to 12-year-old children using the Child Behavior Check List (Achenbach, 1991). Given the geographic unevenness of the distribution of the fallout, the samples were ascertained, not through individual cases, but through schools. The researchers used a targeted ascertainment strategy. The selection of the schools in the affected areas was driven by two considerations: the representativeness of the selected sample and the comparability of the results among the schools. Thus, the researchers selected three schools from highly contaminated areas, five schools from lower contaminated areas, and three matched schools situated in noncontaminated areas of Russia. The researchers' hypothesis was that the frequencies of emotional and behavioral disturbances would be elevated in children living in territories affected by the Chernobyl fallout. This hypothesis was verified by means of multivariate models looking at the effects of the zone of contamination (high, low, or none) on the narrow-band CBCL scores (withdrawal, somatic complaints, anxiety and depression, social problems, aggression, delinquent behaviors, attention problems), and controlling for age and gender of children, parental education, and the degree of urbanization of the schools' regions. The results failed to support the initial hypotheses: The children from the high-contamination areas did not look systematically worse than did low-contamination-zone children or control children, and the children from the low-contamination areas did not look systematically better than did the children from the highly poisoned areas or worse than did the control-sample children. In other words, there was no systematic elevation in the frequencies of maladaptive behaviors among children from the areas contaminated by the Chernobyl fallout. These results are similar to those of Noll et al. (1997)—irradiation does not appear to be impacting the social–behavioral spectrum of functioning.

Indirect Impacts of Irradiation

The main moderator of the impact of radiation is the variable of stress. When danger is unknown and difficult to quantify, the situation becomes stressful. It is well known that the major source of stress is lack of information.

The Chernobyl accident is known to the world not only by its magnitude but also by the way it was mishandled by the Soviet government. Specifically, the delay in the initial acknowledgment by the government that the accident had occurred was frustrating and perturbing. The Soviet officials waited for two days to recognize the accident, repeatedly refusing to cooperate in releasing the details concerning the tragedy. Only on April 28, 2 days after the catastrophe, at 9:02 P.M., did the news commentator on a Moscow television news program read a terse four-sentence statement from the Soviet Council of Ministers: "An accident has taken place at the Chernobyl power station, and one of the reactors was damaged. Measures are being taken to eliminate the consequences of the accident. Those affected by it are being given assistance. A government committee has been set up."

The Soviet refusal to provide timely details of the accident gave rise to increasingly pervasive information-gathering efforts. The U.S. intelligence community and the media raced to report the superficial story and as a result greatly exaggerated the news of the accident, blowing it out of proportion. This combination made a bad situation worse. The Soviet government did not want to talk about the accident, and the American mass media sensationalized the story by reporting many thousands of deaths. Together, these actions had the worst possible impact on the inhabitants of the areas poisoned by the Chernobyl clouds. The stress of these people is readily apparent and can be easily understood. According to an assessment done by 2,000 scientists from 25 countries and 7 multinational organizations for the United Nations International Atomic Energy Agency, stress-related illnesses are caused by lack of public information about the nature of a disaster and the mass evacuations that ensue. The psychological stress that followed in the surrounding areas outside the radioactive hot zones was wholly disproportionate to the biological significance of the radioactive contamination.

Researchers (Havenaar, Rumiantseva, & van den Bout, 1994) summarized some of the observations recorded by Dutch and Russian investigators who collaborated in studying the mental health aftereffects of the 1986 Chernobyl disaster. Among major stress factors mentioned were the unknown scale of the damage and loss of confidence in the local and federal services. Van den Bout, Havenar, and Meijler-Iljina (1995) gave a general overview of the psychological reactions following the Chernobyl disaster as they were encountered in inhabitants living in or near the contaminated areas. They stated that a prominent reaction of the people in these areas was massive health concern. Based on their research, these authors presented arguments for the hypothesis that the health problems of the population living in contaminated zones were the result, not of radiation, but of identifiable psychosocial stressors.

In a study of Havenaar et al. (1999), two samples, exposed and unexposed, were compared. The first sample was drawn from the Gomel region (Republic of Belarus) in the direct vicinity of the damaged Chernobyl nuclear plant. A control sample was taken from the Tver region (Russian Federation), a region not significantly contaminated by fallout from Chernobyl. All participants ($N = 3{,}084$) were asked to complete a self-report questionnaire assessing psychological well-being (assessed with the General Health Questionnaire), subjective health, and health-related behaviors. Selected participants

(N = 449) were comprehensively evaluated physically and psychiatrically. Participants from the Gomel region demonstrated significantly higher levels of psychological distress, poorer subjective health, and higher medical consumption than Tver participants. The researchers found no significant differences in overall levels of psychiatric or physical morbidity between exposed and nonexposed participants, including radiation-related diseases. The results were interpreted as indicating that psychological distress following the Chernobyl disaster had a marked effect upon psychological well-being and perceived health, and on subsequent illness behaviors.

Drottz-Sjoeberg and Sjoeberg (1990) collected data in September 1986 from three regions of Sweden that were exposed to radioactive fallout from the Chernobyl nuclear accident. In these three regions, samples of farmers, adolescents, parents of children born just before or after the accident, and middle-aged men who were not registered as legal custodians of children were surveyed. Attitudes toward nuclear power were predominantly negative. The risks associated with radiation and nuclear power were rated among the worst risks, and residents of the most exposed region (Gaevle) reported being worried about injury from radiation twice as often as others.

Kolominsky and Igumnov (1995) studied the Chernobyl catastrophe as a stressor affecting the psychological functions of children and teenagers living in contaminated areas. The fear of radiation in this population is vivid. The invisible nature of the radiation threat and its long-lasting effects strengthened the radiophobia in some children. Pukhova (1993) studied the perception of radiation as represented in the drawings of schoolchildren living in areas contaminated with radioactive substances. In spite of varying means of pictorial representation of radiation, subjective connotations underlying all the drawings reflect fear and helplessness.

Collins and Bandeira de Carvalho (1993) conducted a multidisciplinary field study in Goiania, Brazil, 3.5 years after a nuclear accident involving stealing radioactive material and distributing it carelessly in laypersons' households. Those whose households were involved were exposed to low levels of ionizing radiation. The "victims" who experienced anticipatory stress from fear of radiation exposure and a nonirradiated control group were compared. Results indicate the presence of chronic stress, as measured by psychological, behavioral, and neuroendocrine indices, in those who were exposed to radiation. Anticipatory stress associated with potential exposure to ionizing radiation resulted in a level of stress similar to that from actual exposure.

Another major source of stress related to potential sequelae of irradiation lies in whether irradiation was voluntary or involuntary and whether, when voluntary, those irradiated are provided with substantial social support. For example, Kroz, Lipatov, and Chinkina (1993) compared the perception of the risks posed by radiation after the Chernobyl catastrophe between specialists in nuclear technology and the general population. Estimation of radiation health risks by the operators of the Chernobyl nuclear plant was significantly lower than that made by nonprofessionals. The specialists judged radiation risk to be similar to other challenges of everyday life (see also Tarabrina & Petrukhin, 1994). Similarly, Collins (1992) noted the importance of the "feeling of control" in managing and adapting to higher radiation danger. Those who volunteered their professional services for the clean-up operation in Chernobyl, willingly and repeatedly exposed themselves to ionizing radiation; they had a modicum of control over whether or not they would be exposed (volunteering or not) and could therefore regulate their exposure. The absence of that perception of control (as was the case for the general populace that just "happened to be" in the zone of accident) created a feeling of victimization and precipitated negative psychological feelings that often were manifested through somatic problems, even though the exposure of the populace to ionizing radiation was far less than that of the Chernobyl workers.

Garcia (1994) explored memories and perceptions of exposure to radiation in open-ended interviews with atomic veterans (i.e., military personnel who participated in above-ground nuclear testing programs or other nuclear-connected events). Findings suggest that resolution of these events involves emotional and cognitive processing of a new perspective that is in contradiction with prior beliefs. Aspects of this emotional work include feeling ineffective and helpless in relation to a potent, unresponsive government, isolation from other atomic veterans, and consequent intensification of self-doubt. Factors involved in the process of resolving or integrating these disparate realities include a willingness to explore and confront images and feelings about radiation exposure and validation of the exposure experience and efforts to cope with the consequences. Another group of researchers (Murphy, Ellis, & Greenberg, 1990) conducted semistructured, videotaped interviews with veterans who were exposed to atomic radiation, along with their families, to explore the psychological effects of such exposure. Themes that emerged were: invalidation of the veterans' experiences by government and other authority figures; family concerns about genetic effects on future generations; family members' desire to protect each other from fear of physical consequences of exposure through defense mechanisms; and the desire to leave a record of their experiences to help prevent future suffering.

In sum, considering the impact of ionizing radiation on human cognitive functioning, we have to take into account not only the physical/biological impact of irradiation but also the stress originating from this impact. The literature has accrued enough evidence to formulate a hypothesis that, overall, the detrimental impact of stress on human mental health is as strong or stronger than that of the ionizing radiation itself.

SUMMARY

Animal, clinical, and epidemiological data on the impact of radiation yield a number of summary statements.

Very high-dose irradiation leads to adverse and immediate somatic outcomes overriding neuropsychological consequences. High-dose irradiation tends to result in both somatic and neuropsychological outcomes. Prenatally, when received during special sensitive periods, high-dose irradiation is linked to serious consequences, including mild and severe mental retardation. Postnatally, high-dose irradiation tends to result in disruption of memory and attention. There is, however, some evidence of progressive deterioration in neuropsychological functioning with age. It is commonly believed that adult mammalian organisms are resistant to low-dose irradiation. Although this is still the dominant assumption, some new evidence has emerged that indicates some behavioral changes in experimental animals in response to low-dose irradiation.

Impacts of nuclear irradiation on large groups of people are difficult to estimate precisely, due to a number of methodological, ethical, and psychological constraints. Among methodological constraints are: difficulties in identifying everybody subjected to irradiation; difficulties in specifying precise doses received; difficulties in finding matched controls; difficulties in separating confounders (i.e., secondary stress and health status prior to irradiation); and difficulties in establishing causal pathways of observed deficits. There are also ethical constraints that interfere with studies of the epidemiology of irradiation (see, e.g., Tatara, 1998).

First, victims of nuclear accidents tend to have difficult lives with multiple problems. Yamada (1995), for example, provides the following story of a Hibakusha women:

> When the atomic bomb fell, she was 25, married, a mother of a one-year old baby. She survived, even though she was badly burned, but she lost the baby. Massive keloid scarring restrained her movements, limited her employability, and led to a divorce. She remarried two years later. Trying to have children, she gave birth to a child who lived only 10 days, to a mentally retarded girl, and a boy with serious chronic illnesses and behavioral problems. Her second marriage did not last long; her husband left, complaining about medical bills he needed to pay for the three of them. Her son ran away from home.

It appears that nuclear accidents trigger a chain reaction of social misfortunes, which themselves are often confounders to the impact of radiation.

Second, perception of possible ill-effects from radiation play a crucial role in the psychological experience of nuclear accident victims and their families. The fear of being ill and transmitting these health problems to subsequent generations creates significant stress and social isolation.

When people talk about Hibakusha Nisei, this makes me nervous that my children cannot marry, because people want to avoid the possibility of an unhealthy baby. However, I know that I cannot keep the fact of being a Hibakusha from people's attention forever. (Esuko, 1972, p. 10)

These fears are often ungrounded, yet they form the psychological reality for victims of nuclear accidents. Unfortunately, nuclear health professionals have not yet been able to separate the impact of these fears from the impact of irradiation itself.

Finally, to process their own experiences psychologically, nuclear accident victims often create collective myths and legends about the event. A women evacuated from Pripyat' (a small satellite town to the Chernobyl Power Plant) was convinced that ". . . right after the reactor exploded, night turned to day, lighting the sky with strange tinges of color, the air became unusually hot, and all the flowers and trees in this cool region suddenly burst into blossom" (Kiev, February 1988). There are also horrifying stories about the lost generation of people affected by the catastrophe and their children, living without faith and according to their own morals. Because they believe it themselves, these storytellers will tell their tale to their children and grandchildren. Perhaps many will tell this story to each other, and it will make its way throughout the world in various versions as an atomic-era legend. These collective memories are impossible to disregard—often they form the basis for group identification, for sharing emotional pain and fear, and for building new communities in place of destroyed ones. However, they certainly make it more difficult to separate the direct impact of atomic irradiation from the secondary impact of stress. It is the task of science to sort fact from mythology.

Yet, despite these methodological, ethical, and psychological difficulties, the field of nuclear health has been growing and will continue to grow. Given the needs of modern society for energy, it is unlikely that societies will stop using nuclear sources. And, if this is the case, it is essential that societies know what the potential consequences of mishandling this source of energy are for human development.

REFERENCES

Abayomi, O., Chun, M. S., & Kelly, K. (1990). Cerebral calcification and learning disabilities following cranial irradiation for muedlloblastoma. *Journal of National Medical Associated, 82,* 833–836.

Achenbach, T. M. (1991). *Manual for the Child Behavior Checklist/4-18 and 1991 Profile.* Burlington, VT: University of Vermont Department of Psychiatry.

Ainsworth, E. J., Fry, J. M., Brennan, P. C., Stearner, S. P., Rust, J. H., & Williamson, F. C. (1976). Life shortening, neoplasma, and systematic injuries in mice after single or fractionated doses of neutron or γ radiation. *Biological and Environmental Effects of Low-Level Radiation* (pp. 77–92). Vienna, Austria: International Atomic Energy Agency.

278   GRIGORENKO

Bailey, C. C. (1989). *The aftermath of Chernobyl. History's worst nuclear power reactor accident.* Iowa: Kendall/Hunt.

Bazylevich, T. F., Aseyev, V. G., Bodunov, M. V., & Guseva, O. V. (1993). Integral individuality under radiation stress. *Psikhologicheskiy Zhurnal, 14,* 25–34.

Bound, J. P., Francis, B. J., & Harvey, P. W. (1995). Down's syndrome: Prevalence and ionising radiation in an area of north west England 1957–91. *Journal of Epidemiology & Community Health, 49,* 164–170.

van den Bout, J., Havenaar, J. M., & Meijler-Iljina, L. I. (1995). Health problems in areas contaminated by the Chernobyl disaster: Radiation, traumatic stress, or chronic stress? In R. J. Kleber, C. R. Figler, & B. P. R. Gersons (Eds.), *Beyond trauma: Cultural and societal dynamics.* Plenum series on stress and coping. (pp. 213–232). New York: Plenum Press.

Brouwers, P. (1987). Neuropsychological abilities of long-term survivors of childhood leukemia. In N. K. Aaronson & J. Beckman (Eds.), *The quality of life of cancer patients* (pp. 153–165). New York: Raven Press.

Brouwers, P., & Poplack, D. (1990). Memory and learning sequelae in long term survivors of acute lymphoblastic leukemia: Association with attention deficits. *American Journal of Pediatric Hematology-Oncology, 12,* 174–181.

Calvo, W., Hopewell, J. W., Reinhold, H. S., Van Den Berg, A. P., & Yeung, T. K. (1987). Dose-dependent and time-dependent changes in the choroid plexus of the irradiated rat brain. *British Journal of Radiology, 60,* 1109–1117.

Calvo, W., Hopewell, J. W., Reinhold, H. S., & Yeung, T. K. (1988). Time- and dose-related changes in the white matter of the rat brain after single doses of X-rays. *British Journal of Radiology, 61,* 1043–1052.

Casarett, L. J. (1968). Role of radioactive substances in effects of smoking. *National Cancer Institute Monographs, 28,* 199–209.

Ciesielski, K. T., Yanofsky, R., Ludwig, R. N., Hill, D. E., et al. (1994). Hypoplasia of the cerebellar vermis and cognitive deficits in survivors of childhood leukemia. *Archives of Neurology, 51,* 985–993.

Chen, E., Zeltzer, L. K., Bentler, P. M., Byrne, J., Nicholson, H. S., Meadows, A. T., Mills, J. L., Haupt, R., Fears, T. R., & Robison, L. L. (1998). Pathways linking treatment intensity and psychosocial outcomes among adult survivors of childhood leukemia. *Journal of Health Psychology, 3,* 23–38.

Chen, Q. M., Lamproglou, I., Poisson, M., Le Poncin, M., & Delattre, J. Y. (1992). Long-term effects of cranial irradiation in the rat: A behavioural study. *Journal of Neurology, 239,* 116.

Chinkina, O. V., & Torubarov, F. S. (1991). Psychological features of patients with acute radiation sickness following the Chernobyl Atomic Power Station disaster. *Human Physiology, 17,* 301–307.

Collins, D. L. (1992). Behavioral differences of irradiated persons associated with the Kyshtym, Chelyabinsk, and Chernobyl nuclear accidents. *Military Medicine, 157,* 548–552.

Collins, D. L., & Bandeira de Carvalho, A. (1993). Chronic stress from the Goiania -1-3-7Cs radiation accident. *Behavioral Medicine, 18,* 149–157.

Christianson, S. A., Neppe, V., & Hoffman, H. (1994). Amnesia and vegetative abnormalities after irradiation treatment: A case study. *Acta Neurologica Scandinavica, 90,* 360–366.

Copeland, D. R., Moore, B. D., III, Francis, D. J., Jaffe, N., & Culbert, S. J. (1996). Neuropsychologic effects of chemotherapy on children with cancer: A longitudinal study. *Journal of Clinical Oncology, 14*(10), 2826–2835.

D'Amato, C. J., & Hicks, S. P. (1965). Effects if low levels of ionizing radiation on the developing cerebral cortex of the rate. *Neurology, 15,* 1104–1116.

Davidson, A., Childs, J., Hopewell, J. W., & Trait, D. (1994). Functional neurological outcome in leukaemic children receiving repeated cranial irradiation. *Radiation Oncology, 31,* 101–109.

Dekaban, A. (1968). Abnormalities in children exposed to x-radiation injury to the human fetus: Part I. *Journal of Nuclear Medicine, 9,* 471–477.

Dennis, M., Spiegler, B. J., Obonsawin, M. C., Maria, B. L., et al. (1992). Brain tumors in children and adolescents: III. Effects of radiation and hormone status on intelligence and on working, associative and serial-order memory. *Neuropsychologia, 30,* 257–275.

Devi, P. U., Hossain, M., & Bisht, K. S. (1999). Effect of late fetal irradiation on adult behavior of mouse: Dose-response relationship. *Neurotoxicology & Teratology, 21,* 193–198.

Diaz-Granados, J. L., Greene, P. L., & Amsel, A. (1994). Selective activity enhancement and persistence in weanling rats after hippocampal X-irradiation in infancy: Possible relevance for ADHD. *Behavioral & Neural Biology, 61,* 251–259.

Drottz-Sjoeberg, B. M., & Sjoeberg, L. (1990). Risk perception and worries after the Chernobyl accident. *Journal of Environmental Psychology, 10,* 135–149.

Dunn, K., Yoshimaru, H., Otake, M., Annegers, J. F., & Schull, W. J. (1990). Prenatal exposure to ionizing radiation and subsequent development of seizures. *American Journal of Epidemiology, 131,* 114–123.

Esuko, S. (1972). Appeal for Hibaku Nisei. In S. Ienaga, H., Odagiri, & K. Kuroko (Eds.), *Hibaku Nisei* (pp. 87–103). Tokyo: Jiji-Tishin Co.

Fletcher, J., & Copeland, D. (1988). Neurobehavioural effects of central nervous system prophylactic treatment of cancer in children. *Journal of Clinical and Experimental Neuropsychology, 10,* 495–538.

Fogarty, K., Volonino, V., Caul, J., Rongey, J., Whitman, B., O'Connor, D., & Accardo, P. (1988). Learning disabilities following CBS irradiation. *Clinical Pediatrics, 27,* 524–528.

Fossen, A. (1995). Sequelae of brain tumor treatment in children. *Tidsskrift for Norsk Psykologforening, 32,* 232–238.

Furchgott, E., Tacker, R. S., & Draper, D. O. (1968). Open-field behavior and heart rate in prenatally X irradiated rats. *Physiological Behavior, 16,* 441–452.

Gaffey, C. T. (1971a). Relation between RBE and LET to inhibit neural impulse conduction. *Radiation Research, 47*(2), 511–525.

Gaffey, C. T. (1971b). The response of maximal and submaximal action potentials from frog sciatic nerve to 200-kV x-rays. *Radiation Research, 45*(2), 311–325.

Garcia, B. (1994). Social-psychological dilemmas and coping of atomic veterans. *American Journal of Orthopsychiatry, 64,* 651–655.

Gigi, A., Mintz, M., Ben-Elyahu, S., & Myslobodsky, M. (1997). Prenatal γ-irradiation alters axial asymmetry in low birth weight pups. *Behavioural Brain Research, 86,* 205–207.

Goff, J. R., Anderson, H. R., & Cooper, P. F. (1980). Distractibility and memory deficits in long-term survivors of acute lymphoblastic leukemia. *Journal of Developmental and Behavioral Pediatrics, 1,* 158–163.

Goldstein, L., & Murphy, D. P. (1929). Microcephalic idiocy following radium therapy for uterine cancer during pregnancy. *American Journal of Obstetric Gynecology, 18,* 189–195, 281–283,

Grigorenko, E. L., & Kunzetsova, I. V. (1999). *Behavioral profiles of children in Chernobyl-contaminated regions of Russia.* Unpublished manuscript.

Gunther, J., & Hug, O. (1974). Acute effects of x-irradiation on membrane potential and membrane resistance of snail neurons. Original in German. *Radiation & Environmental Biophysics, 11*(3), 171–187.

Haupt, R., Fears, T. R., Robinson, L. L., Mills, J. L., Nicholson, H. S., Zeltzer, L. K., Meadows, A. T., & Byrne, J. (1994). Educational attainment in long-term survivors of childhood acute lymphoblastic leukemia. *Journal of the American Medical Association, 272*(18), 1427–1432.

Havenaar, J. M., Savelkoul, T. J. F., van den Bout, J., Boostsma, P. A., & van den Brink, W. (1999). Consequences of the Chernobyl disaster: Illness or illness behaviour? *Gedrag & Gezondheid: Tijdschrift voor Psychologie & Gezondheid, 27,* 84–90.

Havenaar, I. M., Rumiantseva, G. M., & van den Bout, J. (1994). Mental health problems in the Chernobyl area. *Journal of Russian & East European Psychiatry, 27,* 83–91.

Hodges, H., Katzung, N., Sowinski, P., & Hopewell, J. W., Wilkinson, J. H., Bywaters, T., & Rezvani, M. (1998). Late behavioural and neuropathological effects of local brain irradiation in the rat. *Behavioural Brain Research, 91,* 99–114.

Iaconetta, G., Lamaida, E., Rossi, A., Signorelli, F., et al. (1994). Post-radiation cerebral lesions in adults. *Acta Neurologica, 16,* 277–287.

Imperato, J. P., Paleologos, N. A., & Vicky, N. (1990). Effects of treatment on long-temr survivors with malignant astrocytomas. *Annals of Neurology, 28,* 818–822.

Jenkins, J. R. (1991). The MR equivalents of cerebral hemispheric disconnection: A telencephalic commissuropathy. *Computerized Medical Imaging & Graphics, 15,* 323–331.

Jensch, R. P., Eisenman, L. M., & Brent, R. L. (1995). Postnatal neuropsychological effects of prenatal X-irradiation. *International Journal of Radiation Biology, 67,* 217–227.

Joseph, J. A. (1992). The putative role of free radicals in the loss of neuronal functioning in senescence. *Integrative Physiological & Behavioral Science, 27,* 216–227.

Kimler, B. F., & Norton, S. (1988). Behavioral changes and structural defects in rats irradiated *in utero. International Journal of Radiational Oncology, Biology, and Physics, 15,* 1171–1177.

Kolominsky, Y. L., & Igumnov, S. A. (1995). Peculiarities of perception of the radiation threat by children of different ages. *Human Physiology, 21,* 199–201.

Kolominsky, Y., Igumnov, S., & Drozdovitch, V. (1999). The psychological development of children from Belarus exposed in the prenatal period to radiation from the Chernobyl atomic power plant. *Journal of Child Psychology & Psychiatry & Allied Disciplines, 40,* 299–305.

Kroz, M. V., Lipatov, S. A., Chinkina, O. V. (1993). Differences in perception of radiation risks by specialists in the field of nuclear energy and nonspecialists, *Voprosy Psikhologii, 5,* 59–66.

Ladavas, E., Missiroli, G., Rosito, P., Serra, L., & Vecchi, V. (1983). Intellectual function in long-term survivors of childhood acute lemphoblastic leukemia. *Archives of Disease in Childhood, 58,* 906–910.

Lakosina, N. D., Sergeev, I. I., Voskresensky, B. A., Borodin, V. M., et al. (1992). The clinical characterization of mental disorders in the community living in the radiation-polluted area. *Zhurnal Nevropatologii i Psikhiatrii Imeni S - S – Korsakova, 92,* 69–72.

Lamproglou, I., Chen, Q. M., Biosserie, G., Mazeron, J. J., Poisson, M., Baillet, F., Le Poncin, M., & Delattre, J. Y. (1995). Radiation-induced cognitive dynfunction: An experimental model in the old rat. *International Journal of Radiation Oncology, Biology, and Physics, 41,* 65–70.

Lockwood, K. A., Bell, T. S., & Colegrove, R. W. Jr. (1999). Long-term effects of cranial radiation therapy on attention functioning in survivors of childhood leukemia. *Journal of Pediatric Psychology, 24,* 55–66.

MacLean, W. F., Noll, R. B., Stehbens, J. A., Kaleita, T. A., Schwartz, E., Whitt, J. K., Cantor, N. L., Waskerwitz, M. J., Ruymann, F. B., Novak, L. J., Woodard, A., & Hammond, G. D. (1995). Neuropsychological effects of cranial irradiation in young children with acute lymphoblastic leukemia 9 months after diagnosis. *Archives of Neurology, 52,* 156–160.

Maier, D. M., & Landauer, M. R. (1990). Onset of behavioral effects in mice exposed to 10 Gy -6-0Co radiation. *Aviation Space & Environmental Medicine, 61,* 893–898.

Makarenko, N. V., Voronovskaya, V. I., & Sprin', A. B. (1996). Psychophysiological functions of the Chernobyl clean-up crew six years after the accident. *Human Physiology, 22,* 460–465.

Margolin, J. F., & Poplack, D. G. (1997). Acute lymphoblastic leukemia. In P. A. Pizzo & D. G. Poplack (Eds.), *Principles and practice of pediatric oncology* (pp. 409–462). Philadelphia: Lippincott-Raven.

Maurer, H. S., Steinherz, P. G., Gaynon, P. S., Finkelstein, J. Z., Sather, H. N., Reaman, G. H., Bleyer, W. A., & Hammond, G. D. (1988). The effect of initial management of hyperleukocytosis on early complications and outcome of children with acute lymphoblastic leukemia. *Journal of Clinical Oncology, 6,* 1425–1432.

Miller, R. W. (1990). Effects of prenatal exposure to ionizing radiation. *Health Physiology, 59,* 57–61.

Minamisawa, T., & Hirokaga, K. (1996). Long term changes on open-field activity of male mice irradiated with low levels of γ rays at late stage of fetal development. *Journal of Radiation Research, 37,* 117–124.

Mintz, M., Yovel, G., Gigi, A., & Myslobodsky, M. S. (1998). Dissociation between startle and prepulse inhibition in rats exposed to γ-radiation at day 15 of embryogeny. *Brain Research Bulletin, 45,* 289–296.

Miyachi, Y., & Yamada, T. (1996). Head-portion exposure to low-level X-rays reduces isolation-induced aggression of mouse, and involvement of the olfactory carnosine in modulation of the radiation effects. *Behavioural Brain Research, 81,* 135–140.

Moss, H. A., Nannis, E. D., & Poplack, D. G. (1981). The effects of prophylactic treatment of the central nervous system on the intellectual functioning of children with acute lymphocytic leukemia. *American Journal of Medicine, 71,* 47–52.

Mumby, D. G., & Pinel, P. J. P. (1994). Rhinal cortex lesions and object recognition in rats. *Behavioral Neuroscience, 108,* 11–18.

Murphy, B. C., Ellis, P., & Greenberg, S. (1990). Atomic veterans and their families: Responses to radiation exposure. *American Journal of Orthopsychiatry, 60,* 418–427.

Neal, J. V., Morton, N. E., Schell, W. J., McDonald, J. D., Kondani, M., Takeshima, K., Suzuki, M., & Kitamura, S. (1953). The effect of exposure of parents to the atomic bomb on the first generation offspring in Hiroshima and Nagasaki. *Japanese Journal of Genetics, 28,* 211–216.

Noll, R. B., MacLean, W. E. Jr., Whitt, J., Kaleita, T. A., Stehbens, J. A., Waskerwitz, M. J., Ruymann, F. B., & Hammond, G. D. (1997). Behavioral adjustment and social functioning of long-term survivors of childhood leukemia: Parent and teacher reports. *Journal of Pediatric Psychology, 22,* 827–841.

Norton, S., & Kimler, B. F. (1987). Correlation of behavior with brain damage after *in utero* exposure to toxic agents. *Neutoroxicology & Teratology, 9,* 145–150.

Norton, S., Kimler, B. F., & Mullenix, P. J. (1991). Progressive behavioral changes in rats after exposure to low levels of ionizing radiation *in utero. Neurotoxicology & Teratology,* 13, 181–188.

Novikov, V. S., Tsygan, V. N., Borisova, E. D., & Rybina, L. A. (1997). Changes in cerebral bioelectric activity in the Chernobyl NPP accident liquidators. *Human Physiology,* 23, 542–546.

Ochs, J. J., Muhlen, R., Fairclough, D. Parvey, L., Whitaker, J., Ch'ien, L., Mauer, A., & Simone, J. (1991). Comparison of neuropsychological functioning and clinical indicators of neurotoxicity in long-term survivors of childhood leukemia given cranial radiation or parenteral methotrexate: A prospective study. *Journal of Clinical Oncology, 9,* 145–151.

Otake, M., & Schull, W. (1984). *In utero* exposure to A-bomb radiation and mental retardation: a reassessment. *British Journal of Radiology, 57,* 409–414.

Otake, M., Schull, W., & Yoshimaru, H. (1991). Brain damage among the prenatally exposed. *Journal of Radiational Research.* Supplement. 249–264.

Plummer, G. (1995). Anomalies occurring in children exposed *in utero. Hiroshima Pediatrics, 10,* 687–692.

Pukhova, T. I. (1993). Image of radiation as reflected in drawings of schoolchildren living in contaminated areas. *Voprosy Psikhologii, 1,* 40–46.

Radcliffe, J., Bunin, G. R., Sutton, L. N., Goldwein, J. W., et al. (1994). Cognitive deficits in long-term survivors of childhood medulloblastoma and other noncortical tumors: Age-dependent effects of whole brain radiation. *International Journal of Developmental Neuroscience, 12,* 327–334.

Roman, D. D., & Sperduto, P. W. (1995). Neuropsychological effects of cranial irradiation: current knowledge and future directions. *International Journal of Radiation Oncology, Biology, and Physics, 40,* 21–32.

Rowland, J. H., Glidewell, O. J., Sibley, R. F., Holland, J. C., Tull, R., Berman, A., Brecher, M. L., Harris, M., Glicksman, A. S., Forman, E., Jones, B., Cohen, M. E., Duffner, P. K., & Freeman, A. I. (1984). Effects of different forms of central nervous system prohylaxis on neuropsychological function in childhood leukemia. *Journal of Clinical Oncology, 2,* 1327–1335.

Russell, W. J., Keehn, R. J., Ihno, Y., Hattori, F., Kigura, T., & Imamura, K. (1973). Bone maturation in children exposed to the atomic bomb in utero. *Radiology, 108,* 367–370.

Schull, W. J., Norton, S., & Jensh, R. P. (1990). Ionizing radiation and the developing brain. *Neurotoxicology & Teratology, 12,* 249–260.

Sever, L. E. (1993). Neuroepidemiology of intrauterine radiation exposure. In C. A. Molgaard (Ed.), *Neuroepidemiology: Theory and method.* (pp. 241–256). San Diego, CA: Academic Press.

282 GRIGORENKO

Shtemberg, A. S. (1999). The combined effect of hypokinesia and various doses of γ-radiation on the conditioned reflex activity of rats. *Aerospace & Environmental Medicine, 31*, 34–39.

Sienkeiwicz, Z. J., Haylock, R. G. E., & Sounders, R. D. (1994). Prenatal irradiation and spatial memory in mice: Investigation of dose-response relationship. *International Journal of Radiational Biology, 65*, 611–618.

Sienkeiwicz, Z. J., Sounders, R. D., & Butland, B. K. (1992). Prenatal irradiation and spatial memory in mice: Investigation of critical period. *International Journal of Radiational Biology, 62*, 211–219.

Stehbens, J. A., & Kisler, C. T. (1984). Intelligence and achievement testing in childhood cancer: Three years post-diagnosis. *Developmental and Behavioral Pediatrics, 5*, 184–188.

Stehbens, J. A., MacLean, W. E., Kaleita, T. A., Noll, R. B., Schwartz, E., Cantor, N. L., Woodard, A., Whitt, J. K., Waskerwitz, M. J., Ruymann, F. B., & Hammond, G. D. (1994). Effects of two different forms of CNS prophylaxis on the neuropsychological performance of children six years and older with acute lymphoblastic leukemia: Nine months post-diagnosis. *Children's Health Care, 23*, 231–250.

Strigini, P., Sansone, R., Carobbi, S., & Pierluigi, M. (1990). Radiation and Down's syndrome. *Nature, 347*, 717.

Sudakov, K. V., Moroz, B. B., Salieva, R. M., Deshevoy, Yu, B., et al. (1995). Combined effects of chronic γ-irradiation and emotional stress in rats. *Fiziologicheskii Zhurnal SSSR im I.M. Sechenova, 81*, 41–49.

Tamaki, Y., Hoshino, K., & Kameyama, Y. (1989). Avoidance learning deficits in prenatally γ ray irradiated rats. *Congenital Anomalies, 29*, 295–308.

Tarabrina, N. V., Lazebnaya, E. O., & Zelenova, M. E. (1994). Psychological features of post-traumatic stress states in participants in the aftermath of the Chernobyl nuclear disaster. *Psikhologicheskii Zhurnal, 15*, 67–77.

Tarabrina, N. V., & Petrukhin, E. V. (1994). Psychological features of radiation danger perception. *Psikhologicheskii Zhurnal, 15*, 27–40.

Tatara, M. (1998). The second generation of Hibakusha, atomic bomb survivors: A psychologist's view. In Y. Danieli (Ed.). *International handbook of multigenerational legacies of trauma.* The Plenum series on stress and coping (pp. 141–146). New York: Plenum Press.

Terestchenko, N. Y., Lyaginskaya, A. M., & Burtzeva, L. I. (1991). Stochastic and non-stochastic effects and some population-genetic characteristics in children of the critical group in the period of basic organogenesis. In *Scientific and practical aspects of the preservation of health of people exposed to radiation influence as a result of the accident at the Chernobyl atomic power station* (pp. 73–74). Minsk: Publishing House of the Belarussian Committee "Chernobyl Children."

Tkachenko, A. S., & Vlasov, V. N. (1995). Psychological service: Help to children and teenagers from Bryanskaya oblast. *Psikhologicheskii Zhurnal, 16*, 122–128.

UNSCEAR (1993). Radiation effects on the developing human brain. In *Sources and effects of ionizing radiation. Annex H.* (pp. 805–867). United Nations Scientific Committee on the Effects of Atomic Radiation. New York: United Nations.

Upton, A. C. (1959). Ionizing radiation and aging. *Gerontologia, 4*, 162–176.

Wakabayashi, S. (1995). Microcephaly: Children exposed to the atomic bomb *in utero*. In T. Suzuki & Atomic Bomb Suggerers and Counselors Groups (Eds.), *With Hibakusha* (pp. 63–79). Hiroshima: Chugoku Shinbun Newspaper Co.

Walters, T. J., Mason, P. A., Sherry, C. J., Steffen, C. et al. (1995). No detectable bioeffects following acute exposure to high peak power ultra-wide band electromagnetic radiation in rats. *Aviation Space & Environmental Medicine, 66*, 562–567.

World Health Organization (WHO) (1996). *The medical consequences of the Chernobyl catastrophe.* Geneva: WHO.

Yamada, S. (1995). Holding Hibaku Nisei. In T. Suzuki & Atomic Bomb Suggerers and Counselors Groups (Eds.), *With Hibakusha* (pp. 141–145). Hiroshima: Chugoku Shinbun Newspaper Co.

Yamada, M., Sasaki, H., Mimori, Y., Kasagi, F., Sudoh, S., Ikeda, J., Hosoda, Y., Nakamura, S., & Kodama, K. (1999). Prevalence and risks of dementia in the Japanese population: RERF's Adult Health Study Hiroshima subjects. *Journal of the American Geriatrics Society, 47*, 189–195.

Yamazaki, J. N., Wright, S. W., & Wright, P. M. (1954). Outcome of pregnancy in women exposed ot the atomic bomb in Nagasaki. *American Journal of Disabled Children, 87*, 448–463.

Zhavoronkova, L. A., Kholodova, N. B., Zubovskii, G. A., Smirnov, Yu. N., et al. (1995). Electroencephalographic correlates of neurological disturbances at remote periods of the effect of ionizing radiation: Sequelae of the Chernobyl' NPP accident. *Neuroscience & Behavioral Physiology, 25*, 142–149.

III

WORK ENVIRONMENTS

10

Schooling and Cognitive Development

Kate Christian
Grand Rapids Community College

Heather J. Bachnan
Frederick J. Morrison
Loyola University, Chicago

The value of schooling to individuals and to society was recognized almost two centuries ago when compulsory education was legally mandated in the United States for all children under age 16. Yet only in recent decades has more serious consideration been given to the specific impact of schooling on a child's thinking skills. Surprisingly, the answers emerging from contemporary research and theory present a complex picture of the role of schooling in shaping cognitive growth. Nevertheless, the knowledge accumulating from recent scientific work is yielding valuable insights into how children learn and how schooling can best promote intellectual development.

FOCUS OF INQUIRY

Why study the role of schooling in cognitive development? The reasons are both theoretical and practical. First, the focus on schooling permits exploration of some fundamental themes in current psychology: nature–nurture, domain specificity, transfer. A second major reason to study schooling effects on cognitive development is of more practical urgency. In industrialized nations, formal education is a nearly universal experience among young children and is perhaps the most salient environmental influence beyond the family. Nevertheless, there is concern that U.S. students are not developing the skills they need to survive in a global economy (U.S. Department of Education, 1991). National and international investigations have documented inadequate levels of academic achievement among U.S. students in reading, science, and mathematics (International Association for the Evaluation of Educational Achievment, 1988; Mullis & Jenkins, 1990; Stevenson, Chen, & Lee, 1993; Stevenson & Lee, 1990). Moreover, within the United States, individual differences in academic skills have been documented as early as entrance to kindergarten (Morrison, Griffith, Williamson, & Hardway, 1995), suggesting that forces prior to formal schooling are operating to produce substantial variability in literacy even before children start school. Hence, understanding the impact of schooling can provide critical information on how to address the serious literacy problems facing the nation.

CHAPTER OVERVIEW

The first major section of this chapter addresses theoretical issues related to schooling, and begins with an overview of evidence from correlational, cross-cultural, extended year, and "school cutoff" studies that suggests schooling uniquely enhances children's intellectual and academic skills. Nevertheless, these investigations also reveal a striking degree of domain specificity in schooling effects during the early school years. In an attempt to explain the complex pattern of results emerging from schooling research, four major hypotheses are reviewed and evaluated. Finally, current speculation about how domain specific skills may eventually transfer or generalize to new domains is explored.

In the second part of the chapter, a comprehensive review of the nature and sources of early individual differences in cognitive and literacy skills is presented. It will become apparent that a multitude of factors in the child, family, and sociocultural contexts operate on a child's cognitive growth even before formal schooling begins. This conclusion confirms and illuminates the perspective that developmental change is best viewed within a complex, multilevel, interactive, theoretical framework (Bronfenbrenner, 1986, 1996; Sameroff, 1987; Magnusson, 1990). A strategy called *pathway analysis* is presented as a potentially useful approach to operationalize this perspective; the method involves the creation of developmental pathways from unique predictors of cognitive skills. An example demonstrates that the impact of schooling on literacy development differs in complex ways as a function of children's level of intelligence. These findings yield novel insights into the nature of learning and offer practical suggestions about the most effective instructional practices in schools.

Although relevant literature from all ages are considered where appropriate, the dominant focus of this chapter is on schooling and cognitive development during the early elementary grades. This chapter does not explore preschool (prior to kindergarten) influences on children's skills or examination of schooling effects on higher order processes in adolescence.

COGNITIVE GROWTH IN ELEMENTARY SCHOOL CHILDREN: NATURE OR NURTURE?

Where does knowledge come from? This question addresses perhaps the most fundamental debate in developmental psychology: the degree to which development is shaped by nature or nurture. On the one hand, behavioral geneticists have revealed strong heritability estimates for IQ scores (Plomin, 1995; Rowe, 1994), and some contemporary psychologists believe that certain types of intelligence are unaffected by schooling (Eysenck, 1988; Horn, 1978; Jensen, 1980). Alternatively, the particular knowledge and skills a person acquires are clearly molded by specific experiences. Nevertheless, certain skills appear to develop primarily from age-related or non-schooling-related factors. Overall, data from schooling research reveals a complex, intricate pattern of developmental change in children during the early elementary school years.

CORRELATIONAL STUDIES

Early research on the role of schooling in cognitive growth was largely correlational in nature. Scientists examined associations between participation in school and such varied skills as intelligence, perceptual development, concept formation, academic achievement, and memory. Although a complete review of these studies is beyond the scope of this chapter (see Ceci, 1991 and Ceci & Williams, 1997, for earlier treatment of these issues), two current topics highlight the themes emerging from this research: the relation between schooling and IQ test scores, and the effects of summer vacation on children's IQ and academic performance. The first topic documents continued interest in the origins of intelligence and the degree to which it can be altered by the environment; the second topic provides a nice illustration of how children's performance changes during an *absence* of schooling.

Schooling and Intelligence

The positive correlation between schooling and intelligence is strong, generally between .50 and .90 (Ceci, 1991; Herrnstein & Murray, 1994; Neisser et al., 1996), but has been documented in a study of twins reared together to be as high as .96 (Bouchard, 1984). Children with higher IQ scores are less likely to drop out of school and more likely to attend college, have higher incomes, and hold a professional job than children with lower IQ scores (Ceci, 1991). Unfortunately, determining the causal direction of the correlation between schooling and intelligence is difficult. On the one hand, the association may reflect a gene–environment correlation, such that genetically more intelligent students remain in school longer, perhaps due to reinforcement for their intelligence by teachers and parents. On the other hand, as argued by Ceci (1991), direct and indirect school learning may be the key mechanisms behind increases in intelligence. Support for the latter view is that the correlation between full-scale IQ and highest grade in school remains relatively high (between $r = .60$ and $r = .80$) even after other potential influences on IQ (e.g., socioeconomic status) have been controlled (Kemp, 1955; Wiseman, 1966, both cited in Ceci, 1991). Although certainly persuasive, it should be noted that even a semipartial correlation as high as $r = .80$ between schooling and IQ leaves 36% of the variance in intelligence scores unaccounted for (and thus attributable to non-schooling factors). Nevertheless, the strong and consistent link between these variables suggests that the quantity of schooling obtained can substantially affect the kinds of cognitive processes that underscore most intelligence tests.

Summer Vacation

In the majority of Western-style schools, children do not attend school during the summer months (typically June through August). Investigations of changes in performance on intelligence and academic achievement tests across the summer months have revealed a small but consistent *negative* association between IQ scores and time spent out of school (Hayes & Grether, 1982; Heyns, 1978; Jencks et al., 1972). In addition, the deleterious effects of summer vacation appear to depend in part on individual factors such as the child's age, socioeconomic status, or reading ability. In a study of academic achievement among second- to seventh-grade children over the course of a year, children in earlier grades experienced a greater decline in reading, vocabulary, and math performance during the summer than children in later grades (Parsley & Powell, 1962). Other investigations have found that lower socioeconomic status (SES) children show greater decrements in IQ scores (Jencks et al., 1972) and scores on reading and mathematics tests (Entwisle & Alexander, 1996) than children of higher SES, perhaps due to a lack of cognitively stimulating activities from out-of-school sources. Finally, fifth-grade children at the 40th percentile or below in reading ability demonstrated larger losses in reading over the summer than children of higher reading ability (Beggs, 1969, cited in Frazier & Morrison, 1998). In summary, accumulating evidence suggests that lack of schooling during summer may contribute to lower performance on academic and IQ tests, especially among younger, lower ability, or lower SES students.

CROSS-CULTURAL STUDIES

In an attempt to avoid some confounds associated with correlational data, scientists have investigated schooling effects on cognitive skills through direct comparisons between schooled and nonschooled children in other cultures. Cole and Cole (1996) reviewed findings from a number of studies conducted in nonindustrialized areas where schooling is not a universal experience. From this research, major differences have emerged between schooled and nonschooled groups of children in several intellectual domains such as memory, metacognition, and the organization of children's lexicons (Cole, Gay, Glick, & Sharp, 1971; Rogoff, 1981; Scribner & Cole, 1981; Wagner, 1974). For instance, memory performance of schooled children in other cultures was more comparable to American counterparts than to unschooled children in the same village (Cole et al., 1971). Similarly, Wagner (1974) found that Mayan children who attended school demonstrated substantial improvement with age in remembering the location of objects (as American children do), whereas nonschooled children did not. Wagner attributed this finding to rehearsal strategies learned in school. Metacognitive processes may also be enhanced by schooling: Scribner and Cole (1981) found that although both uneducated and educated Vai people in Liberia could identify a sentence as grammatically incorrect, only educated people could identify the particular features that made it so. At least one piece of evidence implies that the organization of children's lexicons may also differ as a consequence of schooling (Sharp, Cole, & Lave, 1979): Mayan adolescents with 1 to 2 years of high school experience were more likely to associate a noun like "duck" with nouns in the same category (e.g., fowl, goose), whereas unschooled adolescents related the noun to things the word did (e.g., it flies, or eats).

Stevenson and his colleagues (Stevenson et al., 1993; Stevenson & Lee, 1990) adopted a slightly different approach to the study of how schooling shapes particular skills. Reading and mathematics achievement was compared among American, Japanese, and Chinese elementary school students in first and fifth grades. In both grades, Japanese and Chinese students outscored American students in mathematics, and Chinese children surpassed American children in reading. Whereas genetic, familial, or cultural variables may all have contributed to discrepancies in performance, a host of specific instructional practices that differed between American and Asian classrooms (e.g., individual vs. group instruction, amount of time spent on a subject) were identified as critical determinants of the superior achievement of Asian students (Stevenson & Stigler, 1992; Stigler & Perry, 1990).

There is also evidence from cross-cultural research that some aspects of cognition may develop independently of schooling. Studies of the acquisition of concrete operational thought have produced mixed results (Dasen, 1977, Dasen, Ngini, & Lavallee, 1979; Greenfield, 1966; Nyiti, 1976), leading some researchers to conclude that differences in performance on conservation tasks are caused by familarity with test taking, not lack of understanding. If so, then concrete operational thinking increases with age and emerges regardless of whether or not a person attends school (Cole & Cole, 1996).

In summary, results from studies of schooling across cultures have demonstrated a positive influence of schooling on a variety of intellectual and academic skills, and a lack of an effect in concrete operational thinking. Unfortunately, investigations of schooled and nonschooled children or children from different cultures suffer from problems of nonequivalent samples, or selection bias. For instance, the advanced intellectual skills of schooled (vs. unschooled) children in non-Western societies may in part be attributable to the phenomenon of choosing the brightest and most likely to achieve children to attend school (Rogoff, 1981). Similarly, ascertaining the degree to which cross-cultural differences in family or societal expectations influence results has proven difficult. Hence, these research endeavors have been limited in their ability to make solid claims about the connection between school experiences and subsequent growth in skills.

QUASI-EXPERIMENTAL DESIGNS

Difficulties associated with correlational and cross-cultural investigations (e.g., causal inference, selection bias) can be greatly reduced through the use of experimental designs. Although promising from a research standoint, it is obviously unethical to assign children to "school" or "no school" experimental conditions in an attempt to isolate schooling as the critical determinant of cognitive change. Thus, even the most innovative designs in schooling research today are quasi-experimental in nature. Still, promising methodologies have been developed recently. Scientists have compared academic performance between students in a traditional versus extended-year school program, between children of different birthdates and cohorts, and between children of the same age in different grades in school. Findings from these studies are generally consistent with results from correlational and cross-cultural studies but have the distinct advantage of minimizing potential confounds.

Extended-Year Schooling

In a unique quasi-experimental design, Frazier and Morrison (1998) examined the influence of additional school days on children's academic and psychosocial skills by comparing the performance of kindergarten children in an extended-year program (210 days) or a traditional program (180 days). Groups were matched on magnet school attendance and 18 background characteristics including parents' education, age, and occupation, child IQ, entrance age, gender, race, and preschool experience. Despite equivalent performance between groups at the fall of kindergarten, children in the extended-year program outscored traditional students in the fall of first grade on the mathematics, reading recognition, and general information (i.e., general knowledge about the world) subtests of the Peabody Individual Achievement Test–Revised (Markwardt, 1989) and displayed higher levels of cognitive competence on the Harter–Pike Pictorial Scale of Perceived Competence (Harter & Pike, 1984). These findings demonstrated a positive effect of additional instruction time during the summer on selected academic skills and cognitive competence. It is noteworthy that no effect of days in school was found on the Peabody Picture Vocabulary Test–Revised (PPVT-R), a measure of receptive vocabulary (Dunn & Dunn, 1981) or on the maternal acceptance, peer acceptance, or physical competence subscales of the Harter–Pike Pictorial Scale of Perceived Competence (Harter & Pike, 1984).

Birthdate Studies

An innovative quasi-experimental technique to explore schooling effects on cognitive change relies upon the relatively unsystematic processes associated with children's birthdates and on the existence of a specified cutoff date for entrance to school. Because children are typically not allowed to enter school after a specified criterion date (determined by the school district), children born during the final 3 months of the year are statistically more likely to enter school a year later than children born during the first 9 months of the year. Neal and Johnson (cited in Heckman, 1995) capitalized on the fact that by age 17 (when adolescents are no longer mandated to attend school), children born in the last part of the year have had one year less school than children born earlier in the cohort's birth year. By comparing average IQ scores between these groups at that time, the impact of one year of schooling on intelligence test scores was estimated. In the study, the approximate gain in IQ score was 3.5 points per year of schooling (cited in Heckman, 1995). Unfortunately, results are subject to alternative explanations for the gains in intelligence, because the groups were not matched on important variables (e.g., differential retention or dropout rates) that may have confounded the obtained positive relation between years in school and intelligence. Furthermore, it is not clear whether the analysis compared the intelligence scores of older versus younger students within the same grade to identify the advantage of being among the oldest at a given grade level.

A Cohort-Sequential Analysis. Although not originally intended as a study of schooling, an investigation by Baltes and Reinhart (1969) minimized at least one potentially salient confound by matching groups on SES. The study consisted of a cohort-sequential analysis with three cross-sections of 8- to 10-year-old children classified by cohort and season of birth. Because of an established cutoff date for school entry, children at each age who made the cutoff date had an additional year of schooling compared to similar-age children who missed the cutoff date. On a measure of intelligence, 8-year-olds with an additional year of instruction actually scored closer on average to the performance of 10-year-olds with less schooling than they did to the 8-year olds with less schooling. This suggested a stronger influence of schooling (vs. maturational) influences on intelligence during this age period. Incidentally, the correlation between length of schooling and intellectual performance among these same-aged, same-SES children was also substantial (Baltes & Reinert, 1969).

Regression Discontinuity Design.   Bentin, Hammer and Cahan (1991) utilized a *between-grades regression discontinuity design* to disentangle age-related and schooling-related influences on children's growth in phonological awareness. This design eliminates from consideration children nearest the school cutoff date in order to avoid potential selection biases such as parents attempting to enroll ineligible children or holding back eligible children. Although these occurrences have been judged unlikely in past research (Morrison, Smith, & Dow-Ehrensberger, 1995), the regression discontinuity design avoids the issue entirely by including large samples of children spanning the range of birthdates within a given grade. By examining the slope of the within-grade regressions of scores on chronological age, the design reveals the impact of years in school through any discontinuity in the lines between grades. In the Bentin et al. investigation, children in kindergarten and first grade were asked to isolate the first and last phonemes in spoken words and in self-generated picture names. Regression analyses revealed both age (within-grade) and schooling (between-grade) effects on growth of phonological awareness, with schooling effects four times larger than age effects.

Table 10.1 organizes results from correlational (including years in school, summer vacation, and birthdate studies), cross-cultural, and extended-year studies reviewed in the previous sections. As shown, these investigations yielded a preponderance of schooling effects. Interestingly, schooling effects on reading and mathematics were obtained in all three types of investigations (possible reasons for this are discussed later). In contrast, schooling did not appear to shape the development of concrete operational thought, receptive vocabulary, or certain aspects of perceived competence (see Table 10.1). These results demonstrate that the influence of schooling is relatively domain specific.

School Cutoff Investigations

Over the past several years, we have exploited our own natural experiment, termed *school cutoff*, to examine the role of early schooling-related experiences in shaping cognitive growth, in contrast to other, so-called age-relat-

TABLE 10.1
Summary of Evidence From Correlated, Cross-Cultural, and Extended-Year Schooling
Investigations

School-Related Effects	Age-Related or Nonschooling Effects
	Correlational Studies
Full-scale IQ[1,2,3] Reading[4,5] Vocabulary[4] Mathematics[4,5]	
	Cross-Cultural Comparisons
Short-term picture memory[6] Short-term verbal memory[8] Metacognition[9] Lexicon organization[10] Reading[11] Mathematics[11]	Conservation Tasks[7]
	Quasi-Experimental Studies *
Reading[12] Mathematics[12] General information[12] Phonological segmentation[13,14]	Receptive vocabulary[12] Physical competence[12] Peer and maternal acceptance[12]

Note. *Excludes cutoff investigation (see Table 10.2). [1]Ceci, 1991; [2]Neil & Johnson, cited in Heckman, 1995; [3]Baltes & Reinhart, 1969; [4]Parsley & Powell, 1962; [5]Entwisle & Alexander, 1996; [6]Wagner, 1974 (short-term picture memory); [7]Cole & Cole, 1996 chap. 12; [8]Cole et al., 1971; [9]Scribner & Cole, 1981; [10]Sharp et al., 1979; [11]Stevenson et al., 1993; Stevenson & Lee, 1990; [12]Frazier & Morrison, 1998; [13]Cahan & Cohen, 1989; [14]Bowey & Francis, 1991.

ed influences, including maturation and general experience. Similar to the Neal and Johnson (cited in Heckman, 1995) and Baltes and Reinart (1969) studies, the methodology takes advantage of the fact that school districts in North America set an arbitrary cutoff date for school entry. However, the difference between the school cutoff method and earlier research utilizing entrance dates is that the cutoff method selects children very close in age who either just make versus just miss the cutoff, such that two groups of children virtually identical in chronological age are obtained. The groups are also equated on a number of important background variables (e.g., IQ, maternal education, preschool experience, and home literacy environment). Yet the schooling experiences of the two groups of children, in principle, are markedly different. Children in the cutoff studies typically have birthdates that fall on either side of the first-grade cutoff date. Hence, cognitive growth has been examined in a series of studies between two groups of children: young first-graders, who just make the cutoff and enter first grade; and old kindergartners, who just miss the cutoff and enter kindergarten. The method has also been used in an investigation of schooling effects on social and referential communication skills using groups of children who just made or missed the cutoff date for *kindergarten*, yielding groups of old prekindergartners and young kindergartners (Christian & Morrison, 2000). In addition, the technique has been used to examine a wide range of literacy, mathematic, visuospatial, language, and memory skills (see Table 10.2).

Using a pre–post design with testing at the beginning and end of the school year, the method permits assessment of the influence of specific schooling experiences on growth of cognitive skills. For example, group differences observed at fall pretest reveal kindergarten schooling influences, because Young first-graders have already been to kindergarten. Group differences at spring posttest reveal specific influences of first-grade schooling experiences. In contrast, similar growth patterns across groups over time reflect a lack of specific influence of schooling on growth of that skill in kindergarten or first-grade. The sources of these effects cannot be specified precisely and may be due to maturational, general experiential, family, or peer influences.

Findings From Cutoff Studies.   The cutoff method has proved to be sensitive to an array of predicted schooling- and age-related influences on a variety of linguistic, quantitative, general cognitive, and social skills. Nevertheless, as shown in Table 10.2, findings across a variety of domains and tasks have yielded a pattern of results characterized by a surprising degree of specificity in the nature and timing of developmental change over the age period studied. As listed in the table, across a number of independent investigations (see table for references), specific schooling effects have been observed in literacy skills (i.e., alphabet, reading, initial consonant stripping, general information, phonemic segmentation), quantitative skills (i.e., addition, standardized math tests), general cognitive skills (i.e., phonological memory, short-term verbal memory, sentence memory, components of narrative production and memory, visuospatial memory) and social skills (referential communication). Nevertheless, age-related effects have been documented for other types of literacy (i.e., receptive vocabulary, subsyllabic segmentation), quantititive (i.e., conservation of number, liquid, and solids), and general cognitive skills (i.e., syntactic constituents, narrative coherence). Finally, neither schooling or maturational effects were found for children's syllabic segmentation skills.

TABLE 10.2
Summary of School-Related and Age-Related Effects From "School Cutoff" Investigations

School-Related Effects		Age-Related or Nonschooling Effects
Literacy Skills		
Grade		
Alphabet recognition[1]	K and 1	Receptive vocabulary[1]
Standardized reading[1]	K and 1	Subsyllabic segmentation[1]
Initial consonant stripping[3]	K and 1	
General information[1]	1	
Phonemic segmentation[2]	1	
Mathematical Skills		
Addition[4]	K and 1	Conservation of number[4]
Standardized math[1]	K and 1	Conservation of solid quantity[4]
		Conservation of liquid quantity[4]
General Cognition		
Phonological memory[7]	K	Knowledge of syntactic constituents[5]
Short-term verbal memory[2]	1	Narrative coherence[8]
Sentence memory[5]	1	
Components of narrative production and memory[6]	K and 1	
Visuospatial memory[7]--matching	K and 1	
Visuospatial memory[7]--explicit	K and 1	
Visuospatial memory[7]--implicit	K and 1	
Social Skills		
Referential communication[9]	K and 1	Receptive vocabulary[1]

Note. [1]Morrison, Griffith, & Frazier, 1997; [2]Morrison, Smith, and Dow-Ehrensberger, 1995; [3]Treiman & Weatherston, 1992; [4]Bisanz et al., 1995; [5]Ferreira & Morrison, 1994; [6]Varnhagen et al., 1994; [7]Massetti & Morrison, 1997; [8]Frazier, Morrison, & Trabasso, 1995; [9]Christian & Morrison, 2000.

Findings from two investigations using the cutoff strategy highlight the specificity of schooling effects across and within task domains. The first investigation focused on children's quantitative reasoning (Bisanz, Morrison, & Dunn, 1985). Groups of children who just made versus missed the cutoff for first grade performed two tasks: a standard conservation of number task and an addition task in which they were asked to add all possible pairwise combinations of numbers 1 through 5 without the use of calculators or writing utensils. Findings revealed that instruction in kindergarten and first grade significantly increased children's performance on the addition task; in contrast, no schooling effects were obtained for the conservation task, suggesting age-related or nonschooling factors were responsible for the change. Thus, even within the same domain (quantitative reasoning), patterns of cognitive growth differed across tasks, with no evidence that skills acquired in one area (e.g., addition) benefited or transferred to performance in the other (e.g., conservation).

An even greater degree of specificity was revealed in an investigation of the impact of schooling on three phonological segmentation skills from kindergarten through second grade (Morrison, Smith, & Dow-Ehrensberger, 1995). In that study, the processing required was virtually identical across tasks (to verbally segment words), differing only in the level of phonological segmentation (syllabic, subsyllabic, or phonemic). Nevertheless, distinctly different patterns of change and influence were observed for the three segmentation tasks. For phonemic segmentation, schooling effects were noted in first grade. For subsyllabic segmentation, only a gradual increase in performance was observed for both groups of children—no schooling effects emerged. Finally, for syllabic segmentation, no changes at all were revealed over kindergarten or first grade. The pattern of results for subsyllabic and phonemic segmentation was also found by Bowey and Francis (1991) in an investigation using an almost identical procedure to the cutoff design (but lacking a longitudinal component). The findings for all three levels of phonological segmentation have been replicated most recently by Bachman, Bagdade, Massetti, Morrison, and Frazier (2000).

Taken together, findings from the phonological awareness study demonstrated that each level of segmentation appeared to follow its own unique developmental or experiential trajectory. Surprisingly, no evidence of transfer across domains could be discerned over a 2-year period, suggesting a high degree of specificity in the nature of developmental change in cognitive skills developing during the early school years.

FOUR VIEWS OF THE INFLUENCE
OF SCHOOLING

The complex, intricate pattern of growth in children's cognitive skills revealed in Tables 10.1 and 10.2 is not easily explained. Moreover, it is interesting that certain skills that seem to be molded by instruction in school were not necessarily those domains hypothesized by theorists to be most affected by schooling (Geary, 1995; Morrison & Massetti, 1997; Skeen & Rogoff, 1987). In the following section, four hypotheses that explore how schooling shapes children's cognitive development are presented and evaluated.

I. Schooling Enhances Verbal–Linguistic Skills to the Exclusion of, or Even to the Detriment of, Visuospatial Skills

This hypothesis dates back to the work of Bruner (1966) but can be seen in more recent theorizing by Skeen and Rogoff (1987), Muir (1985), and Baker-Ward and Ornstein (1988). In essence, the view holds that the typical format for interaction and learning in Western-style school settings places a heavy emphasis on linguistic skills and linear or serial modes of information processing (Skeen & Rogoff, 1987). Muir (1985) asserted that teacher education textbooks rarely apply theories of spatial conceptual development (i.e., Bruner, 1966; Piaget & Inhelder, 1956) to the instruction of map reading and use, hindering children's development in this area. Muir also noted that many adults (most of whom have completed high school or beyond) still have difficulty following simple directions when aided by maps.

Support for this hypothesis can be seen in two empirical investigations of memory for nonverbal information. First, in an investigation involving a complex layout of rooms in a funhouse, 7-year-old children who were told they would be asked to remember the location of rooms after walking through the house actually recalled less about the spatial relations of the rooms than did children who were simply involved with the information but not told to remember (Skeen & Rogoff, 1987). The authors suggested that the instructional emphasis on linear strategies such as rehearsal in typical American elementary schools may actually interfere with children's ability to remember nonlinear spatial arrangements. The teaching of rehearsal strategies has been found to be most evident during second and third grade (Hart, Leal, Burney, & Santulli, 1985), the same age period in which the discrepancy between explicit and incidental memory was found (Skeen & Rogoff, 1987).

Second, in a systematic comparison of performance between college students and children ages 5 to 9 years on "Concentration," a picture memory game, children's performance equaled that of adults on number of trials needed to complete the game, and actually outscored adults on a measure of "perfect" matches—those matches obtained not due to guessing and presumed to involve strategies for remembering the location of cards (Baker-Ward & Ornstein, 1988). The poorer performance among adults may reflect an age-related change in preference for verbal over visual encoding. The verbal–linguistic hypothesis would explain this shift in preference as result of increased focus on verbal processing and on linear rehearsal strategies acquired in school.

2. Relationship Between Instructional Emphasis and Learning

This hypothesis states that cognitive skills change as a function of relatively specific experiences or encounters with the instructional environment. Thus, schooling effects will be observed only on those specific cognitive skills that are enriched or stimulated in the instructional environment. If a particular skill is not explicitly targeted and drilled, it will not improve.

Considerable support exists for this hypothesis. Ceci (1991) argued that it is through direct instruction, ". . . a mechanism so obvious and straightforward as to be overlooked by some researchers" (p. 717) that schooling conveys its influence on IQ tests. The direct instruction approach of reading–literacy is based on the premise that systematic teaching in both reading comprehension and word decoding is critical for the development of reading skills (Gersten & Dimino, 1993). Particularly for students struggling to read, mere exposure to print material is not sufficient to enhance reading ability. Instead, advances in reading occur through direct, well-regulated instruction (Stein, Leinhardt, & Bickel, 1989). In addition, other holistic approaches, such as "whole language," have been criticized for depriving minority students of the explicit tutoring required to succeed (Delpit, 1988). In essence, the instructional emphasis hypothesis implies that growth in a particular cognitive domain can be predicted by the degree of emphasis placed on that domain in the schooling environment.

3. Schooling Enhances Those Cognitive Skills That Are Important for Success in School But Does Not Change General Thinking Ability

This view was recently espoused by Cole and Cole (1996) after reviewing a broad range of schooling and literacy influences, including cross-cultural research reviewed earlier in this chapter. In the authors' words:

> The picture that emerges from extensive research on schooling provides only minimal support for the idea that schooling changes the cognitive processes associated with middle childhood in any deep and general way. In those cases in which schooling *has* been found to affect cognitive performance, the effect appears to be restricted to rather specific information processing strategies or to a specific context that is relevant primarily, if not exclusively, to school itself. (p. 539)

In the case of memory development, Cole and Cole (1996) argued that children in school learn ways to commit material to memory for later testing, but schooling does not increase memory capacity in general. Other theorists have suggested the tasks required of children in school represent "academic" intelligence, somehow different from and irrelevant to "everyday" or "practical" intelligence found in other settings (Neisser, 1976; Scribner & Cole, 1973; Wagner & Sternberg, 1985). Gardner (1983) further suggested that there are *multiple* types of intelligences (e.g., linguistic, musical, bodily-kinesthetic, logical-mathematical, personal) that develop at different ages in different people and that the majority of instruction children encounter in a typical school environment does little to enhance some of these intelligences.

4. A Biocultural Perspective

The final hypothesis to be considered is also the most recent and in many ways the most comprehensive and ambitious. Drawing on evolutionary, neurological, cognitive, developmental, and social perspectives (including schooling effects), Geary (1995) proposed a fundamental distinction between two types of cognitive processes, primary and secondary. Primary cognitive processes comprise those operations and skills considered vital for functioning in the social and ecological world of our ancestors. As such, primary cognitive skills develop in the course of ordinary transactions with the world (i.e., via incidental learning), and motivation to acquire primary cognitive processes are presumed to be universal in all members of the species regardless of particular environmental circumstances (e.g., schooling). A corollary of this view, not explicitly stated by Geary, suggests that individual differences in the rate of acquisition of the primary cognitive processes would be relatively small. Examples of primary cognitive processes include language and facial processing in response to social adaptational pressures and visuospatial skills, including mental images of familiar ecologies and incidental memories for object location and organization in response to ecological pressures.

In contrast, secondary cognitive processes comprise those operations that are not considered vital for evolutionary adaptation but have emerged as important cognitive skills in particular environments. Secondary cognitive processes require effort and explicit learning, and universal motivation and mastery are not guaranteed at this level. Higher level reading and math skills constitute clear examples of secondary cognitive skills acquired in Western-style schooling environments. Primary and secondary cognitive processes do not develop in isolation, however. Secondary skills can build on primary processes through redescription (e.g., converting visuospatial knowledge into verbal form) or cognitive co-optation (essentially adapting skills acquired in one primary cognitive domain for use in a separate secondary domain).

EVALUATING THE HYPOTHESES

Each of the foregoing hypotheses appears to have merit in illustrating how schooling might influence cognitive development. Still, to move beyond conjecture requires evaluation of each proposition within the context of empirical data. The following section examines findings from schooling research that support a particular view as well as those that are problematic or present challenges for the position.

1. Schooling Enhances Verbal–Linguistic Skills to the Exclusion of, or Even to the Detriment of, Visuospatial Skills

Examination of the pattern of effects in Tables 10.1 and 10.2 does reveal a preponderance of schooling effects on verbal processes. For example, alphabet naming, reading achievement, referential communication, general information, phonemic awareness, initial consonant stripping, short-term verbal memory, and sentence memory were all uniquely enhanced by kindergarten and/or first-grade schooling experiences. In addition, cross-cultural investigations have documented unique characteristics in children's associations among words between schooled and nonschooled children (Sharp et al., 1979).

Nevertheless, there is evidence against this hypothesis. First, over the past six decades, substantial gains in IQ have been found on the Raven Progressive Matrices, a test requiring visual analysis and the ability to abstract relations among meaningless figures (Neisser, 1998). One explanation for the gains is that improved school quality has led to the teaching of decontextualized problem-solving skills (Flynn, 1998). However, it should be noted that the linkage between school-taught skills and problem-solving skills used on IQ tests has not been established (Flynn, 1998).

Second, a number of tasks tapping basic verbal skills showed no differential influence of early schooling: receptive vocabulary (in *both* cutoff and extended-year studies), subsyllabic segmentation, knowledge of syntactic constituents and narrative coherence (see Tables 10.1 and 10.2). A final problem for this view is that several *nonverbal* processes were reliably enhanced by exposure to early schooling experiences. Both basic computation in addition and standardized math achievement were sensitive to schooling influences in kindergarten and first grade, not all of which can be attributed to the verbal mode of testing. In addition, on three separate visuospatial processing tasks, kindergarten and first-grade encounters uniquely improved performance both in a concentration-like matching game and in memory for the identity and locations of objects in a dollhouse (in both deliberate and incidental memory conditions). The presence of a kindergarten and first-grade schooling effect in the *deliberate* memory condition of the dollhouse experiment was in direct opposition to the interpretation by Skeen and Rogoff (1987) that children learn linear strategies in school that interfere with their memory for nonlinear spatial arrangements. Nevertheless, to the extent that instruction in rehearsal strategies is concentrated in second and third grade (Hart et al., 1985), a cutoff study during these grades could further determine precisely when and in what manner schooling affects visuospatial memory.

In summary, although many of the cognitive processes found changed by schooling were verbal in nature, other verbal processes developing over the same period were not sensitive to schooling experiences. Further, *non*-verbal processes, both quantitative and visuospatial, showed themselves to be equally sensitive to schooling influences. Overall, although it does seem relevant for understanding some of the findings, the hypothesis that schooling enhances verbal skills and not others is not uniformly supported in the data from current schooling research.

2. Relationship Between Instructional Emphasis and Learning

On the surface, the idea of a connection between instructional emphasis and learning has a lot to recommend it. As shown in Table 10.1, the pattern of results depicted a classic schooling effect on early reading, communication, alphabet, and mathematics skills. Young first graders outperformed Old kindergartners in Fall and Spring, confirming that both kindergarten and first-grade experiences produced unique gains in these domains. In contrast, no schooling effects were found for knowledge of syntactic constituents, conservation, or narrative coherence. These findings were consistent with examination of curricular guidelines in the districts studied; early instructional emphases were placed on alphabet naming, elementary reading skills like decoding, even initial consonant stripping, whereas no mention was made of syntactic knowledge or narrative skills. Likewise, addition skills and elementary math skills were targeted for instruction, whereas conservation was typically not part of the curriculum. Other reading-related skills that showed schooling effects but did not appear to be explicitly taught in the early grades (e.g., phonemic awareness, phonological memory, sentence memory) could improve via transfer or generalization from other *directly* taught skills such as word decoding or memory retrieval. Indeed, memory demands constitute a notable proportion of teacher requests from children (Mercer, 1996). In addition, referential communication skills could be expected to improve as a result of teacher demands for children to be explicit in communicating their needs and answering teacher initiated questions.

Some findings from cross-cultural investigations and research on extended-year schooling also appeared congruent with the instructional emphasis perspective. First, the superior mathematics performance of Asian over American students may result from additional time spent on mathematics instruction and the cultural emphasis on math in Asian culture compared to the United States (Stevenson & Stigler, 1992; Stigler & Perry, 1990). Second, higher math, reading, and general information scores among extended-year (vs. traditional students) at the start of first grade can be interpreted as a result of increased focus on these areas during the additional school days after required material for the traditional school year is completed (Frazier & Morrison, 1998). These results clearly suggest that children's academic performance is strongly influenced by the emphasis placed on specific domains of knowledge.

Nevertheless, other findings seem to pose problems for the instructional emphasis view. Skills like receptive vocabulary and subsyllabic segmentation do not show schooling effects in either kindergarten or first grade, although they are typically identified as curricular emphases by teachers or they could be expected to show transfer effects from other skills. In addition, tacit knowledge of school would suggest that some children may learn material *not* specifically targeted for instruction. The opposite may also be true: Emphasis on a particular skill does not guarantee learning. Although this view can accommodate a wide range of direct schooling effects, as well as appeal to transfer or generalization effects, the evidence is by no means definitive. Indeed, we are currently conducting observations in kindergarten and first grade to ascertain what is actually being taught in the classrooms, with a view to linking instructional emphases to direct and indirect effects on growth of literacy skills.

3. Schooling Enhances Those Cognitive Skills That Are Important for Success in School But Does Not Change Thinking in Any Deep or General Way

This view can clearly accommodate the schooling effects found on a broad range of literacy and mathematical skills in schooling investigations. Further, they correctly predict minimal schooling influences on more general cognitive skills like conservation or the higher order cognitive skills involved in narrative comprehension and storytelling. Nevertheless, there are several problems for this hypothesis. First, triarchic instruction (involving analytical, creative, and practical instruction) has been identified as superior to other instructional methods in fostering the analytic, critical, and practical intelligence of third-grade students (Sternberg, Torff, & Grigorenko, 1998), suggesting that schooling does indeed enhance more general, practical thinking. Second, robust schooling effects have been found on a host of other general cognitive skills: memory for sentences, phonological memory, short-term verbal memory, intelligence, and a variety of visuospatial memory skills. It could be argued that these are really school-related skills with little or no general value outside the schooling environment. Yet it would seem hard to sustain the view that the ability to remember more of what someone said or to remember the location of objects in the environment is without value outside the school environment. Third, to the extent that IQ tests measure important general intellectual skills, the consistent correlation between years in school and intelligence as well as the decline in IQ during summer vacation create problems for this hypothesis. Fourth, the kindergarten schooling effect on referential communication suggested that in school, children increased their ability to take the perspective of others, a skill certainly beneficial beyond the confines of the classroom (Christian & Morrison, 2000). Perhaps the biggest problem for this view is the difficulty of separating cognitive processes important for school from those important in the rest of life. However culturally sensitive it might be, the view that schooling does not improve general thinking skills will turn out to be unsustainable.

4. Biocultural Perspective

Overall, the biocultural perspective fares well when examining the pattern of results from research on schooling effects. Perhaps the most striking confirmation of the view is the distinction between growth of conservation skills and acquisition of addition and general math skills. Conservation of number or solid and liquid quantity would seem to qualify as a primary cognitive process, whose ecological importance would predict relatively uniform and universal acquisition. Indeed, studies using the cutoff method have revealed no evidence for schooling effects on conservation in two separate replications across three conservation domains. In contrast, schooling effects on addition and other related math skills have been found in the same children over the same time period. This pattern in particular seems to confirm the operation of two distinct systems of cognitive processes, developing in different ways and responsive to different sources of influence. Also consistent with Geary's view would be the plethora of schooling effects on literacy skills like alphabet naming, reading achievement, initial consonant stripping, and phonemic awareness, because all would be considered cognitive skills not necessary for basic social or ecological adaptation but important for functional literacy in Western society. As for the development of more general cognitive skills (i.e., short-term memory, sentence memory) and social skills such as referential communication, Geary could explain schooling effects on these processes as the result of secondary processes redescribing or co-opting primary skills to cope with demands of the schooling environment. In a similar fashion, schooling effects on deliberate visuospatial memory tasks could result from verbal redescription of primary visuospatial presentations. In contrast, basic knowledge of syntactic constituents and narrative coherence in the early grades could be viewed as primary cognitive skills.

Notwithstanding its overall explanatory power, there are several results that challenge this view. First, schooling effects were observed on visuospatial memory tasks involving incidental processing, contradicting Geary's claim that primary cognitive processes like visuospatial memory develop automatically as a by-product of interactions with the ecological environment. Second, schooling effects have also been documented on phonological memory (Morrison & Massetti, 1997) which Geary views as a primary cognitive system relatively immune to specific schooling effects. Finally, findings for receptive vocabulary would not appear to fit the picture completely. Although no schooling effects have emerged in the cutoff studies, large individual differences in these skills are evident as early as the beginning of kindergarten. To the extent that vocabulary is considered to be a primary cognitive process, relatively little variation should occur in the rate of acquisition of these skills. The presence of wide individual differences raises the question of the status of these two skills in Geary's theoretical scheme.

Despite some seemingly contradictory results, the theoretical perspective developed by Geary provides an interesting and potentially powerful interpretive framework for identifying the influence of schooling on cognitive growth.

Summary

In summary, although none of the four hypotheses provide a complete understanding of the pattern of results found in investigations of schooling effects, each offers unique insights. First, in accord with Geary, the notion that cognitive processes vary in the degree to which they have been prepared or adapted by evolution represents an important insight. Hence, the ease and universality of acquisition of some cognitive skills (e.g., conservation) must be acknowledged. Second, however, it has been shown that most if not all cognitive skills, regardless of their preparedness, can be modified in significant ways by appropriate instructional emphases or through such lateral processes as transfer, redescription, or co-optation. The challenge for theory-builders is to understand and predict the conditions necessary for transfer or co-optation processes to occur. Third, schooling effects, although not limited to verbal skills, are more widespread in the verbal domain in the cutoff studies, reinforcing the notion that schools place a heavier emphasis on one mode of social discourse over other possible modes. Finally, as to whether schooling really modifies general thinking ability, the data to date have been limited to the early elementary years (kindergarten through second grade). The question can most likely be answered only by following children for a longer period of time through elementary school and beyond.

Thus, when considered independently, each of the four hypotheses is limited. However, taken together, they may provide the elements of an integrative view of the nature and sources of cognitive growth. Further, it is entirely feasible that multiple influences operate simultaneously on cognitive development, such that an attempt to identify one overarching explanation of the impact of schooling will inevitably fail.

CONDITIONS OF TRANSFER

The discussion thus far has emphasized the surprising degree of domain specificity of the effects of schooling. Notwithstanding the continuing evidence of specificity in cognitive skill acquisition, children and adults surely acquire more general or abstract cognitive skills over time, and hence, some consideration of when and how transfer of skills might occur is also necessary. Skills not directly shaped by instruction may advance through the process of re-description or co-optation (Geary, 1995; Karmiloff-Smith, 1992) or as a result of sharing "common elements" with instructed skills (Singley & Anderson, 1989), such that some degree of generalization does occur as children learn novel tasks. The goal for scientists has been to predict when transfer or generalization might be expected.

Fischer and Farrar (1987) specified four conditions that may influence the degree of transfer of a particular skill *within a task domain*. With some elaboration, these conditions can be explored within the context of schooling research. The first criteria is that "the tasks are similar and familiar." The tasks within a given domain (e.g., reading, mathematics) in early elementary grades tend to involve less varied or complex tasks than in later years, such that children would seem to become quickly familiar with a core set of fairly similar tasks (e.g., worksheets, group recitation). The second condition to promote transfer is that "the environment provides opportunities for practice and support." In this case, what environment could better provide a variety of opportunitites for practice than a classroom led by a supportive, challenging teacher? The third condition, "the person has had time to consolidate skills at the relevant developmental level," would seem to be satisfied by schooling, since curricular guidelines outline major emphases of instruction for a particular grade that typically remain in effect for an entire school year, providing ample time to consolidate skills. Finally, the fourth qualification to enhance the possibility of transfer among skills is that "the person is intelligent and in an emotional state facilitative of the particular skill." As discussed later in this chapter, intelligence has been identified as a relevant child variable interacting with the effect of schooling on various cognitive skills (Entwisle & Alexander, 1996; Jencks et al, 1972; Williams, Morrison, & Williams, 1999). In addition, a child's emotional interest in a subject would seem to influence his or her understanding of the material.

Despite the apparent applicability of Fischer and Farrar's conditions to the school environment, the issue of transfer has not yet been explored in relation to schooling research. To date, although the criteria for transfer would seem to exist in elementary school classrooms, data from schooling investigations offer little evidence for generalization or re-description of skills across tasks or domains in the early stages of learning a skill. Further research may provide answers to the apparent discrepancy between theory and empirical results.

PART TWO: PRACTICAL ISSUES

The first section of the chapter systematically reviewed current research on important theoretical issues in the contemporary study of cognitive growth. Equally compelling are a number of very practical concerns about children's cognitive and literacy skills that have emerged in the last two decades. Taken together, these two perspectives (basic and applied) yield some truly novel insights about the nature and sources of children's learning and the influence of schooling.

LITERACY AND ILLITERACY IN AMERICA

National assessments of reading, mathematics, and science achievement have documented that sizable percentages of children and adolescents (20% or more) are not acquiring the literacy skills necessary for academic and vocational success (Applebee, Langer, & Mullis, 1989). Cross-cultural evidence has uncovered significant disparities between Asian and American elementary school children's academic skills, with the Asian children displaying superior performance in mathematics, reading, and problem-solving skills (Stevenson & Lee, 1990; Stevenson, Chen, & Lee, 1993).

Perhaps more striking, mounting evidence has revealed substantial variability in the literacy skills of American children at surprisingly early ages (Alexander & Entwisle, 1988; Morrison, Frazier, Hardway, Griffith, Williamson, & Myazaki, 1999; Stevenson, Parker, Wilkinson, Hegion, & Fish, 1976). In a cross-cultural comparison of U.S., Chinese, and Japanese elementary school children, Stevenson and Lee (1990) found that American children lagged behind their Asian counterparts in first grade, with the gap widening by fifth grade. Stipek and Ryan (1997) uncovered large social class differences in both cognitive and early literacy skills among a sample of preschoolers and kindergartners. In addition, on several of the cognitive measures, such as word knowledge, number memory, conceptual grouping, and letter reading, the disadvantaged kindergartners actually scored lower than the advantaged preschoolers at the beginning of the year. A recent observational study of expressive vocabulary uncovered meaningful social class differences in children's acquisition as early as 18 months of age (Hart & Risley, 1995).

In a separate longitudinal study, Morrison et al. (1999) found substantial variation across children in both early literacy and learning-related social skills at kindergarten entry. Stable individual differences emerged across a wide range of early literacy skills, such as receptive vocabulary, general information, reading recognition, and mathematics. In addition, children's learning-related social skills, such as independence, responsibility, self-regulation, and cooperation, also showed considerable variability. Moreover, children in the Morrison et al. study did not display a mosaic of strengths and weaknesses across literacy and social skills; correlational analyses revealed that children performing relatively poorly in one area tended to perform similarly across all literacy and social domains.

Perhaps even more disconcerting was the stability of these early individual differences over time. Children's scores on early literacy tasks at kindergarten entry consistently predicted academic performance throughout the first 3 years of formal schooling experience (Morrison et al., 1995; Stevenson et al., 1976). Additional literature has pointed to an unbroken line of predictability from 1st-grade reading ability to 11th-grade reading experience and ability, even after accounting for children's cognitive abilities (Cunningham & Stanovich, 1997; Cunningham, Stanovich, & West, 1994). When assessing 11th-graders print exposure to determine how much students voluntarily seek reading experiences outside of school, three measures of 1st-grade reading proficiency continued to significantly predict 11th-graders exposure to print, even after statistically controlling for 11th-graders' reading comprehension ability. In other words, regardless of an individual's eventual level of reading comprehension, early facility with reading acquisition significantly influenced future engagement in reading activities throughout a child's schooling experience. Taken together, a growing body of evidence testifies to the very early emergence and stability of meaningful differences among children in important literacy skills and related social skills.

Two important questions emerge from these findings. First, what are the sources of these early individual differences in cognitive, and specifically, literacy development? And second, what are the implications of these differences when considering the effects of schooling on cognitive development?

SOURCES OF EARLY INDIVIDUAL DIFFERENCES

It is becoming clear that a large number of factors are implicated in shaping the growth of literacy and cognitive skills (Morrison, Frazier, et al., 2000). Due to the growing awareness of this complexity, scientists have increasingly relied on more complicated, multilevel theoretical frameworks. In the present context, the claim that factors at different levels of analysis (child, family, and sociocultural) contribute to literacy acquisition (Bronfenbrenner, 1979, 1986; Bronfenbrenner & Morris, 1998) is particularly useful in reviewing and organizing the sources of early individual differences in literacy skills.

Child Factors

In the past decades, research has pointed to the unique influence of a number of child characteristics on children's cognitive and literacy development (Alexander & Entwisle, 1988; Stevenson et al., 1976; Williams et al., 1999). The factors most heavily implicated in a child's literacy growth include: IQ, social skills, gender, and self-esteem. (For a discussion of other child factors such as personal and motivational constructs that are beyond the scope of this review, refer to Dweck, 1975, 1986; Dweck and Reppucci, 1973; Kalechstein and Nowicki, 1997; Rotter, 1966; Stipek, 1980, 1981.)

IQ. The contribution of IQ to academic achievement has been repeatedly established (Plomin & Neiderhiser, 1991). In recent years, findings from twin studies have revealed substantial genetic influence on cognitive ability and on measures of academic achievement (Chipuer, Rovine, & Plomin, 1990; Thompson, Detterman, & Plomin, 1991). Even within ethnically and socioeconomically diverse samples of children, IQ consistently predicts substantial unique variance in academic performance (Morrison, Frazier, et al., 2000; Oakland, 1983). Overall, although the concept of IQ continues to generate controversy (Sternberg, 1997), as well as criticism (Gardner, 1983), decades of methodologically sound research continues to demonstrate that scores on standardized tests of intelligence remain among the strongest of predictors of cognitive functioning and academic achievement.

Social Skills. Under the broad heading of social skills, researchers have distinguished two components of children's behavior contributing to academic performance: interpersonal skills, namely, the quality of social relations with peers and adults, and learning-related social skills, which involve the degree of independence, responsibility, and self-control exhibited in the classroom.

The academic benefits associated with the quality and maintenance of children's peer relations have been evidenced early in a child's schooling experience. Stable peer relationships have been shown to facilitate school adjustment during the transition from preschool to kindergarten (Ladd & Price, 1987). Furthermore, kindergartners' ability to form new friendships with their classmates during the first 2 months of school yielded significant gains in their academic performance by the end of their first year. Likewise, children who experienced early peer rejection displayed lower patterns of academic performance during the course of the year. This relation between peer interactions and academic achievement was evidenced in third grade as well (Green, Forehand, Beck, & Vosk, 1980), where academically successful third graders interacted positively with their peers and were also liked by their peers.

In addition to children's interpersonal skills, learning-related social skills have also predicted early academic achievement. Wentzel's (1991, 1993) work with adolescents revealed that teacher and peer ratings of students' socially responsible behavior, such as acting in accordance with social rules and role expectations, cooperating, and showing respect for others, were significantly related to academic performance. Among younger children, teacher ratings of first graders' learning-related behaviors, such as their participation, interest, and attention span, correlated significantly with children's report card marks and test scores (Alexander, Entwisle, & Dauber, 1993). However, because these studies did not investigate the role of learning-related social skills until the children already experienced a year or more of schooling, the possibility that these early learning patterns resulted from schooling socialization could not be definitively ruled out.

To address this ambiguity, several studies have investigated the roles of both interpersonal and learning-related skills at kindergarten entry. When attempting to identify maladjusted children, teacher ratings of children's work-related skills, such as disorganization, dependence, distractibility, and noncompliance, proved more important than assessments of their interpersonal skills, which included physical and verbal aggressiveness and disrupting (Cooper & Farran, 1988). Additional research supported Cooper and Farran's findings; children's work-related skills at the beginning of kindergarten were more uniquely predictive of their early academic performance than were their interpersonal skills (Morrison, Frazier, et al., 2000). In addition, teacher ratings of kindergartner's work-related skills have predicted unique variance in parental ratings of academic achievement 3 to 5 years later (Hansen, Morrison, & Holmes, 2000). Children rated low on work-related skills performed significantly worse than the overall sample on a number of early literacy measures (receptive vocabulary, reading recognition, general information, and mathematics) at the beginning of kindergarten and at the end of second grade (McClelland, Morrison, & Holmes, in press).

In summary, the literature demonstrates a clear connection between children's social skills, both work-related and interpersonal, at kindergarten entry and later academic achievement, adaptation and adjustment to school, and peer relationships. However, only learning-related behaviors uniquely predict cognitive development and academic performance.

Entrance Age. Since the 1970s, concerns about the impact of a child's chronological age on academic performance have surfaced regularly. Several studies have suggested that younger children may be at greater risk for poor academic performance (Breznitz & Teltsch, 1989; Davis, Trimble, & Vincent, 1980), grade retention (Langer, Kalk, & Searls, 1984), special education referrals (DiPasquale, Moule, & Flewelling, 1980; Maddux, 1980), and learning disabled labeling (Maddux, 1980). Nevertheless, recent reviews of that literature raised several questions about the validity of the claims about the deleterious impact of a children's entrance age (Morrison, Griffith, & Alberts, 1997; Shephard & Smith, 1988). For instance, many studies failed to control for potentially important background characteristics between the older and younger students or reported small, yet statistically significant, effects when large sample sizes were employed.

In a recent study by Morrison, Griffith, and Alberts (1997) using the cutoff method described earlier, reading and mathematics scores from the fall and spring of the school year were compared among groups of Old Kindergarten, Young First Grade, and Old First-Grade Children. Small but significant differences in reading and math achievement were sustained between the young and old first graders at both time points during the school year; however, both groups also experienced comparable growth. In addition, a significant effect of schooling was revealed by the young first graders who consistently outperformed their same-age kindergarten counterparts. Overall, the findings clearly revealed that young first graders were benefiting from formal instruction as much as their older peers.

Although results of the Morrison et al. (1997) study suggest that entrance age in and of itself, is not a useful predictor of early academic achievement, two issues remain unresolved. First, whereas the early effects of entrance age appeared short-lived, the long-term effects have not been adequately examined. For example, it is possible that although entrance age effects diminish in early elementary school (Morrison, Griffith, & Alberts, 1997; Morrison, Frazier, et al., 2000) the effects of age on cognitive and social domains may reemerge as schooling requirements become more difficult (Crosser, 1991; DeMeis & Stearns, 1992). Second, it is still not clear whether entrance age is an independent risk factor, or whether the risk is produced when young school entry is combined with other factors such as low IQ or social immaturity.

Gender. Although, the role of gender differences in academic achievement has been frequently explored and discussed in the literature, the findings have yielded a confusing picture. Early reviews suggested that although small discrepancies may emerge at younger ages, consistently significant gender differences in verbal, mathematics, and spatial abilities were not generally evidenced until 10 or 11 years of age, with disparities in spatial skills favoring males producing the strongest effects (Maccoby & Jacklin, 1972, 1974). However, later work has displayed girls' superior verbal ability and similar mathematics performance compared to boys' (Entwisle & Baker, 1983;

Stevenson et al., 1976), and no gender differences in cognitive measures such as memory tasks (Stevenson et al., 1976) during the early elementary school years.

Several studies have attempted to uncover the predictive power of gender on academic and literacy task performance. For example, when sex differences in cognitive ability have been examined outside North American culture, gender contributed less than 5% unique variance in cognitive and academic tasks for Peruvian schooled and nonschooled children (Stevenson, Chen, & Booth, 1990). Similar results emerged from longitudinal work conducted in the United States (Morrison, Frazier, et al., 2000), where gender failed to uniquely predict performance on several standardized measures of academic achievement.

A series of recent meta-analyses performed by Hyde and colleagues exploring gender differences in mathematics and verbal ability yielded interesting historical trends. Since 1974, the magnitude of gender differences in math and verbal performance has declined (Hyde, Fennema, & Lamon, 1990; Hyde & Linn, 1988), and the average effect size in math performance actually favored *females* (Hyde et al., 1990). In addition, although prior to age 2, female infants displayed consistently greater rates of vocabulary growth (Huttenlocher, Haight, Bryk, Seltzer, & T. Lyons, 1991), by age of 2, these early differences were no longer apparent, and unlike Maccoby and Jacklin's claims (1972, 1974), later tests of language competence no longer detected gender differences (Hyde & Linn, 1988).

In summary, although the literature has produced contradictory findings, it appears that the size of gender differences in cognitive functioning have diminished over the last few decades, and that existing gender differences tend to diminish with age.

Self-Esteem. The importance of self-esteem or self-efficacy has been widely postulated (Bandura, 1977); however, during the first several years of schooling, self-esteem appears to lack unique, predictive power for children's academic performance (Morrison, Frazier, et al., 2000; Snyder & Michael, 1983). Harter and Pike (1984) proposed four primary domains of self esteem, or self-worth (cognitive competence, physical competence, peer acceptance, and maternal acceptance) and later claimed that children's reports of these domains from ages 4 to 7 were reliable, although the children had difficulty differentiating competence from acceptance (Harter, 1990). In addition, children during this time period appeared to possess an unrealistic conception of their academic adequacy, most often demonstrated by their overrating of abilities (Harter, 1990; Richman & Rescorla, 1995). This phenomenon of inflated self-reports was exemplified in the Greensboro Early Schooling Study (Morrison, Frazier, et al., 2000) where, despite large individual differences in literacy skills at kindergarten entry, little variation was found in the self-esteem scores of the children, who rated themselves quite positively, regardless of actual academic performance.

By around fourth grade, self-esteem scores are not only more stable over time (Granleese & Joseph, 1994), but greater variability in reported self-esteem begins to emerge (Browne & Rife, 1991). However, increased variability does not necessarily signify increased accuracy; children who continue to overrate themselves exhibit greater anxiety and lower self-esteem (Connell & Ilardi, 1987) than peers who could accurately rate their performance.

Although self-esteem is consistently thought by teachers to be an important determinant of academic achievement, research has failed to establish its causal connection to academic achievement (Bohrnstedt & Felson, 1983). As Baumeister (1997) argued, although self-esteem may predict individuals' responses to evaluative feedback, very little research has evidenced greater competence or achievement for people with higher self-esteem than for those with lower self-esteem. Furthermore, low levels of self-esteem are *relatively* low; as reviewed by Baumeister and colleagues (Baumeister, Tice, & Hutton, 1989), most people would be more appropriately labeled with high or moderate self-esteem because few scores are actually low.

Family Factors

In elucidating the nature and sources of early individual differences in literacy skills, it is becoming increasingly evident that aspects of the home environment contribute substantially to a child's cognitive development and school success. In this section, special attention is placed on those parental behaviors and family dynamics occurring in the home, rather than on more distal factors, such as birth order and family size (Sputa & Paulson, 1995), parent configuration (Thompson, Entwisle, Alexander, & Sundius, 1992; Kaiser, 1994), and sibship size (Kuo & Hauser, 1997).

Although examination of parenting styles has been the most frequently employed method of assessing parental influence on child outcomes, the heavy reliance on adolescents' reports of perceived parenting behavior has been problematic. As one solution, Darling and Steinberg (1993) suggested a reconceptualization of parenting styles as a supportive framework for subsequent parenting practices which integrates reports of parenting style with observation of parental behaviors. Therefore, in the discussion that follows, the literature examining the effects of parenting styles on children's academic achievement is supplemented with a review of five specific dimensions of parenting emerging as key sources of influence on children's literacy acquisition: parental beliefs, the home literacy environment, the emotional climate in the home, the rules, standards, and limits in the home, and family organization (Bornstein, 1995).

Parenting Styles. The study of parenting styles has been significantly shaped by the original triadic configuration of authoritarian, authoritative, and permissive styles defined by varying levels of warmth and control developed by Baumrind (1966, 1968, 1971). These delineations were revised by Maccoby and Martin (1983) who claimed that parenting styles could be best understood by exploring the levels of demandingness and responsiveness promoted by parents, yielding four parenting styles: authoritarian, authoritative, indulgent, and neglectful. Authoritative parenting has been frequently associated with the promotion and maintenance of higher levels of academic competence and school adjustment, whereas the detrimental effects of neglectful or nonauthoritative parenting on adolescent outcomes, such as poorer classroom engagement and homework completion, appear to accumulate over time (Dornbusch, Ritter, Leiderman, Roberts, & Fraleigh, 1987; Glasgow, Dornbusch, Troyer, Steinberg, & Ritter, 1997; Lamborn, Mounts, Steinberg, & Dornbusch, 1991; Steinberg, Lamborn, Darling, Mounts, & Dornbusch, 1994).

Parental Beliefs. Clark (1983) conducted case studies of 10 poor, Black, one- and two-parent families of high- and low-achieving students. The parents of high achievers promoted strong values and high expectations for education, fostered children's active participation in school, and felt responsible for their children's performance. In contrast, parents of low achievers communicated a sense of powerlessness about their children's poor academic achievement and behavior, and not only refused to accept responsibility for their children's performance, but viewed academic failure as the fault of the child.

Despite the apparent association between parental beliefs and children's academic achievement, researchers have failed to establish a direct relation (Okagaki & Sternberg, 1993; Richman & Rescorla, 1995). Furthermore, this association between parental beliefs and children's competence seemed varied across different ethnic groups (Okagaki & Frensch, 1998; Steinberg, Dornbusch, & Brown, 1992; Stevenson, Chen, & Uttal, 1990) Okagaki and Frensch (1988) suggested that if a causal relationship exists between parental beliefs and behaviors and children's school achievement, one possible mediator may be children's perceptions of those parental beliefs.

Other work uncovered discrepancies not only between parental beliefs and children's academic outcomes, but between parental educational beliefs and their literacy-promoting behaviors. Robeson (1997) found that after statistically controlling for the child's IQ, entrance age, gender, maternal education, and amount of preschool experience, parental beliefs about the importance of schooling failed to uniquely predict the quality of the home literacy environment provided by parents. More important, after accounting for the unique variance contributed by background variables and the home literacy environment, parental beliefs failed to predict performance on receptive vocabulary, reading recognition, and mathematics, and contributed roughly 2% of the variance on a measure of general knowledge. Taken together, empirical findings to date have revealed a tenuous relationship between measures of parents' educational beliefs and their children's academic achievement that is most likely mediated by a number of other factors, such as parents' subsequent literacy-promoting behaviors and children's perception and internalization of parental beliefs.

Home Literacy Environment. Investigators have begun moving from assessing parental beliefs to measuring parenting practices that enhance or inhibit literacy development and academic achievement. Two primary foci of research have included the quality of language stimulation in the home, and explicit literacy-promoting behaviors.

Maternal speech patterns, such as the amount, quality, and kinds of speech produced, have predicted vocabulary growth during the first 3 years of life (Hart & Risley, 1995) as well as prekindergarten measures of emergent literacy and print-related skills (De Temple & Snow, 1992). Another facet of parental behavior that has attracted increased attention is the deliberate parenting practices which promote children's cognitive and literacy development (Bloom, 1981; Clark, 1983; Morrow, 1989; Stewart, 1995). Researchers have uncovered significant correlations between the home environment measures, which include parental reading habits and children's exposure to print, and a number of child outcomes such as IQ scores at 1 and 3 years of age (Bradley & Caldwell, 1980), 2nd-grade reading competency (Scarborough, Dobrich, & Hager, 1991), and 11th-grade reading comprehension (Cunningham & Stanovich, 1997; Cunningham, Stanovich, & West, 1994).

Griffin and Morrison (1997) created a composite measure of the home literacy environment, consisting of assessments of frequency of library card use, number of child and adult magazine subscriptions, number of newspaper subscriptions, how often someone read to the child, the number of books the child owned, the hours of television viewed per week by the child, and how often the father and mother read to themselves. After taking into account a host of other background characteristics (child IQ, maternal education, entrance age, preschool experience, race, and gender), the measure of the home literacy environment uniquely predicted fall kindergarten scores in receptive vocabulary, general knowledge, and reading, and spring second-grade scores in general knowledge and reading. In summary, both aspects of parenting behavior (language and literacy environments) appear to substantially influence children's cognitive development. Most important, not only can dramatic effects be found at very young ages, but these early parenting practices contribute significantly to children's later academic achievement.

Emotional Climate. In their reconceptualization of the influence of parenting styles on children's development, Darling and Steinberg (1993) argued that recognition of the emotional climate, which provides the context for socialization, must be assessed in order to understand this relationship between parenting practices and child outcomes. Consequently, a number of researchers have examined the effect of the quality of parent–child interaction, and specifically, parental warmth displayed in measures of sensitivity, attachment, cooperation, or acceptance on different aspects of children's socioemotional development, such as compliance (Maccoby & Martin, 1983), adjustment and coping strategies (Herman & McHale, 1993), academic motivation (Radin, 1971), and self-efficacy (Richman & Rescorla, 1995).

Of particular interest in this discussion is the role of parental warmth on children's cognitive development. Observations of parental warmth, such as open displays of affection, physical or verbal reinforcement, and sensitivity to children's requests and feelings, have been significantly associated with academic achievement and cognitive growth (Clark, 1983; Radin, 1971). Other research also documented a consistent relation over time between the affective quality of mother–child interactions and a number of measures of children's cognitive competence: mental ability scores at age 4, school readiness skills at ages 5 and 6, IQ scores at age 6, and vocabulary and mathematics performance at age 12 (Estrada, Arsenio, Hess, & Holloway, 1987). The authors suggested that the affective quality of parent–child interactions influenced children's cognitive development in three ways: through parents' willingness to engage themselves in problem-solving tasks with their children; by regulation of the information shared among adults and children (affecting children's developing social competence); and finally, by encouraging children's exploratory tendencies, thereby enhancing their motivation and persistence in challenging tasks.

Most notable in these studies are the effects of parental influence on social and cognitive domains before kindergarten entry. Not only have patterns of social behavior and cognitive functioning been established before children experience a formal schooling environment, but the affective quality of parent–child relationships apparently contributes to the long-term stability of these effects.

Rules, Standards, and Limits. This parenting dimension reflects the "control" aspect of Baumrind's authoritative parenting style. Although the "warmth," or emotional climate of the home is an important component of parenting, setting and maintaining rules, standards, and limits establishes parental authority and creates a supportive, structured context for children's cognitive development. Although this dimension remains somewhat speculative, recent research has suggested an indirect relation between parental control and children's academic achievement. For example, Clark (1983) observed that parents of low achievers indiscriminately and inconsistently employed physical punishment. In another investigation, the social skills children developed as a result of parental socialization mediated the relation between parental control and children's literacy skills at the beginning of kindergarten (Cooney, 1999). Thus, although more research is necessary to establish causality, there appears to be an important if complex relation between parental rules, standards, and limits and children's cognitive development.

Family Organization. Although not frequently addressed in the literature, there is an additional component of parenting that may influence children's cognitive and literacy development. The effort parents expend to organize the family's schedule into a set of predictable time tables and routines may affect children's school-related social behavior and academic achievement. Family organization refers to the degree of predictability built into a child's schedule (e.g., whether and when a family eats together, the consistency of a bedtime routine, and planning for future events or obligations). It also includes creation and maintenance of rituals and traditions surrounding special occasions, holidays, and birthday. A child who can rely on structured schedules and predictable routines is free to focus energy and time on academic and related pursuits.

Although this dimension has not been heavily investigated, there is evidence that children's work and chores aid the development of behavioral and academic competence. For instance, Clark (1983) found a strong emphasis on family rituals and routinized daily household activities, such as housekeeping, cooking chores, and personal grooming, in the homes of high-achieving students. Household work may have also benefited children's cognitive functioning by enhancing their social cognition and promoting the development of cognitive strategies (Goodnow, 1988). In summary, although not extensively studied, family organization may play a vital, if less direct, role in shaping children's social behavior and cognitive growth.

Sociocultural Factors

A number of sociocultural factors outside the family have been hypothesized to affect children's cognitive development. In the present discussion, broader sociocultural influences, such as neighborhood characteristics or the media are not reviewed. In addition, although the influence of peers becomes increasingly important as children progress through school (Kupersmidt, DeRosier, & Patterson, 1995; Steinberg et al., 1992), primary emphasis will be placed on more immediate factors in children's experience that contribute to early individual differences in literacy development: preschool experience, socioeconomic status, and race and ethnicity.

Preschool Experience. Although preschool attendance is generally considered to be an advantageous experience for enhancing children's developing cognitive and social skills, the literature has been less conclusive about its universally beneficial effects (Gullo & Burton, 1993; Sheehan, Cryan, Wiechel, & Bandy, 1991). Baydar and Brooks-Gunn (1991), for example, found that mother and grandmother care were more favorable than center-based care for poor children's cognitive development than for children not in poverty. Other researchers have also noted SES-specific effects of preschool experience when the roles of additional background variables were considered. Only for the most at-risk children, who had less educated mothers and poorer home literacy environments, did more time in child-care centers significantly relate to academic performance, and this effect was evident only in mathematics scores (Christian, Morrison, & Bryant, 1998). For the other children in the sample, the effects of preschool experience on indices of cognitive functioning were negligible. In another study, after statistically controlling for possible confounds such as family income, maternal education, ethnicity, and HOME scores, day-care attendance in the first year of life resulted in higher reading recognition and mathematics scores for children at ages 5 and 6 from impoverished families, whereas children from more optimal home environments with the same day-care experience actually performed lower on these measures (Caughy, DiPietro, & Strobino, 1994).

In summary, the literature suggests that the effects of preschool on children's cognitive development must be considered in conjunction with a number of other factors, such as the timing of entrance and type of child-care setting, as well as the background characteristics of the families.

Socioeconomic Status. As mentioned throughout this review, SES differences in academic achievement are a common finding in the literature (Alexander & Entwisle, 1988; Morrison, Frazier, et al., 2000; Stevenson et al., 1976; Stipek, 1980; Stipek & Ryan, 1997). Not only do children from lower social classes begin school behind, and display slower rates of growth during the schooling process, but unlike children from more educationally advantaged families, poorer children with less educated parents also appear to lose ground academically over the summer months (Entwisle & Alexander, 1992, 1994). Despite these well-documented social class differences, findings from a number of studies revealed surprisingly low statistical associations among SES indices, such as education level, occupational status, and family income, and academic performance (Miller, 1970; White, 1982). However, if measures of the home atmosphere such as work habits, quality of language, and number of reading materials in the home were included in an SES index, the correlations between the SES indices and measures of academic performance increased substantially (White, 1982).

Additional work has uncovered the predictive power of home environment measures such as language stimulation and literacy promotion over and above the effects of parental education on the early literacy skills of 2 and 3 year-olds (Johnson et al., 1993), preschoolers (Mantzicopoulos, 1997), and kindergartners in the fall of the school year (Bachman, Morrison, & Bryant, 2000). As emphasized by Clark (1983), focusing attention simply on distal social class effects masks the tremendous qualitative variation in more proximal parenting practices and attitudes within families of similar socioeconomic backgrounds. Additionally, among a sample of Indo-Chinese refugees, parents who could not speak English or assist with homework nevertheless made their home environment conducive for school success by promoting at least 2 hours of homework a night, and more than 50% of these parents also reported reading regularly to their children (Caplan, Choy, & Whitmore, 1992). As a result, children newly arrived in this country performed surprisingly well academically, maintaining B averages and demonstrating superior performance in math.

Although the socioeconomic context experienced by a child is undeniably influential in terms of the resources available to the family, levels of parental stress, and psychological well-being, the rather surprising finding emerging from the literature is that while traditional indices of SES are associated with other environmental and family factors, SES measures hold little unique predictability for children's academic outcomes. In contrast, parental literacy-promoting behaviors have consistently emerged as a key source of influence, beyond SES. As detailed by Caplan et al. (1992) and Clark (1983), poor parents, through deliberate structuring of a learning environment at home and involvement in their children's literacy development and academic performance, can raise high-achieving students, despite their low socioeconomic status.

Race and Ethnicity. Asian immigrant students have shown consistently superior reading and math performance, which has been attributed to differences in parenting practices (Chao, 1994), and peer support (Steinberg et al., 1992). In addition, although European Americans display significantly lower academic ability, especially in math, to Asian Americans, both Hispanic and Black students tend to score lower than European Americans on measures of academic achievement (Ortiz, 1986; Stevenson, Chen, & Uttal, 1990).

Perhaps the greatest scientific effort has been devoted to understanding the nature and sources of differences in academic achievement between Euro-Americans and African Americans. One explanation proposed by Ogbu (1983, 1988, 1991) claimed that whereas Black Americans support education, as their children observe their parents' experience with job ceilings and view high levels of unemployment in their communities, Black children's expectations and beliefs about what they can realistically accomplish is lowered. In related work, Steele and colleagues (Steele, 1998; Steel & Aronson, 1995) discussed the deleterious effects of stereotype threat on African Americans' academic performance. Stereotype threat is a self-evaluative process whereby individuals believe their behavior will be perceived according to the negative stereotypes held about their group. Controlling for prior SAT performance, the African American college students who were told their tests were diagnostic for assessing verbal ability performed worse than the White students and the African American students who took nondiagnostic tests.

Although these sociocultural effects would become increasingly evident as children progressed through school, this awareness seems too cognitively sophisticated to explain the racial differences found at kindergarten entry (Bachman, Morrison, & Bryant, 2000; Cooney, 1999; Phillips, Crouse, & Ralph, 1998), or even by the end of first grade (Alexander & Entwisle, 1988; Entwisle & Alexander, 1988), especially because Black children report liking and doing well in school (Stevenson, Chen, & Uttal, 1990).

Although these sociocultural interpretations have been influential in suggesting possible qualitative differences between races as sources of school performance, others have attempted to explain these academic achievement disparities in more quantitative terms. Using structural equations modeling, Rowe, Vazsonyi, and Flannery (1994, 1995) did not find minority-specific developmental processes; instead, Rowe et al. (1994) proposed that inasmuch as racial groups shared similar developmental pathways, the findings of group differences in academic performance resulted from the influence of different levels of developmental antecedents.

Other researchers have examined aspects of the actual schooling experience for possible explanations of racial differences. Despite early similarities in verbal and quantitative skills, a racial gap in children's academic performance had emerged by the end of first grade (Alexander & Entwisle, 1988), which the authors attributed to differential adjustment to full-time schooling. The results of Alexander and Entwisle contrast somewhat with other studies documenting sizable racial differences in academic skills at kindergarten (Morrison, Frazier, et al., 2000) and first grade (Stevenson, Chen, & Uttal, 1990). The discrepancies appear to be explained in part by differing sample characteristics across studies.

In the Greensboro Early Schooling Study, sizable racial differences were evident in the fall of kindergarten across a variety of early literacy measures (receptive vocabulary, general information, reading recognition, and mathematics), and these differences remained consistent through the spring of second grade (Cooney, 1999). Follow-up analyses revealed that significant racial differences in performance at kindergarten entry persisted across levels of parental education (Bachman, Morrison, & Bryant, 1999); increased educational attainment among Black parents did not reduce the racial differences in children's academic skills at higher socioeconomic levels. Recent analysis of national databases also detected a lack of interaction between race and socioeconomic indices for several cognitive and literacy measures (Phillips, Brooks-Gunn, Duncan, Klebanov, & Crane, 1998). Furthermore, Phillips and colleagues demonstrated that that if Black–White skill differences in first grade could be eliminated, half of the Black–White test score gap at the end of 12th grade could be eliminated as well (Phillips, Crouse, & Ralph, 1998). Taken together, social class does not appear to act as a prime determinant of racial differences in academic achievement, and as argued by Jencks and Phillips (1998), increased investigation of more proximal developmental influences is necessary to understand the nature and sources of these early differences. For example, home environment measures have been shown to uniquely predict cognitive functioning (IQ and receptive vocabulary) over and above the effects of SES for White children, but not Black children, as early as 3 years of age (Johnson et al., 1993).

In summary, findings from a number of studies reveal large differences between Black and White children that, in many instances, are established prior to school entry. Although the sources of these racial differences remains controversial, recent findings point to differences in the early experiences of Black and White children, irrespective of social class. In addition, Black children may experience more difficulty in the transition to early schooling, which could independently hamper academic growth.

Toward a More Dynamic Framework: Pathway Analysis

The preceding review reinforces the claim that a complex set of factors in the child, family, and sociocultural context are all implicated in growth of literacy and cognitive skills in early childhood. Yet simple recitation of individual factors does not adequately capture the ongoing interaction among these forces that operates to shape a child's growth over time. Clearly a more dynamic conceptualization as well as a more flexible methodology are needed to fully describe and understand cognitive change.

A first step in that direction was recently taken by Morrison, Ornstein, Hardway, & Pelphrey (2000). Using data from the Greensboro Early Schooling Study, the authors attempted to chart different developmental pathways to literacy arising from the independent and combined contributions of important sources of influence. To create developmental pathways, a two-pronged strategy was employed. First, using a series of forced-entry regressions, the strongest unique predictors of literacy outcomes were determined. For example, IQ and home literacy environment emerged as strong unique predictors. Second, using these variables, a homogeneous grouping strategy was employed in which children were equated on one of the predictor variables so that the impact of a second predictor variable could be examined with the first held constant. In one instance, children were grouped according to IQ, creating two relatively homogeneous groups of high and low IQ children. Then for each of the groups the impact of variation in home literacy environment was assessed on beginning kindergarten literacy scores and on growth of four literacy skills (vocabulary, general information, reading, and math) over the next 2 years. Findings revealed that the impact of IQ and literacy environment depended on the literacy skill being examined. For vocabulary, general information and reading, the effects of IQ and literacy environment were additive, such that low IQ children from high literacy environments performed as well as high IQ children from low literacy environments over the first 2 years of school. A distinctly different pattern emerged for mathematics, where IQ effects predominated over literacy environment and no interactions emerged.

Although the pattern of findings was intriguing, the point to be made here is that a relatively straightforward methodological strategy aimed at charting developmental pathways was successful in demonstrating the dynamic interplay among the individual sources of influence shaping cognitive growth. Clearly future theory and research will benefit from sustained efforts to translate the important insights gained from ecological theory into viable research strategies.

IMPLICATIONS FOR UNDERSTANDING SCHOOLING EFFECTS

The foregoing discussion sets the stage for a clear, if complex, answer to the fundamental question posed in this chapter, namely what is the impact of schooling on cognitive development? To adequately address the question, two conclusions need to be reviewed. First, the impact of schooling on cognitive growth is largely domain specific. Some cognitive and literacy skills are strongly modified by schooling experiences, whereas others show minimal influence of schooling. Second, the impact of schooling will depend greatly on other child, family, and sociocultural factors impinging on the child's growth. Accepting these two conclusions and adopting a dynamic pathway approach, Williams, Morrison, and Williams (2000) examined the independent and combined influence of schooling (using the cutoff method) and IQ on four literacy skills—vocabulary, general information, reading, and math. Findings from that study revealed a complex, intricate pattern of IQ and schooling effects and their interactions across the four literacy skills. Although IQ substantially influenced vocabulary scores, no schooling effects were observed and no schooling × IQ interactions surfaced. Schooling did significantly influence the other three literacy skills, but in unique and revealing ways as a function of IQ. For general information (see Fig. 10.1)

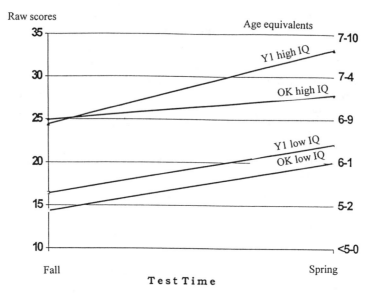

FIG. 10.1.   Raw scores on the PIAT-R general information test as a function of
IQ group (low or high) and school group (Old Kindergarten and Young First
Grade).

first-grade schooling enhanced growth only for high IQ children whereas no
benefits were seen for low IQ children. The result of the interaction was to
increase IQ differences in general information over time. For mathematics,
schooling enhanced performance of both high and low IQ children, but
scores of higher IQ children grew more rapidly, again magnifying the IQ differences in math skills over time. In stark contrast, the opposite effect
merged for reading (see Fig. 10.2). Schooling effects were much more powerful than IQ effects such that low IQ children exposed to kindergarten and
first-grade schooling experiences outperformed matched groups of children
who had not yet experienced formal instruction in these grades. Most striking, by the end of first grade low and high IQ children did not differ statistically in elementary reading scores.

Findings from the study provided a clear and dramatic example of the
complex, dynamic nature of developmental change in important literacy
skills in early childhood. Clearly the effects of schooling on cognitive growth
depended on the skill being assessed and on the measured IQ of the child.
Similar interactions of schooling with other child, family, and sociocultural
factors could be expected and warrant further examination.

The particular pattern of findings from this study appeared to reflect the
degree of instructional emphasis placed on various literacy skills in early

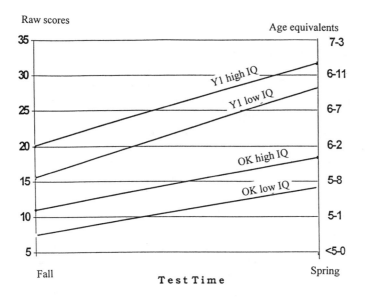

FIG. 10.2. Raw scores on the PIAT-R reading recognition test as a function of IQ group (low or high) and school group (Old Kindergaren and Young First Grade).

elementary classrooms in the United States. Substantial time is devoted to the fundamentals of reading, including alphabet naming and elementary word decoding. Less instructional time appears to be devoted to mathematics (Stevenson & Lee, 1990) and even less to vocabulary and general information. Although speculative, it is plausible that in those subject areas where heavier instructional emphasis is placed, strong schooling effects are produced and individual differences in IQ among children are proportionately reduced. In areas less emphasized in instructional activities, IQ differences persist or are even magnified. The obvious implication is that schooling can help to reduce the size of early individual differences but that large amounts of direct sustained instruction will be required to achieve this goal.

CONCLUSIONS AND IMPLICATIONS

The present chapter attempted to integrate basic and applied work on schooling and cognitive growth, in the belief that each perspective could enlighten the other and together they could provide a fuller, more accurate and insightful account of how schooling shapes intellectual development. Basic research has demonstrated that schooling experiences can dramatically change cognitive skills, but that the influence of schooling depends heavily on the skill in question. The nature, timing, and magnitude of schooling effects are surprisingly domain specific and appear to depend, in part, on instructional emphases operating in the classroom. With notable exceptions (Sternberg et al., 1998), American classrooms tend to emphasize verbal over visual and other kinds of skills or intelligences (Gardner, 1983). Among verbal skills, important literacy skills like reading that are necessary for success in school and workplace are stressed in early classroom instruction. Among literacy skills, elementary reading processes (letter, sound, and word recognition) probably receive the lion's share of instructional emphasis.

From the applied perspective, recent evidence points to the existence of major individual differences in important literacy skills among U.S. children. These differences appear to emerge well before children enter kindergarten, in some cases (e.g., vocabulary) surfacing as early as 18 months of age. Mounting evidence further reveals that full understanding of the nature and source of these individual differences will require adoption of a complex, multilevel interactive framework combining factors in the child, family, and larger sociocultural context. One challenge for future research is discovery of new methodological strategies for capturing the complex, dynamic interplay among forces, including schooling, that shape children's cognitive growth over time.

Parenthetically, realization of the number and complexity of factors influencing early literacy acquisition highlights the difficulty and perhaps futility of "school readiness" discussions. Clearly isolating one aspect of a child (e.g., entrance age) as the sole predictor of academic growth provides an extremely limited perspective on the child's growth potential.

When viewed together, conclusions drawn from basic and applied perspectives yield some novel insights about both learning and schooling. The influence of schooling on cognitive growth is substantial but it depends in part on the cognitive skill or domain being stimulated in the classroom. Furthermore the effects of schooling will vary dramatically with other factors (child, family, and sociocultural) impinging on the child's life at the time. Consequently, the impact of schooling in reducing the power of other individual, family, or sociocultural forces depends in large degree on how directly and heavily a particular cognitive or literacy skill is instructed in the classroom. Direct, sustained instruction can serve to reduce the large individual differences produced by other factors prior to school entry. Nevertheless, it must be admitted that is unreasonable to expect schools to be solely responsible for amelioration of academic problems in every single area of literacy. There are simply not enough hours in the school day to accomplished that goal. Realistically, the burden must fall primarily on parents during the preschool years to ensure that the necessary emergent literacy skills are effectively acquired. Working in concert, both parents and schools can then ensure that children maximize their intellectual potential.

REFERENCES

Alexander, K. L., & Entwisle, D. R. (1988). Achievement in the first 2 years of school: Patterns and processes. *Monographs of the Society for Research in Child Development, 53*(2, Serial No. 218).

Alexander, K. L., Entwisle, D. R., & Dauber, S. L. (1993). First-grade classroom behavior: Its short- and long-term consequences for school performance. *Child Development, 64,* 801–814.

Applebee, A. N., Langer, J. A., & Mullis, N. S. (1989). *Crossroads in American education.* Princeton, NJ: Educational Testing Service.

Bachman, H. J., Bagdade, P., Massetti, G. M., Morrison, F. J., & Frazier, J. A. (1999). *Factors predicting growth of phonological segmentation skills: The influences of schooling and phonemic complexity.* Manuscript submitted for publication.

Bachman, H. J., Morrison, F. J., & Bryant, F. (2000). *Beyond social class: The nature and sources of racial differences in academic achievement at school entry.* Manuscript submitted for publication.

Baker-Ward, L., & Ornstein, P. (1988). Age differences in visual-spatial memory performance: Do children really out-perform adults when playing Concentration? *Bulletin of the Psychonomic Society, 26(4),* 331–332.

Baltes, P., & Reinert, G. (1969). Cohort effects in cognitive development in children as revealed by cross sectional sequences. *Developmental Psychology, 1,* 169–177.

Bandura, A. (1977). Self-efficacy: Toward a unifying theory of behavior change. *Psychological Review, 84,* 191–215.

Baumeister, R. F. (1997). Identity, self-concept, and self-esteem: The self lost and found. In R. Hogan & J. A. Johnson (Eds.), *Handbook of personality psychology* (pp. 681–710). San Diego, CA: Academic Press.

Baumeister, R. F., Tice, D. M., & Hutton, D. G. (1989). Self-presentational motivations and personality differences in self-esteem. *Journal of Personality, 57,* 547–579.

Baumrind, D. (1966). Effects of authoritative parental control on child behavior. *Child Developmental, 37,* 255–272.

Baumrind, D. (1968). Authoritarian vs. authoritative parental control. *Adolescence, 3,* 255–272.

Baumrind, D. (1971). Current patterns of parental authority. *Developmental Psychology Monograph, 4,* 1–103.

Baydar, N., & Brooks-Gunn, J. (1991). Effects of maternal employment and child-care arrangements on preschooler's cognitive and behavioral outcomes: Evidence from the children of the National Longitudinal Survey of Youth. *Developmental Psychology, 27,* 932–945.

Beggs, D. L. (1969, January). The summer vacation- an interruption in learning. *Illinois Journal of Education, 60,* 46–48.

Bentin, S., Hammer, R., & Cahan, S. (1991). The effects of aging and first grade schooling on the development of phonological awareness. *Psychological Science, 2,* 271–274.

Bisanz, J., Morrison, F. J., & Dunn, M. (1995). Effects of age and schooling on the acquisition of elementary quantitative skills. *Developmental Psychology, 31,* 221–236.

Bloom, B. S. (1981). *All our children learning: A primer for parents, teachers, and other educators.* New York: McGraw-Hill.

Bohrnstedt, G. W., & Felson, R. B. (1983). Explaining the relations among children's actual and perceived performances and self-esteem: A comparison of several causal models. *Journal of Personality and Social Psychology, 45,* 43–56.

Bornstein, M. H. (Ed.). (1995). *Handbook of parenting, Vols. 1–4.* Hillsdale, NJ: Lawrence Erlbaum Associates.

Bouchard, T. J. (1984). Twins reared together: What they tell us about human diversity. In S. W. Fox (Ed.), *Individuality and determinism* (pp. 162–184). New York: Plenum Press.

Bowey, J. A., & Francis, J. (1991). Phonologically analysis as a function of age and exposure to reading instruction. *Applied Psycholinguistics, 12,* 91–121.

Bradley, R. H., & Caldwell, B. M. (1980). The relation of home environment, cognitive competence, and IQ among males and females. *Child Development, 51,* 1140–1148.

Breznitz, Z., & Teltsch, T. (1989). The effect of school entrance age on academic achievement and social-emotional adjustment of children: Follow-up study of fourth graders. *Psychology in the Schools, 26,* 62–68.

Bronfenbrenner, U. (1996). *The ecology of human development: Experiments by nature and design.* Cambridge, MA: Harvard University Press.

Bronfenbrenner, U. (1986). Ecology of the family as a context for human development: Research perspectives. *Developmental Psychology, 22,* 723–742.

Bronfenbrenner, U., & Morris, P. A. (1998). The ecology of developmental processes. In W. Damon & R. M. Lerner (Eds.), *Handbook of child psychology: Vol. 1.* (5th ed., pp. 993–1028). New York: Wiley.

Browne, C. S., & Rife, J. C. (1991). Social, personality, and gender differences in at-risk and not-at-risk sixth-grade students. *Journal of Early Adolescence, 11,* 482–495.

Bruner, J. S. (1966). On cognitive growth. In J. S. Bruner, R. R. Oliver, & P. M. Greenfield (Eds.), *Studies in cognitive growth* (pp. 1–67). New York: Wiley.

Cahan, S., & Cohen, N. (1989). Age versus schooling effects on intelligence development. *Child Development, 60,* 1239–1249.

Caplan, N., Choy, M. H., & Whitmore, J. K. (1992). Indochinese refugee families and academic achievement. *Scientific American, February,* 36–42.

Caughy, M. O., DiPetro, J. A., & Strobino, D. M. (1994). Day-care participation as a protective factor in the cognitive development of low-income children. *Child Development, 65,* 457–471.

Ceci, S. J. (1991). How much does schooling influence general intelligence and its cognitive components? A reassessment of the evidence. *Developmental Psychology, 27*(5), 703–722.

Ceci, S. J., & Williams, W. M. (1997). Schooling, intelligence, and income. *American Psychologist, 52*(10), 1051–1058.

Chao, R. K. (1994). Beyond parental control and authoritarian parenting style: Understanding Chinese parenting through the cultural notion of training. *Child Development, 65,* 1111–1119.

Chipuer, H. M., Rovine, M., & Plomin, R. (1990). LISREL modelling: Genetic and environmental influences on IQ revisited. *Intelligence, 14,* 11–29.

Christian, M. K., & Morrison, F. J. (2000). *Kindergarten schooling effect on children's growth in referential communication.* Manuscript in preparation.

Christian, M. K., Morrison, F. J., & Bryant, F. B. (1998). Predicting kindergarten academic skills: Interactions among child care, maternal education, and family literacy environments. *Early Childhood Research Quarterly, 13,* 485–505.

Clark, R. M. (1983). *Family life and school achievement: Why poor Black children succeed or fail.* Chicago: The University of Chicago Press.

Cole, M., & Cole, S. R. (1996). *The development of children (3rd ed).* New York: W. H. Freeman.

Cole, M., Gay, J., Glick, J. A., & Sharp, D. W. (1971). *The cultural context of learning and thinking.* New York: Basic Books.

Cooney, R. R. (1999, April). How early are the racial gaps in academic achievement evident? In F. J. Morrison (Chair), *Racial differences in academic achievement: When and why?* Symposium conducted at the biennial meeting of the Society for Research in Child Development, Albuquerque, NM.

Cooper, D. H., & Farran, D. C. (1988). Behavioral risk factors in kindergarten. *Early Childhood Research Quarterly, 3,* 1–19.

Connell, J. P., & Ilardi, B. C. (1987). Self-system concomitants of discrepancies between children's and teacher's evaluations of academic competence. *Child Development, 58,* 1297–1307.

Crosser, S. L. (1991). Summer birth date children: Kindergarten entrance age and academic achievement. *Journal of Educational Research, 84,* 140–146.

Cunningham, A. E., & Stanovich, K. E. (1997). Early reading acquisition and its relation to reading experience and ability 10 years later. *Developmental Psychology, 33,* 934–945.

Cunningham, A. E., Stanovich, K. E., & West, R. F. (1994). Literacy environment and the development of children's cognitive skills. In E. M. H. Assink (Ed.), *Literacy acquisition and social context* (pp. 70–90). New York: Harvester Wheatsheaf.

Darling, N., & Steinberg, L. (1993). Parenting style as context: An integrative model. *Psychological Bulletin, 113,* 487–496.

Dasen, P. R. (1977). Are cognitive processes universal? A contribution to cross-cultural Piagetian psychology. In N. Warren (Ed.), *Studies in cross-cultural psychology, Vol. 1,* London: Academic Press.

Dasen, P. R., Ngini, L., & Lavallee, M. (1979). Cross-cultural training studies of concrete operations. In L. H. Eckenberger, W. J. Lonner, & H. Poortinga (Eds.), *Cross-cultural contributions to psychology.* Amsterdam: Swets & Zeilinger.

Davis, B. G., Trimble, C. S., & Vincent, D. R. (1980). Does age of entrance affect school achievement? *The Elementary School Journal, 80,* 133–143.

Delpit, L. D. (1988). The silenced dialogue: Power and pedagogy in educating other people's children. *Harvard Educational Review, 58,* 280–298.

DeMeis, J. L., & Stearns, E. S. (1992). Relationship of school entrance age to academic and social performance. *Journal of Educational Research, 86,* 20–27.

De Temple, J. M., & Snow, C. E. (1992, April). *Styles of parent-child book reading as related to mothers' views of literacy and children's literacy outcomes.* In J. Shimron (Ed.), *Literacy and Education: Essays in Memory of Dina Feitelson* (pp. 221–230). Paper presented at biennial Conference on Human Development, Atlanta.

DiPasquale, G. W., Moule, A. D., & Flewelling, R. W. (1980). The birthdate effect. *Journal of Learning Disabilities, 13,* 234–238.

Dornbusch, S. M., Ritter, P. L., Leiderman, P. H., Roberts, D. F., & Fraleigh, M. J. (1987). The relation of parenting style to adolescent school performance. *Child Development, 58,* 1244–1257.

Dunn, L. M., & Dunn, L. M. (1981). *Peabody picture vocabulary test-revised (Form L).* Circle Pines, MN: American Guidance Service.

Dweck, C. S. (1975). The role of expectations and attributions in the alleviation of learned helplessness. *Journal of Personality and Social Psychology, 31,* 674–685.

Dweck, C. S. (1986). Motivational processes affecting learning. *American Psychologist, 41,* 1040–1048.

Dweck, C. S., & Reppucci, N. D. (1973). Learned helplessness and reinforcement responsibility in children. *Journal of Personality and Social Psychology, 25,* 109–116.

Entwisle, D. R., & Alexander, K. L. (1988). Factors affecting achievement test scores and marks of black and white first graders. *Elementary School Journal, 88,* 449–471.

Entwisle, D. R., & Alexander, K. L. (1992). Summer setback: Race, poverty, school composition, and mathematics achievement in the first two years of school. *American Sociological Review, 57,* 72–84.

Entwisle, D. R., & Alexander, K. L. (1994). Winter setback: The racial composition of schools and learning to read. *American Sociological Review, 59,* 446–460.

Entwisle, D. R., & Alexander, K. L. (1996). Family type and children's growth in reading and math over the primary grades. *Journal of Marriage and Family, 58*(2), 341–355.

Entwisle, D. R., & Baker, D. P. (1983). Gender and young children's expectations for performance in arithmetic. *Developmental Psychology, 19,* 200–209.

Estrada, P., Arsenio, W. F., Hess, R. D., & Holloway, S. D. (1987). Affective quality of the mother-child relationship: Longitudinal consequences for children's school-relevant cognitive functioning. *Developmental Psychology, 23,* 210–215.

Eysenck, H. J. (1988). The biological basis of intelligence. In S. Irvine & J. Berry (Eds.), *Human abilities in cultural context* (pp. 87–104). Cambridge, England: Cambridge University Press.

Ferreira, F., & Morrison, F. J. (1994). Children's knowledge of syntactic constituents: Effects of age and schooling. *Developmental Psychology, 30,* 663–678.

Fischer, K. W., & Farrar, M. J. (1987). Generalizations about generalization: How a theory of skill development explains both generality and specificity. *International Journal of Psychology, 22*, 643–677.

Flynn, J. R. (1998). IQ gains over time: Toward finding the causes. In U. Neisser (Ed.), *The rising curve: Long-term gains in IQ and related measures*. Washington, DC: American Psychological Association.

Frazier, J. A., Morrison, F. J., & Trabasso, T. R. (1995, March). *Age and schooling influences on growth of narrative coherence*. Paper presented at annual conference of the American Educational Research Association, San Francisco.

Frazier, J. A., & Morrison, F. J. (1998). The influence of extended-year schooling on growth of achievement and perceived competence in early elementary school. *Child Development, 69*, 495–517.

Gardner, H. (1983). *Frames of mind: The theory of multiple intelligences*. New York: Basic Books.

Geary, D. C. (1995). Reflections of evolution and culture in children's cognition: Implications for mathematical development and instruction. *American Psychologist, 50*, 24–37.

Gersten, R., & Dimino, J. (1993). Visions and revisions: A special education perspective on the whole language controversy. *Rase: Remedial & Special Education, 14*(4), 5–13.

Glasgow, K. L., Dornbusch, S. M., Troyer, L., Steinberg, L., & Ritter, P. L. (1997). Parenting styles, adolescents' attributions, and educational outcomes in nine heterogeneous high schools. *Child Development, 68*, 507–529.

Goodnow, J. J. (1988). Children's household work: Its nature and functions. *Psychological Bulletin, 103*, 5–26.

Granleese, J., & Joseph, S. (1994). Reliability of the Harter Self-Perception Profile for children and predictors of global self-worth. *The Journal of Genetic Psychology, 155*, 487–492.

Green, K. D., Forehand, R., Beck, S. J., Vosk, B. (1980). An assessment of the relationship among measures of children's social competence and children's academic achievement. *Child Development, 51*, 1149–1156.

Greenfield, P. M. (1966). On culture and conservation. IN J. S. Bruner, R. R. Olver, & P. M. Greenfield (Eds.), *Studies in cognitive growth*. New York: Wiley.

Griffin, E. A., & Morrison, F. J. (1997). The unique contribution of home literacy environment to differences in early literacy skills. *Early Child Development and Care, 127–128*, 233–243.

Gullo, D. F., & Burton, C. B. (1993). The effects of social class, class size and prekindergarten experience on early school adjustment. *Early Child Development and Care, 88*, 43–51.

Hansen, E. E., Morrison, F. J., & Holmes, D. L. (2000). *The stability of academic and social skills and cross-domain predictability in elementary school*. Manuscript submitted for publication.

Hart, S. S., Leal, I., Burney, L., & Santulli, K. A. (1985, April). *Memory in the elementary school classroom: How teachers encourage strategy use*. Paper presented at the meeting of the Society for Research in Child Development, Toronto, Canada.

Hart, B., & Risley, T. R. (1995). *Meaningful differences in the everyday experience of young American children*. Baltimore, MD: Paul H. Brookes.

Harter, S. (1990). Causes, correlates, and the functional role of global self-worth: A life-span perspective. In R. J. Sternberg & J. Kolligian, Jr. (Eds.), *Competence considered* (pp. 67–97). New Haven, CT: Yale University Press.

Harter, S., & Pike, R. (1984). The pictorial perceived competence scale for young children. *Child Development, 55*, 1969–1982.

Hayes, D., & Grether, J. (1982). The school year and vacations: When do students learn? *Cornell Journal of Social Relations, 17*, 56–71.

Heckman, J. J. (1995). Lessons from the bell curve. *Journal of Political Economy, 103*, 1091–1120.

Herman, M. A., & McHale, S. M. (1993). Coping with parental negativity: Links with parental warmth and child adjustment. *Journal of Applied Developmental Psychology, 14*, 121–136.

Herrnstein, R. J., & Murray, C. (1994). *The bell curve: Intelligence and class structure in American life*. New York: Free Press.

Heyns, B. (1978). *Summer learning and the effects of schooling.* San Diego, CA: Academic Press.

Horn, J. (1978). Human ability systems. In P. Baltes (Ed.), *Life-span development and behavior.* San Diego, CA: Academic Press.

Huttenlocher, J., Haight, W., Bryk, A., Seltzer, M., & Lyons, T. (1991). Early vocabulary growth: Relation to language input and gender. *Developmental Psychology, 27,* 236–248.

Hyde, J. S., Fennema, E., & Lamon, S. J. (1990). Gender differences in mathematics performance: A meta-analysis. *Psychological Bulletin, 107,* 139–155.

Hyde, J. S., & Linn, M. C. (1988). Gender differences in verbal ability: A meta-analysis. *Psychological Bulletin, 104,* 53–69.

International Association for the Evaluation of Educational Achievement (IEA). (1988). *Science achievement in seventeen countries: A preliminary report.* Elmsford, NY: Pergamon Press.

Jencks, C., & Phillips, M. (1998). *The black-white test score gap.* Washington, DC: Brookings.

Jencks, C., Smith, M., Acland, H., Bane, M. J., Cohen, D., Gintis, H., Heyns, B., & Mitchelson, S. (1972). *Inequality: A reassessment of the effects of family and schooling in America.* New York: Basic Books.

Jensen, A. R. (1980). *Bias in mental testing.* New York: Free Press.

Johnson, D. L., Swank, P., Howie, V. M., Baldwin, C. D., Owen, M., & Luttman, D. (1993). Does HOME add to prediction of child intelligence over and above SES? *The Journal of Genetic Psychology, 154,* 33–40.

Kaiser, J. (1994). The role of family configuration, income, and gender in the academic achievement of young self-care children. *Early Child Development and Care, 97,* 91–105.

Kalechstein, A. D., & Nowicki, S., Jr. (1997). A meta-analytic examination of the relationship between control expectancies and academic achievement: An 11-year follow-up to Findley and Cooper. *Genetic, Social, and General Psychology Monographs, 123,* 27–56.

Karmiloff-Smith, A. (1992). *Beyond modularity: A developmental perspective on cognitive science.* Cambridge, MA: MIT Press.

Kemp, L. (1955). Environmental and other characteristics determining attainments in primary schools. *British Journal of Educational Psychology, 25,* 67–77.

Kuo, H. H. D., & Hauser, R. M. (1997). How does size of sibship matter? Family configuration and family effects on educational attainment. *Social Science Research, 26,* 69–94.

Kupersmidt, J. B., DeRosier, M. E., & Patterson, C. P. (1995). Similarity as the basis for children's friendships: The roles of sociometric status, aggressive and withdrawn behavior, academic achievement and demographic characteristics. *Journal of Social and Personal Relationships, 12,* 439–452.

Ladd, G. W., & Price, J. M. (1987). Predicting children's social and school adjustment following the transition from preschool to kindergarten. *Child Development, 58,* 1168–1189.

Lamborn, S. D., Mounts, N. S., Steinberg, L., & Dornbusch, S. M. (1991). Patterns of competence and adjustment among adolescents from authoritative, authoritarian, indulgent, and neglectful families. *Child Development, 62,* 1049–1065.

Langer, P., Kalk, J. M., & Searls, D. T. (1984). Age of admission and trends in achievement: A comparison of blacks and caucasians. *American Educational Research Journal, 21,* 61–78.

Maccoby, E. E., & Jacklin, C. N. (1972). Sex differences in intellectual functioning. *Proceedings of the invitational conference on testing problems* (pp. 37–55).

Maccoby, E. E., & Jacklin, C. N. (1974). *The psychology of sex differences.* Stanford, CA: Stanford University Press.

Maccoby, E. E., & Martin, J. A. (1983). Socialization in the context of the family: Parent-child interaction. In P. Mussen (Ed.), *Handbook of child psychology* (pp. 1–101). New York: Wiley.

Maddux, C. D. (1980). First-grade entry age in a sample of children labeled learning disabled. *Learning Disability Quarterly, 3,* 79–83.

Magnusson, D. (1990). Personality development from an interactional perspective. In L. Pervin (Ed.), *Handbook of personality: Theory and research* (pp. 193–222). New York: Guilford Press.

Mantzicopoulos, P. Y. (1997). The relationship of family variables to Head Start children's pre-academic competence. *Early Education and Development, 8,* 357–375.

Markwardt, F. (1989). *Peabody individual achievement test-revised.* Circle Pines, MN: American Guidance Service.

Massetti, G. M., & Morrison, F. J. (1997, May). *Cultural and maturational effects on visual-spatial memory development.* Poster presented at the Annual Meeting of the Midwestern Psychological Association, Chicago.

McClelland, M. M., Morrison, F. J., & Holmes, D. L. (2000). Children at-risk for early academic problems: The role of learning-related social skills. *Early Childhood Research Quarterly.*

Mercer, J. G. (1996). *Developing a taxonomy of memory relevant classroom experiences.* Senior Honor Thesis, The University of North Carolina at Chapel Hill.

Miller, G. W. (1970). Factors in school achievement and social class. *Journal of Educational Psychology, 61,* 260–269.

Morrison, F. J., Frazier, J. A., Hardway, C. L., Griffith, E. M., Williamson, G., & Myazaki, Y. (2000). *Early literacy: The nature and sources of individual differences.* In preparation.

Morrison, F. J., Griffith, E. M., & Alberts, D. M. (1997). Nature-nurture in the classroom: Entrance age, school readiness, and learning in children. *Developmental Psychology, 33*(2), 254–262.

Morrison, F. J., Griffith, E. M., & Frazier, J. A. (1996). Schooling and the 5–7 shift: A natural experiment. In A. Sameroff & M. M. Haith (Eds.), *Reason and responsibility: The passage through childhood* (pp. 161–186). Illinois: University of Chicago Press.

Morrison, F. J., Griffith, E. M., Williamson, G., & Hardway, C. L. (1995, April). *The nature and sources of early literacy.* Paper presented at the Society for Research in Child Development, Indianapolis, IN.

Morrison, F. J., & Massetti, G. M. (1997, April). *Schooling and cognitive growth: A search for generalizations.* Paper presented at symposium on Sources of cognitive growth: Toward a biocultural synthesis, Society for Research in Child Development, Washington, DC.

Morrison, F. J., Orrnstein, P., Hardway, C. L., & Pelphrey, K. (2000). *Charting developmental pathways: One methodological strategy.* Manuscript in preparation.

Morrison, F. J., Smith, L., & Dow-Ehrensberger, M. (1995). Education and cognitive development: A natural experiment. *Developmental Psychology, 31*(5), 789–799.

Morrow, L. M. (1989). *Literacy development in the early years: Helping children read and write.* Englewood Cliffs, NJ: Prentice-Hall.

Muir, S. P. (1985). Understanding and improving students' map reading skills. *Elementary School Journal, 86*(2), 207–216.

Mullus, I., & Jenkins, L. B. (1990). *The reading report card, 1971–1988: Trends from the nation's report card.* Washington, DC: U.S. Department of Education.

Neisser, U. (1976). General, academic, and artificial intelligence. In L. B. Resnick (Ed.), *The nature of intelligence* (pp. 135–144). Hillsdale, NJ: Lawrence Erlbaum Associates.

Neisser, U. (1998). *The rising curve: Long-term gains in IQ and related measures.* Washington, DC: American Psychological Association.

Neisser, U., Boodoo, G., Bouchard, T., Boykin, A. W., Brody, N., Ceci, S. J., Halpern, D. F., Loehlin, J. C., Perloff, R., Sternberg, R. J., & Urbina, S. (1996). Intelligence: Knowns and unknowns. *American Psychologist, 51*(2), 77–101.

Nyiti, R. M. (1976). The development of conservation in the Meru children of Tanzania. *Child Development, 47,* 1122–1129.

Oakland, T. (1983). Joint use of adaptive behavior and IQ to predict achievement. *Journal of Counseling and Clinical Psychology, 51,* 298–301.

Ogbu, J. U. (1983). Minority status and schooling in plural societies. *Comparative Education Review, 27,* 168–190.

Ogbu, J. U. (1988). Black education: A cultural-ecological perspective. In H. P. McAdoo (Ed.), *Black families* (pp. 169–184). Newbury Park, CA: Sage.

Ogbu, J. U. (1991). Low school performance as an adaptation: The case of blacks in Stockton, California. In M. A. Gibson, & J. U. Ogbu (Eds.), *Minority status and schooling: A comparative study of immigrant and involuntary minorities* (pp. 249–285). New York: Garland.

Okagaki, L., & Frensch, P. A. (1998). Parenting and children's school achievement: A multiethnic perspective. *American Educational Research Journal, 35,* 123–144.

Okagaki, L., & Sternberg, R. (1993). Parental beliefs and children's school performance. *Child Development, 64,* 36–56.

Ortiz, V. (1986). Reading activities and reading proficiency among hispanic, black, and white students. *American Journal of Education, 95,* 58–76.

Parsley, K. M., & Powell, M. (1962). Achievement gains or losses during the academic year and over the summer vacation period: A study of trends in achievement by sex and grade level among students of average intelligence. *Genetic Psychology Monographs, 66,* 285–342.

Phillips, M., Brooks-Gunn, J., Duncan, G. J., Klebanov, P., & Crane, J. (1998). Family background, parenting practices, and the black-white test score gap. In C. Jencks & M. Phillips (Eds.), *The black-white test score gap.* Washington, DC: Brookings.

Phillips, M., Crouse, J., & Ralph, J. (1998). Does the black-white test score gap widen after children enter school? In C. Jencks & M. Phillips (Eds.), *The black-white test score gap.* Washington, DC: Brookings.

Piaget, J., & Inhelder, B. (1956). *The child's conception of space.* London: Routledge & Kegan Paul.

Plomin, R. (1995). Molecular genetics and psychology. *Psychological Science, 4*(4), 114–117.

Plomin, R., & Neiderhiser, J. M. (1991). Quantitative genetics, molecular genetics, and intelligence. *Intelligence, 15,* 369–387.

Radin, N. (1971). Maternal warmth, achievement motivation, and cognitive functioning in lower class preschool children. *Child Development, 42,* 1560–1565.

Richman, E. A., & Rescorla, L. (1995). Academic orientation and warmth in mothers and fathers of preschoolers: Effects on academic skills and self-perceptions of competence. *Early Education and Development, 6,* 197–213.

Robeson, R. A. (1997, May). Disparity between beliefs about the importance of education and literacy promoting activities. A poster presented at the annual conference of the Midwestern Psychological Association, Chicago, IL.

Rogoff, B. (1981). Schooling and the development of cognitive skills. In H. C. Triandis & A. Heron (Eds.), *Handbook of cross-cultural psychology* (Vol. 4, pp. 233–292). Boston, MA: Allyn and Bacon.

Rotter, J. B. (1966). Generalized expectancies for internal versus external control of reinforcement. *Psychological Monographs: General and Applied, 80*(1, Whole No. 609).

Rowe, D. C. (1994). *The limits of family influence: Genes, experience, and behavior.* New York: Guilford Press.

Rowe, D. C., Vazsonyi, A. T., & Flannery, D. J. (1994). No more than skin deep: Ethnic and racial similarity in developmental process. *Psychological Review, 101,* 396–413.

Rowe, D. C., Vazsonyi, A. T., & Flannery, D. J. (1995). Ethnic and racial similarity in developmental process: A study of academic achievement. *Psychological Science, 6,* 33–38.

Scarborough, H. S., Dobrich, W., & Hager, M. (1991). Preschool literacy experience and later reading achievement. *Journal of Learning Disabilities, 24,* 508–511.

Scribner, S., & Cole, M. (1973). Cognitive consequences of formal and informal education. *Science, 182,* 553–559.

Scribner, S., & Cole, M. (1981). *The psychology of literacy.* Cambridge, MA: Harvard University Press.

Sharp, D. W., Cole, M., & Lave, C. (1979). Education and cognitive development: The evidence from experimental research. *Monographs of the Society for Research in Child Development, 4* (1–2, Serial No. 178).

Sheehan, R., Cryan, J. R., Wiechel, J., & Bandy, I. G. (1991). Factors contributing to success in elementary schools: Research findings for early childhood educators. *Journal of Research in Childhood Education, 6,* 66–75.

Shephard, L. A., & Smith, M. L. (1988). Synthesis of research on school readiness and kindergarten retention. *Educational Leadership, 44,* 78–86.

Singley, M. K., & Anderson, J. R. (1989). *Transfer of cognitive skill.* Cambridge, MA: Harvard University Press.

Skeen, J. A., & Rogoff, B. (1987). Children's difficulties in deliberate memory for spatial relationships: Misapplication of verbal mnemonic strategies? *Cognitive Development, 2,* 1–19.

Snyder, S. D., & Michael, W. B. (1983). The relationship of performance on standardized tests in mathematics and reading to two measures of social intelligence and one of academic self-esteem for two samples of primary school children. *Educational and Psychological Measurement, 43,* 1141–1148.

Sputa, C. L., & Paulson, S. E. (1995). Birth order and family size: Influences on adolescents' achievement and related parenting behaviors. *Psychological Reports, 76,* 43–51.

Steele, C. M. (1998). A threat in the air: How stereotypes shape intellectual identity and performance. In J. L. Eberhardt & S. T. Fiske (Eds.), *Confronting racism: The problem and the response* (pp. 202–233). Newbury Park, CA: Sage.

Steele, C. M., & Aronson, J. (1995). Stereotype threat and the intellectual performance of African Americans. *Journal of Personality and Social Psychology, 69,* 797–811.

Stein, M. K., Leinhardt, G., & Bickel, W. (1989). Instructional issues for teaching students at risk. In R. E. Slavin, N. L. Karweit, & N. A. Madden (Eds.), *Effective programs for students at risk* (pp. 145–194). Boston: Allyn & Bacon.

Steinberg, L., Dornbusch, S. M., & Brown, B. B. (1992). Ethnic differences in adolescent achievement: An ecological perspective. *American Psychologist, 47,* 723–729.

Steinberg, L., Lamborn, S. D., Darling, N., Mounts, N. S., & Dornbusch, S. M. (1994). Over-time changes in adjustment and competence among adolescents from authoritative, authoritarian, indulgent, and neglectful families. *Child Development, 65,* 754–770.

Sternberg, R. J. (1997). The concept of intelligence and its role in lifelong learning and success. *American Psychologist, 52,* 1030–1037.

Sternberg, R. J., Torff, B., & Grigorenko, E. L. (1998). Teaching triarchically improves school achievement. *Journal of Educational Psychology, 90,* 1–11.

Stevenson, H. W., Chen, C., & Booth, J. (1990). Influences of schooling and urbanural residence on gender differences in cognitive abilities and academic achievement. *Sex Roles, 23,* 535–551.

Stevenson, H. W., Chen, C., & Lee, S. Y. (1993). Mathematics achievement of Chinese, Japanese, and American children: Ten years later. *Science, 259,* 53–58.

Stevenson, H. W., Chen, C., & Uttal, D. H. (1990). Beliefs and achievement: A study of Black, White, and Hispanic children. *Child Development, 61,* 508–523.

Stevenson, H. W., & Lee, S. Y. (1990). Contexts of achievement: A study of American, Chinese, and Japanese children. *Monographs of the Society for Research in Child Development, 55*(1–2, Serial No. 221).

Stevenson, H. W., Parker, T., Wilkinson, A., Hegion, A., & Fish, E. (1976). Longitudinal study of individual differences in cognitive development and scholastic achievement. *Journal of Educational Psychology, 68,* 377–400.

Stevenson, H. W., & Stigler, J. W. (1992). *The learning gap: Why our schools are failing and what we can learn from Japanese and Chinese education.* New York: Summit.

Stewart, J. P. (1995). Home environments and parental support for literacy: Children's perception and school literacy achievement. *Early Education and Development, 6,* 97–125.

Stigler, J. W., & Perry, M. (1990). Mathematics learning in Japanese, Chinese, and American classrooms. In J. W. Stigler, R. A. Shweder, & G. Herdt (Eds.), *Cultural psychology: Essays on comparative human development.* New York: Cambridge University Press.

Stipek, D. (1980). A causal analysis of the relationship between locus of control and academic achievement in first grade. *Contemporary Educational Psychology, 5,* 90–99.

Stipek, D. (1981). Social-motivational development in first grade. *Contemporary Educational Psychology, 6,* 33–45.

Stipek, D. J., & Ryan, R. H. (1997). Economically disadvantaged preschoolers: Ready to learn but further to go. *Developmental Psychology, 33*, 711–723.

Thompson, L. A., Detterman, D. K., & Plomin, R. (1991). Associations between cognitive abilities and scholastic achievement: Genetic overlap but environmental differences. *Psychological Science, 2*, 158–165.

Thompson, M. S., Entwisle, D. R., Alexander, K. L., & Sundius, M. J. (1992). The influence of family composition on children's conformity to the student role. *American Educational Research Journal, 29*, 405–424.

Treiman, R., & Weatherson, S. (1992). Effects of linguistic structure on children's ability to isolate initial consonants. *Journal of Educational Psychology, 84*(2), 174–181.

U.S. Department of Education. (1991). *America 2000: An education strategy.* Washington, DC: U.S. Government Printing Office.

Varnhagen, C., Morrison, F. J., & Everall, R. (1994). Age and schooling effects in story recall and production. *Developmental Psychology, 30*(6), 969–979.

Wagner, D. A. (1974). The development of short-term and incidental memory: A cross cultural study. *Child Development, 48*, 389–396.

Wagner, R. K., & Sternberg, R. J. (1985). Practical intelligence in real-world pursuits: The role of tacit knowledge. *Journal of Personality and Social Psychology, 49*, 436–458.

Wentzel, K. R. (1991). Relations between social competence and academic achievement in early adolescence. *Child Development, 62*, 1066–1078.

Wentzel, K. R. (1993). Does being good make the grade? Social behavior and academic competence in middle school. *Journal of Educational Psychology, 85*, 357–364.

White, K. (1982). The relation between socioeconomic status and academic achievement. *Psychological Bulletin, 91*, 461–481.

Williams, S. E., Morrison, F. J., & Williams, M. A. (2000). *Individual differences in early literacy acquisition.* Manuscript in preparation.

Wiseman, S. (1966). Environmental and innate factors and educational attainment. In J. Meade & A. S. Parkes (Eds.), *Genetic and environmental factors in human ability* (pp. 64–79). Edinburgh, Scotland: Oliver & Boyd.

11

Family Environments
and Adult Cognitive Functioning

K. Warner Schaie
Yan-Ling Zuo
The Pennsylvania State University

There is an extensive literature dealing with the relative contribution of inherited predispositions and the influence of both the shared and unique experiences occurring within the family of origin upon cognitive functioning in children. Much of this work is derived from twin studies because behavior geneticists have advocated the twin model as the most desirable paradigm to investigate the heritability of intelligence and many other traits (cf. Bouchard, 1997; Plomin, 1986). However, because twins represent a rather atypical subset of the general population, the role of family environments has also been investigated in parent–offspring and sibling pairs (e.g., DeFries et al., 1976). Most twin studies report that roughly hail of the individual difference variance in cognitive functioning can be attributed to heritability. On the other hand, very little variance has been allocated to shared family environments. In fact, it has been argued that the environment in the family of origin has quite unique influence upon different siblings (Plomin & Daniels, 1987).

Relatively little is known about the origin of individual differences in the later half of the life span as they might relate to inherited predispositions or to early influences transmitted through the family environment. Again, twin studies dominate because of the argument that both age and early shared environment are maximally controlled in such studies (e.g., Jarvik, Blum, & Varma, 1971; Petrill et al., 1998; Plomin, Pedersen, Nesselroade, & Bergeman, 1988; Saudino-Kimberly, Pedersen, & McClearn, 1994). Hence, it is relatively difficult to extrapolate to the more typical case of family similarities among nontwins.

An important objective of behavior genetic studies in adulthood is to address the question why it is that different persons show such vastly different aging patterns. To do so one would like to know what proportions of individual differences variances can be accounted for by genetic and environmental influences (Pedersen, 1996; Plomin & McClearn, 1990). While some might argue that personality variables might well be implicated in such differences (Saudino-Kimberly, Pedersen, Liechtenstein, & McClearn 1997), the same group of investigators have also shown that personality differences do not account for the influences of family environment factors (Chipuer, Plomin, Pedersen, & McClearn, 1993).

In this chapter we present findings from a large-scale longitudinal study of adult intellectual functioning, the Seattle Longitudinal Study (SLS; Schaie, 1996) that may inform us on the relative contribution of familial similarity due to genetic influences of certain cognitive traits as contrasted to the extent to which current cognitive performance may be attributed to family influences that are shared with other family members during early life as well as the influences of the non-shared family setting currently being experienced by our subjects (also see Plomin & McClearn, 1990; Rowe & Plomin, 1981).

THE SEATTLE LONGITUDINAL STUDY

The research to be summarized here capitalizes on the longitudinal-sequential design of the SLS which offers the opportunity to compare young adult and middle-aged offspring with their middle-aged and old parents, as well as to compare sibling pairs from young adulthood to old age. The data for the parents and target siblings come from our inquiry into adult cognitive functioning that began some 42 years ago by randomly sampling 500 subjects equally distributed by sex and age across the range from 20 to 70 years from the approximately 18,000 members of a Health Maintenance Organization (HMO) in the Pacific Northwest (Schaie, 1983, 1996; Schaie & Hertzog, 1986). The survivors of the original sample were retested and additional panels were added in seven-year intervals; a total of over 5000 different individuals have been studied at least once. The sampling frame for the SLS represents a broad distribution of educational and occupational levels, covering the upper 75% of the socio-economic spectrum. This frame has grown to over 400,000 individuals, but the general characteristics of the HMO remain very similar to its structure at the inception of the study. The study design of the SLS is shown in Fig. 11.1.

Throughout the course of the SLS our primary focus has been the investigation of psychometric abilities within the Thurstonian (1938) framework. This view of the structure of intelligence proposes that there is a rather small number of latent constructs (perhaps no more than 10) that suffice to describe virtually all individual differences in intellectual performance. Moreover, the measures of these constructs are presumed to be only mod-

Study Waves

1956	1963	1970	1977	1984	1991
S_1T_1	S_1T_2	S_1T_3	S_1T_4	S_1T_5	S_1T_6
(N = 500)	(N = 303)	(N = 162)	(N = 130)	(N = 92)	(N = 71)
	S_2T_2	S_2T_3	S_2T_4	S_2T_5	S_2T_6
	(N = 997)	(N = 420)	(N = 337)	(N = 204)	(N = 161)
		S_3T_3	S_3T_4	S_3T_5	S_3T_6
		(N = 705)	(N = 340)	(N = 225)	(N = 175)
			S_4T_4	S_4T_5	S_4T_6
			(N = 612)	(N = 294)	(N = 201)
				S_5T_5	S_5T_6
				(N = 628)	(N = 428)
					S_6T_6
					(N =693)

S = Sample
T = Time of Measurement

FIG. 11.1. Basic design of the Seattle Longitudinal Study (SLS). From "The Course of Adult Intellectual Development" by K. W. Schaie, 1994, *American Psychologist, 49*, pp. 304–313. Copyright 1994 by the American Psychological Association. Reprinted with permission.

estly correlated. Thurstone's work identified the dimensions of Verbal Meaning, Spatial Orientation, Inductive Reasoning, Number and Word Fluency to be the most important of these abilities. These are the abilities whose relationship with perceptions of family environment are described in this chapter. Utilization of independent abilities rather than a unitary "*g*" concept of intelligence is also reinforced by recent behavior genetic work stressing the importance of specific cognitive abilities (cf. Pedersen, Plomin, & McClearn, 1995).

In addition, we have also collected data on rigidity–flexibility, lifestyles, some personality traits, as well as the health histories of our participants (cf. Schaie & O'Hanlon, 1990). Of these we also present here relationship with perceptions of family environment three latent constructs derived from our work on rigidity–flexibility because these dimensions can be conceived as measures of cognitive style. The latent constructs involved are Motor–Cognitive Flexibility, the tendency to be able to shift from familiar to unfamiliar responses; Attitudinal Flexibility, the tendency to display attitudes compatible with being comfortable in adapting to change; and Psychomotor Speed, the ability to emit familiar cognitive responses in a speedy manner.

In order to examine perceptions of shared environments we began to add appropriate scales for this purpose beginning with our 1989–1990 data collections. This work is based on the methods developed by Moos and Moos (1986) to describe multiple dimensions of family environments. Details of the measures included in the study reported here are provided in the following methods section.

This chapter first summarizes briefly what we have already learned about familiar similarity of cognitive functioning in adults and about the similarity of perceptions of family environments across generations. Our major focus in this chapter, however, is on the results of our most recent analyses which try to identify the contribution of family environments to adult cognitive functioning. We believe these analyses permit us to identify some of the salient family environment dimensions that influence adult cognitive functioning. They also permit us to provide estimates of the relative importance of familial factors (familial similarity and other parental or sibling characteristics), early shared family environment, early nonshared family environments, and current family environment as they affect adult cognitive performance.

METHODS

Subjects and Procedure

The participants in our family similarity studies consist of the adult offspring and siblings (22 years of age or older in 1990) of members of the SLS panels and their target relatives (i.e., the adult parents or sibling who had previously been studied). Panel members who participated in the fifth cycle of the SLS (1990–1992) had a total of 3,507 adult children. Of these, 1,416 adult children ($M = 701$; $F = 715$) resided in the Seattle metropolitan area. They also had a total of 1,999 siblings including 779 brothers and 1,020 sisters.

The recruitment of the adult offspring and siblings began with a letter containing an update report on the SLS sent to all study participants tested in 1983–1985. This letter also announced the family similarity study and requested that panel members provide names and addresses of siblings and adult offspring. A recruitment letter was then sent to all siblings and offspring thus identified.

Those who agreed to participate in the study were tested in small groups or individually (no differences were found between subjects tested in groups or individually). Approximately 80% of the subjects tested resided in the Seattle metropolitan area. Other subjects were tested preferably when they visited their Seattle relatives, but approximately 150 subjects were tested in other locations throughout the United States. A total of 1,176 relatives of our longitudinal panel members were tested. Of these 776 were adult offspring (465 daughters and 311 sons), and 400 were adult siblings (248 sisters and 152 brothers) of SLS participants.

Data on the target subjects (i.e., individuals who had previously been members of the SLS panel) were obtained during the 1991 longitudinal follow-up (data collection actually continued from mid-1990 to mid-1992). Subsequent to matching target subjects and their relatives, we were able to identify 512 parent–offspring and 294 sibling pairs on whom complete data is available; or a total sample of 1,612 individuals. These consist of 106 father–son, 118 father–daughter, 115 mother–son, 198 mother–daughter, 51 brother–brother, 139 brother–sister, and 104 sister–sister pairings. The reduction in sample size occurred, because of substantial attrition in the number of study members whose relatives we had been able to assess earlier; among the older study members attrition was due primarily to death or sensory and motor disabilities that precluded further assessment or questionnaire response.

Table 11.1 provides a breakdown of parents, offspring, and siblings by age and gender, using the 7-year cohorts conventionally employed in the SLS (cf. Schaie, 1983, 1996).

Average age of the parents was 70.59 years (SD = 10.37) and 41.76 years (SD = 10.46) for the offspring. The parents averaged 14.22 years of education (SD = 2.75) as compared to 15.64 years of education (SD = 2.49) for their children. Total family income averaged \$25,002 for the parents and \$26,841 for the offspring, respectively.

Average ages for the siblings were 60.75 years (SD = 14.42) for the longitudinal study members and 59.62 years (SD = 14.77) for their relatives. The tar-

TABLE 11.1
Age and Gender Distribution of study Participants

	Parents			Offspring			Siblings					
	(Targets)			(Relatives)			(Targets)			(Relatives)		
	(1991)			(1990)			(1991)			(1990)		
Age Range	M	F	T	M	F	T	M	F	T	M	F	T
22–28	–	–	–	19	19	38	–	–	–	1	2	3
29–35	–	–	–	53	76	129	2	11	13	6	13	19
36–42	–	–	–	52	85	137	14	10	24	9	19	28
43–49	–	11	11	50	66	116	19	20	39	10	22	32
50–56	15	29	44	26	37	63	13	21	34	13	15	28
57–63	31	52	83	16	20	36	15	23	38	18	27	45
63–70	41	60	101	3	7	10	28	29	57	22	38	60
71–77	61	67	128	1	5	6	21	27	48	25	28	53
78–84	43	56	99	–	1	1	15	18	34	6	14	20
85–91	14	28	42	–	–	–	2	4	6	2	4	6
92+	9	10	19	–	–	–	2	2	–	–	–	–
Total	224	313	537	221	316	537	129	165	294	112	182	294

get siblings averaged 15.04 years of education (SD = 2.80) as compared to 14.90 years of education (SD = 2.72) for their brothers or sisters. Average incomes were $29,361 for the longitudinal study members, and $25,682 for their siblings.

Procedure. Potential subjects who agreed to participate were scheduled for group assessment sessions. Size of the groups ranged from 5 to 20 participants, depending upon the age of the subjects. The testing sessions lasted approximately 2½ hours plus a "homework" package of questionnaires requiring approximately an additional hour of effort. The homework packages were examined for omissions and obvious errors, with telephone callbacks or mailing of missing pages as appropriate. Each session was conducted by a psychometrist aided by a proctor whenever more than five participants were tested simultaneously. Subjects were paid $25 for their participation.

Measures

Although our data on cognitive functioning are based on formal psychometric assessment of our study participants, we must perforce rely on our subjects' ratings of their perceptions of their family environments. Our efforts to measure these perceptions were motivated by the fact that it is extremely difficult to measure current environments objectively. And it is of course virtually impossible to obtain information directly on the characteristics of family environments that pertained at earlier life stages. We therefore decided that it was necessary. to infer these attributes by asking our subjects to rate both their current environments and their retrospection of the family environment they experienced within their biological family of origin.

Primary Mental Abilities. The test battery administered to the participants in this study included multiple measures of cognitive abilities which broadly sample higher order constructs such as those espoused by Horn and Hofer (1992). Thus fluid intelligence (sometimes referred to as the "mechanics" or procedural aspects of intellectual ability) is represented by the abilities of Inductive Reasoning and Spatial Orientation, whereas Verbal Ability and Numeric Ability stand as representatives of crystallized intelligence (sometimes referred to as the "pragmatics" are culturally acquired aspects of intelligence).

A brief description of these abilities and their measures follows. Test–retest correlations for the ability measures come from a study of 172 individuals tested over a 2-week interval. Similar values for the other measures represent test–retest correlations over a 7-year interval.

Verbal Ability. Language knowledge and comprehension is measured by assessing the scope of a person's recognition vocabulary by matching 1 of 4 synonyms to a stimulus word (Thurstone & Thurstone, 1949; test–retest correlation = .89).

Spatial Orientation.   This is the ability to visualize and mentally manipulate spatial configurations, to maintain orientation with respect to spatial objects, and to perceive relationships among objects in space. The study participant is shown an abstract figure and is asked to identify which of six other drawings represents the model in two-dimensional space (Thurstone & Thurstone, 1949; test–retest correlation = .82).

Inductive Reasoning.   This is the ability to educe novel concepts or relationships. The study participant is shown a series of letters (e.g., a b c c c b a d e f f e) and is asked to identify the next letter in the series (Thurstone & Thurstone, 1949; test–retest correlation = .88).

Numeric Ability.   The ability to understand numerical relationships and compute simple arithmetic functions. The study participant checks whether additions of simple sums shown are correct or incorrect (Thurstone & Thurstone, 1949; test–retest correlation = .88).

Word Fluency.   The ability to recall words easily is measured by asking the study participant to recall freely as many words as possible according to a lexical rule within a 5-minute period (Thurstone & Thurstone, 1949; test–retest correlation = .90).

Two summary scores can be generated from the Primary Mental Abilities (PMA) battery. The first is an Index of Intellectual Ability (an IQ equivalent). It takes the form of IQ = V + S + 2R + 2N + W. The second is an Index of Educational Aptitude (EQ; Thurstone, 1962) and takes the form of EQ = 2V + R.

Rigidity–Flexibility.   The multiple dimensions of this construct are measured by the Test of Behavioral Rigidity (TBR; Schaie, 1955; Schaie & Parham, 1975; Schaie & Willis, 1991). The TBR was designed to measure the three dimensions of Psychomotor Speed (PS; test–retest correlation = .88), Motor–Cognitive Flexibility (MCF; test–retest correlation = .67), and Attitudinal Flexibility (AF; test–retest correlation = .84). Factor scores on these dimensions are estimated from linear combinations of the scores yielded from the three TBR subtests:

The Capitals Test.   Participants copy a printed paragraph that contains some words starting with capital letters, others spelled entirely in capitals, and some starting with a lower case letter and their remainder in capitals. In the second half of the test, the paragraph is copied again, but in reverse form (i.e., substituting capitals for lower case letters, and lower case letters for capitals; adapted from Bernstein, 1924).

The Opposites Test.   Subjects respond to three lists of words (at a third-grade level of difficulty). The first list requires providing the antonym, the second list the synonym of the stimulus word, and the third list contains selected stimulus words from the previous lists that are responded to with an antonym if the stimulus word is printed in lower case letters, but with a synonym if printed in capitals (after Scheier & Ferguson, 1952).

The TBR Questionnaire.   This is a 75-item true–false questionnaire that contains 22 rigidity–flexibility items (attitudinal flexibility) and 44 masking social responsibility items from the California Psychological Inventory (Gough, 1957; Gough, McCloskey, & Meehl, 1952; Schaie, 1959; Schaie & Parham, 1974). It also contains nine (behavioral flexibility) items suitable for adults obtained from the Guttman-scaling of a perseveration scale first used by Lankes (1915), We include findings on the social responsibility scale in this chapter as a control measure of a trait that should not represent familial factors, but should be responsive to family environment influences.

Family Environment.   Moos and Moos (1986) constructed a 90-item true–false family environment scale measuring 10 different dimensions (each measured by 9 items) three of which they described as relationship, five as personal growth and the remaining two as system maintenance an change dimensions. The purpose of these scales was to provide an assessment instrument to examine environmental context of adaptation (Moos, 1985, 1987). We adapted eight of these scales for our purposes by selecting five items per scale and presenting each statement in Likert scale form (1 = *strongly disagree*, 2 = *somewhat disagree*, 3 = *in between*; 4 = *somewhat agree*; 5 = *strongly agree*). The eight dimensions included for our purpose and examples of statements scored in the positive direction on each dimension follow:

a. Cohesion (Relationship). Example: "Family members really help and support one another."

b. Expressivity (Relationship). Example: "We tell each other about our personal problems."

c. Conflict (Relationship). Example: "Family members hardly ever lose their temper."

d. Achievement Orientation (Personal Growth). Example: "We feel it is important to be the best at whatever we do."

e. Intellectual–Cultural Orientation (Personal Growth). Example: "We often talk about political and social problems."

f. Active–Recreational Orientation (Personal Growth). Example: "Friends often come over for dinner or to visit."

g. Organization (System Maintenance). Example: "We are generally very neat and orderly."

h. Control (System Maintenance). Example: "There are set ways of doing things at home."

Two forms of the Family Environment Scale (FES) were constructed: The first asked that the respondents rate their family of origin (i.e., past tense statement with respect to their parental family); the second form requested the same information (in present tense) with respect to their current family. They were then instructed to do the ratings with respect to the family grouping identified by them. In other words, for the parents this implied rating the "empty nest" family. In recognition of the fact that significant numbers of our young adult and older study participants lived by themselves, an alternate form was constructed which allowed defining the current family as those individuals (whether or not related by blood or marriage) that the respondent considered as his or her primary reference group and with whom the respondent interacted at least on a weekly basis.

A confirmatory factor analysis was conducted on a random half of the sample of relatives for both forms to determine whether the retained items clustered on the factors described by Moos. The obtained fit (Family of origin: $X^2(701) = 1235.56$, $p < .001$, GFI = .842, RMS = .084. Current family: $X^2(701) = 1254.48$, $p < .001$, GFI = .839, RMS = .089) was then confirmed on the second random half (Family of origin: $X^2(701) = 1266.05$, $p < .001$, GFI = .842, RMS = .090. Current family: $X^2(701) = 1357.07$, $p < .001$, GFI = .829, RMS = .089).

Although we obtained a good fit for the primary dimensions of the FES, we were unable to reproduce the higher order structure postulated by Moos. Our findings are therefore reported only with respect to Moos' primary dimensions. Means and standard deviations for each scale by separate samples are shown in Table 11.2, and Factor intercorrelations for both scales are shown in Table 11.3.

Family Contact. As a measure of the intensity of family contact we asked respondents to indicate on a set of Likert scales the nature of their relationship, the number of years the respondent and their relative had lived in the same household, their physically visiting, talking on the telephone, writing letters, or obtaining news of their relative via a third party. Item scores were then summed to obtain a single contact score (a high score implying closeness and frequent contact).

Analyses

A general linear regression model was fitted to associate each dependent variable with the significant independent variables. The model was initially chosen by the stepwise model selection procedure. To include all potentially significant independent variables, the level for entering the model was set

TABLE 11.2
Means and Standard Deviations for Family Environment Scale

	Family of Origin				Current Family			
	Parents	Offspring	Target Sibling	Relative Sibling	Parents	Offspring	Target Sibling	Relative Sibling
Cohesion	18.90 (4.38)	17.81 (5.01)	18.62 (4.44)	18.03 (4.64)	21.41 (3.31)	20.32 (4.03)	20.96 (3.48)	20.45 (3.85)
Expressivity	14.76 (3.83)	14.60 (4.05)	15.18 (3.77)	14.36 (4.10)	18.22 (3.39)	18.72 (3.81)	18.35 (3.45)	18.07 (3.64)
Conformity	17.59 (4.44)	16.29 (5.06)	16.60 (4.29)	16.58 (4.77)	19.42 (3.61)	17.98 (4.37)	19.04 (3.93)	18.24 (4.24)
Achievement orientation	18.05 (3.47)	18.14 (3.63)	17.96 (3.54)	18.46 (3.76)	17.60 (3.37)	18.74 (3.20)	17.60 (3.37)	17.76 (3.57)
Intellectual–Cultural Orientation	14.66 (4.76)	16.33 (5.02)	15.20 (5.19)	15.06 (5.11)	18.27 (4.23)	18.59 (4.00)	18.91 (4.24)	18.12 (4.19)
Recreational Orientation	14.74 (4.55)	17.16 (4.45)	15.61 (4.61)	15.00 (4.41)	16.09 (4.41)	17.90 (4.33)	17.28 (4.44)	16.46 (4.34)
Organization	18.99 (3.70)	18.03 (4.30)	18.32 (3.69)	18.92 (3.75)	17.63 (3.84)	16.30 (4.03)	17.59 (3.82)	18.08 (3.96)
Control	17.46 (4.21)	17.07 (4.66)	16.92 (3.99)	18.05 (4.38)	14.14 (3.87)	14.53 (3.99)	14.11 (3.51)	15.08 (4.12)

Note. Parent–Offspring sample: $N = 452$ pairs; Sibling sample: $N = 207$ pairs. Scores can range from 5 to 25. Standard deviations are in parentheses.

TABLE 11.3
Intercorrelation of Family Environment Scales
(Family of Origin Above Diagonal, Current Family Below Diagonal)

	Cohesion	Expressivity	Conflict	Achievement Orientation	Intellectual–Cultural	Active–Recreational	Organization	Control
Cohesion		.860	.664	.372	.434	.524	.272	-.133
Expressivity	.837		.341	.339	.483	.515	.033	-.208
Conflict	.565	.323		.065	.161	.210	.25	-.286
Achievement–Orientation	.274	.239	.009		.430	.369	.333	.289
Intellectual–Cultural	.492	.562	.251	.234		.659	.056	-.130
Active–Recreational	.448	.453	.093	.445	.606		.138	-.038
Organization	.346	.235	.346	.234	.149	.186		.393
Control	-.013	-.121	-.155	.209	-.216	.006	.446	

Note.. From *Adult Intergenerational Relations* (pp. 174–209, Table 2), by V. L. Bengston, K. W. Schaie, and L. Burton (Eds.), 1995. New York: Springer. Copyright 1995 by Springer Publishing Co. Reprinted with permission.

at an alpha of $p < .10$. With independent variables selected from the initial screening step, we fit the linear regression model and then excluded those independent variables with $p > .05$ from the final model.

After selecting the optimal regression models as specified, we conducted several hierarchical regression analyses to assess the proportion of variance explained by several blocks of independent variables. We classified the independent variables into four blocks. Block 1 contains the static familial variables (i.e., parents' or siblings' performance on the corresponding cognitive variable, as well as their level of educational attainment). Block 2 includes the significant variables for characterizing the shared early environment (i.e., parents or siblings' perception of the family of origin of the targeted offspring or sibling). Block 3 includes the significant variables characterizing the non-shared early environment (i.e., the offspring's or targeted siblings' perception of their family of origin). Block 4, finally, includes the significant variables representing the perception of the significant variables characterizing the targeted subjects' perception of their current (non-shared) environment. The proportion of variance accounted for by each block after the first is the increment in R^2. Contrary to the practice of some behavior geneticists, we did not double genetic correlations to estimate heritability. Hence, all proportions of individual differences variances reporting in the result sections should be interpreted as expressions of familial similarity rather than heritability (i.e., as shared correlations between the independent and dependent variables.

RESULTS OF THE FAMILY STUDIES

Family Similarity in Cognitive Performances

We have previously reported our findings on cognitive similarity (Schaie, Plomin, Willis, Gruber-Baldini, & Dutta, 1992; Schaie, Plomin, Willis, Gruber-Baldini, Dutta, & Bayen, 1993). Briefly, we found that significant family similarities were observed for parent–offspring and sibling pairs for all ability measures, except perceptual speed, as well as for cognitive style measures of rigidity–flexibility. However, it should be noted that family similarity was greater for the parent-offspring than for the sibling dyads. Also patterns of similarity coefficient differed across gender combinations in both data sets. The magnitude of correlations for the ability measures were comparable for those found between young adults and their children (DeFries et al., 1976). Our data also strongly supported stability of parent-offspring correlations over as long as 21 years.

We had suspected that cohort effects in parent–offspring correlations would result in higher correlations for earlier cohorts, because of a decline in shared environmental influence attributed to an increase in extrafamilial influences in more recent cohorts. This proposition could be supported only for the attitudinal trait of social responsibility (systematic cohort differences on this variable have previously been reported; e.g., Schaie & Parham, 1974). For the cognitive abilities, once again counterintuitively, there seems to be stability or even an increase in family similarity for more recent cohorts. It may well be that our rough division of our sample into three cohort groups was not sensitive enough to detect a gradual shift. Our previous data suggest the greatest break between cohort groups born before and after World War I. Because both parents and offspring in our younger cohorts were born after this watershed event, there is greater similarity in educational opportunities and lifestyles than for the cohort pairings containing the oldest parents in our sample. Finally, ability level differences within families equaled or approximated differences found for similar cohort ranges within a general population sample (cf. Schaie, 1996; Willis, 1989). When broken down by cohort groupings, such differences, consistent with the earlier findings, became generally smaller for the more recently born parent–offspring pairs.

Perceptions of Family Environments

We analyzed data for our adult siblings with respect to within generation similarities and differences, and we studied parent–offspring pairs to determine these relations across generations. Because of the possibility of shifts in these relationships for successive cohorts we also included a cohort variable, classifying our offspring into those born prior to World War II, those born during the war years and immediately thereafter, and into the early and late baby boomers (Schaie & Willis, 1995).

Our first and most dramatic conclusion was that there is a clear differentiation for parents, offspring, and sibling in the perceived level of all family dimensions between the family of origin and the current family. They see their current families as more cohesive and expressive but also characterized by more conflict than was true for their families of origin. What these changes reflect, of course, may simply express generally greater openness and engagement in family interactions. More intensive family interactions may also be represented by the reported increase in intellectual–cultural and active–recreational orientation from the family of origin to the current family. At the same time we found lower levels of perceived control, family organization, and achievement orientation. Perhaps these judgments are another way of the increasing complexity of modern American families (cf. Elder, 1981; Elder, Rudkin, & Conger, 1995; Hareven, 1982). When our parent–offspring sample is broken down into four distinct cohort groups, we noted further that the shift in perceived family level occurred primarily for perceptions of the family of origin, with much greater stability for the perception of current families.

Second, we found that sibling pairs share substantial variance in the perception of their family of origin (i.e., the family that they shared in childhood and adolescence) over all family dimensions that we examined. However, this commonality does not extend to their perception of their current (nonshared) families. The only exception to this finding was a low correlation for intellectual cultural orientation and family organization. In spite of the lack of similarity of current family environments in siblings, we do find that the best predictor for the level of each dimension of the current family turns out to be the corresponding level reported by each person for their family of origin. Perhaps, perceptions of the family environment of origin may be one of the factors entering into marital assortativity, even though such perceptions may differ for and may differentially affect the perceptions of current family environments by different siblings.

Third, supporting evidence for the continuity of family values and behaviors (cf. Bengtson, 1986) was provided by substantial correlations between the parents' description of their current family environment and their offspring's description of their family of origin. Even though there is a substantial time gap in the period rated, these two rating do refer to the same parental family unit. These relationships were particularly strong for the three dimensions most closely reflective of value orientations (achievement, intellectual-cultural, and active-recreational) and for family organization.

Fourth, we concluded that the intensity (frequency) of contact between parents and offspring has virtually no impact upon the similarity of reported family environments. However, there were family environment dimensions (particularly level of family cohesion) that could predict almost one fourth of the variance in the total family contact scores.

Finally, we suggested that the hierarchy of the magnitude of shared perceptions, from low correlations when describing nonshared environments, to moderately high correlations when describing commonly experienced environments provides at least indirect evidence for the contention that self-descriptions of family environments (perceptions) may well be useful indicators of the actually experienced environments.

Family Environments and Cognitive Performance

In our most recent analyses we combined the two databases to determine the extent to which family environments influence current cognitive performance. We now present findings for the mental abilities, their composites, and the measures of cognitive style, as well as for a Scale of Social Responsibility, for which trait we assume zero familial influences (see Tables 11.4 and 11.5).

TABLE 11.4
Regression Coefficients for Parent–Offspring Study

Predictors	Verbal Meaning	Spatial Orientation	Inductive Reasoning	Number	Word Fluency	IQ	EQ
Parents' Ability	.149	.176	.239	.180	.256	.229	.191
(Familial Similarity)							
Parents' Education		.156	.134			.117	.118
Parents' Perception							
Cohesion	.088						
Expressivity							
Conflict							
Achievement							
Intellectual–Cultural				-.129			
Active–Recreational							
Organization							
Control							
Offspring's Perception of Family of Origin							
Cohesion	-.213	.134	-.163			-.130	-.217
Expressivity							
Conflict				.095	-.146		
Achievement				.090			
Intellectual–Cultural	.141		.107				
Active–Recreational	-.110		-.088				
Organization							
Control	-.131	-.139					-.130
Offspring's Perception of Current Family							
Cohesion	.154	-.134	.110		.115	.126	.168
Expressivity							
Conflict							
Achievement							
Intellectual–Cultural	.099						.119
Active–Recreational							
Organization							
Control		-.109				-.103	

(continued)

TABLE 11.4
(Continued)

Predictors	Motor–Cognitive Flexibility	Attitudinal Flexibility	Psychomotor Speed	Social Responsibility
Parents' Status (Familial Similarity)	.112		.204	
Parents' Education	.142	.129		
Parents' Perception				
Cohesion				
Expressivity				
Conflict				.138
Achievement				
intellectual–Cultural				
Active–Recreational				
Organization	.112			
Control				
Offspring's Perception of Family of Origin				
Cohesion	-.124			.164
Expressivity			-.106	
Conflict				
Achievement				
intellectual–Cultural				
Active–Recreational				-.132
Organization				
Control				
Offspring's Perception of Current Family				
Cohesion				
Cohesion		.148	.146	.082
Expressivity				
Conflict		-.159 .155	.088	.256
Achievement				
intellectual–Cultural	.129		.106	
Active–Recreational				
Organization		-.147		
Control		-.128		.113

TABLE 11.5
Regression Coefficients for Sibling Study

Predictors	Verbal Meaning	Spatial Orientation	Inductive Reasoning	Number	Word Fluency	IQ	EQ
Target Sibling's Ability	.209	.163	.295	.122	.230	.218	.269
(Familial Similarity)							
Siblings' Education		.115	.123				
Target Siblin's' Perception							
Cohesion	-.174				-.252	-.218	
Expressivity							
Conflict			-.155				
Achievement							
Intellectual–Cultural	.194				.171	.205	
Active–Recreational				.158			
Organization		-.179					
Control		.265					
Sibling's Perception of Family of Origin							
Cohesion							
Expressivity	-.119		-.233			-.148	
Conflict							
Achievement							
Intellectual–Cultural			.142		.153	.163	
Active–Recreational				-.126			
Organization							
Control							-.140
Sibling's Perception of Current Family							
Cohesion	.179		.176	.190			.161
Expressivity							
Conflict							
Achievement							
Intellectual–Cultural	.180	.139	.139		.125	.125	.211
Active–Recreational	-.206		-.215			-.191	-.227
Organization							
Control							

(continued)

TABLE 11.5
(Continued)

Predictors	Motor–Cognitive Flexibility	Attitudinal Flexibility	Psychomotor Speed	Social Responsibility
Target Sibling's Status (Familial Similarity)	.241	.226	.268	
Target Siblings' Perception				
Cohesion				
Expressivity	-.150		-.203	
Conflict	.224		.138	
Achievement				
intellectual–Cultural			.173	.159
Active–Recreational				
Organization				
Control	-.147			
Sibling's Perception of Family of Origin				
Cohesion	-.161		-.148	.202
Expressivity				
Conflict				
Achievement				
intellectual–Cultural				
Active–Recreational			.107	
Organization				
Control				-.113
Sibling's Perception of Current Family				
Cohesion				
Cohesion				
Expressivity	.182		.142	
Conflict	-.126		.149	
Achievement	.173	.200		
intellectual–Cultural		-.123		-.166
Active–Recreational				
Organization	-.226	-.194		.372
Control				

Note. All reported values are significant at or beyond the .05 level of confidence.

354

Parent-Offspring Data. In the parent–offspring data set we find significant familial similarity for the five primary mental abilities and the derived summative indices, as well as for Motor–Cognitive Flexibility and Psychomotor Speed. In addition parental education regresses significantly on adult offspring performance on Spatial Orientation, Inductive Reasoning and the composite cognitive induces as well as on Motors–Cognitive and Attitudinal Flexibility. However, only one of the regression coefficients for the abilities and one coefficient for the regression of social responsibility upon the parental perceptions of their current family environment (the estimate of shared environment) are significant. It seems that the time since our adult offspring shared the current family of their parents is simply too long to have the parents' current environment serve as a surrogate for the early shared environment.

Nevertheless, there were a number of significant regressions for the offspring perception of the family of origin (the unique experience of their early environment). These regressions, at least for the cognitive abilities, accounted for as much or more variance then the subjects' perception of their current environment (see later). Cohesion related positively to Spatial Orientation and Social Responsibility. Expressivity was negatively related to Verbal Meaning, Spatial Orientation, Motor–Cognitive Flexibility and Psychomotor Speed, as well as the indices of Intellectual Ability and Educational Aptitude. Perceived conflict related positively to Number and negatively to Word Fluency. Achievement orientation related positively to Number. Intellectual–Cultural orientation related positively to Verbal Meaning and Social responsibility. Organization related negatively to Inductive Reasoning. Finally, perceived Control related negatively to Verbal Meaning, Spatial Orientation, and the index of Educational Aptitude.

Significant regressions for the effect of the current environment of the offspring were also found. Cohesion related positively to Word Fluency and the IQ and EA indices, but negatively to Spatial Orientation. Expressivity related positively to Verbal Meaning, Inductive Reasoning, Attitudinal Flexibility, and Psychomotor Speed. Conflict related positively to Social Responsibility. Achievement orientation related positively to Psychomotor Speed, but negatively to Attitudinal Flexibility. Intellectual–Cultural orientation related positively to Verbal Meaning, Educational Aptitude, Attitudinal Flexibility, Psychomotor Speed, and Social Responsibility. Active-Recreational orientation related positively to Spatial Orientation. Organization related negatively to the IQ index and Attitudinal Flexibility. Control related positively to Social Responsibility but negatively to Attitudinal Flexibility.

Sibling Data. Significant heritabilities were again observed for all Primary Mental Abilities and their composite indices, as well as for Motor–Cognitive Flexibility, Attitudinal Flexibility, and Psychomotor Speed. Siblings' educational level yielded significant regressions for Spatial Orientation and Inductive Reasoning. Substantial regressions were also found for the shared environment in the family of origin. Cohesion influences negatively Word Fluency, Intellectual Ability, and Psychomotor Speed. Expressivity relates negatively to Verbal Meaning, but positively to Psychomotor Speed. Achievement Orientation relates positively to Motor–Cognitive Flexibility and Social Responsibility. Intellectual–Cultural orientation relates positively to Verbal Meaning, Word Fluency, Intellectual Ability, and Motor-Cognitive Flexibility. Active-Recreational Orientation relates positively to Number. Organization relates negatively to Spatial Orientation and Motor-Cognitive Flexibility. Finally, Control relates positively to Spatial Orientation.

Smaller but significant contributions are provided by the siblings' unique perceptions of the family origin. These include a positive correlation of cohesion with Social Responsibility, but a negative correlation with Motor-Cognitive Flexibility and Psychomotor Speed. There is a negative relation between Expressivity and Inductive Reasoning as well as the index of Intellectual Ability, Conflict relates negatively to Verbal Meaning. And the measure of Intellectual Aptitude. Active–Recreational Orientation relates positively to Inductive Reasoning, Word Fluency, and intellectual aptitude, as well as to Psychomotor Speed, and Control relates negatively to Social Responsibility.

Significant regressions were also found for the influences of perceptions of the current family environment. Here Cohesion relates positively to Number. Expressivity relates positively to Verbal Meaning Inductive Reasoning, Educational Aptitude. Motor–Cognitive Flexibility, and Psychomotor Speed. Conflict relates negatively to Motor–Cognitive Flexibility. Achievement orientation relates positively to Motor–Cognitive Flexibility and Psychomotor Speed, but negatively to Social Responsibility. Intellectual-Cultural orientation relates positively to Verbal Meaning, Inductive Reasoning, Word Fluency, the composite indices, Motor–Cognitive Flexibility, and Psychomotor Speed, but negatively to Social Responsibility. Active-Recreational orientation relates positively to Spatial Orientation and Attitudinal Flexibility, but negatively to Verbal Meaning; Inductive Reasoning, and the composite indices. Organization relates negatively to Spatial Orientation, Motor–Cognitive Flexibility, and Attitudinal Flexibility. Control, finally, relates negatively to Attitudinal Flexibility.

PROPORTIONS OF INDIVIDUAL DIFFERENCES ACCOUNTED FOR BY FAMILIAL INFLUENCES, SHARED EARLY ENVIRONMENT, UNIQUE EARLY ENVIRONMENT, AND CURRENT ENVIRONMENT

We now come to the critical issue of the extent to which individual differences in cognitive performance in adulthood can be allocated to familial influences (including genetic influences) and shared early environment, and how much is due to the unique influences of early and current family environments.

Parent–Offspring Data. When we diaggregate perceived environmental from static familial influences we find that the former account for relatively small proportions of variance, ranging from 1.7% for Attitudinal Flexibility to 7.5% for Inductive Reasoning. No such influences can be found for Attitudinal Flexibility and Social Responsibility. As mentioned earlier, the lack of temporal coincidence in the parental ratings for the offspring families of origin, we find only trivial influences for the perceptions of the shared early family environment. Significant, but fairly small proportions of individual differences in cognition in adulthood are accounted for by the unique offspring perceptions of the family origin. These range from 1.7% for the Number ability to 9.5% for Verbal Meaning. No effects of the unique early environment are found for Attitudinal Flexibility. Current family environment influences range from 1.2% for Inductive Reasoning to 10.9% for Attitudinal Flexibility. The only dependent variable not significantly affected is the Number ability. Detailed findings are shown in Table 11.6.

Sibling Data. We first note that static familial influences range from zero for Social Responsibility and Motor–Cognitive Flexibility to a high of 10.2% for Inductive Reasoning. Contributions of early shared environment range from zero for Attitudinal Flexibility to 9.4% for Attitudinal Flexibility. Perceptions of the unique early environment range from zero for Spatial Orientation and Attitudinal Flexibility to 7.4% for Inductive Reasoning. Current environment influences range from 1.6% for Word Fluency 16.6% for Social Responsibility.

TABLE 11.6
Proportion of Variance by Source for Parent–Offspring Study

Variables	Familial Similarity	Shared Early Environment	Unique Early Environment	Unique Current Environment
Verbal Meaning	2.2	0.8	9.5	3.4
Spatial Orientation	5.5	–	3.7	3.0
Inductive Reasoning	7.5	–	4.6	1.2
Number	3.2	1.7	1.7	–
Word Fluency	6.6	–	2.1	1.3
IQ	6.6	–	1.7	2.6
EQ	5.0	–	6.4	4.2
Motor–Cognitive Flexibility	3.3	1.3	1.5	1.7
Attitudinal Flexibility	1.7	–	–	10.9
Psychomotor Speed	2.6	–	1.1	4.0
Social Responsibility	–	1.5	4.4	9.2

The total contribution of all family environment sources ranges from a low of 7.7% for Number to a high of 25% for Motor–Cognitive Flexibility. When we consider the joint effect of static familial influences and early shared environment, the proportion of explained individual differences ranges from a low of 2.5% for Social Responsibility to a high of 16% for Psychomotor Speed.

For the primary mental abilities these values are Verbal Meaning, 11.2%; Spatial Orientation, 14.2%; Number, 4%; and Word Fluency, 12.6%. Table 11.7 shows the detailed breakdown into the various sources of variance.

CONCLUSIONS AND IMPLICATIONS

Given the assumption that individual's perceptions of family environments are reasonable representations of such environments we find that a significant impact of shared early environment upon adult cognitive performance can be demonstrated in sibling but not in parent–offspring dyads. This discrepancy is readily explained by the fact that the parental family perceptions must be measured by inquiring about their current family (which in most cases is the family of origin of the offspring). On the other hand, the siblings' perception of their family of origin involves retrospection to that time interval most of which was shared with the target sibling. By contrast, influences of the unique early environment (involving the subject's own retrospection) and current environment yielded significant proportions of variance in adult cognitive performance in both the parent–offspring and sibling samples.

We once again noted significant differences in both static familial characteristics and shared early environment estimates between same-gender and

TABLE 11.7
Proportion of Variance by Source for Sibling Study

Variables	Familial Similarity	Shared Early Environment	Unique Early Environment	Unique Current Environment
Verbal Meaning	4.4	6.8	1.4	10.7
Spatial Orientation	4.0	10.2	–	5.7
Inductive Reasoning	10.2	2.4	7.4	9.7
Number	1.5	2.5	1.6	3.6
Word Fluency	5.3	9.3	2.3	1.6
IQ	4.8	9.0	4.8	5.2
EQ	7.2	–	2.0	12.2
Motor–Cognitive Flexibility	5.8	9.4	2.6	13.0
Attitudinal Flexibility	5.1	–	–	9.3
Psychomotor Speed	7.2	8.8	3.3	4.2
Social Responsibility	–	2.5	5.4	16.6

cross-gender pairs. Although subsamples were too small to provide stable estimates in this chapter, we observed that familial similarity estimates were generally higher in same gender pairs, while the effect of shared early environment was greater in cross-gender pairs for most (but not all) variables.

What were the family environment dimensions that were most salient in predicting adult cognitive performance? As far- as the early environment was concerned there was a clear positive effect of a strong intellectual–cultural family orientation. On the other hand high levels of family cohesion had a negative effect.

High expressivity estimates from the unique perceptions of the early environment also seemed to have negative effects on several cognitive variables, whereas the unique perception of high active-recreational orientation had positive impact. By contrast, positive influences on cognitive performance and positive cognitive styles of the current family environment involved primarily high levels of cohesion, expressivity, and intellectual cultural orientation coupled with low levels of family organization.

In this chapter we do make somewhat strong assumptions about the utility of perceptions as measures of family environment and further investigations with better estimates of early environment as reported by the adult parents are needed. Nevertheless, we think that it is fair to conclude that we have provided significant evidence for the importance of early family environment (both shared and uniquely experienced) in understanding family similarity in adult cognitive performance. Although we do not wish to deny the important contribution of genetic transmission of individual differences in cognition, and the not insignificant contribution of current family environments, we nevertheless here do call attention to a substantial influence of early family environment in shaping cognitive performance throughout the life span.

ACKNOWLEDGMENTS

This chapter was originally presented as an invited address presented at the biennial meeting of the International Society for the Study of Behavioral Development, August 1996, Quebec City, Canada. Preparation of this chapter was supported by Grant # R37 AG08055 from the National Institute on Aging. We would like to acknowledge the assistance of Scott Maitland and Holly Mack in preparing the data archive on which this report is based, and recognize the contributions of Sherry L. Willis, the principal coinvestigator in the Seattle Longitudinal Study, to the conceptualization and data collection of the main study. We would also like to acknowledge the enthusiastic participation of members and staff of the Group Health Cooperative of Puget Sound and their relatives, without whose support this study would not have been possible.

REFERENCES

Bengtson, V. L. (1986). Sociological perspective on aging, the family and the future. In M. Bergener (Ed.), *Perspectives on aging: The 1986 Sandoz lectures in gerontology.* New York: Academic Press.

Bernstein, E. (1924). Quickness and intelligence. *British Journal of Psychology, 3*(7).

Bouchard, T. J., Jr. (1997). IQ similarity in twins reared apart: Findings and responses to critics. In R. J. Sternberg & E. L. Grigorenko (Eds.), *Intelligence, heredity and environment* (pp. 126–160), New York: Cambridge University Press.

Chipuer, H. M., Plomin, R., Pedersen, N. L., & McClearn, G. E. (1993). Genetic influences on family environment: The role of personality. *Developmental Psychology, 29*, 110–118.

Defries, J. C., Ashton, G. C., Johnson, R. C., Kusi, A. R., McClearn, G. E., Mi, M. P., Rashad, M. N., Vandenberg, S. G., & Wilson, J. R. (1976). Parent-offspring resemblance for specific cognitive abilities in two ethnic groups. *Nature, 261*(5556), 131–133.

Elder, G. H., Jr. (1981). History of the family: The discovery of complexity. *Journal of Marriage and the Family, 43*, 489–519.

Elder, G. H., Jr., Rudkin, L., & Conger, R. D. (1995). Intergenerational continuity and change in rural America. In V. L. Bengtson, K. W. Schaie, & L. Burton (Eds.), *Societal impact on aging: Intergenerational perspectives* (pp. 30–60). New York: Springer.

Gough, H. G. (1957). *The California Psychological Inventory.* Palo Alto, CA: Consulting Psychologists Press.

Gough, H. G., McCloskey, H., & Meehl, P. E. (1952). A personality scale for social responsibility. *Journal of Abnormal and Social Psychology, 42*, 73–80.

Hareven, T. K. (1982). Family history at the crossroads. *Journal of Family History, 12*, ix–xxiii.

Horn, J. L., & Hofer, S. M. (1992). Major abilities and development in the adult period. In R. J. Sternberg & C. A. Berg (Eds.), *Intellectual development* (pp. 44–99). Cambridge, England: Cambridge University Press.

Jarvik, L. F., Blum, J. E., & Varma, A. 0. (1971). Genetic components and intellectual functioning during senescence: A 20-year study of aging twins. *Behavior Genetics, 2*, 159–171.

Lankes, W. (1915). Perseveration. *British Journal of Psychology, 7*, 387–419.

Moos, R. H. (1985). Context and coping: Toward a unifying conceptual framework. *American Journal of Community Psychology, 12*, 5–25.

Moos, R. H. (1987). *The Social Climate Scales: A user's guide.* Palo Alto, CA: Consulting Psychologists Press.

Moos, R. H., & Moos, B. (1986). *Family Environment Scale manual* (2nd ed.). Palo Alto, CA: Consulting Psychologists Press.

Pedersen, N. L. (1996). Gerontological behavior genetics. In J. E. Birren & K. W. Schaie (Eds.), *Handbook of the psychology of aging* (4th ed., pp. 59–77). San Diego, CA: Academic Press.

Pedersen, N. L., Plomin, R., & McClearn, G. E. (1995). Is there G beyond g? (Is there genetic influence on specific cognitive abilities independent of genetic influence on general cognitive ability?) *Intelligence, 18*, 133–142.

Petrill, S. A., Plomin, R., Berg, S., Johansson, B., Pedersen, N. L., Ahern, F., & McClearn, G. E. (1998). The genetic and environmental relationship between general and specific cognitive abilities in twins age 80 and older. *Psychological Science, 9*, 183–189.

Plomin, R. (1986). *Development, genetics, and psychology.* Hillsdale, NJ: Lawrence Erlbaum Associates.

Plomin, R., & Daniels, D. (1987). Why are two children in the same family so different from each other? *The Behavioral and Brain Sciences, 10*, 1–16.

Plomin, R., & McClearn, G. E. (1990). Human behavioral genetics of aging. In J. E. Birren & K. W. Schaie (Eds.), *Handbook of the psychology of aging* (3rd ed., pp. 67–77). San Diego: CA: Academic Press.

Plomin, R., Pedersen, N. L., Nesselroade, J. R., & Bergeman, C. S. (1988). Genetic influence on childhood family environment perceived retrospectively from the last half of the life span. *Developmental Psychology, 24,* 738–745.

Rowe, D. C., & Plomin, R. (1981). The importance of nonshared (El) environmental influences in behavioral development. *Developmental Psychology, 17,* 517–531.

Saudino-Kimberly, J., Pedersen, N. L., Liechtenstein, P., & McClearn, G. E. (1994). The etiology of high and low cognitive ability during the second half of the life span. *Intelligence, 19,* 359–371.

Saudino-Kimberly, J., Pedersen, N. L., & McClearn, G. E. (1997). Can personality explain genetic influences on life events? *Journal of Personality & Social Psychology, 72,* 196–102.

Schaie, K. W. (1955). A test of behavioral rigidity. *Journal of Abnormal and Social Psychology, 51,* 604–610.

Schaie, K. W. (1959). The effect of age on a scale of social responsibility. *Journal of Social Psychology, 50,* 221–224.

Schaie, K. W. (1983). The Seattle Longitudinal Study: A twenty-one year exploration of psychometric intelligence in adulthood. In K. W. Schaie (Ed.), *Longitudinal studies of adult psychological development* (pp. 64–135). New York: Guilford Press.

Schaie, K. W. (1996). *Intellectual development in adulthood: The Seattle Longitudinal Study.* New York: Cambridge University Press.

Schaie, K. W., & Hertzog, C. (1986). Toward a comprehensive model of adult intellectual development: Contributions of the Seattle Longitudinal Study. In R. J. Sternberg (Ed.), *Advances in human intelligence* (Vol. 3, pp. 79–118). Hillsdale, NJ: Lawrence Erlbaum Associates.

Schaie, K. W., & O'Hanlon, A. M. (1990). The influence of social-environmental factors in the maintenance of adult intelligence. In R. Schmitz-Scherzer, A. Kruse, & E. Olbrich (Eds.), *Altern—Ein lebenslanger Prozess der Sozialen Interaktion* [Aging—A lifelong process of social interaction] (pp. 55–66). Darmstadt: Steinkopf Verlag.

Schaie, K. W., & Parham, I. A. (1974). Social responsibility in adulthood: Ontogenetic and sociocultural change. *Journal of Personality and Social Psychology, 30,* 483–492.

Schaie, K. W., & Parham, I. A. (1975). *Manual for the test of behavioral rigidity.* Palo Alto, CA: Consulting Psychologists Press.

Schaie, K. W., Plomin, R., Willis, S. L., Gruber-Baldini, A., & Dutta, R. (1992). Natural cohorts: Family similarity in adult cognition. In T. Sonderegger (Ed.), *Psychology and aging: Nebraska Symposium on Motivation, 1991* (pp. 205–243). Lincoln, NE: University of Nebraska Press.

Schaie, K. W., Plomin, R., Willis, S. L., Gruber-Baldini, A. L., Dutta, R., & Bayen, U. (1993). Family similarity in adult intellectual development. In J. J. F. Schroots (Ed.), *Aging, health and competence: The next generation of longitudinal research* (pp. 183–198). Amsterdam, The Netherlands: Elsevier.

Schaie, K. W., & Willis, S. L. (1991). Adult personality and psychomotor performance: Cross-sectional and longitudinal analyses. *Journal of Gerontology: Psychological Sciences, 46,* P275–P284.

Schaie, K. W., & Willis, S. L. (1995). Perceived family environments across generations. In V. L. Bengtson, K. W. Schaie, & L. Burton (Eds.), *Adult intergenerational relations: Effects of societal change* (pp. 174–209). New York: Springer.

Scheier, I., & Ferguson, G. A. (1952). Further factorial studies of tests of rigidity. *Canadian Journal of Psychology, 6,* 19–30.

Thurstone, L. L. (1938). *The primary mental abilities.* Chicago: University of Chicago Press.

Thurstone, L. L., & Thurstone, T. G. (1949). *Examiner Manual for the SRA Primary Mental Abilities Test (Form 10-14).* Chicago: Science Research Associates.

Thurstone, T. G. (1962). *Primary mental abilities for grades 9–12.* Chicago: Science Research Associates.

Willis, S. L. (1989). Cohort differences in cognitive aging: A sample case. In K. W. Schaie & C. Schooler (Eds.), *Social structure and aging: Psychological processes* (pp. 94–112). Hillsdale, NJ: Lawrence Erlbaum Associates.

12

The Intellectual Effects of the Demands of the Work Environment[1]

Carmi Schooler
Section on Socioenvironmental Studies
National Institute of Mental Health

The focus of this chapter is on how the nature and conditions of the work that people do on their jobs affect their intellectual functioning. In order to provide useful evidence on this question, a study has to face two issues:

1. It has to be able to specify which aspects of the job are the ones that have the intellectual effect.

2. It has to provide evidence that any empirical relationship (e.g., correlation) between the nature of work and intellectual functioning is not completely the effect of selective recruitment or retention. People may be selected into jobs, either by themselves or by their employers, on the basis of their intellectual functioning. In addition, people who have intellectual difficulties in carrying out their work may be subject to relatively high levels of job attrition. Furthermore, individuals' levels of intellectual functioning may affect what they do on their jobs and how they do it. Consequently, any correlation found between a job condition and intellectual flexibility reflects a potential reciprocal causal connection. A causal path from person to job may come about because people fit into their jobs or perhaps mold them; a causal path from job to person occurs because people's job conditions actually affect their intellectual functioning.

---

[1]Although this chapter is new in its purpose and orientation, several sections derive substantially from earlier theoretical and review papers I have written. Among the earlier papers upon which the present chapter relies are: Schooler 1984, 1989, 1998, in press.

Surprisingly, after several searches of what would seem to be the appropriate research literatures, I have been forced to the conclusion that the only research studies that deal with both of these issues, or indeed even with just the second, are those associated with the Kohn–Schooler research project on the psychological effects of occupational conditions (e.g., Kohn & Schooler, 1969, 1973, 1982, 1983; Naoi & Schooler, 1985; Schooler & Naoi, 1988; Naoi & Schooler, 1990; Kohn & Slomczynski, 1990). The findings from this research program appeared primarily in sociology journals and are not all that well known to psychologists. There are, of course, studies in the psychology literature that focus on the usefulness of tests of various aspects of intellectual functioning as a tool for selecting workers for various jobs—personnel psychology has a long interest in such concerns (e.g., Donnay, 1997; Mabon, 1998). Other studies (i.e., Avolio & Waldman, 1990, 1994) do report correlations between certain occupational conditions (i.e., doing complex work) and the intellectual functioning of workers holding them. They do not, however, distinguish between the relative effects of two possible causes of the correlations they find. The first is the degree to which their findings are a function of the effect of the nature of the work on the cognitive functioning of the the worker. The second is the degree to which their findings reflect the relationship between intellectual performance and the likelihood of getting and keeping a job characterized by a given level of intellectual demand.

Research carried out by Melvin Kohn and myself and our colleagues in the United States and abroad does meet both criteria. Our studies, instead of comparing specific jobs (e.g., plumbers vs. surgeons, poultry graders vs. chicken sexers), evaluate job effects in terms of a series of dimensions (e.g., routinization, bureaucratization, time pressure). Dimensionalizing occupational conditions permits us to specify which aspects of a job are having a particular psychological effect. Furthermore, we can determine how strongly a particular occupational condition affects a particular aspect of psychological functioning by estimating the size of its effect when other occupational conditions are controlled.

In order to deal with the possibility of reciprocal effects between occupational conditions and intellectual functioning we employed, from relatively early on, statistical techniques then more commonly used in econometrics (two-stage least squares in Kohn & Schooler, 1973) and sociology (structural equation modeling [SEM] in Kohn & Schooler, 1978). Such statistical procedures permitted us to come to grips with the problem of "whether the relationships between job conditions and personality solely reflect processes of occupational selection and job molding or whether, in addition, the job actually does affect personality" (Kohn & Schooler, 1983, pp. x–xi).

THE KOHN–SCHOOLER STUDIES
ON THE PSYCHOLOGICAL EFFECTS
OF OCCUPATIONAL CONDITIONS

The original purpose of the research that Kohn and I undertook was to test the hypothesis that differences between lower social status and higher social status parents' values for their children arise in substantial part from differences in their work experience (Kohn, 1963). We hypothesized that higher social status parents—whose jobs tend to require self-direction and the manipulation of interpersonal relations, ideas, and symbols—would value self-directedness for their children, whereas lower social status parents—whose jobs tend to require that they conform to rules and procedures established by authority—would value conforming behavior in their children. Thus, the key difference was hypothesized to be the relatively greater degree of occupational self-direction (i.e., the use of initiative, thought, and independent judgment required by higher status occupations).

The data on psychological and occupational functioning on which these hypotheses were first examined came from interviews conducted in 1964 with a sample of 3,101 men, representative of all men employed in civilian occupations throughout the United States (Kohn & Schooler, 1969). Many psychological measures other than parental values were included in the survey questionnaire we designed. This permitted us to examine the relationship of work experience to many aspects of psychological functioning. In terms of the present chapter, the most important addition was the inclusion of measures of intellectual flexibility, but we also added indices of self-conception, and social orientations.

Because occupational conditions determining the level of occupational self-direction were only some of the dimensions of occupational experience that might have psychological effects, questions about the gamut of potentially effective occupational conditions were also included. We found that we could describe jobs in terms of their locations on more than 50 dimensions that we were able to differentiate. After a series of analyses, we were able to isolate a set of 12 occupational conditions which we saw as imperatives of the work, built into the very structure of the job (Kohn & Schooler, 1983, p. 53). This set of "structural imperatives" defines aspects of the work that impinge on the worker directly, insistently, and demandingly. Each is related to psychological functioning independent of other job conditions and education. Central among these structural imperatives are the three job conditions defining occupational self-direction—the substantive complexity of work, closeness of supervision, and routinization. The other structural imperatives of the job fall into three clusters: (a) position in the organizational structure—bureaucratization, position in the hierarchy, ownership, (b) job pressures—time pressure, hours worked, dirtiness and heaviness of work, and (c) job uncertainties—likelihood of dramatic change, risk of loss of job or business, being held responsible for things outside one's control.

We early came to feel that occupational conditions that increased the complexity of the intellectual demands placed on the individual would have the greatest potential for affecting the individual's cognitive functioning. The complexity of an environment was later more formally defined in terms of its stimulus and demand characteristics in a rough-hewn theory of environmental complexity (Schooler, 1984). According to this definition, the more diverse the stimuli, the greater the number of decisions required, the greater the number of considerations to be taken into account in making these decisions, and the more ill defined and apparently contradictory the contingencies, the more complex the environment. The theory postulates that to the degree to which complex environments reward cognitive effort, individuals in such environments should be motivated to develop their intellectual capacities and to generalize the resulting enhanced cognitive processes to other situations. We hypothesized that social-structurally determined occupational conditions that promote occupational self-direction or otherwise involve dealing with complex environments would increase intellectual flexibility whereas conditions that limit occupational self-direction and environmental complexity would decrease intellectual flexibility. Unlike many other researchers, we hypothesized that such intellectual development could take place in the midlife and that intellectual change was not limited to occurring either in childhood or old age.

The occupational dimensions that most clearly reflect the proposed definition of environmental complexity are those of occupational self-direction—routinization, closeness of supervision, and substantive complexity. Substantively complex work is defined as work that in its very substance demands thought and independent judgment and which by its very nature requires making many decisions involving ill-defined or apparently contradictory contingencies (Kohn & Schooler, 1983, p. 106). Routinization and closeness of supervision are each measured by a series of closed-end questions. Substantive complexity of work is measured through a detailed inquiry about precisely what people do when working with data, with things, and with people, the answers to which are coded according to the scales for complexity of work with things, data, and people which first appeared in the third edition of the Dictionary of Occupational Titles (United States Department of Labor, 1965) as well as in a code of overall job complexity that we developed. We also asked our respondents about the number of hours they worked with data, things, and people.

In our early papers (i.e., before 1977), we indexed the three components of occupational self-direction through scores based on exploratory factor analysis (e.g., Kohn & Schooler, 1973). In Kohn and Schooler (1978), we presented a measure of substantive complexity based on SEM confirmatory factor analysis (see Fig. 12.1.). In Kohn and Schooler (1982), the substantive complexity measure was incorporated into a full SEM three-factor occupational self-direction model.

For the index of intellectual flexibility, the intellectual variable hypothesized to be most affected by environmental complexity, a wide variety of indicators were sampled. None was assumed to be completely valid; but all were assumed to reflect, to some substantial degree, men's flexibility in attempting to cope with the demands of a complex situation (see Kohn & Schooler, 1983, p. 112). Its measurement is based on an SEM measurement model with five indicators:

1. a summary score for performance on a portion of the Embedded Figures Test (Witkin, Dyk, Faterson, Goodenough, & Karp, 1962);

2. the interviewer's appraisal of the respondent's intelligence based on his or her impressions during the interview session (rating scale ranged 1 to

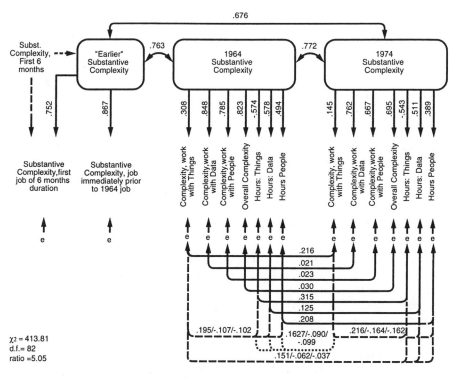

FIG. 12.1.   Measurement model of substantive complexity (from Kohn & Schooler, 1983, Fig. 6.1).

5: 1 = *dull, uncomprehending,* 2 = *slow, needs explaining,* 3 = *average intelligence,* 4 = *somewhat above average intelligence,* and 5 = *much above average intelligence*);

3. the frequency with which the respondent agreed when asked the many agree–disagree questions included in the interview; because some of the questions included in this battery are stated positively and others negatively, an overall tendency to agree suggests that the respondent is not thinking carefully about and is not differentiating among the questions;

4. a rating of the degree to which the answer to the question "What are all of the arguments you can think of for or against allowing cigarette commercials on TV?" provided reasons for both sides of the argument;

5. a rating of the adequacy of the answer to a hypothetical question about how the respondent would decide between two alternate locations for a hamburger stand (adequacy being judged by a concern with potential costs, with potential sales, and with the understanding that profits result from the difference between the two).

In papers published before 1978 these items were combined into a single ideational flexibility measure based on exploratory factory analysis. From 1978 onwards intellectual flexibility was indexed by an SEM measurement model based on ideational flexibility. The basic SEM measurement model that includes both ideational and perceptual flexibility factors is shown in Fig. 12.2. Although initial analyses indicated that the perceptual flexibility factor was affected by work conditions in a manner generally similar to ideational flexibility, the extremely high level of overtime correlations of perceptual flexibility tended to make it intractible to statistical modeling, so that ideational flexibility became the measure of intellectual flexibility upon which we focused our analyses. As I describe more fully later, recent evidence (Schooler, Mulatu, & Oates, 1999) shows that this measure correlates very highly with an SEM cognitive functioning factor based on more standard indices.

We were able to use the data from the original study to derive multiple and partial correlations and estimate reciprocal effect causal models that supported our hypotheses (Kohn & Schooler, 1968, 1973). Nevertheless, it became clear that we needed longitudinal data to definitively evaluate the potential reciprocal causal connections between job conditions and psychological functioning. The longitudinal data necessary to assess these reciprocal effects more adequately were gathered through a 10-year follow-up survey of a representative portion (687 men) of the original sample (for details see Kohn & Schooler, 1983).

The significant paths in the prototypic longitudinal SEM analysis of the effects of substantively complex work on intellectual functioning (Kohn &

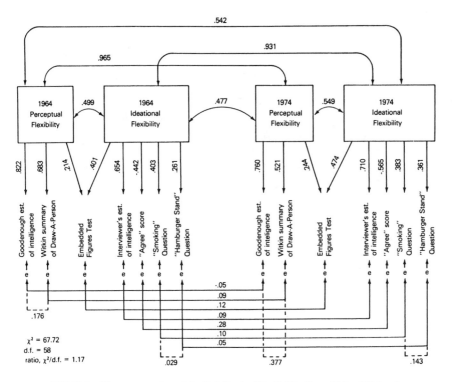

FIG. 12.2. Measurement model of intellectual flexibility (from Kohn & Schooler, 1983, Fig. 5.3).

Schooler, 1978) are shown in Fig. 12.3. Because prior analyses indicated that the contemporaneous path from 1974 intellectual functioning to the substantive complexity of 1974 work was not significant, that path is not shown. On the other hand, the reciprocal contemporaneous path from 1974 substantive complexity to 1974 intellectual flexibility is significant. The effect on intellectual flexibility of the substantive complexity of the work done (the central component of occupational self-direction and a key source of environmental complexity on the job) is real and noteworthy (standardized path = .17)—on the order of one fourth as great as the effect of men's earlier levels of intellectual flexibility on their present intellectual flexibility (standardized path = .71).

Although the contemporaneous reciprocal effect of intellectual functioning on substantive complexity was not significant, the significant lagged path from 1964 substantive complexity to 1974 intellectual flexibility shows that intellectual flexibility does have a significant lagged effect on the substantive complexity of work.

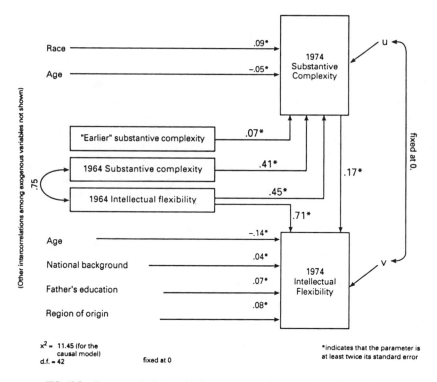

FIG. 12.3. Reciprocal effects of substantive complexity and intellectual flexibility [1964–1974] (from Kohn & Schooler, 1983, Fig. 5.5).

The causal model was later expanded to consider simultaneously all of the structural imperatives of the job (i.e., the essential job conditions that impinge on the worker most directly, insistently, and demandingly) and three major dimensions of personality—intellectual flexibility, a self-directed orientation to self and society, and a sense of distress (Kohn & Schooler, 1982, 1983). The findings from this expanded analysis confirmed that substantively complex work increases intellectual flexibility and indicated that doing routine work results, over time, in a loss of such flexibility. In addition, working under time pressure increased intellectual flexibility, whereas doing heavy work decreased it. Individuals' intellectual functioning was also shown to influence the complexity of the work they do. Over time, workers' levels of intellectual flexibility reciprocally affected the substantive complexity of their work—more intellectually flexible individuals coming to do more substantively complex work.

The overall pattern of findings on American men described in *Work and Personality* (Kohn & Schooler, 1983) indicated that job conditions that facilitate occupational self-direction, particularly substantive complexity, increase men's intellectual flexibility and promote a self-directed orientation to self and society, whereas jobs that limit occupational self-direction decrease men's intellectual flexibility and promote a conformist orientation to self and society. To the extent that the necessity for using initiative, thought, and independent judgment represent complex environmental demands, these findings provide strong empirical support for the hypothesis that environmental complexity on the job increases adult intellectual flexibility as well as generating a self-directed orientation to self and society. (For more full empirical reviews and theoretical discussions of the psychological effect of environmental complaints, see Schooler, 1984, 1998, 1999.) Taken together with the finding that oppressive working conditions lead to psychological distress, the Kohn–Schooler results consistently imply that the principal process by which a job affects psychological functioning is one of straightforward generalization from the lessons of the job to life off-the-job, rather than such less direct processes as compensation and reaction-formation. The demonstration of a strong positive effect of the substantive complexity of their work on the intellectuality of workers' leisure-time activities (K. A. Miller & Kohn, 1983) is powerful further evidence that people generalize from job experience, not only to their psychological functioning off the job, but to the actual activities they perform in their leisure time.

Other studies in the same research program strongly suggest that environmentally complex occupational conditions have similar effects on the intellectual functioning of other adult populations. Miller, Schooler, Kohn, and Miller (1979) found that occupational self-direction is related to intellectual flexibility and self-directed orientations in the same way in employed American women as in employed American men. Although longitudinal data were not available, linear structural equation analyses indicated that working in a substantively complex job increases women's intellectual flexibility, while working in a routinized job decreases it. Replications in Poland (Kohn & Slomczynski, 1990; Miller, Slomczynski, & Kohn, 1985; Slomczynski, Miller, & Kohn, 1981) and Japan (Naoi & Schooler, 1985), also using cross-sectional data, indicated that substantively complex work has the same effects on men in those countries as in the United States. These findings were also replicated on Japanese women (Naoi & Schooler, 1990). More generally, cross-cultural comparisons of the United States, Japan, and Poland (Kohn, Naoi, Schoenbach, Schooler, & Slomczynski, 1990) indicated that in each of these industrialized societies, occupational self-direction plays a crucial role in explaining the higher levels of intellectual functioning of advantaged social positions. This holds true whether such positions are defined in terms of social stratification (aggregates of individuals who occupy broadly similar positions in the hierarchy of power, privilege, and prestige) or social class (conceptualized in Marxian terms by ownership and control of the means of production).

THE COGNITIVE EFFECTS OF SUSBANTIVELY COMPLEX WORK IN OLDER WORKERS

Analyses have not been limited to examining the effects of self-directed substantively complex paid work on intellectual functioning in midlife. Examining the cognitive effects of occupational conditions has also helped our understanding of the nature of intellectual functioning in older people. Older individuals may well be expected to be more adversely affected than younger ones by intellectually demanding environmental conditions. If cognitive speed (Salthouse, 1991) and working memory (Baddeley, 1986) decline with age, older workers may be expected to react particularly poorly to such demanding environmental conditions. On the other hand, the very existence of such deficits might make it more important for older than for younger individuals to be in environments that demand that they continue to practice and develop their intellectual skills (see Schooler, Caplan, & Oates, 1998, for an overview of the psychological literature relevant to issues of aging and work).

Miller, Slomczynski, and Kohn (1985) tested whether the effects of substantively complex work on intellectual flexibility differ as workers age. Using data from the United States and Poland, they found that in both countries, the degree to which substantively complex work increases intellectual flexibility is at least as great in older as in younger workers. Their analyses suggested that, if anything, the intellectual effect of doing substantively complex work may increase with age.

The best evidence on the continuing effects of doing substantively complex paid work on the intellectual functioning of older male and female workers is found in a recently completed analyses of data from a 1994–1995 follow-up of the respondents in the Kohn–Schooler occupation study (Schooler, Mulatu, & Oates, 1999). The male respondents in this follow-up derive from the sample of men interviewed in 1964 in the first wave of the study. The female respondents were the wives of these men in 1974. These women were first interviewed in 1974, when the men were interviewed for the second time.

The analysis under discussion is concerned with those men and women who were working in both 1974 and 1994–1995. Unless they were known to be dead or disabled, we had to interview respondents in 1994–1995 in order to establish whether they were still working. Of the 626 working men in the 1974 sample, 590 (94.2%) were located in 1994–1995; of these, 159 (26.9%) had died, 14 (2.4%) were disabled. Of the remaining 417 cases who might have been working in 1994–1995, 334 (80.0%) were interviewed; of these, 160 (47.9%) were still working. The parallel numbers for the 269 women who were working in 1974 were: 248 (92.2%) found, of these 26 (10.5%) had died and 2 (0.8%) were disabled. Of the 220 women who might have still been working, 182 (82.7%)

were interviewed; of these, 73 (40.1%) were still working. The respondents ranged in age from 41 to 83; their median age was 57. Their median level of education was high school graduate with some technical schooling.

The measures of the substantive complexity of work and of intellectual functioning are substantially the same as those described earlier. The major difference is that we were able to constrain the loadings of their indices to be the same (i.e., they are congeneric) for both time periods (1974 and 1994) and for both genders and still have very well fitting measurement models.

In order to test whether the late career effects of substantively complex work on intellectual functioning differed in relatively old compared to somewhat younger workers, we divided our sample at the median age of 57 years. The factor loadings of the SEM measurement models for both substantive complexity and intellectual flexibility proved the same for the two groups. Our causal analyses (see Fig. 12.4) of the potential reciprocal effects between substantively complex work and intellectual functioning indicated that the path from 1994–1995 Substantive Complexity to 1994–1995 Intellectual Flexibility is significant in both the younger and the older groups. Nevertheless, as the modification indices (Sörbom, 1989) indicated, the paths for the two groups are significantly and markedly different. The impact of Substantive Complexity on Intellectual Flexibility is about twice as great in the older group (b = .50, t = 14.87) than in the younger group (b = .26, t = 3.47).

The reciprocal path from 1994–1995 Intellectual Flexibility to 1994–1995 Substantive Complexity was also significant. There was, however, no evidence of an age difference in its size. Nevertheless, the relative magnitude of the path from 1994–1995 Intellectual Flexibility to 1994–1995 Substantive

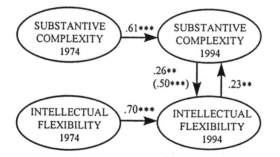

FIG. 12.4. Late career reciprocal effects of substantive complexity and intellectual flexibility (1974–1994/5). *Note.* χ^2 (219) = 142.20, p = 1.00; χ^2 /d.f. =.65; RMSEA = .00; CFI = 1.00. Numbers in the figure are completely standardized coefficients. *p < .05; **p < .01; ***p < .001. Paths from background variables to substantive complexity and intellectual flexibility are not shown. When two coefficients are provided for a path, the one within the bracket is for the older group and the other for the younger group. From Schooler, Mulatu, & Oates (1999). Reproduced with permission.

Complexity (b = .25) compared to its reciprocal was different for the two groups. For the younger group it is about the same size as the reciprocal effect of Substantive Complexity on Intellectual Flexibility; for the older group, it is about half the size. The relative effect of the intellectual demands of workers' jobs on their cognitive functioning is thus twice as great among the older than younger workers, compared to the degree to which the workers' cognitive functioning affects the level of intellectual demandingness of the jobs they hold. Our findings clearly demonstrate that, as workers grow older, substantive complexity of work has a continuing and, in fact, increasing effect on intellectual flexibility.

The confidence with which we can generalize these findings—as well as others based on the Kohn–Schooler Intellectual Flexibility measure—to a broader view of intellectual functioning may well be seen as compromised by the particularities of that measure. The Kohn and Schooler measure, although seemingly face valid and meeting the criteria for an acceptable SEM-based latent concept, had not been linked to more standard measures of intellectual functioning .

To deal with this issue, we also included in the 1994–1995 interview a series of six standard cognitive tasks frequently used as indicators of effective intellectual functioning (Schaie, Maitland, Willis, & Intrieri, 1998). Table 12.1 lists the measures. The bottom part of Fig. 12.5 shows the results of an

TABLE 12.1
Description of the Standard Cognitive Functioning Measures

1	*Immediate Recall* (Zelinski, Gilewski, & Shaie, 1993). Respondents study a list of 20 words for 3 1/2 minutes. They are then given an equal period of time to recall the words in any order;
2	*Category Fluency* (Drachman & Leavitt, 1972; Kozora & Cullum, 1995). Respondents name as many kinds of furniture as they can in 1 1/2 minutes;
3	*Number Series* Adult Development and Enrichment project (ADEPT), Form A (Blieszner, Willis, & Baltes, 1981). A times 15-item test (4 1/2 minutes) in which respondents are shown a series of systematically ordered numbers and are asked to identify the next number that would continue the series;
4	*Verbal Meaning Test* Primary Mental Abilities (Thurstone & Thurstone, 1949). A timed (3 minute) 30-item multiple-choice vocabulary test in which the respondents circle which of five words is the same as the target word.
5	*Identical Pictures Test* from Educational Testing Services' (ETS) Kit of Factor-Referenced Cognitive Tests (Ekstrom, French, Harman, & Derman, 1976). A 1 1/2 minute 48-item test in which the respondents select which of five shapes is exactly the same as target shape;
6	*Different Uses Test* from ETS Kit of Factor-Referenced Cognitive Tests (Ekstrom et al., 1976). There are four trials. In each, respondents are given 1 1/4 minutes to tell the interviewer all the uses they can think of for a common object (e.g., paper clip).

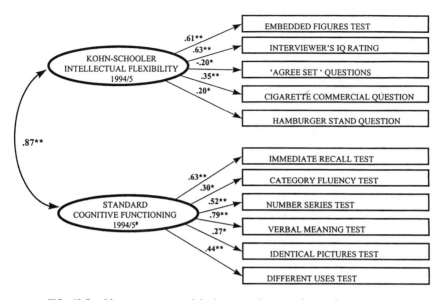

FIG. 12.5. Measurement model showing the correlation between the Kohn–Schooler intellectual flexibility and standard cognitive measures. *Note*. $\chi^2 (42) = 75.86$, $p = 1.00$; $\chi^2 /\text{d.f.} = 1.81$; RMSEA = .059; CFI = .92. Completely standardized coefficients; $*p < .01$; $**p < .001$; # stands for the standard functioning model only: $\chi^2 (9) = 17.09$, $p = .047$; $\chi^2 /\text{d.f.} = 1.90$; RMSEA = .062; CFI = .96.

SEM measurement model in which these measures have been postulated to be indices of a single latent concept—Standard Cognitive Functioning.

As Fig. 12.5 indicates, the model fits the data well. Having developed this Standard Cognitive Functioning measure, we were able to establish that it is very highly correlated with the measure of Intellectual Flexibility we have been using—its correlation with 1994 Intellectual Flexibility being .87 (cf. full Fig. 12.5). The strength of this correlation provides strong evidence that these Schooler, Mulatu, and Oates findings (as well as analogous ones in earlier Kohn–Schooler studies), which demonstrate that doing substantively complex, self-directed work increases Intellectual Flexibility, can be generalized beyond the effects on intellectual functioning as Kohn and Schooler measured it, to more generally used measures of intellectual functioning.

In a further exploration, we ran a 1974–1994/5 longitudinal causal model in which 1994–1995 intellectual functioning was a single comprehensive latent concept that combined the standard cognitive measures together with the original Kohn–Schooler measures. The pattern of significant findings regarding our younger and older age groups remained the same. For both age groups, there were significant reciprocal effects between Substantive Complexity and Intellectual Functioning. As in the analyses based solely on the

Kohn–Schooler measures (cf. Fig. 12.4), the multigroup analysis indexing 1974 intellectual functioning with the Comprehensive Intellectual Functioning factor revealed that, although there was no difference between the two groups in the magnitude of the significant effect of Intellectual Functioning on Substantive Complexity, the effect of Substantive Complexity on Intellectual Functioning was significantly greater in the older than the younger group. Thus, our findings would appear to hold up even if we use a widely inclusive measure to evaluate the intellectual functioning of our sample in 1994–1995.

COGNITIVE EFFECTS OF NONPAID WORK

Besides replication in different populations, there have been other forms of extension of the hypotheses about the intellectual effects of doing self-directed, substantively complex work. These extensions have examined the effects of doing complex work outside of paid employment. Substantively complex housework has been shown to affect women the same way as substantively complex work done for pay (Schooler, Miller, Miller, & Richtand, 1984). SEM-based reciprocal effects causal models indicate that for women, but not for men, doing substantively complex housework increases intellectual flexibility, and doing heavy housework decreases it.

Miller, Kohn, and Schooler (1985, 1986) examined how the substantive complexity of students' school work affects their intellectual functioning. To do this we used SEM on data from interviews conducted in 1974 with a subsample of the children of the respondents in the Kohn and Schooler study of work and personality. The results indicated that educational self-direction, in particular the substantive complexity of school work, has a decided impact on students' intellectual flexibility. Even in competition with the powerful genetic and environmental effects of parental intellectual functioning and social class, measures of which were also included in the model, complex academic environments increase a student's intellectual flexibility. Further analyses indicate that, as with adults' work for pay, doing substantively complex work in school also increases the self-directedness of students' orientations.

Yet another type of generalization is implied by the finding (Schooler, 1976) that men from ethnic groups with a recent and pervasive history of serfdom tend to show the intellectual inflexibility and conformist orientation of men working under the environmental conditions characteristic of serfdom. This finding holds true even when a wide range of potentially confounding variables are controlled (e.g., age, father's education, rurality, religion, region of the country, occupational self-direction). These effects of ethnic background suggest that the restrictive social and occupational conditions that prevailed within European societies may have affected those societies' cultures in a manner analogous to the way in which the lack of occupational self-direction affects an individual's cognitions, values, and orientations.

CONCLUSION

It is clearly a theoretical stretch to argue that the correlation linking the relatively early abolition of serfdom in an American ethnic group's homeland with relatively high levels of intellectual functioning among its members provides strong evidence of the psychological effects of an individual's work. Nevertheless, taken as a whole, the studies I have described provide proof that the immediate conditions and demands of work do affect the intellectual functioning of the worker and that this effect is far from trivial. Furthermore, the pattern of results strongly suggests that what is involved is a generalization of what is learned on the job to what is done off of the job. Unfortunately, the experimental psychological evidence for such generalization is far from ironclad.

Although in the past the experimental evidence for cognitive generalization across situations has not been overwhelming, a goodly number of plausible mechanisms for such generalization have been specifically hypothesized or are readily deducible from various cognitive theories. Some of these involve changes in memory, association, or the storage of information (e.g., similar experiences may lead to more effective superposition of traces at time of storage, resulting in composites that are effective portrayals of what related experiences have in common [McClelland & Rumelhart, 1985]). Other possible modes of generalization involve changes in the way that information is directly processed or linked to performance (e.g., the development, as a result of experience in similar situations, of better initial models with which to deal with ambiguities and uncertainties, as well as of more effective ways of adjusting the models as more evidence becomes available [Einhorn & Hogarth, 1985]). Generalization can also be seen as coming about through the development of relatively context-free forms of information processing that can be used in a variety of structurally similar, but substantively different situations (e.g., the development of appropriately generalized production models [Anderson, 1983]; for a full discussion of possible forms of cognitive generalization see Schooler, 1989).

In recent years interest in experimental research on the processes of cognitive generalization seems to have waned somewhat. Nevertheless, research by Lehman and Nisbett (1990) and Smith, Langston, and Nisbett (1992) does demonstrate that relevant cognitive principles and schemas may be transferred across situations more frequently and appropriately than suggested by earlier reviews of the experimental evidence by even those sympathetic to such generalization (e.g., Ceci, 1990; Schooler, 1989). More recently Caplan and Schooler (1999) reported on how the complexity of within-domain encoding affects the generalization of analogies across domains. In a truly ambitious program, Anderson and his colleagues (e.g., Anderson, Fincham, & Douglass, 1997) are using production rule-based ACT theory and its successors (Anderson, 1983; Anderson & Lebiere, 1998) as a basis for examining the process of generalizing from examples to rules. Nevertheless our understanding of the mechanisms underlying such transfer across domains and situations remains inexact and the likelihood of finding cognitive generalization in experimental investigations uncertain.

As Ceci (1990) noted, the sort of nonexperimental evidence of the intellectual effects of doing complex work that I have described in this chapter actually constitutes some of the strongest empirical evidence both for cognitive generalization and for environmental effects on intellectual functioning. As such, these findings remain a challenge both to social theorists and planners and to cognitive psychologists.

Social theorists and planners face the daunting challenge of deciding whether the gathered evidence of the effects on the intellectual functioning of the individual of the demands of the work environment merits considering some changes in the way work is carried out in a society. Those who conclude that some change is warranted face the still more daunting tasks of figuring out what changes should be made and how they can be implemented.

Cognitive psychologists remain faced with the problem of elucidating the psychological processes through which cognitive approaches and procedures developed to deal with environmental complexity in one situation are transferred to another. Nevertheless, the findings described in this chapter, despite the problems they raise, provide strong evidence that the environment in general and the work environment in particular can notably affect the cognitive functioning of the individual, and that such effects may continue until quite late in the individual's life course. In doing so, these findings rule out the possibility that the individual's cognitive functioning is merely the result of the unfolding of a preprogrammed biological course of development that, given relatively "normal" circumstances, would invariably lead to a particular level of intellectual competence.

REFERENCES

Anderson, J. R. (1983). *The architecture of cognition.* Cambridge, MA: Harvard University Press.

Anderson, J. R., Fincham, J. M., & Douglass, S. (1997). The role of examples and rules in the acquisition of a cognitive skill. *Journal of Experimental Psychology: Learning Memory and Cognition, 23,* 932–945.

Anderson, J. R., & Lebiere, C. (1998). *The atomic components of thought.* Mahwah, NJ: Lawrence Erlbaum Associates.

Avolio, B. J., & Waldman, D. A. (1990). An examination of age and cognitive test performance across job complexity and occupational types. *Journal of Applied Psychology, 75*, 43–50.

Avolio, B. J., & Waldman, D. A. (1994). Variations in cognitive, perceptual, and psychomotor abilities across the working life span: Examining the effects of race, sex, experience, education, and occupational type. *Psychology and Aging, 9*, 430–442.

Baddeley, A. (1986). *Working memory.* Oxford, England: Clarendon Press.

Blieszner, R., Willis, S. L., & Baltes, P. B. (1981). Training research in aging on the fluid ability of inductive reasoning. *Journal of Applied Developmental Psychology, 2*, 247–265.

Caplan, L., & Schooler, C. (1999). On the use of analogy in text-based memory and comprehension: The interaction between complexity of within-domain encoding and between-domain processing. *The Journal of the Learning Sciences, 8*, 41–70.

Ceci, S. J. (1990). *On intelligence . . . more or less: A bio-ecological treatise on intellectual development.* Englewood Cliffs, NJ: Prentice-Hall.

Donnay, D. A. C. (1997). E. K. Strong's legacy and beyond: 70 years of the Strong Interest Inventory. *Career Development Quarterly, 46*, 2–22.

Drachman, D. A., & Leavitt, J. (1972). Memory impairment in the aged: Storage versus retrieval defecit. *Journal of Experimental Psychology, 93*, 302–308.

Einhorn, H. J., & Hogarth, R. M. (1985). Ambiguity and uncertainty in probabilistic inference. *Psychological Review, 92*, 433–461.

Ekstrom, R. B., French, J. W., Harman, H., & Derman, D. (1976). *Kit for factor-referenced cognitive tests* (Rev. ed.). Princeton, NJ: Educational Testing Service.

Kohn, M. L. (1963). Social class and parent-child relationships: An interpretation. *American Journal of Sociology, 68*, 471–480.

Kohn, M. L. (1969). *Class and conformity: A study in values.* Homewood, IL: The Dorsey Press.

Kohn, M. L., & Schooler, C. (1969). Class, occupation, and orientation. *American Sociological Review, 34*, 659–678.

Kohn, M. L., & Schooler, C. (1973). Occupational experience and psychological functioning: An assessment of reciprocal effects. *American Sociological Review, 38*, 97–118.

Kohn, M. L., & Schooler, C. (1978). The reciprocal effects of the substantive complexity of work and intellectual flexibility: A longitudinal assessment. *American Journal of Sociology, 84*, 24–52.

Kohn, M. L., & Schooler, C. (1982). Job conditions and personality: A longitudinal assessment of their reciprocal effects. *American Journal of Sociology, 87*, 1257–1286.

Kohn, M. L., & Schooler, C. (1983). *Work and personality: An inquiry into the impact of social stratification.* Norwood, NJ: Ablex.

Kohn, M. L., Naoi, A., Schoenbach, C., Schooler, C., & Slomczynski, K. M. (1990). Position in the class structure and psychological functioning: A comparative analysis of the United States, Japan, and Poland. *American Journal of Sociology, 95*, 964–1008.

Kohn, M. L., & Slomczynski, K. M., with Carrie Schoenbach. (1990). *Social structure and self-direction: A comparative analysis of the United States and Poland.* Oxford: Basil Blackwell.

Kozora, E., & Cullum, C. M. (1995). Generative naming in normal aging: Total output and qualitative changes using phonemic and semantic constraints. *Clinical Neuropsychologist, 9*, 313–320.

Lehman, D. R., & Nisbett, R. E. (1990). A longitudinal study of the effects of undergraduate training on reasoning. *Developmental Psychology, 26*, 952–960.

Mabon, H. (1998). Utility aspects of personality and performance. *Human Performance, 11*, 289–304.

McClelland, J. L., & Rumelhart, D. E. (1985). Distributed memory and the representation of general and specific information. *Journal of Experimental Psychology, 114*, 159–188.

Miller, K. A., Kohn, M. L., & Schooler, C. (1985). Educational self-direction and cognitive functioning of students. *Social Forces, 63*, 923–944.

Miller, K. A., Kohn, M. L., & Schooler, C. (1986). Educational self-direction and personality. *American Sociological Review, 51*, 372–390.

Miller, J., Schooler, C., Kohn, M. L., & Miller, K. A. (1979). Women and work: The psychological effects of occupational conditions. *American Journal of Sociology, 85,* 66–94.

Miller, J., Slomczynski, K. M., & Kohn, M. L. (1985). Continuity of learning-generalization: The effect of job on men's intellective process in the United States and Poland. *American Journal of Sociology, 91,* 593–615.

Naoi, A., & Schooler, C. (1985). Occupational conditions and psychological functioning in Japan. *American Journal of Sociology, 90,* 729–752.

Naoi, M., & Schooler, C. (1990). Psychological consequences of occupational conditions among Japanese wives. *Social Psychology Quarterly, 58,* 100–116.

Salthouse, T. A. (1991). Mediation of adult age differences in cognition by reductions in working memory and speed of processing. *Psychological Science, 2,* 179–183.

Schaie, K. W., Maitland, S. B., Willis, S. L., & Intrieri, R. C. (1998). Longitudinal invariance of adult psychometric ability factor structure across 7 years. *Psychology and Aging, 13,* 8–20.

Schooler, C. (1976). Serfdom's legacy: An ethnic continuum. *American Journal of Sociology, 81,* 1265–1286.

Schooler, C. (1984). Psychological effects of complex environments during the life span: A review and theory. *Intelligence, 8,* 259–281.

Schooler, C. (1987). Cognitive effects of complex environments during the life span: A review and theory. In C. Schooler & K. W. Schaie (Eds.), *Cognitive functioning and social structure over the life course* (pp. 24–29). Norwood, NJ: Ablex.

Schooler, C. (1989). Social structural effects and experimental situations: Mutual lessons of cognitive and social science. In K. W. Schaie & C. Schooler (Eds.), *Social structure and aging: Psychological processes* (pp. 129–147). Hillsdale, NJ: Lawrence Erlbaum Associates.

Schooler, C. (1998). Environmental complexity and the Flynn effect. In U. Neisser (Ed.), *The rising curve* (pp. 67–79). Hyattsville, MD: American Psychological Association.

Schooler, C. (1999). The workplace environment: Measurement, psychological effects, basic issues. In S. Friedman & T. Wachs (Eds.), *Measurement of environment across the life span* (pp. 229–246). Hyattsville, MD: American Psychological Association.

Schooler, C., Caplan, L., & Oates, G. (1998). Aging and work: An overview. In K. W. Schaie & C. Schooler (Eds.), Impact of work on older adults (pp. 1–19). New York: Springer.

Schooler, C., Miller, J., Miller, K. A., & Richtand, C. N. (1984). Work for the household: Its nature and consequences for husbands and wives. *American Journal of Sociology, 90,* 97–124.

Schooler, C., Mulatu, M. S., & Oates, G. L. (1999). The continuing effects of substantively complex work on the intellectual functioning of older workers. *Psychology and Aging, 14,* 483–506.

Schooler, C., & Naoi, A. (1988). The psychological effects of traditional and of economically peripheral job settings in Japan. *American Journal of Sociology, 94,* 335–355.

Slomczynski, K. M., Miller, J., & Kohn, M. L. (1981). Stratification, work, and values: A Polish–United States comparison. *American Sociological Review, 46,* 720–744.

Smith, E. E., Langston, C., & Nisbett, R. E. (1992). The case for rules in reasoning. *Cognitive Science, 16,* 1–40.

Sörbom, D. (1989). Model modification. *Psychometrika, 54,* 371–384.

Thurstone, L. L., & Thurstone, T. G. (1949). *Examiner manual for the SRA primary mental abilities test (Form 10–14).* Chicago: Science Research Associates.

Witkin, H. A., Dyk, R. B., Faterson, H. F., Goodenough, D. R., & Karp, S. A. (1962). Psychological differentiation: Studies of development. New York: Wiley.

United States Department of Labor Dictionary of Occupational Titles. (1965). Washington, DC: U.S. Government Printing Office. Third ed.

Zelinski, E. M., Gilewski, M. J., & Schaie, K. W. (1983). Individual differences in cross-sectional and 3-year longitudinal memory performance across the adult life span. *Psychology and Aging, 8,* 176–186.

CONCLUSIONS

13

Sociohistorical Changes and Intelligence Gains

Rocío Fernández-Ballesteros
Manuel Juan-Espinosa
With the collaboration of Francisco-Jose Abad
Autonoma University of Madrid

Has intelligence changed over the course of human life on Earth? The scientific study of intelligence is relatively recent,[1] so that we lack data from reliable and valid intelligence testing. Nevertheless, intelligence (however we define it), like life, undoubtedly has an evolutionary pattern (e.g., Bock, 1980; Jerison, 1982).

This pattern not only relates to the fact that human intelligence arose in association with a biological and evolutionary process, but also because intelligence is a cultural and sociohistorical product. In other words, intelligence, as well as being a biological product of life across evolution, is also the product of the synergistic relationships between biological and cultural (environmental) circumstances. Despite the fact that our genome has not changed over the last 50 thousand years, our intelligence has indeed developed over this period.

If we were science fiction writers we would have no problem imagining aliens assessing (even measuring) some type of intelligence in some type of environment. Of course, such analysis would be developed through a variety of procedures. In the case of aliens, or "observers" (O) assessing Earth people, they would assess our physical and cultural productions, from art (from the Altamira cave drawings to Michelangelo, or to Picasso) to political organizations (from primitive patriarchal systems to democracies). O would also measure parameters in our brain, or they might observe other overt behav-

---

[1]Even if intelligence has been considered as a human faculty since the very beginning of the history of the human thought (Aristotle, Juan Huarte de San Juan).

iors as indices of our cognitive operations or intellectual development. Supposing, then, that these O aliens belong to a highly-developed species, observing us over a very long period of time; they might analyze the synergetic relationships between our intelligence and our social and cultural productions.

However, we are not aliens. We must be a little more modest and measure the evolution of human intelligence and human social organization and culture through quite immature methods, such as studying the use of perspective in the Altamira cove drawings (Spain), painted more than fourteen thousand years ago, or the starting point of democratic organization, or by looking at cultural movements: from the agricultural through the industrial to the communication revolution (Toffler, 1980).

In fact, there were no systematic studies about intelligence before the turn of the century (Alfred Binet conceptualized the construct when he published the first test of intelligence in 1905), so that we lack data about synergetic relationships between sociocultural achievement and intelligence through history. However, we can at least try to examine what happened in the last century in this respect.

Although, from a historical perspective, then, we have very little data from systematic studies of the relationships between intelligence shifts and sociohistorical shifts, from cross-sectional intergroups and within-group studies, we do have empirical evidence about consistent relationships between several social and cultural conditions (schooling, profession, income, positive stimulation, rearing practices, nutrition, and so forth) and intelligence. We also have empirical evidence that intelligence has increased during the 20th century, while sociology, political sciences and demography have provided us with data that allow us to analyze sociocultural changes in the same period.

The main objective of this chapter is to look at gains in intelligence and some of its potential sociohistorical influences over the last 100 years. We must begin, however, by saying that, in our opinion, to the same extent that cultural and biological factors interact over the course of the life of a given human being, we must consider the relationships among sociohistorical conditions and human intelligence as synergistic. That is, as the Laboratory of Comparative Human Cognition (LCHC, 1982) stresses "we cannot assume a one-way causal relation between culture and intelligence. If one is willing to assume that some aspect of experience makes individuals more intelligent, then a culture that provides the needed experience is going to produce more intelligent members" (p. 645).

THE SOCIOHISTORICAL PERSPECTIVE

From a theoretical perspective, several authors have recognized the importance of sociohistorical evolution in human development. However, it was in the first third of the 20th century that Vygotsky laid the foundation stone of a sociohistorical understanding of the origin and organizations of human intellectual functioning, through his cultural–historical theory (Vygotsky, 1929, 1978). The main concern of this theory is the study of how individual cognitive processes are dependent upon cultural shifts. Vygotsky's work inspired several research projects that yielded evidence of this over the last century. For example, Luria (1979) said: "for many decades before I met Vygotsky there had been widespread debate on the question of whether people growing up under different cultural circumstances would differ in the basic intellectual capacities" (p. 58). Nevertheless, this issue was, and continues to be, an empirical question.

In attempt to take an empirical step forward, Luria (1931) developed a natural cultural–historical experiment. As is well known, during the 1930s, as a consequence of the Soviet revolution, several important social changes took place. Several populations living in isolated Russian communities received the relative impact of cultural transformations. The results of Luria's study demonstrate the importance of historical changes in cognitive processes and products, and yielded important evidence for a sociohistorical conceptualization of the development of human intelligence. However, they were aware that this natural cultural–historical experiment was a cross-sectional study and not, as they would have preferred, a true sociohistorical investigation (see Luria, 1931). There are, indeed, hundreds of cross-cultural studies that demonstrate the importance of cultures in the so-called human higher functioning, but there are very few studies studying the effect of social and cultural variables across time (see Rosa, 1991).

Intelligence (as well as many other psychological constructs) has been studied from a diversity of points of view and scopes: its nature and components, its development through life, its determinants, its relationships with many other human characteristics or behaviors, and so on. However, perhaps because the scientific study of intelligence is relatively young, and due to its "nativist" conceptualization, very few studies have been conducted that refer to how and to what extent intelligence is linked to historical conditions. Even though there is strong evidence supporting the relevance of biological conditions in intelligence, there are certainly also sound data supporting the notion that environmental factors explain an important degree of variance in intelligence (between 20% and 60%), that the two types of factors interact with one another, and even that there are synergistic relationships between them. In other words, the nature–nurture debate appears to make little sense from an interactive perspective (Staats, 1971).

At this point, though, the most important issue for us is that, if *nature* is more important than *nurture*, several assumptions arise: among others, that there are universal rules governing the nature and structure, individual differences in, and development of intelligence, and—as underscored by Labouvie-Vief (1982)—that Darwinian principles would be the only ones governing intellectual phenomena (e.g., see the next section on Cattell's dysgenic hypothesis).

Nevertheless, although intelligence is a product of biological evolution, it is also influenced by certain environmental conditions and, therefore, has a cultural function related to sociohistorical evolution. In other words, intelligence and cultural evolutionary processes have a synergic interaction across history. Even if there have been no human genetic changes in the last fifty thousand years, it can be hypothesized that human intelligence has increased through learning. As Gould (1981) emphasized:

> Whatever one generation learns, it can pass to the next by writing, instruction, inculcation, ritual, tradition, and a host of methods that humans have developed to assure continuity in culture... Our large brain is the biological foundation of intelligence; intelligence is the ground of culture; and cultural transmission builds a new mode of evolution more effective than Darwinian process in its limited realm -the 'inheritance' and modification of learned behavior. (p. 325)

When a human being is born it receives not only a genetic heritage, but also a cultural one. During the socialization process, the newborn child will incorporate culture into his or her biology. His or her intelligent behaviors will always be a product of the synergistic relationships between nature and nurture. However, just as the human organism is modified through life by social–environmental factors, culture is modified by the effects of human intelligence through time. Inasmuch as sociohistorical evolution is "inherited" through the assimilation of culture, we can state that, to some extent, Lamarckian principles regulate the evolution of intelligence across time.

Applying this perspective of human intelligence to aging, Labouvie-Vief (1982) pointed out:

> The instructional techniques, symbolic products, and behavioral adaptations that shape the intellectual capacities of the young and that form, in effect, the selective context of their adaptation, are, after all, creations of the adults of a culture. This generative role of the adult may be only very loosely related to the growth and decline of those biological parameters that are already subject to Darwinian selection since many of the generative capacities simply lie outside of those models of aging that are primarily tied to the decline of reproductive capacity, biological vigor, and health parameters [. . .] The argument of cultural evolution does not reject the biological nature of intelligence, however, but rather points out that intelligence and its biological roots participate in a bidirectional causal bond. (p. 171)

Although there are important essays regarding these matters from historical and anthropological perspectives, there are very few studies relating human intelligence and sociohistorical conditions (LCHC, 1982; Rosa, 1991).

Psychologists have looked at environmental determinants of intelligence mainly through cross-sectional studies, disregarding the study of human intelligence both as a consequence and as a motor of biological evolution and cultural development.

Several facts justify that sociohistorical factors have been disregarded in the study of intelligence:

1. First of all, cultural changes occur slowly, in a wide time interval and, moreover, the human life span is comparatively short. Thus, it is difficult to observe cultural changes and, at the same time, cognitive changes across generations.

2. Historical studies are mainly retrospective, and science is resistant to such types of design.

3. As already stated, the measurement of intelligence is relatively new. Furthermore, sociohistorical studies of intelligence would require very expensive sequential studies during long periods of time. The only possibility is the use of longitudinal aggregated series and, as Bouchard and Segal (1985) pointed out, such measures and analysis introduce important biases.

4. In order to study intelligence in its relationships with sociohistorical factors, reliable measures of cultural shift would be necessary, as well as the empirical definition of cultural conditions. However, we have very few series of reliable data regarding sociocultural factors collected over long periods of time. Moreover, unfortunately, there are no empirical definitions of the most relevant sociohistorical factors (e.g., "environmental complexity").

5. Finally, such studies would require interdisciplinary collaboration and extensive financial support.

In spite of all these important problems, we present some empirical results about both intelligence shifts through time and parallel changes in some relevant sociohistorical conditions, such as education, family and leisure practices, work demands, health care systems, and so on.

CHANGES IN INTELLIGENCE OVER THE 20TH CENTURY

Cattell (1936, 1937) predicted a decline in the intelligence of the population of the so-called developed countries due to the *dysgenic* hypothesis. In short, the theory is that, if individuals with low IQ reproduce at a greater rate than individuals with high IQ, the result would be an intergenerational decrease in intelligence. Contrary to this prediction, a great deal of research shows quite impressive IQ gains that are difficult to explain by generational inheritance (Vining, 1986).

Clearly, gains in IQ cannot be attributed to genetic changes. In fact, in a study using 11 cohorts of Norwegian male twins conducted by Sundet, Tambs, Magnus, and Berg (1988), the trends over the century for changes in heritability rise and fall in a complex wave pattern that is not easy to explain (see Fig. 13.1). This result shows that heritability estimates may be subject to cohort effects. Heritability changes do not match trends in IQ gains.

This effect of massive gains in intelligence, called the "Flynn effect" in honor of James Flynn, has been found in every country where it has been possible to compare IQs across successive generations. The general ratio of gain in standard broad-spectrum IQ tests amounts to three IQ points per decade, and is even higher on certain kinds of measures, such as Raven's Progressive Matrices.

Flynn (1984) summarized data for the United States that demonstrated increases over the century in IQ. Using data from the Wechsler and Binet tests, he estimated that IQ increased in the United States between 1932 and 1978 by 13.8 points. This analysis was extended from 14 to 20 industrialized countries (Colom, Andrés, & Juan-Espinosa, 1998; Flynn, 1987, 1991, 1994), showing that these massive IQ gains are found throughout the developed world.

There is an exception to this rule of massive and increasing gains: Japan. Lynn and Hampson (1986a) estimated gains of 7.7 points per decade for Japan up to the 1960s, followed by a decline in rate of gain in IQ. Nevertheless, as a

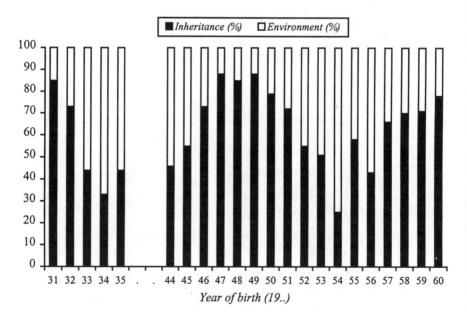

FIG. 13.1.   Secular changes in the heritability and environmentality of intelligence (based on Sundet, Tambs, Magnus, & Berg, 1988).

general rule, the gains are widespread and substantial, and they vary in magnitude for different countries.

Flynn (1984, 1987) considers four different levels of data reliability, ranging from 1 (*verified*) to 4 (*speculative*) according to the number and type of methodological problems (differences in tests, samples, time periods, and so on) involved. Although the results of some of the studies may be doubtful due to the abovementioned problems, there are studies based on very large and relatively representative populations of males (military conscripts) in The Netherlands, Belgium, New Zealand, Spain, and Norway that leave little doubt that increases in tests scores have occurred over the last century (see Fig. 13.2). Whether these test score increments indicate true intelligence gains or reflect an increase in familiarity with tests is a matter for discussion (Flynn, 1996) that we must leave for later.

Age Differences and IQ Gains.   Are there age sample differences in these gains? There is not enough research to answer this question, but the evidence tends to confirm it. For instance, in a study conducted with Danish soldiers, Teasdale and Owen (1989) examined test scores for individuals born between 1939 and 1958 and compared them with individuals born between 1967 and 1969. The results show a significant IQ increase in the 1967–1969 cohort with respect to cohorts born earlier. Lynn and Hampson (1986b) found a similar result: Gains in IQ in Britain varied with the age of the sam-

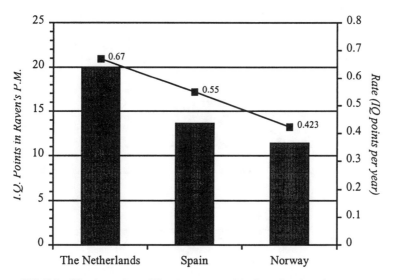

FIG. 13.2.   IQ gains and rate (IQ points per year) in three developed countries with Status 1 (based on Flynn, 1987, and Colom, Andrés, & Juan-Espinosa, 1998).

ple. Nevertheless, this increasing tendency is not the same for all kinds of cognitive abilities. In the "Seattle Longitudinal Study," Schaie (1996) analyzed cohort and period differences in various cognitive abilities. He found differences between earlier-born cohorts and later-born cohorts, and substantial increase and decline gradients. Schaie (1996) summarized his findings on intelligence from the Seattle Longitudinal Study: "systematic cohort trends, which generally favor later-born cohorts for variables such as Verbal Meaning, Spatial Orientation and Inductive Reasoning" (p. 169).

As can be seen in Fig. 13.3, between 1907 and 1966 generations have shown linear and positive gradients in inductive reasoning and verbal memory between earlier-born and later-born cohorts. This indicates an increase in these latent cognitive ability levels, more pronounced from the 1930s. This is also the case for spatial orientation, but to a lesser extent than for the previously mentioned abilities. On the contrary, numerical ability, perceptual speed, and verbal comprehension show a different pattern. There is a concave gradient in generations born in the 1950s that indicates a decline in these cognitive abilities. This increase in indicators of fluid intelligence

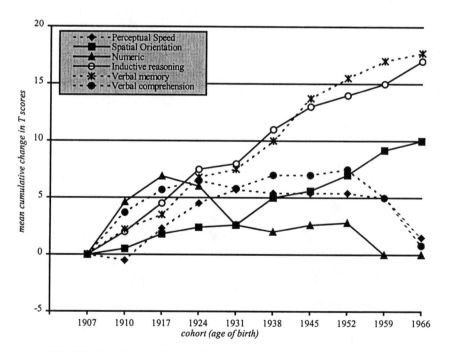

FIG. 13.3. Cumulative cohort gradients for six latent ability construct. From "The Course of Adult Intellectual Development," by K. W. Schaie, 1994, *American Psychologist, 49*(4), p. 305. Copyright 1994 by the American Psychological Association. Reprinted with permission.

(inductive reasoning) and visual–spatial abilities (spatial orientation) contrasts with the decline of indicators of crystallized intelligence (numerical ability and verbal comprehension), with the exception of verbal memory.

IQ Levels and IQ Gains. Another important issue is the possibility of a differential increase related to IQ levels. As in the case of age-related changes, there is not enough evidence to clarify this point, but the tendency indicates that there is a more pronounced gain in low than in high IQ levels. In the abovementioned study by Teasdale and Owen (1989) it was found that the magnitude of IQ increase varied inversely with IQ level. They found that maximum gains occurred at the lower percentiles, and that at the higher percentiles the curves converged. This indicates a continued increase in low (and middle) intelligence levels, with a stable prevalence in the high levels. Lynn and Hampson's (1986b) study, for British subjects, shows similar results. In our studies with Spanish samples (Colom et al., 1998), on comparing scores in the Standard to the Advanced Progressive Matrices of Raven (SPM, APM), the magnitude of increase in the APM is significantly smaller (6 IQ points) than in the SPM (15.3 IQ points). Finally, if there has been an increase in IQ in the lowest percentiles of IQ, then there should have been a reduction in the prevalence of mild mental retardation (50–70 IQ band). As Lynn (1990) pointed out, there is some evidence that this is the case. In a study carried out in Sweden, Hagberg, Lewerth, Olsson, and Westerberg (1987) found only 0.38% of adolescents with mild mental retardation, far fewer than the expected 2.1%.

Changes in Cognitive Abilities. Are the gains equal for all kinds of intelligence indicators? Intelligence is not a unitary concept. Is there a multifaceted structural construct including many cognitive abilities that differ in their generalization level?

Carroll's (1993) "Three-Stratum" theory summarizes the most widely accepted approaches to the structure of intelligence: the Cattell-Horn and Gustafsson models of cognitive abilities (Cattell, 1987; Gustafsson, 1988). All of these models point to a hierarchical structure of intelligence, with General Intelligence or *g* factor at the top. Broad abilities such as crystallized intelligence or Gc (mainly verbal abilities), visual–spatial ability or Gv, and so on, are placed in second position. Fluid intelligence or Gf (as a broad ability) deserves a special mention: Although given a lower status than *g*, many researchers have found it so closely related to the *g* factor that on a number of occasions Gf and the *g* factor have been taken as representing the same latent construct: general intelligence. Finally, the primary abilities are placed at the bottom of the structure. From top to bottom, the theory presents high to low biological influence in performance, the *g* factor being the most biologically influenced ability construct, and the primary abilities the least (except for some speed abilities). All of these considerations are important for potential explanations of changes in cognitive abilities over the century, but the important issue now is whether all kinds of abilities have shown gains (or losses) in the population scores.

There are marked differences among broad cognitive abilities that deserve mention. Although the increments in the g factor or Gf indicators (culture free tests) are impressive, crystallized intelligence gives a different pattern of changes. For gains on verbal tests among 11 nations that allow comparison, there is not one in which verbal gains match nonverbal gains (Flynn, 1996). Furthermore, the SAT scores, considered as indicators of crystallized intelligence, show not only no increments, but a decline of 4.32 IQ points (Flynn, 1984). In a recent study (Colom, Andrés, & Juan-Espinosa, 1997) we found differences between Gf and Gc gains for three European countries that reach Status 1 (in terms of Flynn's classification). As can be seen in Fig. 13.4, all the countries analyzed show increases in both fluid and crystallized intelligence, but the gains in fluid intelligence are much more pronounced.

As far as visual–spatial ability is concerned, the results are far from clear. Some indicators, such as the Performance Scale of the WAIS or the WISC or Raven's PM test, are taken sometimes as an indicator of fluid intelligence (Brody, 1992), and others as an indicator of general visual–spatial ability (Lynn, 1990, Neisser, 1997). This prevents the possibility of clear accounts for historical visual–spatial ability gains or losses.

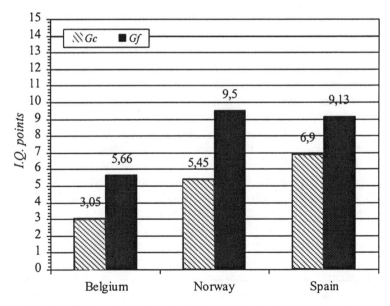

FIG. 13.4.   Fluid and crystallized intelligence gains in three developed European countries (modified from Colon, Andrés, & Juan-Espinosa, 1997).

Regarding the primary mental abilities, the patterns of increase–decline are also varied. As mentioned earlier (see Fig. 13.3), there are systematic increases in cohort level for verbal meaning, spatial orientation, and inductive reasoning. A significant advantage of the later-born cohorts is apparent throughout for spatial orientation. However, the cohort gradients flatten out for verbal meaning, beginning with the cohort born in 1952, and for inductive reasoning with the cohort born in 1945.

The findings for number and word fluency are, however, quite different. For number fluency, positive cohort differences are shown up to around the 1910 cohort, followed by a plateau and a shift to successive reduction in performance level. Thus, the 1924 cohort exceeds both earlier- and later-born ones; the youngest and eldest cohorts are at a disadvantage with respect to those in the middle. As far as word fluency is concerned, there is a successive reduction of cohort level up to the 1931 cohort, but improvement after that. Hence, here earlier cohorts have an advantage over later ones, but from the 1938-born cohort onwards there are successive cohort differences for this variable, too.

Schaie (1996) also reported cohort gradients for the additional ability markers used in the 1984 and 1991 testing cycles, noting that cohort differences for the other additional markers of the *inductive reasoning* factor (PMA reasoning, letter series, word series, and number series) present a similar positive linear shape to that found for the original marker test. Across the cohort range from 1903 to 1966 there is a gain of 1.3 to 1.7 *SD*, the lowest for the number series.

With regard to the *spatial orientation* factor (PMA space, object rotation, alphanumeric rotation, and cube comparison), two of the new markers, object and alphanumeric rotation, present lower cohort differences, 0.4 and 0.8 *SD*, respectively, than the original marker (PMA Space). The cube comparison test, however, shows a cumulative cohort difference of roughly 1.5 *SD* (close to that of the original marker).

Meanwhile, the *perceptual speed* factor (assessed using identical pictures, number comparison, and finding A's) yields a positive and accelerating profile. The cumulative cohort difference for Finding A's, the most specific measure, is only half the magnitude of cohort differences for the more abstract measures: 1 *SD*, as compared to 2 *SD*.

The *verbal ability* factor (tested by PMA verbal meaning, ETS vocabulary, and ETS advanced vocabulary) shows an increase from cohorts born in 1903 through those born in 1924, followed by a plateau period to the 1952 cohort. From this point to the 1966 cohort, verbal ability declines considerably. It would appear that the lexical span component of crystallized intelligence is declining. Also, markers for the *numeric ability* factor (addition, subtraction, and multiplication) attain a peak for the early cohorts, with a modest decline thereafter, which is not explained by Schaie (1996).

Measures of *verbal memory* (immediate recall, delayed recall), however, present marked cohort trends: 2 *SD* for immediate recall and 1.5 *SD* for delayed recall of the word list memorized in the test. In this way, both verbal measures show the same increasing pattern as verbal meaning, although word fluency remains stable across cohorts.

Summarizing, massive gains in IQ have taken place in developed countries. These gains seem to affect younger rather than older generations, and low IQ rather than high IQ levels. Gains are higher in fluid than in crystallized intelligence, and the change differs across abilities. There are also some IQ variations from country to country, due, in part, to the research methodologies (test variations, samples, time periods, and so on), and in part to other potential sociohistorical factors (incomes, ratio of expenditure on education, access to technology, educational resources, and so on). However, in spite of the roughly 20-point IQ gain per generation for tests of fluid intelligence, as Neisser (1997) acknowledged, the cause of this increase remains unknown. Let us review the evidence about some of the covariant sociohistorical factors that might influence intelligence gains.

SOCIOHISTORICAL CHANGE DURING THE 20TH CENTURY AND INTELLIGENCE

When a baby is abandoned at birth to a nonhuman environment, he or she usually fails to develop the two most important human characteristics: two-leg walking and speaking. Once the baby is discovered and transferred to a human group, the process of human socialization begins and the intelligence repertoire increases dramatically (e.g., Leduc, 1988).

Even if the influence of environmental factors in intelligence decreases from infancy to adulthood and, as Baltes (1987) pointed out, growth and decline have relative weights throughout the life span, we must add that they also seem to have relative importance over history and in different living conditions. A biological property of our nervous system, such as plasticity of neural structures, is dependent on physical and social conditions. In other words, society can stimulate or inhibit neural development at different rates throughout the life span (Fernández-Ballesteros, 1996) and, obviously, social and environmental circumstances can also stimulate or inhibit cognitive processes and products over human history.

As we saw in the previous section, intelligence—mainly the *g* factor—has been increasing during this century. What sociohistorical changes have occurred that can contribute to this important change? A first answer to this question is *familiarity with testing*. Let us analyze briefly this possibility.

Testing Familiarity. The easiest and simplest way to understand IQ changes over the century is by considering familiarity with testing. Intelligence testing is a twentieth-century invention. During the past century more and more people have been tested, mainly in developed countries. Without doubt, more and more people have become accustomed to testing, and this fact may influence test performance. So, is testing familiarity a causal factor for the increase in measured intelligence over the century?

Testing intelligence requires a complex situation in which stimuli with several levels of uncertainty or familiarity are presented. Several IQ test materials are very similar to school tasks (e.g., the Binet–Simon Tests); others consist of abstract stimuli that are much more unfamiliar to subjects (e.g., Raven's progressive matrices). Also, the instructions and type of answer required have different levels of familiarity. Finally, as with any human behavior, testing requires the subject's motivation and positive affect.

Familiarity with testing, then, is a dynamic property of the testing situation that can change across time. Without doubt, the percentage of people with experience of testing has increased from close to 0% at the beginning of the 20th century to close to 100% today. Moreover, dozens of studies have been devoted to the question of familiarity with testing, and we know how much performance in a given test increases as an effect of environmental circumstances when egalitarian policies, research factors, or other social conditions promote the implementation of experimental situations for increasing test familiarity. In sum, in order to investigate this phenomenon, three types of strategy, not well distinguished from one another, have been studied: test practice, coaching, and training.

Test-taking practice, by itself, influences test performance. When a subject takes the same test for the second time we can predict that he or she scores higher. In several countries books and booklets have even been published that offer general test-taking suggestions (e.g., U.S. Department of Labor, Employment and Training Administration, 1971), and several international initiatives have been developed to reduce test anxiety (e.g. Spielberger, Gonzalez, & Fletcher, 1978).

Familiarity has been considered as a testing bias (Jensen, 1980). However, the relationship between test-taking effects and testing performance is nonlinear, as the former very quickly reaches its asymptote, producing a ceiling effect (Fernandez-Ballesteros & Calero, 1993). Furthemore, the test-taking effect is so weak that it has been used in control groups for training studies, as it can be tested in several research (see, for a review, Lidz, 1987).

On the other hand, *coaching* has been defined as an intense and concentrated instruction in the test items (Anastasi, 1981) but, despite several attempts to make a distinction, its differences with respect to *training* are not sufficiently clear. Perhaps the most important differential trait is that whereas coaching focuses on the test materials and task instruction, training is focused on teaching intellectual skills or problem-solving strategies tested not only in the items coached but also in other test criteria. In other words, differences between coaching and training depend on the level of generalization the coaching–training has in the coachee–trainee performance. Moreover, the level of generalization depends on the efficacy of a given cognitive manipulation, as well as the subject's learning potential (see Campllonch & Fernandez-Ballesteros, 1981; Fernández-Ballesteros & Calero, 1993, 1995). However, this is not the place to discuss this issue. Our only concern is how much coaching can explain intelligence increase and what types of intelligence tests are most sensitive to coaching.

Several reviews (Anastasi, 1981; Flynn, 1996; Jensen, 1980; Neisser, 1997; Snow & Yalow, 1982) about test-taking familiarity and coaching yielded the following conclusions:

1. Although practice and coaching influence test performance, the gains obtained are from 5 ± points, and these results are not generalizable for either task or time.

2. When Gc tests are compared with Gf tests, Gc tests seems to be less sensitive to practice and coaching (even to training); gains are correlated with intelligence and variability is extremely high.

The general conclusion is that familiarity with testing and coaching cannot fully explain the gains in intelligence over the century.

Framework for Studying Intelligence Gains

If familiarity with testing cannot fully explain gains in intelligence test scores, our question must be, What are the main socioenvironmental conditions influencing intelligence gains?

The human being is an adaptive organism. Living is a continuous and fluid problem-solving task. Intelligence, taken as a cognitive device for solving problems, can be seen as an adaptive structure of the human being. In this sense, the adaptation process can be taken as the trade-off between the environmental or contextual requirements and people's biological or cognitive resources, mediated by social transmitters (such as culture, education, and so forth).

Several variables have been proposed, including *schooling, rearing practices, income, social status, nutrition, motivation, technology*, and so on. All of these could be social factors stimulating (and being stimulated by) intelligence through this century. However, these conditions have been presented in an additive way, and appear to be like the pieces of a jigsaw puzzle. Let us review historical evidence of social progress, on the basis of our *integrative framework of individual differences in intelligence* (see Fernández-Ballesteros, Juan-Espinosa, Colom, & Calero, 1997), but applied to the intelligence gains in populations.

As Fig. 13.5 shows, we consider social progress as the key source for environmental changes impacting IQ gains. As derivations of social progress, we shall review the most important social context conditions: education, work, and family–leisure. Finally, we consider social progress as an important influence on the bioenvironmental changes link with the improvement of intelligence.

CHANGES IN ENVIRONMENTAL CONDITIONS

In general, human life takes place in three main contexts: *educational, work, and family–leisure.* The human being spends approximately the same amount of time in the three environments: one third working or studying, one third spent in family and leisure activities, and one third sleeping. Sleeping is a quasi-biological condition (of course, there are important environmental circumstances involved in sleeping too), but work, study, and family–leisure settings are completely bound up with sociohistorical and cultural circumstances, because they are the three main contexts of human adaptation.

Educational Context

In every culture, every historical period, formal education or schooling is understood as one of the most important tools for preparing people for social life. As stressed by Snow and Yalow (1982), one of the most key aims of education is the development of aptitude and preparedness for later states of human life.

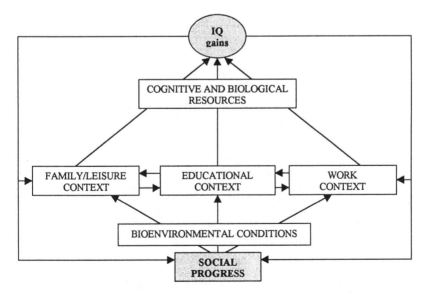

FIG. 13.5.   A framework for studying IQ gains.

Schooling and intelligence have been studied as two faces of the same coin. Intelligence needs some type of schooling for its development, and schooling needs a given level of intelligence in order to be enacted. There is a great deal of empirical data to show that the correlation between the highest grade reached in school and IQ is high, frequently in excess of .8 (Ceci, 1991).

However, formal education has not only increased from a quantitative point of view (years of schooling) but also from a qualitative one. More sophisticated teaching strategies, more idiosyncratic procedures, more technical support systems, more compensatory education programs, and so on, have been implemented over the last 100 years (e.g., Ceci, 1991; Snow & Yalow, 1982).

Recently, Ceci (1991) and Ceci and Williams (1997) have analyzed several types of evidence that demonstrate schooling effects on intelligence: years in school, intermittent school attendance, delayed school start-up, remaining in school longer, discontinued schooling summer vacations, early-year birth dates, and changes in cohort trends. Without doubt, empirical cross-sectional evidence and longitudinal or sequential analyses support the effects of schooling on IQ.

Throughout the history of humanity, schooling has changed greatly. Mandatory education is a nineteenth-century social advance. As we can verify from the UNESCO Statistical Yearbooks (from 1963 to 1997), over the course of the 20th century, worldwide schooling parameters have been considerably modified. All over the world, from 1900 through 1998, there is less illiteracy and there are higher numbers in preschool, primary, secondary, and tertiary education. People born now start school earlier than their parents and grandparents did, stay there longer, and have much more probability of attending higher education. Figures from a new UNESCO (1997) indicator, "school expectancy," available from the 1970s, show an average increase, in developed countries, of 3.5 years of education in 20 years. For example, Japan had in 1970 a school expectancy of 12.1, and in 1993 of 14, while Spain's increase over the same period was 5.5 years of education (from 10.1 in 1970 to 15.6 in 1994).

To start at the beginning, *early educational experience* represents an effective way of promoting increase in intellectual functioning not only at early ages, but also throughout life. As Ramey and Blair (1996) pointed out, "early educational experience might represent an effective way of promoting increases in intellectual functioning at early ages which can be maintained through continued mentoring across a variety of culture-specific domains of knowledge . . . (serving) as priming mechanisms for subsequent self-guided intellectual development" (p. 63). They state that "experience in development, and malleability is understood to be a function of systematic variations in experience operating within a set of *historical, biomedical and socially defined contexts*" (our italics, p. 64).

From a historical point of view, the prevalence of early or preschool education has increased throughout the 20th century not only with preparation for mandatory education in mind, but also as a consequence of important social changes in the first half of the 1990s (e.g., Anastasi, 1958). In other words, preschool programs can be considered not only as educational, but also as social and family programs. The feminist revolution, egalitarian policies, family needs, and so on, have resulted in ever greater growth in preschool programs.

In the course of the past century, in all developed countries, preschool education has taken up more and more extensive periods of time. In other words, not only do more children attend preschool classes, but they begin younger as well. Figure 13.6 shows changes in preschool gross enrollment ratios from 1970 through 1990 for five countries from different geographical regions. Although there are differences between countries, this ratio is exponential in almost all of them.

As has been pointed out by Snow and Yalow (1982), "nursery-school studies found average IQ gains of 6 to 7 points among children attending nursery

Enrollment ratios (preschool)

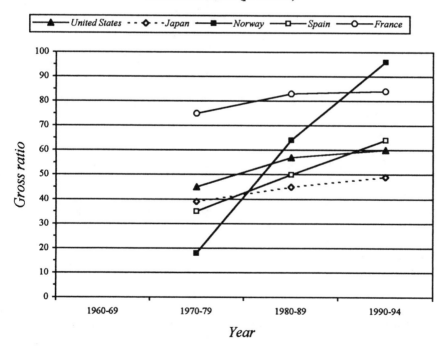

FIG. 13.6.   Preschool gross enrollment ratio from 1970 through 1990 in five developed countries.

school from fall to spring, with continued but diminishing gains over subsequent years" (p. 534). In a study we carried out (Juan-Espinosa & Rosenvinge, 1980) in Spain in 1978–1979, we compared children who had been to nursery school with those who had not. After controlling socioeconomic status and type of school (private or public), differences in intelligence were found to be significant ($F = 32.313$, $p < 0.001$) in favor of those who had been to nursery school. Even if the influence of preschool attendance on intelligence is not totally clear, the increase in preschool programs over the last century must have had a considerable impact on shifts in intelligence.

Regarding mandatory education, even if certain countries (such as Canada or the United States) reached the primary schooling ceiling at the beginning of the 20th century, it is still the case that secondary and tertiary education have been extended in all developed countries. Figures 13.7A and B show enrollment ratios for secondary (A) and tertiary (B) education for several industrialized countries belonging to different regions. As we can see, both levels of education have shown relative increases, even since 1960.

However, we are not presenting these data as a unidirectional explanatory proof that schooling is a causal condition for changes in intelligence. As Bouchard and Segal (1985) pointed out, it makes no sense to conduct correlational analysis with aggregate data (both of intelligence and schooling) with so few countries. Moreover, as stressed by Ceci (1991), "Correlation between IQ and schooling could be seen as an epiphenomenon, a form of gene-environment correlation. Instead of schooling influencing IQ performance, the level of schooling that one attains may itself be influenced by IQ" (p. 705).

Not only have schooling and other formal education strategies increased and improved during the past century. Since the 1960s, cognitive and instructional programs have been developed with the purpose of increasing intelligence—learning-to-learn programs (e.g., Snow & Yalow, 1982). This volume includes two chapters dealing with the effect of training programs on intelligence, so we need not go into detail on the matter here. However, it is worth considering how many subjects have received such educational programs around the world. It has been estimated that in Venezuela alone, one and a half million subjects received programs for training intelligence (Fernández-Ballesteros, 1984). Without doubt, training intelligence programs represent a form of social intervention that should be understood and analyzed from a historical perspective.

Our point is that changes in education have had a functional role in intelligence, but that education and schooling are prerequisites for receiving social interventions and other demanding conditions. In other words, education has a synergistic influence on intelligence, and intelligence influences educational success, while both of them prepare the subject for assuming other health, social, and environmental conditions.

A: Enrollment ratios (secondary level)

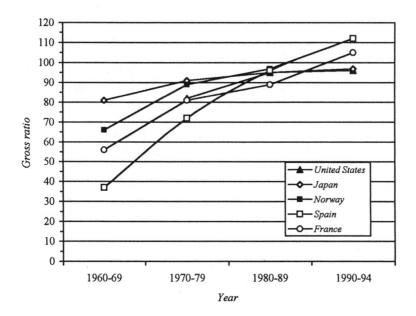

B: Enrollment ratios (third level)

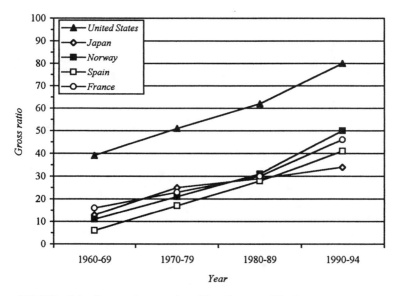

FIG. 13.7.   Schooling rate in secondary (A) and tertiary (B) education.

It appears to be clear that there is an association between intelligence and education, but which intelligence? And, moreover, how is it possible to modify intelligence and not the cognitive products of formal education? Let us look at these questions:

As mentioned earlier, based on the Seattle Longitudinal Study, Schaie (1996) analyzed comparative cohort effects on several mental abilities. At the same time, other cohort characteristics, such as level of education (as well as other social parameters) were examined.

Based on scores reported by Schaie (1996), in his assessment of the shifts in educational level across cohorts, Fig. 13.8 shows cumulative difference mean change in year of education. A correlational analysis of data provided by Schaie, referring to educational and mental ability data from different cohorts, yielded the following results: Inductive reasoning, verbal ability, and verbal memory significantly correlated with education (respectively, .82, .74, and .79), whereas spatial orientation, perceptual speed, and numeric ability (respectively, −.14, .38, and .57) did not. In other words, from a cohort-sequential design, we can establish that, as schooling increased during the 20th century, so have several mental abilities; also, that education is associated with several cognitive abilities, but not with others. Of course, we must be careful about these interpretations, as they come from aggregated data.

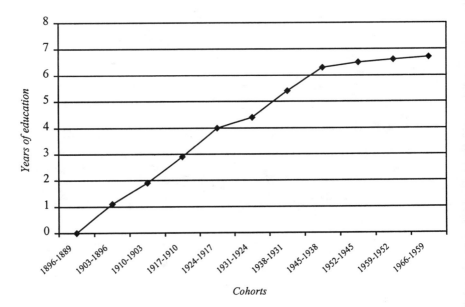

FIG. 13.8. Cohort differences for years of education (based on Schaie, 1996).

Also, as already mentioned, there is a significant decrease in SAT scores, related, as we pointed out, to crystallized intelligence. What happens, then, in the case of crystallized intelligence? In terms of Cattell's (1987) "Investment Theory," it appears that either (a) there has been scarce investment of fluid intelligence in intellectual skills culturally transmitted through formal instruction or, (b) society, through its educational mediators, has decreased its rate of reinforcement or lowered the level of activities that facilitate the conversion of intellectual habits into patterns of cognitive instruments linked to language and mathematics.

On the other hand, the increase in fluid intelligence, associated with years of education, may result in an increase in the development of basic cognitive processes and activities of general reasoning, acquired through *incidental learning*, due to the exposition of individuals to the formal and informal demands provided by the educational context.

In summary:

1. Years of education appear to have influence to the extent of approximately 1 SD in IQ gains.
2. Influence of years spent in education appears to be reflected much more in the development of fluid intelligence than in that of crystallized intelligence.
3. The increase in intelligence appears to be more related to the development of those cognitive skills that are linked to incidental learning than to those linked to intentional learning.

Work Context

The relationship between intelligence and occupation is very well documented in the scientific literature, but the picture of this relationship is not as clear as in the case of education and intelligence (for an excellent analysis, see Hunt, 1995b). Among the many reasons for this lesser clarity are the kinds of intelligence tests used in personal selection contexts, the variety of other predictors of job performance used in conjunction with intelligence test scores for selection purposes, and the variety of criteria for assessing job performance. All of these reasons make difficult the comparison between intelligence gains measured in the "Flynn effect" studies and the measures used for assessing cognitive competence level of the workforce.

The principal studies that relate intelligence and job performance use a composite measure that is akin to the general intelligence factor. This composite measure results from the correlation among cognitive competence indicators. Since these indicators are mainly correlated, any external factor known to influence an intelligence test score (such as the Raven or WAIS IQ score) probably has a similar influence on the general make-up of an industrial test. As a result, it makes sense to consider composite measures of various industrial indicators as measures of the g factor. If this is true, the g factor would be relatively independent of the form of estimating general intelligence. In a massive study conducted by Ree and Earles (1990), a range of correlation between .93 and .99 was found among 14 different forms of estimating g in industrial cognitive competence indicators.

Considering the relationship between composites "general intelligence" and job performance, a meta-analysis conducted by Hunter and Hunter (1984) found corrected (population) validity coefficients for performance within a job to range from .27 to .61. They estimated the mean population validity coefficient to be .53,[2] using supervisor ratings as a criterion. Compared to other predictors, composite general intelligence is the best predictor of job performance, even if we take into account different criteria of job performance, such as promotion, training success, and tenure (Hunter & Hunter, 1984; Juan-Espinosa, 1996; Juan-Espinosa & Giménez, 1996, Schmith, Ones, & Hunter, 1992). In our view, this is an important fact to be taken into account when evaluating the cognitive competence of the workforce.

Another important fact is the differential prediction of composite general intelligence and psychomotor abilities, according to type of job. Arranging the family of jobs in order of decreasing cognitive complexity of job requirements, the validity coefficients of general intelligence decrease correspondingly, with a range from .61 to .27. Meanwhile, the validity of psychomotor ability increases as job complexity decreases (Hunter, 1986; Hunter & Hunter, 1984).

Changes in Work Requirements. In a sense, jobs can be seen as contexts for human adaptation. At this level of analysis, intelligence (in its broadest sense) can be taken as the capacity to adapt to work conditions. Such adaptation can be seen as a trade-off between the job requirements and the cognitive resources of the workforce. As we have seen, some jobs are more cognitively demanding in the sense that cognitive capabilities are critical for problem-solving tasks. Other jobs may demand people's skills where the intervention of psychomotor abilities is crucial. Moreover, even in cognitively demanding problems, the dominant tasks associated with them may place demands on different kinds of general abilities (such as crystallized intelligence or visual–spatial abilities). In this sense, different jobs can be analyzed in terms of the kinds of activities and skills demanded for carrying them out. What changes (if any) have job requirements undergone in the course of this century?

A first glance at the changing nature of work can be taken by considering Katz' (1988) study about the so-called "Information society." Figure 13.9

---

[2]Wigdor and Green (1991) report a lower estimate of .38 for the AFQT (Armed Forces Qualification Test).

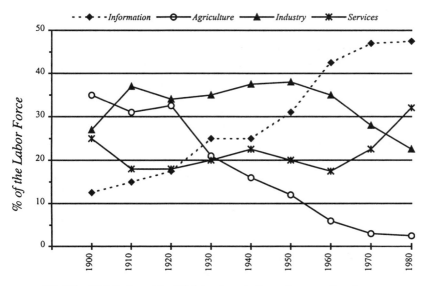

FIG. 13.9.   Distribution of the U.S. labor force in the main occupational groups (modified from Katz, 1988).

shows the relative proportion of the U.S. workforce involved in agriculture, industrial production, physical services, and information services, from 1900 to 1980. As can be seen, agriculture has been declining in relative importance since the 1920s, about 20 years before the move toward a service economy began to pick up. If we take into account that, in this picture, services have been broken down into physical services and information services, we can realize how dramatic the growth in information processing has been with respect to that of physical services. It seems that the work context of adaptation at the beginning of the century was very different from the context of the 1970s or the 1980s. In fact, it would appear that the demands for cognitive ability have increased in the last 100 years.

In accordance with the abovementioned results, in a study by Wegmann, Chapman, and Johnson (1989, cited by Hunt, 1995b), the growth rates of 225 occupations were projected from 1985 to 2000. Five "Top Ten" lists were obtained for: occupations with most employees; occupations with most new jobs; occupations with highest growth rates; occupations with most job losses; and occupations with highest loss rates. Lists 4 and 5 can be seen as indicators of occupations whose requirement for skills are not being reinforced by the work context of adaptation. Occupations included in these lists are identical except for their relative positions: farmers, typists and word processors, clothing workers, moving equipment operators, textile machine operators, data entry key operators, metalworkers, machinists, primary school teachers, and quality control inspectors. Except in the case of primary school teachers, the less demanded abilities seem to be those related to jobs where psychomotor skills are critical, or those we no longer needed because they have been replaced by a technological device (e.g., typists and word processors).

In contrast, List 3, containing occupations with the highest growth rates, seems to be a good indicator of those occupations whose related abilities are being reinforced by the world of work. The occupations included are systems analysts, computer programmers, service sales representatives, health service workers, security guards, computer operators, electrical/electronics workers, repair and service workers, estate agents, registered nurses, and receptionists. With the exception of security guards, all the occupations need at least a first degree from university, and in many cases advanced degrees are an important requirement. Systems analysts and computer programmers are examples of the increasing demand for the highest levels of cognitive resources in the workforce.

The workplace context of adaptation has changed greatly since the last century. The changes appear to be so profound that, as in the case of cross-cultural studies, comparisons of levels of intelligence cannot be made directly, without taking into account the kind of main job requirement in each case. In the last 100 years, technological change has greatly altered the demand for worker skills. Many tasks once carried out manually are now performed by automatic equipment, and the demand for certain abilities (such as perceptual–motor skills) has nearly disappeared, as the demand for more cognitively driven skills has emerged. In parallel, intelligence and the level of education of workers has increased markedly in almost all the advanced countries. Today, as information-based technologies, such as computers and sophisticated machine tools, become more widespread, certain abilities may be less in demand, while the demand for workers capable of maintaining, programming and developing these sophisticated technologies increases.

Changes in Demand for Worker's Ability Resources. The period from the 1980s to the 1990s saw an upskilling in the labor force. A recent work (Colecchia & Papaconstantinou, 1996) demonstrated the change in the educational level of workers. Figure 13.10 represents, in terms of annual percentage change, the evolution of the labor force with high and low education. It shows that the educational level of the workforce has been significantly upgraded, owing to a marked decrease in the portion of the workforce with low education and large increases in the share of workers with high education.

Education is usually categorized by years of schooling or final degree obtained, and is not adjusted for quality. Occupations sometimes provide

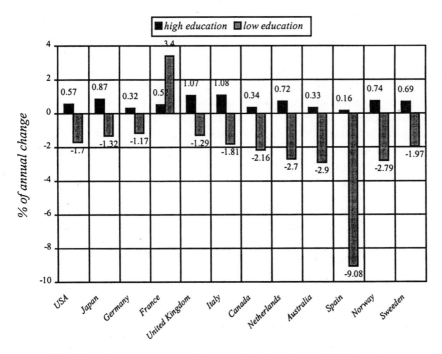

FIG. 13.10.   Percentage of annual change of the labor force with high and low education from 1970s to 1990s (based on Colecchia & Papaconstantinou, 1996).

more information on the abilities required of workers. Usually (but not always), physical, psychomotor, cognitive and interpersonal abilities are taken into account for qualifying the labor force (Wolff, 1996). In terms of the new version of the International Standard Classification of Occupations of the International Labour Office (ISCO-88), occupations were aggregated in the following way:

- *White-collar high skilled* (WCHS): legislators, senior officials and managers, professionals, technicians and associate professionals.
- *White-collar low-skilled* (WCLS): clerks, service workers, shop and market sales workers.
- *Blue-collar high-skilled* (BCHS): skilled agricultural and fishery workers, craftspeople and related trade workers.
- *Blue-collar low-skilled* (BCLS): plant and machine operators and assemblers, elementary occupations.

According to the data from a recent report (Colecchia & Papaconstantinou, 1996), within the white-collar group of occupations, high-skilled jobs have tended to show the fastest growth. Within the blue-collar group of workers, high-skilled jobs have declined in most countries, while blue-collar low-skilled jobs show a more diverse picture, depending on the country. Despite this trend, the majority of occupations remain low skilled, but the share of high-skilled occupations is steadily rising in all countries.

The most important result is that most of the shift away from unskilled and toward skilled employment reflects a true upskilling process, rather than a change in the industrial composition of economies: Shifts have occurred primarily within industries, rather than between them. This is true both in manufacturing and in the services, bur particularly so in manufacturing.

The foregoing authors examined the role of technology in explaining upskilling trends with the help of cross-sectorial regressions for 22 manufacturing industrial sectors in five of the seven[3] most developed countries (G7). The results show that upskilling has occurred faster in industries that have higher than average R&D (research and development) expenditures and growth rates in the number of patents. Moreover, human capital has accumulated faster in those sectors that were more intensive in the use of high skilled workers at the beginning of 1980. This represents an interesting result because "human capital accumulation and innovative effort can be seen as a joint process which reinforces in a cumulative way and can create some phenomena of persistence in industrial performance" (Colecchia & Papaconstantinou, 1996, p. 5).

Furthermore, as Senge (1987) stressed, companies have become converted into contexts of continuous education of the individual. Companies are constantly providing training courses for their employees (both to increase productivity and in response to the demands of unions), and investment in education by such businesses is ever greater.

In summary, since intelligence is the best job performance predictor, it can be taken as an important indicator of human adaptation to work context. The nature of work has changed during the 20th century, showing that the workplace has become more complex and more cognitively demanding. The demand for cognitive ability shows a genuine upskilling process in the labor force. Such upskilling appears to be due mainly to the increase of high technology in the workplaces. Finally, work context has become a mediator of such an adaptation process, providing training courses for the labor force.

Family–Leisure Context

The family context is the common environmental milieu of the human being that acts throughout the entire human life span. Family influence has been reduced mainly to the *rearing practice*, but it is much more than this. We

---

[3]Canada and United Kingdom excluded.

understand the family scenario as a continuous problem-solving situation, ever-present in the life span of the human being.

The child, later to become an adult, is an active organism in an active environment. It is not only the child that responds to the environment, but also the environment that responds to the actions of the child. The family milieu probably constitutes the principal incidental learning context of the human being.

How has the family milieu changed over the course of the 20th century? Obviously, there will have been changes with regard to the roles and practices of upbringing and care in the family (Ramey & Blair, 1996), but we are not concerned with that here. The family environment has become transformed into a world of highly demanding stimuli, where human and social contact and the learning of roles has become mediated by ever more sophisticated technology: electronic toys, child computers, and so forth, are becoming a normal part of the life of a human being from its very beginning. Thus, the family milieu has turned into one of the key scenarios for the development of intelligent behavior.

The pressure of the environment in the demands for higher levels of cognitive resources can be seen in other contexts of human adaptation, such as the family–leisure context. Like the work contexts, the home and leisure milieus can be seen as groups of problem tasks that subjects must solve in order to perform successfully and be reinforced. Have these task requirements changed over the last century? Do these contexts demand higher levels of cognitive resources?

The recent history of scientific discoveries shows that it is during the 20th century that the most important technological changes have occurred, and that these discoveries have changed everyday life for a considerable portion of humanity (e.g., Lleget, 1972). The number of families or people with technological devices such as phones, radios, fax machines, TVs, personal computers, and so on, is increasing dramatically. Since all of these advances are quite well known, let us move on to some theoretical and even speculative discussion.

As in the case of work contexts for adaptation, home and leisure tasks have changed in such a way that, whereas in former times they demanded extensive psychomotor abilities, nowadays the demands seem to be for highly cognitive abilities.

Hunt (1995a, 1995b), Neisser (1997) and Sternberg (1997) coincide in highlighting the importance of technology in everyday contexts. Clearly, such technological devices as the telephone, radio, television, tape-recorder, video, washing machine, dishwasher, microwave oven, electric coffeepot, and sports devices convert daily life, especially in developed countries, where they are commonplace into a demanding context. Recently, a new technological device has been producing even more profound changes in the family and leisure context: the computer. It is even affecting the communication context, with the advent of the Internet.

Recently, some authors (Neisser, 1997) have argued that the arrival of technology in everyday life may be an important explanation factor for intelligence increases. Neisser (1997) pointed out that the greater exposition to more figurative representations of the world may have led to the rise of visual–spatial abilities which explain the score gains in Raven tests. Apart from the fact that the factorial status of Raven's scores refers to fluid intelligence or general intelligence, and not visual–spatial ability, analyses of the relationship between intelligence and hours spent watching TV are not relevant to any intelligence test scores. Our point in considering technology as a source (and a result) of intelligence increases follows a different line.

As a result of the arrival of technology in everyday life, some activities have become automated, so that the abilities previously demanded have become secondary. Some "well defined" tasks (in terms of Anderson's classification of task analysis) have passed over to a "representational model" of such a task, and involve the use of technological devices that subrogate such activities. This does not mean that such tasks are no longer performed. On the contrary, such tasks are performed, but by a technical device that people must operate. What does "operate" mean in cognitive terms? Whereas in former times washing clothes required interaction with the "real" world, nowadays the task requires interaction through a "symbolic" representation of the world: the washing machine instruction program. Whereas previously performing a washing operation demanded psychomotor ability, now the demand has become for a cognitive ability that enables us to perform the same activity through a symbolic model. If this is true for the washing machine, we need only take a look at the symbols through which we operate video, tape-recorder, and so on, to realize the extent of the change.

The arrival of technological devices does not mean simply interacting with the world through the model represented in them. It means that we have to *learn* how to use them. Moreover, computer technology is having a great impact on our mechanical and electronic equipment, and more and more equipment becomes obsolete. According to a recent report of the OECD, the rate of changing home equipment is increasing, and each change to a new TV, video, radio, coffee maker or cycling machine, requires new and more complicated operations. Every time we buy a new electronic device, we must generalize some of our previous knowledge, replace some, and learn some new things. These changes in learning have not only to do with the new equipment, but also with new ways of subrogating representations of the world. For example, some equipment is moving from "analog" to "digital" representations of the operations required. All of these changes are shaping the home environment in a context of continuously changing tasks, where dealing with novelty and with higher rates of learning situations are leading to higher demands on the cognitive resources of the householder. In the words of Reich (1991), we are becoming a "symbol analyst" society.

As far as the computer is concerned, the change in the world representation is much more pronounced. In fact, it is the "main" surrogate of direct manipulation of the world, and the demands for cognitive ability level are higher than for other technological devices (Hunt, 1995b). Only at the user level, the number of software programs to be learned and the rates of program changes are dramatically increasing. This more and more demanding environment requires higher levels of intelligence.

When precise data about technological change and intelligence are available, these environmental conditions may perhaps be considered as one of the most important explanatory factors for present and future intelligence gains.

BIOENVIRONMENTAL CONDITIONS

During the last century, tremendous changes have occurred in human beings' biophysical characteristics (both at population and group levels) as effects of socioenvironmental circumstances. Adult and child mortality, life expectancy, height, etc., have dramatically changed as results of health care systems, nutrition, hygiene, and so on. Changing biophysical characteristics as results of environmental advances are called here *bioenvironmental* conditions.

As stressed by Zigler and Seitz (1982), during the 20th century, social policies have had an important influence on intelligence and on social competence. Intelligence and social competence have been two related concepts during recent decades and throughout the life span (e.g., Schroots, Fernandez-Ballesteros & Rudinger, in press; Zigler & Tricket, 1978).

An indicator of social competence such as life expectancy has increased dramatically. As Fig. 13.11 shows, in European Union countries, life expectancy at birth is 80.5 for women and 74 for men. Although from the Bronze Age through the 19th century life expectancy did not change, over the last 100 years the life expectancy of human beings has more than doubled in the more developed countries (Baltes, Reese, & Lipsitt, 1980). Without doubt, social, cultural and environmental changes that occurred during this past century have determined the extraordinary increase in life expectancy. Medical developments, child and family resources policies, educational, nutritional, hygiene, and health programs have had a clear and obvious effect on decreasing mortality (birth mortality as well as general mortality) and increasing life expectancy. That is, health care systems, good alimentary and hygiene practices, and other social developments are certainly the "cause" of the increment in one of the best indices of human competence, that is, life expectancy.

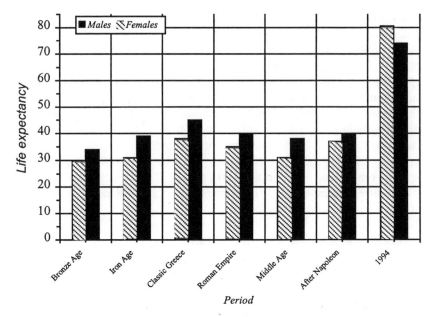

FIG. 13.11. Life expectancy of males and females over history (based on
Baltes, Reese, & Lipsitt, 1980, and EUROSTAT, 1996).

All of the abovementioned environmental conditions can be seen as
indices of *social progress* (Estes, 1988, 1992). As many studies of intelligence
gains are conducted in developed countries (where intelligence assessment
is common practice), in which indicators of social progress have also shown
tremendous increases, some problems arise when we try to disentangle
potential causal factors.

In looking for potential causal factors of intelligence shifts, an important
conceptual problem, as well as two associated methodological problems,
should be dealt with. The main conceptual problem is *multicausality*: that is,
changes in intelligence have many causal factors. However, in addition to
this obvious multicausality, even if a main causal factor is discovered, it may
be different or have different weight (importance) for different aptitudes, different countries, different ages, or in different historical periods.

Methodological problems refer to the difficulty of disentangling, empirically, these causal factors. These problems are "nonlinearity" and "collinearity" (Hunt, 1995a). *Nonlinearity* means that a relation is not the same at all levels of the predictor. For instance, as Earl Hunt (1995a) pointed out,
nonlinearity problems are obscuring the relationship between the poverty
index, SES, and intelligence, decreasing the influence of these social factors
on intelligence. At this point, *collinearity* is the most important for us, because,

in sum, it means that almost everything correlates with almost everything. As we pointed out earlier, at the population level, the entire social progress indicators (intelligence included) tend to correlate highly among themselves. Thus, with these potential problems in mind, in order to disentangle the effects of social environmental from bioenvironmental factors on intelligence gains, we must proceed in a theory-based way, applying systemic and multilevel analysis (Jackson & Antonucci, 1994).

Having made these conceptual and methodological observations, let us return to some theoretical conceptualizations that may throw some light on the multiple coeffects between social progress and intelligence.

Cattell's Hypothesis of Differential Biological Influence. The distinction between fluid and crystallized intelligence (Gf and Gc) has been closely related to the theoretical analysis of two types of intelligence, initially called, by Donald Hebb (1949), "Intelligence A" and "Intelligence B." The former is intended to reflect the basic biological capacity to acquire knowledge, and the latter the ability whose individual differences are influenced by acculturation processes.

Especially important for our proposal is Cattell's theoretical interpretation (1971, 1987) of Gf and Gc (derived from his Theory of Investment), which has several deductive implications. Changes in the biological state of the organism influence Gf more than Gc. Fluid intelligence may be more influenced by brain damage, prenatal events, nutrition and so on, than is Gc. By contrast, changes in the quality of education and other attempts to change intelligence by providing improved intellectual socialization experiences would influence Gc more than Gf. As predicted by modern theoretical accounts of Cattell's Theory of Investment (Juan-Espinosa, 1997), while Gf would be more linked to people's opportunities (provided by the environment) to invest their potential, Gc would be more related to the quality and extent of such opportunities. Finally, Cattell also argued, based on the abovementioned reasons, that there would be age-related changes in the functioning of the brain that would lead to an age-related decline in Gf, while Gc levels would remain constant, and would even increase, throughout the life span.

If this is correct for individuals, and there is evidence to believe so, there is no reason to assume that such a rationale would not apply to the historical changes in fluid and crystallized intelligence. Based on this argument, increases over the century in *g* or fluid intelligence may be influenced by environmental changes that have an impact on the biological resources of the population. If illnesses, prenatal experiences, the effects of birth and delivery, and nutrition are among the biological events that have been assumed to influence fluid intelligence (Brody, 1992), then, changes during this century in the population's health and nutrition quantity–quality balance would have an impact on the average increase in indicators of such kinds of intelligence, and less impact on changes in indicators of crystallized intelligence.

Bioenvironmental Sources of Intelligence Changes. The rationale behind the potential connection among kinds of intelligence and bioenvironmental influences is based on the hypothesis that prenatal events and those related to the birth process would have enduring neurological consequences. This hypothesis has been called the "*the continuum of reproductive casualty*" (Pasamanick & Knoblock, 1966), and derives from the principle of "*sensitivity to the initial conditions*" of living-system development applied to intelligence (Juan-Espinosa, 1997). Taking into account Cattell's arguments, potential environmental factors that have an impact on the biological equipment of individuals may have a correlative impact on fluid intelligence (and less on Gc). If this is true, changes in these environmental factors will lead to changes in biological indicators, and changes in intelligence will mirror such influences. Among early life factors that may influence biological equipment and, therefore, intelligence development, prenatal care, infections, and nutrition are the most important. Richard Lynn (1990), maintains that nutrition may be the main potential factor influencing intelligence gains.

The first clue to the role of nutrition in increases in intelligence in this century lies in the parallel increases that have taken place in height. Even though measurements of body composition during growth and development would provide more detailed information about nutritional status than the measurement of stature (and weight) alone (Zemel, Riley, & Stallings, 1997), anthropometric assessment is nevertheless a rapid, inexpensive, and noninvasive means of determining short- and long-term nutritional status. Thus, because height and weight data are easy to collect, a number of standard publications report series of data over the past century, especially for military service recruits.

The Parallel Increases in Intelligence and Height. As in the case of IQ increases this century, height increase is a well-documented phenomenon in the populations of industrialized countries (Floud, Wachter, & Gregory, 1990; Schmidt, Jørgensen, & Michaelsen, 1995). Richard Lynn, in his seminal article (1990) and in a recent book (1996), took height as an indicator of the nutritional status of a population. His main claim is that, given the parallel increase between intelligence and height in developed countries, and given that nutrition is the main cause of the height increase in a population, changes in nutritional status are the major causal factor in intelligence increase.

Lynn (1990), then, stated that the first clue to nutritional status is the height of population. In a recent paper, Schmidt et al. (1995) described and analyzed average height growth in several European countries. Figure 13.12 shows mean conscript height during the period from 1960 to 1990. In all the countries represented there has been an increment in height, but large differences among countries arise. While the Netherlands, Belgium, France, and Spain show similar rates of increment (and the differences are small), Norway is a different case: Its ratio of increase in height is smaller compared to the other countries. Meanwhile, the Netherlands and Norway reached a plateau during the 1980s, the main heights of Belgium and Spain were still increasing up to 1990. Comparing intelligence increase with height growth in the abovementioned countries, parallel trends are found.

It is widely accepted that adult height is determined by genetic and endocrine factors and modified by the environment. Socioeconomic factors

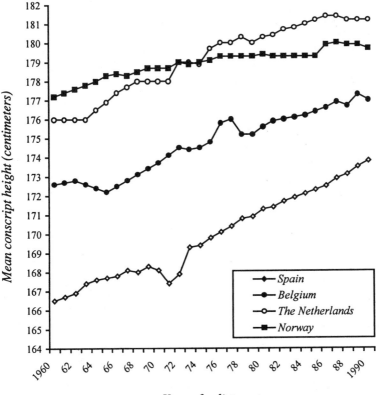

Year of enlistment

FIG. 13.12. Increasing in mean conscript height during the period from 1960 to 1990 in the four European countries that reach Status 1 in studies of IQ gains (modified from Schmidt et al., 1995).

especially, among other environmental variables (social class, income, parental education, overcrowding, hygiene, and war), are suggested as factors that influence adult height (Sandberg & Steckel, 1987). Obviously, socioeconomic factors cannot influence growth directly, but must act through biological factors, such as nutrition and infection. Careful analyses of data have reached the conclusion that improved nutrition and reduced prevalence of infection are the main determinants of the trend toward increasing adult height (Schmidt et al., 1995).

Two sociodemographic indicators are especially important as predictors of adult height: neonatal and postneonatal mortality. Both are regarded as sensitive indicators of infant health for a population in a given country. Infant nutritional status and the prevalence of infections are regarded as the most important determinants of PNM or postneonatal mortality (Stembera, 1990), and neonatal mortality reflects improvements in pre- and perinatal care. Both postneonatal mortality and neonatal mortality decline when socioeconomic conditions improve.

The PNM rates for the abovementioned European countries, analyzed from 1946 to 1990, are shown in Fig. 13.13. As can be seen, the general pattern is a rapid decrease until a low level is reached, after which PNM remains low or decreases very slowly. However, there are large differences between countries regarding the year at which this low level was reached (criterion: 3 per 1000). For instance, while The Netherlands reaches the criterion in 1971 and Norway in 1972, Spain reaches it in 1986.

Trends of neonatal mortality show a different pattern. There is a continuous and slower decrease that reflects the continuous improvement in pre- and perinatal care during recent decades. Schmidt et al. (1995) concluded that it was not until the beginning of the 1980s that the countries with the lowest mortalities reached a low and steady plateau.

With regard to the correspondence between indicators of nutrition and infections (PNM) and height, Schmidt et al. (1995) compared the mean height in 11 European countries with PNM 18 years earlier (when recruits were infants). They found that the general trend is that height increases toward a maximum when PNM approaches zero. That is, the improvement in PNM is reflected by a parallel increase in height. In conclusion, results point to the increase in quality of nutrition and the reduction of infection (PNM) as the main causal factors of height increase.

Height, Anatomical Brain Measures, and Intelligence Gains. Obviously, the foregoing statement about the relationship between intelligence and nutrition must necessarily be tentative. Lynn's (1990) nutrition argument claimed a correspondence between height and intelligence on the basis of the analogous increases in head size, and presumably by increases in the average size of the brain.

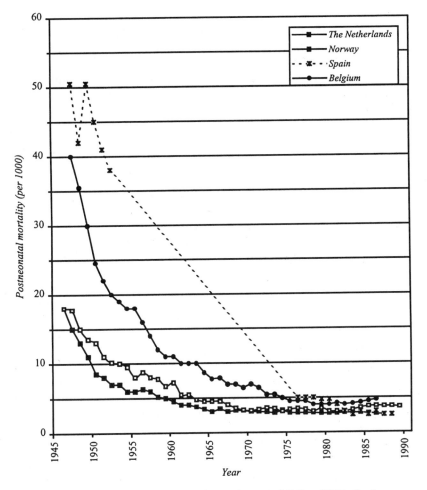

FIG. 13.13.   Postneonatal mortality during the period 1946 to 1990 in the four European countries that reach Status 1 in studies of IQ gains (modified from Schmidt et al., 1995).

Some studies reviewed by Lynn (1990) showed that, over this century, head size has consistently increased in various developed countries (Great Britain, Hong Kong, and Japan). The increases of approximately 1SD over half a century are similar to the gains that have occurred for height and IQ (Davies, Leung, & Lau, 1985; Morita & Ohtsuki, 1973; Whitehead & Paul, 1988). There is also evidence that, in consequence, brain size increases have taken place (Miller & Corsellis, 1973; Pakkenberg & Voight, 1964).

These results are clearly considered on the basis of a relationship between anatomical brain measures and intelligence scores. Lynn's (1990) argument is, "Larger heads contain larger brains, and larger brains have meant higher intelligence" (p. 275). However, as Lynn acknowledges, "Although the correlations between head size and intelligence are consistently positive, they are quite low, and average out at around 0.2" (p. 275). Even though recently more sophisticated measures of brain size (neuroimages measures) have increased the correlation to a mean of 0.44 (Egan et al., 1994; Raz et al., 1993; Wickett, Vernon, & Lee, 1994), many methodological problems still remain (Andrés, 1993; Juan-Espinosa, 1997).

Intelligence and Improvement of Nutrition.   Although there is some evidence of the link between malnutrition and low height (Martorell, Rivera, Kaplowitz, & Pollitt, 1992), small brain size (Naeye, Diener, & Dellinger, 1969; Parekh, Pherwani, Udani, & Mukherjee, 1970), and low intelligence (Winick, Meyer, & Harris, 1975), some of these studies give contradictory results, especially about famine and intelligence (Stein, Susser, Saenger, & Marolla, 1972). The establishment of a direct connection between nutrition and intelligence demands an experimental approach where, with adequate controls, dietary manipulation takes place.

Recently, Eysenck (1995) reviewed the evidence from 10 such studies. All of these involved children who were considered to be adequately fed, and none involved deprived inner-city children, or children in third-world countries. The results show that in all 10 studies, the dietary supplementation group scored better than the placebo on group performance IQ (fluid intelligence). Meanwhile, none found a significantly increased verbal IQ (crystallized intelligence) in the supplementation group, as compared with the placebo control group. The mean IQ gain in the supplementation group was 3.5 IQ points.

As we expected from the Cattell's Gc/Gf differential hypothesis on biological resource influence, nutrition has more to do with Gf changes than Gc changes. If intelligence gains over the past century reflect more Gf than Gc increases (as we have seen in a previous section), changes in nutrition may provide a potential explanation for this differential gains. Sound support for such an explanation has come from the results of experimental studies, but nevertheless, much more research effort must be made in order to overcome the related methodological problems (too small groups, too short periods of supplementation, and so on) which lead to difficulties in replicating results due to insufficient statistical power. Up to now, nutrition must remain as a "potential" causal factor of intelligence gains, behind which sociohistorical changes (educational, socialeconomic, and cultural) still act as distal influences.

One of the most important problems in the field of intelligence is that, when biological factors are emphasized as potential explanatory conditions, *nature* emerges immediately as an opposite domain to *nurture*. In our understanding, nature and nurture are not opposite but synergistic sources for the explanation of intelligence variance.

CONCLUSIONS

Intelligence test scores have changed during the 20th century, there has been an extremely high increase in IQ and g factor, and there have been differences between the shifts of different cognitive abilities. At the same time, several sociohistorical changes have occurred with similar profiles to the intelligence shifts: increase in education, in the demands of the work, leisure, and home contexts, and improvements in bioenvironmental conditions. Several kinds of empirical evidence have been reviewed in order to test potential relationships between these two types of variable.

Nevertheless, both qualitative and quantitative sociohistorical and intellectual changes cannot have a bivariate relationship. As Staats (1971), Bandura (1986), and others interactive psychologist pointed out, intelligence is a human characteristic developed through a synergistic process between intelligence behavior, socioenvironmental, and biological factors. *Nature* and *nurture* are tightly linked: Human intelligence contributes to a more complex and developed society, at the same time that complex environment is more and more demanding of general cognitive ability, that is, the g factor. Our developed society is producing biological changes, and these changes can also be considered as cumulative environmental (or, as we call them here, bioenvironmental) effects on the biological bases of intelligence.

In accordance with what has been said up to now, if changes in intelligence have been produced without the existence of genoma changes linked to verifiable mutations that explain the increase in intelligence of the human species, we would then be assuming that there has been an "inheritance" of acquired characters. However, we can still suggest two types of hypotheses:

1. From Gould's (1981) perspective, there would be produced a cultural inheritance of acquired characteristics, learned in earlier generations and transmitted both formally and informally by society. This would mean that each individual, throughout his or her life cycle, could "become" more intelligent.

2. The second possibility is that proposed by Storfer (1990), in which bioenvironmental changes, to which we referred earlier, are transmitted to successive generations through colinergic changes, as a vehicle of transmission.

Further research should clarify the relationship between socioenvironmental and historical factors and changes in intelligence, reviewed in this chapter, as a vehicle of transmission.

It is extremely difficult to study such complex interactive phenomena. Interdisciplinary studies must be planned and systematic data series on intelligence must be available. International research organizations should perhaps be more concerned with one of the most genuinely human expression. As thousands of sociodemographic and socialeconomic characteristics and indicators are measured and studied through time by international organizations, intelligence must also be taken into consideration as an important expression of the human progress. Our proposal is that an International Observatory of Intelligence must be founded in order to assess human intelligence, through history, as well as others societal conditions and their relationships.

REFERENCES

Anastasi, A. (1958). *Differential psychology: Individual and group differences in behavior.* New York: Macmillan.

Anastasi, A. (1981). Coaching, test sophistication, and developed abilities. *American Psychologist, 36,* 1086–1093.

Andrés, A. (1993). *La inteligencia como fenómeno natural [Intelligence as a natural phenomenon].* Valencia: Promolibro.

Baltes, P. (1987). Theoretical propositions of life-span developmental psychology: On the dynamics between growth and decline. *Developmental Psychology, 23,* 611–626.

Baltes, P. B., Reese, H. W., & Lipsitt, L. P. (1980). Life-span developmental psychology. *Annual Review of Psychology, 31,* 65–100.

Bandura, A. (1986). *Social foundation of thought and action: A social cognitive theory.* Englewood Cliffs, NJ: Prentice-Hall.

Bock, P. K. (1980). *Continuities in psychological anthropology.* San Francisco: Freeman.

Bouchard, T. J., & Segal, N. L. (1985). Enviroment and IQ. In B. Wolman (Ed.), *Handbook of intelligence: Theories, measurements and applications* (pp. 391–464). New York: Wiley.

Brody, N. (1992). *Intelligence.* New York: Academic Press.

Campllonch, J. M., & Fernandez-Ballesteros, R. (1981). La evaluación del potencial de aprendizaje [Learning Potential Assessment]. In R. Fernandez-Ballesteros (Ed.), *Nuevos avances en evaluación conductual [Advances in behavioral assessment]* (pp. 678–715). Valencia: Alfaplus.

Carroll, J. B. (1993). *Human cognitive abilities.* Cambridge, England: Cambridge University Press

Cattell, R. B. (1936). Is our national intelligence declining? *Eugenic Review, 28,* 181–203.

Cattell, R. B. (1937). *The fight for our national intelligence.* London: King.

Cattell, R. B. (1971). *Intelligence: Its structure, growth, and action.* Boston: Houghton-Mifflin.

Cattell, R. B. (1987). *Intelligence: Its structure, growth and action.* New York: North-Holland.

Ceci, S. J. (1991). How much does school influence general intelligence and its cognitive components? A reassessment of the evidence. *Developmental Psychology, 5,* 703–722.

Ceci, S. J., & Williams, W. M. (1997). Schooling, intelligence, and income. *American Psychologist, 52,* 1051–1059.

Colecchia, A., & Papaconstantinou, G. (1996). The evolution of skills in OECD countries and the role of technology. *STI Working Papers Series.* OECD, Paris.

Colom, R., Andrés, A., & Juan-Espinosa, M. (1997, November). Cambios generacionales de rendimiento en los tests de inteligencia [Generational changes in intelligence tests performance]. Paper presented to the *First Congress of the SEIDI [Spanish Society for Research on Individual Differences],* Madrid.

Colom, R., Andrés, A., & Juan-Espinosa, M. (1998). Generational IQ gains: Spanish data. *Personality and Individual Differences, 25*, 927–935.

Davies, D. P., Leung, S. F., & Lau, S. P. (1985). Secular trends in head growth. *Archives of Diseases of Childhood, 60*, 623–624.

Egan, V., Chiswick, A., Santosh, C., Naidu, K., Rimmington, J. E., & Best, J. J. K. (1994). Size isn't everything: A study of brain volume, intelligence and auditory evoked potentials. *Personality and Individual Differences, 17*, 357–367.

Estes, R. (1988). *Trends in world social development.* New York: Praeger.

Estes, R. (1992). *At the crossroads: Dilemmas in social development toward the Year 2000 and beyond.* New York: Praeger.

EUROSTAT, Statistical Office of the European Communities (1996). *Demographic statistics 1996.* Luxemburg: Office for Official Publications.

Eysenck, H. J. (1995). Can we study intelligence using the experimental method? *Intelligence, 20*, 217–228.

Fernández-Ballesteros, R. (1984). *Evaluation of the programs for developing intelligence in Venezuela.* Paris: UNESCO.

Fernández-Ballesteros, R. (1996). *Psicología del envejecimiento [Psychology of aging].* Madrid: Autonoma University of Madrid.

Fernández-Ballesteros, R., & Calero, M. D. (1993). Measuring learning potential. *International Jounal of Cognitive Education and Mediated Learning, 3*(1), 9–21.

Fernández-Ballesteros, R., & Calero, M. D. (1995). Training effects on intelligence of older persons. *Archives of Gerontology and Geriatrics, 20*, 135–148.

Fernández-Ballesteros, R., Juan-Espinosa, M., Colom, R., & Calero, M. D. (1997). Contextual and personal sources of individual differences in intelligence: Empirical results. In J. S. Carlson, J. Kingma, & W. Tomic (Eds.), *Advances in cognition and educational practice: Reflections on the concept of intelligence.* Greenwich, CT: JAI Press.

Floud, R., Wachter, K., & Gregory, A. (1990). *Height, health and history.* Cambridge, England: Cambridge University Press.

Flynn, J. R. (1984). The mean IQ of Americans: Massive gains 1932–1978. *Psychological Bulletin, 95*, 29–51.

Flynn, J. R. (1987). Massive IQ gains in 14 nations: What IQ tests really measure. *Psychological Bulletin, 101*, 29–51.

Flynn, J. R. (1991). *Asian Americans: Achievement beyond IQ.* Hillsdale, NJ: Lawrence Erlbaum Associates.

Flynn, J. R. (1994). IQ gains over time. In R. J. Sternberg (Ed.), *The encyclopedia of human intelligence* (pp. 617–623). New York: Macmillan.

Flynn, J. R. (1996). What environmental factors affect intelligence: The relevance of IQ gains over time. In D. K. Detterman (Ed.), *Current topics in human intelligence. Vol. 5: The environment* (pp. 17–30). Norwood, NJ: Ablex.

Gould, S. J. (1981). *The mismeasure of man.* New York: Norton.

Gustafsson, J. E. (1988). Hierarchical models of individual differences. In R. J. Sternberg (Ed.), *Advances in the psychology of human intelligence* (Vol. 4). Hillsdale, NJ: Lawrence Erlbaum Associates.

Hagberg, G., Lewerth, A., Olsson, E., & Westerberg, B. (1987). Mild mental retardation on Gothenburg scales: 1980 compared to 1966–1970. *Uppsala Journal of Medical Science, 44*, 52–57.

Hebb, D. O. (1949). *The organization of behavior.* New York: Wiley.

Hunt, E. B. (1995a). The role of Intelligence in modern society. *American Scientist.* August.

Hunt, E. B. (1995b). *Will we be smart enough?* New York: Russell Sage Foundation.

Hunter, J. E. (1986). Cognitive ability, cognitive aptitudes, job knowledge, and job performance. *Journal of Vocational Behavior, 29*, 340–362.

Hunter, J. E., & Hunter, R. F. (1984). Validity and utility of alternative predictors of job performance. *Psychological Bulletin, 1*, 72–98.

Jackson, J. S., & Antonucci, T. C. (1994). Survey methodology in life-span human development research. In S. H. Cohen & H. W. Reese (Eds.), *Life span developmental psychology: Methodological contributions*. Hillsdale, NJ: Lawrence Erlbaum Associates.

Jensen, A. R. (1980). *Bias in mental testing*. New York: Free Press.

Jerison, H. J. (1982). The evolution of biological intelligence. In R. J. Sternberg (Ed.), *Handbook of human intelligence* (pp. 723–791). Cambridge, England: Cambridge University Press.

Juan-Espinosa, M. (1996). Selección de personal para puestos de alta complejidad técnica [Personnel selection for complex high-technology posts]. In M. Juan-Espinosa, B. R. Colom, & M. A. Quiroga (Eds.), *La práctica de la psicología diferencial en industria y organizaciones* [The practice of differential psychology in industry and organizations]. Madrid: Pirámide.

Juan-Espinosa, M. (1997). *Geografía de la inteligencia humana* [Geography of human intelligence]. Madrid: Pirámide.

Juan-Espinosa, M., & Giménez, L. F. (1996). Diferencias individuales en selección de recursos humanos [Individual differences in selection of human resources]. In M. Juan-Espinosa, B. R. Colom, & M. A. Quiroga (Eds.), *La práctica de la psicología diferencial en industria y organizaciones* [The practice of differential psychology in industry and organizations]. Madrid: Pirámide.

Juan-Espinosa, M., & Rosenvinge, A. (1980). *La investigación diferencial a la entrada de la EGB* [Differential research at the beginning of Primary Education]. Premio de Investigación de la Sociedad Española de Psicología [Research Award of the Spanish Society of Psychology]. April, Zaragoza. Unpublished report.

Katz, R. L. (1988). *The information society: An international perspective*. New York: Preager.

Labouvie-Vief, G. (1982). Dynamic development and mature autonomy: A theoretical prologue. *Human Development, 25*, 161–191.

LCHC, Laboratory of Comparative Human Cognition (1982). Cultural intelligence. In R. J. Sternberg (Ed.), *Handbook of human intelligence*. Cambridge, England: Cambridge University Press.

Leduc, A. (1988). *L'histoire d'appentissage d'une enfant "sauvage"* [Story of the learning of a "wild" child]. Broussard, Quebec: Edition Behavioral.

Lidz, C. S. (Ed.). (1987). *Dynamic assessment*. New York: Academic Press.

Lleget, M. (1972). *Grandes inventos* [Great inventions]. Barcelona: Plaza y Janes.

Luria, A. R. (1931). Psychological expedition to Central Asia. *Science, 74*, 383–384.

Luria, A. R. (1979). *The making of mind*. Cambridge, MA: Harvard University Press.

Lynn, R. (1990). The role of nutrition in secular increases in intelligence. *Personality and Individual Differences, 11*, 273–285.

Lynn, R. (1996). *Dysgenics: Genetic deterioration in modern populations*. Westport, CT: Praeger.

Lynn, R., & Hampson, S. (1986a). Intellectual abilities of Japanese children: An assessment of 2–8· derived from the McCarthy scales of children's abilities. *Intelligence, 10*, 41–58.

Lynn, R., & Hampson, S. (1986b). The rise of national intelligence: Evidence from Britain, Japan, and the U.S.A. *Personality and Individual Differences, 7*, 23–32.

Martorell, R., Rivera, J., Kaplowitz, H., & Pollitt, E. (1992). Long-term consequences of growth retardation during early childhood. In M. Hernandez & J. Argente (Eds.), *Human Growth: Basic and clinical aspects*. Amsterdam: Elsevier.

Miller, A. K. H., & Corsellis, J. A. N. (1973). Evidence for a secular increase in human brain weight during the past century. *Annals of Human Biology, 4*, 253–257.

Morita, S., & Ohtsuki, T. (1973). Secular changes in the main head dimensions in Japanese. *Human Biology, 45*, 151–165.

Naeye, R. L., Diener, M. M., & Dellinger, W. S. (1969). Urban poverty: Effects on prenatal nutrition. *Science, 166*, 1206.

Neisser, U. (1997). Rising scores on intelligence tests. *American Scientist*, September–October.

Pakkenberg, H., & Voight, J. (1964). Brain weight and the Danes. *Acta Anatomia, 56*, 297–307.

Parekh, U. C., Pherwani, A., Udani, P. M., & Mukherjee, S. (1970). Brain weight and head circumference in fetus, infant, and children of different nutritional and socio-economic groups. *Indian Pediatrics, 7*, 347–358.

Pasamanick, B., & Knoblock, H. (1966). Retrospective studies of the epidemiology of reproductive casualty, old and new. *Merrill-Palmer Quarterly, 12*, 7–26.

Ramey, C. T., & Blair, C. (1996). Intellectual development and the role of early experience. In D. K. Detterman (Ed.), *Current topics in human intelligence. Vol. 5: The environment*. Norwood, NJ: Ablex.

Raz, N., Torres, I. J., Spencer, W. D., Millman, D., Baertschi, J. C., & Sarpel, G. (1993). Neuroanatomical correlates of age-sensitive and age-invariant cognitive abilities: An *in vivo* MRI investigation. *Intelligence, 17*, 407–422.

Ree, M. J., & Earles, J. A. (1990). *Estimating the general cognitive component of the armed services vocational aptitude battery (ASVAB): Three faces of G*. Brook Air Force Base, TX: Air Force Human Resources Laboratory.

Reich, R. (1991). *The work of nations: Preparing ourselves for 21st century capitalism*. New York: Knopf.

Rosa, A. (1991). Inteligencia en contexto [Intelligence in context]. In M. R. Martínez Arias & M. Yela (Eds.), *Pensamiento e inteligencia* [Thinking and intelligence]. Madrid: Alhmabra.

Sandberg, L. G., & Steckel, R. H. (1987). Heights and economic history: The Swedish case. *Annals of Human Biology, 14*, 101–110.

Schaie, K. W. (1994). The course of adult intellectual development. *American Psychologist, 49*(4), 304–343.

Schaie, K. W. (1996). *Intellectual development in adulthood: The Seattle Longitudinal Study*. Cambridge, England: Cambridge University Press.

Schmidt, I. M., Jørgensen, M. H., & Michaelsen, K. F. (1995). *Annals of Human Biology, 22*(1), 57–67.

Schmith, F. L., Ones, D. S., & Hunter, J. E. (1992). Personnel selection. *Annual Review of Psychology, 43*, 627–670.

Schroots, J. J. F., Fernández-Ballesteros, R., & Rudinger, G. (1999). *Aging in Europe*. Amsterdam: IOS Press.

Senge, P. M. (1987). *The fifth discipline*. New York: Bantam.

Snow, R. E., & Yalow, E. (1982). Education and intelligence. In R. Sternberg (Ed.), *Handbook of human intelligence*. Cambridge, England: Cambridge University Press.

Spielberger, C. D., Gonzalez, H. P., & Fletcher, T. (1978). Test anxiety reduction, learning strategies, and academic performance. In C. D. Spielberger and I. G. Sarason (Eds.), *Stress and anxiety (Vol. 5)*. New York: Hemisphere.

Staats, A. W. (1971). *Child, learning, intelligence, and personality*. New York: Harper & Row.

Stein, Z., Susser, M., Saenger, G., & Marolla, F. (1972). Nutrition and mental performance. *Science, 178*, 708–713.

Stembera, Z. (1990). Prospects for higher infant survival. *World Health Forum, 11*, 78–84.

Sternberg, R. J. (1997). Technology changes intelligence: Societal implications and soaring IQs. *Technos Quarterly for Education and Technology, Vol. 6*(2), *Summer*.

Storfer, M. D. (1990). *Intelligence and giftedness: The contributions of hereditary and early environment*. San Francisco: Jossey-Bass.

Sundet, J. M., Tambs, K., Magnus, P., & Berg, K. (1988). On the question of secular trends in the heritability of intelligence scores: A study of Norwegian twins. *Intelligence, 2*, 47–59.

Teasdale, T. W., & Owen, O. R. (1989). Continuing secular increases in intelligence and a stable prevalence of high intelligence levels. *Intelligence, 13*, 255–262.

Toffler, A. (1980). *The third wave*. New York: William Morrow.

U.S. Department of Labor, Employment and Training Administration (1971). *Doing your best on aptitude tests*. Washington, DC: U.S. Government Printing Office.

UNESCO (1963–1997). *Statistical yearbooks*. Paris: UNESCO.

UNESCO (1997). *http://unescostat.unesco.org*. Division of Statistics. Paris: UNESCO.

Vining, D. R. (1986). Social versus reproductive success: The central theoretical problem of human sociogiology. *The Behavioral and Brain Sciences, 9*, 167–216.

Vygotsky, L. S. (1929). The problem of the cultural development of the child. *Journal of Genetic Psychology, 36*, 415–434.

Vygotsky, L. S. (1978). *Mind in society.* M. Cole, V. John-Steiner, S. Scribner, & E. Souberman (Eds.). Cambridge, MA: Harvard University Press.

Wegmann, R., Chapman, R., & Johnson, M. (1989). *Work in the new economy.* Alexandria, VA: American Association for Counseling and Development.

Whitehead, R. G., & Paul, A. A. (1988). Comparative infant nutrition in man and other animals. In R. G. Whitehead & A. A. Paul (Eds.), *Proceedings of the International Symposium of Comparative Nutrition.* London: Libbey.

Wickett, J., Vernon, P. A., & Lee, D. H. (1994). In vivo brain size, head perimeter, and intelligence in a sample of healthy adult females. *Personality and Individual Differences, 16*, 831–838.

Wigdor, A. K., & B. F. Green, Jr. (1991). *Performance assessment in the workplace.* Washington, DC: National Academy Press.

Winick, M., Meyer, K. K., & Harris, R. C. (1975). Malnutrition and environmental enrichment by early adoption. *Science, 190*, 1173–1175.

Wolff, E. (1996). Technology and the demand for skills. *STI Review No. 18*, OCDE, Paris.

Zemel, B. S., Riley, E. M., & Stallings, V. A. (1997). Evaluation of methodology for nutritional assessment in children: Anthropometry, body composition, and energy expenditure. *Annual Review of Nutrition, 17*, 211–235.

Zigler, E., & Seitz, V. (1982). Social policy and intelligence. In R. Sternberg (Ed.), *Handbook of human intelligence.* Cambridge, England: Cambridge University Press.

Zigler, E., & Tricket, P. K. (1978). IQ, social competence, and evaluation of early childhood intervention programs. *American Psychologist, 33*, 789–798.

14

Epilogue: Is There a Heredity–Environment Paradox?

Robert J. Sternberg

Yale University and Moscow State University

The chapters in this volume make an ostensibly appealing case regarding the power of the environment in affecting intellectual functioning. Large numbers of variables have been shown to make a difference. The list seems almost endless and the case for their power irrefutable. Yet, there seems at first glace to be something of a paradox.

Analyses of the relative contributions of heredity and environment to intellectual functioning typically yield relatively high coefficients of heritability, often in the .4 to .8 range, with heritability increasing as a function of age (see chapters in Sternberg & Grigorenko, 1997; see also, in particular, Bouchard, 1997; Mackintosh, 1998; Plomin, 1997; Scarr, 1997). Moreover, these same analyses suggest that to the extent that environment matters in producing variability in intellectual functioning, it seems to be within-family rather than between-family factors that make the lion's share of the difference. This finding becomes especially puzzling when we consider that many of the environmental variables presumed to affect intelligence—lead, serious undernutrition, certain diseases such as HIV infection—would seem as likely to operate between families as within families.

Is there a paradox? How could so many environmental variables matter, yet matter so little in analyses of the heritability versus environmentality of intellectual abilities?

Some of the issues may revolve around limitations in the operationalization of heritability, although it is not my intention here to engage in a lengthy analysis of this operationalization (see, however, Sternberg & Grigorenko,

1999). Rather, other factors seem to be particularly relevant, some of whose operation we can observe but not fully understand.

Individual-Difference Versus Stimulus-Difference Analysis

Analyses of heritability are based on a consideration of variation that contributes to differences in performance among individuals. Thus, a heritability of, say, .5, refers not to 50% of intelligence being inherited, but to 50% of the individual-difference variation in scores being associated with hereditary factors. This issue is important, for several reasons.

First, the absence of a rational zero point in the analysis of intellectual abilities leaves scientists unable to compute how much "total" variance there is. Clearly, an IQ of 0 does not signify "no intelligence": IQ is not on a ratio scale. As a result, we have no way of quantifying "how much" intelligence an IQ of 100 or anything else represents. Effects attributed to genes are within a given range of variation within a particular population, not within the total range of variation possible with respect to intelligence or even human intelligence.

Second, heritabilities of attributes can and do vary from one population to another. There is no one heritability of height, intelligence, or of anything else. The heritability of a trait can vary over time and space as a function of the respective amounts of individual-difference variation in inheritance and in environment, respectively.

Third, the use of a narrow conception of intelligence may overestimate the contribution of heredity to individual differences in intelligence. Our own research suggests that family transmission of analytical abilities—those grounded in traditional theories—tends to be higher than family transmission of creative or practical abilities (Grigorenko & Sternberg, in press), and these latter abilities may be as important to intelligence as the former (Sternberg, 1997). Moreover, to the extent genes even matter for the creative abilities, much of the effect may be emergenic—due to unpredictable combinations of genes—rather than to additive genetic variance (Lykken, 1998).

Fourth, heritability tells us nothing about modifiability. An attribute can be highly heritable and either weakly or highly modifiable. The question of modifiability simply is just a different question. For example, height is highly heritable, with estimates of heritability typically between .90 and .95, yet heights have been rising over the past several generations in many countries, especially in Japan (Van Wieringer, 1978). If everyone's height were suddenly to rise 6 inches, it would represent a substantial change in mean height, but the heritability of height would remain exactly the same because the pattern of individual differences would not have been altered.

WHY DO WE FOCUS ON INDIVIDUAL DIFFERENCES?

The preoccupation of many psychologists studying intelligence with individual differences may be, to a large extent, an historical accident. Galton (1883, 1892), who devised some of the earliest (and least successful) purported tests of intelligence, was especially interested in questions of individual differences and particularly of inheritance. Binet and Simon (1916) were commissioned to detect individual differences among school children in their abilities to profit from normal instruction in schools. Spearman (1904, 1927), perhaps, was most responsible for the association of the study of intellectual abilities with the study of individual differences, because his invention of the method of factor analysis based the identification of factors of intelligence on individual differences. But as Piaget (1972), Hunt, Frost, and Lunneborg (1973), Sternberg (1977), and many others have pointed out, the study of intelligence can equally well originate in the study of stimulus variation or situational variation (Fiedler & Link, 1994), or cultural variation (Serpell, 2000), or even species variation (Pinker, 1997).

The type of variation that serves as the focus of intelligence tends to lead to different questions about intelligence and variability in it. Scholars who study individual differences are likely to ask what variables affect individual differences and thus may easily be led to the study of hereditary and environmental sources of such variation. Scholars who study stimulus or situational variation are more likely to ask what stimulus or situational variables affect mean levels of intelligence. The effects of these variables may be difficult to discern because they may be higher order interaction effects rather than simple main effects.

If the study of individual-difference variation rather than stimulus or situational variance has seemed to predominate in the study of intellectual abilities, the fault lies not just with differential psychologists. Cognitive psychologists early on began to validate their models using correlations with psychometric tests as primary (Deary & Stough, 1996; Hunt et al., 1973) or secondary (Sternberg, 1977, 1983) criteria. Even biologically oriented psychologists sometimes have ended up using such correlations as the basis for their claims (e.g., Haier et al., 1995). Thus, psychometric tests, whose metatheoretical claim to be the arbiters of intelligence always has been weak at best, have taken on a prominence in analyses of intelligence that may exaggerate their importance.

Environmental variables have tended to seem more powerful when their effects on means are studied than when their effects on correlations are studied. The predominance of differential methodologies thus may have given undue emphasis to the importance of hereditary variables in the understanding of intelligence.

STARTING WITH ENVIRONMENTAL INDEPENDENT VARIABLES VERSUS STARTING WITH SCORE-BASED DEPENDENT VARIABLES

The trend in the study of environmental variables has been to start with one or more such variables, and to examine their effects on mean levels of intelligence. When such effects are examined only qualitatively, these examinations have given rise to the complaint that the more quantitative analyses are more compelling and in some sense more believable (Hunt, 1997). Probably, however, there is adequate room both for quantitative and for qualitative analyses.

An interesting alternative approach is to start with one or more dependent variables rather than with one or more independent variables. Consider, for example, weight. Hardly a month goes by without some study indicating the insidious role of heredity in influencing weight. People with an external orientation (Rotter, 1990) or with a fatalistic attitude may take comfort in the fact that their excessive weight is somehow largely outside their control. This barrage of genetic analyses, however, fails to explain a simple and inescapable fact. People in the United States are among the heaviest in the world, on average, although this trend is relatively recent. It is too recent for there to have been some inexplicable genetic mutation. Rather, the puzzle is easily solved in terms of not altogether known factors that affect weight. Although the issue would seem to be a straightforward matter of calorie consumption, recent high-protein, low-carbohydrate diets and well as "sugar-buster" diets suggest that some people, at least, believe that more than carbohydrates affect weight gain. We can blame genes all we want, but they cannot account for the rapid expansion of American waistlines above and beyond those of members of, say, the European Community or of Asian cultures.

Most relevant to this discussion, of course, is not the analysis of weight but rather the analysis of intelligence, or at least, aspects of it. Flynn (1987, 1998; see also Neisser, 1998) observed dramatic increases in levels of measured intelligence over the course of the past several decades. These increases amount to roughly 3 points per 10-year period, or 9 points per generation, a staggering increase in an index with a standard deviation of 15 points.

The increases become even more impressive when we consider that those aspects of intelligence (as conventionally defined) that have risen the most are exactly the aspects that most scholars initially would have thought would have risen the least. In particular, scores on measures of fluid abilities (such as are used in abstract reasoning) have risen substantially more than scores on measures of crystallized abilities (such as are used in tests of vocabulary and general knowledge). On the one hand, the brief time window for the increase shows that the effects must be environmental. On the other hand, the greater rise in fluid than in crystallized abilities is puzzling because the mechanism by which knowledge-based measures would show increases is more transparent than the mechanism by which abstract-reasoning-based measures would show increases.

A number of analyses have speculated on the sources of the increases, and they are summarized in Neisser (1998). They include better nutrition, video games, exposure to computers, improved parenting, and improved schooling. But the wide range of explanations are not accompanied by data that enable scholars, at this point, to go beyond speculation in identifying the sources of the increases.

What is of particular interest here is that these effects show enormous power of the environment, but again, the effects are shown through analyses of means rather than of correlations and the particular independent variables underlying them are not clearly identifiable at this time. Had the analyses started with the known independent variables rather than the dependent variable of IQ, and instead asked what the combined effects of the independent variables are, there is no way scholars could have concatenated the known independent variables to predict such massive gains. These analyses thus suggest that, for all our knowledge of the power of the environment, we are still close to clueless in terms of what really matters.

We are similarly locked in a state of speculation with regard to the greater power of within-family than of between-family variation as sources of individual differences in IQ. Scholars can speculate, as did Harris (1998), that peers or any other factors are responsible, but these explanations tend to be ones of default (no other obvious factors come to mind) or of speculation rather than ones of established fact.

The increases noted by Flynn (1987), of course, are secular. But research described in this volume by Ramey as well as our own research suggests that it is possible to obtain meaningful increases both in cognitive abilities and in school achievement based on cognitive abilities. To the extent that interventions have been unsuccessful, it may be because they were based on inadequate models of intelligence. Our own interventions based on the theory of successful intelligence have shown meaningful gains in both abilities and achievement (Sternberg, 1997). They are based on skills and subject matter not only being taught in traditional ways, but for analytical, creative, and practical thinking (Sternberg, Ferrari, Clinkenbeard, & Grigorenko, 1996; Sternberg, Grigorenko, Ferrari, & Clinkenbeard, 1999; Sternberg, Torff, & Grigorenko, 1998).

CONCLUSION

To the extent there is a heredity–environment paradox, it appears to be due to our still profound lack of understanding as to what variables substantially affect intellectual abilities, and as to how these effects take hold (Serpell, 2000). Studies of environmental variables, as presented in this volume, tend to examine mean differences rather than correlations, and to show environmental effects in this way. When one starts with dependent variables such as weight or IQ, the environmental effects appear to be far more powerful than when we start with specific independent variables and try to concatenate their effects.

There are those who will argue that tradition somehow favors the study of correlations. But as people in the United States grow fatter and fatter, and their rates of diabetes, heart disease, and other factors show substantial increases, it is not clear we can afford the false confidence that we obtain when we attribute it all to "the genes." Some of it may be in the genes, but that fact does not account for why other countries do not show similar effects—until they adopt the same unhealthy diets that have become so popular in the United States.

As massive environmental insults become more and more prevalent in a world whose population is growing at an almost unchecked rate, whether the insults be of lead or radiation or other forms of pollution or contamination, we may find the study of heritabilities in restricted ranges of populations to be something of a luxury. It is estimated that more than a billion children in the world are infected with intestinal parasites, and there is reason to believe that parasitic infections decrease cognitive abilities (Sternberg, Powell, McGrane, & Grantham-McGregor, 1997). Such infections can be combated rather easily through environmental interventions. It may be that some day in the distant future, it will also be possible to manipulate genes, although the collateral effects may be much more complex than we now can imagine in our optimism about genetic interventions. The world can implement environmental interventions right now, and the evidence presented in this book suggests that the importance and value of such interventions is incontestable, whatever may be the heritability of intelligence as traditionally measured.

ACKNOWLEDGMENTS

Preparation of this chapter was supported under the Javits Act Program (Grant No. R206R950001) as administered by the Office of Educational Research and Improvement, U.S. Department of Education. Grantees undertaking such projects are encouraged to express freely their professional judgment. This chapter, therefore, does not necessarily represent the position or policies of the Office of Educational Research and Improvement or the U.S. Department of Education, and no official endorsement should be inferred.

REFERENCES

Binet, A., & Simon, T. (1916). *The development of intelligence in children.* Baltimore: Williams & Wilkins. (Originally published in 1905).

Bouchard, T. J., Jr. (1997). IQ similarity in twins reared apart: Findings and responses to critics. In R. J. Sternberg & E. L. Grigorenko (Eds.), *Intelligence, heredity, and environment* (pp. 126–160). New York: Cambridge University Press.

Deary, I. J., & Stough, C. (1996). Intelligence and inspection time: Achievements, prospects, and problems. *American Psychologist, 51*(6) 599–608.

Fiedler, F. E., & Link, T. G. (1994). Leader intelligence, interpersonal stress, and task performance. In R. J. Sternberg & R. K. Wagner (Eds.), *Mind in context: Interactionist perspectives on human intelligence* (pp. 152–167). New York: Cambridge University Press.

Flynn, J. R. (1987). Massive IQ gains in 14 nations. *Psychological Bulletin, 101,* 171–191.

Flynn, J. R. (1998). WAIS-III and WISC-III gains in the United States from 1972 to 1995: How to compensate for obsolete norms. *Perceptual & Motor Skills, 86,* 1231–1239.

Galton, F. (1883). *Inquiry into human faculty and its development.* London: MacMillan.

Galton, F. (1892). *Heredity genius: An inquiry into its laws and consequences* (2nd ed.). London: MacMillan.

Grigorenko, E. L., & Sternberg, R. J. (in press). Analytical, creative, and practical intelligence as predictors of self-reported adaptive functioning: A case study in Russia. *Intelligence.*

Haier, R. J., Chueh, D., Touchette, R., Lott, I. et al. (1995). Brain size and cerebral glucose metabolic rate in nonspecific mental retardation and Down syndrome. *Intelligence, 20,* 191–210.

Harris, J. R. (1998). *The nurture assumption: Why children turn out the way they do.* New York: Free Press.

Hunt, E. (1997). Nautre vs. nurture: The feeling of *vujà dé.* In R. J. Sternberg & E. L. Grigorenko (Eds.), *Intelligence, heredity, and environment* (pp. 531–551). New York: Cambridge University Press.

Hunt, E., Frost, N., & Lunneborg, C. (1973). Individual differences in cognition: A new approach to intelligence. In G. Bower (Ed.), *The psychology of learning and motivation* (Vol. 7, pp. 87–122). New York: Academic Press.

Lykken, D. T. (1998). The genetics of genius. In A. Steptoe (Ed.), *Genius and mind: Studies of creativity and temperament* (pp. 15–37). New York: Oxford University Press.

Mackintosh, N. J. (1998). *IQ and human intelligence.* Oxford, England: Oxford University Press.

Neisser, U. (Ed.). (1998). *The rising curve.* Washington, DC: American Psychological Association

Piaget, J. (1972). *The psychology of intelligence.* Totowa, NJ: Littlefield Adams.

Pinker, S. (1997). *How the mind works.* New York: W. W. Norton.

Plomin, R. (1997). Identifying genes for cognitive abilities and disabilities. In R. J. Sternberg & E. L. Grigorenko (Eds.), *Intelligence, heredity, and environment* (pp. 89–104). New York: Cambridge University Press.

Rotter, J. B. (1990). Internal versus external control of reinforcement: A case history of a vriable. *American Psychologist, 45,* 489–493.

Scarr, S. (1997). Behavior-genetic and socialization theories of intelligence: Truce and reconciliation. In R. J. Sternberg & E. L. Grigorenko (Eds.), *Intelligence, heredity and environment* (pp. 3–41). New York: Cambridge University Press.

Serpell, R. (2000). Intelligence and culture. In R. J. Sternberg (Ed.), *Handbook of intelligence* (pp. 549–580). New York: Cambridge University Press.

Spearman, C. (1904). 'General intelligence,' objectively determined and measured. *American Journal of Psychology, 15*(2), 201–293.

Spearman, C. (1927). *The abilities of man.* London: MacMillan.

Sternberg, R. J. (1977). *Intelligence, information processing, and analogical reasoning: The componential analysis of human abilities.* Hillsdale, NJ: Lawrence Erlbaum Associates.

Sternberg, R. J. (1983). Components of human intelligence. *Cognition, 15,* 1–48.

Sternberg, R. J. (1997). *Successful intelligence.* New York: Plume.

Sternberg, R. J., Ferrari, M., Clinkenbeard, P. R., & Grigorenko, E. L. (1996). Identification, instruction, and assessment of gifted children: A construct validation of a triarchic model. *Gifted Child Quarterly, 40*(3), 129–137.

Sternberg, R. J., & Grigorenko, E. L. (Eds.). (1997). *Intelligence, heredity, and environment.* New York: Cambridge University Press.

Sternberg, R. J., & Grigorenko, E. L. (1999). Myths in psychology and education regarding the gene environment debate. *Teachers College Record, 100,* 536–553.

Sternberg, R. J., Grigorenko, E. L., Ferrari, M., & Clinkenbeard, P. (1999). A triarchic analysis of an aptitude-treatment interaction. *European Journal of Psychological Assessment, 15,* 1–11.

Sternberg, R. J., Powell, C., McGrane, P. A., & McGregor, S. (1997). Effects of a parasitic infection on cognitive functioning. *Journal of Experimental Psychology: Applied, 3,* 67–76.

Sternberg, R. J., Torff, B., & Grigorenko, E. L. (1998). Teaching triarchically improves school achievement. *Journal of Educational Psychology, 90*(3), 1–11.

Van Wieringer, J. C. (1978). Secular growth changes. In F. Falker & J. M. Tanner (Eds.), *Human growth* (Vol 2). New York: Plenum.

Author Index

Subject Index